WORDSWORTH

The Chronology of the Middle Years

1800–1815

Wordsworth

The Chronology of the Middle Years

1800–1815

MARK L. REED

HARVARD UNIVERSITY PRESS

Cambridge, Massachusetts

1975

Publication of this book has been aided by a
grant from the Hyder Edward Rollins Fund

Library of Congress Catalog Card Number 74–77179
ISBN 0–674–95777–6

Printed in the United States of America

Preface

THE present volume chronologizes the life and work of Wordsworth during the period from the early days of his residence at Grasmere through the consolidation of his achievement manifested in the publication of the first collected edition of his verse, *Poems by William Wordsworth*, and the long-delayed *White Doe of Rylstone*. The calendar demarcation that has seemed to me the most appropriate point of conclusion occurs at the end of the first half of the year 1815, when the poet departed London after the long visit in the course of which had appeared the *White Doe*, and which had in turn immediately followed the appearance of the collected *Poems*.

Stylistic and organizational methods generally conform to those in *Wordsworth: The Chronology of the Early Years, 1770–1799*, as discussed in the introduction to that volume; they are in any case, I hope, largely self-explanatory. I have, however, altered a few procedures. One change has been the confinement of *Prelude* line citations to the 1805 text in instances where no misunderstanding seems likely to result from omission of reference to the 1850 version.

A perhaps more obvious difference will be found in frequency of employment of square brackets, which in the first volume were used as a standard indication of inference or extensive editorial organization. Experience in compiling chronologies, though no empiric or sceptic philosophies were in this world, would suffice to teach that most facts must be counted in some degree as subjective. The typographic complication of the square brackets in the first volume now seems to me an equivocal contribution to precision, and I have employed this punctuation in the chronological reports below only in a relatively small number of instances where the information seems virtually certain, but where in my opinion its inferential character ought not be forgotten entirely.

With regard to another aspect of method, it has appeared useless, or counter to the object of clarity, to assign explicit *termini a quo* and *ad*

v

quem to each incident or poem or part thereof; I have supposed the logic of context, in many instances, sufficiently obvious demarcation.

I should repeat that certain subjects, although often reported in detail, are by nature too large and complex for exhaustive treatment here—notably, the health of Wordsworth and his family, letters received by the Wordsworths, letters of the Wordsworths that do not survive, and the Wordsworths' reading in other authors or in newspapers and ephemeral publications.

A few other procedures may be specified:

(1) Where dates have seemed most usefully presented in terms of seasons or other even less exact indices, the significance of the terms employed must of course be interpreted on the basis of content and context. A date of "early spring" would not be used, for example, if a date like "Mar 21–Apr 4" appeared equally justified.

(2) Dates of publication of journal reviews of Wordsworth's works have been conjecturally assigned, when advertisements of publication have not been found, to a time about the first day of the month following that printed on the journal itself (where one is present).

(3) With respect to the Wordsworths' financial dealings as recorded in Richard Wordsworth's accounts, when account entries for payment of drafts are accompanied by a note indicative of the period preceding the date that payment became due, the original draft is backdated accordingly. When this information is not present, normally only the date of final payment is recorded.

(4) Only minimal report is made of household activities during the poet's absences from home. Individual dates of attendance at church during periods when churchgoing was a regular family activity are unrecorded except where specifically documented. The same procedure has been followed with regard to visits to the Wordsworths by the Coleridge boys and Algernon Montagu during the time of their attendance at the school of Mr. Dawes in Ambleside. No attempt is made to supply exhaustive information about the normal daily comings and goings of the Wordsworth children around the house and to and from school; nor are minute speculations regularly presented concerning the

children's and long-term visitors' participation in household activities such as calls, walks, and brief excursions.

(5) Except where evidence has directly indicated a date within the last ten days of 1799, I have assigned Grasmere poems to 1800 or after (see *CEY* 283–86; 1800:1n).

(6) For the sake of consistency poems are usually designated by latest authorized titles Many of Wordsworth's verses were of course written before he had conceived the final form of the work with the title by which they are now associated, or in some cases had conceived the work itself. I have assumed that the reader does not need frequent reminding that specified lines are those lines as they stood in the state of advancement of their final context indicated by the discussion at hand.

(7) Copies made by the Wordsworths of writings of other authors are not listed in the General Chronological List.

(8) The spelling "Rydal" is employed throughout, although the Wordsworths commonly wrote "Rydale" during the period treated; and I have regularly recorded the "Black Quarter" of Dorothy's journal "Easedale."

(9) Where no description is given of a family letter other than the fact that it was written at a particular time, it may be assumed that the letter is not known to have survived.

(10) In 1815 the Mail made the journey from Kendal to London in about forty-four hours, from Penrith in about forty-eight and a half, and from Keswick in slightly under fifty-two (Cary's *Roads*, 1815, 328–35, 419, and Coach Directory entry no. 453). I have regularly assumed that a London postmark on a letter posted in the Lake area was stamped no earlier than the third day after the writing of the letter. (See also *Shelley and His Circle* III, ed. K. N. Cameron, Cambridge, Mass., 1970, 25–26; and *The Letters of Percy Bysshe Shelley*, ed. F. L. Jones, Oxford, 1964, I, 241–42n.)

(11) A critic has recently remarked of the "Poems Dedicated to National Independence and Liberty":

The captions often include a date, either month and year or year alone. It would be needlessly matter-of-fact to take such

vii

a date as either the time of the action recorded or the date of composition. In origin the dates are sometimes those of publication and sometimes Wordsworth's later error concerning date of composition, but either fact is incidental. He tried to convey in the date a particularly intense emotional reference. To achieve the full sublimity of each sonnet, you are to imagine yourself present at the date he assigns.

> (Carl Woodring, *Politics in English Romantic Poetry*, Cambridge, Mass., 1970, 123.)

The concluding advice might be extended to the dates in the titles of many of Wordsworth's other poems. But the poet seems in fact to have entitled a number of his works, for all that can be told to the contrary, with the actual dates of their composition—for example, eight of the first fourteen "Poems Dedicated to National Independence and Liberty": *Composed by the Sea-side, near Calais, August, 1802; Calais, August 1802; Composed near Calais . . . August 7, 1802; Calais, August 15, 1802; September 1, 1802; September, 1802, near Dover; Written in London, September, 1802; London, 1802.* Each case must, of course, be weighed on its own account. Where other and more cogent evidence does not apply, title dates have been regarded as indicative of dates of composition.

(12) Entry headings for longer and more complex entries are occasionally abbreviated by omission of some of the specific dates noted in the entry itself.

Compilation of a chronology is by necessity a cooperative venture, and no effort to express my gratitude for the aid I have received could fairly detail the extent to which this book is indebted to the work of others. Foremost thanks go to Frederick A. Pottle, originator of the project, for continuing his substantial assistance, advice, and encouragement in the preparation of this, as of the preceding, volume. The first studies covering the years treated here were compiled under Professor Pottle's direction by Boylston Green (1800–04), Chester A. Soleta, C.S.C. (1805–09), George L. Sixbey (1810–14), and George Kellogg (1815). Robert Daniel, Professor Pottle's successor and my predecessor in the project, has remained an engaged contributor.

Preface

My obligations to Professor Pottle, to Herschel C. Baker, to Walter Jackson Bate, to Cecil Y. Lang, and to David Perkins have been continuously accumulative from the time that I was their student. To Professor Baker I am particularly grateful for invaluable and timely assistance in the late stages of preparation of this volume. My indebtedness for the scholarship and unstinting assistance and encouragement, over many years, of Paul F. Betz, Stephen C. Gill, Robert G. Kirkpatrick, Mary Moorman, Stephen M. Parrish, Basil Willey, and Jonathan Wordsworth is immeasurable. Repeated, generous, and gracious assistance has been given by Beth Darlington, Alan Hill, Carol Landon, W. J. B. Owen, and Donald P. Sewell. I am indebted to Professor Owen for providing photocopies of page proof of various sections of his and Jane W. Smyser's edition of Wordsworth's *Prose Works*, which appeared too late for me to use as a standard reference. I have been able to incorporate some references to their first volume (on the basis of proof), as *Prose*. The late George Harris Healey, John Alban Finch, and A. Lionel Stevenson not only gave much to the content of this book but much to me in personal help and inspiration: in my, as in many students', work and feelings for Wordsworthian scholarship and for literature generally they have played no small part.

My primary institutional debt is to the Trustees of Dove Cottage, to whom I am most grateful for permission to examine, use, and quote from manuscript materials at the Dove Cottage Library, necessarily the center of research for a study like this one. The unfailing help of the former librarian, Nesta Clutterbuck, has been invaluable.

Many other institutions have made important contributions to this volume. For permission to quote and draw on unpublished materials in their possession, and for aid of a more general order, I am indebted especially to: Bodleian Library; Bristol University Library; British Museum; Carlisle Public Libraries; Cornell University Library; Fitzwilliam Museum; Folger Shakespeare Library; Harvard University Library; Henry E. Huntington Library; University of Keele Library; Lilly Library, University of Indiana; Longmans, Green, & Co.; McGill University Library; Pierpont Morgan Library; Rosenbach Foundation; St. John's College Library; Swarthmore College Library; University College, London; Victoria and Albert Museum; Wedgwood Museum;

ix

Washington University Library; Dr. Williams's Library; and Yale University Library. For help of many kinds I am grateful to: the Alderman Library, University of Virginia; Amherst College Library; Arizona State University Library, Tempe; Armitt Library; Berg Collection, New York Public Library; Boston Public Library; Brown University Library; Library of the University of California, Davis; Cambridge University Library; University of Chicago Library; Colgate University Library; Joint Archives Committee for the Counties of Cumberland and Westmorland; Duke University Library; University of Illinois Library; Lambeth Palace Library; Liverpool Public Library; Library of the University of Missouri, Kansas City; Norfolk and Norwich Record Office; University of North Carolina Library; Princeton University Library; and Royal Institution. Documents at the University of Texas have been examined and quoted by courtesy of the Humanities Research Center Library, the University of Texas at Austin.

I am indebted to Mrs. Basil Marsden-Smedley for permission on behalf of the Pinney family to examine and quote from materials in the Pinney family papers, on deposit at the University of Bristol; to Lord Abinger for permission to quote from the Godwin Diary; to Jonathan Wordsworth for permission to examine and quote from papers of the Wordsworth, Hutchinson, and Monkhouse families in his possession. For various kindnesses I am especially grateful to: John Alden, Helen Bennett, W. A. Billington, Margaret G. Brander, Mary Booth, Bruce M. Brown, Victoria Burkhart, James Butler, Herbert Cahoon, Eric and Jane Clay, Norman Colbeck, Katherine Hershey Cosby, John Creasey, Donald Eddy, Lawrence G. Evans, Ian H. C. Fraser, Mary Isabel Fry, E. L. Griggs, Holly Hall, George Mills Harper, Norman Higham, C. Carroll Hollis, Bishop C. Hunt, Michael Jaye, Phoebe Johnson, B. C. Jones, Martha Keever, Hilton Kelliher, Carl Ketcham, Donald Kunitz, Sally Leach, Lawrence F. London, George Maby, James B. Meriwether, Adolph Meyer, June Moll, the Rev. Canon J. P. S. Morton, Russell Noyes, Robert Osborn, Michael Papantonio, Stephen Park, Lewis Patton, Janet Percival, J. Richard Phillips, Gordon N. Ray, James Rieger, Anthony Rota, Mr. and Mrs. A. E. Sanderson, Stuart Sherman, Robert Siegfried, Michael Simball, Kenneth Smith, Frances Stephens, G. A. Stollard, William A. Strutz, the Rev. Canon R. C. Tait, R. P. Taylor, John E. Via, Robert Voitle, Sir John Wedgwood, George

Whalley, Joan Whitworth, Robert S. Woof, Marjorie Wynne, and Paul M. Zall.

That the *Chronology* has reached this stage of completion is in most essential degree the result of aid through fellowships from the John Simon Guggenheim Memorial Foundation (1965–66, 1970–71), a Fulbright Scholarship (1960–61), a Frank Knox Memorial Travelling Fellowship (1960–61), a grant from the University of North Carolina–Duke Cooperative Program in the Humanities (1964), grants from the University of North Carolina Research Council, and grants from the American Philosophical Society (from the Penrose Fund, 1964; and from the Johnson Fund, 1968).

No help has matched, in quantity or quality, that of my wife Martha.
M.R.

Contents

Short Forms of Citation

AB	Allan Bank
Acland	*The Political Poetry of William Wordsworth*, ed. A. H. D. Acland (Oxford, 1915)
AM	*The Ancient Mariner*
App crit	*Apparatus criticus*
Ariel discussion	R. S. Woof, "John Stoddart, 'Michael,' and *Lyrical Ballads*," *Ariel* I (1970), 7–22; Jonathan Wordsworth, "A Note on the Ballad Version of 'Michael,'" *Ariel* II (1971), 67–71; "Mr. Woof's Reply to Mr. Wordsworth," *Ariel* II (1971), 72–79; Mark Reed, "The Development of Wordsworth's 'Michael,'" *Ariel* III (1972), 70–79; Stephen Parrish, "'Michael,' Mr. Woof and Mr. Wordsworth," *Ariel* III (1972), 80–83
B	(used alone) Beaumont
Betz *BN*	Paul F. Betz, "Wordsworth's First Acquaintance with Blake's Poetry," *Blake Newsletter* III (1970), 84–89
Betz *PB*	Paul F. Betz, "The Dates of *Peter Bell* MSS. 5 and 6," forthcoming
Blake, Etc.	*Blake, Coleridge, Wordsworth, Lamb, Etc.*, ed. E. J. Morley (Manchester, 1922)
Blanshard	Frances Blanshard, *Portraits of Wordsworth* (Ithaca, 1959)
BM	British Museum
BNYPL	*Bulletin of the New York Public Library*
C	(used alone) *Coleridge*
CC	*Concerning the Relations of Great Britain, Spain, and Portugal . . . as Affected by the Convention of Cintra*
CCl	Catherine Clarkson
CCS	*The Life and Correspondence of Robert Southey*, ed. Charles Cuthbert Southey (London, 1849–50). 6 vols
CEY	Mark L. Reed, *Wordsworth: The Chronology of the Early Years, 1770–1799* (Cambridge, Mass., 1967)

CL	Charles Lamb
Cl	Clarkson
Cornell	*The Cornell Wordsworth Collection*, comp. G. H. Healey (Ithaca and New York, 1957)
Courier	*The Courier* (London)
Curry	*New Letters of Robert Southey*, ed. Kenneth Curry (New York, 1965). 2 vols
Curry *RES*	Kenneth Curry, "Uncollected Translations of Michelangelo by Wordsworth and Southey, *RES* XIV (1938), 193–99
Curtis	Jared R. Curtis, *Wordsworth's Experiments with Tradition. The Lyric Poems of 1802* (Ithaca and London, 1971)
Curtis Diss.	Jared R. Curtis, "Wordsworth's Poetry: Spring, 1802. Essay and Critical Edition," Diss. Cornell, 1967
CW; CW Jr.	Christopher Wordsworth, brother of W; Christopher Wordsworth, Jr., nephew of W
DC; DCP	Dove Cottage; Dove Cottage Papers
DeQ	Thomas De Quincey
DNB	*Dictionary of National Biography*
DS	*Descriptive Sketches*
Duppa 1806; Duppa 1807	Richard Duppa, *The Life and Literary Works of Michel Angelo Buonarroti* (London, 1806); *The Life of Michel Angelo Buonarroti* (London, 1807), 2nd edn
DW	Dorothy Wordsworth. Except where indicated otherwise, refers to the sister of W
DWJ	*Journals of Dorothy Wordsworth*, ed. Ernest de Selincourt (London, 1959). 2 vols
DWJ M	*Journals of Dorothy Wordsworth*, ed. Mary Moorman (Oxford, 1971)
Eaton	H. A. Eaton, *Thomas De Quincey* (London, 1936)
EdS	Ernest de Selincourt
EdS *DW*	Ernest de Selincourt, *Dorothy Wordsworth, A Biography* (Oxford, 1933)
EKC	E. K. Chambers, *Samuel Taylor Coleridge* (Oxford, 1938)
ER	*The Edinburgh Review*
EW	*An Evening Walk*
Exc	*The Excursion*

EY	The Letters of William and Dorothy Wordsworth, The Early Years, 1787–1805, ed. Ernest de Selincourt, rev. Chester L. Shaver (Oxford, 1967)

Farington	Joseph Farington, *The Farington Diary*, ed. James Greig (London, 1922–28). 8 vols

Finch HG	John A. Finch, "On the Dating of *Home at Grasmere*: A New Approach," *WBS* 14–28

Finch THE	John A. Finch, "Wordsworth's Two-Handed Engine," *WBS* 1–13

FQ	*The Faerie Queene*

Friend R	Samuel Taylor Coleridge, *The Friend*, ed. Barbara E. Rooke (Princeton, 1969). 2 vols

FV	*The Female Vagrant*

G	W's *Guide through the District of the Lakes* (pub. so titled Kendal and London, 1835). When used without accompanying date, refers to state of work indicated by context.

G 1810; G 1820;	W's letterpress for Joseph Wilkinson, *Select Views in*
G 1822; G 1823;	*Cumberland, Westmoreland and Lancashire* (London,
G 1835	1810); *Topographical Description of the Country of the Lakes*, in *RD* (1820); *A Description of the Scenery of the Lakes* (London, 1822); the same (London, 1823); for G 1835, see G

G&SG	Dorothy Wordsworth, *George & Sarah Green, A Narrative*, ed. Ernest de Selincourt (Oxford, 1936)

GCL	General Chronological List of Writings, below

GGW	Gordon G. Wordsworth, grandson of the poet

GH	Greta Hall

Gillies	R. P. Gillies, *Memoirs of a Literary Veteran* (London, 1851). 3 vols

Godwin Diary	Diary of William Godwin, microfilms of Abinger Collection, Duke University Library

Grosart	*The Prose Works of William Wordsworth*, ed. A. B. Grosart (London, 1876). 3 vols

H	(used alone) Hutchinson

Hale White	*A Description of the Wordsworth and Coleridge Manuscripts in the Possession of Mr. T. Norton Longman*, ed. W. Hale White (London, 1897)

Hayden	John O. Hayden, *The Romantic Reviewers, 1802–1824* (Chicago, 1969). Unless described otherwise, infor-

	mation from this source is taken from the list of reviews of W pp. 296–98.
Haydon *Diary*	*The Diary of Benjamin Robert Haydon*, ed. W. B. Pope (Cambridge, Mass., 1960–63). 5 vols
HC	Hartley Coleridge
HCR	Henry Crabb Robinson
HCR *Diary*	*Diary, Reminiscences, and Correspondence of Henry Crabb Robinson*, ed. Thomas Sadler (New York, 1877). 2 vols
HCRBW	*Henry Crabb Robinson on Books and Their Writers*, ed. E. J. Morley (London, 1938). 3 vols
HCRNB	Notebooks of Henry Crabb Robinson, at Dr. Williams's Library
HCRWC	*The Correspondence of Henry Crabb Robinson with the Wordsworth Circle*, ed. E. J. Morley (Oxford, 1927). 2 vols
HEH	Henry E. Huntington Library
HG	*Home at Grasmere*
Hogg *Autobiography*	*Autobiography of the Ettrick Shepherd*, in *The Works of the Ettrick Shepherd*, ed. Thomas Thomson (London, 1865), 441–68
Howe	*The Complete Works of William Hazlitt*, ed. P. P. Howe (London, 1930–34). 21 vols
HUL	Harvard University Library
IF; IF note(s)	Isabella Fenwick; note(s) dictated to her by W
ISHS	*[Inscription] for the Spot Where the Hermitage Stood on St. Herbert's Island, Derwent-water*
Japp	A. H. Japp, *Thomas De Quincey: His Life and Writings* (London, 1890)
JEGP	*Journal of English and Germanic Philology*
JFP	John Frederick Pinney
JFW Papers	Wordsworth, Hutchinson, and Monkhouse family papers in the possession of Jonathan Wordsworth
Jordan	John E. Jordan, *De Quincey to Wordsworth* (Berkeley and Los Angeles, 1963)
JPM	Jane Pollard Marshall
JW; JW Sr.	John Wordsworth, brother of W; father of W
JWL	*The Letters of John Wordsworth*, ed. Carl H. Ketcham (Ithaca, 1969)
Kirkpatrick	Robert G. Kirkpatrick, "*Lines Addressed to a Noble*

	Lord: Wordsworth's and Mary Barker's Retort to 'Satanic' Criticism" (forthcoming)
L	(used alone) Lamb
Lady B	Lady Beaumont
Landon *RES*	Carol Landon, "Wordsworth, Coleridge, and the *Morning Post*: An Early Version of 'The Seven Sisters,'" *RES* N.S. XI (1960), 392–402
LB	*Lyrical Ballads*
LB 1800	*Lyrical Ballads, with Other Poems* (London, 1800). 2 vols
LB 1802; *LB* 1805	*Lyrical Ballads, with Pastoral and Other Poems* (London, 1802); the same (London, 1805). Each 2 vols
LdL	Sir William Lowther; from 24 May 1802 Viscount and Baron Lowther; from 7 Apr 1807 Earl of Lonsdale
LG	*The Leech Gatherer* (see General Chronological List, 68)
Life of Bell	Robert Southey and C. C. Southey, *The Life of the Rev. Andrew Bell* (London and Edinburgh, 1844). 3 vols
LL	*The Letters of Charles Lamb, to Which Are Added Those of His Sister Mary Lamb*, ed. E. V. Lucas (London, 1935). 3 vols
LLSYT	*Lines Left upon a Seat in a Yew-tree*
Losh Diary	Diary of James Losh, in Tullie House Library, Carlisle
LY	*The Letters of William and Dorothy Wordsworth, The Later Years*, ed. Ernest de Selincourt (Oxford, 1939). 3 vols
M	(used alone) Monkhouse
Masson	*The Collected Writings of Thomas De Quincey*, ed. David Masson (Edinburgh, 1889–90). 14 vols
MC	*The Morning Chronicle* (London)
Mem	Christopher Wordsworth, *Memoirs of William Wordsworth* (London, 1851). 2 vols
Memorials	*De Quincey Memorials*, ed. A. H. Japp (London, 1891). 2 vols
MH	Mary Hutchinson, from 4 Oct 1802 Mary Wordsworth, wife of W
Minnow	*Minnow among Tritons, Mrs. S. T. Coleridge's Letters to Thomas Poole, 1799–1834*, ed. Stephen Potter (London, 1934)
ML	Mary Lamb

MLN	*Modern Language Notes*
MLR	*Modern Language Review*
MM, MMH	Mary Monkhouse, from 2 Nov 1812 Mary Hutchinson, wife of Thomas Hutchinson
Moore Memoirs	*Memoirs, Journals, and Correspondence of Thomas Moore,* ed. Lord John Russell (London, 1853–56). 8 vols
Moorman I; Moorman II	Mary Moorman, *William Wordsworth, A Biography, The Early Years. 1770–1803* (Oxford, 1957); Mary Moorman, *William Wordsworth, A Biography, The Later Years. 1803–1850* (Oxford, 1965)
MP	*The Morning Post* (London)
Mrs. Gordon	Mrs. Gordon, *"Christopher North," A Memoir of John Wilson* (Edinburgh, 1862). 2 vols
Mus Hum	Jonathan Wordsworth, *The Music of Humanity* (London, 1969)
Musgrove	S. Musgrove, "Unpublished Letters of Thomas De Quincey and Elizabeth Barrett Browning," *Auckland University College Bulletin,* no. 44, English Series no. 7 (1954)
MW	Mary Wordsworth, wife of W
MWL	*The Letters of Mary Wordsworth 1800–1855,* ed. Mary E. Burton (Oxford, 1958)
MY I	*The Letters of William and Dorothy Wordsworth, The Middle Years, Part I, 1806–1811,* ed. Ernest de Selincourt, rev. Mary Moorman (Oxford, 1969)
MY II	*The Letters of William and Dorothy Wordsworth, The Middle Years, Part II, 1812–1820,* ed. Ernest de Selincourt, rev. Mary Moorman and Alan G. Hill (Oxford, 1970)
N&Q	*Notes and Queries*
NB	Notebook
OCB	*The Old Cumberland Beggar*
OMT	*Old Man Travelling. Animal Tranquillity and Decay*
Owen *Anglistica*	*Wordsworth's Preface to Lyrical Ballads,* ed. W. J. B. Owen (*Anglistica* IX) (Copenhagen, 1957)
Owen CSP	W. J. B. Owen, "Costs, Sales, and Profits of Longman's Editions of Wordsworth," *The Library* N.S. XII (1957), 93–107
Owen LLW	"Letters of Longman & Co. to Wordsworth, 1814–36," *The Library* N.S. IX (1954), 25–34

P 1815	*Poems by William Wordsworth* (London, 1815). 2 vols
P 1820	*The Miscellaneous Poems of William Wordsworth* (London, 1820). 4 vols
Parrish *WBS*	Stephen Parrish, "*Michael* and the Pastoral Ballad," *WBS* 50–75
PB	*Peter Bell*
Pearson	*Papers Letters and Journals of William Pearson*, ed. by his widow (London, 1863)
PELY	*Poems, Chiefly of Early and Late Years* (London, 1842)
Penrith	*The Parish Registers of St. Andrew's, Penrith*, comp. J. F. Haswell (Cumberland and Westmorland Antiquarian and Archaeological Society, 1938–). 5 vols pub
PH	Park House
PL	*Paradise Lost*
PML	Pierpont Morgan Library
Pottle *YULG*	Frederick A. Pottle, "An Important Addition to Yale's Wordsworth-Coleridge Collection," *YULG* XLI (1966), 45–59
PP	Papers of the Pinney family on deposit in the Bristol University Library
PR	Parish Register
Prel	*The Prelude*, ed. Ernest de Selincourt, rev. Helen Darbishire (Oxford, 1959)
Prel	*The Prelude*; unless otherwise described or indicated by context, version of 1805, text of Prel
Prel$_2$	*The Prelude*, version of 1850, text of Prel
Prose	*The Prose Works of William Wordsworth*, ed. W. J. B. Owen and Jane W. Smyser (Oxford, 1973), I. See Preface.
P2V	*Poems, in Two Volumes* (London, 1807). 2 vols
P2V H; *P2V* HD	*Poems in Two Volumes*, ed. Thomas Hutchinson (London, 1897), 2 vols; ed. Helen Darbishire (Oxford, 1914)
PW	*Poetical Works*. Where used alone, refers to *The Poetical Works of William Wordsworth*, ed. Ernest de Selincourt and Helen Darbishire (Oxford, 1940–49). 5 vols. Where accompanied by date, refers to edition of W's *PW* of that year, between 1827 and

	1850 (*PW* 1836 refers to the edition of 1836–37; *PW* 1850 refers to the edition of 1849–50).
PW Dowden	*The Poetical Works of William Wordsworth*, ed. Edward Dowden (London, 1892–93). 7 vols
PW Knight, 1882–89	*The Poetical Works of William Wordsworth*, ed. William Knight (London, 1882–89). 11 vols
PW Knight, 1896	*The Poetical Works of William Wordsworth*, ed. William Knight (London, 1896). 8 vols
PW Smith	*The Poems of William Wordsworth*, ed. N. C. Smith (London, 1908). 3 vols
R &C	P. W. Clayden, *Rogers and His Contemporaries* (London 1889). 2 vols
R &I	*Resolution and Independence* (see General Chronological List, 68)
RC	*The Ruined Cottage*
RD	*The River Duddon. A Series of Sonnets: Vaudracour and Julia: and Other Poems. To Which Is Annexed, A Topographical Description of the Country of the Lakes* (London, 1820)
Reed *N &Q*	Mark Reed, "The Wordsworth Letters: New Items, 1810–1815," *N &Q* N.S. XIX (1972), 93–96
RES	*Review of English Studies*
RLP	Thomas De Quincey, *Recollections of the Lake Poets*, ed. Edward Sackville-West (London, 1948)
RM	Rydal Mount
RM Sale Catalogue	*Catalogue of the . . . Library of . . . William Wordsworth . . . Which Will Be Sold by Auction* [19, 20, 21 July 1859], reproduced *Transactions of the Wordsworth Society*, no. 6 (1884), 195–257
Robberds	J. W. Robberds, *A Memoir of the Life and Writings of the Late William Taylor of Norwich* (London, 1843). 2 vols
Rogers *Table-Talk*	*Recollections of the Table-Talk of Samuel Rogers* [ed. Alexander Dyce] (New York, 1856)
RS	Robert Southey
RW	Richard Wordsworth, brother of W
S	(used alone) Southey
SC; SC *Mem*	Sara Coleridge, daughter of STC and SFC; *Memoir and Letters of Sara Coleridge*, ed. Edith Coleridge (London, 1873). 2 vols

8

SEL	*Studies in English Literature*
SFC	Sara Fricker Coleridge, wife of STC
SH	Sara Hutchinson
SHL	*The Letters of Sara Hutchinson*, ed. Kathleen Coburn (London, 1954)
Simmons	Jack Simmons, *Southey* (London, 1945)
Sir GB	Sir George Beaumont
SMJ	Sara Hutchinson's Journal of the 1814 Scotch Tour and/or Mary Wordsworth's derivative journal of the same tour, DC MS 77 (see 1814:44n)
Some Letters	*Some Letters of the Wordsworth Family*, ed. L. N. Broughton (Ithaca and New York, 1942)
SP	*Salisbury Plain*
STC	Samuel Taylor Coleridge
STCL	*Collected Letters of Samuel Taylor Coleridge*, ed. E. L. Griggs (Oxford, 1956–71). 6 vols
STCNB	*The Notebooks of Samuel Taylor Coleridge*, ed. Kathleen Coburn (New York, 1957–). 3 vols (each in 2 parts) pub
STCPW	*The Complete Poetical Works of Samuel Taylor Coleridge*, ed. E. H. Coleridge (Oxford, 1912). 2 vols
Stud Phil	*Studies in Philology*
TA	*Lines Composed a Few Miles above Tintern Abbey*
TCl	Thomas Clarkson
TLS	*Times Literary Supplement* (London)
TofP	*The Tuft of Primroses*
UKL	University of Keele Library
UTL	University of Texas Library
V &A	Victoria and Albert Museum
Venn	J. A. Venn, *Alumni Cantabrigiensis* (Cambridge, England, 1922–54). Unless otherwise stated, information from this source is taken from the article on the person being discussed.
W	Wordsworth. Used alone, except where context indicates otherwise, refers to William Wordsworth (1770–1850).
W and Reed	*Wordsworth and Reed*, ed. L. N. Broughton (Ithaca and New York, 1933)
Ward	William S. Ward, *Literary Reviews in British Periodicals 1798–1820. A Bibliography* (New York, 1972).

	Unless described otherwise, information from this source is taken from the list of reviews of W II, 572–75.
Warter	*Selections from the Letters of Robert Southey*, ed. John Wood Warter (London, 1856). 4 vols
WBS	*Bicentenary Wordsworth Studies in Memory of John Finch*, ed. Jonathan Wordsworth (Ithaca and London, 1970)
WD	*The White Doe of Rylstone*
WDQR	*Written with a Slate Pencil upon a Stone, the Largest of a Heap Lying near a Deserted Quarry, upon One of the Islands at Rydal*
Wells *CC*	J. E. Wells, "The Story of Wordsworth's 'Cintra,'" *Stud Phil* XVIII (1921), 15–76
WofRM	Frederika Beatty, *William Wordsworth of Rydal Mount* (London, 1939)
Woof *Ariel*	R. S. Woof, "John Stoddart, 'Michael,' and *Lyrical Ballads*," *Ariel* I (1970), 7–22
Woof *Inward Eye*	R. S. Woof, "Wordsworth in the North East (a New Light)," *The Inward Eye*, North Now pamphlet no. 1, ed. George Stephenson (Ashington, Northumberland, 1970), 26–38
Woof *SB*	R. S. Woof, "Wordsworth's Poetry and Stuart's Newspapers: 1797–1803," *Studies in Bibliography* XV (1962), 149–89
WSIG	*Written with a Pencil upon a Stone in the Wall of the House (an Out-house), on the Island at Grasmere*
YUL	Yale University Library
YULG	*Yale University Library Gazette*

General Chronological List of Wordsworth's Writings with Their First Published Appearances

Concerning the composition of the following, see also *CEY: The Brothers, The Borderers, A Character, Ellen Irwin, Exc, The Farmer of Tilsbury Vale,* "I Would Not Strike a Flower," *A Night-piece, Nutting*[1], [*Ode to Lycoris, Sequel*] 42–48, *OCB, PB, Prel, Prospectus, Redundance, The Reverie of Poor Susan, RC*

1. *The Prelude* (See also esp. *CEY* 29–31. Except where stated otherwise, dates assigned are based on Appendix V.)

   a. *Prel* I–V

      (1) *Prel* I–II[2]

         a. I.1–54: Possibly composed on or shortly after 18 Nov 1799; perhaps composed c Jan 1800. Fairly certainly completed by 13 Feb 1804. (See Finch THE; *CEY* 30n; Appendix V.)

         b. Two-part stage of *Prel* as MSS U, V, RV (U–V Part I contains what became I.271–304, 310–524, 535–663, V.450–72, and XI.258–65, 274–316, 345–89; U–V–RV Part II contains substantially *Prel* II but includes *Prel*₂ VIII.458–75): RV probably revised, U, V probably written between 26 Nov and 17 Dec 1799. (Appendix V; Jonathan Wordsworth and Stephen Gill, "The Two-part *Prelude* of 1798–9," forthcoming *JEGP*.)

         c. I.55–271, and possibly other passages (unidentified) for final

---

[1] *Nutting* work includes *Travelling* ("This Is the Spot"), composed between possibly 14, probably 21 or 28 Dec 1798 and 4 May 1802, lines 6–9 composed by c 5 June 1800 (see *PW* IV, 423–24; *CEY* 35, 331–32; 1802:118).

[2] On materials contributive to II.321–41, see *CEY* 30. (These materials contributed also to *Prel* VII.716–29. See also *Prel* 566.) On materials contributive to *Prel* II.416–34 see esp. *CEY* 30. Texts of the 1799 two-part stage of the poem (see 1. *a.* (1). *b.*) are forthcoming in editions by Jonathan Wordsworth and Stephen Gill, in *JEGP* and in a Norton Critical Edition of *The Prelude*; by Stephen M. Parrish, in the Cornell Wordsworth Series; and by Michael Jaye.

1805 version of I–II: Possibly composed c early 1801, by 3 Apr; more probably between c 14 Jan and 13 Feb 1804.

    d. MSS U–V–RV stage probably corrected between 29 Sept and 3 Apr 1801. Corrections to MS V possibly c early 1801; probably between 29 Sept 1800 and early 1804.

(2) *Prel* III[3]: Some composition toward opening of book (esp. in DC MS 16) probably 1801; some composition possibly esp. c Apr–May 1801; other composition perhaps 26 Dec, 27 Dec, possibly also 28 Dec 1801. Other composition perhaps 1803, including possibly 11 Jan 1803. Probably largely composed by 13 Feb 1804. Certainly completed as MS M by 18 Mar 1804.

(3) *Prel* IV[4]

    a. IV, including c183–92, 201, 204–c21 as MS WW; 270–345 [see PREL 535], 353–65 as MS W: Probably mostly composed, except 363–504, between c 14 Jan and 18 Mar 1804.

    b. Prose draft, basis of *Prel*$_2$ IV.354–70, DC MS 28: Probably composed between c late June and early Sept 1806. (Appendix VI.)

(4) *Prel* V[5], including 17–37, 44–60, 103, 113, 121–35, 149–65, 301–02, c313–18, 322–25, 329–33, 336–37, 349, 473–500, 538–48, 551–57, c588–c607 as MS WW; 1–7, 10, 19–25, 28–48, 294–376, 445–515, 590–94, 630–37, lines quoted PREL 620–28 as MS W; *Prel* V as MS M: Probably mainly composed between c 14 Jan and 18 Mar 1804. Organized as MS M probably between 6 and c 12 Mar 1804.

(5) *Prel* I–V, MS M: Probably written between c but by 6 Mar and 18 Mar 1804.

b. *Prel* VI–XIII

(1) *Prel* VI[6]

    a. VI.220–30, c323–c27, 347–54, 426–27, 469–c86, 494–97,

---

[3] On III.124–67 see *CEY* 30.

[4] On IV.363–504 see *CEY* 29–30.

[5] On V.370–88 and lines quoted PREL 545–46, and *PW* V, 345–46, see *CEY* 326. On V.389–422 see *CEY* 30. On V.450–72 see above, I. a. (1). *b.*

[6] On VI.553–72 see *CEY* 31 and below, 641–42, 652.

500–19, 524–30 as MS WW: Probably written between c 14 Jan and 29 Apr 1804 (on c323–c27 see *c* below).

b. Bulk of VI; VI.1–54 and probably other lines as MS X: Bulk of book perhaps organized, MS X materials perhaps written between late Mar and 29 Apr 1804.

c. VI.246–331: Probably composed late Mar, by 29 Mar 1804.

d. VI.61–62, and probably surrounding lines, including 55–69: Probably composed between 1 and 14 Apr 1804.

e. *Prel*$_2$ VI.420–88 (see PREL 556–57): Perhaps basically composed between 6 Apr and early autumn 1808. (See *PW* V, 483.)

(2) *Prel* VII

a. Drafts contributive to VII.699–706 ("Shall He Who Gives His Days to Low Pursuits"; see PREL 566): Probably composed 1800 between c early Oct, certainly a time by 11 Oct, and perhaps 9 Dec, certainly by 19 Dec. (1800:149.)

b. VII.75–740 as MS X: Perhaps written between late Mar and 13 June 1804; possibly between early Oct and late autumn 1804.

c. VII.43–c50 as MS Y; VII.1–74: Probably written between early Oct and late autumn 1804.

(3) *Prel* VIII[7]

a. VIII.222–311 ("The Matron's Tale"): Perhaps composed between c early Oct 1800 and c Apr 1801. DC MS 31 draft probably written between early Feb and c Apr 1801. (1800:148; 1800:149n.)

b. VIII.711–17, 720–24, 727 as MS WW; 860–70 as MS W: Probably composed between c 14 Jan and 13 June 1804.

c. VIII.736–38, 742–51 as MS X: Probably written between late Mar and 13 June 1804.

d. Bulk of VIII; lines in MS Y, replaced by VIII.159–72, quoted PREL 571–78 ("Two feelings have we"); lines in MS Y originally following VIII.497, quoted PREL 581; VIII.[68–405], [406–35], 436–661, materials toward 802–15, 824–59 as MS Y: Probably composed between early Oct and late autumn 1804.

(4) *Prel* IX, including 293–[c521] as MS Y, and the lines pub. *P* 1820 as *Vaudracour and Julia* (IX.555–934): Indeterminate amount of

[7] On *Prel*$_2$ VIII.458–75 see above, I. a. (1) *b*.

composition perhaps between late Mar and 13 June 1804; other, including specified, composition probably between early Oct and late autumn 1804.

(5) *Prel* X

    a. X, including materials toward X.445–66, 568–74 as DC MS 74: Indeterminate amount of composition possibly between late Mar and 13 June 1804; other, including specified, composition possibly between early Oct and late autumn 1804.

    b. X.933–34, and many surrounding lines, including 922–41: Probably composed shortly after 2 Dec 1804.

(6) *Prel* XI[8]

    a. Large part of XI, including 42–44, 121–64, c176–85, 199–257, 274–77, 316–45 as MS W: Perhaps written between late Mar and 13 June 1804; perhaps not organized as book until late 1804 or early 1805.

    b. XI.9–14, c48–c56 as MS Y: Probably written between early Oct and late autumn 1804.

    c. XI.1–41 as MS Z: Perhaps written late 1804 or early 1805.

    d. XI.42–397 as MS Z: Perhaps written late Apr or early May 1805.

    e. Draft toward XI.164–90, Windy Brow NB: Perhaps written late Apr or early May 1805, but certainly before MS Z.

(7) *Prel* XII[9]

    a. Drafts contributive to 185–204 in DC MS 31: Probably written 1800 between c early Oct, certainly a time by 11 Oct, and perhaps 9 Dec, certainly by 19 Dec. (See 1800:148; 1800:149.)

    b. Bulk of XII: Probably largely composed between early Oct 1804 and early 1805.

    c. XII.112–277, 300–04 as MS Y: Probably written between early Oct and late autumn 1804.

    d. XII as MS Z: Perhaps written late Apr or early May 1805; certainly completed by c 19 May 1805.

---

[8] On XI.15–22, 214–21, see *CEY* 31. On XI.258–65, 274–316, 345–89, see above 1. a. (1). *b.*, and note 2.

[9] On materials toward XII.194–201 (see *PW* V, 344–45) see *CEY* 30–31.

(8) *Prel* XIII[10]

    a. XIII.1–128, including 1–38, 66–90, 93–94 [see p. 641], Prel 623–28 lines 1–7, 31–47, as MS WW, and all, including Prel 620–29, as MS W: Probably composed between c 14 Jan and c 12 Mar 1804.

    b. XIII.154–84 as MS W: Perhaps written between 6 Mar and 13 June 1804.

    c. XIII.334–67, 374–85 as MS Y: Probably written between early Oct and late autumn 1804.

    d. Bulk of XIII: Probably finally organized early 1805, perhaps c early May.

c. I–XIII

(1) I–XIII probably finished in early complete form c 20 May 1805.

(2) Early completed MSS

    a. MS A: First five books probably written between late Nov and 14 Dec 1805; eight books written by 25 Dec; remainder written by 2 Mar 1806.

    b. MS B: Probably written between c early Jan and 2 Mar 1806.

I.213–19 pub. as epigraph to *Composed at Cora Linn, P* 1820. I.428–89 pub. *The Friend* 28 Dec 1809. V.389–422 ("There Was a Boy") pub. *LB* 1800. *Prel₂* VI.448–50 pub. *Essay, Supplementary, P* 1815. VI.553–72 (*The Simplon Pass*) pub. *Kendal and Windermere Railway*, 1845. Drafts contributive to VII.699–706 pub. *PW* Knight, 1882–89 IX, 381–82. VIII.221–311 ("The Matron's Tale") as DC MS 31 pub. *PW* Knight, 1882–89 IX, 382–87. IX.555–934 pub. as *Vaudracour and Julia, P* 1820. X.690–711 pub. *The Friend* 26 Oct 1809. XII.223–77 pub. *Postscript* 1835. *Prel₂* pub. 1850.

2. *On Seeing Some Tourists of the Lakes Pass by Reading: a Practise Very Common*
    Probably composed between 1800 and early Apr 1807, possibly c late July 1800. (Appendix VII; *STCNB* 760.)[11]

---

[10] On XIII.211–45 also see below GCL 8.

[11] *STCNB* 760, probably dating from July 1800 and from a time when STC was with W (see 1800:74), notes an instance of the sort about which W complains; but a connection between this entry and the verses remains only a remote possibility.

Pub. Hale White.

3. "Orchard Pathway" (*PW* IV, 374)
Probably composed between 1800 and late Feb 1807. (See 1800:122n; Appendix VII.)
Pub. Hale White.

4. *The Affliction of Margaret*
The Forsaken
Probably composed between c 1800 and c early Jan 1807; perhaps esp. c 1800, spring 1802, or between late Mar 1804 and c early Jan 1807. (Appendix V; Appendix VII.)[12]
The Affliction of Margaret pub. *P2V*. Introduction to *The Affliction* pub. Hale White. *The Forsaken* pub. *PELY*.

5. *The Recluse* I. *Home at Grasmere* (Dates assigned are based on Appendix VI.)
a. First stages of composition (see 1800:14): Some parts, including portions of 71–79, 170–92, 238–68, 471–90, 502–44, 648–63 perhaps begun c early 1800. *HG* 648–63 perhaps composed between late Jan and late Feb 1800.

---

[12] There seems no cause to doubt W's statement in the IF note to *The Affliction* that *The Forsaken* was an overflow from that poem; but the date of 1804 there (and in editions 1836–1850) assigned to *The Affliction* may be late. W's note in the *P2V* MS, "Written for the Lyrical Ballads" (see Hale White 63) implies an earlier date. W is not known to have composed new poems for introduction into *LB* after 1800. The rejected introduction to the poem (see Hale White 63; *PW* II, 476) exemplifies a structural practice esp. common in W's poems between late 1798 and 1800 (employed in *Address to the Scholars*, "'Tis Said That Some Have Died for Love," *The Pet Lamb*, *The Oak and the Broom*, the last part of *The Waterfall and the Eglantine*). Two of the three works in *P2V* that employ the device are methodically imitative of the traditional rather than "Lyrical" ballad (*Rob Roy* and *Song at the Feast of Brougham Castle*; *The Emigrant Mother*, of which the introductory stanzas do not in fact appear in the earliest MS, DC MS 41, is not). The possibility remains that the subtitle "Written for the Lyrical Ballads" might have been used for a poem written after 1800 but deliberately in the style of *LB*. Curtis 222 (*q.v.*), noticing similarities to *The Sailor's Mother*, *Alice Fell*, and *Beggars*, "all poems in the mode of *Lyrical Ballads*," suggests spring 1802. *P2V* H suggests a date "some years earlier" than 1804; *P2V* HD suggests "probably 1801"; EdS suggests "1801?" Neither poem, however, appears in MS M, of early 1804 (see Appendix III). The evidence does not appear to justify a very exact dating.

HG 170–92 perhaps composed c but after 10 Mar 1800, possibly in form resembling *PW* V, 319–20 *app crit* for lines 170–71.

    b. MS A (DC MS 58), including basis of *Water Fowl* (as *HG* 203–29 and *PW* V, 321 *app crit*): Probably written between c late June and early Sept 1806.

    c. MS R (DC MS 28): Probably written, except for 75–77 and 597–607 (which are toward late MS D), between c late June and early Sept 1806 but before MS B.

    d. MS B (DC MS 59): 1–116 probably written between c late June and early Sept 1806; 117–end probably written between July and early Sept.

    HG 122–25 pub. *G* 1810. *HG* 80–125 ("On Nature's Invitation"), 152–68 ("Bleak Season Was It"), 703, 705–08, 708–13 pub. *Mem. Water Fowl* pub. *G* 1823 (cf *PW* V, 477).

6. Motto for *Poems on the Naming of Places* (*PW* II, 486)
    Probably composed between 1800 and 6 Mar 1804. (Content; Appendix III.)

7. "I Have Been Here in the Moonlight" (*PW* IV, 365)
    Probably composed between 1800 and 6 Mar 1804; perhaps c 22 Apr 1802. (Content; 1802:104; Appendix III.)[13]

8. Fragment: "Witness thou/The dear companion of my lonely walk" (*PW* V, 347, VII, ii)
    Probably composed between 1800 and 4 Oct 1802, fairly certainly by 18 Mar 1804. (*STCNB* 2429 & n; *PW* Knight, 1896 VIII, xi–xii; Appendix V.)[14]

[13] The content of the lines is possibly connected with events, and DW's description of them, of 22 Apr 1802; cf *DWJ* M 114. The verses fairly certainly date from W's Grasmere residence, and since they appear in MS M, they were probably written by 6 Mar 1804.

[14] The fragment was almost certainly written before STC departed from London for Malta and is likely to have been composed at Grasmere (*STCNB* 2429 & n). More specifically, the content and possible priority of the lines to *Prel* XII.211–45 suggest that the lines were intended for *Prel* but composed before W's marriage. *STCNB* 2429n states that the lines were printed by Knight as "'extracted from Dorothy Wordsworth's Grasmere Journal, 1802': *WPW* (Knight) VIII 234." *PW* Knight, 1896 VIII, 233 does state that the fragment is among ones "extracted from [W's] sisters' Grasmere Journal," but mentions the date only in the index, VIII, xi–xii. Knight's first publication of the fragment (1882–89 IX, 389) is unaccompanied by date.

9. "There Is an Eminence,—of These Our Hills"
Probably composed 1800, certainly by 18 Dec 1800; possibly basically c Jan. (1800:1.)
Pub. *LB* 1800.

10. Fragments: Blank verse drafts concerning characters named Mary and Lennox, a yew-tree, and the composing effect of the yew-tree on Mary's thoughts, in DC MS 33.
Probably written 1800 by 15 Oct. (1800:2.)

11. "It Was an April Morning: Fresh and Clear"
Probably composed 1800, certainly by 15 Oct 1800: perhaps between Apr and 13 Oct. (1800:3.)
Pub. *LB* 1800.

12. *Rural Architecture*
Probably composed 1800, certainly by 10 Oct 1800. (1800:4.)
Pub. *LB* 1800.

13. *The Childless Father*
The Pet Lamb
Probably composed 1800, certainly by 15 Sept 1800. (1800:5.)
Pub. *LB* 1800.

14. *For the Spot Where the Hermitage Stood on St. Herbert's Island, Derwentwater*
Probably composed in *LB* 1800 form 1800, certainly by 13 Aug 1800; extensively revised toward *P* 1815 version probably c early Nov, certainly by 16 Nov, 1811; further revised by 20 Nov 1811. (1800:6; 1811:61; 1811:63.)
Pub. *LB* 1800.

15. *Song for the Wandering Jew*
"'Tis Said, That Some Have Died for Love"
Probably composed 1800, certainly by 13 Aug 1800. (*CEY* 325–26.)
Pub. *LB* 1800.

16. *Written with a Pencil upon a Stone in the Wall of the House (an Out-house), on the Island at Grasmere*
Probably composed 1800 by early June, certainly by 13 Aug 1800. (1800:8.)
Pub. *LB* 1800.

17. *Written with a Slate Pencil upon a Stone, the Largest of a Heap Lying near a Deserted Quarry, upon One of the Islands at Rydal*
    Probably composed 1800, certainly by 4 Aug 1800, except final version of lines 1–9, probably composed c but by 13 Aug. (1800:8.)
    Pub. *LB* 1800.

18. *The Oak and the Broom*
    The Waterfall and the Eglantine
    Probably composed 1800, certainly by 4 Aug 1800. (1800:10.)
    Pub. *LB* 1800.

19. *The Two Thieves*
    Probably composed 1800 by 29 July. (1800:11.)
    Pub. *LB* 1800.

20. *The Idle Shepherd-boys*
    Probably composed 1800, certainly by 29 July 1800. (1800:12.)
    Pub. *LB* 1800.

21. *Hart-leap Well*
    Probably composed early 1800, certainly by c early June 1800. (1800:13.)
    Pub. *LB* 1800.

22. *Preface* to *LB* 1800
    Probably basically composed between 29 June and 27 Sept 1800. MS corrections toward *LB* 1800 readings by 1 Oct 1800. Further corrections 5 Oct (not surviving), 6, possibly 7 Oct, 18 Dec. (1800:74; 1800:154; 1800:155; 1800:229. See GCL 37, 43.)
    Pub. *LB* 1800.

23. Preface to *The Borderers*, as DC MS 27
    Perhaps written between mid-July and 29 Sept 1800. (1800:78.)

24. "A Narrow Girdle of Rough Stones and Crags"
    Probably composed between 23 July and 6 Nov 1800, perhaps in part between 23 July and 26 Sept. Probably composed in part 10 Oct. (1800:83; 1800:142.)
    Pub. *LB* 1800.

25. *The Seven Sisters*
Probably composed c but by 17 Aug 1800. (1800:108.)
Pub. *MP* 14 Oct 1800.

26. *To Joanna*, and Note
To Joanna probably composed c but by 23 Aug 1800. Note probably written between that time and 15 Oct. (1800:115.)
Pub. *LB* 1800.

27. "When to the Attractions of the Busy World"
A first version composed 29–30 Aug 1800. Some parts, probably including most or all of lines 67–110, probably composed between that time and 6 Mar 1804. MS 2 (DC MS 46) possibly between c mid-Feb 1804 and late 1805. Drafts toward *P* 1815 version, DC MS 80, and completion of *P* 1815 version, probably between 9 Sept and late Oct 1814. (1800:122; 1800:123; 1804:22; 1814:94.)
Pub. *P* 1815.

28. A Character[15]
Probably completed in 1800 *LB* form between 13 Sept and 15 Oct 1800. (See *Ariel* discussion; 1800:135; *CEY* 323–27.)

29. *FV*: Corrections as *EY* 322–24
Probably composed between 29 Sept 1800 and 9 Apr 1801. (1800:146.)

30. *Michael*
a. *Michael*, *LB* 1800 version
Rhymed verses associated with *Michael* (see *WBS* 72–75)
Fragments of blank verse associated with *Michael* quoted *PW* II, 479–84: these include lines drawn on for *Musings near Aquapendente* 47–52 and for *Prel* VII.699–706, VIII.222–311 ("The Matron's Tale"), and XII. 185–203
Probably composed between c early Oct, certainly a time by 11 Oct, and perhaps 9 Dec, certainly by 19 Dec, 1800, except for lines used *Prel* VIII.222–311, on which see above GCL 1.b.(3). (1800:149.)
b. *Michael* lines transcribed *EY* 324 in letter to Poole of 9 Apr 1801: Probably composed between early Feb and 9 Apr 1801. (1801:12.)
Associated verses quoted *PW* II, 482–83 (b), 1–25, 27–28, pub. *PW*

---

[15] On early composition see *CEY* 29, 323.

Knight, 1882–89 IX, 388. *Musings near Aquapendente* pub. *PELY*. *Michael* pub. *LB* 1800. Rhymed verses pub. Parrish *WBS*.

31. Fragments: Drafts in Christabel NB quoted *PW* V, 342–44, i–viii; other drafts in same NB possibly describing water droplets on moss; others in same NB concerning the Niger
    Probably written about the general time of the composition of *Michael* (see GCL 30).

32. Notes to *The Thorn*, *AM*, as *LB* 1800
    Probably written late Sept, certainly by 30 Sept, 1800. (1800:147.)

33. "I Travelled among Unknown Men"
    Probably composed c but by 29 Apr 1801. (1801:41.)
    Pub. *P2V*.

34. *Peter Bell*[16]
    a. MS 2 (DC MS 33)
       MS 3 (DC MS 34)
       Probably written between 9 Nov 1801 and 22 Jan 1802, possibly between 16 and 26 July or 24 Sept and 2 Oct 1802. (1801:91.)
    b. MS 4 (in DC MS 44): Part 2 written 17 Feb 1802; Part 3, 18 Feb; Part 1, 20 Feb; Second Prologue, 21 Feb; First Prologue, later on 21 Feb. (1802:38–1802:42.)
    c. MS 5 (DC MS 60): Probably written between 30 Oct 1806 and mid-Apr 1807. (1806:93.)
    d. MS 6 (DC MS 72): Probably written c but by 29 Mar 1812. (1812:17.)
       Pub. 1819.

35. *Repentance*
    Probably basically composed between 24 Nov 1801 and mid-1802, perhaps c Apr 1802. Perhaps heavily revised c 1815 but not before c Mar 1815; fairly certainly completed between c Mar 1815 and c early 1820. (1801:108; GCL 222n.)
    Pub. *P* 1820.

36. *Troilus and Cressida* (adaptation from Chaucer; only a fragment of MS, lines 47–91, survives)
    Perhaps composed c Dec 1801. (1801:115.)
    Pub. *Chaucer Modernized* 1841.

[16] On *PB* MS 1 see *CEY* 32–33.

37. Essay for second volume of *LB* 1800 (surviving only in a fragment, if at all, and probably never complete, but perhaps contributive to 1802 Appendix and 1815 *Essay, Supplementary*.
    Draft perhaps toward this essay in DC MS 28.
    Probably written between 3 Oct and 18 Dec 1800. (Appendix IV; 1800: 74; 1800:152.)

38. *The Manciple's Tale* (adaptation from Chaucer; *PW* IV, 358–65)
    Probably composed 2–c 3 Dec 1801; some correction perhaps 28 Apr 1802. (1801:117.)

39. *The Prioress's Tale* (adaptation from Chaucer)
    Probably composed 4–5 Dec 1801; some correction perhaps 28 Apr 1802. (1801:119.)
    Pub. *P* 1820.

40. *The Cuckoo and the Nightingale* (adaptation of work assumed by W to be by Chaucer)
    Probably composed 7–9 Dec 1801. (1801:122; 1801:123; 1801:124.)
    Pub. *Chaucer Modernized* 1841.

41. *The Ruined Cottage*[17]
    a. Addenda iv, v (*PW* V, 405–09): Probably written between 21 Dec 1801 and 6 Mar 1802. (Appendix VI.)
    b. MSS E, E$_2$ (DC MS 37): MS E perhaps written late 1803 or early 1804; MS E$_2$ probably written c early Mar 1804. (Appendix VI.)
    c. MS M: Probably written between 6 and 18 Mar 1804. (Appendix VI.)

42. *The Excursion* (Except where stated otherwise, dates assigned are based on Appendix VI.)
    a. Summary by books[18]
        I. *a.* Drafts toward I.66–111 in DC MS 69: Probably written between c Dec 1809 and Mar 1812, esp. between c Dec 1809 and c late May 1810, between c early May and c early July 1811, or between late Aug 1811 and Mar 1812, before MS P (DC MS 71).
        b. As MS P, DC MS 71: Probably written between c Dec 1809 and Mar 1812, esp. within periods cited I.*a.*

[17] On the early development of *RC* see also *CEY* 27–28. On MS P see GCL 42 and Appendix VI.
[18] For summary of dates of MSS see Appendix VI.

II. *a.* II.1–26 as DC MS 48: Probably written between early Oct and late autumn 1804. (Appendix V.)

   b. II.1–c725, 741–63 as DC MS 47, and Tale of Old Man (c730–826, 881–95): Remotely possibly written in basic form c Sept 1806; probably written between c Dec 1809 and c late May 1810, before MS P (DC MS 71).

   c. II.153–320 as DC MS 70: Probably written between c Dec 1809 and Mar 1812, esp. in periods cited I.*a.*, before MS P.

   d. Basic MS of MS P: Probably written between c Dec 1809 and Mar 1812, esp. in periods cited I.*a.*

   e. II.39–319, inserts in MS P (including first account of Solitary's marriage): Probably written between 3 Jan 1813 and c late May 1814.

III. *a.* III.367–405 in *TofP* form: Probably written between 6 Apr and early autumn 1808. (1808:36.)

   b. III.20–22, 30–47, 143–64, 303–24, 367–78, probable draft for most of III, in DC MS 69: Probably written between c Dec 1809 and Mar 1812, esp. in periods cited I.*a.*, before MS P. (DC MS 71.)

   c. III.967–88 as DC MS 73. As III.*b.*, before MS P.

   d. III.1–324 as MS P: Probably written between c Dec 1809 and Mar 1812, esp. in periods cited I.*a.*

   e. III.325–991 as MS P, including inserts, with materials later drawn upon for *Characteristics of a Child Three Years Old* and *Maternal Grief*: Probably written between 3 Jan 1813 and c late May 1814. 584–98 (*PW* V, 95 *app crit*, lines 2–6): Probably written c but not before 8 Jan 1813.

IV.[19] *a.* IV.402–12, 763–65 as DC MS 48: Probably between early Oct and late autumn 1804. (Appendix V.)

   b. IV.332–72 as DC MS 28: Probably written basically between July and early Sept 1806.

   c. IV.332–825, 851–1119, 1130–47, 1307–15 as DC MS 70: Probably written between c Dec 1809 and Mar 1812, esp. in periods cited I.*a.*

   d. IV.83–91, 1158–1290, including materials *PW* V, 429–30 (1), (2) as DC MS 60: Probably written between 3 Jan 1813 and c late May 1814.

   e. IV.9–c26, c108–329, 676–[?758], 759–62; probably most of 1–762

---

[19] Concerning VI.958–68, 1207–75 see *CEY* 28.

as DC MS 69 (all but 759–62 indicated by stubs only): Perhaps written between 3 Jan 1813 and c late May 1814.

V. *a.* V.1–10, c100–104, 168–c225 as DC MS 70: Probably written between c Dec 1809 and Mar 1812, esp. within periods cited I.*a.*

b. V.264–365, 485–557, c897–921, c978, 1002–16 as DC MS 74: Probably written between 3 Jan 1813 and c late May 1814.

c. V.308–672, as indicated by stubs, DC MS 69: Perhaps written between 3 Jan 1813 and c late May 1814. Materials corresponding to materials in DC MS 74 are later than MS 74.

d. V.922–43 as DC MS 75: Probably written c but by 6 Mar 1813.

e. V.1–1016 as DC MS 74A: Perhaps written c early 1814.

VI. *a.* VI.1080–1187 as DC MS 28: Basically composed between July and early Sept 1806.

b. VI.787–805 as DC MS 75: Probably written between 3 Jan 1813 and c late May 1814.

c. VI.573–1267 as DC MS 74: Probably written between 3 Jan 1813 and c late May 1814. Materials corresponding to materials in DC MS 75 are later than MS 75.

d. VI.1–211, 275–521 as DC MS 73: Probably written between 3 Jan 1813 and c late May 1814. Materials corresponding to materials in MS 74 are later than MS 74.

VII. *a.* VII.242–91 in *TofP* form: Probably written between 6 Apr and early autumn 1808. (1808:36.)

b. VII.395–481 as *Essays upon Epitaphs*: Probably composed c Dec 1809 or early 1810 by 28 Feb.

c. HUL MS of VII.535–c575[20]: Possibly written between c Dec 1809 and c late May 1810; fairly certainly between c Dec 1809 and c late May 1814.

d. VII.30–58, 201–36, 252–85, c529, c780–816, 821–30, c849–58 as DC MS 75: Probably written between 3 Jan 1813 and c late May 1814. Draft for VII.c529 probably c but by 6 Mar 1813. Materials up to line 285 corresponding to materials in DC MS 74 are later than MS 74; other corresponding materials precede MS 74. Materials up to line 285 perhaps copied early 1814.

e. VII.1–268, 302–400, 482–695, 878–1057 as DC MS 74: Probably written between 3 Jan 1813 and c late May 1814. Materials

---

[20] This draft MS, which precedes the corresponding lines in MS 74, is written on the cover of a letter addressed to "Capt. Luff / &c- &c- &c- / Patterdale / Penrith." No indication of the date of the letter remains. Luff departed the Lakes area c early 1812 (see SHL 46), but W could of course have written on this cover after that time.

corresponding to materials in DC MS 75 follow MS 75, except for drafts toward 1–268, which precede corresponding materials in MS 74.

VIII.[21] *a.* VIII.459–571 as DC MS 75: Probably written between 3 Jan 1813 and c late May 1814.

   b. VIII.1–486, [487–591], 592–601 as DC MS 74: Probably written between 3 Jan 1813 and c late May 1814. Materials corresponding to materials in DC MS 75 are later than MS 75.

IX.[22] *a.* IX.437–48 as DC MS 48: Probably written between early Oct and late autumn 1804. (Appendix V.)

   b. IX.57–92, 105–c130, c156–78, as DC MS 75: Probably written between 3 Jan 1813 and c late May 1814.

   c. IX.3–c397 as DC MS 74: Probably written between 3 Jan 1813 and c late May 1814. Materials corresponding to materials in DC MS 75 are later than MS 75.

   d. IX.293–796 as DC MS 73: Probably written between 3 Jan 1813 and c late May 1814. Materials corresponding to materials in DC MS 74 are later than MS 74.

b. Materials quoted or described:

   1. *PW* V, 429–30 as DC MS 73: Probably written between 3 Jan 1813 and c late May 1814.

   2. *PW* V, 432–41 as DC MS 74 ("The Peasant's Life"): Probably written between 3 Jan 1813 and c late May 1814.

   3. *PW* V, 461–62 as DC MS 74 ("The Shepherd of Bield Crag"): Probably written between 3 Jan 1813 and c late May 1814, but possibly earlier—probably not in any case before c Dec 1809.

   4. *PW* V, 466, in DC MS 75: Probably between 3 Jan 1813 and c late May 1814.

c. Lines not otherwise accounted for probably composed between c Dec 1809 and c late May 1814, esp. within periods cited I.*a.* For more detailed comment see Appendix VI.

   Exc I.500–02 pub. *The Friend* 25 Jan 1810. *Exc* I.626–34 pub. *The Friend* 16 Nov 1809. *The Excursion* pub. 17 Aug 1814. (*MC.*)

43. Additions to Preface to *LB* for *LB* 1802
   Appendix, 1802
   Revision and copy for *LB* 1802
   Perhaps composed early 1802, by 6 Apr. (1802:1.)

[21] Concerning VIII.276–334 as DC MS 16 see *CEY* 35, 326–27.
[22] Concerning IX.1–26, 124–52 as DC MS 16 see *CEY* 35, 326–27; *PW* V, 286–91.

44. *Louisa*
    To a Young Lady Who Had Been Reproached for Taking Long Walks in the Country
    Perhaps composed 1802 between 23 and 27 Jan, certainly by 9 Feb. (1802:13.)
    Louisa pub. *P2V. To a Young Lady* pub. *MP* 12 Feb 1802.

45. *To a Sky-lark* ("Up with Me!")
    Probably composed between c Mar and 29 July 1802. (1802:50.)
    Pub. *P2V.*

46. *The Sparrow's Nest*
    Probably composed c Mar–Apr, certainly by 7 May, 1802. (1802:50.)
    Pub. *P2V.*

47. *The Sailor's Mother*
    Composed 11, 12 Mar 1802. (1802:61; 1802:62.)
    Pub. *P2V.*

48. *Alice Fell*
    Composed 12, 13 Mar 1802. (1802:62; 1802:63.)
    Pub. *P2V.*

49. *Beggars*
    Composed 13, 14 Mar 1802. (1802:63; 1802:64.)
    Pub. *P2V.*

50. *To a Butterfly* ("Stay near Me")
    Composed 14 Mar 1802. (1802:64.)
    Pub. *P2V.*

51. *The Emigrant Mother*
    Composed 16, 17 Mar 1802. (1802:66; 1802:67.)
    Pub. *P2V.*

52. *To the Cuckoo*
    Perhaps largely composed 23–26 Mar 1802; further composition possibly c and on 14 May, and possibly c and on 3 June. (1802:73; 1802:128; 1802:155.)
    Pub. *P2V.*

53. "My Heart Leaps Up"
    Probably composed 26 Mar 1802. (1802:76.)
    Pub. *P2V.*

54. *Ode. Intimations of Immortality*
    Probably some or all of stanzas I–IV composed 27 Mar 1802. Further
    composition—possibly including some or, less probably, all of stanzas
    V–VIII—on 17 June 1802. Most of last seven stanzas probably composed,
    and the poem completed, probably early 1804, by 6 Mar. (1802:77;
    1802:167; 1804:3.)
    Pub. *P2V.*

55. *To H.C. Six Years Old*
    Possibly composed between 27 Mar and c 17 June 1802, or, more prob-
    ably, early 1804, by 6 Mar; fairly certainly between the earliest and latest
    of these dates. (1802:77; 1802:167.)
    Pub. *P2V.*

56. *The Glow-worm* ("Among All Lovely Things My Love Had Been")
    Composed 12 Apr 1802. (1802:92.)
    Pub. *P2V.*

57. *Written in March*
    Composed 16 Apr 1802. (1802:96. Cf *PW* II, 539.)
    Pub. *P2V.*

58. *The Green Linnet*
    To the Daisy ("In Youth")
    Perhaps composed between 16 Apr and 8 July 1802. (1802:97.)
    Pub. *P2V.*

59. *To the Daisy* ("Bright Flower!")
    To the Daisy ("With Little Here")
    Perhaps composed at least in part between 16 Apr and 8 July 1802.
    Possibly not fully developed or written until between 6 Mar 1804 and c
    Mar 1805. (1802:97; Appendix VII.)
    Pub. *P2V.*

60. *The Redbreast Chasing the Butterfly*
    Composed 18 Apr 1802. (1802:99.)
    Pub. *P2V.*

61. *To a Butterfly* ("I've Watched You Now")
   Composed 20 Apr 1802. (1802:101. See 1802:64.)
   Pub. *P2V*.

62. *The Barberry Tree*
   Probably composed between late Apr and June 1802. (1802:102.)
   Pub. *The New Statesman* 31 July 1964.

63. "These Chairs They Have No Words to Utter" (*PW* IV, 365)
   Half an Hour Afterwards ("I Have Thoughts That Are Fed by the Sun")
   (*PW* IV, 365–66)
   Probably composed c but by, "I Have Thoughts" certainly by, 22 Apr
   1802. (1802:104. See also GCL 7.)

64. *The Tinker*
   Composed 27, 28, 29 Apr 1802. (1802:109–1802:112.)
   Pub. Hale White.

65. *Foresight*
   Composed 28 Apr 1802. (1802:110.)
   Pub. *P2V*.

66. *To the Small Celandine* ("Pansies, Lilies")
   Probably composed 30 Apr–1 May 1802. (1802:113; 1802:114.)
   Pub. *P2V*.

67. *To the Same Flower* ("Pleasures Newly Found")
   Probably composed 1 May 1802. (1802-114.)
   Pub. *P2V*.

68. *Resolution and Independence* (referred to in *DWJ* as *The Leech Gatherer*;
   referred to in *Chronology* as *LG* through 5 July 1802, as *R &I* thereafter)
   A first version (see *PW* II, 539–41) composed 3–7 May 1802; revised 9
   May. Heavy revision, probably basically to *PW R &I* "MS" form,
   perhaps between 14 June and 4 July 1802. Probably completed basically
   in *PW R &I* "MS" form 4 July 1802. (1802:116; 1802:118; 1802:121;
   1802:164; 1802:183; 1802:184.)
   Pub. *P2V*.

69. *Travelling* (*PW* II, 543; *PW* IV, 423–24)
   Perhaps composed in form of *PW* II, 543 c but by 4 May 1802; certainly

between completion of long form of *Nutting* (see *CEY* GCL 83) and 4 May 1802; in form of *PW* IV, 423–24, by 6 Mar 1804. (1802:117.)

70. *Stanzas Written in My Pocket-copy of Thomson's "Castle of Indolence"*
    Probably composed 9, 10, 11 May 1802. (1802:123–1802:125.)
    Pub. *P* 1815.

71. *1801* ("I Grieved for Buonaparté")
    Probably composed 21 May 1802. (1802:136.)
    Pub. *MP* 16 Sept 1802. (See Woof *SB* 183.)

72. *On the Extinction of the Venetian Republic*
    Probably composed between 21 May 1802 and early Feb 1807. (1802:136; 1803:15n; Appendix VII.)
    Pub. *P2V*.

73. "How Sweet It Is, When Mother Fancy Rocks"
    Personal Talk:
      i. ("I Am Not One Who Much or Oft Delight")
      ii. ("'Yet Life,' You Say, 'Is Life; We Have Seen and See'")
      iii. ("Wings Have We,—and as Far as We Can Go")
      iv. ("Nor Can I Not Believe but That Hereby")
    "Pelion and Ossa Flourish Side by Side"
    "The World Is Too Much with Us; Late and Soon"
    To the Memory of Raisley Calvert
    "Where Lies the Land to Which Yon Ship Must Go?"
    "With How Sad Steps, O Moon, Thou Climb'st the Sky"
    "With Ships the Sea Was Sprinkled Far and Nigh"
    Probably composed between 21 May 1802 and 6 Mar 1804. (1802:137; Appendix III.)
    Pub. *P2V*, except "Pelion and Ossa," pub. *P* 1815.

74. "It Is No Spirit That from Heaven Hath Flown"
    Probably composed between 21 May 1802 and 6 Mar 1804; perhaps between 8 Nov 1802 and 7 Jan 1803, or between 1 and 28 Apr 1803. (1802:138; Appendix III.)[23]
    Pub. *P2V*.

---

[23] Although "It Is No Spirit" has seventeen lines, its form is sufficiently sonnet-like to suggest a date about the time of composition of the sonnets copied in MS M, where "It Is No Spirit" also appears. The IF note states that the poem was prompted by and composed immediately after a remark of SH's made at DC in 1803. The appropriate periods are 8 Nov 1802–7 Jan 1803, and 1–28 Apr 1803. W also dated the poem 1803 *PW* 1836–*PW* 1850.

75. "I Find It Written of Simonides"
Probably composed between 21 May 1802 and 7 Oct 1803. (1802:139.)
Pub. *MP* 10 Oct 1803.

76. "Methought I Saw the Footsteps of a Throne"
Probably composed between 21 May and c late 1802, possibly by 25
Dec, possibly by late July 1802. (1802:140; Appendix III.)
Pub. *P2V*.

77. "'Tis Six Miles from Our Dwelling Place" (revised before MS M to
"There Is a Trickling Water"; before *P* 1815 to "There Is a Tiny Water";
and before *P* 1820 to "There Is a Little Unpretending Rill")
Probably composed between 21 May and c late 1802, possibly by 25 Dec;
revised to *P* 1820 form perhaps after late Oct 1814. (1802:141; Appendix
III; GCL 222n.)
Pub. *P* 1820.

78. "Are Souls Then Nothing?" ("What If Our Numbers Barely Could
Defy")
"'Beloved Vale!' I Said, 'When I Shall Con'"
"Brook That Hast Been My Solace Days and Weeks" ("Brook! Whose
Society the Poet Seeks")
"Dear Native Brooks Your Ways I Have Pursu'd" ("Return, Content!
for Fondly I Pursued")
"England! the Time Is Come When Thou Should'st Wean"
"Great Men Have Been among Us; Hands That Penned"
"It Is Not to Be Thought of That the Flood"
"There Is a Bondage Worse, Far Worse, to Bear"
To Sleep ("A Flock of Sheep")
To Sleep ("Fond Words Have Oft")
To Sleep ("O Gentle Sleep")
"When I Have Borne in Memory What Hath Tamed"
Probably composed between 21 May and c late 1802, possibly by 25 Dec.
(1802:142.)
"It Is Not to Be Thought of" pub. *MP* 16 Apr 1803. "When I Have
Borne" pub. *MP* 17 Sept 1803. "Are Souls Then Nothing" pub. as
"What If Our Numbers" *PW* 1836. "Brook That Hast Been" pub.
as "Brook[!] Whose Society" *P* 1815; "Dear Native Brooks" pub.
as "Return, Content!" *RD*. Others pub. *P2V*.

79. *A Farewell*
    Probably basically composed late May, certainly by 29 May, 1802; developed further between 30 May and 14 June. (1802:135.)
    Pub. *P* 1815.

80. "The Sun Has Long Been Set"
    Composed 8 June 1802. (1802:160.)
    Pub. *P2V*.

81. "The Owl as If He Had Learn'd His Cheer" (DC MS 44; basis of *Waggoner* III.120–25)
    Possibly composed between 13 and c 20 June, esp. 15 June 1802. (1802: 163.)

82. Lines about the night-hawk and other images of the evening perhaps contributive to *Waggoner* MSS 1, 2 (see 1802:165)
    Possibly composed 15 June, c 7, 8 July 1802. (1802:165.)

83. *Composed upon Westminster Bridge, September 3, 1802*
    Perhaps begun 31 July 1802; probably completed 3 Sept 1802. (1802:202.)
    Pub. *P2V*.

84. *Calais, August, 1802* ("Is It a Reed That's Shaken by the Wind")
    Composed by the Sea-side, near Calais, August 1802 ("Fair Star of Evening, Splendour of the West")
    "It Is a Beauteous Evening, Calm and Free"
    Probably composed between 1 and 29 Aug 1802. (1802:203.)
    Calais, August, 1802 pub. *MP* 13 Jan 1803. (See Woof *SB* 184.) Others pub. *P2V*.

85. *To Toussaint l'Ouverture*
    Possibly composed between 1 and 29 Aug 1802. (1802:203.)
    Pub. *MP* 2 Feb 1803. (See Woof *SB* 184.)

86. *Composed near Calais, on the Road Leading to Ardres, August 7, 1802* ("Jones! as from Calais Southward You and I")
    Probably composed 1 or 7 Aug 1802. (1802:203.)
    Pub. *P2V*.

87. *Calais, August 15, 1802* ("Festivals Have I Seen That Were Not Names")
    Probably composed 15 Aug 1802. (1802:203.)
    Pub. *MP* 26 Feb 1803. (See Woof *SB* 184.)

88. *September 1, 1802* ("We Had a Female Passenger Who Came")
    Perhaps composed between 29 Aug and 1 Sept 1802, and perhaps completed on 1 Sept. (1802:206.)
    Pub. *MP* 11 Feb 1803. (See Woof *SB* 185.)

89. *Composed in the Valley near Dover, on the Day of Landing* ("Here, on Our Native Soil, We Breathe Once More")
    Probably composed 30 Aug 1802. (1802:207.)
    Pub. *P2V.*

90. *September, 1802. Near Dover* ("Inland, within a Hollow Vale, I Stood")
    Probably composed 30 Aug 1802 or shortly after. (1802:207.)
    Pub. *P2V.*

91. *Tale, Imitated from Gower* (DW)
    Possibly written c Sept 1802, more probably c late 1802. (Appendix V.)

92. *London, 1802* ("Milton! Thou Shoulds't Be Living at This Hour")
    Written in London, September, 1802 ("O Friend! I Know Not Which Way I Must Look")
    Probably composed Sept, by 22 Sept, 1802. (1802:207.)
    Pub. *P2V.*

93. "Nuns Fret Not at Their Convent's Narrow Room"
    Perhaps composed c late 1802. (Appendix III.) [24]
    Pub. *P2V.*

94. *Composed after a Journey across the Hambleton Hills, Yorkshire*
    Probably composed 4 Oct 1802. (1802:224.)
    Pub. *P2V.*

95. "Those Words Were Uttered as in Pensive Mood"
    Probably composed between 4 Oct 1802 and 6 Mar 1804. (1802:225.)
    Pub. *P2V.*

[24] The content of "Nuns Fret Not" suggests that W had already written a considerable number of sonnets.

96. "Hard Was Thy Durance, Queen, Compared with Ours" (sonnet of which only first line is known to survive)
Probably composed between 6 and c 8 Oct 1802. (1802:227.)

97. "A Plain Youth, Lady, and a Simple Lover" (see *PW* III, 577), translation from the Italian of Milton
Translations from the Italian of Metastasio (see *PW* IV, 369–70; Woof *SB* 185–87):

"Gentle Zephyr"
"I Will Be That Fond Mother"
"Laura, Farewell My Laura!"
"Oh! Bless'd All Bliss Above"
"The Swallow, That Hath Lost"
"To the Grove, the Meadow, the Well"

Perhaps composed between c Nov 1802 and early Jan 1803. (1802:246.) "A Plain Youth, Lady, and a Simple Lover" pub. *MP* 5 Oct 1803 see Woof *SB* 185); "Laura, Farewell My Laura!" pub. *MP* 17 Oct 1803 (see Woof *SB* 185–86); "To the Grove, the Meadow, the Well" pub. *MP* 22 Oct 1803 (see Woof *SB* 186–87); "The Swallow, That Hath Lost" pub. *MP* 2 Nov 1803 (see Woof *SB* 187–88); "Gentle Zephyr" pub. *MP* 15 Nov 1803 (see Woof *SB* 187); "Oh! Bless'd All Bliss Above" pub. *MP* 12 Dec 1803 (see Woof *SB* 188–89); "I Will Be That Fond Mother" pub. *PW*.

98. Translation from the Italian of Ariosto (see also *CEY* 26)
Two books, including the materials quoted *PW* IV, 367–69, from the *Orlando* I.v–xiv (otherwise not surviving), probably composed 7–perhaps c 19 Nov 1802. Additions perhaps made between this time and early 1808. (1802:253.)

99. *The Small Celandine*
Possibly composed 1803 or early 1804, by 6 Mar. (Appendix III.)[25]
Pub. *P2V*.

[25] W dated the poem 1804 in editions 1836–1850. It appears to have no immediate connection with the 1802 Celandine poems. But while content and W's other preoccupations of early 1804 do not strongly encourage speculation that it was composed in Jan or Feb of that year, the verses are copied in DC MS 44, and so were complete by 6 Mar 1804.

100. *At the Grave of Burns. 1803*
     First two stanzas, perhaps other parts, including lines 60–63, possibly
     composed 18 Aug 1803 or shortly after. Earliest finished version, *Ejacu-
     lation at the Grave of Burns* (see Hale White 57, 63, 69; *PW* III, 65 *app
     crit*), probably composed between late Mar 1804 and early Apr 1807.
     Not certainly completed before preparation of *PELY* 1842. (IF note;
     Appendix V; Appendix VII.) [26]
     Pub. *PELY*.

101. *Thoughts, Suggested the Day Following, on the Banks of the Nith, near the
     Poet's Residence*
     Some conception possibly formed 19 Aug 1803. Perhaps composed in
     part within a few years of that date, but not completed until late 1839.
     (*At the Grave of Burns* IF note; *W and Reed* 13–14.) [27]
     Pub. *PELY*.

102. *Address to Kilchurn Castle, upon Loch Awe*
     Lines 1–3 composed 31 Aug 1803; the remainder probably composed
     between 1820 and 1827. (1803:79.)
     Lines 1–3 pub. G 1820; entire poem pub. *PW* 1827.

103. *Sonnet Composed at ——— Castle*
     Probably basically composed 18 Sept 1803. (1803:98.)
     Pub. *P2V*.

104. "Fly, Some Kind Harbinger, to Grasmere-dale"
     Probably partly or wholly composed 25 Sept 1803; fairly certainly
     completed by 21 Nov 1803. (1803:105.)
     Pub. *P* 1815.

---

[26] The IF note comments that the lines were "actually composed at the time." But
not even the *Ejaculation at the Grave of Burns* appears in MS M, and these lines are thus
unlikely to have been written by 6 Mar 1804.

[27] W remarked to Henry Reed on 23 Dec 1839 that the verses belonged to the year
1803 although they were "not actually composed till many years afterwards." The IF
note to *At the Grave of Burns* comments that the lines "though then felt" on the 1803
tour, were not put into words "till several years afterwards." The significance of the
difference between "many" and "several" is indeterminate. The last stanza was not
written before late 1839 (*W and Reed* 13–14).

105. Prose fragment: description of a baby, probably Johnny, in MS 48 (see Appendix V; 1803:108)
> Probably written late 1803 or early 1804. (Content. See esp. 1804:36; 1804:54; 1804:57; Appendix IX.)

106. *Recollections of a Tour Made in Scotland A.D. 1803* (DW)
> Composed basically through entry for 2 Sept probably between late Sept and 20 Dec 1803; perhaps some part of entries for 3–5 Sept, probably 2 Feb 1804 and perhaps a day or so following; probably some part of entries for 3–5 Sept, up to conclusion of Part II, c 29 Mar 1804; Part III, and a copy of *Recollections*, between 11 Apr and 31 May 1805. (1803:107; 1804:16; 1804:49; 1805:37.)
> MS A (copied by CCl) probably written between early Sept and 1 Nov 1805. (1805:81.)
> MSS B (copied by DW), C i, ii (copied by SH) probably written between 29 Dec 1805 and 21 Feb 1806. MS C ii follows revision by DW; DW's copy is probably made after SH's; both copies of Part III are probably made between late Jan and 21 Feb 1806. (1805:119.)
> A version of a part of the entries for 27 Aug (top *DWJ* I, 276-mid-278) and 22 Aug (*DWJ* I, 233-top 235) pub. *Yarrow Revisited* 1835, 38–43. Extensive selections pub. *Mem.* Pub. entire 1874.

107. *To the Men of Kent. October, 1803*
> Probably composed between 25 Sept and 14 Oct 1803. (1803:106.)
> Pub. *P2V.*

108. *Anticipation. October, 1803*
> Perhaps composed between 1 and 14 Oct 1803. (1803:109.)
> Pub. *Courier* 28 Oct 1803. (See Woof *SB* 187.)

109. *To a Highland Girl*
> *Yarrow Unvisited*
> Probably composed between 14 Oct 1803 and 6 Mar 1804; possibly by 21 Nov, esp. probably early or mid-Nov, 1803. (1803:117.)
> Pub. *P2V.*

110. *At Applethwaite, near Keswick*
> "She Was a Phantom of Delight"
> Probably composed between 14 Oct 1803 and 6 Mar 1804, perhaps early 1804. (1803:118.)
> *At Applethwaite* pub. *PELY.* "She Was a Phantom" pub. *P2V.*

111. *Lines on the Expected Invasion, 1803* ("Come Ye—Who, If [Which Heaven Avert!]")
     October, 1803 ("One Might Believe That Natural Miseries")
     October, 1803 ("When, Looking on the Outward Face of Things")
     October, 1803 ("These Times Strike Moneyed Wordlings with Dismay")
     Probably composed (*Lines* at least in basic form) between 14 Oct 1803 and early Jan 1804, possibly by 31 Oct 1803. (1803:119.)
     Lines pub. *PELY*. Others pub. *P2V*.

112. *Sonnet. In the Pass of Killicranky. October, 1803* ("Six Thousand Veterans")
     Perhaps composed between 14 and 31 Oct 1803. (1803:121.)
     Pub. *P2V*.

113. *Ode to Duty*
     Probably basically composed, except first stanza, in MS M version, early 1804 by Mar 6. First stanza probably added between late Mar 1804 and early Dec 1806. *P2V* MS probably written between 30 Oct 1806 and mid-Jan 1807. (1804:3; Appendix VII.)
     Pub. *P2V*.

114. Fragment: "Along the Mazes of This Song"
     Possibly composed between c 14 Jan 1804 and c Jan 1805. (Content.)[28]
     Pub. *PW* Knight, 1882–89.

115. Prose fragment: psychological analysis of daughter of a blind man (perhaps Idonea-Matilda), DC MS 45
     Possibly written c Mar–Apr 1804. (See Appendix VI.)

116. Letter on the Education of a Daughter
     Perhaps written c Mar–Apr 1804. (1804:29.)
     Pub. *Mem*.

117. *Admonition*
     "Who Fancied What a Pretty Sight"
     Probably composed between late Mar 1804 and early Apr 1807. (Appendix III; Appendix VII.)[29]
     Pub. *P2V*.

---

[28] The fragment apparently speaks of a time when *Prel*, *Recluse*, or *Exc* was well advanced, but its concluding phrases ("if my lot be joy/More joyful if it be with sorrow mixed") make a time after JW's death unlikely.

[29] W dated "Who Fancied" 1803 *PW* 1836–*PW* 1850, but neither poem appears in MS M.

118. "I Wandered Lonely as a Cloud"
Probably composed between late Mar 1804 and early Apr 1807; possibly by end of year 1804. (1804:43.)
Pub. *P2V*.

119. *Prospectus* (see also *CEY* 29)
a. MSS 1, 2 (2 called 3 by EdS) (DC MSS 45, 24)
Probably written between late Mar 1804 and early Sept 1806. (Appendix VI.)
b. MS 3 (called 2 by EdS) (DC MS 59)
Probably written between c late June and early Sept 1806. (Appendix VI.)
Pub. *Exc* 1814.

120. *The Blind Highland Boy*
Probably composed between late Mar 1804 and c Mar 1806. (Appendix VII.) [30]
Pub. *P2V*.

121. *The Matron of Jedborough and Her Husband*
Probably composed between late Mar 1804 and 1 Nov 1805. (Appendix III; *DWJ* I, ix.)
Pub. *P2V*.

122. *Address to My Infant Daughter, Dora, on Being Reminded That She Was a Month Old That Day, September 16*
Probably basically composed 16 Sept 1804. (1804:103.)
Pub. *P* 1815.

123. *Yew-trees*
Lines 1–13 composed possibly 24 Sept 1804 or shortly after. Other composition possibly between that time and June 1811. Probably completed as DC MS 74 between June 1811 and c late Mar 1814. Finished by late Oct 1814. (IF note and date *PW* 1836–1850; 1804:107; DC MSS 74, 80; Appendix VI.) [31]
Pub. *P* 1815.

[30] The headnote "A Tale Told by the Fire-side, after Returning to the Vale of Grasmere" (*PW* 1827–*PW* 1850) may be supposed a device for fitting the poem among "Memorials of a Tour in Scotland, 1803."

[31] W's own date was 1803, both in the IF note and *PW* 1836–*PW* 1850, but EdS's conclusion that the poem would have been present in MS M had it existed when that

124. "O Mountain Stream! the Shepherd and His Cot" (later *The River Duddon* XIV)

>   Possibly composed between 27 Sept and early Oct 1804. Fairly certainly completed by c Mar 1806. (1804:107.)
>   Pub. *P2V.*

125. *The King of Sweden*
>   Probably composed between late 1804 and early Feb 1807. (Andrew

---

MS was being made up (it would have been written by 6 Mar 1804) appears sound in this case. The only surviving MSS seem to date much later than 1803. The first of these, in MS 74 (not mentioned by EdS), consists of copy of lines 1–3, 14–33, and lines represented by *PW* II, 210 *app crit.* No work in the main body of the NB can be assigned to a time before June 1811, when "Praised Be the Art," which immediately preceded the *Yew-trees* copy in the NB, was composed. The *Exc* drafts now surrounding it are unlikely to date before early 1813. Although lines 20–24 are heavily corrected, the MS generally is plainly not first draft, and the absence of lines 4–13 suggest that a satisfactory copy of that part was already in existence. The first three lines are later than the readings of the two MSS of DC MS 80, which are clearly written in the process of preparation of *P* 1815. One of the copies in MS 80 contains the conclusion of *PW* II, 210 *app crit,* cancelled, while the other, copied off from the earlier MS 80 copy, omits it. Corrections to the MS 74 copy are integrated in the MS 80 copies.

One suggestion from the available facts is that the poem was not begun, nor its first thirteen lines composed, before W and DW visited the Lorton Vale yew-tree in late Sept or early Oct 1804 (see *EY* 507). But taking W's own remarkably early date into account, one may speculate that the opening section, lines 1–13, was possibly composed at about that time. No other evidence provides grounds for supposing that the poem was completed until some time between June 1811 and late 1814.

It would be pleasant to think that a pertinent connection existed between (1) W's sight of the Lorton Vale yew, (2) the unidentified Cowper poem recommended by Lady B, which "set [W] on to writing after a pause sooner than he otherwise would have done," probably in early Oct 1804 (see *EY* 508), and (3) Cowper's *Yardley Oak,* of which the first 124 lines are copied by SH in DC MS 26 (see Appendix IX). Cowper's poem was published in the first week of May 1804 in the third volume of Hayley's *Life and Posthumous Writings* of Cowper, a book which DW said on 11 Apr 1805 that she was planning to read and which the Ws had apparently possessed long enough for her to dip into earlier (*EY* 577). The extract from *Yardley Oak,* however, immediately precedes extracts from Barrow's *Travels in China,* unlikely to date before 27 Feb 1807 (see Betz *BN*).

G 1810, p. 42, where W describes the Borrowdale yews, would have been a likely place, in view of the work's general style, for W to have quoted some portion of these lines had they existed when he wrote in late 1810.

Hilen, "The Date of Wordsworth's 'The King of Sweden,'" *English Studies* XXIV, 1953, 156–60; Appendix VII.)
Pub. *P2V*.

126. *The Kitten and the Falling Leaves*
Possibly between early Oct 1804 and early 1805; perhaps late 1805 or early 1806. (1805:79.)
Pub. *P2V*.

127. *Vaudracour and Julia* (as part of *Prel* IX)
Fragment: "There Was a Spot" (*PW* V, 342, III)
Probably composed between early Oct and late autumn 1804. (Appendix VI.)
Vaudracour and Julia pub. *P* 1820.

128. *French Revolution as It Appeared to Enthusiasts at Its Commencement* (composed as part of *Prel* X)
Probably composed c late Nov or Dec 1804. (1804:120; Appendix V.)
Pub. *Friend* 26 Oct 1809.

129. "No Whimsey of the Purse Is Here"
Probably composed c but by 25 Dec 1804. (1804:130.)
Pub. *Memorials of Coleorton*, ed. William Knight (Boston and New York, 1887).

130. *From the Italian of Michael Angelo. I* ("Yes, Hope May with My Strong Desire Keep Pace")
Probably composed 1805, by 24 Aug. (1805:1.)
Pub. Duppa 1806.

131. "Grateful Is Sleep" (two versions; *PW* IV, 370–71; translation from the Italian of Michaelangelo)
"Come, Gentle Sleep" (translation from the Latin of Thomas Warton the Younger)
Possibly composed between 1805 and 1807, not certainly before c 1836– c 1840. (1805:1.)
Pub. *PW* Knight, 1882–89.

132. "And Sweet It Is to See in Summer Time," translation from the Italian of Michaelangelo
Probably composed between 1805 and early May 1807. (1805:1.)
Pub. Duppa 1807.

133. "Distressful Gift! This Book Receives" (*PW* IV, 372–73)
     To the Daisy ("Sweet Flower!")
     Perhaps composed between c 20 May and 5 July, possibly shortly before
     5 July, 1805. (1805:46.)
     To the Daisy pub. P 1815.

134. *Glen Almain*
     Probably composed between c 20 May and 11 June 1805. (1805:46.)[32]
     Pub. *P2V*.

135. *Stepping Westward*
     Probably composed 3 June 1805. (1805:48.)
     Pub. *P2V*.

136. *Elegiac Verses, in Memory of My Brother, John Wordsworth*
     Probably composed 8 June 1805. (1805:50.)
     Pub. *PELY*. Some rejected stanzas and lines pub. *PW* IV, 263–65.

137. *Fidelity*
     Probably composed between 14 Aug and 10 Nov 1805, certainly by 2
     Mar 1806. (1805:71.)
     Pub. *P2V*.

138. *Incident Characteristic of a Favorite Dog*
     Tribute to the Memory of the Same Dog
     Probably composed between 14 Aug 1805 and 23 Dec 1806, but after
     Fidelity. (1805:71. see GCL 137.)
     Pub. *P2V*.

139. *Rob Roy's Grave*
     Probably composed between early Sept 1805 and 21 Feb 1806. (1805:80.)
     Pub. *P2V*.

140. *To the Sons of Burns*
     Stanzas 2, 3, 4, 8 probably composed between early Sept 1805 and 21
     Feb 1806. Other stanzas added between 1820 and 1827. (1805:80.)
     Stanzas 2, 3, 4, 8 pub. *P2V*; the other stanzas pub. *PW* 1827.

[32] W apparently intended to correct the spelling of the title name to "Glenalmond"
PW 1850, but failed to do so (see Charles W, *Annals of My Life, 1847–1856*, London,
1893, 50).

141. *The Solitary Reaper*
Probably composed 5 Nov 1805. (1805:95.)
Pub. *P2V*.

142. "Rid of a Vexing and a Heavy Load" (early version of *At Florence*
[ii]; *PW* III, 500; translation from the Italian of Michaelangelo)
Perhaps begun 1805; probably completed between 7 Nov 1805 and
early Apr 1807. (*EY* 640; 1805:1; 1805:98; Appendix VII.)
Pub. *PW* Knight, 1896.

143. *From the Italian of Michael Angelo. II* ("No Mortal Object Did These
Eyes Behold")
Perhaps begun 1805; probably completed between 7 Nov 1805 and 8
Sept 1806. (1805:1; 1805:98.)
Pub. *P2V* and shortly after in Duppa 1807. (Cf *PW* III, 15.)

144. *From the Italian of Michael Angelo. III* ("The Prayers I Make Will Then
Be Sweet Indeed")
Perhaps begun 1805; probably completed between 7 Nov 1805 and
early 1806, certainly by 1 Aug. (1805:1; 1805:98.)
Pub. *P2V* and shortly after in Duppa 1807. (Cf *PW* III, 15.)

145. *Excursion on the Banks of Ullswater* (DW)
Perhaps composed shortly after 12 Nov 1805. (1805:103.)
Pub. in revised form *G* 1823; pub. in original form *DWJ*.

146. *Address to a Child during a Boisterous Winter Evening* (DW)
The Cottager to Her Infant (DW's portion)
Probably composed between 28 Nov and c 6 Dec 1805. W's third and
fourth stanzas for *The Cottager* possibly between this date and early
1815. (1805:109.)
Pub. *P* 1815, except third and fourth stanzas of *Cottager* which were pub.
PW Knight, 1896.

147. *The Character of the Happy Warrior*
Probably composed between c 6 Dec 1805 and early Jan 1806. (1805:
112.)
Pub. *P2V*.

148. "Through Cumbrian Wilds, in Many a Happy Cove" (*PW* III, 409)
Perhaps composed between 1806 and late Oct 1814. (See *PW* III, 574.)[33]
Pub. *PW* Knight, 1896.

149. *Song for the Spinning Wheel*
Possibly 1806 or, more probably, 1812. (1812:1.)
Pub. *P* 1820.

150. *The Waggoner* (see also 1802:118; 1802:163; 1802:165)
   a. Basic version
      Probably composed between 1 and 14 Jan 1806. (1806:2.)
   b. Drafts in DC MS 28 toward II.145–48, III.1–2, and in DC MS 47
      toward IV.99–108
      MS [1] (BM Ashley MS 4637)
      MS [2] (DC MS 56)
      Probably written between early Jan and 29 Mar 1806. (1806:2.)
   c. MS 3
      Probably written early 1812, perhaps c, certainly by 29 Mar. (1812:4.)
      Pub. 1819.

151. *Star-gazers*
Probably composed between 4 Apr and 14 Nov 1806. (1806:17.)
Pub. *P2V*.

152. *The Power of Music*
Stray Pleasures
Probably composed between 4 Apr and 10 Nov 1806. (1806:17.)
Pub. *P2V*.

153. *A Fragment* ("Peaceful Our Valley") (DW)
A Fragment ("There Is One Cottage") (DW)
Perhaps composed c mid-Apr 1806; probably composed between that
time and c end May 1808. (1806:19.)
"Peaceful Our Valley" pub. *The Academy* 9 Nov 1878 (10 stanzas);
Monthly Packet Feb 1892 (entire).

---

[33] EdS points out that the sestet of this sonnet was used as the sestet also of "Grief,
Thou Hast Lost" and suggests that this poem was a preliminary working of the other.
The sestet clearly draws on the same tradition that formed the basis of "Song for the
Spinning Wheel," possibly 1806 or 1812, and shares phrasing with that poem. "Grief,
Thou Hast Lost" was probably completed by late Oct 1814 (see 1814:112).

154. *Elegiac Stanzas Suggested by a Picture of Peele Castle*
Probably composed between c 20 May and 27 June 1806. (1806:37.)
Pub. *P2V*.

155. "Yes, It Was the Mountain Echo"
Composed 15 June 1806 or shortly after. (1806:47.)
Pub. *P2V*.

156. *To the Evening Star over Grasmere Water, July 1806* (*PW* V, 347)
Probably composed July 1806. (1806:56; Appendix VI.)
Pub. *PW* Knight, 1882–89.

157. *To the Spade of a Friend*
Probably composed between 18 Aug and 26 Oct 1806. (1806:74.)
Pub. *P2V*.

158. Fragment: "The Rains at Length Have Ceas'd" (*PW* IV, 456)
Lines. Composed at Grasmere ("Loud Is the Vale")
Probably composed c early Sept 1806, "Loud Is the Vale" following
"The Rains at Length." (1806:82.)
Lines. Composed at Grasmere pub. *P2V*; "The Rains at Length" pub. *PW*
Knight, 1882–89.

159. *Song at the Feast of Brougham Castle*
"Though Narrow Be That Old Man's Cares, and Near"
A Complaint
Probably composed between 30 Oct 1806 and early Apr 1807. *A
Complaint* possibly composed by 7 Dec 1806. (1806:93; 1806:94.)
Pub. *P2V*.

160. *Thought of a Briton on the Subjugation of Switzerland*
November, 1806 ("Another Year!—Another Deadly Blow!")
Probably composed between 30 Oct 1806 and late Feb 1807. *November,
1806* perhaps composed by 7 Dec 1806. (1806:94.)
Pub. *P2V*.

161. *The Horn of Egremont Castle*
Possibly composed between 30 Oct and early Dec 1806. (1806:94.)
Pub. *P2V*.

162. *A Prophecy. February, 1807*
     Probably composed Feb 1807. (1807:7.)
     Pub. *P2V*.

163. *To Lady Beaumont* ("Lady! the Songs of Spring Were in the Grove")
     Probably composed c early Feb 1807. (1807:6.)
     Pub. *P2V*.

164. "O Nightingale! Thou Surely Art"
     Probably composed between early Feb and early Apr 1807. (1807:8.)
     Pub. *P2V*.

165. *Gipsies*
     Probably composed c but not before 26 Feb 1807. (1807:15.)
     Pub. *P2V*.

166. *To Thomas Clarkson*
     Probably composed 26 Mar 1807 or shortly after. (1807:21.)
     Pub. *P2V*.

167. *The Plain of Donnerdale* ("The Old Inventive Poets, Had They Seen")
     Probably composed between Apr 1807 and late Oct 1814, but possibly
     1817. (*PW* III, 254; GCL 222n.) [34]
     Pub. *RD*.

168. "Grief, Thou Hast Lost an Ever Ready Friend"
     "Mark the Concentered Hazels That Enclose"
     "The Shepherd, Looking Eastward, Softly Said"
     "Weak Is the Will of Man, His Judgment Blind"
     Perhaps composed between Apr 1807 and late Oct 1814. (1807:22;
     Appendix VII; GCL 222n; *PW* III, 422.)
     All except "Grief, Thou Hast Lost" pub. *P* 1815. ("Weak Is the Will of
     Man" also pub. shortly after in *WD*.) "Grief" pub. *Waggoner* 1819.

---

[34] The *terminus a quo* is suggested from the poem's absence from *P2V*. MW wrote c
but by 1 Dec 1818 (in a letter so franked) that W had lately written "21 sonnets
(including 2 old ones) on the river Duddon" (MS; *PW* III, 506; cf *MWL* 41). "O
Mountain Stream" was one of the "old ones"; *The Plain of Donnerdale* seems likely to
have been the other (see GCL 222n).

169. *To the Poet, John Dyer*
      Perhaps composed between Apr 1807 and early 1811. (*MY* 521.)
      Pub. *P* 1815 (cf *PW* III, 10).

170. *The Mother's Return* (DW)
      Perhaps composed 5 May 1807. (1807:40.)
      Pub. *P* 1815.

171. *Composed by the Side of Grasmere Lake. 1807* ("Clouds, Lingering Yet, Extend in Solid Bars")
      Possibly composed 1807 after 10 July; fairly certainly by late Oct 1814. (1807:60.)
      Pub. *Waggoner* 1819.

172. *The Force of Prayer*
      Perhaps composed c 18 Sept 1807. (1807:82.)
      Pub. *P* 1815 (also pub. shortly after in *WD*).

173. *The White Doe of Rylstone* (Dates assigned are based on Appendix V.)
      Introduction (not known to survive) composed probably between 16 Oct and 8 Nov 1807; 500 lines composed by 1 Dec; about half the poem by c 19 Dec; over 1200 lines by 3 Jan 1808; completed in a 1700-line version by 16 Jan 1808.
      MS 1 (DC MS 61), MS 2 (DC MS 62) and Advertisement probably written between 16 Oct 1807 and late Jan 1808.
      A full MS probably written shortly after 16 Jan 1808. Alteration and revision c Apr, including 19 Apr, 1809. Organization in final form perhaps between c Nov 1814 and late Jan 1815. (Appendix VIII.)
      Pub. 2 June 1815. (*Courier.*)

174. Fragment: *On Milton* ("Amid the Dark Control of Lawless Sway") (*PW* III, 409)
      Probably written c early 1808. (1808:2.)

175. "Press'd with Conflicting Thoughts of Love and Fear" (A View of St. Paul's; *PW* IV, 374–75)
      The Tuft of Primroses (*PW* V, 348–62)
      To the Clouds
      Probably composed between 6 Apr and early autumn 1808. (1808:36.)
      To the Clouds pub. *PELY.*

176. *Narrative Concerning George and Sarah Green*
W writes a first account of the Green disaster probably between 6 and
11 Apr 1808. (1808:37.)
DW's *Narrative* probably written between 22 Apr and 4 May 1808.
(1808:55.)
Pub. *G&SG*.

177. *George and Sarah Green*
Composed perhaps 7 or 8 Apr 1808 or shortly after. (1808:38.)
Pub. *Tait's Edinburgh Magazine*, Sept 1839.

178. *Pelayo* (*PW* III, 415)
Possibly composed c late June, perhaps c early July 1808. (1808:77.)

179. *Concerning the Relations of Great Britain, Spain, and Portugal . . . as
Affected by the Convention of Cintra*
Probably composed between c mid-Nov 1808 and 26 Mar 1809. First
Courier installment probably completed c but by 15 Dec 1808, and
second installment within a day or so thereafter. (1808:114.) A third and
fourth installment completed, and a fifth installment probably completed, except for final corrections, by 28 Dec. A revised second installment, partly by STC, prepared 2–3 Jan 1809, possibly sent off 8 Jan.
(1808:114; 1809:2.) A decision to publish only in pamphlet form
reached between c 10 Jan and probably 26 Jan, certainly 3 Feb 1809.
Bulk of composition completed by 26 Mar 1809. (1808:114; 1809:4.)
On details of preparation of pamphlet see 1809:4–1809:86 *passim*.
First *Courier* installment pub. 27 Dec 1808. Second *Courier* installment
pub. 13 Jan 1809. *CC* pub. 27 May 1809. (*Courier*.)

180. *Composed While the Author Was Engaged in Writing a Tract Occasioned by
the Convention of Cintra. 1808.*
Composed at the Same Time and on the Same Occasion
Probably composed between c mid-Nov 1808 and 24 Mar 1809,
possibly between c mid-Nov and 31 Dec 1808. (Title; 1808:114.)
Pub. *P* 1815.

181. "Avaunt All Specious Pliancy of Mind"
The French and the Spanish Guerillas. 1811
"Say, What Is Honour?—'Tis the Finest Sense"

46

Perhaps composed between c Mar 1809 and some time in 1810. (1809:
23.)
Pub. *P* 1815.

182. "Ah! Where Is Palafox? Nor Tongue nor Pen"
"Hail Zaragossa! If with Unwet Eye"
"Is There a Power That Can Sustain and Cheer"
Perhaps c late Mar, after 14 Mar, 1809; fairly certainly between 14 Mar
1809 and some time in 1810. (1809:23n.)
Pub. *P* 1815.

183. "Call Not the Royal Swede Unfortunate"
"Look Now on That Adventurer Who Hath Paid"
Perhaps composed c early Apr 1809, probably not before 30 Mar.
(1809:23n.)
Pub. *P* 1815.

184. Classifications of Poems:
List in DC MS 24
Lists in Yale (Tinker) copy of *P2V*
Probably written between 5 May 1809 and late Oct 1814, esp. near the
later date; but possibly c 27 Dec 1811. (See 1809:75; 1811:72.)

185. "Brave Schill! by Death Delivered, Take Thy Flight"
Perhaps composed c but not before 19 June 1809. (1809:23n.)
Pub. *P* 1815.

186. "Alas! What Boots the Long Laborious Quest?"
"And Is It among Rude Untutored Vales"
Feelings of the Tyrolese ("The Land We from Our Fathers Had in
Trust")
"O'er the Wide Earth, on Mountain and on Plain"
"Alas!" probably composed between 22 June and 16 Nov 1809,
certainly by 16 Nov; the others probably composed between 22 June
and 21 Dec 1809, certainly by 21 Dec; any or all possibly composed
between 22 and 29 June. (1809:23n.)
"Alas!" pub. *Friend* 16 Nov 1809; the others pub. *Friend* 21 Dec 1809.

187. John Wilson, *The Angler's Tent*, four lines beginning "The placid lake
that rested far below" (see *Isle of Palms*, 1812, 187), esp. second line.

W assists in composition possibly c 29 June 1809 or shortly after, or possibly between 8 and 13 Sept 1809. (1809:100.)

188. Translations from the Italian of Chiabrera
   a. "Weep Not, Belovèd Friends! Nor Let the Air"
      "True It Is That Ambrosio Salinero"
      Possibly composed in part late 1809 or early 1810, by c late Feb. Not certainly completed until c but by 1837. (1807:117.)
      Pub. *PW* 1836.
   b. "Torquato Tasso Rests within This Tomb"
      Probably composed late 1809 or early 1810, by c late Feb. (1809:117.)
      Pub. Grosart.
   c. "O Lelius, Beauteous Flower of Gentleness"
      Probably composed late 1809 or early 1810, certainly by 28 Feb. (1809:118.)
      Pub. Grosart. Pub. revised to form of "O Flower of All That Springs from Gentle Blood" *PW* 1836.
   d. "Perhaps Some Needful Service of the State"
      "O Thou Who Movest Onward with a Mind"
      Probably composed late 1809 or early 1810, certainly by 22 Feb. (1809:119.)
      Pub. *Friend* 22 Feb 1810.
   e. "There Never Breathed a Man Who, When His Life Was Done"
      "Destined to War from Very Infancy"
      Probably composed late 1809, by 22 Dec. (1809:120; 1809:143.)
      Pub. *Friend* 28 Dec 1809.
   f. "Not without Heavy Grief of Heart"
      "Pause, Courteous Spirit!—Balbi Supplicates"
      Probably composed late 1809, by 11 Dec. (1809:121; 1809:143.)
      Pub. *Friend* 4 Jan 1810.

189. "Advance—Come Forth from Thy Tyrolean Ground"
   Hofer ("Of Mortal Parents Is the Hero Born")
   Probably composed 10 Oct 1809. (1809:123.)
   Pub. *Friend* 26 Oct 1809.

190. *On the Final Submission of the Tyrolese*
   Probably composed between 24 Oct and 21 Dec 1809. (1809:125.)
   Pub. *Friend* 21 Dec 1809.

191. *A Guide through the District of the Lakes*
    a. Letterpress for Joseph Wilkinson's *Select Views of Cumberland, West-moreland, and Lancashire*
        "Introduction" probably composed between mid-June and early Nov, completed c early Nov 1809, by 17 Nov. (Appendix VI.)
        "Section I," "Section II": Some materials probably written c June 1810. "Section I" and "Section II" probably composed between c but by 3 Sept and c mid-Nov 1810. (Appendix VI.)
    b. Expanded guide (incomplete), including Essay on the Sublime
        Probably composed c late Nov 1812. (Appendix VI; 1812:99.)
        "Introduction" pub. between c early Nov 1809 and 10 May 1810; probably c early 1810. (Appendix VI.)

192. Reply to Mathetes
    Probably basically composed between early Nov and early Dec, by 11 Dec 1809. (1809:129.)
    Pub. through "direct as that of the Roman road with which we began the comparison" *Friend* 14 Dec 1809. The remainder pub. *Friend* 4 Jan 1810.

193. Essays upon Epitaphs
    Probably composed between c Dec 1809 and 22 Feb 1810. (1809:136.)
    Sentence "If then in a creature" (*Exc* 1814, p. 434) perhaps added to first published essay early 1814. (Appendix VI.)
    One Essay, "It needs scarcely be said . . ." pub. *Friend* 22 Feb 1810. Other two essays pub. Grosart.

194. *1810* ("O'erweening Statesmen Have Full Long Relied")
    Indignation of a High-minded Spaniard. 1810
    "In Due Observance of an Ancient Rite"
    Feelings of a Noble Biscayan . . . 1810
    The Oak of Guernica . . . 1810
    Perhaps composed 1810. (1809:23n.)
    Pub. *P* 1815.

195. "The Martial Courage of a Day Is Vain"
    Perhaps composed c but not before 15 Mar 1810. (1809:23n.)
    Pub. *P* 1815.

196. *Characteristics of a Child Three Years Old*
Possibly composed 1811; probably composed between 3 Jan 1813 and c
late May 1814. (IF note; Appendix VI. See 1811:1.)
Pub. *P* 1815.

197. *Conclusion. 1811* ("Here Pause: the Poet Claims at Least This Praise")
1811 ("The Power of Armies Is a Visible Thing")
Spanish Guerillas. 1811 ("They Seek, Are Sought; to Daily Battle Led")
Perhaps composed 1811. (1811:2.)
Pub. *P* 1815.

198. *On a Celebrated Event in Ancient History*
Upon the Same Event ("When, Far and Wide, Swift as the Beams of
Morn")
Probably composed between c 20 Mar and 30 Mar 1811. (1811:13.)
Pub. *P* 1815.

199. *Upon the Sight of a Beautiful Picture*
Perhaps composed c early June 1811. (1811:25.)
Pub. *P* 1815.

200. *Epistle to Sir George Howland Beaumont, Bart.*
Departure from the Vale of Grasmere. August 1803 (originally part of
Epistle)
Probably mainly composed c 26–c 28 Aug 1811. *Epistle* probably not
completed until preparation for 1842 publication. (1811:42.)
Departure pub. *PW* 1827; *Epistle* pub. *PELY.*

201. *Written with a Slate Pencil on a Stone, on the Side of the Mountain of Black
Comb*
View from the Top of Black Comb
Probably composed between late Aug 1811 and c 1813. One poem
probably composed by c Nov 1812. (1811:45.)
Pub. *P* 1815.

202. *In the Grounds of Coleorton* ("The Embowering Rose, the Acacia, and
the Pine")
Written at the Request of Sir George Beaumont, Bart. ("Ye Lime-trees,
Ranged before This Hallowed Urn")

Perhaps basically composed c mid-Oct, probably by 26 Oct, 1811;
alterations probably c but by 30 Oct; other alterations to "Ye Lime-
trees" by 16 Nov. (1811:53; 1811:60; 1811:63.)
Pub. *P* 1815.

203. *In a Garden of the Same* [Coleorton] ("Oft Is the Medal Faithful to Its
Trust")
  Probably composed c but by 29 Oct 1811. (1811:59.)
  Pub. *P* 1815.

204. *For a Seat in the Groves of Coleorton* ("Beneath Yon Eastern Ridge, the
Craggy Bound")
  Composed 19 Nov 1811. (1811:64.)
  Pub. *P* 1815.

205. "The Fairest, Brightest Hues of Ether Fade"
  Probably composed 28 July 1812 or shortly after; possibly early Sept,
  by 8 Sept, 1812. (1812:65; 1812:80.)
  Pub. *P* 1815.

206. "Even as a Dragon's Eye That Feels the Stress"
  "Hail, Twilight, Sovereign of One Peaceful Hour"
  Perhaps composed c but by 8 Sept 1812. (1812:80.)
  Pub. *P* 1815.

207. *Composed on the Eve of the Marriage of a Friend in the Vale of Grasmere,
1812*
  Perhaps composed 1 Nov 1812. (1812:93.)
  Pub. *P* 1815.

208. "Surprised by Joy—Impatient as the Wind"
  Probably composed between some time in 1813 and c mid-Oct 1814.
  (1813:1.)
  Pub. *P* 1815.

209. Fragments:
  a. "As When upon the Smooth Pacific Deep" (*PW* V, 346)
  b. "Come Ye That Are Disturb'd" (*PW* V, 429–30)
  Maternal Grief

51

Fragments perhaps composed between 3 Jan 1813 and c late May 1814.
Maternal Grief probably basically composed within that period. (Appendix VI. See also GCL 196.)
Maternal Grief pub. *PELY.*

210. *November, 1813* ("Now That All Hearts Are Glad, All Faces Bright")
Perhaps composed c mid-Nov 1813, not before 6 Nov. (1813:104.)
Pub. *Courier* 1 Jan 1814.

211. *Composed in One of the Valleys of Westmoreland, on Easter Sunday*
Possibly basically composed 10 Apr 1814. (1814:20; GCL 222n.)
Pub. *Waggoner* 1819.

212. "Oft, through Thy Fair Domains, Illustrious Peer!" (Dedicatory Verses
for *Exc*)
Probably c June, possibly 29 June, 1814. (1814:33.)
Pub. *Exc.*

213. *Composed at Cora Linn* ("Lord of the Vale! Astounding Flood")
Possibly composed in part 25 July 1814 or shortly after; probably not
completed until c but by 1820. (1814:52.)
Pub. *P* 1820.

214. *The Brownie's Cell*
Possibly composed in part 5 Aug 1814 or shortly after; probably not
completed until c but by 1820. (1814:63.)
Pub. *P* 1820.

215. *Effusion. In the Pleasure-ground on the Banks of the Bran, near Dunkeld*
Possibly composed in part 19 Aug 1814 or shortly after; probably not
completed until between 1820 and 1827. (1814:77.)
Pub. *P* 1827.

216. "From the Dark Chambers of Dejection Freed"
Perhaps composed between 25 and 30 Aug 1814; possibly c early Oct,
fairly certainly by late Oct. (1814:83.)
Pub. *P* 1815.

217. *Yarrow Visited*
Probably mostly composed between 2 and 16 Sept 1814; certainly
between 1 and 16 Sept. (1814:89.)
Pub. *P* 1815.

218. *Laodamia*
    A 130-line version composed probably c mid-Oct, certainly by 27 Oct,
    1814. Probably organized in *P* 1815 form by early Feb 1815. Lines 115–
    20 perhaps composed c early Feb. (See 1814:112; 1815:11.)
    Pub. *P* 1815.

219. Mary Barker, *Lines Addressed to a Noble Lord*
    Some composition by W possibly c early Oct 1814.
    Revision and additions (see 1814:124) perhaps written c Nov, probably
    by 10 Dec, 1814. Other revisions c 19 Feb 1815. (See 1814:103; 1814:
    111; 1814:124; 1815:21.)

220. *Lines Written November 13, 1814, on a Blank Leaf in a Copy of the Author's
    Poem " The Excursion"*
    Composed 13 Nov 1814. (1814:129.)
    Pub. *P* 1815.

221. *Preface* to *P* 1815
    Essay, Supplementary to the Preface
    Probably mostly composed c Jan, certainly by early Feb 1815. *Essay,
    Supplementary* perhaps draws on work dating between 3 Oct and 18 Dec
    1800. (GCL 37; 1815:1.)

222. *Artegal and Elidure*
    Possibly composed c 1815, but not before Mar 1815. (*Laodamia* IF note;
    DC MS 80.)[35]
    Pub. *P* 1820.

---

[35] Much of DC MS 80 is filled—or was at one time filled—with copy and draft for
P 1815. Remaining also are copies by SH of *View from the Top of Black Comb* and
Written with a Slate Pencil on a Stone, on the Side of the Mountain of Black Comb that
appear earlier than the main body of the copying. Other materials, some written after
preparations for *P* 1815, some written out seemingly for *P* 1815 but not published until
later, are also present.
    Materials fairly certainly connected with the preparations for *P* 1815, and hence
probably written in between 9 Sept and late Oct 1814, include *The Plain of Donnerdale*
(here entitled *To the River Duddon*); *Composed by the Side of Grasmere Lake. 1807*;
Composed in One of the Valleys of Westmoreland, on Easter Sunday; *Grief, Thou Hast Lost
an Ever Ready Friend*; and *"There Is a Little Unpretending Rill"* (here commencing
"There Is a Tiny Water"). All of these were published in 1819 or 1820. Materials
possibly somewhat later include drafts of blank verse concerning age and death

223. "In Trellis'd Shed with Clustering Roses Gay" (Dedicatory Verses for
WD)

    Perhaps composed c and probably concluded on 20 Apr 1815. (1815:53.)
Pub. *Courier* 17 May 1815 (also pub. shortly after in *WD*).

---

loosely resembling *Exc* VII.c285; *Laodamia* 7–12 (1820 readings; these lines were
written in before the blank verse); *Repentance* (EdS MS 2, certainly written after the
Laodamia lines); and drafts for *Artegal and Elidure*. The *Epistle Dedicatory* to *WD* is also
present and seems of about the same time as the *P* 1815 materials.

    The *Artegal and Elidure* drafts are spread out widely through the NB and must have
been written later than most of the rest of the drafts just cited—certainly later than the
Laodamia and *Epistle Dedicatory* drafts, and probably, though less certainly so, later than
the *Repentance* drafts. At one point such draft has been copied in after this note:

Postage of Proofs for White Doe

Feb 24   2 Proofs [?11½] . . . . . 1–1.

The *Artegal and Elidure* draft, clearly very early in the development of the poem, can
thus hardly in any case all have preceded 24 Feb 1815. W obviously did not write the
Laodamia revision in time for it to be included in *P* 1815; so that that entry probably
dates after early Feb (see 1815:21). While the *Epistle Dedicatory* may have been among
the last printed portions of *WD*, and must have been written by 20 Apr, it was not
necessarily all written about that date, and most or all of the drafts might conceivably
have been entered c Mar 1815. Further indications of a date this early for work on
Artegal and Elidure are found in W's IF note date of 1815 for the poem and in his statement in the IF note to *Laodamia* that that poem, *Artegal and Elidure*, and *Dion* were
written "at the same time." What is clearly early draft for *Dion*, however, is found in
DC MS Verse 66, otherwise containing work closely related to the preparation of W's
main publications of 1819 and 1820; and the subject matter of *Dion* strongly suggests a
time of origin, as remarked by J. P. Pritchard, about early 1816 ("On the Making of
Wordsworth's 'Dion,'" *Stud Phil* XLIX, 1952, 66), or in any case not before the
second half of 1815. W's IF note recollection may thus have been overinclusive.

    A date of possibly c 1815 but not before c Mar would seem justified for basic work
on *Artegal and Elidure*. Possibly some work on *Dion* took place that early, but the likelihood is not strong. This MS of *Artegal and Elidure* precedes the MSS in MS 72 and MS
Verse 66, which were certainly written by 1820—by which time the revision of
Repentance had of course also been written.

54

Chronology, 1 8 0 0 — 1 8 1 5

1 8 0 0

[On writings of W possibly of this year, see below and GCL 1–32.]

1. Probably this year, certainly by Dec 18; possibly basically c Jan

W composes "There Is an Eminence." (DC MS 25. See 1800:3n; 1800:229.)[1]

2. Probably this year, by Oct 15

W writes blank verse drafts concerning characters named Mary and Lennox, a yew-tree, and the composing effects of the recollections of the yew-tree on Mary's thoughts. (DC MS 33. See 1800:89n.)[2]

3. Probably this year, certainly by Oct 15; perhaps between Apr and Oct 13

W composes "It Was an April Morning." (Content; DC MS 25. See 1800:89n; 1800:164.)[3]

[1] As remarked in the Preface, I have uniformly assumed, except where evidence directly indicates a date within the last ten days of 1799 (see *CEY* 283–86), that W's Grasmere poems in fact do not date before 1800. Noteworthy here is a comment by W for his nephew John, dated 6 Mar 1844, on the flyleaf of a copy of the second volume of *LB* 1800 (DCP): "This 2nd volume consists exclusively of Poems composed by me either during my residence in Germany or in the course of a few months after my Sister and I came to live in the Vale of Grasmere."

[2] These fragments are found in DC MS 33 between the draft for *The Brothers*, with which they appear contemporary, and a copy of the note for *Joanna*. The draft toward *The Brothers* cannot have been written before late Dec 1799 (see *CEY* 36, 285), and the note to *Joanna* probably dates between a time c but by 23 Aug and 15 Oct 1800.

[3] Drafts for lines 38–47 appear in DC MS 25 along with numerous drafts for *The Brothers*, *To M.H.* (the MS mentioned *PW* II, 488; see *CEY* 36), and "There Is an Eminence" (lines 12–17). All the drafts appear to have been written at about the same time.

4. Probably this year, certainly by Oct 10

W composes *Rural Architecture*. (*DWJ* M 44; *EY* 306–07; content. See 1800:89n; 1800:159; Appendix II.)

5. Probably this year, certainly by Sept 15

W composes:
The Childless Father
The Pet Lamb
(IF note; Hale White 14; *CEY* 324. See 1800:89n; 1800:138.)[4]

6. Probably this year, certainly by Aug 13 (and 1811 Nov)

W composes *For the Spot Where the Hermitage Stood on St. Herbert's Island, Derwent-water*. (He revises the poem in Nov 1811: see 1811:61; 1811:63.) (Content; *EY* 291; *STCL* I, 617. See 1800:89n.)

7. Probably this year, certainly by Aug 13

W composes:
Song for the Wandering Jew
"'Tis Said That Some Have Died for Love"
(*CEY* 326. See 1800:89n; 1800:99; Appendix I.)[5]

8. Probably this year, by early June, certainly by Aug 13

W composes *Written with a Pencil upon a Stone in the Wall of the House (an Out-house), on the Island of Grasmere*. (Appendix II. See 1800: 89n; 1800:99.)

---

[4] *The Pet Lamb*, subtitled "A Pastoral," would seem fairly certainly a Grasmere "pastoral" associated with the other poems similarly subtitled composed in this year— *The Brothers, The Oak and the Broom, The Idle Shepherd-boys, Michael* (see esp. 1800:31n). JW remarked on 24 Feb 1801 that W had Joanna [H] in mind when he wrote *The Pet Lamb*. (*JWL* 94. See also *Pet Lamb* IF note, where W denies that Barbara Lewthwaite prompted the poem.)

[5] The poet's introduction of the subject of "'Tis Said," esp. the statement that "There is one whom I five years have known" (line 6), is probably not factually accurate.

9. Probably this year, certainly by Aug 4; and c but by Aug 13

Probably by 4 Aug, W composes *Written with a Slate Pencil upon a Stone, the Largest of a Heap Lying near a Deserted Quarry, upon One of the Islands at Rydal.* The final *LB* 1800 version of lines 1–9 is completed probably c but by 13 Aug. (*EY* 291–92; *STCL* I, 617. See 1800:89n; 1800:99; Appendix I.)

10. Probably this year, certainly by Aug 4

W composes:
The Oak and the Broom
The Waterfall and the Eglantine
(*CEY* 324; Hale White 10. See 1800:89n; 1800:94; Appendix I.)

11. Probably this year, by July 29

W composes *The Two Thieves.* (Appendix I; Appendix II; 1800: 89.)[6]

12. Probably this year, certainly by July 29

W composes *The Idle Shepherd-boys.* (Appendix I; Appendix II; 1800:89.)[7]

13. Probably early this year, fairly certainly by Apr 5

W completes *The Brothers.* In a period of c 3 days during composition of *The Brothers,* W composes *Hart-leap Well.* (*Hart-leap Well* IF note; Appendix II; 1800:48n. See 1800:18.)

14. Perhaps c early this year (and 1806)

W possibly composes lines used in *The Recluse* I, *Home at Grasmere.* (Main composition is unlikely to precede 1806.) The poem in any case probably largely describes Grasmere, and W's and DW's response

---

[6] Neither content nor style nor other evidence offers conclusive indication of composition during the Grasmere residence, but nothing is known of the existence of the poem before 1800, the date assigned in editions from 1836 through 1850.

[7] The IF note to *The Idle Shepherd-boys* dates the poem 1800, the year also assigned in editions 1836–1850. The content strongly implies that this poem is a Grasmere "pastoral" (see 1800:5n).

to it, in the early months of 1800. Among passages of which the content is esp. suggestive of conception in 1800 are:

  71–79 ("On Nature's Invitation")
  170–92 (Possibly in form resembling *PW* V, 319–20 *app crit* for lines 170–71): Possibly c but after 10 Mar. (See *PW* V, 475.)
  238–68 (The two swans)
  471–90 (Prospects opening to the newcomer)
  502–44 (Dwellers in sight of the Vale)
  648–63 (JW): Perhaps between late Jan and late Feb. (See 1800:18.) (See Appendix VI.)

15. Probably c very early this year, by Feb 4–early 1803

Probably c very early 1800, W entrusts to Basil Montagu delivery of a letter to [JFP] concerning his financial affairs and Montagu's involvement in them. Montagu does not deliver the letter, despite JFP's remonstrances, until perhaps shortly after 4 Feb. (*STCL* I, 567–68. See *CEY* 282.)

By 11 Mar JFP undertakes to pay W's annuity for Montagu, but perhaps subsequently makes no direct payments. For at least the next three years Montagu pays approximately £13 a quarter. (*EY* 281, 336, 383.)[8]

16. Probably Jan (–1808 June 5)

W, DW commence filling a Commonplace Book, now DC MS 26. For contents and probable time of entry see Appendix IX. (The last entry probably dates from 5 June 1808.)

17. Jan 1

RW's accounts credit DW with £100, a legacy from Christopher Crackanthorpe, under this date. (RW accounts, DCP. See *CEY* 273, 275.)[9]

---

[8] *CEY* 172, 184, 186 indicate that Montagu's indebtedness to W, on which either annuity payment or interest and insurance regularly came due, was £400. Montagu was £50 in arrears at the time of W's arrival at Grasmere (*EY* 398).

[9] A note below one record of this credit (the substance is repeated in a later draft) states that RW is to inquire into a sum of £136 received from William Cookson, of which the time or exact sum cannot now be accounted for. In the final accounts W's and DW's share is credited under the date of May 1792 (see *CEY* 130–31).

18. c end of Jan–Sept 29

JW arrives at DC c end of Jan for a visit. He remains until Sept 29. (*EY* 272, 649; 1800:145. See *EY* 563; 1800:21.)

Lines 76–77 of *The Brothers* perhaps draw on circumstances of his arrival, when he twice fails to find courage to knock at the door and finally sends word from the inn. (*EY* 272.) On this visit see esp.: *EY* 559–60, 562–63; *JWL* 24; Moorman I, 471–74. W refers to the visit in "When to the Attractions." (See esp. 1800:26.)[10]

19. Feb 3

RW's accounts credit W with £7/10/–, half-year dividend on W's 3 percent consols, under this date. (RW accounts, DCP.)

20. Probably c Feb 14

W draws on RW for £10/14/– by a bill in favor of J. Halhead, and for £8/16/6 by a bill in favor of Robinson and Wilson. (RW accounts, DCP.)[11]

21. c late Feb–probably Apr 4 or 5

W fetches MH from Penrith for a visit c late Feb. She remains at DC until probably 4 or 5 Apr. (*EY* 282. See 1800:28.)

On the relationship between JW, W, MH during this visit see esp. *EY* 560, 563; *MWL* 3; *JWL* 24; Moorman I, 472–74.[12]

22. Possibly c but after Mar 10

W composes *HG* 170–92, possibly in a form resembling *PW* V, 319–20 *app crit* for lines 170/171. (See 1800:14; *PW* V, 475.)

[10] DW stated that JW arrived before she and W had been six weeks in the house (*EY* 649). A later remark of W's to Harriet Martineau recorded in Mrs. Martineau's *Autobiography* (Boston, 1877) II, 235, has little specific relevance to JW, but may be noted under the date of the first known arrival of a guest who dined at DC: "When you have a visitor you must do as [DW and I] did [in our early days at Grasmere]; you must say 'if you like to have a cup of tea with us, you are very welcome; but if you want any meat;—you must pay for your board.'" (See also R. W. Emerson, *English Traits*, Boston, 1856, 295, and Lady Charnwood, *An Autograph Collection*, London, 1930, 245.)

[11] RW's accounts record payment of both drafts, due at 40 days, under 25 Mar.

[12] W later stated that at this time he had "no thoughts of marrying" (*EY* 563).

23. Mar 11

W writes to RW: JW asks for £20 by return of post. Pinney has undertaken to pay the Montagu annuity [see 1800:15]. (*EY* 281.)

24. Mar 22

RW's accounts charge W £-/2/- for postage for "a foreign letter" under this date. (RW accounts, DCP. See 1800:27; *EY* 282.)

25. Probably c early Apr

John Stoddart and James Moncrieff probably visit at DC, arriving c but by 5 Apr, and departing after 6 Apr. (Woof *Ariel* 7; *JWL* 90; Stoddart, *Remarks on Local Scenery & Manners in Scotland*, London, 1801, General Map and II, 216–17, 252, 265–75, 287, 332.)[13]

26. Possibly Apr

W discovers a forest path which he believes to have been worn by JW. The discovery forms the subject of "When to the Attractions of the Busy World," esp. lines 43–66 [see also *PW* II, 120–21 *app crit*]. ("When to the Attractions," line 45.)

DW probably receives a letter from Charles Lloyd. It perhaps inquires about the possibility of obtaining a house in the neighborhood. (Letter, Lloyd to Thomas Manning, 9 May 1800, Cornell Collection, Cornell 2904.)[14]

[13] JW remarked to MH on 16 Feb 1801 that he called upon "S[t]oddart [in London] very often on purpose to have the pleasure of talking about you—" (*JWL* 90). MH was not at DC when Stoddart visited later in the year. Stoddart's tours of Scotland of 1799–1800 apparently included two returns into England near the Lake area, the first in the spring of 1800 (see *Remarks* as cited). Robert Woof has published confirming evidence in a transcript of a portion of a letter of 20 Sept 1854 from Stoddart to I. Richardson (Woof *Ariel* 7). Stoddart there explains that in his walk from Edinburgh to London in 1800 he took Moncrieff to visit Wordsworth. "Hence," he continues, "we found Coleridge; and I have the general impression of having been much gratified by their poetical communications." Stoddart's other comments express doubt that W contributed substantially to STC's translation of *Wallenstein*. "Hence" apparently means "thus" or "there," rather than "elsewhere from there."

[14] The early MSS of the poem make no mention of the month in which the path apparently worn by JW was discovered; but the discovery itself no doubt really took place. Lloyd observes, without further comment, "I have, as yet received no answer to my letter to Miss Wordsworth—."

27. Apr 2

RW's accounts charge W payment of £-/1/- for postage for "a foreign letter" under this date. (RW accounts, DCP. See 1800:24; *EY* 282.)

28. Probably Apr 4 or Apr 5 ff

MH departs from DC, probably for Penrith, and perhaps accompanied by W. W probably returns to DC within a day or so at most. (*EY* 282; letters, Joanna H to John M, postmark 9 Apr 1800, and to John M [26 Apr 1800], JFW Papers.)[15]

29. Apr 6–Apr 22; May 4

STC arrives for a visit, his first to DC, on 6 Apr. He remains until 4 May. (*STCNB* 719; *STCL* I, 588.)

Probably during this visit STC translates the second part of Schiller's *Wallenstein*, completing the work by 22 Apr. Perhaps at this time W is impressed by a passage possibly now *Piccolomini* II, iv, 83ff. (*STCL* I, 585–87; *HCRWC* 402; *STCPW* II, 598; *LL* I, 179; 1800:25; 1800:36.)[16]

---

[15] DW wrote on 11 Apr that MH "left us a week ago" (*EY* 282; cf *EY* 560). Joanna H wrote to John M from Penrith (post office stamp) in a letter fairly certainly written by 6 Apr: "[MW] is now with Miss Wordsworths at Grasmere. we expect her home to night. Mr. W. came for her . . . ." The remarks suggest that MH is unlikely to have remained at DC much beyond the time at which Joanna's letter was written. Since W came to Penrith for her, he perhaps accompanied her on her return as well.

Joanna later wrote to John M in a letter dated "Saturday night"—probably 26 Apr (postmark 29 Apr): "Mary and my sister left us on friday, Poor Honeys . . . . My Sister Mary was very much delighted indeed with Grasmere, and the Wordsworth way of living, she says she n[*seal*] so compleat a Cottage in he [*sic*] life, and e[*seal*]ng [? so] very comfortable as they have."

[16] STC writes to Josiah Wedgwood from DC on 21 Apr that he will send off the last sheet of his translation of Schiller "tomorrow morning." W is recorded by HCR as saying that it was at "about" the time of STC's translation of Part II of *Wallenstein* that he saw the "passages of the Astronomical Times and the antient Mythology, which, as treated in Coleridge's professed [?] translat[i]on, were infinitely superior." The superiority is presumably that of STC's adaptation over the original.

30. Apr 8 or Apr 9–Apr 11 and shortly after

Richard Cooke arrives at DC for a visit on 8 or 9 Apr. He remains until at least 11 Apr, probably departing shortly thereafter. (*EY* 282.)

31. Apr [10]

STC writes to RS that W has decided to publish "a second Volume of Lyrical Ballads, & Pastorals," and is meditating a novel. (*STCL* I, 585.)[17]

32. Apr 11

DW writes to RW: Cooke, JW, STC visit. Requests RW to forward some items to be sent him for STC, with his old clothes and a parcel to be sent him by Montagu. (*EY* 282.)

33. Apr 19

RW's accounts charge W for remittance of a £20 Bank of England note to him at Grasmere under this date. (RW accounts, DCP.)

34. Perhaps May 1

A review of *LB* 1798 [by William Heath] appears in the *Antijacobin Review* (V, Apr 1800). (See Hayden; Ward.)

35. May 1

W draws on RW for £25/18/– by bill in favor of Thomas Lady-man. (RW accounts, DCP; bill, DCP.)[18]

---

[17] STC's full comment is: "Wordsworth publishes a second Volume of Lyrical Ballads, & Pastorals. He mediates a novel—& so do I—but first I shall re-write my Tragedy." The sort of novel W was meditating is not known. (Concerning an earlier plan see C. L. Shaver, "Wordsworth's *Vaudracour* and Wilkinson's *The Wanderer*," *RES* N.S. XII, 1961, 55–57; *CEY* 138.) STC's phrasing makes clear that W's plan for a "series of pastorals, the scene of which [is] laid among the mountains of Cumberland and Westmoreland" was firmly conceived by this time. See *The Brothers* n; *CEY* 285; 1800:5n.

[18] RW records payment under 13 June.

36. May 4 (–June 29)

STC departs from DC for Bristol and Stowey. He probably takes with him MSS of W's poems, including *Hart-leap Well*, "There Was a Boy," *Ellen Irwin*, *The Brothers*. (*STCL* I, 588. See also *STCL* I, 585, 587, 589.)

37. May 14–June 7, 8; –1806 Sept 8

On 14 May W, JW depart from Grasmere for a visit to the H farm at Gallow Hill. DW accompanies them on their departure as far as the turning in Lowwood Bay. W returns to DC 7 June, JW 8 June. The trip to Gallow Hill includes visits to Gordale, Yordas, and probably neighboring areas. The visit to Yordas probably contributes to *Prel* VIII.711–41. This visit to Gordale and the area perhaps contributes also to "Pure Element of Waters!," *Malham Cove*, and *Gordale*, although it is not the immediate occasion of any of these. Possibly at this time W also visits St. Robert's Chapel near Knaresborough. (He later refers to the visit in *Effusion. In the Pleasure-ground . . . near Dunkeld*, 46–72.)

On 14 May DW begins her Grasmere Journal. (*DWJ* M 15.)

W, JW probably arrive at Gallow Hill c 19 May, and depart probably c but by 5 June. Probably during this visit, and perhaps c 22 May or c 28 May, W writes a letter to DW of which only a sentence survives, asking DW to "say all that is affectionate to A. and all that is fatherly to C." (*EY* 282.) Perhaps during this visit W visits Whitby. He also visits Whitby several times between now and 8 Sept 1806, on one such occasion seeing from the pier an apparition, produced by mist, of huge faces with fantastically prominent noses in profile. (*MY* I, 79.) (On this visit see also 1800: 49.)[19]

[19] Whether this was W's first visit to Gordale and Yordas is not known (see esp. *CEY* 84, 93). The brothers were absent from DC from 14 May till 7–8 June, or three weeks and three days, despite DW's later statement they were absent a "whole month" and W's that they visited at Gallow Hill itself for three weeks (*EY* 298, 317–18). A fairly direct route to Gallow Hill would have measured something like 150 miles each way; but the journey plainly included side excursions.

The time suggested for the visit near Knaresborough, which possibly occurred as early as summer 1788 or 1789, is highly conjectural. W is not known to have gone near Knaresborough, however, between this time and that of the composition of the

38. May 16

DW writes to MH. (*DWJ* M 16–17.)

39. May 17

DW reads *A Midsummer Night's Dream*, [LB]. Ashburner brings coals. (*DWJ* M 17.)

40. May 18, 19

On 18 May DW walks to Ambleside, where letters arrive from STC and Cottle.

On 19 May she reads *Timon of Athens*. (*DWJ* M 17–19.)

41. May 21

STC writes to William Godwin from Nether Stowey, stating an intention of settling at Keswick if he is unable to procure a suitable house at Stowey. (*STCL* I, 588. See 1800:60.)

42. May 24 (–June 8)

RW's accounts credit W with £104/17/– received from Charles Douglas under this date. This sum completes Douglas's payment of his debt to W [see esp. *CEY* 177, 184, 190], including interest to date. (RW accounts, DCP. See *EY* 283; 1800:52; 1800:56.)[20]

[20] W on 8 June urged RW to "accept the 100 £ which Douglas is ready to pay and discharge him from any obligation for the other 100 £"—that is, the rest of the £200 hitherto owed jointly by Douglas and Montagu. The sum recorded under 24 May can hardly be a repayment of some other debt; so probably either the account is misdated, or RW already had a bill so dated, or the money in hand, from Douglas. See also 1800:52.

Effusion. The times of W's several visits to Whitby are also unrecorded. He probably did not visit eastern Yorkshire between his marriage (4 Oct 1802) and 1806. W's description of the faces recalls grotesque faces drawn in his schoolboy notebooks.

W's letter mentioning "A." and "C." probably reached DW on 24 or 30 May (see *DWJ* M 20, 22).

On 21 May 1800 Joanna H wrote to John M: "You will be glad to hear that Tom, George, and Mary are safe arrived at Gallow Hill and like their farm very well." (JFW Papers.)

Letters arrive from W, MH, Douglas. DW writes to W. (*DWJ* M 20.)

43. May 25

DW reads *Macbeth*, writes to CW. Letters arrive from STC, Charles Lloyd. (*DWJ* M 20.)

44. May 26

DW writes to Joanna H, STC, Charles Lloyd, W. (*DWJ* M 20–21.)

45. May 27

A beggar woman calls at DC. Later DW, on her way to Ambleside with letters [see 1800:44], meets other members of the woman's family, including two boys who deny that she is their mother. DW's description of the incident later forms the basis of W's *Beggars* [see 1802:63; 1802:64]. A letter arrives from STC. (*DWJ* M 21, 26–27.)

46. May 29

DW reads *King John*; fishes with a party of the Sympsons'. (*DWJ* M 21.)

47. May 30

A letter arrives from W. (*DWJ* M 22.)

48. Probably c early June; perhaps between c early June and June 29

Probably c early June STC leaves with Humphry Davy, in Bristol, MSS of *Hart-leap Well*, "There Was a Boy," and other of W's poems, possibly including *Ellen Irwin*; reads *The Brothers* to him. He probably leaves *The Brothers* with Thomas Poole in Stowey. (*STCL* I, 611; *EY* 289; *The Rowfant Library*, 1886.)[21]

[21] On 26 Nov 1800 Davy wrote to STC of his regrets that "Christobel is not to be published in the lyrical ballads," remarking that he would have liked to see the whole poem because of a wish induced by the first part. (Letter, Davy to STC, PML. Cf *STCL* I, 649.) It thus appears likely that Davy saw or heard *Christabel* I at the time of

49. Probably c very early June

W, Thomas H call on Francis Wrangham at Hunmanby, W intending a two-day visit; but Wrangham is not at home. (*EY* 317–19. See 1800:37.)

50. June 1

A letter arrives from STC. (*DWJ* M 22–23. See 1800:51.)

51. June 2, 3

On 2 June DW inquires about lodgings for STC; writes to him. The letter is sent off 3 June. (*DWJ* M 23.)

52. June 4, 5

RW's accounts credit W with £10 from Charles Douglas received through Richard Cooke under 4 June. (RW accounts, DCP. See 1800:42.)

On the same day DW writes to [William] Jackson [at Keswick].

On 5 June she receives a letter from Jackson and writes to STC. The correspondence probably concerned the possibility of renting GH for STC. (*DWJ* M 23–24. See 1800:50; 1800:51.)

53. Probably c but by June 5

W, JW depart Gallow Hill for Grasmere. (See 1800:37.)

54. June 6

DW writes to Aunt Cookson; posts a letter to STC [see 1800:52]; receives letters from John H and Montagu (who has enclosed a £3 note). (*DWJ* M 24.)

STC's visit. A MS of *The Brothers* described in *The Rowfant Library* (1886) contains a flyleaf endorsement, in the autograph of Thomas Poole, "Manuscript of Wordsworth left here by Coleridge in 1800." Poole's "here" is undoubtedly Stowey. The bulk of the MS is in the autograph of MH, and W has corrected the MS throughout; so MW would have written it before her departure from Grasmere, probably by 5 Apr.

55. June 7 (–June 8)

W arrives at DC at 11 PM, having left JW at Greta Bridge. He and DW retire at 4 AM. (*DWJ* M 25–26; *EY* 283–84.)

56. June 8

W, DW rise at 10. W and DW write to STC, Montagu, Douglas, RW. Mr. and Miss Sympson call; W and DW walk them home. JW returns. (*DWJ* M 35.)

W's letter to RW is the only letter written today known to survive: W encloses Montagu-Douglas note for £200; RW should accept the £100 that Douglas offers [see 1800:42n] and discharge him from further obligation, and obtain security from Montagu for the remaining £100. Other financial matters. Plans for a new edition of *LB*. (*EY* 283–84. See also 1800:42; 1800:52; 1800:54.)

57. June 9

W cuts down the winter cherry tree; he and DW go fishing. A girl calls begging. (*DWJ* M 25.)

58. June 10

JW carries letters to Ambleside; fishes. W, DW work about the house; W lies down after dinner. W, DW walk to Ambleside to search for lodgings for STC. (*DWJ* M 25–26.)

59. June 11

W, DW, JW fish; catch two pike; visit the island. Sympson calls. (*DWJ* M 27.)

60. June 12

W, DW, JW fish; walk to Rydal. (*DWJ* M 27.)

On this day STC writes to Josiah Wedgwood from Bristol indicating an intention to settle in the North. (*STCL* I, 591.)

61. June 13

W, DW, JW fish; catch a 7½-lb pike. [William] Gell and a party call. (*DWJ* M 27.)

62. June 14

W, JW go upon the lake. All drink tea at Mr. Sympson's. (*DWJ* M 27.)

63. June 15 (–June 16)

On 15 June JW walks to Coniston; W, DW walk. (JW returns next day.) Parker the tanner and the blacksmith from Hawkshead call. (*DWJ* M 27.)

64. June 16

W, DW walk to Brathay via Little Langdale. They drink tea at J. C. Ibbetson's; look at his pictures. They lend £3/9/– to the potter at Kendal; meet JW on their return home at about 10. (*DWJ* M 27–28; *EY* 494.)[22]

65. June 17

W, DW install a new window; walk to Rydal for letters in the evening; find one for STC. (*DWJ* M 28.)

66. June 18

W, DW walk around the lake and to the lower fall at Rydal. A poor hatter calls begging. (*DWJ* M 28.)

67. June 19

W, DW walk to Mr. Sympson's. W and Mr. Sympson go fishing in Thirlmere. W catches a 4¾-lb pike. JW, DW, Miss Sympson walk to meet them. (*DWJ* M 28.)

---

[22] This call on Ibbetson, at Brathay, is probably the occasion described by DW in 1804 as that when early in their residence at Grasmere they "called upon him and looked at his pictures" and the artist "was very civil" (*EY* 494). (On Ibbetson see esp. Mary R. Clay, *Julius Caesar Ibbetson*, London, 1948.)

68. June 20

W, DW garden. (*DWJ* M 28.)

69. June 21

W, DW walk to Ambleside for dental work for W. Young Mr. Sympson calls, drinks tea, sups. W, JW, and he fish at Rydal Water. Miss Sympson and three children call. DW walks with them to Rydal. DW walks also to Rydal Water; probably returns with the fishermen. (*DWJ* M 28–29.)

70. June 22

W, DW walk toward Rydal; walk for letters in the evening; find none. Jimmy Benson comes home drunk beside them. (*DWJ* M 29.)

71. June 23

Mr. Sympson calls in the morning. W, DW go into Langdale; W fishes. W also fishes in the evening at Rydal. DW, JW take tea to him, but meet him returning. (*DWJ* M 29–30.)

72. June 24

W goes to Ambleside. DW works; JW walks. W, DW, invited earlier by Barth Sympson, drink tea at Mr. Sympson's. (*DWJ* M 30.)

73. June 25

W, DW fish in Langdale; DW makes a shoe. (*DWJ* M 30.)

74. June 29 and shortly after (–c July 13, –July 23, 24); between June 29 and Oct 1

On 29 June STC, SFC, HC arrive at DC for a visit. (STC departs 23 July; the others 24 July.) A group including DW goes sailing on Grasmere. Within a few days STC becomes very ill. He is confined to bed for part of the time before c 13 July. (*DWJ* M 30; *STCNB* 749; *STCL* I, 603–04, 607, 615.)

STCNB 749–62 possibly reflect observations or conversations of this visit, on which see also esp. Moorman I, 477.

Probably during this visit W determines, at the urging of STC, esp. at a deserted quarry during a walk, to write a Preface for *LB* and perhaps begins work on it. He completes basic composition of the *Preface* on 27 Sept, and final basic MS corrections are completed by 1 Oct. (*EY* 292, 302; *DWJ* M 41; *LY* II, 910, III, 1248–49; BM Add. MS 41, 325, opp. p. 112; Appendix IV.)[23]

Probably during this visit, but by early July, STC, DW, W write two letters to Biggs and Cottle giving directions and corrections for *LB* vol. I:

(First letter:) (STC:) The order of the poems [*STCL* I, 593]. Alterations and other directions: (STC:) for *Expostulation and Reply, The Tables Turned, OMT, Complaint of a Forsaken Indian Woman, The Last of the Flock, LLSYT*; (DW:) *LLSYT* (continued) [*EY* 285–86]; *The Foster Mother's Tale* [*STCL* I, 594]; *Goody Blake and Harry Gill, The Thorn, We Are Seven, Anecdote for Fathers, Lines Written at a Small Distance, FV* [*EY* 286–87]; *The Dungeon* [*STCL* I, 594]; *Simon Lee, Lines Written in Early Spring* [*EY* 287]; *The Nightingale* [*STCL* I, 594]; *Lines*

---

[23] STC'S remarks of 29 July 1800 (*STCL* I, 615) suggest that the indisposition that attacked him shortly after 29 June 1800 was only just overcome when he wrote; but he appears to have been able to engage in correspondence or work on *LB* by c 13 July (*STCL* I, 603).

Concerning the origins of the Preface to *LB*, a note by W in BM Add. MS 41, 326, quoted in part Moorman I, 492, states: "In the foregoing [Memoir] there is frequent reference to what is called Mr W's theory, & his Preface. I will mention that I never cared a straw about the theory, & the Preface was written at the request of Mr Coleridge out of sheer good nature. I recollect the very spot, a deserted Quarry in the Vale of Grasmere where he pressed the thing upon me, & but for that it would never have been thought of." The deserted quarry was possibly that at Rydal (not strictly in the Vale of Grasmere), mentioned in the title of *WDQR*; but Grasmere, like many areas of the Lakes, abounds in small disused quarries. There can be little doubt, anyhow, that the present visit by STC was the occasion. (See also *LY* II, 910.) STC may have been too ill to walk out during the earlier part of his visit, but was apparently not so from the very first, and evidence is in any case so indeterminate that no more exact date seems justified. W's remark in his letter to Biggs and Cottle of c but by 13 Aug that the preface is "not yet ready" (*EY* 292) implies that some work had perhaps been done by that time. Composition was well advanced by mid-Sept (*DWJ* M 40; *EY* 302).

Written when Sailing in a Boat at Evening, Lines Written near Richmond.
(W:) Instructions to begin the printing immediately. (*EY* 285–88;
STCL I, 592–94.)

(Second letter:) (STC:) Correction for *The Idiot Boy* [*EY* 288]; copy
of *Love* [*STCL* I, 595–97]; correction for *The Mad Mother* [*EY* 288];
corrections for *AM* [*STCL* I, 598–602]; corrections for *TA* [*EY* 288];
advice to printer [*STCL* I, 602]. (*EY* 288; *STCL* I, 595–602.)[24]

75. July 11

RW's accounts charge W for remittance of a £30 bank note to
him at Grasmere under this date. (RW accounts, DCP.)

76. July 13

W writes to Josiah Wedgwood from Grasmere: Ill success, until
now, in obtaining repayment of loans from friends [see esp. 1800:42]
that would allow him to repay Wedgwood [see *CEY* 266–68]: RW
will pay Wedgwood £110/13/–. Poor health. (*EY* 284–85.)[25]

77. July 15

STC reports in a letter to Daniel Stuart that W's health is at present
such as to preclude all possibility of writing for a paper. (*STCL* I, 603.)

[24] While the letters might seem unlikely to date from the period of STC's illness
(see *STCL* I, 603, 607), the onset of the illness was probably not coincident with his
arrival at Grasmere, and its length remains uncertain. One may assume the arrival on
29 July of news that Biggs was ready to print vol. II of *LB* to be a fair indication that
the printing of vol. I was well advanced; the likelihood that W supervised the writing
of the second letter and the presence of DW's autograph in the first letter make it
probable that both were finished after STC's arrival at DC. The order of the contents
of the letter is not fully apparent in *EY* or *STCL*.

On the printing of *LB* 1800 see esp.: R. W. Chapman, "*Lyrical Ballads, 1800*,"
Book Collector's Quarterly II (1932), 25–26; E. L. McAdam, "The Publication of
Lyrical Ballads, 1800," *YULG* VIII (1933), 43–46; J. E. Wells, "*Lyrical Ballads, 1800*:
Cancel Leaves," *PMLA* LIII (1938), 207–29; J. E. Wells, "*Lyrical Ballads 1800*: A
Paste-In," *The Library* XIX (1939), 486–91.

[25] The money—at least £100 of it—was repaid to Wedgwood in Nov, apparently
after intervention by JW. See 1800:190.

78. Probably between mid-July and late in the year; perhaps between mid-July and Sept 29 (–1842)

Probably between mid-July and late in the year W sends a copy of *The Borderers*, or allows a copy to be sent, to Sheridan for consideration for presentation at Drury Lane. William Linley probably suggests revisions. W does not revise. (Nothing further is done with the play until it is prepared for its 1842 publication.)

Perhaps between mid-July and 29 Sept JW and DW make a copy (DC MS 27) of W's Preface to *The Borderers*. (E. J. Morley, "Coleridge in Germany [1799]," *Wordsworth and Coleridge. Studies in Honor of George McLean Harper*, Princeton, 1939, 234–35; *STCL* I, 603–04, 622–24, 646; *LL* I, 199, 245; *CEY* 254n.)[26]

---

[26] Sheridan apparently requested a tragedy from W and perhaps also from STC—possibly a revision of *Osorio*—through Stuart c early July 1800, evidently not having seen *The Borderers* earlier (*STCL* I, 603–04, 623, 624; see *CEY* 211–12). Evidence concerning subsequent events appears inconsistent. G. B. Greenough remarks (see Morley reference), fairly certainly referring to events of 1800: "Wordsworth showed *his* play to Linley who proposed several alterations. Wordsworth said he would not submit to having one syllable altered, that if in its present form it was not fit for the stage, he would try the experiment whether it was adopted for the closet."

W had submitted the play to Covent Garden in 1797; Linley was at Drury Lane; and W did alter the play in 1797 (*CEY* 26, 211); so, as far as this evidence is concerned, the time referred to by Greenough would appear to be the present. The play is mentioned elsewhere, however, in the coming months. On 6 Aug CL wrote (*LL* I, 199) that he would pay "five-and-forty thousand carriages to read W.'s tragedy, of which [he had] heard so much and seen so little—only what [he] saw at Stowey." On 17 Sept STC wrote that W "will set about adapting his Tragedy for the Stage" after the *LB* volumes have been published (I, 622–23); but on 22 Sept STC's expectations had changed: "[M]y Tragedy will remain at Keswick, and Wordsworth's is not likely to emigrate from Grasmere. Wordsworth's Drama is in it's present state not fit for the stage, and he is not well enough to submit to the drudgery of making it so." Then on 1 Nov he wrote: "Sheridan has sent to [W] requesting him to write a Tragedy for Drury Lane. But W. will not be diverted by anything from the prosecution of his Great Work" (*STCL* I, 646).

Stoddart wrote to STC on Monday 12 Jan 1801 requesting him to bring W's play for him to read (letter, PML). CL writes in his famous letter to Manning of 15 Feb 1801 (*LL* I, 245) that he has received from W a copy of the second volume of *LB* "accompanied by an acknowledgement of having received from me many months since a copy of a certain Tragedy"—which can only have been *The Borderers* (which

79. July 16 (and thereabouts)

On 16 July STC writes a letter to Davy in which he discusses a chronic illness of W's, clearly the pain which afflicted him when composing intently. (*STCL* I, 606. See *CEY* 73.)

80. Probably July 18

The Ws and Cs perhaps drink tea on the island in Grasmere. (*DWJ* M 30. See Moorman I, 478n; 1800:81.)[27]

81. Probably July 20

The Ws and Cs, perhaps also the Sympsons, possibly, but not probably, drink tea on the island in Grasmere. With the Sympsons they make a bonfire; possibly also drink tea in Bainriggs. (*STCL* I, 612; *STCNB* 758; *DWJ* M 30. See 1800:80.)

82. July 21

The Farmer of Tilsbury Vale is published in *MP* with the subtitle *A Character*, unsigned. (See Woof *SB* 173.)

83. Probably July 23 (–July 24, –1812 Mar 26); probably between July 23 and Dec 18

---

[27] *STCL*'s report to Davy (I, 612) may have condensed events of two days (tea on the island, and a bonfire and tea on shore probably on 20 July) into a synthesized description of events of "the night before [he] left Grasmere."

Manning had read earlier—*CEY* 254n).

One may infer that W was ready to submit the tragedy on 15 July (*STCL* I, 603–04); that the tragedy, probably in original form, did in fact emigrate from Grasmere; that it was seen by Linley between 15 July and 17 Sept; and that it was returned to W, perhaps by CL, who in any case saw it in London. The exact MS concerned is unidentified, although it was probably the "one perfect copy" to which STC refers on 15 July. It may be supposed to have corresponded in most respects to MS B. STC's remark on 22 Sept that the tragedy was not "likely to emigrate" would hence, in the case just described, refer to emigration in a revised state.

The copy of the Preface to *The Borderers* now DC MS 27 presents JW's autograph in an unusually small and neat form, but the writing shows a persuasive number of the characteristics of his hand (see esp. Appendix IX).

Probably on 23 July W, DW, STC perhaps all walk out together at an early hour. They meet an aged man fishing, an admonitory incident that later forms the basis of "A Narrow Girdle of Rough Stones and Crags" and of parts of *R &I*. W probably accompanies STC to Keswick. (He returns next day.) They perhaps arrive at GH at 5 PM. STC takes up residence at GH. (He last departs GH 26 Mar 1812.) (*STCNB* 761–62; *EY* 289; *STCL* I, 613; *DWJ* M 30; "A Narrow Girdle of Rough Stones and Crags" content and IF note; *R&I* content; 1800:142&n.)

Probably between 23 July and 18 Dec, perhaps in part between 23 July and 26 Sept, W composes "A Narrow Girdle of Rough Stones and Craggs." The poem is probably completed between 26 Sept and 6 Nov; probably composed in part 10 Oct. (See 1800:142n.)[28]

84. July 24

DW accompanies SFC and HC to Wythburn on their way to Keswick. Probably she meets W there. They drink tea at Mr. Sympson's. (*DWJ* M 30.)

85. July 25

DW bakes; unpacks Somersetshire goods. She and W sit in the orchard. (*DWJ* M 30.)[29]

86. July 26

W, DW sit in the orchard. DW makes shoes. (*DWJ* M 30–31.)

---

[28] W's statement on Tuesday 29 July (*EY* 289) that STC had departed "last Wednesday" and SFC and HC on Thursday, looks like an exact recollection, despite contrary indications in *STCL* I, 607–08, 610, 613, which imply that STC did not arrive at GH till 24 July. *STCNB* 762, however, appears to imply arrival at GH on 23 July: the "Jackesson's house" of that entry, although STC corrected the spelling from "Jackson," is almost certainly GH, of which William Jackson was owner and cotenant.

[29] It would be interesting to know what "our Somersetshire goods" included, esp. in the way of literary materials (see *CEY* 327n). On this day, one may note here also, STC complained in a letter to Humphry Davy of W's laziness (*STCL* I, 611; cf *STCL* I, 657–58).

87. July 27

DW copies out *Ruth;* reads Knight's *The Landscape.* W, DW row on, walk near the lake; hear a raven. The incident, and esp. DW's description of it, later contribute to *Exc* IV.1175–87. They meet Mr. and Miss Sympson; return to supper at 10. (*DWJ* M 31.)

88. July 28

W receives a note from STC enclosing one from Davy advising that Biggs is ready to print *LB* vol. II. W alters poems in the woods. (*DWJ* M 31; *EY* 289–90; *STCL* I, 611–12.)

89. July 29

W, DW gather peas for dinner; walk in the evening to find Hewetson's cottage, but darkness prevents them. (*DWJ* M 31–32.)

W writes to Humphry Davy: Sends MSS for *LB* 1800. Requests Davy to look over punctuation of the MS, and to look over proof sheets of the second volume of *LB*. DW copies *Hart-leap Well,* "There Was a Boy," *Ellen Irwin, The Brothers* 1–37. This is the third sheet of copy for *LB* 1800. (*EY* 289–90; Hale White 5–9; MS, YUL. See 1800: 48; 1800:91.)[30]

90. July 30

W intends to go to Keswick, but does not. In the evening he sails on the lake with DW till at least 10. (*DWJ* M 32.)

RW's accounts credit W with £7/10/–, half-year dividend on W's 3 percent consols, under this date. (RW accounts, DCP.)

[30] How many of W's poems STC had previously handed over to Davy (see 1800:48) in addition to at least two of the first three poems here forwarded by W is not known, nor is the immediacy of the relationship between that delivery and plans for the publication of a new edition of *LB*. A sufficient number of poems seems to have been involved in the earlier transfer for W to feel that printing could have been started in late July were Davy not asked to wait. It is remotely possible that any poem for vol. II, unless specifically shown by other evidence to date later, had been virtually completed by early June. A final date cannot ordinarily be fixed with confidence before the sending off of the MS of the particular poem in question. On W's sending of copy and proof corrections, probably esp. in his early years at Grasmere, see esp. H. A. L. Rice, "Wordsworth in Easedale," *Ariel* I (1970), 37. See also 1800:99&nn.

91. July 31 (–Aug 2)

On 31 July DW copies poems. STC arrives at DC bringing vol. II (1800) of RS's *Annual Anthology*. (He remains till 2 Aug.) The men go bathing. Probably all read poems while boating; walk. (*DWJ* M 32.)

92. Aug 1 (–Aug 4)

On 1 Aug DW copies *The Brothers*, commencing the fourth sheet of copy for *LB* 1800. (This sheet is completed on 4 Aug.) W, STC walk to the lake; all walk to Mary Point; read W's poems; "A Whirl-blast" and perhaps other poems are altered, perhaps cooperatively. Mr. Sympson comes to tea, and Barth Sympson comes afterward. (*DWJ* M 32.)

93. Between Aug 1 and Aug 4, and Aug 1 or 2

Between 1 and 4 Aug DW and STC complete the fourth sheet of copy for *LB* 1800. By 2 Aug DW completes copy of conclusion of *The Brothers* begun 1 Aug from line 38; STC adds directions about the printing of *The Brothers* and the order of the poems in II;[31] DW copies "Strange Fits of Passion." By 4 Aug STC copies "She Dwelt among the Untrodden Ways," "A Slumber Did My Spirit Seal"; writes the printer's directions, a memorandum concerning the order of the first seven poems in the volume. (*STCL* I, 611; *EY* 290; Hale White 9; *DWJ* M 32–33; MS, YUL. See *STCNB* 768–69.)

94. Between Aug 2 and Aug 4, and Aug 4 (–Aug 6)

STC and W complete the fifth sheet of MS copy for *LB* 1800, STC writing the main copy. The sheet contains *The Waterfall and the Eglantine, The Oak and the Broom, The Fly* [*Written in Germany*, cancelled

---

[31] The instruction to print *The Brothers* first confirms a plan first mentioned in STC's letter to Davy of 25 July (*STCL* I, 611); but the advice apparently did not reach the printer before the first sheet had been set in type from copy presumably sent on 29 July. *The Brothers* became the third poem in the volume (and remained third in the subsequent editions of *LB*).

without note by W]; *Lucy Gray; The Idle Shepherd Boys.* STC adds a memorandum probably written on 4 Aug.[32]

On 2 Aug W and STC walk to Keswick. (W returns on 6 Aug.) JW accompanies them to Wythburn, where he fishes; DW accompanies them as far as [Grove Cottage]; returns to DC; papers W's room. Probably on 2 Aug W writes to DW asking her and JW to come to Keswick (letter not known to survive). On 3 Aug DW receives the letter and writes a reply. (*DWJ* M 32–33; *EY* 291; *STCL* I, 616–17; Hale White 10; MS, YUL.)

95. Aug 4–possibly c Aug 6

JW travels to Keswick by chaise. He possibly returns c 6 Aug. (*DWJ* M 33.)[33]

96. Aug 6

W returns from Keswick at 11 PM, possibly with JW. (*DWJ* M 33. See 1800:95.)

97. Aug 7

DW packs up and sends a mattress to Keswick; boils gooseberries. W composes in the woods. He, DW walk to Mary Point in the evening. (*DWJ* M 33.)

The DCP Longman accounts charge W's account for two copies of Withering's *Botany* and two microscopes under this date. One of the microscopes, as well as one of the copies of Withering, probably goes to STC and becomes the microscope referred to in W's *Stanzas, Written in*

---

[32] The sheet is dated "Monday" and postmarked 7 Aug; so it was probably finished Monday 4 Aug.

[33] JW is not specifically stated by *DWJ* to be present at DC again until 18 Aug. In the absence of other evidence it is reasonable to assume that he returned from the place that W had been visiting at about the time that W returned, and that he returned to Keswick when W and DW did on 8 Aug.

My Pocket Copy of Thomson's Castle of Indolence 59–63. (See *EY* 321&n; Moorman I, 514n.)[34]

98. Aug 8 (–Aug 17)

W, DW, perhaps JW, delayed in starting by heat, walk via Watend-lath to Keswick, reaching GH at 11 PM. They drink tea at Mr. Sympson's on the way. (They return to DC on 17 Aug.) On the visit see esp. *EY* 298–99. (*DWJ* M 33.)

99. Between Aug 8 and Aug 13

W, DW, STC prepare and send off the sixth and seventh sheets of printer's copy for *LB* 1800. Sheet six, in the autograph of DW, with notes by W and STC, contains "'Tis Said That Some Have Died for Love," *Poor Susan*, *To a Sexton* (W adds note concerning its placement), *ISHS*, *WSIG*, *WDQR* (first seven lines cancelled and STC adds a note that new lines will be sent in the next sheet), *Andrew Jones* (numbered "18th poem" by STC), *A Whirl-blast*, *Song for the Wandering Jew*, *The Two Thieves*[35] (W adds a note asking that *The Two Thieves* be placed here [see below]), *Ruth*, lines 1–102.

Sheet seven, probably written c but by 13 Aug, in the autograph of DW, with notes by W and a note by STC, contains the remainder of *Ruth* (from line 103), a new beginning for *WDQR*, *Lines Written on a Tablet* ("If Nature, for a Favorite Child"; introduced by a note in W's hand), *The Two April Mornings*, *The Fountain*, *Nutting* (with a note in W's hand), "Three Years She Grew in Sun and Shower." W and STC add notes to the printer (STC's note begins "Be careful . . ."). (*EY* 291–93; *STCL* I, 617; Hale White 10–13; MS, YUL.)[36]

---

[34] The accounts record a charge of £2/16/0 for the copies of Withering and £1/7/0, with £-/1/4 wharfage, for the microscopes. All the items were probably sent off to the north at about this time. See also George Whalley, *Coleridge and Sara Hutchinson and the Asra Poems* (London, 1955) 27n.

[35] Stanzas 4 and 5 of *The Two Thieves* were probably copied by JW.

[36] It is possible that the sixth sheet was sent off before the seventh: DW in the seventh refers to the uncancelled portion of *Lines Written with a Slate Pencil* in the sixth as in "the last-sent sheet." Both received postmarks of 16 Aug (morning duty). As it is improbable that either was kept at Keswick long after completion, the fifth sheet may be dated c but by 13 Aug.

100. Aug 9

DW, STC walk in the Windy Brow woods. (*DWJ* M 33.)

101. Aug 10

W, DW, perhaps JW and one or more of the Cs sail upon Derwent Water in the evening. (*DWJ* M 34.)

102. Aug 11

DW, possibly W, JW walk with STC to Windy Brow. (*DWJ* M 34.)

103. Aug 12

DW, perhaps W, JW, and one or more of the Cs drink tea with the Cockins. W, DW walk along the Cockermouth road. W alters his poems. (*DWJ* M 34.)

104. Aug 13

DW and possibly others possibly make a sofa of sods out of the Windy Brow seat. Perhaps DW simply walks as far as the Windy Brow seat. (*DWJ* M 34; *STCNB* 830&n.)[37]

105. Aug 14

DW, perhaps W and JW and one or more of the Cs call at John Spedding's; they see Mary Spedding. W, DW walk in the woods in the evening. (*DWJ* M 34; *EY* 299.)

---

[37] The conjecture that the remark in *DWJ* "made the Windy Brow seat" refers to the "sopha of sods" mentioned *STCNB* 830 is supported by the appearance of *Inscription for a Seat by a Road Side*, a revision, fairly certainly by STC, of W's earlier *Inscription for a Seat by the Pathway Side Ascending to Windy Brow* in *MP* on 21 Oct (see *CEY* 25, 27; *STCNB* 830n). DW's phrasing is odd, however, for a reference to a seat that had in fact been in existence many years. She is perhaps using the word "made" in the sense of "went as far as" or "reached."

106. Aug 15

W probably works on poems. DW, HC go to see the Cockins; buy bacon. In the evening DW and others walk to Water End; feast on gooseberries at Silver Hill. (*DWJ* M 34.)[38]

107. Aug 16

DW works for SFC; walks with STC intending to gather raspberries. They are joined by Mary Spedding. (*DWJ* M 34; *EY* 299.)

108. Probably c but by Aug 17

W composes *The Seven Sisters*. (*DWJ* M 34. See Landon *RES* 393–94; Woof *SB* 176–78.)[39]

109. Aug 17

W, DW, perhaps JW return to DC, perhaps via Watendlath. They dine in Borrowdale; see Bassenthwaite and Bristol prison (unidentified) at the same time. W reads *The Seven Sisters*. (*DWJ* M 34.)[40]

110. Aug 18

DW, JW walk to Mr. Sympson's; meet W in returning. (*DWJ* M 34.)

[38] DW states simply that W was "in the wood." That he was composing is likely (see *DWJ* M 32, 33, 45). DW describes her purchase as "Bacon," but the chance of reference to Lord Verulam is slight.

[39] W appears to have read the poem to DW and probably JW on 17 Aug after several days of work at composition. The poem was probably written within those days. The note, undoubtedly by STC, that accompanied the poem on its publication in *MP* on 14 Oct acknowledges the poem's debt to Mrs. Robinson's *Haunted Beach*, mentioning the publication of Mrs. Robinson's poem in both *MP* (where it appeared on 26 Feb) and in the second volume of *The Annual Anthology*, which *DWJ* records STC's bringing to DC on 31 July (see *DWJ* M 32).

[40] DW states, "Wm. read us the 7 Sisters on a stone." The audience and place are uncertain, but it would appear that the Ws were on their way home, and that the "us" was DW and JW.

III. Aug 19

Mr. and Mrs. Sympson dine at DC; Miss Sympson and probably Barth Sympson drink tea in the orchard. (*DWJ* M 34.)

112. Aug 20

DW works. Apparently no one walks out. (*DWJ* M 34.)

113. Aug 21

DW reads, sends off (perhaps to Keswick) STC's translation of *Wallenstein*; she and JW walk around the lakes; meet W in Bainriggs. (*DWJ* M 34–35.)

114. Aug 22

W walks in the woods; DW, JW walk to Rydal, find the papers. W walks with JW. (*DWJ* M 35.)

115. Probably c but by Aug 23; probably between that time and 15 Oct

Probably c but by 23 Aug W composes *To Joanna*. Probably between that time and 15 Oct W composes the note for *To Joanna*. (See 1800:116; 1800:164.)[41]

116. Aug 23

W composes; walks in the woods with DW. Probably with JW they walk to Ambleside; see Mr. Partridge's house. W reads *To Joanna* by the roadside. They reach home about 7. W reads *PB*. (*DWJ* M 35.)

117. Aug 24

[Richard] Twining [2nd] calls. DW writes to Mrs. Rawson and her Aunt Cookson. (*DWJ* M 35; Stephen H. Twining, *The House of Twining*, London, 1956, 52.)

---

[41] The chronology in the poem is plainly the product of W's judgment concerning the needs of the poem rather than literal history. (See 1800:122n.)

118. Aug 25

DW, perhaps W and JW walk in the morning in the wood and to the fir grove; walk to Mr. Sympson's in the evening. (*DWJ* M 35.)

119. Aug 26

DW, probably W and JW walk to Ambleside. W is not quite well. They sit a long time on the far side of Rydal. (*DWJ* M 35.)

120. Aug 27

Probably W, DW, JW walk in the morning; are passed by Mr. Palmer. DW, probably W and JW walk along the shore of Grasmere in the late afternoon; go over into Langdale and down to Loughrigg Tarn. (*DWJ* M 35–36.)

121. Aug 28

DW, probably JW walk around Grasmere Lake and on by Rydal. Mr. Sympson comes to fish, probably in Grasmere Lake. (*DWJ* M 36.)

122. Aug 29 (–Aug 30)

W, DW, JW walk to Rydal to inquire for letters; walk over the hill by the fir grove, and through the woods over the stepping-stones. DW, JW leave W composing. The composition is probably toward "When to the Attractions of the Busy World" (of which a version is probably completed on the following day). (*DWJ* M 36.)[42]

---

[42] *DWJ* states in the entry for 29 Aug that after the walk by the fir grove W worked on "an Inscription—that about the path"; under 30 Aug DW records that W this day "finished his Inscription of the Pathway"; and under 1 Sept she records that W "read Joanna and the Firgrove." All these statements probably refer to the same poem. W's own comments never place "When to the Attractions" so early as 1800 (it is dated 1802 upon its publication in 1815, and in *P* 1820; is undated in 1827 and 1832; then dated 1805 in editions 1836–1850 and the IF note). But W can hardly have worked two days on the six lines of "Orchard Pathway" (cf *PW* II, 488–89). Chances are that "When to the Attractions" was substantially composed at this time, although parts, esp. most or all of lines 67–110, may have been written in at any time between now and 6 Mar 1804 in the form of MS M (EdS MS 1). DC MS 46 (EdS MS 2) appears to

123. Aug 30 (–Aug 31)

W probably this day completes a version of "When to the Attractions of the Busy World." He walks in the woods; goes bathing with JW. DW reads Boswell. Anthony Harrison arrives. (He departs next day.) Perhaps all drink tea, row, walk. Thomas Ashburner brings their eighth load of coal since 17 May. (*DWJ* M 36; *EY* 300.)

124. Aug 31

Anthony Harrison and JW depart at 7:30 AM. JW returns after a ride around Coniston. STC arrives for a visit at 11 PM. (He departs 3 Sept.) W, who had retired, arises, chats with DW and STC till 3:30 AM. STC reads a part of *Christabel*. (*DWJ* M 36–37. See *STCNB* 798, 798f41n.)

125. Sept 1

DW, probably W, JW walk. W reads *To Joanna* and probably "When to the Attractions of the Busy World" to STC. The men go

---

follow MS M, although its variants from MS M are not of major significance. Variations from the 1815 version are numerous. A date near MS M, or possibly in 1805, at no great distance of time from JW's death, is a possibility. Drafts for lines 1–15, probably written in anticipation of the 1815 edition of the Poems, appear in DC MS 80. W's date of 1802 might recall a reworking of the poem or additions made some time after JW's departure from Grasmere (29 Sept 1800): lines 67–110, as suggested by Knight (*PW* Knight, 1882–89 III, 58–59; 1896 III, 71–72), are the most likely to represent such work.

The suggestion that this is the "Silver How" poem which W attempted to alter on 26 Mar 1802 (see *PW* II, 489; *DWJ* M 106) is forced. The statement that JW has gone "back to the joyless Ocean" need not, of course, be factually accurate: compare the precise comment of *Joanna*, written probably c but by 23 Aug, that Joanna had been absent from the W household "for two long years," a statement which has no clear relevance to the Ws' recent contacts with Joanna H; and see also *WBS* 12–13n.

"Orchard Pathway" (*PW* IV, 374) is in fact an "Inscription," and its phrase "huge store" is reminiscent of "plenteous store," used several times in the poetry of the early 1800's. A date within this general period of vigorous production of Inscriptions is thus not impossible; but the verses do not appear in MS M and nothing is seen of them before the MS for the 1807 poems. They cannot be dated at any precise time before late Feb 1807 (see Appendix VII).

bathing. STC discovers a rock-seat in the orchard; probably he, with or without help, clears away the brambles; retires to bed after tea. W walks. DW, JW follow. DW and JW and/or W borrow some bottles from Mr. Sympson to bottle rum. W retires before the others. (*DWJ* M 37. See *STCNB* 799&n.)

126. Sept 2

Probably W, JW, STC walk to Stickle Tarn, returning at 6 PM. At Stickle Tarn they hear their laughter echoed surprisingly. DW walks to Grasmere Fair with Mr. and Miss Sympson. W, DW, STC walk by the church. (*DWJ* M 37–38; *STCL* II, 827; *STCNB* I, 800.)

127. Sept 3 ff

W, JW, STC, Mr. Sympson walk up Helvellyn. DW goes to a funeral. Her description afterward contributes to *Exc* II.370–402, 546–92. STC probably leaves the company to go on to Keswick. W, JW return at 10 PM. (*DWJ* M 38; *STCNB* 801–02&nn.)

128. Sept 4

W walks in the woods in the morning. He, DW, perhaps JW walk in Easedale in the evening. A letter arrives from CCl. (*DWJ* M 39. See *DWJ* I, 40n.)[43]

129. Sept 5

James Losh and Mrs. Losh call at DC while W, JW are out walking. DW shows them the house. (*DWJ* M 39; *EY* 300; Losh Diary.)[44]

----

[43] James Losh had tea and supped with STC and William Calvert today. To much information of his own plans which he told Losh, STC apparently added concerning W (whom he considered the first poet now living): "[He] is about to publish another Vol: of [*LB*], which have had great success. he is also engaged in a great moral work in verse." (Losh Diary.)

[44] Losh noted that he learned that the Ws paid £5 per year rent and 6 shillings taxes.

130. Sept 6 (–Sept 8)

W, DW, JW breakfast with the Loshes at Ambleside. TCl and CCl arrive at DC for a visit. (They depart 8 Sept.) All walk around Rydal Water. (*DWJ* M 39; *EY* 300–01; Losh Diary.)

131. Sept 7

DW, probably W, JW, and the Cls walk to Langdale. W does not feel well. DW and some or all of the others walk into Easedale. (*DWJ* M 39. See *DWJ* I, 40n.)

132. Sept 8

The Cls depart from DC after dinner. DW, probably W, JW walk toward Rydal, and to Olliff's gate. (*DWJ* M 39.)

STC this day writes to Godwin that the title "Lyrical Ballads" is to be dropped from the new edition of W's poetry, and a title of W's "Poems" substituted. (*STCL* I, 620–21.)

133. Sept 9 (–Sept 10)

W goes to the inn to welcome John Marshall. (Marshall departs Grasmere next day.) After a walk around the lakes with JW they dine with DW. W, DW, Marshall row to the island on the Lake. In the late afternoon W, unwell, remains at home as the others walk. After supper probably all talk about W's poems. (*EY* 293–94; *DWJ* M 39.)

134. Sept 10–Sept 12 (–Sept 13)

On 10 Sept, W, JW, Marshall depart on horseback for Keswick and elsewhere. (W returns 11 Sept; JW 13 Sept.) They walk halfway around Thirlmere; dine at the Royal Oak in Keswick; drink tea and sup at GH; perhaps pass the night there. DW pays Mr. Bousfield £8/2/11. (*EY* 294–95, 301; *DWJ* M 39–40.)[45]

On 11 Sept W is unable, because of illness in his side and stomach,

---

[45] It may here be noted that the Charles Lloyds moved to Ambleside between 10 Sept and 23 Sept. (*EY* 296; *DWJ* M 40.)

to continue his tour with JW and Marshall; parts from them in Borrow-dale; returns to DC. In Borrowdale he notes a decaying house and its inscription, architectural curiosities. (*EY* 301; *DWJ* M 40.)

On 10, 12 Sept DW writes a letter to JPM: (10 Sept:) Marshall's visit; DC, Grasmere; the family; W's unsatisfactory health, esp. when writing. Friends, visitors. (12 Sept:) W's return; his and JW's tour with Marshall. (*EY* 293–301.)[46]

On 12 Sept DW works; walks, perhaps with W. (*DWJ* M 40.)

135. Sept 13–Sept 26, –Oct 15

On 13 Sept W works on the *Preface*. Robert Jones and Mr. Palmer come to tea; W, DW walk with them to Borwick's. Apparently after the visitors' departure W walks out. JW returns to DC. DW sends a message to CCl. (*DWJ* M 40.)

Jones's visits between 13 and 26 Sept probably prompt W to include characteristics of Jones in *A Character*. W probably completes *A Character* in *LB* 1800 form between 13 Sept and 15 Oct, esp. probably in early Oct, by 15 Oct. (See *A Character* IF note; *CEY* 323–27; 1800: 149n; *Ariel* discussion.)

136. Sept 14

DW reads Boswell. (*DWJ* M 40.)

Derwent Coleridge, third son and third child of STC and SFC, is born at Keswick at 10:30 PM. (*STCL* I, 622–23.)

137. c mid-Sept–c early Oct

STC regards and reports W as being in indifferent and declining health. (*STCL* I, 623, 627, 634–35.)

138. Sept 15

W, DW complete the eighth sheet of printer's copy for *LB* 1800. DW copies *The Pet Lamb, Written in Germany, The Childless Father*. W

---

[46] It seems fairly plain that the letter to the middle of p. 301 was written on Wednesday 10 Sept, then concluded on "Friday."

adds a note to the printer: These poems are to be placed before *Christabel* even if the type for *Christabel* is already composed. He would have sent these poems earlier had he known that the setting of *Christabel* would proceed without further instructions from STC. Preface will follow within four days. (*EY* 302; Hale White 14–15.)[47]

139. Sept 19 (–Sept 26)

Robert Jones arrives at DC for a visit. (He had called on 13 Sept; he departs on this occasion on 26 Sept.) (*DWJ* M 40.)

140. Sept 21

The Rev. Thomas Myers and his son Tom call at DC. (*DWJ* M 41.)

141. Sept 23 (–Sept 26); perhaps within a few months

STC arrives at DC for a visit. (He remains until 26 Sept.) Charles Lloyd calls. (*DWJ* M 40–41.)

Perhaps within a few months STC, in DW's presence, terms Lloyd a rascal, and DW refutes the description. (*STCNB* 4006. See *CEY* 211; 1803:1.)

142. Sept 26; probably between Sept 26 and Nov 6

On 26 Sept Robert Jones, STC depart from DC; W, DW probably accompany them part way to Keswick; return in the evening. On returning they meet the old man who gives W his primary suggestion for the character of the leech-gatherer in *R&I*. (*DWJ* M 40–42.)[48]

[47] The note to *Written in Germany* and that to the printer and its signature are in DW's autograph (MS, YUL).

[48] DW's phrasing is that STC "went home with Jones"; so Jones, indeed, seems to have gone on to GH with STC. He probably there received from STC a sermon written three or four years earlier for his brother to preach at Oxford (letter, Jones to W, 7 Feb 1815, DCP).

DW states that W and she met the leech-gatherer when they "returned" after "accompanying Jones," and places the time of the meeting "late in the evening." Although the IF note of *R&I* indicates that the poet met the old man "a few hundred yards" from DC, and that the account of him was "taken from his own mouth,"

Probably between 26 Sept and 6 Nov W completes a basic version of "A Narrow Girdle of Rough Stones." (See 1800:186.)

143. Probably c but by 27 Sept; probably between this time and Sept 30; Sept 27

Probably c but by 27 Sept DW completes the ninth sheet of MS copy for *LB* 1800, containing the Preface through "but likewise that some of the most interesting parts" (*LB* 1800 I, xxiii). The sheet contains corrections and additions by STC and a concluding note to the printer, probably written by DW, instructing that the rest of the Preface will be sent by the next post and that the printing may begin immediately. (*EY* 302; Hale White 18–20; MS, YUL.)[49]

Probably between this time and 30 Sept the tenth sheet of MS copy for *LB* 1800 is written. It contains the Preface from "of the best poems" through "it is only upon condition" (*LB* 1800 I, xxiii, xliv). (1800:147.)

---

[49] The corrections and additions by STC may have been added after his departure from DC; but in any event, in view of the postmark of 30 Sept, the sheet is not likely to have been posted after 27 Sept (cf *STCNB* 818n, 829n).

DWJ gives no hint that W or she immediately derived significant monition from the event. That essential feature of the poem probably may be attributed to another meeting of which an IF note asserts that "the fact took place strictly as recorded," the encounter that is the subject also of "A Narrow Girdle of Rough Stones." The same IF note to "A Narrow Girdle" remarks that STC and DW were with the poet at the time. The statement is intended to clarify the sixth line of the poem, which records that the speaker was with "two beloved friends" (see also line 75). The seventh line dates the incident in Sept, but the old man of "A Narrow Girdle" is of course fishing, unlike the old man met today. *STCNB* 761 would also seem to record the meeting with the old fisherman, and seems definitely to have been written into the NB at about the same time as 762, "July 23, 1800" (BM Add. MS 47,502 fols. 6ᵛ–7ʳ). It looks probable that both "A Narrow Girdle" and *R&I* synthesize elements of encounters that occurred with STC and DW in July and with DW and possibly with, but more likely without, STC (and after leaving Jones) on 26 Sept. W's later remark to HCR, 11 Sept 1816 (*HCRBW* I, 191), was that he met the leech-gatherer "near Grasmere, except that he gave to his poetic character powers of mind which his original did not possess."

W was certainly at work on "A Narrow Girdle" on 10 Oct, and the poem was apparently complete by 6 Nov.

144. Sept 28

Mr. and Miss Smith (perhaps George Smith and his daughter Elizabeth, of Coniston) call at DC. DW, probably W and JW drink tea, sup at Charles Lloyd's. News comes of the arrival of JW's ship, the *Earl of Abergavenny*. (*DWJ* M 41.)[50]

145. Sept 29

JW departs from DC on his way to join the *Earl of Abergavenny*. W, DW accompany him as far as Grisedale Hause. This is JW's last departure from Grasmere. (*DWJ* M 41.)[51]

This parting is a subject of *Elegiac Verses in Memory of My Brother* and the MS quoted *PW* IV, 263–65 *app crit.*

146. Probably between Sept 29 and 1801 Apr 3

Probably between 29 Sept and 3 Apr 1801 W corrects *FV* as *EY* 328–29. He corrects *Prel*, MS U–V stage. (*EY* 328–29; *JWL* 119, 124. See Appendix V.)[52]

147. Sept 30 (–Oct 1)

Charles Lloyd dines at DC; W, DW walk homeward with him.

DW writes the eleventh (tenth surviving) sheet of copy for *LB* 1800, concluding copy of the Preface from "abandoning his old friends" (*LB* 1800 I, xliv), and including a description of a new title page and notes for *The Thorn* and *AM*. (W helps correct the sheet next day.) (*DWJ* M 41; *EY* 303–04; MS, YUL.)

148. Between c early Oct and 1801 c Apr; probably between early Feb and Apr 1801

[50] Mr. Smith was possibly William, M.P. for Sudbury, a friend of TCl's, but Mrs. Moorman's conjecture, repeated in the text, appears more probable.

[51] On the set of Anderson's *British Poets* possibly left behind by JW at this time see 1802:256.

[52] The first definite evidence of *FV* correction is W's letter of 9 Apr 1801 to Miss Taylor. JW states on 22 Apr that he has not yet read the *FV* with corrections; these would appear most probably to have been contained in the sheets of copy containing the *Prel* corrections which probably reached him between 2 and 7 Apr, and were hence probably sent off by 3 Apr (*JWL* 111–113).

W composes *Prel* VIII.221–311, as draft in DC MS 31 ("The Matron's Tale"). The MS 31 copy is probably made between early Feb and Apr. (1800:149n.)

149. Probably between c early Oct, certainly a time by Oct 11, and perhaps Dec 9, certainly Dec 19; probably about this time

Probably between c early Oct and 9 Dec W composes *Michael* in basic form. He is certainly giving thought to the poem by 11 Oct. The version used by the printer for *LB* 1800 was completed by 19 Dec. (*DWJ* M 41–54; 1800:160.) W composes the fragments, or drafts toward them, quoted *PW* II, 479–84, including lines drawn on in *Musings near Aquapendente* 47–52, and drafts used *Prel* VII.699–706 ("Shall he who gives his days"; see PREL 566) and *Prel* XII.185–204 ("There are those who think"). (Content; DC MSS 30, 31.) W writes rhymed draft lines associated with *Michael*. (Parrish *WBS; Ariel* discussion.)[53]

53 The drafts for or associated with *Michael* in DC MS 30 (quoted and described *PW* II, 479–82 as MS 1) are clearly closely related to those in DC MS 31 (EdS's MS 2) and include work on various of the materials of MS 31, which they precede. These, overlapped by materials in MS 30, include EdS fragments (b), (c), *Prel* XII.185–204, and *Prel* VII.222–[43], here followed integrally by *PW* II, 479, lines commencing "Then onwards" and (d) lines 1–18 (see *PW* II, 479). MS 1 also includes lines used for *Michael*, including 61–77 and 151–203.

Thus this draft work was certainly being developed before the completion of the poem as published. The only evidence that appears to place any of these materials in fact later than the completion of the poem as published is the quotation to Poole by DW on 9 Apr 1801 of the passage commencing "Murmur as with" (*EY* 324)—which appears in draft (without the first line) in MS 31—preceded in the letter by DW's remark that "My Brother has written the following lines to be inserted Page 206 [of *LB* II] after the 9th line" and followed by W's request for Poole to tell him whether he thinks "the insertion of these lines an improvement." The draft here appears to have been copied in at a time quite distinct from that of those preceding. The MS 31 "Matron's Tale," corresponding to PREL VIII.223–311, is the only passage following that just cited in MS 31, and, from its appearance, is the only one likely to have been copied into the NB subsequently.

Hence all other materials in MS 30, in the absence of further evidence, may be dated between the commencement of *Michael*, c early Oct, and perhaps 9 Dec, certainly 19 Dec, 1800, and those of MS 31 between the commencement of the poem and 9 Apr, except for the lines quoted to Poole which seem probably of a time between early Feb and 9 Apr, and the "Matron's Tale" draft, which, however, appears of the same general period of copying and unlikely to be later than Apr 1801. Although NB

Probably about this time W composes fragments of verse quoted *PW* V, 342–44, i–viii, in the Christabel NB; also, possibly, lines in the same NB possibly describing water droplets on moss; and lines mentioning the Niger. (Appendix II.)

150. Oct 1 and Oct 1 or Oct 2

On 1 Oct W, DW correct the concluding sheet of the *Preface*. The sheet is probably sent off today or 2 Oct. (*DWJ* M 41; *STCL* I, 602n; MS, YUL. See 1800:143.)

151. Oct 2

W, DW walk to Rydal, W to Butterlip How. The Lloyds call at DC, are greeted by DW. Probably all walk to see Easedale, Sour Milk Ghyll. They converse about disagreeable qualities of the rich. W, DW walk. (*DWJ* M 41.)

152. Oct 3; probably between Oct 3 and Dec 18

W walks to Ambleside after dinner, DW with him part way. He talks much about the object of his essay for vol. II of *LB* 1800. DW

---

placement does not here seem strong chronological evidence, the fragments, or drafts toward them, of *PW* II, 479–84, (α), (b), (c), lines 1–18, are in fact found along with the *Michael* drafts in MS 1 of the poem, and thus are esp. likely to date by 9 Dec 1800.

The search for the sheepfold on 11 Oct would appear to indicate an already established interest most readily explained by work on or thought about a poem like *Michael*. *DWJ* states under 15 Oct that "Wm. again composed at the sheep-fold after dinner." In view of the search on 11 Oct and W's route to Keswick on 15 Oct, and esp. DW's entry for 11 Nov, *DWJ*'s "sheep-fold" may well involve a geographic location; but the general manner of use of the phrase (see 1800:167–1800-171; 1800: 189; 1800:191) leaves little doubt that DW is referring consistently to a poem; and the poem must be *Michael*. I have interpreted all such references accordingly. See *Ariel* discussion *passim*.

Knight's statement that the lines in MS 31 drawn on for *Prel* VII.699–706 (see PREL 566), commencing "Shall he who gives his days," are of the same date as an adjacent note dated 29 May [1802] (see *PW* Knight, 1882–89 IX, 381–82; *PW* Knight, 1896 VIII, 257 although less precise, continues to assign a date of 1802) is contradicted by the appearance of the MS, which suggests that the lines date from the same time as most of the rest of the drafts related to *Michael* in the same NB.

returns to DC to await the Sympsons, who do not come. W returns after 10. News of Amos Cottle's death arrives in *MP*. DW writes to Sally Lowthian. (*DWJ* M 41–42.)

Probably between 3 Oct and 18 Dec W composes an essay perhaps contributive to the 1802 *Appendix* (which included before publication the materials quoted Hale White 47–50) and possibly to the 1815 *Essay, Supplementary*. A prose fragment surviving in DC MS 28 perhaps belongs to this work. (Appendix IV; 1800:224.)

153. Oct 4 (–Oct 7)

DW reads a part of CL's *Pride's Cure* (*John Woodvil*). STC arrives at dinnertime for a visit, possibly brought by reports of W's ill health. (He remains until 7 Oct.) He probably reads the second part of *Christabel*, by which W and DW are delighted. (*DWJ* M 42–43; *STCL* I, 628, 632.)[54]

154. Oct 5

STC reads the second part of *Christabel* again. W and DW are even more pleased. W, DW work on an addition to the *Preface*, probably concerning *Christabel*. W goes to bed, ill from work. DW, STC post the letter, which probably contains the addition to the Preface. This is the twelfth sheet of copy for *LB* 1800 (it is not known to survive). (*DWJ* M 43; *EY* 304. Cf *STCNB* 769&n.)

155. Oct 6, possibly Oct 7

Probably W, DW, STC walk to Rydal after dinner. After tea they read *The Pedlar*. They decide not to print *Christabel* with *LB*, and probably also now decide to print *The Pedlar* and *Christabel* together in a separate volume.

On 6 Oct (possibly 7 Oct) W writes to Biggs and Cottle (part of the letter is in the autograph of STC): The paragraph sent by the last post is not to be inserted in the Preface as directed. The first sentence is to be corrected. If the title page was altered according to direction, the

---

[54] Perhaps this visit is that in the course of which STC sees W reluctant to make a serious trial of prescriptions sent by Dr. Beddoes (see *STCL* I, 632).

paragraph of the Preface beginning "For the sake of variety" down to "do almost entirely coincide" is to be cancelled and replaced by a new reading here supplied. (The letter from "Reader that the poems" is in STC's hand.) Any pages of *Christabel* already printed are to be cancelled. Substitute poems will be supplied by the next post. (*EY* 304–05; *STCL* I, 631.)[55]

This is the thirteenth (eleventh surviving) sheet of copy for *LB* 1800.

156. Oct 7

STC departs from DC at 11 AM. W apparently walks out during the day, possibly accompanying STC part way to Keswick. DW, perhaps accompanying them, walks as far as the Sympsons'; returns with Mary [Jameson?], Miss Sympson, Mrs. Jameson. W has returned before her arrival. Mary drinks tea. (*DWJ* M 43.)

157. Oct 8

£5 arrives from Montagu. DW copies part of *OCB*. W walks to Rydal; walks again later. (*DWJ* M 43. See 1800:159.)

158. Oct 9

W, DW walk, intending to call at the Lloyds'; are prevented by rain. They shelter at Fleming's. A former soldier stops at DC. (*DWJ* M 43–44.)

159. Oct 10 ff; probably between Oct 10 and Oct 13

The Cockermouth traveller (a female pedlar) calls. W, DW, Miss Sympson, Mrs. Jameson walk toward Rydal and to Gell's. W goes to bed after dinner; DW reads a letter from RS. Miss Sympson and Mrs. Jameson come to tea. DW and probably W and the others walk to the Lloyds'; they are not at home. DW writes to CCl.

On this day a sheet of MS copy for *LB* 1800 is sent off to Biggs and

---

[55] The title page was not printed in accordance with W's first wish (see *EY* 303), and the original reading of the paragraph here altered remained through *LB* 1805.

Cottle. It contains *OCB, Rural Architecture, A Poet's Epitaph* 1–11. The sheet is lost in transit. It is the fourteenth sheet of copy for *LB* 1800.

W works on "A Narrow Girdle of Rough Stones." (*DWJ* M 44; *EY* 306–07, 312; Hale White 25; 1800:162; 1800:164.)

160. Oct 11

W composes. Probably he and DW walk after dinner up Greenhead Ghyll in search of a sheepfold. They find it falling apart. On their way they enjoy the view from a field of Mr. Olliff's where DW supposes that they are to build a house. They drink tea at Mr. Sympson's. (*DWJ* M 44–45. See 1800:149&n; *Michael* IF note.)

161. Oct 12

W composes in the woods. DW writes letters to JW, Mrs. Rawson; copies poems for *LB*. Mary Jameson and Sally Ashburner dine. DW and some or all the others pick apples after dinner; walk. W composes in the later afternoon. (*DWJ* M 45.)

162. Oct 13 ff

DW copies some or all of *Poems on the Naming of Places* [see 1800: 164]. She and perhaps W walk in Easedale at night. (*DWJ* M 45.)

The Voice from the Side of Etna; or, The Mad Monk appears in *MP* over the signature "CASSIANI jun." The poem is probably by STC, but W possibly contributed to it. It certainly later influences the phrasing of the *Ode*. (See esp. Stephen M. Parrish and David Erdman, "Who Wrote the Mad Monk? A Debate," *BNYPL* LXIV, 1960, 209–37; Woof *SB* 174–76.)[56]

---

[56] Further debate about the authorship of *The Mad Monk*, as far as W's own poetry or development is concerned, hardly seems necessary. It is easily conceivable that STC, drawing on a fresh encounter with *LB* 1798 during the preparation of the second edition, might have produced such a work, which appears to draw not only on "'Tis Said, That Some Have Died for Love" of *LB* vol. II, but also at least *The Thorn* and *The Mad Mother* of vol. I. It is possible that W, who was not above joking at his own work about this time (see *Ariel* discussion), took a hand. But W was probably too much occupied with other concerns now to contribute extensively, and can scarcely have been responsible for publication.

163. Oct 14

W lies down after dinner; DW reads RS's [*Letters Written during a Short Residence in Spain and Portugal*]. They walk to Rydal. W walks again about bed time.

The Seven Sisters is published in *MP* under the title *The Solitude of Binnorie, or the Seven Daughters of Lord Archibald Campbell, a Poem*, unsigned. (See Landon *RES*; Woof *SB* 176–78.)

164. Oct 15–Oct 17

On 15 Oct W composes a little, probably toward *Michael*; walks with DW; works on *Michael*. W, DW walk to Wythburn, whence W goes on to Keswick. (He returns 17 Oct.)

He probably takes with him the fifteenth (twelfth surviving) sheet of MS copy for *LB*, containing in DW's autograph, *A Poet's Epitaph* from line 12, *A Character*, *The Danish Boy* (W writes one line, "In clouds above the lark is heard," and a note), "It Was an April Morning," *To Joanna*. At Keswick W finds that STC has done nothing for *LB*, having been at work for Stuart. STC adds to the sheet a note to the printer, probably at W's dictation, including the *Advertisement* to *Poems on the Naming of Places*.

The sheet of MS is probably posted before W returns to DC.[57] (*DWJ* M 45–46; *EY* 305–06. See *STCL* I, 631n, 637&n; 1800:149.)

165. Oct 16

DW writes to Miss Nicholson; walks to Rydal; writes to Mr. Griffith. A letter arrives from TCl. (*DWJ* M 46.)

166. Oct 17

DW walks around the lake; writes to MH; walks to the Lloyds' with her letters to Miss Nicholson [see 1800:165] and MH. They are not in; she waits, and evidently sees them. She probably picks up letters from MH, Biggs, and JW. W arrives at DC shortly after her departure. (*DWJ* M 46.)

---

[57] The next MS sheet is not sent off until, probably, 18 Dec. See 1800:229n.

167. Oct 18

W works unsuccessfully on *Michael*. (*DWJ* M 46.)

168. Oct 19

W, DW walk by Rydal and on Loughrigg Fell. W works. They dine late (5:30). Mr. Sympson dines and drinks tea. (*DWJ* M 46–47.)

169. Oct 20

W works on *Michael*. W, DW walk to Rydal; meet the Lloyds; all walk together till 8. W is disturbed in the night by rain falling in the room. (*DWJ* M 47.)

170. Oct 21

W works unsuccessfully on *Michael*. He, DW walk past Gell's; drink tea at the Lloyds'. (*DWJ* M 47.)

Inscription for a Seat by a Road Side, Half Way up a Steep Hill, Facing the South is published in *MP* over the signature "VENTI-FRONS." (See Landon *RES*; Woof *SB* 178–80; 1800:104n.)

171. Oct 22 (–Oct 23, Oct 29–Nov 4)

W, DW walk to Gell's. W works on *Michael* with little success. STC arrives before dinner, still having done nothing [for *LB*; see 1800: 164]. (He departs next day.) They are very merry. John Stoddart arrives at tea. (He probably stays the night.) Mr. and Miss Sympson call. W reads *Ruth* and other poems after supper; STC reads *Christabel*. (*DWJ* M 47.)

(For a comment by Stoddart probably referring to his visits at DC this day and 29 Oct–4 Nov see Woof *Ariel* 11. See also Wilfred Partington, *Sir Walter's Post-bag*, London, 1932, 12.)[58]

---

[58] On STC's recitation of *Christabel* to Stoddart and Stoddart's repetition of portions of the poem to Scott see esp. Woof *Ariel* 11. Some chance may exist that this day's merry moods contributed to the writing of the rhymed stanzas connected with *Michael*. See *Ariel* discussion, esp. Reed article.

172. Oct 23

STC and Stoddart depart for Keswick. W, DW accompany them to Wythburn. W, DW call on Mrs. Sympson. W composes unsuccessfully. (*DWJ* M 47–48.)

173. Oct 24

W, DW walk to Rydal Hill before dinner; around Rydal and up Loughrigg after. W composes with only partial success. (*DWJ* M 48.)

174. Oct 25

W composes unsuccessfully. W, DW read Rogers, Miss Seward, Cowper, and others. (*DWJ* M 48.)

175. Oct 26

W composes a good deal in the morning. The Lloyds dine at DC; W reads some of his poems after dinner. Sympson calls in for a glass of rum [see 1800:125]. (*DWJ* M 48.)

176. Oct 27

W, DW walk in the fir grove. DW carries some cold meat to W there; meets Lloyd; walks homeward with him past Rydal. W is unable to compose much; fatigues himself with altering. (*DWJ* M 48.)

177. Oct 28

W, DW walk. The Lloyds call in the evening. W, DW drink tea, play whist, sup with them at Borwick's. (*DWJ* M 48.)

178. Oct 29 (–Oct 30, –Nov 4)

W works [at *Michael*] all morning. TCl arrives for a visit after dinner. (He departs next day.) All walk to Borwick's; he and the Lloyds, including Priscilla, return to DC for tea. They meet Stoddart, who arrives for a visit at DC. (He departs 4 Nov.) They play cards. (*DWJ* M 48–49.)

179. Oct 30

TCl departs over Kirkstone. W talks all day and most of the night with Stoddart. Mrs. and Priscilla Lloyd call. (*DWJ* M 49.)

180. Oct 31

W, Stoddart remain abed till 1 PM. W is ill. DW, Stoddart drink tea at the Lloyds'. (*DWJ* M 49.)

181. Nov 1

W is better [see 1800:180]. DW, probably W and Stoddart, on their way to Rydal, meet a boy coming from Lloyd for *Don Quixote*. Ashburner brings the tenth cart of coals. (*DWJ* M 49.)

182. Nov 2

DW, probably W, Stoddart walk into Easedale; drink tea at the Lloyds'. (*DWJ* M 49.)

183. Nov 3

DW, probably W, Stoddart walk to Rydal. W, Stoddart continue talking vigorously. The Speddings stop at the door. (*DWJ* M 49.)

184. Nov 4

Stoddart departs, accompanied on his way by W, DW. W walks to Grisedale Tarn and the top of Seat Sandal. DW walks with [Priscilla] Lloyd. (*DWJ* M 49.)[59]

185. Nov 5

W is unwell. DW walks to the Lloyds' after dinner; makes tea for W. (*DWJ* M 49–50.)

---

[59] *DWJ* speaks only of "the Tarn," but the walk up Seat Sandal leaves no doubt of which tarn was visited.

186. Probably c but by Nov 6; Nov 6

Probably c but by 6 Nov DW writes to JW (letter not known to survive): The contents include information that W has progressed well with [*Michael*]; perhaps include an inquiry about the propriety of JW's use of the £100 owed by W to Wedgwood. (*JWL* 75, 191, 193. See 1800:76.)[60]

On 6 Nov Charles and Priscilla Lloyd call. W reads "A Narrow Girdle of Rough Stones." (*DWJ* M 50.)[61]

187. Nov 7

DW reads *Amelia*. W is unwell. A poor woman and child from Whitehaven drink tea. (*DWJ* M 50.)

188. Nov 8

W, DW walk out at 4 as far as Rothay Bridge; meet the butcher's man with a letter to W from Monk Lewis. (*DWJ* M 50.)

189. Nov 9

W, DW walk to Rydal after dinner. Newspapers arrive by agency of Mr. Sympson, Molly, or both. W possibly burns a MS of *Michael*. (*DWJ* M 50. See *Ariel* discussion.)

190. Nov 10

W, DW walk to Rydal after dinner. (*DWJ* M 50.)
JW writes to DW from Forncett advising that he has instructed RW to let Wedgwood be paid £100 at once [see 1800:186], and discussing his own financial and family affairs. (*JWL* 73–75.)[62]

---

[60] DW did not know when she mailed the letter that JW had gone from London to Forncett. The letter would have taken a day to follow him thither, and he replied on 10 Nov.

[61] I read *DWJ* M's "said Point Rash Judgment" as commencing "read" in MS.

[62] The £100 was apparently paid by 17 Nov (*JWL* 75). The discrepancy between this sum and the £110/13/– which W supposed on 13 July that he owed to Wedgwood remains unexplained.

191. Nov 11

W works on *Michael*. He and DW walk to Rydal for letters. The Lloyds drink tea, play cards at DC, after which W, DW walk. (*DWJ* M 50–51.)

192. Nov 12

Mr. Sympson calls, sups at DC. (*DWJ* M 51.)

193. Nov 13

Mr., Miss Sympson, Mrs. Jameson call at dinner, drink tea, sup, play cards at DC. A poor woman from Hawkshead calls begging, as do also, apparently, a Grasmere widow and a merry African from Longtown. (*DWJ* M 51.)

194. Probably c but by Nov 14

DW writes to JW (letter not known to survive): Informs JW of £80 sent to RW for him. (*JWL* 75, 193. See 1800:17.)

195. Nov 14

Two letters arrive from STC, who is ill; a letter arrives from SH, from whom arrives, probably enclosed, £3; and a letter from Sally Lowthian. DW writes to SH. (*DWJ* M 51.)

196. Nov 15 (–Nov 22)

W departs for Keswick at 5 PM. (He returns on 22 Nov.) DW walks over Dunmail Raise with him. (*DWJ* M 51.)

197. Nov 16

Letters arrive from STC, Stoddart. [William] Jackson calls at DC as DW is at tea, bringing a letter from W, STC. The letter perhaps asks DW to come to GH. (*DWJ* M 51. See 1800:198.)

198. Nov 17 (–Nov 22)

DW walks to Keswick, finds all well at GH. (She returns to DC on 22 Nov.) (*DWJ* M 51.)

199. Nov 18

STC and W walk toward Penrith. W meets SH at Threlkeld. They return to GH at teatime. (*DWJ* M 51–52.)[63]

200. Nov 19

DW and others walk by Derwent Water; others go to Mr. Denton's. DW calls on the Misses Cockin. (*DWJ* M 52.)

201. Nov 20

DW and others spend the morning in Keswick. Messrs. Jackson and Peach dine with the GH party. (*DWJ* M 52.)

202. Nov 21

DW and perhaps others go to Mrs. Greaves'. DW, SFC call on the Speddings. (*DWJ* M 52.)

203. Nov 22 (–possibly Dec 10, possibly 1801 Jan 2, certainly by Jan 14)

W, DW, SH, perhaps others view Mr. Peach's Chinese pictures. W, DW, SH depart GH, come to Grasmere. (SH departs possibly 10 Dec, possibly 2 Jan, certainly by 14 Jan.) W arrives not quite well. (*DWJ* M 52.)

204. Nov 23

W is unwell. Mr. Gawthorpe, whom DW and SH meet on a walk, drinks tea at DC. They pay his bill, and if it is not the same bill, probably also £5 for Mr. Bousfield. (*DWJ* M 52.)

---

[63] *STCNB* 838, describing DW's touching Derwent's face with cold hands, apparently refers to this day.

205. Nov 24

DW, SH walk to Rydal, and to the Lloyds'. DW has a toothache, takes laudanum. (*DWJ* M 52.)

206. Probably shortly before, certainly by Nov 25

DW writes to JW (letter not known to survive): Asks JW to find a place for Henry H as fourth or fifth mate. (*JWL* 76.)

207. Nov 25

DW is ill; reads *Tom Jones*. (*DWJ* M 52.)

208. Nov 26

W, DW, probably SH walk into Easedale. A letter arrives from MH. The Lloyds drink tea at DC; all walk with the Lloyds to somewhere near Ambleside. W is described by *DWJ* as being very well and "highly poetical" this day. (*DWJ* M 52.)

209. Nov 27

DW writes to Thomas H (letter not known to survive): Desires him to bring MH with him from Stockton. (*DWJ* M 52.)

210. Nov 28 (–Dec 2)

STC arrives at DC for a visit. (He remains until 2 Dec.) Miss Sympson drinks tea; W walks home with her. STC is unwell; retires before W's return. During this night W awakens STC from a nightmare by calling out to him. (*DWJ* M 52; *STCNB* 848.)

211. Nov 29

DWJ records only the fine weather of this day. (*DWJ* M 53. See *STCNB* 849.)

212. Nov 30

DW, SH walk; return because of snow. Perhaps later all walk by moonlight. (*DWJ* M 53.)

213. Dec

The Longman records for *LB* 1800 commence with this date. (See Owen CSP 94.)

214. Dec 1

STC is unwell. Some or all the household walk by moonlight. (*DWJ* M 53.)

215. Dec 2

STC departs for Keswick. DW, SH meet Charles and Priscilla Lloyd. DW walks around the lake with Charles; Priscilla drinks tea at DC. All walk to Ambleside. (*DWJ* M 53.)

216. Dec 3

DW writes to JW, MH. W, DW, SH walk to Rydal; W, SH walk around the other side of the lake. (*DWJ* M 53.)

217. Dec 4 (–Dec 6)

STC arrives at DC for a visit. (He departs 6 Dec.) A gift of pork arrives from the Sympsons. All walk after tea to look at Langdale; sit up till 1:30 AM. (*DWJ* M 53.)

218. Dec 5

STC, W depart for Keswick. The weather forces them to return. All are very merry in the evening; go to bed at 12. (*DWJ* M 53.)[64]

219. Dec 6

STC departs for Keswick. W accompanies him to the foot of Dunmail Raise; DW, SH accompany him halfway to Keswick; drink tea at the Sympsons'. During their absence Lloyd calls. On their return they find W unwell, having been composing unsuccessfully. A letter arrives from MH. (*DWJ* M 53–54.)

[64] On this day JW wrote to MH that he was to be sworn in as captain of the *Earl of Abergavenny* in a few weeks, and that he was often told that in eight or ten years he would be a "very *rich man*" (*JW L* 76–77).

220. Dec 7

W writes to MH, DW to SFC, SH to HC (letters not known to survive). All walk, W and SH to the falls at Rydal. DW goes to bed till 8, again at 12. Miss Sympson calls. (*DWJ* M 54.)

221. Dec 8
DW writes to Mrs. Cookson, Miss Griffith. (*DWJ* M 54.)

222. Dec 9

W finishes [*Michael*]. DW dines, and W drinks tea at the Lloyds'; they reach home at 1 AM. (*DWJ* M 54.)[65]

223. Dec 10 (–Dec 14)

W, DW, SH walk to Keswick. (They remain until 14 Dec.) They have bread and ale at John Stanley's [Thirlspot]. They find STC in better health. (*DWJ* M 54.)[66]

224. Probably between Dec 10 and Dec 14, Dec 18

Probably between 10 Dec and 14 Dec STC tells W of a plan which he has conceived; or he, with W, develops the plan, of presenting to eminent persons copies of *LB* 1800 accompanied by complimentary letters from W. (See *STCL* I, 654; 1800:229; 1801:6.)[67]

STC copies out lines 1–206 of *Michael* for W, as part of what becomes the seventeenth (fourteenth surviving) sheet of MS copy for *LB* 1800. (1800:223; 1800:229.)

---

[65] DW's phrasing is that W "finished his poem," which does not, of course, ensure that the poem is *Michael*; but there cannot be much doubt about the matter in view of the comments of *DWJ* on W's composition from 11 Oct.

[66] On this day Charles Lloyd wrote to Thomas Manning: "We have little society except W. Wordsworth & his Sisters. The former is very much altered since I last saw him by indisposition—but we are pleased with their company. W[e hea]r a good deal of Coleridge, but we never see hi[m]." (Letter, Cornell Collection, Cornell 2906.) The most recent recorded meeting of Lloyd and W took place 6 Nov. On W's health see esp. 1800:137.

[67] The "persons of eminence" in STC's mind as of 15 Dec were Mrs. Jordan, Mrs. Barbauld, and William Wilberforce.

Probably between 10 Dec and 18 Dec W, SH, DW complete the seventeenth sheet and write the eighteenth (fifteenth surviving) sheet of copy for *LB* 1800, containing the remainder of *Michael* and the notes for vol. II. The copy of *Michael* is written by SH except for line 272 ("He quickly . . . "), written by W. W adds corrections. The note "NB This must begin . . . " and the notes for vol. II are written by DW. (1800: 223; 1800:228; 1800:229; *EY* 308–09; Hale White 29–34; MSS, YUL.)

225. Dec 14

W, DW, probably SH return to DC. (*DWJ* M 54.)

226. Dec 15

DWJ records only baking and starching at DC this day. (*DWJ* M 54.)

227. Dec 16

The Lloyds call. (*DWJ* M 54.)

228. Dec 17

DW, perhaps SH also copy for W all morning [see 1800:229]. (*DWJ* M 54.)

229. Probably Dec 18; Dec 18

SFC, Derwent arrive at DC for a visit. (The length of their visit is unknown; but they possibly depart 2 Jan, probably depart by 14 Jan.) They probably bring a printed sheet (probably sig. K) that indicates to W that the [eighth] sheet of copy has reached Biggs and Cottle; a letter is perhaps brought at the same time that leads W to fear that the [fourteenth (see 1800:159)] may have miscarried. (*DWJ* M 54.)

W writes to Biggs and Cottle: Inquires about their receipt of MS copy for *LB* from [15 Sept]; sends copies of "There Is an Eminence," "A Narrow Girdle of Rough Stones," *To M.H.*; corrections and directions. The first poem is in the autograph of DW, the second in the autograph of DW and W, with a paste-on slip probably in the autograph of STC, of the three lines beginning "Nor did we fail to see," and the last is in the autograph of W. The letter itself, except for the conclusion from "I am sorry" to "W Wordsworth" (*EY* 308), is written by DW. This sheet is the sixteenth (thirteenth surviving) sheet of MS copy for *LB* 1800. W writes to Longman and Rees: He has sent off last sheet of copy for *LB* 1800. He has decided not to include *Christabel* or an introductory essay for vol. II [see 1800:155]. His understanding of the financial arrangements for vol. II: £80 for W for two editions of vol. I, one of 750 copies, one of 1000; two editions of vol. II, each 1000 copies, at the end of which the publisher's copyright ceases. His wish to send copies of the book to some half-dozen persons of eminence in letters or in the state [see 1800:224]. JW is to receive three copies of *LB*; CL one. W wishes a few sets sent to him in any monthly parcel.

The sixteenth, seventeenth, and eighteenth sheets of MS and a letter are probably sent off together this day. (*EY* 306–10; Hale White 29–34; MSS, YUL.)[68]

230. Probably Dec 19

DW bakes. (*DWJ* M 54.)

W writes to Joseph Cottle: Cottle's domestic distresses. Instructions for forwarding a box to STC. SFC and Derwent visiting. Ws have not seen Cottle's *Alfred*. W's inability to present a copy of *LB* to Cottle.

Instructions for Biggs: Has sent off yesterday the last three sheets of copy for *LB* 1800. Alterations for "A Narrow Girdle," *Michael*. Has determined that one sheet of copy, containing *OCB* and other materials [see 1800:159] has been lost in transit. (*EY* 306, 311; information from Professor James Butler; MSS, YUL and Rosenbach Foundation.)[69]

[68] All of these sheets have a 23 Dec postmark. Since W states in his letter of 18 Dec to Longman and Rees that he has "this day sent off the last Sheet of the second Volume of the Lyrical Ballads," it is likely that all four sheets went off together.

[69] Professor James Butler has kindly supplied conclusive evidence that the letter excerpted *EY* 306 and that quoted *EY* 311–12 were originally a single letter. My description of the portion from which the quotations of *EY* 306 are taken is made with permission of the Rosenbach Foundation and Professor Butler. The letter is the nineteenth (sixteenth and last surviving) sheet of copy for *LB* 1800. DW does the writing from the words "In the poem of Michael." *EY* omits the opening line of the address, "To Joseph Cottle."

231. Probably late Dec

W sends off MS to replace copy lost in miscarriage of fourteenth sheet of copy of *LB* 1800. (See 1800:159; 1800:229.)

232. Dec 20 (–1801 Jan 2)

STC arrives for a visit at DC. (He departs 2 Jan.) He arrives wet through; is ill. (*DWJ* M 54; *STCL* II, 662–63.)

233. Dec 21–1801 Jan 2

On 21 Dec or shortly after STC is obliged to go to bed, ill. He probably remains bedridden till 2 Jan. (*STCL* II, 662–63.)

234. Dec 22

W and probably SH go to the Lloyds'; probably W dines there. (*DWJ* M 54.)[70]

235. Probably shortly before, certainly by 29 Dec

W writes to John Stoddart asking him to review *LB*. (Letter, Stoddart to STC, 1 Jan 1801, PML. See Woof *Ariel* 18.)

1 8 0 1

[On writings of W possibly of this year see below and GCL 1–4, 6–8, 27, 29, 30, 33–36, 38–41.]

1. Probably this year; possibly c early this year, by Apr 3

Probably during this year W composes some lines toward the opening of *Prel* III. (See esp. 1801:141–1801:143; Appendix V.)

---

[70] This meeting with the Lloyds, as the last recorded about this time, is an appropriate occasion for noting Lloyd's comment to Manning about the Ws on 26 Jan 1801 (letter, Cornell Collection, Cornell 2907): "We have not any society except the Wordsworth's. they are very unusual characters. indeed Miss Wordsworth I much like. but her Brother is not a man after my own heart. I always feel myself depressed in his society. Coleridge & I have seen each other twice." On W's present opinion of Lloyd see *JWL* 86.

Possibly c early this year, by 3 Apr, W composes *Prel* I.55–271 and possibly other unidentified passages for *Prel* I–II; possibly makes corrections in MS V; but see Appendix V.

2. Jan

RW's accounts credit W with £7/10/–, half-year dividend on W's 3 percent consols, under this date. (RW accounts, DCP.)

3. Jan 2

STC departs DC for Keswick in a chaise, possibly accompanied by SFC, Derwent, and also SH. (*STCL* II, 662–63.)

4. Jan 6

As of this date STC owes £20 to W. (*STCL* II, 661. See 1801:9.)

5. Jan 7

JW is sworn in as Captain of the *Earl of Abergavenny*. (*JWL* 29, 197.)

6. Between Jan 12 and Jan 14, and shortly after (–Jan 19, –Feb 12, –Feb 22)

Between 12 and 14 Jan W, DW travel to Keswick. (W, DW, perhaps SH, depart GH 19 Jan, return to DC by 12 Feb.)

Probably during this visit STC writes or dictates letters, with DW as amanuensis for at least several letters, to accompany presentation copies of *LB* 1800, to a number of eminent personages. At least two of these letters, one to Sir James Bland Burges, are copied on 14 Jan. Probably all the letters are written over W's signature. Other addressees include the Duchess of Devonshire, Mrs. Jordan, William Wilberforce, John Taylor, probably Mrs. Barbauld and M. G. Lewis. A letter probably goes to CL, whether or not as an eminent personage.

On 14 Jan W himself writes to Charles James Fox: Presents *LB* 1800. W's feelings that Fox's concern with the dignity and values of the individual and life in the lower orders of society coincides with W's objects in *LB* 1800, esp. as expressed in *The Brothers* and *Michael*.

Probably on 14 Jan or shortly after, the letters are sent to JW, who delivers them to Longman to be forwarded to the addressees.

Perhaps during this visit to Keswick William Calvert proposes to W that he take the new house that he is finishing, Windy Brow; in which case Calvert will build a little laboratory so that he, STC, and W may study chemistry. (On 3 Feb STC reports W interested in the scheme; but by 22 Feb W has given up all thought of removing to Keswick.) (*EY* 310, 312–15, 325, 683–85; *STCL* I, 654, II, 664–66, 670–71; *LL* I, 246–47; *JWL* 95–96, 103–04.)[1]

7. Probably Jan 19–probably c but by Feb 12

W, DW, perhaps SH travel, probably from Keswick, to Eusemere Hill for a visit with the Cls. They return to DC probably c but by 12 Feb. Possibly along the way they stop at a public house at Dockray or Thornythwaite. (*STCL* II, 664–66, 672–73; *HCRWC* I, 41; Moorman I, 512–513; 1801:144.)

STC and possibly SFC join the party for a time, probably between 3 and 7 Feb, STC returning to Keswick on 7 Feb. Perhaps during this period W receives a letter from, writes to CL about his response to *LB*: Discusses CL's range of sensibility and the character of his own verse. Perhaps during STC's visit W sees Joanna H. The Ws perhaps see her

---

[1] W's letter to Fox reports a remark made to his "Servant two days ago" (*EY* 314). W's object may be rhetorical immediately only; but in absence of other evidence the statement may be taken as a basis for a date after which the remark was made to Molly Fisher, at Grasmere. The date of the letters to Fox and Burges, 14 Jan, indicates a time by which W was in Keswick, despite the fact that the letters are dated from Grasmere. STC says on 19 Jan that he dictated all the presentation letters to distinguished personages except that to Fox. Of these letters that to Wilberforce is partly in the autograph of STC and the remainder in that of DW, and the letter to Fox in that of DW (*STCL* II, 667; MS, HEH). STC's statement that W wrote to Fox "while" STC dictated likewise suggests that he and W were together while the letter-writing proceeded. All this writing was probably completed in a concentrated effort.

W had received replies from all the addressees except Fox by 13 Feb (*STCL* II, 676).

A transcript of another of STC's letters, also dated 14 Jan, to someone addressed by STC as having a mind "acute . . . in the detection of the ludicrous and faulty" will be published in an appendix of the forthcoming new edition of W's later letters, edited by Alan Hill. The addressee was possibly Monk Lewis (see 1800:188).

during their visit. (*STCL* II, 672–74; *LL* I, 246–47; *EY* 316; letter, Joanna H to John M, 2 May 1801, JFW Papers.)[2]

Probably on this visit W shows CCl MSS of poems in *LB* 1800 II, including *The Brothers*. (*HCRWC* I, 41.)

Probably W pays a call on or makes a more lengthy visit to Thomas Wilkinson at Yanwath. (Mary Carr, *Thomas Wilkinson*, London, 1905, 18; copy of letter, Thomas Wilkinson to Mary Leadbeater, 15 Feb 1801, Tullie House Library; Moorman I, 519n.)

Possibly during this visit the Ws dine with [John?] Slee and members of his family. (*STCL* II, 749; *STCNB* 1329&n.)[3]

---

[2] It is likely that CL—despite his assertion that W replied instantly to CL's letter of 30 Jan (*LL* I, 239–42)—wrote his celebrated letter to Manning of 15 Feb only very shortly after receipt of W's. Thus, unless W's letter was delayed unusually on the road, it would have been sent off c but by 12 Feb. CL's letter, addressed to Grasmere (MS, UTL) would not have reached W at Eusemere before 2 or 3 Feb. While the letter shows no physical sign of having been forwarded, CL's report of STC's starting from his sickbed to add four pages of reproof in reply makes his letter the more likely to have gone on to Eusemere, and by 7 Feb. It is possible that STC came to Grasmere on or about 13 Feb (*STCL* II, 672–73), but a letter written by STC no earlier than that day can not have been in CL's hands by 15 Feb. Unless W sent CL's letter (on which see also 1801:22n) off to Keswick about 11 or 12 Feb (unlikely if STC were expected on the 13th) or STC came to Grasmere earlier (on a visit for which there is no other evidence), both W's and STC's comments probably emanated from Eusemere.

[3] On 12 Feb CCl wrote to the Rev. R. E. Garnham that the Ws had left after a visit of "more than three weeks" (*HCRWC* I, 41). It thus appears likely that the Ws travelled directly from Keswick to Eusemere Hill, and did not depart long before 12 Feb. JW writes from London to W at Eusemere on 6 Feb; and he writes to MH on 9 Feb (the letter is dated "Monday 8th of Jan"—the month is clearly wrong, and the Monday in question was the 9th) from London of having heard that morning from DW, and that "they are still staying at Mr Clarkson's" (*JWL* 89). DW's letter would probably have been written by 6 Feb, and perhaps described future plans. STC wrote to DW at Eusemere on 9 Feb.

Wilkinson wrote to Mary Leadbeater on 15 Feb 1801 (the date on a copy at Tullie House Library, Carlisle; the year of the letter is given clearly incorrectly as "Eleventh month 22nd 1799" by Mary Carr, *Friends Quarterly Examiner* 1882, 18, and is undated in Carr's 1905 biography of Wilkinson; this copy is taken from that at Tullie House): "I had lately a young Poet seeing me that sprung originally from the next village. He has left the College, turned his back on all Preferment, and settled down contentedly among our Lakes with his sister and his Muse. He is very sober and very amiable, and writes in what he conceives to be the language of Nature in opposition to the finery of

8. Jan 23

The Longman accounts record on W's account under this date, without charge, delivery or forwarding of three copies of *LB* 1800 for RW, seven copies for W, and one copy of vol. II for Stoddart. (Longman accounts, DCP. See 1801:19; 1801:22.)

9. c Jan 25 ff

LB 1800 is published in London c 25 Jan. The agreed payment to W from Longman is £80, of which W later loans £30 to STC [see 1801:36]. (*EY* 321, 336; Moorman I, 501; *STCL* II, 665; *LL* I, 239; *JWL* 84–86, 92, 98. See also 1801:32.)[4]

10. Jan 26–Jan 30

The Longman accounts record on W's account under 26 Jan, without charge, delivery or forwarding of *LB* 1800 for "Mr. Hutchinson." The accounts record (also without charge) one copy for "Mr Lambe," who has previously borrowed a copy, under 29 Jan. JW forwards a copy to Capt. and Mrs. W probably c but by 29 Jan, and a

---

[4] On W's income from *LB* 1800–1805 see esp. Owen *CSP* 95n.

our present poetry. He has published 2 vols. of Poems mostly of the same character. His name is William Wordsworth." On Wilkinson see also esp. H. D. Rawnsley, *Literary Associations of the English Lakes* (Glasgow, 1894) II, 21–41; Daniel Scott, *Old Time Papers, Chiefly about Lakeland* (Penrith, 1906), 142–46.

The dinner with Slee was the occasion referred to in *STCL* II, 749; *STCNB* 1329&n (*STCNB* 795n, however, implies doubt that the Slee was John) when Slee's little girl, after eructating, announced, "Yan belks [that is, belches] when yan's fu', & when yan's empty"—a remark which became, according to STC, "a favorite piece of Slang at Grasmere & Greta Hall—whenever we talk of poor Joey, George Dyer, & other Perseverants in the noble Trade of Scriblerism."

Joanna H, who is not known to have visited DC by 2 May 1801, wrote from Penrith on that day as if she had seen W and STC lately. Her letter, after praising *LB* 1800, continues: "I shall I am afraid neither see, nor hear anything of the Wordsworths now Sara is gone. They are very nice folks. I love them dearly. I dont admire Mr Coleridge half so much as William Wordsworth. Sara thought I would have liked him better he is not half so *canny* a man, Dorothy is a *sweet* woman: is not so handsome but has auncommon [*sic*] good countenance, and is very lively . . . ." (JFW Papers.)

copy to MH on 30 Jan. Copies probably go off to STC about this time. (Longman accounts, DCP; *LL* I, 239; *JWL* 83, 84, 88, 96.)[5]

11. Probably between Feb and 1802 c May; esp. c Feb–early Oct 1801

W revises poems, esp. those of *LB*, and composes toward *Prel*. He is probably at work on *Prel* esp. c Feb–early Oct 1801. (*EY* 337; 1801:29; 1801:30; Appendix V.)[6]

12. Probably between early Feb and Apr 9

W composes the passage for *Michael* quoted by DW in her letter to Poole of 9 Apr. (*EY* 324. See 1800:149n.)

13. Probably between c Feb 1 and Feb 3

DW writes to JW (letter not known to survive) asking him to send money to Peggy. (*JWL* 86.)

14. Probably c but by Feb 6

DW writes to JW from Eusemere. (*JWL* 89.)

15. Probably c but not before Feb 9

W receives a letter from JW asking for his money in the funds, and advising that Tobin has sent Bartram's *Travels*. (*JWL* 86–87. See 1801: 26.)

---

[5] The date of the postmark of JW's letter mentioning the forwarding of the copies of *LB* is probably, as noted Woof *Ariel* 11n, 29 Jan. JW wrote the letter "at different times and in great haste." The Longman accounts charge W £ -/9/6 for a copy of "Davy's Researches" under 26 Jan, and note delivery of another copy of *LB* under 10 Feb (without charge; recipient not named).

[6] The absence of allusion in *DWJ* (of which the only portion surviving from the period between now and the publication of *LB* 1802 dates from 10 Oct 1801 and after) to corrections for *LB* 1802, except for the alterations to *Ruth* mentioned in entries for 7–8 Mar 1802, suggests that much of this work may have been carried out during this spring—certainly a period of hard work—or in any case by early Oct. W had been directed by Longman by 23 June to prepare a new edition. See esp. Pottle *YULG* 55; Hale White 44–50.

16. Probably c but by Feb 12

W, DW, SH walk to Grasmere, probably over Grisedale. (*JWL* 91; *HCRWC* I, 41; *STCL* II, 672–73. See 1801:7.)

17. Probably c but by Feb 13

W writes to JW (letter not known to survive) informing him of the return from Eusemere [see 1801:16] and their intended visit at Keswick. (*JWL* 90–91.)

18. Probably Feb 13 or Feb 14 and thereabouts–23 Feb (–Mar 2)

Probably on 13 or 14 Feb SH travels to Keswick for a visit. STC possibly comes to DC to fetch her. W, DW probably travel to GH at the same time or shortly after. W, DW return probably c but by 23 Feb. (SH probably returns on 2 Mar.) (*STCL* II, 672–73; *JWL* 96.)

Possibly at this time W copies into DC MS 31 quotations from Descartes and Daniel Sennertus used also by STC in his letter to Wedgwood of 18 Feb 1801. (DC MS 31.)[7]

19. Probably late Feb

W writes to Francis Wrangham, probably from Grasmere: His delay in answering Wrangham's last letter. Disappointment at having

[7] As of 9 Feb STC planned to walk halfway to Grasmere to meet SH on her way to Keswick on 13 Feb, or, should SH be unable to walk so far comfortably, to walk on to Grasmere and accompany her to GH next day. What actually occurred appears uncertain. *EY* 319n states that SH reached Keswick "presumably" on 14 Feb. *JWL* 91 indicates that the Ws were planning to proceed to Keswick after returning home from Eusemere, and they were almost certainly absent from Grasmere later in the month: on 25 Feb JW remarked that he supposed that "by this time *they* will be thinking of returning to Grasmere." They appear to have returned already, however, for on "Thursday morning" JW adds that he has "recd a letter from Dorothy this morning. Sara is staying at Keswick but will return to Grasmere where she will remain about a month . . . " (*JWL* 96).

The quotations copied by W correspond to (1) *STCL* II, 684–85, from "cum enim ait"; (2) *STCL* II, 683, second Descartes quotation at top of page, from "pro omni" (introduction by "The word idea used by Descartes"); (3) *STCL* II, 683, quotation "2"; (4) *STCL* II, 684, quotation "4." The copies, which include the mistake "potestates" at the end of (3), appear to have been taken from STC's own transcriptions.

failed to see Wrangham last summer [see 1800:49]. Has not yet seen second volume of *LB* although it has been out about a month. (*EY* 317–19. See also *STCL* I, 657–58; 1801:9.)[8]

20. Probably c but by Feb 23

DW writes to JW (letter not known to survive) informing him that SH will return to Grasmere and stay about a month. (*JWL* 96.)

21. Probably between Feb 26 and 27 and May 19

JW arranges for an allowance of £10 to be paid to DW every six months from the East India House. (*JWL* 97. See 1801:46; 1801:51.)

22. Perhaps Mar 2 (–Mar 4, –probably late Mar, after 24 Mar); Mar 2

Perhaps on 2 Mar W, DW write to SH and STC: (DW:) Their disappointment at not having received a letter from SH, and at her not having arrived. (W:) Copy of criticisms of *LB* in "harmonies." (*EY* 319–20.)

Perhaps this day SH, STC come to DC for a visit. (STC departs 4 Mar; SH departs probably late Mar, after 24 Mar.) Charles Lloyd probably calls at DC; or STC and perhaps others possibly call on Lloyd. (*EY* 319–20; letter, Lloyd to Manning, 5 Mar 1801, Cornell Collection, Cornell 2908.)[9]

[8] Charles Lloyd stated on 5 Mar that he had not yet seen *LB* 1800 II (letter, Lloyd to Manning, Cornell Collection, Cornell 2908).

[9] The "harmonies of criticism" letter was probably written on the same day that the addressees came to Grasmere. It was certainly written on a Monday and sent off instantly ("But here comes the Waggon!"). *JWL* 96 indicates that SH was at Keswick in late Feb but intended returning to DC shortly to stay for a month; *JWL* 113, 116 indicate that she had left Grasmere finally by early Apr. The remarks quoted from Stoddart are not from his review of *LB*, published in the *British Critic* on 2 Mar, and would seem unlikely to have been made after W had had news of that review, which probably arrived c 5 Mar and was sent on to STC at Keswick (see *JWL* 99). STC was with the Ws, however, on 2 Mar, as Lloyd's remarks to Manning on 5 Mar make plain: "I saw Coleridge on monday. he was with the Wordsworths, & left them yesterday. he looks in very indifferent health—I don't think that he is busied in any literary production. except it be finishing the ballad, part of which you heard him

On 2 Mar a review of *LB* 1800 [by John Stoddart] appears in *The British Critic* (XVII, Feb 1801). (*JWL* 99. See Ward; Hayden.)[10]

23. Probably Mar 4

STC departs DC. (1801:22&n.)

24. Probably c but by Mar 5

W writes to James Losh. (Losh Diary.)[11]

25. Probably c but by Mar 7

DW writes to JW (letter not known to survive): Sends complimentary letters from M. G. Lewis and others, copied by SH, also copy of verses that Lewis sent to W, perhaps *The Felon*. (*JWL* 103–06, 205.)

26. Mar 12

JW signs a promissory note to W for £357/10/–, due in 18 months, at 5 percent. The note probably acknowledges a loan of £277/10/– from W, from his investment in the funds, plus £80 from DW. (Bond, DCP; RW accounts, DCP. See *EY* 337n.)[12]

---

[10] JW thought that the end of the review, from "When the art of poetry," was not by Stoddart (*JWL* 99–100).

[11] Losh received a letter from W at Newcastle on 6 Mar.

[12] JW bonded himself to W in the amount of £550 for £277/10/– under the date of 19 May. RW's accounts record that JW so dated a separate promissory note for £80 to DW. This record is cancelled on another account and corrected to a notation of the £100 Crackanthorpe legacy to DW (see 1800:17); but the correction perhaps is only designed to assure DW full credit for the original legacy, fairly certainly the source of the £80 loan to JW.

RW's accounts with JW contain the following summary record under the date of 13 Mar: "To cash advanced you paid into hands of Mr Stewart in a sum of £910 namely from me in cash £27:10 Bill £175 on Slade & Co as below fr Dr Cookson £350 from William £277/10 from Dorothy £80."

---

repeat .... Lamb has sent an eloquent, but not very flattering, critique of [*LB* 1800, II] to W. Wordsworth." Since SH did arrive at DC about this time, she and STC probably travelled together.

27. Mar 16

STC writes to Poole that he has intermitted the pursuit of philo-sophical study at W's entreaty; that he has traced the whole history of the causes that effected the reputation of Locke, Hobbes, Hume entirely to W's satisfaction, that W means to write to Poole and send lines omitted by the printer from *Michael*, along with errata. (*STCL* II, 707. See 1801:45.)

28. Perhaps c late Mar–early Apr

CW visits DC; stays in Ambleside courting Priscilla Lloyd. (*EY* 321n; *JWL* 106, 119, 212; letter, CW to J. Walton, 16 Apr 1801, DCP.)[13]

29. Probably c late Mar, by Apr 3, c Apr 9

Probably c late Mar SH copies two large sheets of unpublished verse by W, the second being the last such task performed by her before her departure. Her copies include *Prel* materials, probably for I and perhaps II, and possibly some version or portion of I.1–271.

The sheets, with two letters by DW, are sent off to JW by 3 Apr. One of DW's letters contains the story of *The Sailor's Mother*, which possibly describes an event that took place only shortly before the writing of the letter, and bad news about W's health. Corrections for *FV* are probably included in one of the letters or sheets. (*JWL* 109–24; Appendix V; 1801:37; 1800:146n.)

30. Mar 24

DW writes to JW (letter not known to survive): SH is to depart from DC; *LB*; Stoddart; STC's health; W is (in JW's paraphrase) "*going on* with the recluse." (*JWL* 109–10.)

---

[13] CW writes: "I returned last night from a visit to the North where I have been spending the Easter vacation jointly between my brother & Sister, & the Lloyds" (DCP). JW complained on 29 Mar of having written to CW—apparently recently— and having received no reply (and he supposes that CW will be visiting the Lloyds). He evidently had news of CW and his courtship of Priscilla Lloyd by 22 Apr.

31. Probably late Mar, after Mar 24

SH departs DC. (*JWL* 103–04, 109. See 1801:22&n.)[14]

32. Probably Mar 25–probably Mar 26; Mar 25; Mar 26; Mar 26 or shortly after

W probably walks to Keswick on 25 Mar, talks with STC. W perhaps encourages STC to prepare and publish *Christabel*; probably agrees to assume debt of £30 advanced to STC by Longman. Probably today W writes Longman and Rees (letter not known to survive). He probably returns to DC next day. (*STCNB* 925, 926&nn; *STCL* II, 716; *EY* 321, 335–37.)

On 25 Mar STC writes to Godwin asking him to send a copy of Campbell's *Pleasures of Hope* belonging to him. W wishes to see it. (*STCL* II, 714.)

On 26 Mar a letter from Longman and Rees, and copies of cancelled sheets of *LB*, and six copies of *LB* are received by W. (*EY* 321.)

Probably on Mar 26 or shortly after W writes to William Calvert: Sends copy of *LB* 1800. CW is living in Ambleside and courting Priscilla Lloyd. (*EY* 321n.)

33. Mar 27 ff

On 27 Mar W writes to Longman and Rees: Arrival of letter, cancelled sheets, copies of *LB* [see 1801:32]. The £30 advanced to STC to be considered as advanced to W's own account [see 1801:9]. £80 due for *LB* he considers paid. (*EY* 321.)

The amount of W's loan is retained by Longman. (*EY* 336.)

W sends the letter, along with the letter from Longman and Rees, to STC, who adds a letter of his own to W's sheet this evening. (*STCL* II, 715.)

[14] On 10 Mar JW wrote that he understood that George H was to take SH away from Grasmere in "about a fortnight." In response to a letter from DW of 24 Mar referring to SH's approaching departure he indicated on 29 Mar that he supposed that she would have departed by the time of the arrival of his letter.

34. Probably shortly after Mar 27

W probably writes to Longman and Rees concerning errors in *LB* 1800, esp. lines omitted in *Michael* (letter not known to survive). Longman and Rees probably within a few days print a half sheet with omitted lines, and a page of errata. (*EY* 323, 326.)

35. c Apr–May

W probably composes toward *Prel*, possibly toward Book III. (Appendix V.)

36. Perhaps c Apr 5

STC visits at DC. (*EY* 322–24. See 1801:45.)

37. Apr 9

W writes to Thomas Poole: *Michael*. DW copies lines omitted by the printer. (*EY* 322–24. See 1801:27.)

W writes to Anne Taylor: Autobiographical comment; *EW, DS*; corrections for *FV*. (*EY* 326–29.)

W writes to John Taylor: Taylor's praise of *LB* [see 1801:4]; STC's reputedly Jacobinical writings. (*EY* 325–26.)

38. Apr 17

DW writes to SH (letter not known to survive): STC is in better health. (*EY* 229–30; 1801:40.)

39. Apr 18

News arrives at DC that STC is in ill health. (*EY* 329–30.)

40. Apr 19–Apr 27

On 19 Apr W, DW travel to Keswick for a visit, departing at 1, arriving about 6. They find STC unwell. His condition improves next day and remains better during the visit. Plans are formed during this visit for STC and HC to visit at DC, and for HC to go to school at Grasmere.

W, DW return to DC on 27 Apr, departing Keswick at 5:30. They find a letter from JW; read it by moonlight. (*EY* 329–31.)[15]

41. Probably c but by Apr 29

W composes "I Travelled among Unknown Men." (See 1801: 42&n.)

42. Probably Apr 29

DW copies poetry for, writes a letter to JW. The poetry probably includes the Prologue to *PB*. (*EY* 332; *JWL* 119. See 1801:40&n.)

W, DW write to MH: STC; SFC; W's health; copy of "I Travelled among Unknown Men." (*EY* 329–33.)[16]

DW [writes to] Mr., Miss Griffith, Mrs. Rawson. (*EY* 332.)

43. Probably c May–June, by June 23

Samuel Rogers and Richard Sharp visit the Lake District. They see and converse with W and STC, to whom they bring a note of introduction probably from Josiah Wedgwood. This meeting is probably W's first with either man, and STC's first with Rogers, who impresses W and STC favorably. (*STCL* II, 675–76, 737, 744; *STCNB* 961–69 &nn.)[17]

44. Probably May 4, 5

JW writes to DW requesting, among other things, W's advice concerning readings in a newly purchased copy of Anderson's *British Poets*. (*JWL* 122–24, 213. See 1802:256.)

---

[15] The letter from JW was probably that of 22–23 Apr (see *JWL* 117–19) in which he requests the "preface" to *PB*. See 1801:42.

[16] Probably the poem was written shortly before it was copied here. It was transcribed by MH in a copy of *LB* 1800 presented to Isabella Addison 13 May 1802 (see 1802:127).

[17] The amount of time that the travellers spent with either poet is uncertain. STC felt that they were with W long enough to reach a high opinion of him. *EY* 615 (DW to Lady B 16 June 1805) states that Sharp "visits this country every summer." W's contacts with Sharp are, however, noted hereafter only when specifically documented.

45. May 7–May 15, June 23; possibly between June 18 and June 23

STC, probably HC, travel to DC. He visits till 15 May. His health improves progressively until 12 May, when he takes a six-mile walk and suffers a relapse. Possibly during this visit, and shortly before STC's relapse, occurs an incident in which STC has a brief vision and tells DW that he is sure that he will be ill.

HC perhaps returns to GH between 18 and 23 June, fairly certainly by 23 June. While at Grasmere he probably attends the grammar school. (*EY* 329–30, 335; *STCL* II, 730–32, 737. See 1801:49.)[18]

46. May 19 (–1802 Sept 5)

The *Earl of Abergavenny*, Captain John W, sails from Portsmouth for China. (It arrives off Portland upon return 5 Sept 1802.) JW's investment totals between £9,000 and £10,000, including £80 from DW and £277/10/– from W. (Log, East India Office. See *JWL* 30–33; 1801:26.)

47. Probably c but by May 22

W agrees, because of the distressing effects upon him of recent composition, that his MS poems are to be put away and that DW is not to give them to him even if he asks for them. (*EY* 335.)

48. Probably May 22

W, DW drink tea at the Luffs'. They accompany the Lloyds, who are also present, to Rydal. W, DW write to STC: (W:) A parcel of bread and trout being sent to STC. (DW:) JW's sailing; HC; W's health. (*EY* 333–35.)

49. June 18 and thereabouts; and by June 23

STC visits at DC. He is present on 18 June. He returns to Keswick by 23 June, probably accompanied by HC. (*STCNB* 948–49&nn; *STCL* II, 733–38.)

---

[18] STC's visionary instant cannot be dated confidently, but this visit would appear to be the last contact between STC and DW "before his last seizure," as described in *STCL* II, 737.

50. Probably c late June

STC receives a letter from James Tobin proposing to pay him a month's visit, and to bring along with him Underwood and Dyson. The proposal to bring the uninvited and unwished guests surprises W and STC. (*STCL* II, 739, 744.)

51. Probably c but by June 23

W, DW write to RW: (W:) A box, containing W's books in London, old clothes, a new silk hat, and some presents for STC that RW's clerk was to have forwarded. RW should have it dispatched immediately. £30 borrowed by W from RW to be repaid on publication of *LB* now loaned to STC, who will repay shortly, when W will repay RW [see 1801:54]. The Montagu debt. W has received above £50 from him in last year. Please send any small sums now due W. Reception of *LB*; Longman has directed him to prepare another edition, (DW:) Gifts of £10 and a barrel of flour from [Robert] Griffith. A £10 half-yearly payment she is to receive from JW; gifts received and hoped for from CW. Requests for pens and paper. (*EY*, 335–38.)

52. Probably c but by June 24

W writes to James Losh. (Losh Diary.)[19]

53. Probably c July 1

A review of *LB* 1800 appears in *The Monthly Mirror* (XI, June 1801). (Ward; Hayden.)

54. Probably between July 1 and July 5

STC pays to W a portion of the £30 debt of his lately transferred [see 1801:33] by Longman from his to W's account. (*STCL* II, 739.)[20]

55. Probably c early July; and c but by July 18; and July 21

Probably c early July W mentions to STC his intention to request

---

[19] Losh received a letter from W at Newcastle on 25 June.
[20] STC states only that the sum is "sufficient for W's present necessities."

financial aid toward a trip for STC. He is possibly not explicit about his exact intentions.

Probably c but by 18 July W writes to Thomas Poole: Asks Poole to lend £ 50 to STC for a trip to the Azores. (*EY* 338–40.)

On 21 July Poole writes directly to STC offering £ 20. (*STCL* II, 755.)

56. July 9 (ff)

On 9 July James Losh gives letters of introduction for STC and W to, probably, James Barry. (Whether Barry uses them is uncertain.) (Losh Diary. See *STCNB* 1531&n.)

57. Aug 12–Aug 13

On 12 Aug James Losh visits, passes the night at DC, departing next day. He passes what he terms a "rational evening" with W, DW. (Losh Diary. See *LY* I, 56n.)

58. Perhaps last week of Aug

Samuel Ferguson, Martha Ferguson, Mary Threlkeld visit at DC. With W, DW, they probably build a fire and make tea on the island in Grasmere. (*EY* 442–43&nn.)[21]

59. Aug 29

RW pays and under this date charges to W's account £ 7/10/6, premium on £ 300 policy on Montagu's life. (Receipt, DCP; RW accounts, DCP.)

60. Perhaps a few days before Sept 3–between Sept 22 and Sept 30

Perhaps a few days before 3 Sept W joins Basil Montagu, Sir

[21] Perhaps between late Aug and a date by 21 Sept Uvedale Price visited Sir George and Lady Beaumont at Benarth, N. Wales. Price, in a letter to Sir GB of 18 Mar 1815, later recalled the visit as one when he brought "Wordsworth's two little volumes to you . . . , neither of you having ever seen them," and when, upon Price's reading "the woman in the red cloak" to them, they were "a good deal surprised" at the description of "the thorn and hill of moss." (Letters, Price to Sir GB, 16 Aug and 21 Sept 1801, 18 Mar 1815, PML.)

William and Lady Rush, and their six daughters; travels with them to Scotland, where he witnesses the wedding of Montagu to Laura Rush on 6 Sept. He remains with Montagu and probably most or all the others on a tour, returning to DC probably between 22 and 30 Sept. The party probably travels to Glasgow via Longtown, Ecclefecchan, Douglas Mill, Hamilton. W notices the heather along the road from Longtown; writes to DW from Douglas Mill; visits Corra Linn; visits the Duke of Hamilton's picture gallery at Hamilton; probably visits some of the Scotch Lakes. (*DWJ* I, 217, 229–31; EdS *DW* 406–07; *Composed at Cora Linn* IF note; *LY* I, 40; *STCL* II, 757, 763; 1801:62; *Gentleman's Magazine* LXX, 1801, 859.)

Returning southward W probably visits Alnwick, where he sees and dislikes Alnwick Castle. He and the Montagus perhaps pass the night of 15 Sept at Morpeth. They are in Morpeth on the morning of 16 Sept; there see James and Catherine Mackintosh. Later the same day W and Montagu see James Losh for a few minutes, probably at Losh's Newcastle home, The Grove, Jesmond. (*EY* 624; Losh Diary; Woof *Inward Eye* 31–33.)[22]

61. Probably Sept 2–perhaps c mid-Sept; perhaps very early Oct–Oct 7

RS visits at Keswick; spends two days with the Lloyds. (*STCL* II, 757, 766; Curry I, 247–48; CCS II, 161–63; Warter I, 168–72; letter, Lloyd to Manning, 2 Oct 1801, Cornell Collection, Cornell 2910.)[23]

62. Oct 1–Oct 2

STC passes the night of 1 Oct at DC. Early on the morning of 2

[22] STC states on 7 Sept that the marriage of Montagu to Miss Rush was to have taken place on "Thursday last," which would have been 3 Sept. The wedding fairly surely took place on 6 Sept, but it is possible, in view of STC's remark, that W had departed in time for a 3 Sept wedding. I know no reason for supposing that the tour was a foot-tour, or that beyond Glasgow W went by the same route that he and DW followed in 1803 (cf *PW* II, 538).

[23] Lloyd's letter states: "Southey has been spending some time at Keswick with Coleridge—he spent two days with us, on his way from thence to North Wales. . . ."

Oct STC writes *An Ode to the Rain.* (*STCL* II, 763–66; Mary Moorman, "Wordsworth's Commonplace Book," *N&Q* N.S. IV, 1957, 403–04.)[24]

63. Probably between Oct 7 and Oct 9 (–Oct 10)

STC arrives for a visit at DC. (He departs 10 Oct.) (*STCL* II, 766; *DWJ* M 55.)[25]

64. Oct 10 (–1802 Feb 14)

Probably W, DW, STC build "Sara's seat." STC departs for Keswick. (*DWJ* M 55. See *STCL* II 792.) (The portion of *DWJ* written in DC MS 25 covers the dates 10 Oct–1802 Feb 14.)

65. Oct 11

Mr. and Miss Sympson sup at DC. (*DWJ* M 55.)

66. Oct 12

W, DW drink tea at Mr. Sympson's. (*DWJ* M 55.)

67. Oct 13, 14

Wet weather is the only fact about this day noted in *DWJ*. No information is noted for 14 Oct. (*DWJ* M 55.)

68. Oct 15 (–Oct 19)

W, DW dine at the Luffs'. STC arrives during dinner. W, DW walk up Loughrigg Fell. DW is ill, takes laudanum. STC perhaps now comes on to DC. (He remains until 19 Oct.) (*DWJ* M 55.)

---

[24] STC's headnote accompanying the poem upon its publication in *MP* reports that the poem was "composed before daylight, on the morning appointed for the departure of a very worthy, but not very pleasant, visitor; whom, it was feared, the rain might detain," and thus suggests the presence of another visitor besides STC. While the visitor would appear unlikely in any case to be RS, in view of the warmth of STC's feelings towards him at this time, the poem itself clearly addresses the rain as the unwelcome visitor. DC is apparently the location, and W would seem to have returned from his tour with Montagu, inasmuch as the speaker of the poem wishes to be alone with a "dear old Friend" and his "sister dear."

[25] STC would probably not have come to DC before RS's departure from GH (see 1801:61).

69. Oct 16 (–between Oct 26 and Nov 9)

Thomas H arrives at DC for a visit. (He departs between 26 Oct and 9 Nov.) (*DWJ* M 56.)

70. Oct 17

DW, probably W, Thomas H, STC walk into Easedale. (*DWJ* M 56.)

71. Oct 18

DWJ makes no record of this day, DW having forgotten it by the time of writing. (*DWJ* M 56.)

72. Oct 19

STC departs. W, Thomas H walk to Rydal; DW is ill; Mr. Sympson drinks tea and sups at DC. (*DWJ* M 56.)

73. Oct 20 (–Oct 22)

DW, probably W, Thomas H go to the Langdales and Colwith. They perhaps pass the night at Colwith. (They return to DC on 22 Oct.) (*DWJ* M 56.)

74. Oct 21

DW, probably W, Thomas H dine at Bowness. They go boating upon Windermere, come in danger of being cast away. They sleep at Penny Bridge. (*DWJ* M 56.)

75. Oct 22

DW, probably W, Thomas H breakfast at Penny Bridge; dine at Coniston; return to DC. (*DWJ* M 56.)

76. Oct 23 (–probably Nov 6)

DW, Thomas H plant. W, Thomas H ride to Hawkshead; bring back two shrubs from Curwen's nursery. (*DWJ* M 56.)

On this day MH arrives at GH for a visit. (She departs, going to DC, probably 6 Nov.) (*STCNB* 999.)

77. Oct 24

Probably W, DW, Thomas H attempt to climb Fairfield, but only reach the sheepfold up Greenhead Ghyll. W, Thomas H put the boat out on the lake; bring a coat from Luff's. Mr. Sympson comes at dinner-time; drinks tea, plays cards. (*DWJ* M 56.)

78. Oct 25

DW, Thomas H ride to Legburthwaite, expecting to meet MH, who does not come. They go on Helvellyn. (*DWJ* M 56.)[26]

79. Oct 26; and between Oct 26 and Nov 9

On 26 Oct probably W, Thomas H go to Buttermere; perhaps return to DC. Thomas H departs DC between this day and 9 Nov. (*DWJ* M 56. See 1801:78n.)

80. Oct 27

DW, probably W, drink tea at the Sympsons'. (*DWJ* M 56.)

81. Oct 28 (–probably between Nov 5 and Nov 9, perhaps Nov 5)

The Cls arrive for a visit. (They depart probably between 5 and 9 Nov, perhaps 5 Nov.) (*DWJ* M 56; 1801:78n.)

82. Oct 29, 30

Rain all day both days. *DWJ* records no other information. (*DWJ* M 57.)

83. Oct 31

Some or all members of the household walk to Rydal. (*DWJ* M 57.)

[26] The dates of arrival and departure of several visitors in the coming weeks—Thomas H, MH, STC, the Cls—are less certain than the visitors' identities. The Cls came to DC on 28 Oct, but the time of their departure is obscure. On the basis of the stub fragments, which read "Thursday/left us," *DWJ* M 75 conjectures "[The Clarksons] left us" for Thursday [the 5th]. Both Thomas H and the Cls had departed by 9 Nov.

84. Nov 1

Some or all members of the household walk to Butterlip How in the evening. (*DWJ* M 57.)

85. Nov 2

A very rainy day. (*DWJ* M 57.)

86. Nov 3

Some or all members of the household dine at the Lloyds'. (*DWJ* M 57.)

87. Nov 4

W, TCl ride out. (*DWJ* M 57.)

88. Between Nov 5 and Nov 8

The Cls, Thomas H depart DC. One or both possibly depart on 5 Nov. (*DWJ* M 57; 1801:78n.)

89. Nov 6

STC arrives at DC for a visit, probably accompanied by MH. (He departs 9 Nov.) (*Mem* I, 177; *DWJ* M 57.)

90. Nov 9

On 9 Nov W, DW, STC, probably MH, walk to Keswick, arriving just before dark. They sup at Jackson's. SFC and the children have by this day departed for Eusemere. (*DWJ* M 57; *STCL* I, 774.)

91. Probably between Nov 9 and 1802 Jan 22; possibly between July 16 and 26 or Sept 24 and Oct 2

W, DW write *PB* MS 2 (DC MS 33). MH and an unidentified copyist write *PB* MS 3 (DC MS 34).[27]

---

[27] The two MSS were fairly certainly written about the same time and in close connection. On their relationship see esp. John E. Jordan, "The Hewing of Peter Bell," *SEL* VII (1967), 562–63. MS 2 was written by DW and W in what is now DC MS 33

92. Nov 10 (–Dec 28, –1802 Jan 22, –Mar 14)

STC departs Keswick for Eusemere and the South. W, DW, MH depart Keswick at 2; arrive at Grasmere at 9. (MH visits at DC till 28 Dec; remains with the Ws till 22 Jan 1802. STC reaches DC on his return on 19 Mar 1802.) DW, uneasy about STC, weeps; W accuses her of nervous blubbering. (*DWJ* M 57.)

93. Nov 11

W reads; MH writes to SH. (*DWJ* M 57–58.)

94. Nov 12

W walks near John's Grove; DW, MH follow him; W, DW walk before tea, W returning before DW. (*DWJ* M 58.)

95. Nov 13

W, DW, MH pass a happy evening and a restless night. (*DWJ* M 58.)

96. Nov 14

DW is unwell. W, DW, MH pass a quiet evening by the fire. (*DWJ* M 58.)

97. Nov 15

DW lectures little John Dawson for telling lies. Probably W, DW read Chaucer, Bishop [Joseph] Hall; MH reads Thomson. Letters arrive from SH, CCl. (*DWJ* M 58–59.)

---

around a group of materials including the *To Joanna* note, which was probably entered shortly prior to 23 Aug 1800. MS 3 through Part 2 was written by MH, who remained with the Ws till 22 Jan, and who wrote at the back of the NB on part of a double sheet that has served as a wrapper for the NB: "Mary Hutchinson. Gallow-hill. Galu-hill." She is not likely to have had an opportunity to assist in the copying of MS 3 while resident at Gallow Hill at any time between late Aug 1800 and 9 Nov 1801. MS 3 may thus be assigned to the period suggested and MS 2 accordingly to the same date. The Ws' brief visits to Gallow Hill in July and early autumn 1802 remain possible but unlikely occasions.

98. Nov 16

Peggy Ashburner speaks to MH of the good behavior of gay old men toward young wives. DW, perhaps W, MH walk. The Luffs pass. W is weakish but not unwell; reads Spenser. Two beggars call. (*DWJ* M 58–59.)

99. Nov 17

W, DW, MH walk in Easedale before dinner. Miss Sympson comes in before dinner; DW, perhaps all walk to Gell's cottage. They drink tea and sup at the Sympsons'. (*DWJ* M 59.)

100. Nov 18 ff

Probably all sit in in the morning and read Spenser. DW is unwell; lies in bed all afternoon. W, MH walk to Rydal. W writes some lines about [Grasmere] church which possibly later contribute to *Exc* VI.1105–08.[28] DW, MH walk to Sara's Gate before supper; W stays at home, sickish. (*DWJ* M 59–60.)

101. Nov 19

Charles and Olivia Lloyd call in the morning. No one walks. (*DWJ* M 60.)

102. Nov 20

Probably W, DW, MH walk in the morning to Easedale. Letters arrive from SH, STC. (*DWJ* M 60.)

103. Probably c but by Nov 21

W writes to RW: The box, paper [see 1801:51]; requests an account of sums received from RW since 1799; DW requests RW to send a portion of her £20 yearly allowance from JW. (*EY* 341.)

[28] The appearance of the first surviving MS of these lines, in *HG* MS B, is, however, as of draft, and suggests that they can have been composed only in quite unfinished form, if at all, at this time.

104. Nov 21

Probably W, DW, MH walk in the morning; pay £1/–/4 for letters. W is dispirited. Mr. Sympson drinks tea at DC, helps W out with the boat; W, MH walk homeward with him as far as the Swan. (*DWJ* M 60.)

105. Nov 22

W, DW, perhaps MH write to STC. Mr. and Miss Sympson come in at teatime. Probably all walk with them to the blacksmith's and return by Butterlip How. (*DWJ* M 60–62.)

106. Nov 23

W unwell; does not walk. DW, MH sit in the orchard; both are later unwell also. (*DWJ* M 60.)

107. Nov 24 ff

DW reads Chaucer. All walk to Gell's cottage; look at their favorite birch tree on the way. Send some of the goose that they have for dinner, on their return, to Peggy Ashburner, who sends back honey. DW goes to set matters right; has a conversation with her that probably provides W with the story that serves as the basis of *Repentance*. MH reads a poem on Learning by Daniel [probably *Musophilus*]; W reads Spenser. A note arrives from SFC reporting STC ill. W walks to John's Grove. DW walks to meet him. He has been frightened by, as *DWJ* describes it, "a sudden rushing of winds which seemed to bring earth sky and lake together, as if the whole were going to enclose him in." (*DWJ* M 60–62.)

108. Probably between Nov 24 and mid-1802, perhaps 1802 c Apr

W composes a basic version of *Repentance*. (*DWJ* M 60–62; DC MS 41. See GCL 224n.)[29]

---

[29] The poem is copied into DC MS 41 (see *PW* II, 535–43) between *To a Butterfly* ("I've Watched"), composed 20 Apr 1802, and "Among All Lovely Things," composed 12 Apr. *To a Butterfly* is the latest-composed poem of W's preceding *Repentance* in the NB. It is likely that the copy was made not long after composition.

109. Nov 25

W, MH visit the Lloyds. DW writes to SH, STC. (*DWJ* M 62.)

110. Nov 26

Mr. Olliff calls before W is up to say that they will drink tea later in the day at DC. They walk into Easedale to gather mosses and fetch cream. The Olliffs call at 5. They play cards; depart at 11. (*DWJ* M 62–63.)

111. Nov 27

A woman calls begging; tells her story. W walks to Charles Luff's (Ambleside), accompanied part way by DW, MH. They meet a soldier, wife, and child; give them halfpennies. MH writes to her aunt. A letter arrives from SH but not one which they hope for from STC. W sleeps poorly. (*DWJ* M 63–64.)

112. Nov 28

Soldiers go by. W remains abed till 1 PM. DW, MH walk to the Sympsons' to ask them not to come; probably W, DW, MH drink tea, sup at Olliff's. (*DWJ* M 64.)[30]

113. Nov 29

George Olliff brings W's stick. The household remains awake till after 1 AM awaiting letters; but none arrives. (*DWJ* M 64.)

114. Nov 30

Letters arrive from STC, Montagu. W, DW, MH walk; look at Langdale and the Pikes. MH writes to Joanna; DW to RW, SFC. (*DWJ* M 64.)

[30] It is possible that W was not of the party at the Olliffs'; but his presence seems the best explanation of George Olliff's bringing him his stick next day.

115. Perhaps c Dec

W works at a translation of Chaucer's *Troilus and Cressida*, of which only a fragment survives [see *PW* IV, 228–33, esp. 230–31]. (1801:117n.)

116. Dec 1

W is unwell; stays home, reads, as DW, MH walk to Rydal for letters. On the way home DW, MH pass two soldiers, drunk, merry, civil, and excited by the mountains. They meet W at Sara's Gate. He sets out to go around the lake but cannot cross the Rothay and comes back. Mr. and Miss Sympson drink tea, sup at DC. W is poorly and dispirited. (*DWJ* M 64–65.)

117. Dec 2 (–c Dec 3)

W rises late. DW reads Chaucer's *Manciple's Tale*. W translates a large part of it. (He probably finishes his work on it by c 3 Dec.) Mrs. Olliff brings yeast. All promise to meet the Luffs at her house next day. Charles and Olivia Lloyd call; W, MH walk to Rydal with them. DW writes part of a letter to STC. (*DWJ* M 65.)[31]

[31] On the specific copy of Anderson used by W for his translations, and probably for much of the family's reading earlier this year, see 1802:256n.

Most of the surviving MSS of W's work on Chaucer are found in the dismantled set of leaves now DC MS 13, with which once belonged the PML *OCB* sheet (see *CEY* 346). Draft work on *The Manciple's Tale* appears on what is now the inner page of an outer leaf of the NB, and similar draft probably once stood on the now-missing conjugate leaf (/e /ay appear on a stub—cf *Manciple's Tale* 186–87; T/ A/ The/ appear in the autograph of MH—cf lines 156–58). The inner leaves were used, consecutively, for copies of *The Prioress's Tale*, *The Cuckoo and the Nightingale*, and then, after a page left blank except for the title "The Manciple's Tale," a full copy of *The Manciple's Tale* as *PW* V, 358–65, lines 21–244. The first twenty lines of the full copy are in the autograph of MH, the rest in the autograph of W except for a part of the conclusion, lines 235–44, in the autograph of Dora W, clearly written, like many of the draft corrections, much later. The copy of *The Prioress's Tale* here survives only from line 149. The basic copy is in DW's hand. *The Cuckoo and the Nightingale* is in the hands of W and MH. It would appear that the copies of *The Prioress's Tale* and perhaps *The Cuckoo and the Nightingale* were begun before the fair copy of *The Manciple's Tale*. Possibly the page originally intended for the beginning of the fair copy of the last was left blank in anticipation, upon reflection following the writing of the title, of those

118. Dec 3

W walks into Easedale. DW is unwell in the morning; goes to bed after dinner till 7:30. She writes part of her letter to STC [see 1801:117]. [All] sup at the Olliffs' with the Luffs. (*DWJ* M 65.)

---

copies', esp. *The Cuckoo and the Nightingale*'s, requiring more space than they actually did in the event. No reason is evident why the blank space should have been left if those copies were already complete. It would seem that other Chaucer copies were expected to precede *The Manciple's Tale* in the NB, and it is possible that *The Prioress's Tale* was begun before the surviving draft of *The Manciple's Tale* was completed. More certain is that the MS of *The Prioress's Tale* probably dates shortly after 5 Dec, that of *The Cuckoo and the Nightingale* from 6–9 Dec or after, and the other MSS from about the same time. *DWJ* for 5 Dec states that W finished, and that he and MH made a copy of, *The Prioress's Tale*, whereas the copy of the poem in DC MS 13, which survives only from line 149, is basically in DW's autograph throughout. W's basic work on *The Manciple's Tale* almost certainly dates 2–c 3 Dec, and this copy is likely to have been made about that time, as is the copy of *The Cuckoo and the Nightingale*, basically composed about 7 and 8 Dec.

Copies of *The Prioress's Tale* and lines of *The Manciple's Tale*, lines corresponding to published lines 21–86, both entirely in the autograph of MH, and fairly certainly of this time, survive as DC MS 35 and 36 respectively. Both are shown by comparative readings to be later than the corresponding copies in the dismantled set of leaves. *The Prioress's Tale* has at some time been folded into a small packet as if for mailing. Both perhaps represent portions of the copying of the tales from Chaucer that MH was engaged in on 23 Dec.

Another leaf of Chaucer material survives from another dismantled set of leaves containing work otherwise dating from as early as 1799 and as late as 1820 (see Appendix VI). The lines correspond to *Troilus and Cressida* as quoted *PW* IV, 230–31, lines 47–91, and are in the autograph of W and MH. In absence of other evidence one may conjecture that this copy also dates from c Dec 1801.

On a leaf of similar paper, on the reverse side of a fragment of the *Prospectus* (DC MS 24) appear two quotations concerning Chaucer: one the couplet from *Il Penseroso* used as an epigraph for W's *The Prioress's Tale* from its publication in 1820, the other a quotation from Drayton's *Elegy to Henry Reynolds* (see *PW* IV, 471). W was certainly familiar with Drayton's *Poly-Olbion* before 23 Aug 1800, by which date he had written *To Joanna*. DW probably read *L'Allegro* and *Il Penseroso* on 3 June 1802, but these poems were probably as familiar to W as any in existence. The couplet is also quoted in DW's 1820 Tour Journal (*DWJ* II, 43). The Drayton lines are used as the epigraph on the title page of the 1841 *Poems of Geoffrey Chaucer, Modernized* (where they are attributed to W). The copied quotations appear fairly certainly to have been intended for use in connection with Chaucer translations, and perhaps as epigraphs for

119. Dec 4 (–Dec 5)

Mrs. Luff calls. Mr. Sympson and Lloyd call for the yeast recipe. W works at a translation of *The Prioress's Tale* (which he finishes next day). He and MH walk to Rydal after tea. DW finishes a letter to STC [see 1801:117; 1801:118]; letters arrive from STC, SH, CL (about Dyer). (*DWJ* M 65.)

120. Dec 5

Luff calls. W finishes his translation of *The Prioress's Tale*. He, MH copy it out. W is unwell. (*DWJ* M 66.)

121. Dec 6

W works on Chaucer. Walks with DW and probably MH into Easedale. They meet the Olliffs, with whom they walk for a time. DW reads Chaucer aloud; MH reads the first canto of *FQ*. DW, MH walk to Ambleside for letters; return with a melancholy letter from STC that prevents them from sleeping. (*DWJ* M 66.)

122. Dec 7 (–Dec 9)

W, DW, MH depart for Keswick at 9; meet Miss Bancroft along the way. They reach GH at 1; see SFC; write to STC; drink tea and converse with HC; depart at 4; reach home at 7. W works on *The Cuckoo and the Nightingale* (which he finishes by 9 Dec). DW writes to STC. (*DWJ* M 66–67.)

123. Dec 8, and shortly after

W works on Chaucer, probably *The Cuckoo and the Nightingale*. DW reads Michael Bruce's *Lochleven* and his biography [in Anderson's

---

a set of such translations. They possibly date from as early as c Dec 1801 or as late as preparations for *P* 1820.

What MS—if any—is being referred to in the *DWJ* entry for 5 Feb 1802, when "the Chaucer" came in a parcel from SH "not only misbound, but a leaf or two wanting" and when DW wrote about it to MH and also to Soulby (see 1802:26n), remains unclear, as do the identity and fate of the copies of *The Prioress's Tale* and *The Manciple's Tale* made by DW on 28 Apr 1802.

British Poets, XI]. They put up bookcases sent by Lloyd. W, MH walk to the boathouse at Rydal. A letter arrives from RW with news of JW, probably as of 7 Aug. (*DWJ* M 67.)

Perhaps shortly after 8 Dec DW writes to JW in care of RW (see *EY* 343).

124. Dec 9

DW reads "Palamon and Arcite" (probably Chaucer's *Knight's Tale*, but possibly Dryden's paraphrase, also in Anderson's *Poets*). W writes out at least part of his translation of *The Cuckoo and the Nightingale*. DW, MH walk into Easedale after dinner; see and hear many streams and falls. (*DWJ* M 67–68.)

125. Dec 10

DW, probably W, MH walk into Easedale; visit Aggy Fleming; search for mosses. TCl calls at DC, apparently stopping only briefly. W, DW, MH play at cards. (*DWJ* M 68.)

126. Dec 11 (–Dec 12)

The Luffs dine at DC. Mrs. Luff possibly stays the night; the Olliffs drink tea and sup at DC. (*DWJ* M 68.)

127. Dec 12 (–Dec 13)

Probably W, DW, MH walk with Mrs. Luff to Rydal. W goes to look at the Langdale Pikes. TCl arrives before tea for a visit. (He departs next day.) All play cards. (*DWJ* M 68–69.)

128. Dec 13

TCl departs. DW, MH go to Brathay, probably call at the Lloyds' and the Luffs'. W is unwell but improves by the time of their return. Letters arrive from STC, SH. (*DWJ* M 69.)

129. Dec 14

W, MH walk to Ambleside to buy mousetraps. MH falls, hurts her wrist. DW writes to STC. (*DWJ* M 69.)

130. Dec 15

W, DW walk to Rydal for letters; find one from Joanna H. (*DWJ* M 69.)

131. Dec 16

W, DW walk twice to the Swan and back; meet Miss Sympson, with whom they walk. (*DWJ* M 69.)

132. Dec 17

DW, probably W, MH go to the Luffs' to dine; meet Mrs. King; return home after 12. (*DWJ* M 69–70.)

133. Dec 18

W, MH walk around the two lakes. MH goes to look at the Langdale Pikes. DW meets W at Benson's. DW writes to ask STC for money. (*DWJ* M 70.)

134. Dec 19

DW, probably W, MH walk to Ambleside via Brathay; call at the Lloyds', who are not at home. They dine with the Luffs; come home in the evening. (*DWJ* M 70.)

135. Dec 20

DW, probably W, MH, drink tea at Thomas Ashburner's; remain till after 9. Peggy Ashburner talks about the Queen of Patterdale. (*DWJ* M 70, 72–73.)

136. Dec 21; between Dec 21 and 1802 Mar 6 ff

On 21 Dec MH walks to Ambleside for letters. W reads *The Pedlar*; is full of hope about what he should do with it; goes to meet MH, who has brought two letters from STC, one from SH, one probably from Annette. W writes to STC; W reads *The Pedlar*. DW, MH pack (to go to the Cls'); MH writes to SH, Joanna H. (*DWJ* M 70–71.)

On the same day W writes to Daniel Stuart: He had written STC to ask for £10; but STC is out of town. Will Stuart lend him the money, and consider STC his debtor? W will supply articles for *MP* to the value of the amount if Stuart prefers. (*EY* 342.)

Probably between 21 Dec and 6 Mar W reorganizes *RC* and/or portions of it descriptive of the Pedlar, independently from the *RC* narrative. DW possibly during succeeding months refers to these descriptive materials as *The Pedlar*. W probably at this time writes Addenda iv, v to MS D (*PW* V, 405–08). (Appendix VI; *PW* V, 405–10.)

137. Dec 22

W, DW go to Rydal for letters; receive a melancholy one from STC. W composes a few lines for *The Pedlar* on the way home. They also talk about CL's [*John Woodvil*]; pass an ex-sailor; overtake old Fleming and his grandchild at Rydal. W clears the path to the necessary, but snow at once falls back on the path from the top of the house. They discuss going to Ambleside to borrow money from Luff; but decide to postpone their visit to Eusemere for a day. DW reads aloud from Chaucer's *Prologue* and *The Man of Law's Tale*. (*DWJ* M 71–73.)

138. Dec 23

DW bakes; MH writes out tales from Chaucer for STC [see 1801: 117n]. W makes himself ill working on *RC*. Two beggars call. (*DWJ* M 73.)

139. Dec 24

W, DW, MH walk to Rydal; leave patterns for Mrs. King at Thomas Fleming's. They read Chaucer in the evening. DW takes out her old journal, probably that for the preceding year. (*DWJ* M 73.)[32]

140. Dec 25

DW, probably W, MH, drink tea at John Fisher's; receive a letter from STC which makes them uneasy about him. (*DWJ* M 73.)

[32] DW says: "Thoughts of last year. I took out my old Journal."

141. Dec 26

DW, probably W, MH call at the Olliffs', but they are not at home. W, DW call at Tom Dawson's to speak about his grandchild. [All] walk to Rydal. After returning, DW reads *The Miller's Tale* aloud; writes to STC. W writes lines for *Prel*, probably for Book III. (*DWJ* M 74. See 1801:142; Appendix V.)[33]

142. Dec 27

TCl's man probably calls. They write to TCl, probably sending the letter on. W, DW walk in view of Rydal; W goes to take in his boat. W perhaps writes some lines probably toward *Prel* III which MH copies. Mr. Sympson comes, probably helps W bring in his boat. (*DWJ* M 74. See Appendix V.)

143. Dec 28 (–1802 Jan 23)

W, DW, MH set off on foot for Keswick. (W, DW return to DC 23 Jan 1802.) They dine at Thirlspot. W, often alone, composes, perhaps toward *Prel*, possibly Book III. W forgets his gloves and a spencer at different resting places; the gloves are gone when he returns; MH recovers the spencer.[34]

They reach GH about 5:30. [Joshua L.] Wilkinson invites W to supper at the Royal Oak, where W meets a predestined marquis, Johnston[35], who speaks familiarly of *LB*, who has seen a copy presented by the Queen to Mrs. [William] Harcourt, and who wonders why the book does not sell better. (*DWJ* M 74–75; *EY* 344; Appendix V.)

[33] DW states that "Wm wrote part of the poem to Coleridge." He was fairly plainly engaged in basic composition rather than correction. The most convenient supposition, in view of the state of the poem then, and of *DWJ*'s record for 27 Dec, is that the work is toward Book III; but see Appendix V.

[34] DW writes "Spenser," and the reference is possibly to a copy of Spenser; but their copy of Spenser is likely to have been the bulky Anderson volume, and a spencer jacket would seem a more likely article.

[35] Possibly John Lowther Johnstone of Westerhall, 1783–1811 (see *The Complete Peerage*, I, ed. G. E. Cokayne, rev. Vickary Gibbs, London, 1910, 168n).

144. Dec 29–1802 Jan 22, 23

W, DW, MH depart GH; are accompanied by [Joshua L.] Wilkinson to the top of the hill; probably proceed along the old bridle road toward Dockray; dine at a public house, perhaps at Dockray or Thornythwaite, where they have stopped before [see 1801:7]. The landlady is curious and talkative; speaks of Mr. Walker of Grasmere, who has become rich. They reach the Cls', after a difficult walk, at teatime. (MH departs finally on 22 Jan; W on 23 Jan.)

During the visit CCl tells many amusing and interesting stories. During the visit W, DW call at RW's farmer's at Sockbridge; hear a good character of him. (*DWJ* M 75–76; *EY* 344.)

145. Dec 30

DW, probably W, MH, perhaps one or both Cls walk on Dunmallet. (*DWJ* M 76.)

146. Dec 31

DW, probably W, and perhaps CCl accompany MH to Stainton Bridge. They meet TCl with a calf's head in a basket; part from MH; turn back with TCl. (*DWJ* M 76.)

1802

[On writings of W possibly of this year see below and GCL 1–4, 6–8, 27, 34, 35, 37–39, 41, 43–97.]

1. Perhaps early this year by Apr 6

W writes the additions to the Preface to *LB* for *LB* 1802; composes in final form the 1802 *Appendix*. W prepares and sends off revisions and copy for *LB* 1802. (1800:152; 1802:88; Owen *Anglistica* 180–181; Appendix IV.)

2. Jan 1

W, DW walk, probably toward Matterdale. (*DWJ* M 76.)[1]

3. Jan 2

DW, probably W, and perhaps others walk nearly to Dalemain in the snow, which continues all day. (*DWJ* M 76.)[2]

4. Jan 3

MH brings letters from STC, SH to Eusemere; W, DW walk with her toward Penrith as far as Sockbridge, where they part. Thomas Wilkinson dines and sups at Eusemere. (*DWJ* M 76.)

5. Jan 4–Jan 14

W, DW remain at Eusemere. They walk every day during this period. (*DWJ* M 76–77.)

6. Jan 15–possibly Jan 16

Probably on 15 Jan W and DW dine at Thomas Wilkinson's and walk to Penrith for MH, who possibly returns to Eusemere with them and passes the night there, returning to Penrith next day. (*DWJ* M 77.)[3]

7. Jan 16

W, DW walk. (*DWJ* M 77.)

8. Jan 17 (–Jan 22)

W, DW go to meet MH, who comes to Eusemere for a visit. (She departs 22 Jan.) (*DWJ* M 77.)

[1] As recorded *DWJ* M, DW has written "Martindale." Martindale is a possible direction; but it appears that DW's "Martindale" in her entry for 29 Dec was an error for "Matterdale," and she probably erred similarly here.

[2] DW's actual phrase is "near to Dalemain."

[3] *DWJ* says that they "walked to Penrith for Mary" on 15 Jan, and implies that they were at Eusemere next day and went "to meet Mary" on 17 Jan.

9. Jan 18–Jan 20

Probably W, DW, and MH walk every day. (*DWJ* M 77.)

10. Jan 21

A stormy day. W dines at the Rev. Thomas Myers's, probably at [Brow,] Barton. DW rides there after dinner. (*DWJ* M 77; *EY* 344. See Moorman I, 449.)

11. Jan 22

MH departs Eusemere Hill. Probably W, DW accompany her toward Penrith as far as a field above Stainton Bridge. (*DWJ* M 77.)

12. Jan 23

W, DW, TCl depart from Eusemere Hill at 10, probably carrying with them a turkey, a gift from TCl. They part from TCl at 1; make a dangerous descent into Grasmere from Grisedale Tarn; reach DC after dark. They find £5 from Montagu and £20 from CW. They talk of Como, read *DS*, think of MH. (*DWJ* M 77–79. See *MY* I, 252.)

13. Perhaps between 23 and 27 Jan, certainly by Feb 9

W composes:
Louisa
To a Young Lady Who Had Been Reproached for Taking Long Walks in the Country
(*To a Young Lady* IF note; advice from Dr. Carol Landon; *DWJ* M 78–81, 85–86.)[4]

---

[4] *To a Young Lady* was published 12 Feb 1802 (*MP*) and was thus sent off by 9 Feb; and it is likely to have been among the poems being prepared for Daniel Stuart on 27 Jan (*DWJ* M 80), although *DWJ* mentions only sonnets. Although *DWJ* does not record that DW had been directly "reproached" yet for her walk over Grisedale, the circumstances of publication seem to favor the likelihood that the poem was finished at this time (see also *CEY* 153–54, which draws on the suggestion of Dr. Landon). *DWJ* M 85–86 records perhaps the most direct admonishment, an event of 8 Feb, but this was hardly aimed exclusively at DW. The IF note of *To a Young Lady* makes fairly certain that this poem and *Louisa* were composed together, despite the fact that

14. Jan 24

In the orchard W, DW lay out the plan of a new room; W walks. DW writes to STC. (*DWJ* M 79.)

15. Jan 25

W, DW walk to Rydal at dusk. W tires himself with composition. DW writes to CW, CCl, SFC; probably sends a letter from STC to MH. (*DWJ* M 79.)[5]

16. Jan 26

DW writes some portion of her journal. She and W walk, survey damages caused by the storm of 21 Jan. W works on composition— probably *RC*. A letter arrives from MH giving an account of STC's arrival in London. W writes out part of his poem, attempts alterations, makes himself ill; DW copies the remainder. He writes to Annette; DW writes part of a letter to MH. (*DWJ* M 79–80. See Appendix VI.)

17. Jan 27

DW finishes her letter to MH [see 1802:16]; W writes to Daniel Stuart; DW copies sonnets and perhaps other poems [see 1802:13]; Olliff calls with an invitation to tea next day. W, DW walk out, probably to Rydal; receive a letter from SH with an account of James Patrick the pedlar; drink tea at Frank Baty's. DW calls in at the Nab, where surprise is expressed at the Ws' trip over Grisedale [see 1802:13]. DW has calculated expenses for letters since 1 Dec as £1/11/3. W, DW

---

[5] DW's somewhat ambiguous statement is that she "sent off C.'s letter to Mary." CW writes to RW on 10 Feb [1802]: "I heard about a fortnight ago from Grasmere. They were tolerably well there—both William & Dorothy. I am vexed to hear that even yet the sale of the Lyrical Ballads is not so rapid as it ought to be." (DCP.)

W dates *Louisa* 1805 in editions 1836–1850 and *To a Young Lady* 1803 in the same editions (*To a Young Lady* IF note dates the poem 1805); and it seems probable that *Louisa* would have been included in *LB* 1800 had the poem been composed by then (see Hale White 46–47). *Louisa* of course hardly seems a winter's poem, but cf the circumstances of composition of *To Lady Beaumont* ("Lady! the Songs of Spring Were in the Grove") (see *MY* I, 134).

work in the garden; W reads magazines. DW writes to STC, SFC, perhaps someone else. (*DWJ* M 80–81.)[6]

The poems copied for Stuart probably include "If Grief Dismiss Me Not to Them That Rest," *To a Young Lady Who Had Been Reproached*, and *Written in Very Early Youth*. (See 1802:23, 1802:33; 1802:34.)

18. Jan 28

W perhaps writes an epitaph, and alters another written when a boy. He and DW walk to Olliff's for tea and cards [see 1802:17]. W is dispirited, insomniac. (*DWJ* M 81.)[7]

19. Jan 29

W is unwell. DW reads to him. They walk to Ambleside; find the Lloyds at Luff's; drink tea there by themselves. They receive a letter that DW describes as "heart-rending" from STC; W writes a reply. They discuss the possibility of W's visiting London. On their return they both write to STC. (*DWJ* M 81.)

20. Jan 30

W chops wood; asks DW to set down the story of Barbara Wilkinson's turtledoves. W works intensively on *The Pedlar*; sleeps badly. (*DWJ* M 81–82.)

21. Jan 31

W, DW walk around the two lakes, sitting at various places. W works at cutting MH's name more deeply in the Rock of Names. They find William Calvert at DC on their return; he dines; takes away the Encyclopedias. Mr. Sympson drinks tea with them. They pay the rent to Benson. W has a headache; sleeps badly; DW begins a letter to SH. (*DWJ* M 82–83.)

[6] DW makes a partly illegible statement "closed the letters up to [?Samson]." SH's account of Patrick perhaps contributes to W's work on the *Pedlar* and *RC* in coming days (through 6 Mar), to the comments of *Exc* IF note about the Wanderer, and the characterization of the Wanderer himself.

[7] The new epitaph can hardly be "I Travelled among Unknown Men," as suggested *P2V* H I, 177 (see 1801:42). See *CEY* 314.

22. Feb 1

W works hard at *The Pedlar*; tires himself; walks with DW toward the Sympsons'; parts from her; goes to Rydal, later works a little. A box of clothes with books arrives from London [see 1801:51]; DW reads from Campbell's *The Pleasures of Hope*, which comes in the box. (*DWJ* M 83.)

23. Feb 2

W chops wood. Lloyd brings flower seeds. W, DW walk into Easedale, change path upon meeting a cow. W wishes, but is unable, to break off composition; harms himself. He works at *The Pedlar* after dinner. DW reads *PL* XI aloud; both are moved to tears. Papers arrive; W reads them. (*DWJ* M 84.)[8]

"If Grief Dismiss Me Not to Them That Rest," translation from the Italian of Petrarch, is published (a second time), unsigned, in *MP*. (See Woof *SB* 181; *CEY* 23, 303–06.)

24. Feb 3

W, DW walk to Rydal for letters; find ones from Mrs. Cookson, MH. W does not compose; retires, but is insomniac. DW writes to MH, STC; reads to W. (*DWJ* M 84.)

25. Feb 4

W remains at home all day; thinks about *The Pedlar*. DW lies in bed till 3, reads Smollett's Life. (*DWJ* M 84.)

RW notes receipt of £10 on JW's account as "one months absent money for JW." The sum is to be used for an allowance for DW in JW's absence. (RW accounts, DCP; *EY* 337–38, 341, 343, 345; 1802:42.)[9]

---

[8] Presumably W was working at *The Pedlar* before dinner also, but DW's phrasing allows no certainty.

[9] RW notes "The like" received on 5 Apr, with the two sums applied "as above"— seemingly in reference to the charging to DW's account, against JW's allowance, a draft for £20 from Thomas H to John H dated Stockton, 10 Nov 1802. There seems no reason to suppose that the sums received in Feb and Apr did not go directly to DW.

26. Feb 5

W cuts wood; DW reads the story of Old or Young Snell in *Wanley Penson*. A parcel arrives from SH containing a waistcoat and a copy of Chaucer misbound and wanting a leaf or two. DW writes about it to MH and Soulby. W works late at *The Pedlar*. (*DWJ* M 84–85; Walter B. Crawford, "A Three-Decker Novel in Wordsworth's Library, 1802," *N&Q* N.S. XI, 1964, 16–17.)[10]

27. Feb 6

W goes to Rydal for letters; finds two from STC, who is resolved to try another climate. The letters make DW ill; W has a headache; neither can sleep. DW translates two or three of Lessing's *Fables*. (*DWJ* M 85. See Curry I, 271–72.)

28. Feb 7

W works, probably on *The Pedlar*. Sympson calls. W, DW, possibly with Sympson, sit by the fire, read *The Pedlar*, thinking it done; but W finds it uninteresting and in need of alteration. (*DWJ* M 85.)

29. Feb 8

W works, probably on *The Pedlar*; DW reads in Lessing and probably a German grammar [see 1802:44]; W, DW go toward Rydal for letters; stop at Park's for some straw for W's shoes; talk of Ellis the Carrier and the Ws' walk over Grisedale [on 23 Jan]. They meet the letter-carrier on the way; find letters from STC, Montagu. The wind roars and the trees toss at John's Grove. STC's letter contains prescriptions, speaks with less confidence of France [see 1802:27]; W, DW write to him. Montagu's letter encloses £8. DW writes to MH, Montagu, Calvert, SFC. (*DWJ* M 85–87.)

---

[10] *DWJ* did not record that DW read the story of "Isabel" in *Wanley Penson* as stated and discussed by William Heath, *Wordsworth and Coleridge* (Oxford, 1970), 32–33. DW clearly wrote "Snell." "Soulby" was probably A. or M. Soulby of Penrith, listed in *Jollie's Cumberland Guide & Directory* (Carlisle, 1811) I, xxxi, as "printer and bookseller" and "bookseller" respectively.

30. Feb 9

W works, makes himself unwell. The funeral procession of a woman who has drowned herself passes by. W and DW [probably translate] a little from Lessing. W tires himself, probably with composition for *The Pedlar*. (*DWJ* M 84.)

31. Feb 10

W, DW send Fletcher the carrier for letters, writing paper; he apparently finds that no letters have come; a letter arrives later from Eusemere as DW is writing out *The Pedlar*. DW pays Jackson's bill, sends letter to Montagu. W, DW read *The Pedlar*, are delighted with the first part; W then comes to what he regards an ugly place, and goes to bed tired out. (*DWJ* M 87–88.)

32. Feb 11

W works on *The Pedlar*. Miss Sympson calls; W remains in his own room till her departure, when DW walks out with her. DW reads P. or G. Fletcher, and, to W, the Life of Jonson and some of Jonson's short poems, including *On My First Daughter*, probably, and *To Penshurst*. W sleeps. Charles Lloyd calls concerning lodgings for his children, probably with the object of helping them escape whooping cough. W goes to bed unwell from further work. (*DWJ* M 88.)

33. Feb 12

W works; DW recopies *The Pedlar* as W continues working. A poor woman whom DW has met before, and her son, whom W and DW first met at Skelwith Bridge at an unknown time, call. W rubs a table. DW almost finishes copying *The Pedlar*; W wears himself and DW out with labor. They have an affecting conversation. (*DWJ* M 89–90.)

To a Young Lady Who Had Been Reproached is published, unsigned, in *MP* under the title *To a Beautiful Young Lady, who had been harshly spoken of on account of her fondness for taking long walks in the country.* (See Woof *SB* 181–82.)

34. Feb 13

W, DW continue work at *The Pedlar*. Letters arrive from SH and a correspondent whom *DWJ* calls "the Frenchman in London." DW writes to SH; W looks at old newspapers; new ones arrive. W reads parts of *The Recluse* to DW. (*DWJ* M 90.)

Written in Very Early Youth ("Calm Is All Nature as a Resting Wheel") is published, unsigned, in *MP* under the title *Sonnet. Written at Evening.* (Woof *SB* 182–83. See *CEY* 22.)

35. Feb 14–Feb 16 (and Mar 12–Mar 13)

On 14 Feb DW probably works at altering passages of *The Pedlar*; DW reads a letter from CCl to W. W resolves to go to Penrith, and sets off, travelling over Kirkstone. Before his departure DW readies MSS, writes to CCl, puts up some letters for MH. After W's departure DW reads Jonson's *Penshurst*, walks out, meets a carman with an attractive family, reads German, writes to STC. (*DWJ* M 90–91.)

During his trip W sees MH for about two hours between Eamont Bridge and Hartshorn Tree; probably stays at Eusemere; alters *The Pedlar*. Probably during this trip, perhaps at the Cls', W hears from Robert Grahame of Glasgow [see also 1806:50] the story of his meeting with Alice Fell. (The story later prompts W's poem *Alice Fell*, which he writes on 12–13 Mar.) (*DWJ* M 90, 100–01; *Alice Fell* IF note. See 1802:62; 1802:63.)[11]

36. Feb 15

Letters arrive from STC, Annette. DW reads German; writes part of a letter to STC. (*DWJ* M 91–92.)

37. Feb 16

W returns to DC at teatime, having travelled via Threlkeld. Possibly today, between Eamont Bridge and Hartshorn Tree, he sees MH. (*DWJ* M 92. See 1802:35.)

---

[11] No record appears to survive of W's having met Grahame before this time, or between this time and c 19 June 1806; so that the present visit at Eusemere was probably that during which W heard the story of Alice Fell.

38. Feb 17 (–Feb 21)

A short letter arrives from MH. DW copies Second Part of *PB*. (DW probably finishes MS 4 of *PB*, which this work begins, on 21 Feb.) (*DWJ* M 92.)

39. Feb 18

W goes to tea at Mrs. Sympson's; DW copies Third Part of *PB*; starts letter to STC. W comes with letter from STC. W works, perhaps on *The Pedlar*, and is the worse for it. (*DWJ* M 93.)

40. Feb 19

Williamson cuts W's hair; DW writes to STC; W or Williamson carries the letter to Ambleside. DW also writes to MH, SH. (*DWJ* M 93.)

41. Feb 20

W, DW walk to Rydal, find no letters there. DW writes out the First Part of *PB*. (*DWJ* M 93.)

42. Feb 21

DW writes out the Second Prologue to *PB*, and after a call at Mrs. Olliff's and dinner writes out the First Prologue, completing it about 5:30. This copying probably completes MS 4 of *PB*.[12] W walks to the tailor's. DW writes to CCl, RW. W, who has probably been composing, retires exhausted. (*DWJ* M 93; DC MS 44.)

DW's letter to RW [misdated 22 Feb]: Thanks for the box [see 1802:22]. W has been ill but is better. Has RW forwarded a letter to JW addressed to Staple Inn about two months ago [see 1801:123]? JW's safe arrival at the Cape of Good Hope. DW expecting £10 which RW was to receive from the India House [see 1802:25]. Their recent visit at the Cls'; CW. (*EY* 342–44.)

---

[12] For DW's note on the title page of the MS see *PW* II, 528.

43. Feb 22

DW is unwell. Letters arrive from Annette and Caroline, MH, SH, STC. W, DW walk. Mr. Sympson calls. W reads part of *PB* to him, calls DW to read Third Part. Sympson shows them his first engraving. W goes to bed in bad spirits. (*DWJ* M 93–94.)

44. Feb 23

DW reads German grammar. W, DW walk into Easedale, and to John's Grove and Rydal. W reads Bishop Hall; DW perhaps reads German. (*DWJ* M 94.)

45. Feb 24

W, MH are by now known, at least by their intimate friends, to intend to marry. (*STCL* II, 788.)

W writes to Annette, STC, the Frenchman [see 1802:34]; DW receives, answers, letter from CCl. The letter, not known to survive, speaks of her intention to go to Eusemere when W goes to Keswick. DW writes a letter to STC. W takes letters for the post. (*DWJ* M 95.)

46. Feb 25

W writes to Montagu, goes to the Lloyds', DW accompanying him to the turning of the Vale. DW reads in Lessing's "Essay" (perhaps the *Laokoon*). W returns between 9 and 10. (*DWJ* M 95. See Owen *Anglistica* 181.)

47. Feb 26

The Lloyd children call with Mrs. Luff. W, DW accompany them to the gate in their departure for Mrs. Olliff's. DW finds *PB*; they walk; meet Lloyd. Other Lloyds, and possibly the Luffs, call. The Lloyds remain until 8. The conversation concerns Mrs. King, Mrs. Olliff. DW writes to MH; W closes his letter to Montagu [see 1802:46]; writes to Calvert, SFC. (*DWJ* M 95–96.)[13]

---

[13] *DWJ* 125 remarks, "We always get on better with conversation at home than elsewhere—discussion about Mrs. King and Mrs. Olliff." The evening appears to have been exceptionally gossipy.

W's *Personal Talk* sonnets are possibly based in some degree on recollection of this day.

48. Feb 27

W, DW walk toward Rydal. Barth Sympson calls, tipsy. W is not very well. (*DWJ* M 96.)

49. Feb 28

W is ill; employs himself with *The Pedlar*. Papers arrive; DW writes to SH, CCl.

Under this date *DWJ* notes: "Disaster Pedlar." (*DWJ* M 96.)[14]

50. Probably between c Mar and July 29; probably c Mar–Apr, certainly by Mar 7

Probably between c Mar and 29 July, W, according to STC, writes thirty-two poems, of which the longest is 160 lines (probably *R&I* much as the transcription *STCL* II, 966–70, [*PW* "MS"] which contains 154 lines). One of the poems is probably *To a Skylark*. (*STCL* II, 830. See Moorman I, 542; *EY* 583; George Whalley, *Coleridge and Sara Hutchinson and the Asra Poems*, London, 1955, 23–24.)[15]

For poems possibly or definitely among these see below to 29 July *passim*.

Probably c Mar–Apr, certainly by 7 May, W composes *The Sparrow's Nest*. (*STCL* II, 799–801.)[16]

51. Mar 1

W, DW walk to Rydal. DW goes ahead, finds letters from MH,

---

[14] In view of DW's proposal on 3 Mar to rewrite *The Pedlar*, it would appear that the "disaster" was some sort of accidental destruction of a primary MS.

[15] As *To a Skylark* is copied in DC MS 41, it is likely to be contemporary with the bulk of the copies there, which were fairly certainly made soon after composition.

[16] STC's letter of 7 May seems to imply that this poem was composed recently. Its close similarity in stanza form, theme, and tone to *To a Butterfly* ("Stay near Me"), composed 14 Mar, suggests that the two poems were written within a short time of each other. W dated the work 1801 from 1836 through 1850 and in the IF note. See Curtis 197.

SH; meets Mrs. Lloyd. DW writes to MH, twice to SH; W to STC. Mrs. Lloyd calls when DW is in bed. (*DWJ* M 96.)

52. Mar 2

DW works, reads German; W reads also. Mrs. Lloyd rides by without calling. (*DWJ* M 96.)

53. Mar 3

On 3 Mar DW proposes rewriting *The Pedlar*. W goes to work, tires himself. (*DWJ* M 96–97.)

54. Mar 4–Mar 7

Calvert's man brings horses for W. W, DW pack, make pens, arrange poems for writing. W departs for Keswick, with all the pens but two, at 11:30. He returns 7 Mar.

DW writes to W. (*DWJ* M 97.)

During his trip W composes corrections for *Ruth*, including two new stanzas. These corrections are probably those copied in DC MS 31. (See *PW* II, 227–35, 509–10; Pottle *YULG* 53–55.)

55. Mar 5

DW writes to W. This evening W, in Keswick, and DW both observe a curious appearance of the moon. (*DWJ* M 97–99.)

56. Mar 6

DW writes out *The Pedlar*, sends off a letter, perhaps that written the day before, to W. Letters arrive from W, MH, STC. DW writes to STC. (*DWJ* M 98.)

57. Mar 7

DW stitches up *The Pedlar*; writes out *Ruth*; writes to MH. W arrives home, bringing two new stanzas of *Ruth* [see 1802:54]. (*DWJ* M 98.)

58. Mar 8

W, DW walk to Rydal, find letters from MH, Montagu. DW sends probably a single letter to MH, STC, SH; rewrites and sends off *Ruth*, as altered [see 1802:57]. (*DWJ* M 98–99. See Pottle *YULG* 53–55.)

59. Mar 9

W reads in Jonson; reads what *DWJ* describes as "a beautiful poem on love" to DW. They walk; sit in Sara's seat; walk into Easedale; in the evening read *The Pedlar*; W makes a few alterations. (*DWJ* M 99.)[17]

60. Mar 10

W reads in Jonson; DW reads in German. They walk to Rydal. W considers publishing what *DWJ* calls the "Yorkshire Wolds Poem" (probably *PB*) with *The Pedlar*. (*DWJ* M 99.)

61. Mar 11 (–Mar 12)

W works at what *DWJ* calls "The Singing Bird" (*The Sailor's Mother*). TCl arrives for a visit on a fine horse, which W admires greatly. (TCl departs next day. W finishes his poem next day.) All of them walk. (*DWJ* M 99–100.)

62. Mar 12 (–Mar 13)

W, DW see TCl off; walk toward Easedale, are driven back by a shower. W finishes "The Singing Bird" (*The Sailor's Mother*) [see 1802:61].

DW reads Lessing [see 1802:46]. W works on *Alice Fell* (which he

---

17 *Written in a Grotto* (see *PW* III, 413–14) was published in *MP* on this day. Resemblances between this uningenious quinzaine and W's "With How Sad Steps" are seemingly too numerous for chance, even if one takes into account a mutual indebtedness to Sidney, but are too superficial to confirm W's authorship. See Woof *SB* 183; *P2V* H II, 187–88; *PW* III, 575–76. If by W, the poem can be dated only with rough conjecture: possibly c early 1802, certainly by 6 Mar 1802.

finishes next day), written to gratify Robert Grahame [see 1802:35]. (*DWJ* M 100–01; *Alice Fell* IF note.)

63. Mar 13 (–Mar 14)

W finishes *Alice Fell* [see 1802:62]; works on *Beggars* (which he finishes next day). W, DW walk to Rydal. After tea DW reads to W her original account of the incident on which *Beggars* is based [see 1800:45]. W is inhibited by her words and cannot complete the poem; goes to bed tired; sleeps badly. (*DWJ* M 100–01.)

64. Mar 14

W finishes *Beggars* [see 1802:63] before rising. At breakfast he writes *To a Butterfly* ("Stay near Me"). Sympson calls. DW copies *To a Butterfly*, probably *Alice Fell*, *Beggars*, and perhaps other poems; reads them out. They call at Olliff's. DW begins a letter to Mrs. Rawson. W attempts to revise *To a Butterfly*; tires himself. (*DWJ* M 101.)[18]

65. Mar 15

W, DW read poems, probably those copied the previous day. DW reads a little German; Charles Luff calls, talks with W, departs, returns for tea. Isaac Chapel, a sailor closely resembling JW, calls; tells of horrifying experiences aboard a slave ship. A letter arrives from MH; DW writes to MH; writes to SH about Olliff's gig; writes to Longman and Rees; and to CCl. (*DWJ* M 101–02.)

66. Mar 16 (–Mar 17)

Mrs. Luff calls. W writes a part of *The Emigrant Mother* (which he completes next day). DW reads him to sleep with Spenser after dinner; they walk. (*DWJ* M 102.)[19]

[18] A possible stage of interconnection and revision of *To a Butterfly* ("Stay near Me") and *To a Butterfly* ("I've Watched You") is discussed by William Heath, *Wordsworth and Coleridge* (Oxford, 1970), 59–63. The MSS in question possibly date c Mar–Apr 1805, but more probably c Mar 1806 (see Appendix VII).

[19] W's qualified recollection that *The Emigrant Mother* was written at Sockburn (*Emigrant Mother* IF note) is clearly erroneous.

67. Mar 17

W finishes *The Emigrant Mother* [see 1802:66]. Mrs. Luff, Mrs. Olliff call; DW walks with Mrs. Olliff; they meet Mr. Olliff, who offers manure for the garden at DC. W reads his poem to DW; rests; DW reads to him. Miss Sympson calls, drinks tea; DW walks with her to Rydal, later meets W in the road. W writes a poem (unidentified), finishing it and reading it to DW after she has retired. (*DWJ* M 102–03.)

68. Mar 18 (–Mar 19)

W possibly goes to Keswick. He is probably in any case absent from DC this night. DW attempts to write verses. (*DWJ* M 103–04. See Moorman I, 530.)[20]

69. Mar 19

STC arrives at DC for a visit, probably shortly after 4. (He remains until 21 Mar.) W arrives soon after. A letter arrives from SH via MH. W, STC dispute about Ben Jonson. STC retires late; W, DW retire at 4 AM. (*DWJ* M 104–05.)

70. Mar 20

W, STC walk to Borwick's. On returning they discuss going abroad [see 1802:27; 1802:29]. W reads *The Pedlar*. They discuss various subjects, including christening the children [see esp. 1803:128]. (*DWJ* M 105.)

71. Mar 21

W, STC lie abed late. W, DW accompany STC to Borwick's, where STC leaves them to go on to Keswick. W is unwell; has a

---

[20] DW's verses are, if surviving, unidentified. (See 1805:109.)

DW expected W to return the same day, but he apparently did not, returning rather on the next day, when STC also came. But the two did not arrive together, and the times of arrival are uncertain. STC had slept at Scotch Corner on his way home from Gallow Hill on the night of 14 Mar (*STCNB* 1151), and so was fairly surely at Keswick on 18 Mar.

sweet and tender conversation with DW; DW starts letters to MH, SH. (*DWJ* M 105.)

72. Mar 22

W is unwell. Charles Luff brings two letters from SH, one from Annette. DW finishes two letters to MH, SH [see 1802:71], writes to RW. W, DW talk about STC; resolve to see Annette, and that W shall go to MH. W writes to STC that he is not to expect them till Thursday or Friday [25 or 26 Mar; see 1802:78]. (*DWJ* M 105.)

73. Mar 23 (–early June, esp. Mar 24–Mar 26)

On 23 Mar W works on *To the Cuckoo*, which is perhaps begun this day. DW reads German. W joins her in the orchard; they talk about STC. W repeats his poem; attempts further composition after DW goes in; reads Jonson.

To the Cuckoo is perhaps largely written between this day and 26 Mar; but is perhaps not finished before May or early June. (*DWJ* M 105–06, 124–25, 130–31.)[21]

74. Mar 24

W, DW walk to Rydal, find letters from MH. DW vows that they will not leave this country for Gallow Hill. W alters *To a Butterfly* [see 1802:64]. DW writes to MH in the evening. W walks out, writes to Peggy Ashburner. (*DWJ* M 106.)

75. Mar 25

W, DW do not walk. Mr. Sympson drinks tea at DC. (*DWJ* M 106.)

[21] Whether W continued work on *To the Cuckoo* or worked at another poem after DW went in is uncertain. Further work on *To the Cuckoo* seems likely, however [see 1802:76]. DW's first reference to the poem, "William worked at the Cuckow poem," possibly suggests earlier work on these verses, but might equally well result from DW's having written the entry at a later time. W's search for an epithet for the cuckoo on 14 May and their reading in and about Logan on 3 June after hearing a cuckoo sing suggest that the poem may still have been in the foreground of W's mind after 26 Mar, when *DWJ* last mentions the poem.

76. Mar 26

W writes to Annette; works on *To the Cuckoo* [see 1802:73]; writes a conclusion to what *DWJ* calls the "Silver How poem." W, DW walk; DW returns; writes out poems; goes to seek W; finds him at Olliff's, where he has probably been since their parting. He has tried to alter a passage in the Silver How poem. After their return he writes *The Rainbow* (fairly certainly "My Heart Leaps Up"). (*DWJ* M 106.)[22]

77. Mar 27 (–June 17, –early 1804 by Mar 6)

On 27 Mar W writes part of an ode, probably the *Ode. Intimations of Immortality*—probably some part or all of stanzas I–IV. Olliff sends dung [see 1802:67]. W works in the garden; sits in the orchard with DW. (W perhaps adds to the poem—possibly some part or all of stanzas V–VIII—on 17 June. Probably most of the last seven stanzas are written, and the poem completed, in early 1804, by 6 Mar.) Possibly between this date and c 17 June, or, more probably, early 1804, by 6 Mar, W composes *To H.C., Six Years Old*. (*DWJ* M 106; *Ode* IF note; 1802:167n.)[23]

78. Mar 28 (–Apr 5, –Apr 16)

W, DW go to Keswick. (They depart for Eusemere 5 Apr; return to DC 16 Apr.) They are probably met along the way by STC; find a letter from MH on arrival at GH. (*DWJ* M 106–07; *EY* 346.)

[22] DW's statement that W wrote a conclusion to the Silver How poem "before he went out" I have supposed to refer to his departure from DC and not from Olliff's, as her phrasing might imply. The Silver How poem remains unidentified. *PW* II, 489 states that "it has been conjectured" that "When to the Attractions" is the poem in question; but Silver How plays an incidental role there (see line 91), and the suggestion is uncompelling. An independent version of *The Recluse* 1–45 would appear an equal—but equally remote—possibility.

[23] W's brief description of the development of the *Ode* in *Ode* IF note is unambiguous: the first four stanzas are there said to have been written at least two years before the remaining part. W plainly wrote some part of some ode on 27 Mar and went to Keswick next day. STC's *Dejection*, written mostly or all on 4 Apr, appears to contain clear allusions to the opening portions of the *Ode*, and the phrasing "I too will crown me with a coronal" (see *STCL* II, 793) seems a direct reference to what is now the fourth stanza of W's poem. (*STCNB* 1830 possibly looks back to this occasion.) W is not known to have worked on another ode about this time.

79. Mar 29 (–Mar 30)

DW goes to Miss Crosthwaite's to unpack a box. W, STC go to Armathwaite (returning to GH the same day or next). (*DWJ* M 107.)[24]

80. Mar 30

DW, others, perhaps including W, go to Calvert's. (*DWJ* M 107.)

81. Mar 31

DW, probably W, and others walk to Portinscale. Calvert and [the Rev. and Mrs. Joseph] Wilkinson dine at GH. DW walks with Mrs. Wilkinson to the Quaker meeting, then meets W. They walk in the field. (*DWJ* M 107.)

82. Apr

The Longman records for *LB* 1802 commence with this date. (Pottle *YULG* 49n. See 1802:88n.)

83. Apr 1

W, DW, STC, SFC go to the How, come home by Portinscale. (*DWJ* M 107.)[25]

84. Apr 2

W, DW sit all evening in the field. DW, possibly W also, drinks tea with the Misses Cockin. (*DWJ* M 107.)

85. Apr 3; probably Apr 3

W, STC go onto Skiddaw. W, DW, and probably the Cs dine with the Calverts. (*DWJ* M 107.)
Probably this night W and STC converse lengthily about matters relating to W's plan to marry MH. (*STCNB* 3304 & n; 1802:86.)

---

[24] *DWJ* gives no clue to the time of return of W and STC to Keswick.
[25] The How concerned, in view of their route, is probably Seat How, above Thornthwaite.

86. Apr 4

Probably W and DW drive in a gig to Water End. DW walks to GH. SFC evidently joins the company at Greta Bank for tea. W walks with her, either coming or going. DW repeats W's verses to the group. (*DWJ* M 107.)[26]

STC writes the first version of *Dejection. An Ode* in a letter to SH. (*STCL* II, 790–98.)

87. Apr 5 (–Apr 16)

W, DW travel to Eusemere for a visit, probably taking a horse of William Calvert's with them; STC accompanies them to Threlkeld. (They depart 16 Apr. W is also absent 7–13 Apr.) DW probably sees a schoolmistress and her scholars at Dacre.[27] They arrive at Eusemere for tea. (*DWJ* M 107; 1802:89.)

RW notes receipt of £10 on JW's account, to be used for allowance for DW, under this date. (See 1802:25.)

88. Apr 6; possibly Apr 6, probably Apr 7 or Apr 8

On 6 Apr W, DW, CCl walk to Waterside; W, DW walk in the evening toward Dalemain. (*DWJ* M 107.)

Possibly on 6 Apr, probably on 7 or 8 Apr, DW writes to RW from Eusemere: Seeks information about money that was to be paid her during JW's absence [see 1802:25; 1802:87]. Asks RW to take care of four copies of *LB* that are to come to him from Longman [see

---

[26] DW's entry is enigmatic. After the report of their trip to Water End, a property on the west side of the lake belonging to Lord William Gordon (Peter Crosthwaite's *Accurate Map of the Matchless Lake of Derwent*, 1783, rev. 1800), she continues: "I walked down to Coleridge's. Mrs C. came to Greta Bank to Tea. Wm walked down with Mrs C. I repeated his verses to them. We sate pleasantly enough after supper." As Mrs. Calvert lived at Greta Bank, the Mrs. C. who came to tea was probably SFC. The phrase "walked down" would logically apply to a walk down from Greta Bank to GH; so that W perhaps walked home with SFC. Probably, as *EY* 347n suggests, the Ws supped at Greta Bank.

[27] *DWJ* states simply: "The schoolmistress at Dacre and her scholars."

1802:166]: send one to CW, await word on others (for JW, Mr. Griffith, Miss Threlkeld of Halifax). (*EY* 345–46.)[28]

89. Apr 7 (–Apr 13)

W departs Eusemere Hill for Middleham on William Calvert's horse. (He returns to Eusemere on 13 Apr.) DW walks six miles with him. (*DWJ* M 108; *EY* 347.)

This is possibly the day when W experiences the feelings that he later assigns, in *R&I* IF note, to a journey from Eusemere to Askham, and observes the hare on or near the ridge of Barton Fell as described in the note. (See Moorman I, 540.)

90. Probably Apr 8 or Apr 9; Apr 8

Probably on 8 or 9 Apr W arrives at Middleham. Probably soon after his arrival he and SH write to DW. (1802:91.)

On 8 Apr DW, CCl walk to Wood Side. DW writes to MH, SH[29]; marks what she calls "our" names on a tree in Dunmallet. (*DWJ* M 108.)

91. Probably Apr 10 or Apr 11; Apr 10

Probably on 10 or 11 Apr W, MH write to DW. (1802:92.)

On 10 Apr DW writes to STC. A letter arrives from W and SH. (*DWJ* M 108.)

92. Apr 12

DW walks to Thomas Wilkinson's, where she receives a letter

---

[28] DW's letter is dated "6th April," and while one supposes that DW would be particularly conscious of the date of the day before W's birthday, *DWJ* is clear that W departed for Middleham on his birthday, 7 Apr; and his departure is referred to in this letter in the past tense. A slim possibility that DW was anticipating may remain. The 12 Apr postmark perhaps implies that this was among the letters sent off on 9 Apr (*DWJ* M 108). See also Pottle *YULG* 49n. Although DW appears to have been much too hopeful concerning the imminence of publication of *LB* 1802 (see 1802:166), her remarks allow inference that all copy for the volumes had gone to the printer by this time. See also 1802:124.

[29] The letters, at least that to SH, were evidently posted next day. (*DWJ* M·108.)

from W, MH. Wilkinson walks with DW to Barton, troubling her with a series of questions.

W departs from Middleham; parts from MH about 6, a little west of Rushingford. Losing his way once, he travels to Barnard Castle. His horse stumbles badly once also. Between the beginning of Raby Park and 2½ miles beyond Staindrop W composes [*The Glow-worm*] ("Among All Lovely Things My Love Had Been") [see *CEY* 170]. At Barnard Castle he attempts to find the inn where he and STC passed the night [see *CEY* 274]; mistakes another for it and passes the night there. (*DWJ* M 108, 113; *EY* 346–47.)

93. Apr 13

CCl wakes DW from an afternoon sleep to bring her a letter from STC.

W, on his way from Barnard Castle, discovers from a chaise driver that his horse needs shoeing; makes his way to Eusemere slowly; arrives there between 8 and 9. DW walks after tea, returns to find W arrived. (*DWJ* M 108; *EY* 346–47, 350.)

94. Apr 14

W rises at dinnertime. DW is ill, out of spirits, disheartened; walks with CCl. W, DW take a long walk in the rain. (*DWJ* M 109.)

95. Apr 15

W, DW depart Eusemere after dinner. They walk along Ullswater, resting frequently. Beyond Gowbarrow Park they notice daffodils, then more and more daffodils, finally a long belt of them. This incident and DW's description of it later form the basis of "I Wandered Lonely as a Cloud" [see *GCL* 118]. Rain comes on. They call at Luff's, where all is dark; put on dry clothes at Dobson's Inn, where they spend the night. At the inn W takes down Enfield's *The Speaker* and an odd volume of Congreve's plays. (*DWJ* M 109–10.)

96. Apr 16

W, DW depart the inn about 10:30; walk up Patterdale. At the foot of Brothers Water, between 1 and 2, DW leaves W sitting on the bridge, walks to the west of the lake. When she returns, she finds W writing *Written in March*, about the surrounding scene. He finishes the poem before they reach the foot of Kirkstone, where they dine. At Ambleside they call at the Luffs' but do not go in (the Boddingtons are there); ride in Jane Ashburner's cart from near Rydal Lake to Tom Dawson's. At home they find a letter from STC. (*DWJ* M 110–12; *EY* 347.)

W writes to STC (DW adds a note): W's return to Eusemere; walk to Grasmere; verses of STC; transcripts of [*The Glow-worm*] and *Written in March*. W has sent Thel[wall]'s book. (*EY* 346–49.)[30]

DW writes to MH: Concern for MH's health; W's return to Eusemere; the walk to Grasmere; the letter from STC. (*EY* 349–52.)

97. Perhaps between Apr 16 and July 8

W composes:
The Green Linnet
To the Daisy ("In Youth")
He perhaps at the same time also composes, at least in part:
To the Daisy ("Bright Flower!")
To the Daisy ("With Little Here")
("In Youth" and "Bright Flower!" IF notes; "In Youth" and "With Little Here" notes, *P2V* I, 155–56; form and content.)[31]

---

[30] *EY* reasonably conjectures Thelwall's *Poems Chiefly Written in Retirement* (Hereford, 1801).

[31] Of the Daisy poems only "In Youth" appears in MS M, and it remains possible that the other two were not fully composed before 6 Mar 1804. The first *P2V* note, however, assigns all to 1802, and stylistic affinities as well as W's IF notes tend to fix this as the most likely date. In editions from 1836 the first listed is dated 1802, the second 1805, and the third 1803.

The Green Linnet is dated by W in 1803 in editions from 1836. Although more complex and ambitious than the Daisy poems, it is equally genial, and its content suggestive of spring composition. Dowden (*PW* Dowden, II, 266), while not questioning W's date of 1803, notes the resemblance between the poems and the phrasing of *DWJ* for 28 May 1802. Curtis 208 suggests May on the basis of the *DWJ* reference and the poem's own allusions to May. W's phrasing may either anticipate or derive from *DWJ*, but it is probably significant that the stanza corresponds to that of the Daisy poems except for tail-rhyme lines of seven rather than five syllables. The Daisy poem stanza was used by Jonson in *Underwoods* and the *Green Linnet* stanza in Drayton's *Nymphidia* (see *P2V* HD 465).

98. Apr 17

W, DW sit, work in the garden; DW notices a robin chasing a butterfly. This incident probably forms the subject of *The Redbreast Chasing the Butterfly* [see 1802:99]. W, DW rest, walk after tea below Rydal and below Olliff's. Letters arrive from STC, SH. (*DWJ* M 112.)

99. Apr 18

W, DW sit in the orchard. W writes *The Redbreast Chasing the Butterfly*. DW probably walks to and drinks tea at the Luffs'; is accompanied by Aggy [Fisher] to Rydal, where W, probably with the conclusion of the poem, meets her. After W retires, DW reads the poem to him, assists in excising some lines. (*DWJ* M 112.)

100. Apr 19

W works in the garden; DW bakes. W walks to the Luffs'; returns home pale and tired. DW is unwell. (*DWJ* M 112-13.)

101. Apr 20 (–Apr 23)

W writes a conclusion to *To a Butterfly* ("I've Watched You Now"), then probably the remainder of the poem. After tea STC arrives for a visit, having, on his way, cut his and DW's initials over the "SH" on the Rock of Names. (He remains until 25 Apr.) Probably all three clean out the well. (*DWJ* M 113-14; *STCNB* 1163.)

102. Probably 1802 between late Apr and June

W composes *The Barberry Tree*. ("An MS of Mr. Wordsworth" [including commentary by Jonathan Wordsworth], *New Statesman* 1964, 156-58; correspondence, *New Statesman* 1964, 214, 245, 399; Jonathan Wordsworth, "A New Poem by Wordsworth?" *Essays in Criticism* XVI, 1966, 122-23; Jonathan Wordsworth, "The New Wordsworth Poem," *College English* XXVII, 1965-66, 455-65; Mark L. Reed, "More on the Wordsworth Poem," *College English* XXVIII, 1966-67, 60-61.)

103. Apr 21

STC repeats *Dejection* to W, DW. DW is unwell, dispirited; reads probably the Life of Fergusson; all sit comfortably in the evening. (*DWJ* M 113–14.)

104. Perhaps c Apr 22; probably c but by Apr 22; Apr 22

Perhaps c 22 Apr W composes "I Have Been Here in the Moonlight." (See GCL 7.)

Probably c but by 22 Apr W composes "These Chairs They Have No Words to Utter." Perhaps a half-hour afterwards, and certainly by 22 Apr, he composes *Half an Hour Afterwards* ("I Have Thoughts That Are Fed by the Sun"). (*DWJ* M 114; *PW* IV, 365. See Ford Swetnam, "The Controversial Uses of Wordsworth's Comedy," *The Wordsworth Circle* III, winter 1972, 37–39.)[32]

On 22 Apr probably W, DW, STC walk into Easedale. STC talks of his plan to sow laburnum in the woods. W, STC walk probably to some place near Sour Milk Ghyll. W flings rocks into the stream.

Joseph or Thomas Wilkinson calls while they are at dinner. (*DWJ* M 114.)

105. Apr 23

W, DW, STC walk under Nab Scar. W sits; DW, STC walk on, sit. W rejoins them; repeats poems, possibly *The Waterfall and the Eglantine* and *The Oak and the Broom*. STC finds a lovely bower; they find another attractive resting place; resolve to plant flowers in both places next day. After dinner W, DW work in the garden; STC reads; probably a letter arrives from SH. (*DWJ* M 114–15.)[33]

[32] The title and content of "These Chairs" would fairly plainly suggest composition before rising from bed.

[33] EdS identifies the poems recited as *The Waterfall and the Eglantine* and *The Oak and the Broom*, presumably because the rocky seat where DW and STC were sitting before W's arrival has just been described as "a Couch it might be under the Bower of William's Eglantine, Andrew's Broom"; but this evidence does not appear quite decisive.

106. Apr 24

W calls DW to see a waterfall behind the barberry tree. W, DW, STC walk to Rydal in the evening; look at Glow-worm Rock and a primrose there. The rock and its primrose much later form the subject of *The Primrose of the Rock*. (*DWJ* M 115–16. See *The Primrose of the Rock* IF note.)

107. Apr 25

W, DW accompany STC part of the way to Keswick. Probably Joseph or Joshua L. Wilkinson overtakes them, interrupts their conversation, near the potter's. STC climbs into a gig with Mr. Beck, drives away. W, DW spend the morning in the orchard; read Spenser's *Prothalamion*. Mr. (probably Barth) Sympson drinks tea; sends quills, and his brother's book (probably Joseph Sympson's *Science Revived*). The Luffs call at the door. (*DWJ* M 116.)

108. Apr 26

DW copies W's poems for STC. Letters arrive from Peggy [Ashburner], MH. DW writes to Peggy and STC. (*DWJ* M 116.)

109. Apr 27 (–Apr 28, 29)

Mrs. Luff calls; DW walks with her to the boathouse. W, with his fishing rod, joins DW. They sit; DW leaves. W returns home after discovering his lines unfit for use. Miss Sympson calls. W, John Fisher clean out the well; Fisher sods around the bee-stand. W commences composing *The Tinker*. (He continues and completes the poem 28, 29 Apr.) A letter and verses arrive from STC. (*DWJ* M 116.)

110. Apr 28

DW copies *The Prioress's Tale*. W continues work on *The Tinker*. DW remarks to him that when a child she would not have pulled a strawberry blossom. This remark probably forms the basis for *Foresight*. DW copies *The Manciple's Tale*. W composes [*Foresight*].[34]

[34] DW's title "Children gathering flowers" would appear a fairly clear reference to *Foresight*.

DW writes a few lines to STC. She, W walk, discuss Thomas H, Isabella Addison. On returning they correct the Chaucer poems. (*DWJ* M 116–17.)

111. Perhaps Apr 28–Apr 29; possibly between this time and June 14

DW copies out *Foresight, The Tinker* in MS now DC MS 40. (See R. S. Woof, "A Coleridge-Wordsworth Manuscript and 'Sara Hutchinson's Poets,'" *SB* XIX, 1966, 229–30; 1802:110; 1802:112.)

112. Apr 29

W, DW send off their parcel to STC. Mr. Sympson hears the cuckoo today. W finishes, DW copies, *The Tinker*. Luff calls. W, DW walk to John's Grove, lie in the trench. W imagines lying thus in the grave. They walk to Mr. Sympson's after dinner. A letter arrives from STC. (*DWJ* M 117–18.)

113. Apr 30 (–May 1)

W begins, probably, *To the Small Celandine* ("Pansies, Lilies"), (he finishes the poem the next day). W repeats his poem to DW, falls to work again. W, DW walk; return at 8; (probably both) write to STC. DW writes a part of a letter to CCl. They retire at 11:20 with prayers that W may sleep well. (*DWJ* M 118. See 1802:114.)

114. May 1

W finishes *To the Small Celandine*. W, DW walk out after dinner; rest. Return to tea at 8; become aware of their loss of the poem; return to the place that they rested after tea; probably find the poem. They walk more. Probably tonight W writes *To the Same Flower* ("Pleasures Newly Found"). W, DW hear the cuckoo. (*DWJ* M 119.)[35]

[35] DW's phrasing is that W "wrote the Celandine" and also, below, that he wrote the "Celandine 2nd part tonight." It may be supposed, from their resemblances to each other, that "Pansies, Lilies" and "Pleasures Newly Found" are the materials, now two poems, referred to; and that "Pansies, Lilies" was the first of the poems to be written; but some possibility remains that other organizations of these materials preceded the versions now known. Other information shows little consistency. W's IF note for *To the Small Celandine* dates the poem 1805, while the same poem and

115. May 2

A letter arrives from STC. (*DWJ* M 119.)

116. May 3 (–May 7, –July 4)

W begins composition of *LG*. (He probably completes a first version of the poem on 7 May, and a version basically that of *PW* "MS" on 4 July. (*DWJ* M 120; 1802:121; 1802:183. See Jared R. Curtis, "Two Versions of 'Resolution and Independence,'" *The Cornell Library Journal* no. 11, spring 1970, 45–75; Curtis 97–113.)

117. Perhaps c but by May 4

W composes *Travelling* in the form of the DC MS 41 copy. (See *PW* II, 543.)[36]

118. May 4 and about this time, esp. by c early June

On 4 May W writes several stanzas of *LG* before rising. DW copies the portions of the poem that he has written. W, DW walk; repeat the poem. They meet STC near Wythburn; walk; dine. W, STC repeat verses; DW drinks a little brandy and water. They part from STC at the Rock of Names after looking at letters that STC had carved in the morning. W deepens the "T." On Dunmail Raise W and DW meet a poor woman with two children. The Lloyds call in their absence. They reach home at 10. DW repeats verses, including "This Is the Spot" (*Travelling*) over and over to W as he lies in bed. Some portion of the Rock of Names passage in *The Waggoner*

---

[36] *Travelling* (see *PW* IV, 423; II, 543) would have been developed by this time from materials in the latest MS of *Nutting* (dating probably between late Apr 1799 and c 5 June 1800—see *CEY* 331–32; the MS is written probably in the autograph of MH rather than SH as stated in *CEY*). But DW's recitation on 4 May (see 1802:118) indicates that W had possibly been at work on the poem lately; and the appearance of the poem in *Sara's Poets* (DC MS 41), in which all the copies of W's poems but one ("Praised Be the Art") appear to have been copied soon after composition, tends likewise to confirm final composition about this time.

"Pleasures" are dated 1803 in editions from 1836 through 1850. "There Is a Flower" is dated 1804 from 1836 through 1850. When JW speaks on 16 Apr 1803 of the poems that he has received from W, he mentions, among his favorites, only one poem with a "Celandine" title (*JWL* 140).

(see *PW* V, 499–500) is perhaps composed about this time, esp. by c early June. (*DWJ* M 120–21; information from Professor Paul Betz. See 1802:163n; 1802:165.)[37]

119. May 5

W, DW work in the house and garden; plant three-quarters of the bower. DW writes to the Hs, STC; sends off *Thalaba*, perhaps to the Hs. W, DW walk; W begins composition near bedtime. DW reads [Shakespeare's] *The Lover's Complaint* to him as he lies in bed. (*DWJ* M 121.)

120. May 6

W, DW finish their bower [see 1802:119]. They walk in the evening to Tail End; inquire about hurdles for the orchard shed and about Mr. Luff's flower: no hurdles; the flower is dead. W goes to Benson's; joins DW. Ladies have moved into Gell's cottage. Upon return they find a magazine and review; a letter from STC with verses to Hartley and to SH. They read the review. (*DWJ* M 121–22.)

121. May 7

W finishes *LG* (early version). He and DW sit in the garden. He digs and cleans the well. W, DW walk. A letter arrives from CCl. W goes to bed tired with thinking of a poem. (*DWJ* M 122–23.)

122. May 8

W, DW work in the orchard; DW reads *Henry V*; W rests. DW, perhaps W, reads in the review [see 1802:120]. (*DWJ* M 123.)

123. May 9 (–May 10, 11)

W works on *LG*; DW copies it and other poems for STC. W writes two stanzas in the manner of Thomson's *Castle of Indolence*. (The poem is probably continued on 10 May, and finished 11 May.) (*DWJ* M 123. See 1802:124; 1802:125.)

[37] The initials which STC carved this day were perhaps "WW," "MW," and "JW" (*STCNB* 1163&n). He had probably carved "STC" and "DW" on 20 Apr. This carving would have completed the initialing of the rock.

124. May 10

W works at composition, probably of the *Castle of Indolence* lines; also works at other verses, perhaps revision. Old Joyce spends the day. DW writes to MH. Mrs. Jameson, Miss Sympson call. DW writes to STC, sends reviews and poems. W stays awake till 3. (*DWJ* M 123.)

125. May 11

W finishes *Stanzas Written in My Pocket-copy of Thomson's "Castle of Indolence."* Miss Sympson comes to tea. W completely finishes poems, in DW's and perhaps his own opinion; the identity of the poems is uncertain. (*DWJ* M 123–24.)[38]

126. May 12 (–May 13)

W, DW walk into Easedale; pick and buy flowers. STC arrives in the evening. (He departs next day.) All sit up till 1; then STC with DW till 2:15. DW writes to MH. (*DWJ* M 124.)

127. May 13

W, DW accompany STC as far as Wythburn on his way to Keswick; sit at Mr. Sympson's. (*DWJ* M 124.)

MH inscribes a copy of *LB* 1800 to Isabella Addison with this date. (St. John's College Library.)[39]

[38] DW possibly, if not very probably, refers to late revision for *LB* 1802 (see 1802:88; 1802:166).

[39] The St. John's copy of *LB* 1800 contains MS corrections to *The Idiot Boy* and the remains, from a binder's cuttings, of a transcription of "I Travelled among Unknown Men." Both are in the autograph of MH. The corrections to *The Idiot Boy* correspond to ones published in the poem in 1827, and may be supposed to date after the 1820 edition of the poems (they are for lines 87–88, 146, 149–50 as recorded *PW* II, 70–72 *app crit*). Surviving lines of "I Travelled" are 1–4, 8–12, 15–16. The version contains differences both from the copy sent to MH on 29 Apr 1801 and from published versions (line 2 has the phrase "paths beyond"; line 4 reads "How dear thou wast to me"); but it also contains the reading of the 29 Apr 1801 letter for line 10 ("The gladness of desire"), subsequently changed before publication. Thus this copy of the poem, which is written in on pp. 52–53 after "She Dwelt among th' Untrodden Ways," would appear to date in any case between 29 Apr 1801 and mid-Jan 1807 (see Appendix VII). It was probably copied in from memory before the presentation.

128. May 14; c May 14

W, DW walk. W tires himself seeking an epithet for the cuckoo; he and DW bring home and plant a great load of [daisies]. DW walks to Rydal, finds a letter from SH. W plants potatoes with Molly; meets DW at the top of White Moss. They walk. W, DW write to STC; send off a letter to Annette. W probably attempts to alter *The Rainbow* ("My Heart Leaps Up"). W possibly works on *To the Cuckoo* on this day and about this time. (*DWJ* M 124–25.)

129. May 15

Miss Sympson calls. DW reads Shakespeare. A letter arrives from STC. (*DWJ* M 125–26.)

130. May 16

W works all morning, much of it in the orchard with DW. (*DWJ* M 126.)

131. May 17 (–May 19)

W, DW walk to Wythburn Water, where DW perhaps mounts a post chaise to travel to Keswick. At GH she finds the Bancrofts, and a letter from MH. (*DWJ* M 126.)[40]

132. May 18

DW is at Keswick, where [the Rev. R. H.] Froude, the [Joseph] Wilkinsons call. STC, DW walk in the garden; DW writes to MH, SH. (*DWJ* M 126.)

133. May 19

DW, STC depart toward Grasmere; meet W near the 6-mile stone. They sit, drink tea at John Stanley's. STC returns to Keswick. At DC DW packs books for STC. (*DWJ* M 126.)

[40] It is possible that W took the chaise instead of DW, who states that "[h]ail showers snow and cold attacked" her after W "left [her] in a post chaise." And she states also that W had been "not well." DW perhaps rode outside despite her "in," but W may have been too unwell to walk home the shorter distance, if in fact he returned home.

134. May 20

W works. A letter arrives from Keswick asking them not to come there. (*DWJ* M 127.)

135. Probably late May, certainly by May 29; between May 30 and June 14, 17

W completes a version of *A Farewell* probably c late May, certainly by 29 May, but works further between 30 May and 17 June. The poem probably reaches much its present form by 14 June. (*DWJ* M 129, 135; *EY* 365–66; *PW* II, 23, 470, 537. See 1802:152; 1802:164; 1802:167.)[41]

136. May 21 (–May 28)

On 21 May DW reads Milton's sonnets to W. W writes two sonnets on Bonaparte, one of which is "I Grieved for Buonaparté." W probably on this day also composes, but does not write down, another sonnet.

Probably on this day DW catches a cold which proves to be the most severe of her life to that time. (No improvement is noted until 28 May.) (*DWJ* M 127–28; *Miscellaneous Sonnets* IF note; *LY* I, 71; *EY* 358.)[42]

---

[41] *DWJ* implies rather clearly, under 29 May, that W finished the poem on that day, but is more ambiguous about the matter on 31 May (see 1802:152). The corrections which W sent to MH and SH on 14 June indicate that the poem had then reached a late state. W's attempted alterations on 17 June apparently did not succeed.

[42] W's later recollection in his letter of 20 Apr 1822 to Landor (*LY* I, 71) and in the *Miscellaneous Sonnets* IF note is that he composed three sonnets in an afternoon after hearing DW read from Milton's sonnets; in his IF note W identifies one of the poems ("I Grieved"), professes incapacity to particularize another, and recalls that the third remained unwritten. *DWJ* appears to leave little room for doubt that 21 May was the date of the event described. It also indicates that Bonaparte was the subject of a second sonnet; but its identity, if it survives, is uncertain. The IF note plainly errs in stating that the sonnets composed on 21 May were the first he had written since "an irregular one at school": DW had recently been copying out sonnets, fairly certainly W's, on 27 Jan, probably for Daniel Stuart. These works, insofar as they can be identified, however (see 1802:17), were not written recently; and while they certainly

137. Probably between May 21 and 1804 Mar 6

W composes:
"How Sweet It Is, When Mother Fancy Rocks"
Personal Talk:
    i. ("I Am Not One Who Much or Oft Delight")
    ii. ("'Yet Life,' You Say, 'Is Life; We Have Seen and See'")
    iii. ("Wings Have We—and as Far as We Can Go")
    iv. ("Nor Can I Not Believe but That Hereby")
"Pelion and Ossa Flourish Side by Side"
"The World Is Too Much with Us; Late and Soon"
To the Memory of Raisley Calvert
"Where Lies the Land to Which Yon Ship Must Go?"
"With How Sad Steps, O Moon, Thou Climb'st the Sky"
"With Ships the Sea Was Sprinkled Far and Nigh"
(See 1802:136n.)

138. Probably between May 21 and 1804 Mar 6; perhaps between Nov 8 and 1803 Jan 7 or between 1803 Apr 1 and Apr 28

W composes "It Is No Spirit That from Heaven Hath Flown." (1802:136n; Appendix III; GCL 74n.)

---

do not include all of W's youthful sonnets (see *CEY* 19, 22, 23, 25), there appears no evidence to invalidate 21 May 1802 as the earliest likely date for sonnets of W's maturity.

Any sonnet appearing in MS M that is not datable from other evidence may be assumed to have been written between this date and 6 Mar 1804 (see Appendix III). With regard to the possible dates of the "To Sleep" series it may be remarked that W was soon to experience severe insomnia: on the nights of 24, 25, and probably 26 May, and on 5, 6, 10, and 14 June (line 9 of "A Flock of Sheep" is "Even thus last night, and two nights more, I lay"); but the condition was hardly a rare one for him. All these sonnets were probably composed by c late 1802, although only two appear in DC MS 38. "I Grieved" is given the title *1801* in editions from 1815; a similar title for "Pelion and Ossa" in editions from 1836 may slightly increase the chance of that poem's having been written at a time not greatly distant.

Line 8 of "With Ships the Sea Was Sprinkled" is reported in W's *P2V* note to have been derived from Skelton's *Bowge of Court*. The time of W's first acquaintance with that work remains uncertain.

139. Probably between May 21 and 1803 Oct 7

W composes "I Find It Written of Simonides." (1802:136n; 1803:116.)

140. Probably between May 21 and c late this year, possibly by Dec 25, possibly by late July

W composes "Methought I Saw the Footsteps of a Throne." (*DWJ* M 144; Appendix III; 1802:136; *P2V* HD 394.)[43]

141. Probably between May 21 and c late this year

W composes "'Tis Six Miles from Our Dwelling Place" (revised before *P* 1820 to "There Is a Little Unpretending Rill"). (Content; *PW* III, 4 *app crit*; *CEY* 151; GCL 77.)

142. Probably between May 21 and c late this year, possibly by Dec 25

W composes:
"Are Souls Then Nothing?" ("What If Our Numbers Barely Could Defy")
"'Beloved Vale!' I Said, 'When I Shall Con'"
"Brook That Hast Been My Solace Days and Weeks" ("Brook! Whose Society the Poet Seeks")
"Dear Native Brooks Your Ways I Have Pursu'd" ("Return, Content! for Fondly I Pursued")
"England! the Time Is Come When Thou Should'st Wean"
"Great Men Have Been among Us; Hands That Penned"
"It Is Not to Be Thought of That the Flood"
"There Is a Bondage Worse, Far Worse, to Bear"
To Sleep ("A Flock of Sheep That Leisurely Pass By")
To Sleep ("Fond Words Have Oft Been Spoken to Thee, Sleep")

---

[43] *P2V* HD 394 points out the indebtness of the poem to Milton's "Methought I Saw My Late Espoused Saint." This, with what seems a plain debt also to Walter Raleigh's "A Vision upon This Conceipt of the Faery Queene," might suggest composition by some time in the summer, although probably before the departure for France (31 July). W was reading in Spenser, according to *DWJ*, as late as 1 July.

To Sleep ("O Gentle Sleep! Do They Belong to Thee")
"When I Have Borne in Memory What Hath Tamed"
(1802:136n; 1802:264; 1803:15n; Appendix III.)

143. May 22 (–May 24)

W, DW meet STC sitting under the Rock of Names. All sit under the wall of a sheepfold; STC talks of private affairs; all drink tea at a farmhouse. STC comes on to DC. (He departs 24 May.) Letters arrive from SH, MH. (*DWJ* M 127.)

144. May 23

DW sits with STC in the orchard in the morning. Probably all walk in Bainriggs after tea. STC goes to Sara and Mary Points; joins W, DW on White Moss. (*DWJ* M 127.)

145. May 24

Miss Taylor, Miss Stanley call. W, DW, STC walk to the top of Dunmail Raise, where STC departs for Keswick carrying a letter, probably written this day, for MH. At DC DW probably writes another letter to MH, and one to STC. W is awake till 5 AM. (*DWJ* M 127–28.)

On this day Sir James Lowther, Earl of Lonsdale, dies at Lowther Hall. His principal heir is his cousin Sir William Lowther, on whom devolve the Viscountcy and Barony of Lowther of Whitehaven. The Earldom and Viscountcy of Lonsdale and other titles received by Sir James Lowther in 1784 become extinct (but see 1807:24). (*The Complete Peerage* VIII, ed. H. A. Doubleday and Lord Howard de Walden, London, 1932, 134. See *CEY* 61.)

146. May 25

W, DW walk. Papers and a short note from STC arrive. W is again sleepless. (*DWJ* M 128.)

147. May 26

W, DW walk. (*DWJ* M 128.)

148. May 27; perhaps c May 27

W writes to RW, CW, Cooke. W sleeps downstairs, and sleeps better. W's letters probably concern the death of Lord Lonsdale, and announce, at least to RW, W's intention of marrying MH. (*DWJ* M 128; *EY* 358–59; 1802:145.)

Perhaps c 27 May W writes to his Uncle William Cookson asking him to press RW to send them a statement on the Lowther debt. (*EY* 368.)

149. May 28

W tires himself with intense work on a passage, possibly of *A Farewell.* (*DWJ* M 128. See 1802:150.)

150. May 29

W finishes, DW writes out, a version of *A Farewell.* A letter arrives from MH; DW writes to her. (*DWJ* M 128.)[44]

151. May 30

DW writes to CCl and to her Aunt Cookson. The Sympsons call in the evening. (*DWJ* M 129.)[45]

---

[44] On a blotter page of her journal (DC MS 31) DW writes:

> Dorothy Wordsworth
> William Wordsworth
> Mary Wordsworth
>   May 29th 6 O clock
> Sitting at small table by window
>   Grasmere 1802

[45] A note inside the cover of the first volume of the DC 1796 edition of Withering's *Arrangement of British Plants* (see 1800:97) in DW's autograph, reads: "Lysimachia nemorum. Yellow Pimpernell of the Woods. Pimpernell loose strife May 3 30th 1802." The first "3" is written at the edge of the page; it probably represents a false start on a "30." The plant concerned is treated on pp. 237–38 of vol. II of this edition of Withering. DW's often very detailed descriptions of flora in *DWJ* during the spring suggest that she consulted her Botany frequently. The *lysimachia nemorum* is the "pretty little waxy-looking Dial-like yellow flower" that she notices in her entry for 28 May (*DWJ* M 128).

152. May 31

Mary Jameson dines with the Ws. DW writes out *A Farewell*, evidently revised from the 29 May version. In the evening Miss Sympson brings a letter from MH and one from John Wilson. One of DW's teeth breaks. (*DWJ* M 129.)[46]

153. June 1

DW writes to MH. W, DW walk; meet John Dawson. A short note and gooseberries arrive from STC. An old soldier calls begging. (*DWJ* M 129–30.)

154. June 2

W walks to the Swan with Aggy Fisher, who tells W of a woman who buried four grown children within a year and took more pleasure from her memory of them than she took in her four living children, because (according to the woman) as children grow and have families of their own, their duty to their parents weakens. W, DW walk. (*DWJ* M 129–31.)

155. June 3; c June 3

W, DW walk into Easedale, hear the cuckoo, are wet by rain. They read the life and writings of John Logan [in Anderson's *British Poets*]. An affecting letter arrives from MH as DW is reading *Il Penseroso* to W. DW writes to MH. W sleeps badly. W possibly works on *To the Cuckoo* on this day and about this time. (*DWJ* M 130–32; *EY* 363.)

156. June 4

W, DW walk. DW reads *Mother Hubberd's Tale*. (*DWJ* M 132.)

[46] *DWJ* for 29 May states that W "finished," and DW wrote out, the poem "on Going for Mary"; for 31 May, that "I wrote out the poem on 'Our Departure' which [W] seemed to have finished." It is likely that the poem is the same in both cases and that DW is recording the emergence of the, to her, all too predictable revision. On the reply to Wilson see 1802:157–1802:159.

157. June 5 (–June 7)

W, DW walk. Mr. Sympson drinks tea; Mrs. Smith calls with her daughter. W, DW (probably taking W's dictation) begin a letter to John Wilson. (The letter, for which see *EY* 352–58, is completed by 7 June.) DW's letter to MH of 3 June is sent off by Fletcher the carrier. W sleeps badly. (*DWJ* M 132.)[47]

158. June 6 (–June 10)

W, DW continue work on the letter to Wilson. Ellen Bewsher arrives at DC for a visit. (She departs 10 June.) She brings letters from STC, CCl, SH. W sleeps badly. (*DWJ* M 132–33; *EY* 473.)

159. June 7

DW writes to MH; sends *Stanzas Written in a Pocket Copy of Thomson's Castle of Indolence*; writes to RW, SFC; copies letter to Wilson. W walks; letters arrive from Annette, MH, Cooke. DW's letter to SFC perhaps reassures her that the Ws are not going to live at GH. (*DWJ* M 132; *EY* 362.)

160. June 8; possibly c June 8

On 8 June DW, Ellen ride to Windermere; return at 3. DW's letter to MH of 7 June is sent off. W walks, writes, probably in DW's presence, "The Sun Has Long Been Set." He sleeps badly. (*DWJ* M 133–34; "The Sun Has Long Been Set" IF note; note *Yarrow Revisited* 1835, 175; *EY* 363.)[48]

Possibly c 8 June W composes some lines eventually used in lines 1–25 (1806 version) of *The Waggoner*. (See 1802:165.)

[47] Knight, in *Letters of the Wordsworth Family* (Boston, 1907) 435n, states that the letter was a joint production. He is no doubt drawing on DW's phrasing for 5 and 6 June: "We began the letter" and "We were writing the letter." The contents of the letter imply, however, that DW can have originated very little of it.

[48] The IF note makes plain the identity of the "friend" in whose presence both that note and the 1835 note (retained through 1850) agree that the poem was "thrown off."

161. June 9

W, DW, perhaps Ellen Bewsher, walk to Mr. Sympson's after tea. The Lloyds call, evidently while the Ws are absent. DW writes to CW, MH. (*DWJ* M 133–34; *EY* 362–63.)

162. June 10–June 12

On 10 June DW writes to CCl, Luff; goes with Ellen to Rydal, whence, apparently, Ellen returns to Eusemere via Kirkstone. STC arrives from Eusemere via Grisedale with a sack of books. (He departs 12 June.) Mr. Sympson drinks tea. DW sends off a letter to MH, SH, or both. W sleeps badly.

During STC's visit, he tells W, DW of an old woman who used to attend the empty Quaker meeting house at Keswick alone regularly on Sundays. DW and STC discuss SFC; DW tells him of their determination not to live at GH; STC expresses an intention of investigating the availability of Brow Top. (*DWJ* M 134; *STCNB* 1197, 1204; *EY* 361–63.)[49]

W, DW write to RW from Grasmere: (DW:) Her cold. W's approaching marriage. Her financial needs are for £60 per annum as free as possible from risk from the death of her brothers. They have been advised to send a statement of their case to Lord Lonsdale's heirs. Their projected trip to Yorkshire. (W:) Questions concerning procedures to be followed in presenting their claims to the Lonsdale estate. (*EY* 358–61.)[50]

On 11 June W and STC walk. (*DWJ* M 134.)

On 12 June STC departs. W, DW accompany him as far as Dunmail Raise. W, DW walk, finally to Mr. King's. Miss Sympson and Robert call in the Ws' absence. Letters arrive from Annette, SH. (*DWJ* M 134–35; *EY* 362, 364.)

[49] *STCNB* uncharacteristically misdates STC's crossing of Grisedale "Thursday, June 8, 1802." This Thursday was 10 June.

[50] CW writes to RW on a "Tuesday," probably 8 or 15 June, asking what should be done in regard to the Lowther debt and advising that he has had an account of the letters between DW and RW. He remarks: "I shall be ready with my £20, though as to a fixed settlement I do not know how I should be competent to it, as I have no fixed property." (DCP.)

163. June 13; possibly between June 13 and c June 20, esp. June 15

On 13 June W works at altering *A Farewell*; DW writes out poems for their journey; writes to her Uncle Cookson. Mr. Sympson calls, brings a drawing that he has done. W, DW walk. (*DWJ* M 135; *EY* 365–66.)

Possibly between 13 and c 20 June, esp. 15 June, W composes "The Owl as If He Had Learn'd His Cheer" (basis for *The Waggoner* III.120–25). (Information from Professor Paul Betz.)[51]

164. June 14; perhaps between June 14 and July 4

On 14 June DW, ill, retires before tea. A letter arrives from MH. W reads the letter to DW. W, DW write a letter to MH and SH. The haircutter calls; W reads *LG* to him. DW writes also to Annette, STC. DW, better, walks with W. W remains out after she goes in; remains awake all night. (*DWJ* M 135–36; *EY* 364.)

The letter from W and DW to MH and SH: (DW:) Her health; possibility of living at Keswick [see 1802:162]; visit from STC; STC and SFC; projected visit to [Yorkshire and France]. W's reading of *LG* to the haircutter. (W:) Corrections for *A Farewell*; defense of *LG* against criticisms of MH and SH. (DW:) SH must refrain from hasty criticism of W's poetry. W has asked Uncle Cookson to press RW to send statement about the Lonsdale case. (*EY* 361–68.)

Perhaps between 14 June and 4 July W revises *LG*. (See 1802:183.)

165. June 15–possibly c July 7, 8

On 15 June W, DW walk. W composes a few lines about the

[51] Professor Betz has called my attention to the similarity of these lines in mood and style to such works of spring 1802 as *The Tinker*, "The Sun Has Long Been Set," and *The Barberry Tree*. He notes also the trip made by DW to Windermere on 8 June, her notice of the owl's hooting and hallooing on 13 June, and her further notice of the owls' hooting and W's "writing a few lines about the night-hawk and other images of the evening" on 15 June. The lines appear not unlikely to have been among or connected with lines composed that day perhaps later used for the opening of *The Waggoner* (see 1802:165). Professor Betz further suggests that current family interest in the Rock of Names may also have evoked some part of the *Waggoner* lines (see *PW* II, 499–500) on that subject, although the date of that composition remains uncertain (see 1802:118).

night-hawk and other images of the evening. These materials, with others of possibly c 7, 8 July, perhaps eventually become the basis for the opening of *The Waggoner*, esp. lines 1–21 as MSS 1, 2 (see *PW* II, 177–78 *app crit* and 498). Letters arrive from MH and Wade, and one from SH to STC. W does not read them. Probably DW sends off her and W's joint letter to MH, SH today. (*DWJ* M 136; *EY* 363. See 1802:163; 1802:186.)[52]

166. June 16, and probably c June 16

On 16 June W, DW walk; receive an expected letter from MH. DW writes to MH (letter not known to survive), at least partly on the subject of having a cat at DC (probably expressing disinclination to have one there). This morning a bird hops on W's leg in the garden. Swallows are exploring DC for nesting places. Mr. Sympson drinks tea. A letter arrives from STC. DW reads the first canto of *FQ* to W. (*DWJ* M 136–37.)

Twelve copies of *LB*, a lot of eight and a lot of four, are entered on W's account with Longman under this date (without charge; recipients not recorded). Probably *LB* 1802 is published about this date. (Longman accounts, DCP; Pottle *YULG* 49n. See 1802:169; 1802:173.)[53]

---

[52] The similarity of the first twenty-one lines of *The Waggoner*, esp. in the readings of MSS 1 and 2, to "The Sun Has Long Been Set" (composed 8 June), as Professor Betz has suggested to me, would give grounds for supposing that at least some of the *Waggoner* lines were composed about this time; and the *DWJ* statement concerning W's composition on 15 June solidifies the case. But DW's note under 7 July— "Glow-worms. Well for them children are in bed when they shine"—and her reference to the glow worms the next night would appear to have more than a chance connection with the MSS 1 and 2 readings of lines 7–12 of Canto 1 (*PW* II, 177 *app crit*). While the debt is most likely W's to DW, and the lines possibly of c 7, 8 July, DW may instead be drawing on W.

[53] The copy for the volumes was probably in the hands of the printer by 6 Apr (see 1802:88); but the copies of *LB* noted by Longman under 16 June 1802 are the first noted since 10 Feb 1801, and were fairly certainly copies of the 1802 edition. Advertisements for *LB* in the *London Chronicle* of 19–22 and 24–26 June, the only advertisements discovered which perhaps concern publication of *LB* 1802, are apparently the first for *LB* since a notice in the same journal on 26–28 Jan. The lot of four copies perhaps was sent to RW (see 1802:88), the lot of eight perhaps to W (see 1802:173).

Probably between 16 June and 1805 Mar 11 W presents copies of
LB 1800 and *LB* 1802 to Ann Wordsworth. (See John D. Gordan,
William Wordsworth, 1770–1850. An Exhibition, New York, 1950, 9;
copy of *LB* 1802, JFW Papers.)[54]

167. June 17

W works a little; injures himself; Miss Hudson of Workington
calls. W attempts alteration of a stanza of *A Farewell,* is dissuaded by
DW. A short letter arrives from STC.

W adds a little to the *Ode.* The amount is uncertain, but possibly
includes some or all of stanzas V–VIII [see 1804:3]. (*DWJ* M 137;
Curtis 164; Curtis Diss.)[55]

[54] Inscriptions in both sets of *LB* read: "Ann Wordsworth[.] the gift of the Author[.]
Bath. Feby 1802." The inscriptions are not in W's hand, and appear to have been made
at the same time—presumably retrospectively, since *LB* 1802 was not published till
after Feb 1802. W had three cousins named "Ann Wordsworth" in 1802: Ann W,
1771–1841, daughter of RW of Whitehaven (married the Rev. Charles Favell 11 Mar
1805); Ann W, bapt. 26 Dec 1788–1828, daughter of RW of Branthwaite (married
George Ritson in 1813); and Ann W, née Gale, 1758–1815, wife of Capt. W. A
letter of 16 Feb 1804 written in the same autograph survives in DCP. This letter is
addressed to RW by a plainly unmarried Ann W who asks RW, in a tone of arch
familiarity unlikely in a girl just turned fifteen, to be her escort during a trip that she
is shortly to make to London. The writer was probably the Ann born in 1771. I am
indebted for information concerning the several Anns to Mr. Donald P. Sewell and
Professor Carl Ketcham.

[55] DW's phrasing, that W "added a little to the Ode he is writing" suggests that
W had been thinking about, if not actually composing, the *Ode* since 27 Mar. Thus
W's statement in the *Ode* IF note that "two years at least passed between the writing
of the first four stanzas and the remaining part" may be imprecise. (See 1802:77.)

The close affinities in style and content between stanzas V–VIII of the *Ode,* some
part of which may have been composed 17 June, and *To H.C. Six Years Old,* as most
recently pointed out in Curtis Diss., argue a close connection, perhaps chronological,
although composition c or on 19 Sept, the day when HC became six, is unlikely (see
entries for Sept *passim*). While the title suggests birthday verses, HC was six until
19 Sept 1803, and early 1804 appears a more probable time of composition for *To
H.C.* The poem could have been based on materials composed for the *Ode* at that time
with the immediate object of inclusion in MS M, then being made up for STC, where
it is entitled simply *To H.C.* The phrase "Six Years Old" was added upon publication
in 1807, and may have been subjoined by W to the title as a deliberate parallel to the
title used by STC on 22 Sept 1803 for his own poem to HC, *The Language of the*

168. June 18; perhaps shortly after

On 18 June Charles Luff arrives with news that LdL intends to pay all debts of his predecessor; brings with him a letter from TCl on the subject. After Luff's departure W, DW write to STC, MH, RW. W determines to go to Eusemere on Monday [see 1802:172]. W, DW walk, post letters. W does not sleep. (*DWJ* M 137–38.)

W's letter to RW: TCl's information about LdL. Requests exact history of the case at the earliest moment. (*DWJ* M 137–38; *EY* 368–69.)

Perhaps shortly after 18 June W writes to RW again (only the opening phrase survives). (See *EY* 371.)

169. June 19

DW writes to MH; reads Churchill's *Rosciad*. Charles Lloyd calls. (*DWJ* M 138–39.)

170. June 20

W, DW walk. Mr. and Miss Sympson call. W, DW tell them of their hopes for the Lowther affair. Sympson receives the news coldly, while Miss Sympson seems glad. W is insomniac. DW writes to Montagu. (*DWJ* M 139.)

171. This summer

Montagu pays £50 of the arrears of his debt to W. (*EY* 383.)

Birds—that is, "Extempore—to a Child of Six Years Old" (see *STCL* II, 998)—or simply for its appropriateness to the content.

One might also speculate concerning the *Ode* that DW's reading of *FQ* I to W on 16 June played some part in suggesting to W his central metaphor of the journey and the discussion of truth, error, divine and primal unity, and related subjects in stanzas V–VIII of the *Ode*. But the evidence is indecisive, and without firmer indication of the nature of the work done on 17 June, composition of most of the "remaining part" must be supposed an event of early 1804.

Curtis Diss. also cites as a possible indication that stanzas IV and V were composed at once the fact that the Longman MS for *P2V* contains a note to the printer to commence a new paragraph at the beginning of what is now stanza V, as if the division had not previously existed. This note actually precedes stanza IV. Stanzas IV and V are divided in MS M.

172. June 21–June 24

W departs for Eusemere on 21 June, probably travelling over Grisedale, to consult with [the Rev. Thomas] Myers and [William] Lowther about the Lonsdale debt. He and DW part above the blacksmith's. DW dines at Mr. Sympson's.

Probably by 23 June W writes to DW (letter not known to survive) advising of safe arrival at Eusemere. He consults with Myers regarding methods of claiming the Lowther debt. Myers consults with Mr. Lowther and conveys advice. W perhaps also consults with TCl, who perhaps draws up a paper for W. W returns to DC on 24 June. (*DWJ* M 139, 141; *EY* 368–71.)

173. June 22

Letters arrive from Montagu, RW. DW forwards these to W at Eusemere; writes to RW, CW; reads *A Midsummer Night's Dream*; begins *As You Like It*. Letters arrive from MH, STC. News comes that a house has been taken for Betsy [H]. DW writes to MH, puts up a parcel for STC. A copy or copies (perhaps a lot of eight) of *LB* 1802 arrive. (*DWJ* M 140–41. See 1802:166.)

174. June 23 (–June 24)

DW reads *As You Like It*; meets Charles Lloyd, perhaps Charles Lloyd Sr., Mrs. Lloyd; writes a line to W by the Lloyds. STC, John Leslie arrive at DC after dinner, STC bringing a letter from W [see 1802:172]. DW, STC, Leslie walk to the boathouse. Leslie probably departs; STC stays the night. (*DWJ* M 141; *STCL* II, 876, 1011–12.)

175. June 24

W writes to RW from Eusemere: Thanks for letter [see 1802:168]; does not understand RW's advice to delay. Dr. Lowther says that the most proper method of making a claim is to send it to [John] Richardson. W's uneasiness about LdL's possible unwillingness to pay interest; his wish to stay out of court. (*EY* 369–71.)

STC departs DC. DW accompanies him halfway up Dunmail Raise. W returns to DC from Eusemere. He and DW sit up till dawn. (*DWJ* M 141–42.)

176. June 25 (–June 30); probably between June 25 and June 29

DW, Miss Sympson, probably W work on rooms. DW finds that the swallows' nest by her window has fallen [see 1802:166]. (*DWJ* M 142.)

Probably between 25 and 29 June William Sotheby, with his wife, brother, son, and daughter, accompanied by STC, call at DC. This is probably the first meeting of W and Sotheby. (STC probably stays on until 30 June.) (*DWJ* M 142; *STCL* II, 808–13. See *EY* 456n; 1802:191; 1802:201.)[56]

177. June 26 (–Oct 8)

RW writes to John Richardson, agent of LdL: Advises that the balance of the debt of the late Earl of Londsdale to the estate of JW Sr. is, as detailed in the account delivered to Lowther Hall on 30 Aug 1786, £4660/4/10¾. (A full account of the debt, including interest, is submitted 8 Oct.) (*EY* 688. See *EY* 369; *CEY* 68; 1802:189; 1802:229.)[57]

178. June 29 (–June 30)

On 29 June DW writes to MH (the letter is probably finished 30 June). She also writes to CW, Miss Griffith. STC and W come in about 11:30; talk till 12. W sleeps badly. (*DWJ* M 142–43.)

179. June 30

W, DW accompany STC part way up Dunmail Raise on his way to Keswick. Probably after they have parted from STC they meet an

[56] A gap divides *DWJ* between the entry for 25 June and perhaps a part of the entry for 29 June. *DWJ* re-commences with the phrase "that they would not call here," the conclusion of a sentence. The subject remains a mystery but seems unlikely on balance to have been the Sothebys' failure to call. The Sothebys were visiting the Lakes, and apparently came to GH about this time. They and STC travelled from Keswick to Grasmere in a carriage, and STC finally parted from them only between Grasmere and Ambleside. It is improbable that the party simply drove past DC. (*STCL* II, 808–14.) W had met Sotheby before visiting London later this year. See also 1802:191.

[57] The statement delivered on 8 Oct describes the account originally delivered as for £4625/3/7¾.

old man, an ex-servant of the Marquis of Granby. After tea DW writes to STC, closes letter to MH [see 1802:178]. (*DWJ* M 143–44.)

180. Probably c July 1

A review of *LB* 1800 appears in the *Monthly Review* (XXXVIII, June 1802). (See Ward; Hayden.)

On 1 July W, DW walk in the evening, W reads Spenser, DW *As You Like It*. Saddlebags arrive from Keswick with letters from MH, STC, and drawings of [Joseph] Wilkinson's. (*DWJ* M 144.)

181. July 2

W, DW walk in the evening. DW writes a short letter to MH and to STC; transcribes alterations for *LG*. (*DWJ* M 144.)

182. July 3

Letters arrive from MH, Annette; the letter from Annette, written in Blois on 23 June, had first gone to Gallow Hill. The letters make DW sleepless. (*DWJ* M 144.)

W, DW write to RW from Grasmere: (W:) Letters received from RW of 26, 29 June. RW's tone is not acceptable. Approves of RW's letter to Richardson; cautions RW against the viewing the matter of the Lowther debt exclusively with an attorney's eye. The necessity of prompt action. (DW:) Plans for the journey to Gallow Hill. (*EY* 371–73.)

183. July 4

W walks, finishes what are probably revisions for *LG* [see 1802:116; 1802:121; 1802:164]. (*DWJ* M 144–45.)

184. July 5

DW copies *LG*, probably basically in *PW R&I* MS form, for STC and for themselves; writes to Annette, CCl, MH, STC. (*DWJ* M 145.)

185. July 6

W, DW walk toward Rydal. DW is driven in by rain at Nab Cottage, later meets W near Rydal with a letter from CW. Other letters arrive from MH, STC. W sleeps badly. (*DWJ* M 145.)

186. July 7; possibly c July 7

On 7 July DW writes to JW, Molly Ritson, and STC. She walks, perhaps with W. (*DWJ* M 145.)

Possibly c 7 July W writes some lines used for the opening of *The Waggoner*, including the first two lines of the MSS 1, 2 readings of lines 7–12 (*PW* II, 177 *app crit*). (1802:165n.)

187. July 8

DW notices a post chaise with a little girl in a ragged cloak behind [see 1802:62; 1802:63]; reads *The Winter's Tale*. W arranges, DW writes out *The Pedlar* (280 lines). W carries coat to the tailor; engages a horse from George Mackereth. An affecting letter arrives from MH; also letters from RW, STC; from SH to STC. W, DW walk. (*DWJ* M 145–46.) On the *Pedlar* copy see Appendix VI.

188. July 9 (–July 12, –Oct 6)

W, DW set off for Gallow Hill. Meet STC at the Rock of Names. All go on to Keswick. (They remain at Keswick until 12 July; return to DC 6 Oct.) (*DWJ* M 146. See 1802:191; 1802:227.)

189. July 10

W, STC, perhaps others have a view of the Lodore and Borrowdale mountains that impresses W as perhaps unequalled by any view that he had seen in the Alps. This evening probably W, DW, STC, and others call on the Calverts. (*STCL* II, 809; *DWJ* M 146.)

RW writes to Messrs. Graham, Lincoln's Inn, restating to them the substance of his letter to Richardson of 26 June [see 1802:177]. (*EY* 688. See 1802:229.)

190. July 11

W, DW remain at Keswick. (*DWJ* M 147.)

191. July 12 (–July 14)

W, DW walk from Keswick to Eusemere (where they remain until 14 July). STC accompanies them to the seventh milestone. W asks to be remembered to William Sotheby [see 1802:176]. W, DW turn aside to explore the country near Hutton John. They come into the road to the Cls' a little above Dacre; reach Eusemere Hill at about 8. (*DWJ* M 147; *STCL* II, 811; *EY* 528.)

192. July 13

W, DW remain at Eusemere. (*DWJ* M 147.)

193. July 14

W, DW depart Eusemere, walk to Eamont Bridge; mount the coach between Bird's Nest and Hartshorn Tree. DW is driven inside the coach by rain at Bowes; returns to the top at Greta Bridge, having been annoyed by Mr. Lough of Penrith. They pass the night at Leeming Lane. (*DWJ* M 147–48.)

194. July 15

W, DW ride in the post chaise to Thirsk. Walk on to Rievaulx in heat and haze; view the Abbey briefly; reach Helmsley at dusk, where they pass the night. Probably on this day they see two little boys dragging a log, and a team of horses struggling under a load of timber. (*DWJ* M 148–49, 156.)

195. July 16 (–July 26)

W, DW walk through Kirby Moorside, Pickering; meet MH, SH seven miles from Gallow Hill. All reach Gallow Hill at 7. (W, DW remain at Gallow Hill until 26 July.) (*DWJ* M 149; *EY* 374. See 1801: 90n.)

196. Between July 16 and July 26

W, DW, MH, SH visit Scarborough; walk in the Wykeham Abbey pasture and visit Wykeham. (*DWJ* M 149–50.)

197. July 17

DW writes to RW from Gallow Hill: Arrival at Gallow Hill; Lonsdale affair; money that DW was to receive on JW's account [see 1802:25; 1802:42]. She has borrowed £20 from STC; would like to tell STC to draw on RW for the sum. Samuel Ferguson's marriage; is to send DW half a dozen silver spoons. (*EY* 374–75.)

198. July 26

W, DW depart from Gallow Hill in a post chaise with MH. DW, MH become ill. MH leaves them, probably before they reach Beverley. They pass the night at Hull. (*DWJ* M 149–50.)

199. July 27

W, DW depart from Hull at 4 in a coach; proceed to Lincoln, where they sup and pass the night. (*DWJ* M 150.)

200. July 28

W, DW depart Lincoln at 6 AM; proceed to Peterborough, where they view the Minster. They note that a fellow passenger's little girl has bought [Bloomfield's] *The Farmer's Boy*. They do not stop their journey this night. (*DWJ* M 150.)

201. July 29, 30 (–July 31)

W, DW arrive in London on the morning of 29 July. (They remain there until 31 July.)

Probably this day or next in London they see William Sotheby, their first encounter (if more than one took place) occurring while some or all the parties concerned are sheltering from a rainstorm. (*DWJ* M 150; *STCL* II, 849, 858; *EY* 456.)

202. July 31 ff, esp. perhaps Sept 3

At 5:30 or 6:30 AM W, DW depart London on the Dover coach, which they mount at Charing Cross. The scene from Westminster Bridge is impressively lovely, with the city free of smoke. This scene, and perhaps DW's description of it in her journal, form the basis of W's *Composed upon Westminster Bridge, September 3, 1802*, composition of which is perhaps begun today, but probably completed on 3 Sept.

They ride, walking up the steep hills, to Dover. DW is disappointed by Canterbury. They see Dover Castle, and the sea through a long vale. This sight perhaps forms the basis of W's *September, 1802. Near Dover* ("Inland, within a Hollow Vale"), and possibly contributes to *Composed in the Valley near Dover, on the Day of Landing*. They reach Dover near dusk; make arrangements for embarkation; drink tea with the Honorable Mr. Knox and his tutor. They set sail for Calais. (*DWJ* M 150–52; *Composed upon Westminster Bridge* IF note; 1802:207.)[58]

[58] The year of composition of *Composed upon Westminster Bridge* is incorrectly given as "1803," in editions from 1807 through 1836. The year is given as 1802 from 1838, and the IF note states that the poem was "[c]omposed on the roof of a coach, on my way to France Sept. 1802." W had, of course, just returned from France on 3 Sept. One reconciliation of W's statements is that of EdS: "It is possible that the sonnet was inspired and drafted on July 31, 1802, and rewritten on Sept. 3, when W was again in London" (*PW* III, 431). The poem does not now appear in MS M, perhaps through oversight, or through the loss of a leaf of the MS: Farington II, 209–10 records that STC, for whom the portions of MS M containing W's shorter poems were copied by 6 Mar 1804, "read some lines [by W] on Westminster Bridge & the scenery from it" along with "the Maid of Loch Lomond" (*To a Highland Girl*) to a company on 25 Mar 1804. See Appendix III. One might note also the close similarity between line 6 of the sonnet and drafts in *Prel* MS X, probably written between late Mar and 13 June 1804, toward *Prel* VIII.736–38 (see Appendix V):

<pre>
                                 lands
                   with rivers & with lakes in [? spots]
        Ships   temples   trees
        Whole   visible in maps
        Ships tower & trees
        Ships trees whole territories   visible in maps
        Domes   islands   ship   tree   cloud
</pre>

But the resemblances hardly seem to justify an assumption that *Composed upon Westminster Bridge* was uncompleted before 1804. (On a possible source of such images

203. Aug 1–Aug 29; between Aug 1 and Aug 29; Aug 15

   1 Aug: W, DW arrive at Calais, where they remain till 29 Aug, at 4 AM; remain aboard the boat till 7:30, when W goes for letters. W probably pays 2½ or 3 shillings to the customs officer for the trunk. They find Annette and Caroline at the house of Madame Avril in the Rue de la Tête d'Or at about 8:30 or 9. They enter lodgings. W probably on this day or on 7 Aug composes *Composed near Calais* ("Jones! as from Calais Southward You and I").

   During this visit W, DW, Annette, and Caroline, or W and one or two of the others, probably usually including DW, walk by the shore almost every evening. W and DW (after she recovers from a cold) bathe; view Dover Castle and the English coast, the evening star, the fort at Calais. One evening W, DW, alone, observe the sky remarkably gloomy and exciting in appearance. Caroline is delighted on one or more hot nights to observe the tracks of light formed by the boats. (*DWJ* M 152–53; *MY* II, 159; *Composed near Calais* title.)[59]

   On this visit see esp. Moorman I, 562–68.

   Events or considerations prompted by this visit probably form the basis of the following sonnets, composed at this time:

[59] The first surviving MS of *Composed near Calais* in MS M (see Appendix III) concludes the title with the date "August 1st 1802." In the Longman *P2V* printer's copy the word August is followed by a number, too heavily cancelled to be discernible, which has been replaced with "7th." All editions of the poem in W's lifetime assign the date 7 Aug; but the date assigned in MS M, 1 Aug, would not appear inherently impossible.

   The MS fragments DC MS 63, containing respectively fragmentary accounts of the journeys to Goslar and Calais written on paper watermarked with a crowned horn-in-shield and countermarked "1798," have been shown by Professor Betz to date perhaps from 1810 or 1811 (see Betz *PB*). If the fragmentary sonnet on Milton "Amid the Dark Control of Lawless Sway" is in fact by W (on this problem see 1808:2n), however, journal fragments are more likely to date by 1808. On the basis of present evidence a date more limited than between c early 1806 (as the time of earliest use of paper with such watermarks, albeit the earlier paper is of lighter texture) and 1811 would seem unjustified.

see Moorman I, 563.) The specificity of the "Sept. 3, 1803" subtitle would appear meaningless except as a date for composition or completion of the poem. (See also *CEY* 243.)

Calais, August, 1802 ("Is It a Reed That's Shaken by the Wind") (Title and content.)

Composed by the Sea-side, near Calais, August 1802 ("Fair Star of Evening, Splendour of the West") (Title and content.)

"It Is a Beauteous Evening, Calm and Free" (Content.)[60]

Possibly during this visit W composes *To Toussaint l'Ouverture.* (Content.)[61]

Probably on 15 Aug W composes *Calais, August 15, 1802* ("Festivals Have I Seen That Were Not Names"). (Title.)

204. Probably between mid-Aug and early Sept

CL and ML visit for a day or two at DC with the Cls. (*LL* I, 315; letter, CL to Sarah Stoddart, 9 Aug 1802, PP; *STCL* II, 855; 1802:210.)[62]

205. Aug 28

RW pays, and charges to W's account under this date, £7/10/6, premium on £300 policy on Montagu's life. (Receipt; RW accounts, DCP.)

[60] Knight (*PW* Knight, 1882–89 II, 289; *PW* Knight, 1896 II, 331) assigns "Is It a Reed" to 7 Aug; but unless he has confused the poem with *Composed near Calais* ("Jones!"), I cannot guess why.

[61] EdS has assigned both this poem and *On the Extinction of the Venetian Republic* to "probably August, 1802." an opinion apparently accepted by Moorman I, 567–68, 571–72, and reflecting the earlier judgments, variously confident, of Knight, Dowden, and Smith. While the fact that *On the Extinction of the Venetian Republic* is absent from MS M is hardly indicative of time of composition (see Appendix III), it is distinguished from sonnets more certainly of this time by the historical distance of the subject. The poem does not seem on balance certainly assignable to this month.

The imprisonment of Toussaint would have been an appropriate subject for composition at any time in the late summer or autumn, but this period of composition of political sonnets, when Toussaint's whereabouts and treatment were much in doubt (see the *Times* 16, 20–22, 24, 25, 31 July, 30 Aug, 1 Sept), seems particularly likely.

[62] In his letter to Sarah Stoddart CL announces that he and ML are "about to undertake tomorrow" a journey into Cumberland, and are to be "a month out" (PP). They spent "three full weeks" at GH (*LL* I, 315). STC remarks on Thursday 26 Aug (*STCL* II, 855) that "Mr Lamb . . . goes to Penrith next week." The Ls probably, thus, reached GH about 14 Aug and arrived back in London only a day or so before their meeting with the Ws on 7 Sept.

206. Aug 29–Aug 30, perhaps Sept 1

On 29 Aug W, DW depart from Calais at 12 for Dover. They arrive next day. A fellow passenger forms the subject of *September 1, 1802*, which is perhaps composed between this day and 1 Sept, and perhaps completed 1 Sept. (*DWJ* M 153; *September 1, 1802*, title.)[63]

207. Aug 30–Aug 31 and shortly after; between Aug 31 and Sept 22; possibly c Sept, more probably c late 1802

W, DW arrive at Dover from Calais at 1 AM 30 Aug. They bathe, sit on the cliffs; see the French coast plainly. This view possibly contributes to *September, 1802. Near Dover*, which W probably composes this day or shortly after. They observe a cricket match. They mount the coach for London next day at 4:30 PM and arrive in London at 6 AM next morning. (They depart London on 22 Sept.)

Probably today W composes *Composed in the Valley near Dover, on the Day of Landing*. (*DWJ* M 153; *DWJ* II, 8; *Composed in the Valley* title.)[64]

W and DW lodge at the Temple, probably in Montagu's rooms. (*EY* 375.)

While in town W discusses with RW the desirability of W's raising between £1000 and £2000 on JW's account on their bond. (*EY* 691–92.)

W probably now composes:

London, 1802 ("Milton! Thou Should'st Be Living at This Hour")

Written in London, September 1802 ("O Friend! I Know Not Which Way I Must Look") (Titles; 1803:15n. See also 1802:136n.)[65]

---

[63] The title of the poem on its first publication (*MP* 11 Feb 1803; see Woof *SB* 185) was *The Banished Negroes*. The present title was first used in *P2V* and retained through 1850.

[64] *DWJ* states that they landed at Dover "at 1 on Monday the 30th"; that the "next day," when they saw the French coast, was hot; that they mounted the coach at "½ past 4"; and that they "arrived in London at 6 the 30th August." Probably "30th" is a slip for "31st."

[65] The similarity of the sentiments of the sonnets to those of the Aug sonnets and to each other makes Sept the likely time for both.

It is probably this visit to which Richard Sharp refers in a letter to Tom Wedgwood of 5 Jan 1803 (UKL):

Possibly c Sept, more probably c late 1802, DW writes *Tale, Imitated from Gower* in what is now DC MS 38. (Appendix V.)

208. Sept 3

W perhaps on this day composes or completes *Composed upon Westminster Bridge, September 3, 1802.* (Title. See 1802:202.)

209. Sept 5–Sept 7

The *Earl of Abergavenny* arrives off Portland from China on 5 Sept; anchors in Nob Channel on 7 Sept. (It had sailed 19 May 1801.) (Log, East India Co.)

210. Sept 7

W, DW dine with the Ls. CL shows them around Bartholomew Fair. (*LL* I, 312.)[66]

211. Probably c Sept 8 and shortly after

CW arrives in London at RW's chambers; hears of the safe arrival of the *Earl of Abergavenny* in the Downs, and of the presence of

---

[66] Moorman I, 569 reasonably suggests that the visit to Bartholomew Fair supplied W with material for *Prel* VII. He was perhaps drawing on earlier visits as well. He had been in London in early Sept, when the Fair was held, in 1798 and perhaps in 1791 (see *CEY* 120, 246).

> I am almost sorry for the querulous passage in my letter that related to Wordsworth, but I beg you to believe that I am very slow to take any offence, although my surprise at his not calling me, was improper
>
> Your description of the nature of his visit to London accounts for his not seeing anybody. I very sincerely esteem & admire him, and it was natural for me, who had actively sought him at Grasmere [see 1801:43], to expect that he should not come to London without returning my advances.

After commending Tom Wedgwood's religious creed, he continues: "I like you for being so good a hater of priests & of their craft. Wordsworth I see too is a good liker [*sic*],—I judge, from your interesting little anecdote." This anecdote unfortunately remains unknown. The singular "nature" of W's visit was no doubt its connection with private affairs related to W's approaching marriage.

W and DW in London. W, DW, and he soon meet. (Letter, CW to Jonathan Walton, 13 Sept 1802, DCP.)[67]

212. Sept 8

W, DW, CW learn this evening that JW is to be delayed a few days longer near Margate on account of the Neap Tides. (1802:211n.)

213. Sept 9–Sept 11

W, DW, CW set off on the morning of 9 Sept to visit the Cooksons at Windsor. W, DW return to London on 11 Sept. (1802:211n.)

214. Sept 11; between Sept 11 and Sept 22

On 11 Sept JW leaves his ship at Gravesend; travels to London.

W, DW return to London from Windsor this afternoon [see 1802:213]. DW catches cold in the coach. On arrival, they go at once to Staple Inn, where they hear of JW's arrival. They find RW, JW, probably in the Temple Court. All go to W's lodgings. Before their departure from London on 22 Sept W and DW probably visit one or more times at the Ls'. (*EY* 375–76; 1802:211n; *LL* I, 383.)

---

[67] CW's letter, written from Windsor, records:

On my arrival at my brother's Chambers in Staple Inn the first news I heard was that dispatches had been received that very morning announcing the safe arrival in the Downs of the Ship E. of Abergavenny. The next piece of intelligence, even more unexpected, was that my brother William & Sister were in Town, having arrived a few days before from Calais. They had been spending about a month in the neighbou[r]hood of that place, and seemed very glad to get home again. William is not yet married: but the ceremony will take place, we expect, in about ten days time. We continued in London till the Thursday morning expecting daily & almost hourly to hear of John's arrival at the India House. But finding on the Wednesday Evening that the Ship, which he could not on any account be permitted to leave, was likely to be detained a few days longer, near Margate, by the Neap Tides, my brother Wm, my sister & myself set off for Windsor on Thursday morning, as they wished, in their confined allowance of time, to avail themselves of that interval to see my Uncle & his family. On Saturday afternoon they returned to London. By this time we expect that John may have reached them. When we shall have heard that this is the case, I mean to return for a day or two again to London, unless we find that he can pay us an early visit at Windsor.

215. Probably Sept 12; probably between Sept 12 and Sept 19

Probably on 12 Sept DW writes to MH from London: Their visit at Windsor [see 1802:213]; their meeting with JW [see 1802:214]; their plans for departure from London. (*EY* 375–76.)

JW writes to MH from London: Is deeply affected by a letter from MH. (*JWL* 125–26, 215.)

Probably between 12 and 19 Sept W dines with Daniel Stuart. (Letter, Daniel Stuart to STC, postmark 23 Sept 1802, PML.)[68]

216. Sept 16 (and 1803 Jan 29)

"I Grieved for Buonaparté" is published in *MP*, unsigned. (It is published in *MP* again on 29 Jan 1803.) (See Woof *SB* 183; *STCL* II, 869. Cf Moorman I, 571.)

217. Sept 22–Sept 24 (–Oct 4)

W, DW sets off from London for Gallow Hill on 22 Sept. They reach their destination on 24 Sept. They are met in turn by MH, SH, and Joanna H. (W, DW, and MH, who is then MW, depart 4 Oct.) (*DWJ* M 153–54.)

218. Probably c late Sept

DW writes to JW. (See *JWL* 126, 215.)

219. Sept 29

DW writes to JPM from Gallow Hill: Regrets having missed JPM at Scarborough [see 1802:196] and Gallow Hill; their visit in London; W's wedding plans; MH; visit to the Cooksons' [see 1802: 213]; the Lowther debt settlement. (*EY* 376–78.)

---

[68] Stuart writes in the postscript to the letter, of which various parts are dated Monday night, Tuesday morning, and Thursday morning (the Thursday would have been the 23rd): "Wordsworth dined with me last week. I dont know if he has left town not having seen him since." See Woof *SB* 155.

220. Perhaps c late 1802

W composes "Nuns Fret Not at Their Convent's Narrow Room." (GCL 92; Appendix III.)[69]

221. Oct 1

John and George H arrive at Gallow Hill. (*DWJ* M 154.)

222. Oct 2

W, DW, George H, Thomas H, John H, SH ride to Hackness. (*DWJ* M 154.)

W signs a marriage license affadavit; he and Thomas H sign a marriage bond in the amount of £200 that no impediment, by consanguinity or otherwise, exists to a marriage with MH. The documents are sealed and delivered in the presence of John Kirk, Surrogate. (Copies of Marriage License affadavit and marriage bond, DCP.)

223. Oct 3

MH, SH pack. This evening W presents a copy of *LB* 1802 to SH.[70] DW sleeps wearing the wedding ring which W is to use next day. (*DWJ* M 154; *The Athenaeum* 1896, 714; copy of *LB* 1802, DCP.)

224. Oct 4

William Wordsworth and Mary Hutchinson are married at Brompton Church shortly after 8 AM. The officiating minister is John Ellis; witnesses are Thomas H, Joanna H, and John H. SH does not

---

[69] It may be noticed here that the review of *LB* 1800 in the *Literary and Masonic Magazine* for Sept 1802 (I, 462) is a reprint of the notice in the *Monthly Review* (see 1802:180). (See Ward; Woof *Ariel* 18n.)

[70] The copy of *LB* presented to SH is inscribed by the receiver on the title page of vol. I, "Sara Hutchinson|Octobr 3d 18[02]" ("1802" has been rewritten below). MW has written, evidently many years later, on the facing page of the fly-leaf, "Given by W. W. to S. H. at Gallow Hill, the Evening before our marriage Octr 3 1802. M.W." A similar inscription appears on the title page of vol. II, and MW has begun a facing note in pencil, "Given by WW to SH at G."

attend the ceremony because she is preparing the breakfast for the wedding party; DW does not attend, apparently because of nervous uneasiness. DW meets W on his return, is led back to the house by W and John H.

After breakfast W, MW, DW depart together. They stop two hours at Kirkby, where DW, also W or MW or both, write to SH; send a letter to the *York Herald* [about the wedding]; visit the church-yard, read epitaphs.

They depart Kirkby about 2:30, proceed to Helmsley, where their driver leaves them. They stop for a time at the inn where W and DW had stayed on 15 July. W, DW visit the Castle ruins. All set forward with a new driver, pass Rievaulx, the Hambleton Hills. Probably after passing the Hambleton Hills W this day composes *Composed after a Journey across the Hambleton Hills, Yorkshire*. Before reaching Thirsk they see a bonfire. They find no room at the inn, it being John Bell's birthday. They ride on to Leeming Lane, where they pass the night. (*DWJ* M 154–57; Brompton PR; M-W Book of Common Prayer, DCP; *Composed after a Journey* IF note.)[71]

225. Probably between Oct 4 and 1804 Mar 6

W composes "Those Words Were Uttered as in Pensive Mood." (1802:224; Appendix III.)[72]

226. Oct 5

W, MW, DW depart Leeming Lane about 8:30; stop at Leyburn,

[71] Notices of the wedding appeared in the *York Herald* on 9 Oct and the *York Courant* on 11 Oct (*DWJ* M 155n); and an absurd announcement was printed in *MP* on 9 Oct (see Moorman I, 574–75; *EY* 615). Professor Ketcham suggests that the author of the paragraph in *MP* was STC or CL (*JWL* 218). CL, in view both of style and of his recent visit to the Lakes, appears the more likely culprit.

P2V H I, 197–98 expresses doubt, because of the resemblance between phrasing of *DWJ* and *Composed after a Journey*, that W composed the poem on his wedding day; but it seems quite probable that W, although he may have revised the poem after reading *DWJ*, would remember accurately in this instance, and thus that *DWJ* was drawing on W's poem. Concerning John Bell's birthday see *DWJ* M 157n.

[72] The poem is obviously a sequel to *Composed after a Journey*. It appears in MS M, and thus was written before 6 Mar 1804. See *PW* III, 428.

whence they set off in a post chaise up Wensleydale. They are obliged to wait in the carriage as the postboy replaces a restive horse. This incident forms the subject of "Hard Was Thy Durance, Queen, Compared with Ours." They stop to see Aysgarth Falls. MW and DW are frightened by a cow. They proceed to Hawes, where they pass the night. (*DWJ* M 157–59. See 1802:227.)

227. Oct 6; probably between Oct 6 and c Oct 8

On 6 Oct W, MW, DW proceed from Hawes to Sedbergh, which they reach at midday, and on to Kendal, which they reach at about 2. MW, DW visit the house where SH had lived as a child; buy jugs, a dish, some paper. When they return to the inn, W, who has possibly been conducting some business or composing, is almost ready for them. They depart Kendal; visit Ings Chapel. They arrive at DC at about 6. (*DWJ* M 159–61.)

Probably between 6 Oct and c 8 Oct W composes "Hard Was Thy Durance, Queen" (only the first line is known to survive). (*DWJ* M 158, 161.)[73]

228. Oct 7

MW, DW unpack boxes. (*DWJ* M 161.)

229. Oct 8

MW, DW bake, walk. (*DWJ* M 161.)

RW this day submits to James Graham an itemized account of the debt of the late Lord Lonsdale to the estate of JW Sr. The account totals £10,388/6/8. (*EY* 688; RW accounts, DCP. See 1802:177; 1802:189.)

230. Oct 9

W, DW walk to Mr. Sympson's. (*DWJ* M 161.)

[73] W wrote the poem at a time other than immediately after the incident, but before DW wrote up her journal. It would appear likely, in absence of evidence to the contrary, that the writing of the journal occurred soon after the return from the trip, although the appearance of the journal MS does not encourage confident conjecture of a more exact time.

231. Oct 10

Rain all day. The Ws' activities are presumably confined to the house. (*DWJ* M 161.)

232. Oct 11 (–Oct 13)

W, MW, DW walk to the Easedale hills to hunt waterfalls. W, MW walk to Easedale Tarn; DW follows. STC arrives at DC after dinner for a visit. (He departs 13 Oct.) (*DWJ* M 161.)

233. Oct 12

W, MW, DW, STC walk to Rydal. (*DWJ* M 161.)

234. Oct 13 (–Oct 16, 17)

W, MW, DW, STC set forward toward Keswick. STC persuades the others to come on to GH. *DWJ* records that the Ws consent to do so because SFC is not at home. (MW, DW return to DC on 16 Oct; W on 17 Oct.) Probably DW, perhaps others, write to Annette. (*DWJ* M 161; *STCL* VI, 1015.)

235. Oct 14

W, MW, DW, STC visit, sup with William Calvert. (*DWJ* M 161.)

236. Oct 15

W, MW, DW, STC walk to Lord William Gordon's.[74] (*DWJ* M 161.)

237. Oct 16

MW, DW return to Grasmere. W accompanies them part way, turning back before they reach Naddle Fell. They reach home at about 5. (*DWJ* M 161. See 1802:234.)

[74] Possibly Water End, which W and DW had visited on 4 Apr.

238. Oct 17

MW, DW have thirteen neighbors to tea. W arrives home just as tea begins. (*DWJ* M 162. See 1802:234.)

239. Oct 18

DW walks to the Sympsons'. (*DWJ* M 162.)

240. Oct 19

The Sympsons drink tea, sup at DC. W is much oppressed. (*DWJ* M 162.)

241. Oct 20

W, MW, DW walk on Butterlip How. (*DWJ* M 162.)

242. Oct 21

W, DW walk to Rydal. (*DWJ* M 162.)

243. Oct 23–Oct 30

On 23 Oct W, DW walk to see Langdale, Rydal, foot of Grasmere. DW returns with a toothache that confines her to her room till 30 Oct. No *DWJ* entries are made for this period. Perhaps during this time DW writes to JW. (*DWJ* M 162; *JWL* 128, 217n.)

244. Oct 30

W sets off to Keswick. MW accompanies him to Dunmail Raise. W meets John Stoddart at the bridge at the foot of Legburthwaite. The two return to DC; dine. Stoddart reads to them from Chaucer. (*DWJ* M 162.)

245. Oct 31 (–Nov 2)

John M calls at DC. W, Stoddart depart for Keswick. (W returns 2 Nov.) MW, DW look over old letters. (*DWJ* M 162.)

246. Perhaps between c Nov and 1803 early Jan

W translates Italian verse including:
"A Plain Youth, Lady, and a Simple Lover," from Milton
Six poems from Metastasio: "Gentle Zephyr," "I Will Be That Fond Mother," "Laura, Farewell My Laura!" "Oh! Bless'd All Bliss Above," "The Swallow, That Hath Lost," "To the Grove, the Meadow, the Well." (Woof *SB* 185–89; *PW* IV, 369–70, 472–73 [1970 issue, 473–74]; 1802:254. See also 1802:253; *DWJ* M 166.)[75]

247. Perhaps Nov 1802 or within a few months thereafter

W sees Jeffrey's review of *Thalaba* [in *ER* I (Oct 1802)]; sets Jeffrey down as a poor creature. (*MY* I, 191.)

248. Nov

During this month DW enters into the 1800 Commonplace Book (DC MS 26) an inventory of household linen that has arrived for MW from Penrith. (DCP. See Appendix IX.)[76]

249. Nov 1

DW writes to ML. MW walks to Mr. Sympson's. Letters arrive from Cooke, Wrangham, SFC. (*DWJ* M 162–63.)

250. Nov 2

W returns from Keswick. Barth Sympson comes in at teatime. W is unwell in the evening. (*DWJ* M 163.)

251. Nov 3

Charles Luff comes to tea. (*DWJ* M 163.)

[75] It seems likely that a number of Italian poems were sent off to Stuart in Jan 1803 (see 1803:9). These would seem to have included the Italian translations published between 5 Oct and 12 Dec 1803 and "I Will Be That Fond Mother," which is copied with four others of the translations from Metastasio, in the Fitzwilliam copy of Isola's *Italian Poets* (see *PW* IV, 472–73).

[76] Another inventory of linen appears on a separate page, without date, below in the Commonplace Book.

252. Nov 4; probably c Nov 4, and Nov 5

On 4 Nov DW scalds her foot with coffee; does not sleep till 4 AM. (*DWJ* M 163.)

Probably c 4 Nov W and/or DW write to CL and STC. On 5 Nov DW writes to Montagu and Cooke. Probably all the letters, certainly those to CL and STC, are sent off on 5 Nov. (*DWJ* M 163.)

253. Nov 7–perhaps c Nov 19; perhaps between this time and early 1808

On 7 Nov letters arrive from STC with the news that he has gone to London and that SH is at Penrith. DW writes to CCl. W begins translating Ariosto. He probably continues translating until c 19 Nov at the rate of nearly 100 lines per day, perhaps completing translation of two books of the *Orlando Furioso*. This material probably included the lines quoted *PW* IV, 367–69. (*DWJ* M 163; *EY* 628; *LY* II, 999.)

By early 1808 W perhaps determines to publish the translation, to which he has perhaps added since this time. (Jordan 89–90.)[77]

254. Nov 8; between Nov 8 and Dec 24 (–1803 Jan 7)

W continues work on his translation of Ariosto; writes out stanzas; is ill, but better in the evening. DW reads a canto of Ariosto. (*DWJ* M 163.)

Between 8 Nov and 24 Dec, SH arrives for a visit at DC. (She departs 7 Jan 1803.) (*DWJ* M 163.)[78]

---

[77] The MS quoted *PW* IV, 367–69 is plainly a part of the now dismantled fragmentary NB probably referred to by W *LY* II, 999 (see *CEY* 346). That MS, which contains Chaucer translation dating from early Dec 1801 and possibly late Apr 1802, may reasonably be supposed to have been in use later in 1802. The physical appearance of the leaves of the NB indicates that it was dismantled before completion of the copying of the translation from Ariosto, which, as surviving here, appears to be early draft. The loose speculation made here regarding the amount of time that W spent translating Ariosto is based on a division of the number of lines in the first two books of the *Orlando Furioso* (1248) by W's recollected daily rate of "nearly 100 lines."

[78] *DWJ* remarks under 7 Nov that "Sara [is] at Penrith" and under 8 Nov, "Sara is at Keswick I hope." It is unlikely that in STC's absence from GH (4 Nov–24 Dec) she would have lingered at Keswick; but her whereabouts before 19 Dec remains uncertain.

255. Perhaps between Nov 9 and 1803 June 29

Richard Sharp tells W of Charles James Fox's having been hurt by STC's letters to Fox, *MP* 4 and 9 Nov 1802. (*STCL* II, 954.)

256. Nov 10 ff; probably Nov 10 or shortly after; and perhaps Nov, after Nov 10

On 10 Nov Thomas H writes a draft at Stockton to John H for £20, due at one month. This draft is apparently drawn against DW's £20 yearly allowance from JW. (RW accounts, DCP. See 1802:25.)[79]

Probably on 10 Nov or shortly after, DW receives a letter from JW written in London on 7 Nov: Seeks advice about books to take on next voyage. He will send Anderson's *Poets* to W. He wishes only Spenser from it, and will buy that in London. (*JWL* 128–30.)

Probably during this month, after 10 Nov, W writes to an unknown correspondent, perhaps CW (only a fragment is known to survive): Advice to JW to purchase a copy of Spenser containing the *State of Ireland* even though such an edition is probably scarce. W's opinion of Milton's sonnets. (*EY* 378–79.)[80]

---

[79] A copy by DW of RW's memorandum on the subject reads: "The above [draft] was paid on account of a present or allowance for my Brother John to Dorothy, being received by me at the India House under the power of an Attorney as an allowance for wages when absent. R.W." See *EY* 337–38.

[80] *EY* 378n conjectures that W's letter was addressed to CL or STC. STC had departed London by 12 Nov (*STCL* II, 882), although W possibly did not know that; and CL probably had already lately sent off, perhaps on 5 Nov, some books to W via GH (*LL* I, 328) and was later to advise W himself about the rarity of editions of Spenser containing the *State of Ireland* (*LL* I, 419). W also abruptly tells his correspondent to transcribe his comments on Milton for JW "as said by me to him." The request would seem inappropriate for a correspondent actually in London with JW, and peremptory as a request to STC or CL. A close member of the family would seem a more likely recipient; and while a letter to RW might have contained such remarks, CW, whom JW was planning on 7 Nov to visit in Cambridge (*JWL* 128), appears the most likely choice of all.

W plainly had access to a copy of Anderson before this time. *Joanna* (probably c but by 23 Aug 1800) is clearly indebted to Drayton's *Poly-Olbion* (see *PW* Knight, 1896 II, 161), which W probably came to know through Anderson; and the Chaucer translations of late 1801 fairly certainly draw on the Anderson edition, as do many poems, and much of the reading, of the spring of 1802. The annotations in the

257. Perhaps c mid-Nov

W receives from CL, via George H, some books and a pair of thick-soled shoes. (*LL* I, 328.)

258. Probably c but by Dec 14

DW writes to JW (letter not known to survive). (*JWL* 134.)

259. Dec 18

DW dines at Mr. Sympson's. (*DWJ* M 164.)

260. Dec 19

W, MW, DW, SH walk, DW to Rydal. W returns with DW; sits with her; goes to meet MW, SH. (*DWJ* M 164.)

261. Dec 20

A frosty day. (*DWJ* M 164.)

---

copy of Anderson presently at DC inscribed "Wm Wordsworth | from | his dear Brother John" are probably throughout exclusively by STC. The Folger copy of Anderson contains marginalia in W's hand, but apparently in vols. I and II only. The few notations in vol. I of the Folger copy, however, strongly suggest that this was the volume used by W when translating: On p. 123 appear, in W's autograph, "soon as" and "Then sped themselves," draft for lines 217 and 187 of W's translation of *The Prioress's Tale*. In vol. II W has written numerous evaluative comments, many now erased, particularly in the Spenser portion, seemingly for a person not familiar with the poems (at the top of page 358, for example, at the beginning of *FQ* VI.ii, appears the phrase "very well worth reading"). In light of present evidence it would appear that the comments were for the guidance of JW (cf *EY* 379), and thus that this and the other volumes, with the exception of vol. I, may have gone off for JW, about the time of JW's departure, in 1800; that W then used a set from GH, and the retained vol. I, in JW's absence; that JW in 1802 sent back to W the volumes that he had taken earlier; that the full set re-formed by JW's sending back the books was then taken to GH and subsequently annotated by STC, RS, and HC (see esp. 1803:128n) (STC could have annotated both sets earlier and W's later as well); and that the DC copy was inscribed later and somewhat forgetfully. See also Moorman I, 101, 515; *JWL* 213–14; George Whalley, *Coleridge and Sara Hutchinson and the Asra Poems* (London 1955), 31n.

262. Dec 23

Sara Coleridge, fourth child and only daughter of Samuel Taylor Coleridge and Sarah Fricker Coleridge, is born at GH, probably between 6 and 6:30 AM. (*DWJ* M 164; *EY* 381; *STCL* II, 902.)[81]

263. Dec 24

STC, Tom Wedgwood stop by DC in the morning; the Ws inform STC of the birth of SC on the preceding day. W is struck by Wedgwood's deplorable change of appearance. W accompanies STC and Wedgwood as far as Wythburn in their chaise. DW, MW meet W at Dunmail Raise. Back at DC, W, DW sit; they repeat some of W's sonnets; read some of Milton's, also *L'Allegro* and *Il Penseroso*. W looks at Charlotte Smith's sonnets. SH is bedridden from a toothache. (*DWJ* M 163–64; Litchfield 127.)

264. Dec 25

DW dresses to go to Keswick in a return chaise, but does not go. (*DWJ* M 164.)

DW draws on RW for £15 by a draft in favor of SH. (RW accounts, DCP; *EY* 379.)

DW writes to RW and JW in a single letter from Grasmere: (to RW:) She has drawn on him for £15; their pleasure in JW's good prospects for his voyage; their happiness in the hopeful appearance of the Lowther case. (to JW:) Will write to ML about the Dictionary [see *JWL* 134]; asks JW as soon as he receives it to send off the box [see 1802:256]. The visit of STC and Wedgwood [see 1802:263]; old Molly, local acquaintances of JW. W has written some more sonnets, which will possibly appear in *MP*; if not, she will send them.[82] (*EY* 379–81.)

265. Dec 30 (–1803 Jan 2)

DW goes to Keswick. W takes her to the foot of the hill nearest

---

[81] SC supposed herself born on Thursday 22 Dec (see SC *Mem* I, 2), but the Thursday concerned was the 23rd.

[82] The character of the sonnets that appeared in *MP* in 1803 makes it probable that DW here refers to political sonnets. See 1803:15n.

Keswick on a horse. They stop on the way to admire a tuft of primroses; decide not to pick the flowers. It is probable that W's recollections of this tuft contribute to *The Tuft of Primroses*. (DW returns to DC on 2 Jan 1803.) (*DWJ* M 164–65; SC *Mem* I, 20.)

266. Dec 31 (–1803 Jan 4)

STC walks from the Luffs' in ratterdale to DC via Kirkstone. (He departs 4 Jan 1803.) (*STCNB* 1319; *DWJ* M 165.)[83]

1803

[On writings of W possibly of this year see below and GCL 1–4, 6–8, 55, 69, 72–76, 92, 95, 97–112.]

1. Early this year, esp. c Jan 11; possibly c early this year

W perhaps composes lines for *Prel*, possibly for *Prel* III, in addition to those composed on 11 Jan [see 1803:9]. (See Appendix V.)
Possibly c early this year DW becomes annoyed at Charles Lloyd as a result of his having pronounced STC a greater poet than W. (*STCNB* 4006; *STCL* II, 651, 654, 846; 1800:141.)

2. Jan 2

William Mackereth fetches DW home from Keswick. W meets her within three miles of Keswick; MW, SH, STC await her at John Stanley's, Thirlspot. All probably return to DC. DW notices the primrose she had observed on her way to Keswick [see 1802:265]. (*DWJ* M 165; *STCL* II, 908–09, 911; SC *Mem* I, 20.)

3. Jan 4

W, DW walk with STC to George Mackereth's, where STC, evidently unsuccessfully, tries to hire a horse. They walk to Ambleside,

[83] STC says on 8 Jan (*STCL* II, 911) that the walk took place on New Year's Day; but this probably earlier NB entry almost certainly presents the most accurate record. See also *STCNB* 1333.

whence STC departs to proceed via Kirkstone to Charles Luff's. He somewhere obtains a horse to take him to the top of the pass. (*DWJ* M 165; *STCL* II, 911. See 1802:266.)

4. Jan 6 (–Jan 7)

STC arrives at DC from Luff's. (He departs next day.) (*DWJ* M 165; *STCL* II, 912, 914–15.)

5. Jan 7

SH, STC go to Keswick. W accompanies them to the foot of Wythburn. DW, who perhaps accompanies them a shorter distance, dines at Mrs. Sympson's, calls on Aggy Fleming. She and W, whom she evidently meets on her way, return home before sunset. (*DWJ* M 165; *STCL* II, 912–15.)

6. Jan 8

W, DW walk to Rydal. (*DWJ* M 165.)

7. Jan 9

W, DW walk to Brother's Wood. DW writes to ML. (*DWJ* M 165.)

8. Jan 10

W, DW walk to Rydal; find letters from SH, Annette, and [Peggy Ashburner]. (*DWJ* M 165.)

9. Jan 11

MW reads the *General Prologue* to the *Canterbury Tales* to DW. W works on *Prel*, possibly Book III. A letter arrives from Keswick indicating that STC is contemplating a voyage to the Canaries, and one from Taylor, concerning W's marriage. DW reads part of *The Knight's Tale*; MW copies Italian poems, probably including all but one, or all, of W's translations from Metastasio [see 1802:246], for Daniel Stuart. (*DWJ* M 165–66.)[1]

[1] The identity of "Taylor" is uncertain. Cf *EY* 277.

10. Jan 13

Calais, August, 1802 ("Is It a Reed That's Shaken by the Wind") is published in *MP* without title and unsigned, with date "August, 1802." A headnote states that the lines are by "one of the first poets of the present day." (See Woof *SB* 184; Moorman I, 571; 1803:15.)

11. Jan 16

W has a fancy for gingerbread. DW, probably with W, walks to Matthew Newton's, where DW buys 6d-worth of gingerbread. (*DWJ* M 166.)

12. Jan 17

A woman (probably Matthew Newton's wife or sister) brings gingerbread to DC—just as the household is baking (probably gingerbread). They buy 2d-worth. (*DWJ* M 166.)

13. Probably between Jan 18 and c Feb 9

DW visits the Cls at Eusemere. She returns to DC c 9 Feb. (*EY* 383.)[2]

14. Jan 20–Apr 8

STC is absent from GH on a trip to Etruria, Bristol, Stowey, [Tarrant] Gunville, London. (*STCNB* 1336&n; *STCL* II, 942. See *STCL* II, 918–42 *passim*.)

15. Jan 29

MP contains an editorial announcement of receipt of a dozen "Sonnets of a Political nature" by "one of the first Poets of the age." Nos. I and II are published therewith (the others will follow in succes-

---

[2] All that is plain is that DW departed almost certainly after 17 Jan and returned (according to W's statement) "a fortnight" before 23 Feb.

sion). *Sonnet. No. I* is "I Griev'd for Buonaparté" [see also 1802:216]. *Sonnet. No. II* is *Calais, August, 1802* ("Is It a Reed") [see also 1803:10]. Each sonnet is signed "W.L.D." (See Woof *SB* 155, 184; Moorman I, 572.)[3]

[3] "Is It a Reed" is here titled *August, 1801*.

Only five other sonnets known to be by W and of "a political nature" appear to have been published in *MP* hereafter in 1803: *To Toussaint l'Ouverture*; "We Had a Fellow Passenger"; "Festivals Have I Seen"; "It Is Not to Be Thought of"; "When I Have Borne in Memory." These may be assumed to have been received by *MP* among the dozen sonnets announced. The remaining five sonnets cannot be confidently identified. Woof *SB* 156 lists ten sonnets later classified among W's "Poems Dedicated to National Independence and Liberty" and "which could have been written by January, 1803":

1. *Composed by the Sea-side, near Calais* ("Fair Star of Evening")
2. *Composed near Calais* ("Jones!")
3. *On the Extinction of the Venetian Republic*
4. *The King of Sweden*
5. *Composed in the Valley near Dover* ("Here on Our Native Soil")
6. *September, 1802* ("Inland, within a Hollow Vale")
7. *Written in London, September, 1802* ("O Friend! I Know Not")
8. *London, 1802* ("Milton! Thou Shoulds't Be Living")
9. "Great Men Have Been among Us"
10. "England! the Time is Come"

Moorman I, 572, suggests nos. 1, 3, 7, 8, 9, and 10 of the works listed. Woof *SB* assigns no. 10 to "probably 1803" without explanation. W gave the poem no date in published editions, but its similarity in style and sentiment to poems probably composed in Sept 1802, esp. nos. 7 and 8 above, would appear to make an earlier date not improbable. *The King of Sweden* was probably composed between late 1804 and 1807 (see Andrew Hilen, "The Date of Wordsworth's 'The King of Sweden,'" *English Studies* XXI, 1953, 156–60). No. 5 is perhaps too personal a reference to fit well the *MP* note's description of the dozen poems as forming "little Political Essay[s], on some recent proceeding." Nos. 1 and 3 seem to lack immediate reference to "some recent proceeding." The fact that neither 3, 6, nor 8 (nor, of course, 4) appears in MS M is probably not a decisive indication of date (see Appendix III). Nos. 6, 7, 8, 9, and 10, which share a common concern with the moral failings of France, thus appear the five most likely choices, although the dates of composition of 1, 2, and 5 require that these be considered possibilities. "There Is a Bondage Worse" is not named above, but would appear on the grounds of content to be yet another possibility.

If STC had a hand in the introductory note for *MP*, as seems possible (see Moorman I, 271), "dozen" may exaggerate the number of poems. DW's remarks *EY* 381 may imply that the sonnets received by *MP* had been written by 25 Dec.

16. Feb 2; probably c but by Feb 3

On 2 Feb *To Toussaint l'Ouverture* is published in *MP* under the heading and title *Sonnet. No. III. To Toussaint l'Ouverture*, and signed "W.L.D." (See Woof *SB* 184; 1803:15.)

Probably c but by 3 Feb Charles Luff sees the Ws, who tell Luff that they wish to hear from Tom Wedgwood. (Letter, Luff to Tom Wedgwood, 3 Feb 1803, UKL.)

17. Feb 11

September 1, 1802 is published in *MP* under the heading and title *Sonnet. No. IV. The Banished Negroes*, and signed "W.L.D." (See Woof *SB* 185; 1803:15.)

18. Feb 14 (–c but by Feb 18)

RW, JW write to W from Staple Inn: (RW:) Has written to LdL on 4 Feb requesting an appointment, and has accidentally met LdL at Graham's chambers; LdL has promised that part of the debt to the JW Sr. estate shall be paid immediately, and authorized RW and Graham to decide upon terms of a final settlement. [James] Graham advises that £8000 or £8500 should be accepted as full payment, and proposes that about £3000 or £4000 should be paid in a short time. Certain portions of the full claim made by the Ws on LdL, £10,388/6/8, are not recoverable in law, and the amount suggested by Graham may be all that can be obtained. Requests the opinion of W and DW.

It is desirable that W raise between £1000 and £2000 on JW's account on their bond. As much as possible should be obtained from Montagu before settlement of the Lowther debt. Please send an account of Montagu's debts.

(JW:) The hopeful appearance of the Lowther affair. Will write tomorrow about his own concerns. (*EY* 688–92.)

(This letter probably reaches W c but by 18 Feb.)

19. Probably c but by Feb 18

DW writes to JW. (*JWL* 136–38.)

20. Probably a few days before Feb 23

The Ws see Richard Cooke, who probably calls at DC. They probably discuss the Lowther debt together [see 1803:21]. (*EY* 383–85.)

21. Feb 23

RW's accounts record receipt of £3000 from LdL on the account of the debt of the late Earl of Lonsdale to the estate of JW Sr. under this date [see 1803:18]. (*EY* 384n. See 1803:26; 1803:49; 1803:54.)[4]

Richard Cooke visits at DC for at least part of this day. The Ws perhaps today give him copies of poems of W's to take to JW. These include *To the Cuckoo, The Sparrow's Nest,* a *To a Butterfly* poem, a *To the Small Celandine* poem, and *LG.* (*EY* 383; *JWL* 140.)

W writes to RW while Cooke is at DC: He and DW rely confidently on RW's judgment in the settlement of the Lowther debt; the proposed settlement of £8500 [see 1803:18] or even £8000 appears, on balance, satisfactory. Montagu's debt to W is £454: £300 the annuity, £54 arrears on the annuity payments; £100 unsecured. Montagu has paid £13 per quarter for the last three years; paid £50 last summer; has promised £50 more next. W hopes to obtain £50 from him; but is not hopeful about the repayment of the £300 [see also 1803:51]. (*EY* 382–83.)[5]

22. Probably c but not before Feb 24

A letter arrives from JW. (*JWL* 136–38.)

23. Feb 26

Calais, August 15, 1802 is published in *MP* under the heading and title *Sonnet. No. V. August 15, 1802,* and signed "W.L.D." (See Woof *SB* 185; 1803:15.)

24. Feb 28

RW's accounts charge DW £15, payment of bill in favor of SH, due this day, under this date. (RW accounts, DCP.)

---

[4] James Graham's draft is dated on the same day. (DW copy in accounts, DCP.) RW deducted £100 expenses before distributing credit in the accounts.

[5] Montagu was at least £17 further in arrears by early Apr 1804 (see 1804:15n).

25. c early Mar (–perhaps Apr 1)

Probably c early Mar MW departs for a visit at Penrith and Eusemere. (She returns to DC perhaps 1 Apr.) (*EY* 384–85, 387–89.)[6]

26. Mar 1

RW's accounts credit to W and DW under this date a nine-twentieths share of £2900, the sum paid to the estate of JW Sr. by LdL on 23 Feb less £100 expenses, divided according to the custom of York: £1305. (RW accounts, DCP. See 1803:21.)[7]

27. Perhaps c Mar 24

The Ws receive a letter from Cooke advising that LdL sent a £3000 draft to RW [see 1803:26] and will conclude the settlement upon his return to town. (*EY* 384.)

28. Mar 28

DW writes to RW: She seeks news of the settlement of the Lowther debt; Cooke's letter [see 1803:27]. Seeks news of JW. Widespread illness. W has applied unsuccessfully for £1500 for JW's use [see 1803:18]. (*EY* 384–85.)[8]

29. Perhaps Apr 1 (–probably Apr 28)

MW returns to DC, accompanied by SH (who remains until probably 28 Apr). (1803:25.)

30. Apr 16

"It Is Not to Be Thought of That the Flood" is published in *MP*

[6] As of Monday 28 Mar MW, who had been absent from DC "almost a month," was expected home, along with SH, on "Friday." It may here be noticed that STC remarks in a letter to RS on 12 Mar that "Wordsworth means to reside ½ a mile from" Keswick (*STCL* II, 937).

[7] The entire £2900 was advanced to JW, who signed a bond for £2247/10 (the total less his own share) dated 2 May 1803.

[8] RW wrote to W on 26 Mar advising that since the payment of the £3000 he had seen Graham and asked for £500 within six weeks. (DCP.)

under the heading *Sonnet. No. VI*, and signed "W.L.D." (See Woof *SB* 185.)

31. Apr 22

DW writes to RW: She concludes that RW intends to give security for DW's share of the £3000 [see 1803:21] in order that the whole sum may be given to JW. (*EY* 386.)

32. Probably Apr 28

SH departs from DC. (*EY* 389.)

33. Apr 30–May 1

DW writes to RW, JW in a single letter: (to RW:) Summary of her sentiments regarding the circumstances in which it would be proper for her to lend to JW her share of the sum received from LdL. (to JW:) Her feelings about the loan. Illness—of STC, and at DC. (*EY* 387–90. See 1803:34.)

34. May 7 (–1804 Aug 6)

The *Earl of Abergavenny*, JW captain, departs past St. Alban's Head on a voyage to China. (The ship arrives off Portland on its return on 6 Aug 1804.) Concerning this voyage, which includes an encounter with a French fleet under the command of Admiral Linois, see esp. *JWL* 37–40.

Investment in the voyage by the W family circle possibly totals as much as £7827. (Log, East India Co.; *JWL* 37. See also 1801:26.)

35. May 22

DW writes to RW: Seeks news of JW. Local news, including visits by the Cookes at Ambleside and Keswick. Inquiry whether JW has made any provision for payment of interest on her loan to him [see 1803:33]. (*EY* 390–91.)

36. Probably between May 22 and June 5 or June 12

DW visits the Cls at Eusemere Hill for an unknown period. She probably returns to DC on 5 or 12 June. On her return she is accompanied part way by TCl; and they probably call at the Luff's, where DW obtains some lettuces for the DC garden. (*EY* 391–93. See 1803:38.)[9]

37. Perhaps c early June

W perhaps asks STC to write to him, "at large," as STC reports, "on a poetic subject, which he has at present sub malleo ardentem et ignitum." W is, hence, possibly considering development of *The Recluse*. (*STCL* II, 950. See Appendix VI.)[10]

38. Probably June 7 or June 14

DW writes to CCl: Her return from Eusemere on the preceding Sunday; the beauty of their garden, and Grasmere; CCl's health. They expect to move into their new house next week. Errands for CCl. (*EY* 391–93.)[11]
W, DW probably walk. (*EY* 393.)

39. June 15, 19

DW writes to RW: (15 June:) With regard to the £20 that she had before W's marriage asked RW and CW each to allow her per year, she drew last half-year on RW for £15; now wishes to draw for £10 on 25 June, by draft due at two months.[12] (19 June:) Birth of Johnny [see 1803:40]; asks RW to be godfather. (*EY* 394–95.)

[9] On 28 May CL wrote that he had ordered STC's *Imitation of Spenser* restored to STC's *Poems* on W's authority.

[10] STC states on 10 June that he has made an unsuccessful attempt to comply with W's request. No evidence survives to confirm that composition for *The Recluse* went forward about this time.

[11] The "new house" plainly has no connection with STC's statement on 12 Mar that Wordsworth meant to reside half a mile from Keswick (*STCL* II, 937–38). DW states that they "are now working very hard to put the last finishing stroke to [their] work that [they] may have nothing to do when the dear Baby comes but to take care of it and its mother" (*EY* 392–93). Her remarks suggest that the family may have been temporarily encamped somewhere near DC while redecoration or renovation was in progress there.

[12] No record of this draft by DW appears in RW's accounts.

40. June 18

John Wordsworth (d. 25 July 1875), first child of William Words-worth and Mary Hutchinson Wordsworth, is born at Grasmere, probably between 6:10 and 6:25 AM. (*EY* 395, 485; *STCNB* 1404; M-W Book of Common Prayer, DCP.)[13]

41. Between June 18 and June 26

Robert Buck and perhaps Charles Luff possibly pass by DC, but do not see DW or the baby, and perhaps see no one. (*EY* 392–97.)

42. During the summer

DW visits the island in Grasmere Lake at least once. (*EY* 442–43.)

43. Perhaps shortly before June 26, and June 26

Perhaps shortly before 26 June STC arrives at DC for a visit. He departs on 26 June. (*EY* 395.)
On 26 June DW writes to CCl from Grasmere: The baby. (*EY* 395.)

44. Probably c early or mid-July ff –by 1804 June 24

The Cl family departs from Eusemere in permanent removal to Bury. TCl probably remains alone at Eusemere for a time. By 24 June of the following year the house is sold to LdL. (*EY* 395–96, 485. See Moorman II, 15.)

45. Probably between c early July and Aug 9

W possibly composes some verses (unidentified) for *Prel.* (Appendix V.)

---

[13] The Prayer Book gives the time as 6:20, *EY* as 6:10, and *STCNB* as 6:25.

46. Perhaps a few days before July 9

DW writes to CL, ML (letter not known to survive): Birth of Johnny. (*LL* I, 352.)

47. Probably c July 7

RW receives two promissory notes of £2000 each, at least one dated 6 July 1803, and both probably due at one year, bearing interest at 5 percent.

He perhaps also now receives a note for £1500 due on 20 July. (RW accounts, DCP; 1804:81; 1803:52. See 1803:21.)

48. Probably c mid-July, by July 22, by Oct 1, by Oct 24; and Oct 24–Dec 14

Probably c mid-July, and again by 24 Oct, William Hazlitt visits in the Grasmere-Keswick area. By 22 July he paints portraits of W and STC. W pays Hazlitt 3 guineas for his portrait. By 1 Oct Hazlitt takes both portraits away with him, perhaps to Manchester. (*STCL* II, 957–58, 960, 1004.)[14]

Probably during one of his visits Hazlitt sails with W on Grasmere Lake. W denies a suggestion by Hazlitt that he borrowed the idea of *Poems on the Naming of Places* from *Paul et Virginie* (Howe XVII, 115). Many or most of the following allusions by Hazlitt to W's conversation perhaps date from these visits, which would seem to have offered by far the most extended opportunities for conversation between the two that ever occurred: Howe IV, 381n; V, 161; IX, 5; XI, 91–92 (W characterizes Shakespeare's dialogues, or perhaps his plays, as

---

[14] On the portraits generally see esp. *EY* 446–47nn and Blanshard 44–46, 142. On the reactions of W, STC, and their intimates to these works see esp. *STCL* II, 957–58; *EY* 593–94, 600; CCS II, 238; W. Carew Hazlitt, *Memoirs of William Hazlitt*, I, 403n. W's evidently lugubrious portrait appears to have been destroyed (see *Memoirs of Hazlitt* as cited); but see Blanshard 142.

DeQ's statement that Hazlitt proposed marrige to DW (Masson II, 294) seems insufficiently verified by intrinsic probability or external report for inclusion in the text. If the story contains any truth, however, the event probably occurred during one of Hazlitt's 1803 visits.

"interlocutions between Lucius and Caius" or the like); VI, 309 (Daniel's *Epistle to the Countess of Cumberland* a favorite; cf *MY* I, 520); IX, 5 (House of Commons, Newton, Shakespeare, Milton); XI, 91–92 (various major poets and painters); XII, 203 (physical qualities of great artists); XII, 303 (the sleep of infants).[15]

49. Probably c July 16

W, DW probably receive word from RW that an agreement has been reached for completion of payment to the JW Sr. estate of a total sum of £8500 in settlement of the Lowther debt, the sum to be paid within one year; and that £1500 has lately been paid. (*EY* 397–98. See 1803:21; 1803:47.)

50. Probably July 16 (–by July 19)

Charles Luff calls at DC. Probably later in the day STC arrives for a visit. (He departs by 19 July.) (*EY* 397; *STCNB* 1412, 1416; *STCL* II, 957–58.)

---

[15] Two allusions by Hazlitt to W's conversation seem to me more likely to date from Hazlitt's other extended visit in W's neighborhood, between 20 May and 10 June 1798, than a later occasion, and should thus properly have been noted *CEY* 237–39: (1) Howe VII, 133 (W's anger at Commons for compliance with the King's wish to pursue the war against the French Revolution. Hazlitt dates the incident 1800, when in fact Commons did vote, 260–64, on 3 Feb, for continuance of the war. But W and Hazlitt are not likely to have met during that year. On the development of W's feelings toward the Revolution about that time see esp. J. C. Maxwell, "Wordsworth and the Subjugation of Switzerland," *MLR* LXV 1970, 16–18.) (2) Howe IX, 5 (W wishes Tierney had shot out Pitt's tongue. The duel referred to took place 27 May 1798.)

Allusions to conversations possibly of 1803 but more probably of 1798 include: (1) Howe IX, 4 (W describes arguments like those later published in Hazlitt's *On the Principles of Human Action* as "what every shoemaker must have thought of." See *CEY* 238.) (2) Howe VI, 130 (W recites, or Hazlitt reads, from *The Borderers*, the six lines commencing "Action is transitory" [1539–44]. See also IX, 92.)

Hazlitt apparently alludes to the *Prel* passages concerning the Bedouin on the dromedary and the climbing of Snowden in remarks quoted Howe VII, 118, and XIX, 357n; but both the critic's own vague phrasing and the probable time of composition of the lines concerned (see Appendix V) suggest that his knowledge was secondhand.

51. July 17

On 17 July John Wordsworth, son of W and MW, is baptized at Grasmere. The godparents are STC, RW (the Rev. Joseph Sympson proxy), DW. MW is churched. In the afternoon a christening party is held [at DC]. (Grasmere PR; *EY* 396, 399; *STCNB* 1412.)[16]

On this day DW writes to CCl from Grasmere: Johnny; the christening. The Scotch tour. Payment of Lowther debt assured. (*EY* 396–97.)

On the same day W, DW write to RW: (W:) Their pleasure in the settlement of the Lowther debt. Disposal of the £1500 just paid [see 1803:47]; vexation at Montagu for applying for a £30 advance from the money [see 1803:67]. Montagu continues to owe W £450: £300 for annuity, £100 unsecured, £50 arrears owing before W's Grasmere residence. The Scotch tour. Johnny's christening. (DW:) Thanks for RW's help in Lowther affair. (*EY* 397–99.)

52. July 20

RW's accounts record receipt of £1500 cash from LdL through James Graham under this date. (RW accounts, DCP. See 1803:47. Cf *EY* 398n.)[17]

53. Probably between c July 22 and Aug 9, and about this time

Probably c 22 July W departs DC, travels to Patterdale, where he calls on or visits Charles Luff. He takes leave of Luff on 23 July; probably goes on to Eusemere, where he visits TCl, and perhaps to Keswick. He meets Sir George and Lady Beaumont for the first time, perhaps at Keswick. (*STCL* II, 957–58; *EY* 409; letter, Luff to Tom Wedgwood, 23 July 1803, UKL.)[18]

---

[16] The PR reads: "[Baptism:] July 1803. 17th John Son of William Wordsworth of Townend Grasmere."

[17] The Longman accounts (DCP) charge W £-/-/9 for "Postage" (without other comment) under this date.

[18] Luff writes to Wedgwood from Patterdale: "Wordsworth has just left me in his way to Mr Clarksons, he is become a Father, and I consider it as a very favorable event for him. Coleridge I believe is well tho I have not seen him: Wordsworth says, that

Probably about this time, but before the meeting, Sir GB arranges the purchase and presentation to W of a property at Applethwaite. (Moorman I, 586–87; *EY* 406–09; *STCL* II, 973; letter, Sir GB to W, 24 Oct 1803, DCP. See *Memorials of Coleorton* xii–xiii.)[19]

54. July 27, 29, 30

R W's accounts credit to W and DW a purchase of 2500 3 percent consols for £1315/12/6 (including £3/2/6 commission) under the date of 27 July. The accounts credit to W and DW £675, nine-twentieths share of £1500 received from LdL toward settlement of the Lowther debt to the JW Sr. estate on 20 July, under the date of 30 July. (RW accounts, DCP. See 1803:21; 1803:52. Cf *EY* 398n.)

On 27 July a letter arrives from DeQ. On 29 July W writes to DeQ in reply: Gratitude for DeQ's appreciation of his work. Cautions DeQ against ranking his work too high. His defects as a correspondent. Encourages DeQ to write or to visit him. (*EY* 399–401.)

55. Perhaps early Aug (–c 1807 May)

W borrows probably £60 from Daniel Stuart for his Scotch tour. (The sum is possibly repaid c May 1807.) (*STCL* III, 13, 17. Cf *STCL* III, 15. See 1807:36.)

56. Aug 6

STC draws on W and DW for £12/12/– by a bill on William Calvert due at one month. (RW accounts, DCP.)[20]

---

[19] The property probably consisted of two diagonally situated plots, the larger near, the smaller next to, Applethwaite Gill on the north side of the east-west road above the town (information from Mr. B. C. Jones). Sir GB comments, "[Y]ou will recollect when the business was settled, I never had seen you . . . ."

[20] RW's accounts charge payment to W under 6 Aug, but in the accounts concerned most bills seem entered about the time of date, rather than of date due. A memorandum by DW in another account notes that the "copy of Coleridge's draft is dated Augt 6. 1803." The charge is recorded on another memorandum under 9 Sept, where it is also noted that £10 of the sum was to be regarded as DW's (probably in account with JW) and the rest to be considered W's debt.

---

they are about to make the tour of Scotland accompanied by his sister Dorothy." *EY* 396–97 implies that TCl was the only member of his family now remaining at Eusemere.

57. Aug 8 or Aug 9 (–Aug 11)

On 8 or 9 Aug STC, HC, Derwent, probably Mary Stamper, travel from Keswick to DC. (They depart 11 Aug.) (*STCL* II, 960, 964, 974–75. See 1803:59.)[21]

On 8 Aug Samuel Rogers, probably accompanied by his sister, rides by DC. He possibly sees W. He probably receives an invitation to tea the next day. (*R&C* I, 9. See *DWJ* I, 198.)

On 9 Aug Samuel Rogers and probably his sister drink tea, pass the evening at DC in company with STC. STC is perhaps saddened, W amused by what they regard as the petty feelings displayed by Rogers. (*STCL* II, 964; *R&C* I, 9. See *DWJ* I, 198.)

58. Aug 10

The Ws, STC, HC, Derwent, probably Mary Stamper prepare in the afternoon to set off for Keswick. DW becomes ill, and the party remains at DC for the night. (*STCL* I, 964. See 1803:59.)

59. Aug 11 (–Aug 14, –Sept 25)

The Ws, STC, HC, Derwent, probably Mary Stamper travel from DC to Keswick with the jaunting car.[22] (MW, Johnny return 14 Aug; W, DW return 25 Sept.) (*STCL* II, 975; *Departure* IF note.)

Departure possibly reflects feelings associated with this occasion.[23]

---

[21] STC writes on 14 Aug that the group that returned to GH included "our Mary," who would have been the Cs' servant. He perhaps alludes to Cowper's *Lines to Mary Unwin* published in Jan 1803 in Hayley's *Life of Cowper*, and misquoted, probably soon after, in STC's NB (*STCNB* 1441&n) and in the W Commonplace Book (see Appendix IX). STC refers below in the same letter to Cowper's letters (*STCL* II, 965).

[22] To judge from the doubtful state of the arrangements for purchasing their jaunting car, as of probably 23 July, the vehicle had probably arrived from Devonshire only within the last few days (see *STCL* II, 957). The exact nature of the arrangements for their "aged but stout & spirited" horse, whose stoutness and spirit were too often uncreatively organized during the tour itself, remains uncertain also (see *STCL* II, 957, 975).

[23] W's placement of the poem among the *Memorials of a Tour in Scotland* from *PW* 1827 is the chief indication of a connection between these events and the work. But the lines were not written until 1811, and certainly refer esp. to the departure from Grasmere of 31 July 1811.

The party arrives at GH about an hour and a half after the departure of the Bs. W probably now learns of Sir GB's gift to him of the estate at Applethwaite [see 1803:53]. He probably receives two drawings left for him by Sir GB. (*EY* 406–09.)[24]

60. Perhaps Aug 12 or Aug 13; Aug 12; Aug 13

Perhaps on 12 or 13 Aug STC receives the documents relating to the sale of the Applethwaite estate. (*STCL* II, 973.)[25]

On 12 Aug the Ws, SFC visit Applethwaite, probably to view the property lately purchased for W by Sir GB. Possibly on this day DW copies out part of *R&I* for the Bs. (*STCL* II, 964–66.)

On 13 Aug DW completes a copy of *R&I* for the Bs. (*STCL* II, 966–70.) W walks with Samuel Rogers in a grove by Derwent Water. (*R&C* I, 10.)[26]

61. Aug 14 (–Nov 13)

On 14 Aug the Ws, Mary Stamper, SFC, HC, Derwent travel seven miles toward Grasmere. Probably at Legburthwaite W, DW, and the Cs turn back to Keswick. (*STCL* II, 975; *Memorials of a Tour in Scotland, 1803*, IF note; *DWJ* I, 195.)[27]

During the absence of W and DW, Joanna H visits MW at Grasmere, probably for much or all of the time. (She perhaps finally departs DC between 22 Oct and 13 Nov.) Probably John M visits

[24] On the drawings, of a waterfall (Lodore?), and Keswick Church, see Leslie Parris, *Landscape in Britain c. 1750–1850* (London, Tate Gallery, 1973), 72, and *Sir George Beaumont* (Leicester Museum and Art Gallery, n.d.), 65–66.

[25] STC makes no mention of the documents in his letter to the Bs of 12 Aug, but reports their arrival in his letter to the Bs of 13 Aug.

[26] In his letter to the Bs of 12 Aug STC states that DW "has copied out" the poem (*STCL* II, 965). But DW's date of "Saturday Night" (*STCL* II, 966; the copy accompanying STC's letter is in her autograph) implies either that STC was anticipating (Saturday was the 13th) or that the copy was made over two days.

[27] STC indicates that the party was to set MW seven miles on her way on to Grasmere. (*STCL* II, 975.)

for a day or two at DC during the latter part of this period. (Letter, John M to Thomas M, n.d., JFW Papers; 1803:125.)[28]

62. Aug 15 (–Sept 15, –Sept 25)

W, DW, STC set off with their jaunting car from Keswick at 11:20 AM for a tour in Scotland. (STC returns home 15 Sept; W, DW return home 25 Sept.)

They travel to Hesket Newmarket, where they pass the night at Younghusband's public house. In the evening they walk to Caldbeck Falls. (*DWJ* I, 195, 441–42; *STCNB* 1426; *STCL* II, 975n, 990, 993.) This tour is the subject of DW's *Recollections of a Tour Made in Scotland A.D. 1803.*[29]

[28] John M wrote [from Penrith]: "I should have wrote to you before now had not a visit which I have been paying at Grasmere prevented me. I spent a day or two very pleasantly Joanna is there as a companion for Mrs W. during the absence of her Husband and Miss Wordsworth who are on a tour into Scotland they are expected home soon and then Joanna returns here to be present at the races."

[29] Spellings of place names mentioned in connection with the tour have been silently corrected or modernized, normally to accord with spellings in the *Ordnance Gazetteer of Scotland*, ed. Francis H. Groome (Edinburgh, 1901), or the *Three Miles to One Inch Road Atlas of Great Britain* (W. & A. K. Johnston & G. W. Bacon Ltd., Edinburgh & London, 1963).

W later remarked to Richard Sharp that he and DW were indebted to Sharp for a "world of pleasure" on their tour. The significance of this comment (*EY* 469) remains undetermined. Some indication of Sharp's taste in Scottish scenery survives in a letter from him to Lady Holland (BM Add. MS 51,593), d. "Mark Lane. Wednesday," and endorsed "?1806" but probably written in 1807 before Lady Holland made her first tour in Scotland (see 1807:73). Sharp advises Lady Holland to obtain The Hon. Mrs. Murray's *Companion* [*and Useful Guide to the Beauties of Scotland*, etc., London, 2 vols., 1799–1803]. He particularly advises that she notice the following sights: the Tay at Dunkeld (both sides, and the falls); the rumbling bridge on the Bran; the falls of the Moness at Aberfeldie; Fascally; the torrent and falls at Blair Athol; the walk from the Castle into Glen Shira at Inverary; a fall about two miles toward Dalmally from Inverary; the road from Dalmally to Bonawe; the first six miles of Glen Coe from Ballachulish; the road from Appin House to Ballachulish; a field a quarter of a mile behind the Manse, the torrent, and the burying ground in Killin; the road through Glenalmond to Crieff; Ochtertyre; the road from Crieff to Callander by Dunira and Lochearnhead; Loch Katrine.

Sharp's recommendations seem to show a debt to Mrs. Murray, and W and DW

63. Aug 16

W, DW, STC proceed past Rose Castle to Carlisle. They visit the court, where STC startles those assembled there by calling "Dinner!" to W, in a window across the hall. They dine; walk on the city walls; visit the jailer's house, where STC, apparently on DW's urging, visits the forger Hatfield, who is this day condemned. DW converses with a former shipmate of JW's, imprisoned for debt. They travel on to Longtown; pass the night at the Graham's Arms. (*DWJ* I, 195–97; *STCNB* 1427, 1429, 1432. Cf Masson II, 178; and see also *EY* 534n.)

64. Aug 17 (–Aug 18)

W, DW, STC cross the Sark into Scotland; proceed through Springfield and Gretna Green, where they visit the churchyard; dine at Annan. They proceed to Dumfries, where they pass the night in the same inn with Samuel Rogers and his sister (whom they do not see until the next morning). (*DWJ* I, 197–99; *STCNB* 1433, 1443.)

65. Aug 18, and shortly after

On 18 Aug W, DW probably seek out and speak with Rogers and his sister for about a quarter of an hour. With a bookseller from whom DW has bought some little books for Johnny, W, DW visit Burns's house (outside) and his grave. Parting from the bookseller, they return to Burns's house and are shown inside by a servant.

W, DW, STC depart Dumfries, pass by Burns's farm Ellisland,

---

in fact visited most of the places that he mentions (the rumbling bridge on the Bran, the field back of the Manse in Killin, and Ochtertyre appear the only exceptions). But none of the places concerned is sufficiently unfrequented to reveal clear obligation, and the broader character of the Ws' itinerary does not appear to derive either from Sharp, Mrs. Murray—or, for that matter, yet another work recently published which the Ws fairly certainly knew, John Stoddart's *Remarks on Local Scenery and Manners in Scotland* (London, 1801) (see *EY* 320n). The Ws' inquiries and decisions about route along their way (see, for example, *DWJ* I, 305, 310–13, 360) show that they were not following a minutely predetermined plan. W remarks to DeQ in 1804 that the tour was "nothing more than what is commonly called the Short Tour, with considerable deviations" (*EY* 453).

DW's Journal of her second tour in Scotland (*DWJ* II, 337–97) makes a number of casual references to the 1803 tour.

reach the Brownhill inn, where they pass the night. W, DW walk out after dinner, talk of Burns, STC's family, Burns's family in terms afterwards reflected in W's *To the Sons of Burns.* (*DWJ* I, 198–202, 211; *STCNB* 1434, 1436, 1443. See also *STCNB* 1435&n; Rogers *Table-Talk* 205.)

W possibly today or shortly after composes the first two stanzas, and perhaps other parts, including lines 60–63, of *At the Grave of Burns. 1803.* (See GCL 100.)

66. Aug 19

W, DW, STC proceed through Thornhill; stop for a walk at a turnpike house about one and a half miles beyond Drumlanrig; stop later, to feed the horse, at another, where DW converses with the keeper. DW, STC eat a little; STC gives the keeper [James Stephens's] *The Crisis of the Sugar Colonies.* They travel up the valleys of the Nith and Mennock; meet three boys with honeysuckle in their hats, one carrying a fishing rod; meet other schoolchildren; pass Wanlockhead; note a strange building containing a pump for the mines. They spend the night at Mrs. Otto's inn at Leadhills, where after tea W, DW walk, look at the mansion of the Hopetouns, visit the graveyard. DW perhaps today begins a letter to MW. (*DWJ* I, 203–12; *STCNB* 1438&n, 1443. Cf *The Idle Shepherd Boys* IF note. See also *Mem* I, 447–48; *LY* II, 708.)

Possibly today W forms a conception of the verses that became *Thoughts, Suggested the Day Following.* (See GCL 101.)

67. Perhaps c Aug 19

Montagu draws on W for £30 through RW by a bill due at two months. (RW accounts, DCP.)[30]

68. Aug 20

W, DW, STC depart northward from Leadhills at 9 AM; note a group of decaying trees and a decaying cottage; are struck by the sight

---

[30] RW's accounts charge the payment to W under 19 Aug. In the account in question most entries appear to be recorded with the date of the bill rather than date due.

of a woman sitting motionless and alone in a field. W repairs the cart with assistance from a man whom they suspect to be the minister at Crawfordjohn, perhaps the Rev. John Aird. They proceed through Crawfordjohn to Douglas Mill, where DW finishes a letter to MW [see 1803:66]. They dine; W, DW sit by a mill race. All depart Douglas Mill at about 3; continue along Douglas Water to the Clyde, which they cross. W turns aside to see Corra Linn; loses his way; is taken by a boy to see the upper falls, Bonnington Linn, thence to the lower falls. In the meantime DW, STC proceed to the New Inn at Lanark, where all pass the night. DW returns to seek W, fails to find him. He rejoins her and STC at the Inn. (*DWJ* I, 212–21; *STCNB* 1438–39.)[31]

69. Aug 21

W, DW, STC visit Corra Linn; walk; see Wallace's Tower, [Bonnington] Linn; return to the inn at Lanark for dinner. Sending the cart on, they depart with a guide toward Hamilton on foot; hear a remarkably distinct echo; turn aside to visit Cartland Crags; visit Wallace's Caves. W returns to Lanark for the cart cushions. They visit Stonebyres Linn; meet crowds coming from the kirk; at 9 reach Hamilton, where they pass the night. (*DWJ* I, 221–29; *STCNB* 1449–53, 1513.)

70. Aug 22

W, DW, STC are refused admittance to the Duke of Hamilton's picture gallery; are told to return. They visit Barncluith; return to the Duke's palace, where they are again refused admittance. They depart Hamilton at 11; visit Bothwell Castle and the Douglas grounds. At 4 they reach Glasgow; go to the Saracen's Head, where they pass the night. After dining, W, DW walk to the post office, where they receive a letter, probably from MW; walk; read the letter. (*DWJ* I, 229–36; *STCNB* 1453, 1454.)

71. Aug 23

W, DW, STC visit the public laundry and bleaching ground at

---

31 W had visited Corra Linn on his journey to Scotland in 1801. See 1801:60.

Glasgow. They dine, depart Glasgow at 3; allow four boys to ride in the cart; see an impressive view of the Clyde, Dunglass Castle, Dumbarton Rock. They reach Dumbarton before dark; pass the night there. (*DWJ* I, 236–40; *STCNB* 1457–59, 1461. See also *STCL* II, 977.)

72. Aug 24–Aug 28

On 24 Aug W, DW walk to Dumbarton Rock; STC joins them. They walk up the Rock; are shown a sword reputed to have been Wallace's, and an old trout in a well. They depart Dumbarton at about 11; proceed along Leven Water to Loch Lomond; see a monument to Smollett; proceed up the west side of the lake to Luss, where they pass the night. After dinner W, DW walk, view the lake and the town; meet a travelling beggar woman and her child; drink tea at the inn. W, STC are disturbed at night by a drunken man. (*DWJ* I, 240–50; *STCNB* 1459–61; *STCL* II, 977.)

Between 24 and 28 Aug DW rests by the lake in a seat with an inscription announcing that the road was built by Colonel Lascelles's regiment. (*DWJ* I, 291–92.)

73. Aug 25

W, DW walk out in Luss; STC joins them. They are rowed out to Inchtavannach, where they walk. They depart from Luss at about 12; proceed to Tarbet, where they pass the night at the inn. They walk after dinner; decide to visit the Trossachs. (*DWJ* I, 250–58, II, 353; *STCNB* 1462–68; *STCL* II, 977.)

74. Aug 26 (–Aug 28)

W, DW, STC depart from Tarbet between 10 and 11 on their way to the Trossachs. They are rowed in a small boat to a larger. W drops their food in the water, spoiling some. They visit Rob Roy's Cave; land at Inversnaid; set off for Loch Katrine. (They return to Loch Lomond on 28 Aug.)

A Highland woman who had been a fellow passenger in the boat accompanies them part of the way to Loch Katrine. At the lake, which is discouragingly desolate, W sets off to explore; is later joined by the others. They receive directions from a courteous Highlander; reach a gentleman's house between 5 and 6; are offered accommodation; learn that their hostess, Mrs. MacFarlane, is the daughter of the man who had directed them; pass the night there. (*DWJ* I, 259–67, II, 353–54; *STCNB* 1469. See also *STCL* II, 977–78; STC, *Lay Sermons*, ed. R. J. White, Princeton, 1972, 210–11.)[32]

75. Aug 27

W, DW, STC breakfast with the MacFarlane family; are told that Rob Roy is buried in the next farm. Mrs. MacFarlane shows them the burial place of the lairds of Glengyle. They depart at 10. W, DW eat and rest at the hut of a ferryman, Gregor MacGregor, who rows them down to the Trossachs; STC walks along beside the lake. A rain comes on. W sleeps in a plaid; is awakened later by DW. MacGregor shows them many fine views. They reach the landing; find STC; view the Trossachs and Loch Achray; return to the landing; share their food with MacGregor and a young artist just arrived. All return to Mac-Gregor's hut, where they sup and pass the night. (*DWJ* I, 267–78; *STCNB* 1470–71, 1666&n; *STCL* II, 977–78.)[33]

76. Aug 28 ff

MacGregor rows W, DW, STC to the point where they first arrived at the lake. W, DW, STC set off for Loch Lomond. W, DW visit the Garrison House. The travellers meet two Highland girls, the elder of whom impresses all three as being very beautiful. All go to the

---

[32] On Mrs. MacFarlane see also *Rob Roy's Grave* IF note, and 1803:75n. (She is not the Scottish widow of whom STC speaks in the *Lay Sermons* reference; cf *ibid* 210n.) On the sights of this day see also "This Lawn a Carpet All Alive" IF note. The report of *Recollections* differs in small details from that of *STCNB*, esp. concerning the later events of the day. I have followed DW's account, which although written later is more circumstantial. STC's notes evidently reflect growing irritation with W as companion and leader (see esp. *STCNB* 1435, 1461&nn).

[33] The IF note for *Rob Roy's Grave* remarks that Mrs. MacFarlane was the source of W's information about the location of the grave; but *Recollections* implies that W's determination of the spot was finally based on advice from MacGregor as well, and not fixed before 12 Sept. STC possibly recorded the name of the artist as "Wilson" (*STCNB* 1471).

ferry house (the elder girl is the sister of the Loch Lomond ferryman); the girls attend the travellers. The travellers are rowed to Tarbet, where they pass the night. (*DWJ* I, 278–87, II, 353; *STCNB* 1471; *STCL* II, 978.)

The older girl later becomes the subject of *To a Highland Girl*.

77. Aug 29

STC, probably seizing on a suggestion of W's, determines to send his clothes on to Edinburgh and make his way thither. DW, STC set off for Arrochar; DW shelters, awaiting W. When all three are together again, they turn in to the New Inn at Arrochar. They dine but cannot obtain rooms; walk on toward Cairndow. After a little way they divide the contents of their purse, STC taking six guineas and W and DW twenty-nine. STC goes his own way. W, DW walk along Loch Long, enter Glen Croe, thence Glen Kinglas; reach Cairndow Inn, where they pass the night. (*DWJ* I, 287–93, II, 362–63; *STCL* II, 978, 994, 1010; *STCNB* 1471. See also *Sara Coleridge and Henry Reed*, ed. L. N. Broughton, Ithaca, 1937, 100; *EY* 453.)

RW pays and under this date charges to W's account £7/10/6, premium on £300 policy on Montagu's life. (Receipt, DCP; RW accounts, DCP.)

78. Aug 30

W, DW set off at 9, walk to Inverary; see the Castle; go to the inn, where they pass the night. They walk to the Duke of Argyll's pleasure grounds before dinner, and probably again shortly before sunset; walk a short way along the Aray. (*DWJ* I, 293–98.)

79. Aug 31 (and between 1820 and 1827)

W, DW set off at 9 up Glen Aray; turn aside to view a fall; stop for refreshment at Cladich; attempt unsuccessfully to hire a ferryman to take them to an island in Loch Awe; admire Ben Cruachan; overtake a man and boy; the boy rides in the cart, takes cart up a hill alone. W, DW send the man and boy on with the cart to Dunmally; walk to view Kilchurn Castle. W composes the first three lines of *Address to*

Kilchurn Castle (the poem is probably completed between 1820 and 1827). They probably meet a gentleman who advises them to travel to Glen Coe via Loch Etive. Shortly before sunset they reach the inn at Dalmally, where they pass the night. (*DWJ* I, 298–306.) [34]

80. Sept

RW's accounts charge W £7/-/-, cash payment "in the North" under this date. The debit is not included in the final accounts. (RW accounts, DCP.) [35]

81. Sept 1

W, DW arise at 6; proceed through the Pass of Brander; reach Taynuilt, where they spend the night. After refreshment walk to the mouth of the Awe; see Bonawe [see *CEY* 297; *Exc* IF note, *PW* V, 467]; are rowed across the river to the ferry; walk along the river. W arranges for a boat to take them across the lake. W and the owner of the boat inquire unsuccessfully at a farmhouse, then from a member of a crew of tinkers, about a short route to Glen Coe. They obtain the information from a hay-maker. They return down Loch Etive in a heavy rain, from this point apparently abandoning the plan of taking the short route to Glen Coe. They land at a ferry-house opposite Bonawe; are rowed across to the mouth of the river behind the ferry; return to the inn. (*DWJ* I, 306–14.)

82. Sept 2

W, DW set off at about 7 AM; proceed west along the south shore of Loch Etive; cross by ferry to the Moss of Anachree; the horse is badly frightened in the crossing. They proceed to the ferry at Loch

---

[34] W remarks in the IF note to the *Address to Kilchurn Castle* that the poem from the fourth line was finished "many years after" the first three lines, which there is no reason to doubt were, as he here says, composed "at the moment" when he first caught sight of the ruin from a small eminence by the wayside. No clue is given with the publication of these lines in G 1820 as to whether more of the verses existed then; but the poem would probably have appeared in *P* 1820 had it been complete. No date is attached in editions during W's life.

[35] The entry is endorsed, on one copy, "not charged in the account delivered."

Creran, noticing a burying ground along the way. As they wait to make the crossing, the horse again becomes frightened, runs away with the car, but causes no damage. W and the ferryman decide that the horse will swim over. They cross; proceed to Portnacroish accompanied part way by a Highlander. At Portnacroish they dine; W attempts unsuccessfully to purchase the remainder of a fine cheese, but is presented a large portion of it. They proceed along Loch Linnhe to Ballachulish, at the foot of Loch Leven. The horse becomes frightened crossing a river; W is aided by several men, for whom he afterward buys whiskey. They pass the night at the ferry-house. (*DWJ* I, 315–25. See also *LY* I, 194; 1814:68.)[36]

83. Sept 3

W, DW rise at 6; set off toward Glen Coe. The horse becomes frightened, falls partly into the lake with the cart; a man helps W to extricate him. W leads the horse to the next village, probably Glencoe, where the blacksmith makes repairs while DW converses with the women at the blacksmith's house and elsewhere. DW, probably with W, visits a quarry; they climb the hill that appears to terminate the Loch; visit a house where the Glen Coe massacre began. Having hired a man to drive the car, with DW, up Glen Coe, they set off at about 1; travel up the Glen. They part from their companion at a whiskey-house; proceed to the Kingshouse Inn, where they pass an uncomfortable night. (*DWJ* I, 336–41. See *LY* I, 194; 1814:69.)[37]

84. Sept 4

After further inconveniences W, DW set off for Loch Tulla, where they breakfast at Inveroran. They proceed to Tyndrum, which they reach at about 2; dine, learn that STC had dined there a few days previously. They proceed past Loch Dochart; pass the night at an inn

---

[36] As remarked *PW* III, 449, this visit to Loch Leven probably did not directly suggest to W *The Blind Highland Boy*. DW later came to suppose that STC had stayed at the same inn three nights previously (*DWJ* I, 325). *STCNB* 1487 f48v indicates only that STC dined there.

[37] STC had passed the night at the Kingshouse Inn on 1 Sept (*STCNB* 1482–85; cf *DWJ* I, 336).

by the Dochart about eight miles from Killin, perhaps at Luib. (*DWJ* I, 336–41.)

85. Sept 5

W, DW set off shortly after 6 to Killin, where they breakfast. They walk a little way up Glen Lochay; depart Killin at 11; travel along the south side of Loch Tay; visit the Falls of Acharn, which they view from an apartment decorated like a hermit's cell. They arrive after sunset at Kenmore, where they pass the night. (*DWJ* I, 341–45, 443.)

86. Sept 6, 8

On 6 Sept W, DW walk before breakfast in Taymouth Park; after breakfast proceed along the Tay; view the Falls of Moness; dine at Logierait. DW sees a ruinous mansion reputed to have been the palace of a king of Scotland (probably Robert III). They turn up the Tummel; are directed at twilight to a public house at Faskally. W drinks a glass of whiskey there, but they are refused beds. They continue north in the dark through the Pass of Killiecrankie; reach Blair, where they pass the night at the inn. (*DWJ* I, 345–49, 353; Samuel Lewis, *Topographical Dictionary of Scotland*, London, 1851, II, 210.)

W's trips through the Pass of Killiecrankie today and on 8 Sept probably suggest to him the sonnet *In the Pass of Killicranky* [see 1803:121].

87. Sept 7

W, DW visit the gardens and pleasure grounds at Blair Atholl before breakfast. The gardener guides them. After breakfast they set off with a guide for Loch Rannoch. They visit the Falls of the Bruar; part with their guide at a point where the road leads downward to Loch Rannoch. Eventually discouraged by the road, they decide to turn off down to the River Tummel; proceed past Loch Tummel to Faskally, where they are again refused lodgings [see 1803:86]. They meet a poor woman who allows them to sleep at her house. (*DWJ* I, 349–56, 403. See also *EY* 625–26.)

On this day RS, Mrs. S, and probably Mary Fricker Lovell arrive at GH for a visit. This event in fact commences the Ss' permanent residence at GH. (Curry I, 324; CCS II, 226; *STCL* II, 992.)

88. Sept 8

W, DW walk before breakfast to the Pass of Killiecrankie [see 1803:86], through Lady Perth's grounds, to the Falls of the Tummel, and back to Faskally. After breakfast W fetches the car; the master of their host and hostess rails at them for having lodged W and DW. They set off down the Tummel; continue down Strath Tay; arrive at Dunkeld, where they pass the night, at about 3 PM. After dining, they visit the pleasure grounds of the Duke of Atholl, where they walk to the Falls of the Bran, which they view from a mirrored room. (*DWJ* I, 356–59, 443.)

The visit to the falls helps suggest to W *Effusion. In the Pleasure-ground on the Banks of the Bran, near Dunkeld*; but see 1814:77.

89. Sept 9

W, DW are conducted by the gardener about the gardens of the Duke of Atholl. After breakfast they set off up Strathbraan; visit the Rumbling Brig; proceed through the Sma' Glen of Glenalmond and on to Crieff, where they pass the night. (*DWJ* I, 359–62.)

W's memories of the Sma' Glen probably contribute to *Glen Almain*, although W does not at this time know of the tradition that Ossian is buried there.

RW's accounts charge W £2, payment of a draft by STC in favor of William Calvert, under this date. (RW accounts, DCP.)

90. Sept 10

W, DW set off up Strath Earn; breakfast at a public house; view Dunira, the seat of Mr. Dundas; proceed to upper end of Loch Earn, where they dine. They walk about a half-mile up Glen Ogle, return southward and proceed down Strathyre past Loch Lubnaig, where they see the house of the traveller Bruce, and through the Pass of Leny to Callander, where they pass the night at the inn. (*DWJ* I, 362–65.)

91. Sept 11

W, DW set off after breakfast for the Trossachs with a boy to take the car and horse back to Callander from Loch Achray. They proceed past Loch Venachar, where they leave behind the car as planned, and thence through the Trossachs to Loch Katrine. They sit in Lady Perth's shed, walk. W climbs a hill, views the lake and river. They set off up the lake on the north side. About a quarter-mile from the MacGregors' cottage [see 1803:75; 1803:76] they meet two women walking, one of whom asks, "What! you are stepping westward?" They reach the MacGregors' cottage, where they are warmly received and pass the night. (*DWJ* I, 365–68; *STCNB* 1470; *EY* 605–06.)

The incident of the woman's query inspires *Stepping Westward*. (*Stepping Westward* note. See *DWJ* and *EY* references already cited.)

92. Sept 12

MacGregor rows W, DW across the lake to the point where DW, STC dined upon their first arrival at the lake on 26 Aug. All walk on to Inversnaid, where DW is given milk by a woman at the ferry-house; she speaks of STC, who had returned here to recover his watch on [30 Aug]. They are rowed across the lake; walk northward toward Glen Falloch. They note Pulpit Rock, which after W's 1814 visit becomes the subject of *The Brownie's Cell* [see 1814:63]. They reach Glen Falloch at about 1 or 2; after refreshment, set off eastward over the mountains; descend into Glen Gyle; pass through Mr. MacFarlane's grounds [see 1803:74; 1803:75]. MacGregor leaves them in order to fetch the boat; W, DW call at Mr. MacFarlane's house (only a servant is at home); visit the burying ground [see 1803:75], where they had been told by MacGregor that Rob Roy was buried. They row down the lake to MacGregor's cottage, where they pass the night.

The burying ground and the information they receive there, coupled with the information received 27 Aug, probably help suggest to W *Rob Roy's Grave*. (*DWJ* I, 368–78; *STCNB* 1470, 1474–75. See *Rob Roy's Grave* note.)[38]

[38] The actual burial place of Rob Roy was of course at Balquhidder (see *DNB*; *DWJ* I, 268n).

93. Sept 13

DW strolls, talks to a paralytic old woman. W, DW, MacGregor set off over the mountains northward; MacGregor turns back probably somewhere near the crest of the climb. W, DW proceed forward toward Loch Voil. W composes a stanza for the beginning of an ode (unidentified) upon "the affecting subject of those relics of human society found in that grand and solitary region."[39] At the foot of the mountain DW drinks whey; W inquires about the road; they wade the river; cross the vale; see the burial place of the MacGregors as Gregor MacGregor had wished. They walk along the north shore of Loch Voil, and into Strathyre. They stop at a public house in a village near but not in sight of Loch Lubnaig—probably Strathyre village (DC MS 43: "Strath Eger")—where they pass the night. (*DWJ* I, 378–82. Cf *HCRBW* I, 274.)

94. Sept 14

W, DW rise early; stroll to Callander, where they breakfast and recover their car and horse [see 1803:91]. They proceed through Doune and via Kincardine to Stirling, where they find no accommodations for the night. They visit the castle; buy Burns's poems in one volume. They proceed to Falkirk, where they likewise find no accommodations. They pass the night there in a private house. (*DWJ* I, 382–84. See *Yarrow Unvisited*, first line.)[40]

95. Sept 15

W, DW depart Falkirk, breakfast at Linlithgow; see the remains

[39] The subject of the evidently stanzaic ode would appear closely connected with the three blank verse lines composed on 31 Aug about Kilchurn Castle.

[40] That W and DW did not travel from Doune to Stirling via Bridge of Allan, another possible route, is implied by DW's statement that they crossed the Teith a little beyond Doune.

The volume of Burns (Dundee, 1802), which was subsequently presented by DW to Lady B on 10 Sept 1807, is presently in the Cornell Wordsworth Collection (see Cornell 2224). On the front endpaper appears a note in DW's autograph: "This book was bought at Stirling in September 1803 The price two shillings bound." The inscription is followed by a short account of the story of Tam O'Shanter differing slightly from Burns's version.

of the Palace; proceed to Edinburgh. On the way they pass an hour sitting on the bank reading Burns's poems. On reaching Edinburgh they go to the White Hart, Grassmarket, where they pass the night. They walk up to the Castle. (*DWJ* I, 384–85. See also *DWJ* II, 396.)[41]

96. Sept 16

W, DW walk to Holyrood House and on Arthur's Seat to St. Anthony's Well and Chapel; listen to the noise of the city; see the city overhung impressively by smoke; walk about the city, which interests them. At about 6 they set off for Roslin, where they probably pass the night at the inn. (*DWJ* I, 382–86.)

97. Sept 17–Sept 23

On 17 Sept W, DW arise early, walk through the Glen of Roslin past Hawthornden and on to Lasswade, where they go to the house of Walter Scott; arrive before the Scotts have arisen. They breakfast with the Scotts, remain with them till 2 PM. W probably sees the Scott's baby. Scott accompanies them back almost to Roslin; promises to meet them at Melrose two days later. Their discussion includes the subjects of *Christabel* and *The Lay of the Last Minstrel*. W shows Scott an attack on STC and RS by Tytler in the *Scots Magazine*. W, DW view the chapel at Roslin; set forward to Peebles, which they reach after dark, and where they pass the night in a public house. (*DWJ* I, 386–88; *EY* 413; *LY* I, 217.)

On the Ws' impressions of Scott, and their visits and travels with him between 17 and 23 Sept, see esp. *EY* 590–91; *LY* I, 205, 484; *STCNB* 1775&n.

On 17 Sept "When I Have Borne in Memory" is published in *MP* under the heading and title *Sonnet. No. VIII. England*, and signed "W.L.D." (See Woof *SB* 185.)[42]

[41] W appears less likely to have met David Wilkie in Edinburgh at this time than in London in 1806 (see 1806:32; cf *MY* I, 79n).

[42] The exact nature of W's introduction to Scott is unknown. A likely source is their mutual friend Stoddart. No. VI of W's 1803 *MP* political sonnets had been published on 16 Apr. No. VII was apparently omitted.

98. Sept 18

W, DW walk after breakfast to Neidpath Castle, which evokes from W on this day a first version of *Sonnet Composed at* ———— *Castle* ("Degenerate Douglas!"). In Peebles a person questions W about his nationality. W, DW proceed along the banks of the Tweed; pass the house of Lord Traquair; turn northeast from the Tweed about one and one-half or two miles from Clovenford. Probably on this day they consider the possibility of visiting the Yarrow, but decide to postpone the visit for another trip. They pass the night at Clovenford.

The decision to postpone the visit to Yarrow forms the subject of *Yarrow Unvisited*. The Tweed prompts the couplet beginning "More pensive in sunshine" quoted *DWJ* I, 393. (*DWJ* I, 388–93.)

99. Sept 19

W, DW set out along Gala Water; proceed through Galashiels to Melrose, where they breakfast. After breakfast they meet Scott, who shows them the Abbey, accompanies them to Mr. Riddel's gardens and orchards; dines with them at the inn. All pass the night at the inn, W and Scott sharing a room. (*DWJ* I, 394–95.)

100. Sept 20

Scott sets off early for Jedburgh. W, DW follow soon; breakfast in Dryburgh; visit the Abbey, where they are shown about by a crooked old woman. Rain obliges them to cancel plans to visit Kelso. They proceed directly to Jedburgh. They ford the Tweed; cross the Teviot by bridge; on reaching Jedburgh they find no room and are lodged in a private house. Their hostess and her husband later form the subject of *The Matron of Jedborough and Her Husband*. Scott sits an hour or two with W, DW; repeats part of *The Lay of the Last Minstrel*. (*DWJ* I, 395–401. See *EY* 529; *LY* I, 205.)[43]

101. Sept 21

After Scott is finished with his work at court W, DW walk with

[43] The map facing *DWJ* I, 195 incorrectly shows W and DW making a visit to Kelso. On Scott's recitation, continued 21 Sept, see Rogers *Table-Talk* 205–06n.

him and William Laidlaw up the Jed to Ferniehirst; return to Jedburgh. W, DW have dinner and wine sent in; Scott dines and sups with them; repeats more of the *Lay* [see 1803:100]. (*DWJ* I, 402–03.)

102. Sept 22

Scott and Dr. Somerville, the minister, call on W, DW after breakfast. All go to the manse, visit the church. W, DW, possibly Somerville, go into the court to hear the judge's charge. DW discovers that her hostess and her husband are from Cumberland and know Capt. and Mrs. W. Scott travels with W and DW in the car to Hawick; points out objects of interest in the Vale of Teviot. They dine and pass the night at Hawick. (*DWJ* I, 403–06.)

103. Sept 23

W, DW walk before breakfast to the top of a hill; view the Cheviots. After breakfast they part from Scott; proceed along the Teviot past Branxholme, and on to the Mosspaul Inn, where they feed the horse. They proceed to Langholm, where they arrive at 5 PM, and pass the night. After tea they walk out; see Langholm House. (*DWJ* I, 406–08; *EY* 412.)

104. Sept 24

W, DW arise early and proceed to Longtown, where they breakfast at the Graham's Arms. They view the place where Hatfield was executed [see 1803:63]; dine at Carlisle; pass the night at a village six miles south from Carlisle, probably Dalston. W repeats verses of Mickle. (*DWJ* I, 408, 443. See also *EY* 412; "Fly, Some Kind Harbinger" IF note.)

105. Sept 25; possibly between Sept 25 and Nov 21, certainly by 1806 Feb 21

W, DW breakfast at a public house; probably proceed down St. John's Vale; dine at Threlkeld; arrive home between 8 and 9. They find MW in perfect health, Joanna with her, and Johnny asleep.

"Fly, Some Kind Harbinger, to Grasmere-dale" refers to this

homecoming, and is probably partly or wholly composed this day between Dalston and Grasmere. It is fairly certainly completed by 21 Nov. (*DWJ* I, 408–09. See "Fly, Some Kind Harbinger" IF note.)[44]

106. Probably between 25 Sept and 14 Oct

W writes *To the Men of Kent. October, 1803.* (*EY* 409–11.)[45]

107. Probably between late Sept and 20 Dec

DW writes a basic version of *Recollections* through the entry for 2 Sept. (*DWJ* I, viii–ix, 439.)[46]

108. Probably late 1803 or early 1804

DW copies RC MS E. (Appendix VI.) W writes a description of a baby, probably Johnny. (DC MS 48. See Appendix V.)[47]

109. Perhaps between Oct 1 and Oct 14

W composes *Anticipation. October, 1803.* (Title; *EY* 409–11.)[48]

110. Oct 3; about this time and through early 1804

On 3 Oct W, with the majority of the men of Grasmere, goes to Ambleside to enlist for military service with the Grasmere Volunteers;

[44] The sonnet does not appear in MS M (see Appendix III), but W's IF note is precise. Cf 1803:106; 1803:117n. The lines are perhaps one of the two "little" poems which DW mentions to CCl on 21 Nov as written on subjects suggested by the tour.

[45] In a letter to Sir GB of 14 Oct the poem is said by W to be, along with *Sonnet Composed at ——— Castle* and the three lines composed upon seeing Kilchurn Castle (see 1803:79) and *Anticipation. October 1803*, to be his only work since seeing the Bs—that is, since some time between 22 July and 9 Aug.

[46] EdS's statement, *DWJ* I, ix, that DW had by 20 Dec brought her record down to "the entry for September 2" is correct. DW's reference in her first note quoted *DWJ* I, 439 from MS B is to her page 149, the conclusion of the 2 Sept entry. A memorandum inserted into DC MS Journal 12 repeats that the *Recollections* "as far as page 149" were written before the end of the year 1803.

[47] The remaining fragment of the description is brief, but notes the apparent strength of the child. Cf *EY* 399, 420, 429; also Howe XII, 303.

[48] The title in the first surviving MS (*EY* 411) is simply *Anticipation*; but there appears no reason in this case to leave out of account the evidence of the title.

meets TCl and William Smith in Ambleside; returns home at about 10. (*EY* 402–03.)

W probably refers to this time of military preparation in late 1803 and early 1804 in *Exc* VII.757–816. (See esp. *EY* 430.)

111. Oct 4

A note arrives from TCl, in which he asks to borrow W's horse for a journey to Muncaster with Smith. (*EY* 403. See 1803:110.)

112. Oct 5

"A Plain Youth, Lady, and a Simple Lover" is published, unsigned, in *MP* under the title *Translated from the Italian of Milton. Written during his Travels.* (Woof *SB* 185. See Moorman I, 571.)

113. Oct 7 (–Oct 8)

TCl arrives at DC, probably with W's horse [see 1803:111]. He stays for the night. During this evening Joanna H suffers an attack later described by DW as a "hysteric and fainting fit." (*EY* 402–04.)

114. Oct 8 (–between Oct 22 and Nov 13)

TCl departs DC after breakfast. John M brings a whiskey to carry Joanna H to Penrith, but she is too ill to leave, and John M probably takes the whiskey away. W rides to Keswick to consult Mr. Edmondson about Joanna. Edmondson sends medicine. W remains at Keswick, probably at GH, for the night. (Joanna perhaps departs between 22 Oct and 13 Nov.) (*EY* 402–04; *STCL* II, 1012.)

115. Oct 9.

DW writes to CCl: The return from the Scotch tour; TCl; Grasmere Volunteers; Joanna H and her recent illness; eviction of Thomas H from Gallow Hill; Johnny and MW; W and herself; the Scotch vs the English Lakes. (*EY* 402–05.)

W converses with STC and RS, probably at GH. W is more pleasantly impressed by RS than he expected to be. He arrives back at

DC probably after 8 PM. (*EY* 402–05, 409, 412; *STCL* II, 1011–12.
See also *STCNB* 1523n.)[49]

116. Oct 10

"I Find It Written of Simonides" is published in *MP* unsigned,
under the heading *Sonnet*. (See Woof *SB* 185; *STCL* II, 1013.)

117. Probably between Oct 14 and 1804 Mar 6; possibly by Nov 21,
esp. probably early or mid-Nov

W composes:
To a Highland Girl
Yarrow Unvisited
(*EY* 409; *DWJ* I, 283, 391; Appendix III.)[50]

118. Between Oct 14 and 1804 Mar 6; perhaps early 1804

W composes:
At Applethwaite, near Keswick
"She Was a Phantom of Delight"
(1803:117n; 1803:60; "She Was a Phantom of Delight" IF
note; Appendix III; *EY* 409. W's notes, *PELY-PW* 1850, *PW* 1836–
PW 1850.)[51]

[49] On one possible subject of conversation see *STCL* II, 1011–12.

[50] It is fairly plain that the three sonnets and the three lines on Kilchurn Castle
quoted to Sir GB on 14 Oct (*EY* 410–11) are all that W had composed by then since
early Aug; and that, although other composition, esp. of political sonnets, perhaps
occurred in later Oct, "two little poems" on subjects "suggested by the Scotch Tour"
were all that W had done "lately" as of 21 Nov. "Fly! Some Kind [Spirit]" (see
1803:105) would fit the description "little poem" nicely, and, although not copied
in MS M, is probably one of the two. (See Appendix III.) *To a Highland Girl*, which
DWJ I, 283 quotes as written "not long after our return from Scotland," and *Yarrow
Unvisited* (more simply described as written "after our return") are present in MS M,
but are not in any obvious sense "little."

[51] W is not known to have visited Applethwaite between 12 Aug 1803 and the
time that *At Applethwaite* was copied into MS M—probably about late Feb, certainly
by 6 Mar 1804—although he visited Keswick in late Nov. But the likelihood that the
poem was composed before 14 Oct is slight (see *EY* 409). W consistently dated the

119. Probably between Oct 14 and 1804 early Jan; possibly by Oct 31

W composes:
Basic version of *Lines on the Expected Invasion, 1803* ("Come Ye—Who, If [Which Heaven Avert!]") (Title and content; *EY* 409, 430; Appendix III. See 1803:110.)

October, 1803 ("One Might Believe That Natural Miseries") (Title and content; *EY* 409, 430; Appendix III.)

October, 1803 ("When, Looking on the Outward Face of Things") (Title and content; *EY* 409, 430; Appendix III.)

October, 1803 ("These Times Strike Moneyed Worldlings with Dismay") (Title and content; *EY* 409, 430; Appendix III.)[52]

120. Oct 14

W writes to Sir GB: Apologies for delay in writing to thank Sir GB for the gift of the Applethwaite estate [see 1803:53]. Chances are against W's building there; he wishes to be regarded as steward of the land. The drawings left for W by Sir GB [see 1803:59]. STC; RS. The military situation in Grasmere and Keswick. Transcriptions of *Sonnet Written at —— Castle*; *To the Men of Kent*; *Anticipation*; first three lines of *Address to Kilchurn Castle*. (*EY* 406–11.)[53]

[52] W used the title *October. 1803* consistently in MS M and the published editions from 1807 through 1850 for "One Might Believe," "When Looking," and "These Times" as well as for the *Sonnet. In the Pass of Killicranky.* The general similarity in tone and content of these works to *To the Men of Kent* and *Anticipation*, which were certainly composed by 14 Oct, makes a date not long after those sonnets likely. It seems improbable in any case that W would have composed in the spirit reflected in these verses at a time when the family had "given over even thinking about Invasion," as was the case on 15 Jan 1804 (*EY* 430).

[53] On STC's statement of this day that W "has made a Beginning to his Recluse" (*STCL* II, 1012–13; cf *STCNB* 1546) see Appendix VI.

poem 1804 from its publication in 1842, and the longer period is perhaps a safer suggestion. W likewise dated "She Was a Phantom of Delight" 1804 *PW* 1836–*PW* 1850. In the IF note he records that the poem derived from *To a Highland Girl* (see 1803:117). Evidence is so obscure as to justify deference to W's own dates.

121. Probably between Oct 14 and Oct 31

W composes *Sonnet. In the Pass of Killicranky. October, 1803.* (Title; *EY* 409, 437–38.)[54]

122. Perhaps c mid-Oct, certainly by Oct 24; between Oct 27 and Dec 14, 1804 Mar 5

Perhaps c mid-Oct, but certainly by 24 Oct, William Hazlitt returns to the area of Keswick [see 1803:48]. At some time between 27 Oct and 14 Dec he departs precipitately from the Lake District, probably fleeing vengeful local reaction to his behavior toward a young woman. W probably assists in the escape, perhaps taking Hazlitt in at midnight and giving him clothes and money (between £3 and £5). Among the items that Hazlitt leaves behind him somewhere is a sketch of HC which is in the Ws' possession by 5 Mar 1804. (*STCNB* 1610, 1618; *EY* 446–47; *HCRBW* I, 169–70; *MWL* 24; Haydon *Diary* II, 469–70; *Minnow* 64; Herschel Baker, *William Hazlitt*, Cambridge, Mass., 1962, 136–39; *TLS* 1968, 789, 825, 928, 945, 997, 1062.)[55]

[54] W includes a copy of the poem in his letter to Wrangham of between late Jan and 11 Feb 1804 along with *To the Men of Kent* and *Anticipation*, saying that he had earlier sent them to Sir GB, who had advised him of his intention of sending them to the newspapers. It seems fairly certain that W was thinking of his letter to Sir GB of 14 Oct, which included a permission for publication of *To the Men of Kent* and *Anticipation*, but did not in fact contain a copy of *In the Pass*, which was probably not yet written (*EY* 409). W's comment, however, encourages conjecture that the sonnet was written not much later. The copy in MS M is entitled "October 1803."

[55] STC sat for Hazlitt again (see 1803:48) (*STCNB* 1619); this portrait was perhaps that commissioned by Sir GB (see CCS II, 238). The July portrait might have been so commissioned (if, indeed, any portrait was), but Sir GB's admiration for STC would have been a very recent development (see Farington II, 172). References by W and DW in 1805 to what was apparently the first of Hazlitt's two portraits of STC indicate that that portrait was then still in existence (*EY* 594, 600) although not in W's possession (cf *EY* 447n). Whether the second was ever completed is unknown. A "rude sketch" of STC, possibly made together with that of HC, was perhaps given to SH (see *STCL* II, 1025).

RS was apparently also an accomplice in Hazlitt's escape: see Curry II, 92–93.

123. Oct 16

W, DW write to RW: (DW:) The Scotch tour; the family; letter from Cooke asking for loan on good security. (W:) Is willing to loan money to Cooke if RW concurs. W owes £60 to Cooke; would like RW to repay but is concerned at possible loss of use of the debt as a spur to Montagu.

W also writes to Cooke. (*EY* 414–16.)[56]

W writes to Walter Scott: The return from Scotland; STC; RS, who is to review Tytler, Bayley. Invitation to Grasmere. (*EY* 411–14.)[57]

W perhaps goes to Ambleside to be mustered and put on military apparel. (*EY* 409. See 1803:110.)

124. Oct 17

"Laura, Farewell My Laura," translation from the Italian of Metastasio, is published, unsigned, in *MP*. (See Woof *SB* 185–86.)

125. Perhaps c but by Oct 22; between Oct 22 and Nov 13; probably Oct 22–Oct 23

Thomas H perhaps visits at DC for an unknown length of time between c but by 22 Oct and 13 Nov; he is probably present on 22 Oct, and probably departs between that date and 13 Nov. On his departure he perhaps takes with him Joanna H. (*STCNB* 1607–08&nn. See 1803:114; *EY* 418.)

STC visits DC, probably arriving on 22 Oct and departing next day. While there he hears from Thomas H that he has taken Hazel's farm Park House, near Ullswater. (*STCNB* 1607–08&nn; *EY* 417.)

On 22 Oct "To the Grove, the Meadow, the Well," translation from the Italian of Metastasio, is published, unsigned, in *MP*. (See Woof *SB* 186–87; *PW* IV, 369.)

RW's accounts charge W £30, cash payment for a draft by

---

56 On repayment of the debt to Cooke see 1804:38; 1804:67.

57 RS's review was published in the *Annual Review for 1803* (1804), 546–52. (See also Warter I, 245, 254.)

Montagu due at two months, under 22 Oct. (RW accounts, DCP. See 1803: 51.)[58]

126. c Oct 26; Oct 26

W probably visits Keswick c 26 Oct, and is probably there on 26 Oct. On that afternoon W, STC, Hazlitt engage in a dispute disturbing to STC: W and Hazlitt seem to him to speak irreverently of the Divine Wisdom; W to speak of the pedantry of Ray, Durham, Paley. (*STCNB* 1614–16; 1803:48.)

127. Oct 28

Anticipation is published in the *Courier*, under the heading "*Anticipation.—A Sonnet. By Wm. Wordsworth, Esq.*" The poem was probably sent to the *Courier* by Sir GB. (See Woof *SB* 187; *EY* 410–11.)

128. Nov 2

"The Swallow, That Hath Lost," translation from the Italian of Metastasio, is published, unsigned, in *MP*. (See Woof *SB* 187.)

HC, Derwent, and SC are baptized. W, DW do not attend the ceremony. (*EY* 418.)[59]

129. Nov 13

DW writes to CCl: CCl's health; Dr. Beddoes. Thomas H has taken Hazel's farm above Dalemain. Joanna H is recovered; is at Mrs.

---

[58] W appears to have agreed to the loan even though Montagu had earlier irritated him by making an unauthorized application for it to RW (see *EY* 398–99). The upshot was evidently displeasing to W also: of this item, originally omitted from the final account between W and RW, 1816, W writes in a note on one account copy, "It is now admitted into the general accounts though Mr W never received the money from Montagu." See 1814:31.

[59] DW on Sunday 13 Nov records the event as having taken place "last Tuesday," implying a date of 1 Nov; but the date of 2 Nov recorded in the Crosthwaite PR (see *EY* 418n) is confirmed by a marginal note, addressed to HC, in the Folger copy of Anderson's *British Poets* (II, 665–68) including the statement "Today thou art to be christened," and dated "Greta Hall, Keswick, Wed. morning, ½ past 3, Nov 2. 1803.—"

Addison's [at Penrith]. Johnny; SC; Grasmere; a cat obtained to fight rats. DW is writing her recollections of the Scotch tour. (*EY* 416–21.)

130. Nov 15

W's "Gentle Zephyr," translation from the Italian of Metastasio, is published, unsigned, in *MP*. (See Woof *SB* 188.)

131. Nov 20

TCl calls at DC at dinnertime; dines; departs at 4:30. (*EY* 422.)

132. Nov 21

DW writes to CCl: A visit from TCl [see 1803:131]; Johnny. W has written two little poems on subjects suggested by the tour in Scotland [see 1803:117]. (*EY* 422–23.)

133. Nov 24 (–probably Nov 26, possibly Nov 27)

W goes to Keswick to see STC, drawn by news of STC's ill health. (He returns to DC probably on 26 Nov, possibly 27 Nov.) (*STCL* II, 1019–20; 1803:134.)

134. Probably Nov 26, possibly Nov 27

John Thelwall dines at DC with DW and MW. W arrives from Keswick as Thelwall is about to depart. After some delay Thelwall sets off to Keswick. (*STCNB* 1690, 1696; *STCL* II, 1018, 1019; letter, Thelwall to Mrs. Thelwall, 29 Nov ff, 1803, PML. Cf *EY* 431; Curry I, 336.)[60]

---

[60] On "Tuesday 29th Nov," Thelwall wrote to his wife from Penrith that he stayed at Keswick twenty-four hours longer than he had intended. His comments make plain that he arrived at Keswick during an evening. *STCNB* 1690 shows Thelwall with STC on 28 Nov (STC misdates Monday as the 29th), and W was almost certainly with STC on the night of 25 Nov. Thelwall can hardly have arrived at Keswick, remained significantly longer than twenty-four hours, then travelled to Penrith, all by the 29th unless he had reached Keswick by the night of 27 Nov. The night of the 26th looks more probable.

135. Probably Dec 9

DW writes to STC: Colds; a parcel (probably sent by STC) has not arrived. W would prefer to pay nothing toward STC's projected trip to Madeira until next summer when JW returns. Bayley [see 1803:123]. (*EY* 423&n, 426.)

136. Dec 12

W's "Oh! Bless'd All Bliss above," translation from the Italian of Metastasio, is published, unsigned, in *MP*. (See Woof *SB* 188.)

W, DW write to RW: (DW:) Seeks information about money owing to her from Lowther payment or JW's sales; asks RW to discharge a £10 draft which she will make on him next week, due in one month; asks RW to send Peggy Marsh £1. (W:) Has received application for £10/15/3½ from the Rev. James Wood for university expenses [see *CEY* 133], asks RW to pay. Sir GB's gift of the Applethwaite estate. (*EY* 426–28.)[61]

137. Perhaps between Dec 18 and Dec 25

DW draws on RW for £10 by a bill in favor of J. Sympson. (*EY* 426. RW accounts, DCP.)[62]

138. Dec 20–1804 Jan 14 (–Feb 3)

STC and Derwent arrive at DC in a post chaise. STC remains, usually in ill health, until 14 Jan 1804. (Derwent returns home 3 Feb.) W perhaps at this time promises to lend £100 to STC. (*STCNB* 1761, 1843; *STCL* II, 1035, 1040, 1049; *EY* 441, 455–57. Cf *EY* 424.)[63]

[61] RW's accounts charge the Ws £1 for cash sent to Mrs. Marsh under the date of 13 Feb 1804.

[62] RW's accounts charge the sum to DW under the date of 13 Feb, and in an early copy, 18 Jan. See also *EY* 426n. DW's remarks *EY* 426 do not leave much doubt about the time of her draft.

[63] W made out a promissory note to Sotheby on 12 Mar 1804 for £100 and legal interest (5 percent) (see *STCL* II, 1049, 1059, 1086–87) at ten months. The sum was probably repaid to Sotheby on or shortly after 10 May 1806 (see 1806:34) and repaid to W between 3 and 24 Nov 1807 (*STCL* III, 34–35, 39). See also 1804:36; 1805:30; 1805:40.

On this visit see esp. *STCNB* 1761–1842, which probably in large part refers to conversations, thoughts, and other events during STC's visit at Grasmere; also see *STCL* II, 1025–50.

139. Dec 31

W, STC walk up Greenhead Ghyll; visit the sheepfold, where W reads *Michael* to STC. (*STCNB* 1776–82. See also *STCNB* 1783–85.)

1804

[On writings of W possibly of this year see below and GCL 1–4, 6, 7, 41, 54, 55, 59, 69, 72–75, 92, 94, 95, 97–99, 104–06, 109–11, 113–29.]

1. Perhaps c early 1804

W expresses to CL an interest in acquiring important old books, and in effect requests CL's aid in building up a library of older writers, esp. of poets and dramatists. (*LL* I, 369–70, 377–78.)

2. Early this year–mid-1805, esp. by 1804 Mar 6; 1805 June 3; by 1806 early Sept

The period early this year–mid-1805 appears to be that in which W may be most clearly documented as carefully considering the project of a long narrative poem. He arranges the plan of such a poem by 6 Mar 1804. On 3 June 1805 he states that the envisioned narrative poem is to be of the "Epic kind." The plan for such a work is abandoned by early Sept 1806. (*EY* 436, 454, 594; Appendix VI. See also esp. *Prel* I.116–271; Appendix V.)[1]

---

[1] How early in W's maturity the bare intention to write such a poem may have been present in his mind remains uncertain, the answer to the problem depending in part on the ambiguous question of whether the "Was it for this" openings of *Prel* MSS U and V were originally conceived as following an expression, like that of *Prel* I.116–271, of inability to proceed in either the writing of verse on a heroic subject or the writing of "some philosophic song"—and, of course, the question of when *Prel* I.55–271 was written. The period here noted is that in which the plan seems to have stood at its most definite.

3. Perhaps early this year, by Mar 6; between 1804 late Mar and 1806 early Dec

Perhaps early this year, by 6 Mar, W composes most of the last seven stanzas of *Ode. Intimations of Immortality*, completing the MS M version of the poem. Perhaps at the same time W composes *To H. C.* (*Ode* IF note; 1802:76; 1802:167; Appendix III.)

Perhaps during the same period W composes *Ode to Duty*, except for the first stanza, in the form of MS M copy. (Appendix V; Appendix VII. See 1804:44.)[2]

4. Jan 4

W reads *Prel* II to STC in what *STCNB* describes as "the highest & outermost part of Grasmere." (*STCNB* 1801.)[3]

5. Jan 6

STC, probably W, and perhaps others walk into Easedale and back towards Rydal. (*STCNB* 1812.)[4]

6. Probably Jan 11

W, STC walk by Grasmere Lake; see a reflection of mountains in the water with flakes of ice which STC supposes the reflection of clouds. (*STCNB* 1836.)[5]

[2] *STCNB* 1830n reasonably suggests that *STCNB* 1830, dating from early Jan 1804, perhaps refers to the *Ode* or the *Ode to Duty*.

The connection made by Moorman II, 4–5, between the *Ode to Duty* and STC's early Jan speculations about duty (see esp. *STCNB* 1832–33) is attractive, as is the suggestion by the same authority of a debt of the third stanza of the *Ode* to STC's letter to the Ws of 8 Feb (see *STCL* II, 1060)—although a possibility remains that the debt was in the other direction (cf *STCL* I, 334). The first stanza was not completed in time for inclusion in MS M, although space is carefully marked out for it in the MS. It appears in the basic copy for *P2V*, and thus was probably composed by early Dec 1806 (see Appendix VII).

[3] The location is not clear from STC's description. Moorman II, 1, suggests Grisedale Tarn. Easedale, Far Easedale, and Greenhead Ghyll are other possibilities.

[4] The date recorded in *STCNB* is "Friday, Jan. 5," but the Friday in question would have been the 6th.

[5] STC's date is simply "Wednesday morning," but the placement of the entry in the NB leaves little doubt of the day.

7. Possibly between c Jan 14 and c Jan 1805

W writes the fragment "Along the Mazes of This Song." (GCL 114.)

8. Probably between c Jan 14 and Apr 29, and in part before c Mar 12

W writes lines in MS WW used for *Prel* VI, VIII, XIII. (For detailed description see Appendix V.)

9. Probably between c Jan 14 and Feb 13, c Mar 12, Mar 18

Probably between c 14 Jan and 18 Mar W composes *Prel* I.55–271 and *Prel* III–V, subsuming various passages composed from 1798 onward. *Prel* I.55–271 is fairly certainly, and *Prel* III probably largely completed by 13 Feb. W probably composes c 1500 lines toward the poem between c 14 Jan and c 12 Mar. (Appendix V.)[6]

10. Jan 14 (–1806 Oct 25, 26)

STC departs Grasmere for a visit to Liverpool, London, the West Country, and travel to and residence in Malta and Italy. (He next returns to the Lake District 25 Oct 1806; next meets the Ws 26 Oct 1806.) (*EY* 428–29; *STCNB* 1843–49; *STCL* II, 1034, 1040.)

11. Jan 15

DW writes to CCl: STC's departure; life at DC, esp. with the baby; CCl. (*EY* 428–31.)

---

[6] Worth notice here is Farington's record of Sir GB's remarks of 21 Mar 1804 (Farington II, 207): "Wordsworth continues in Westmorland. He has chosen to forego professional views, preferring retirement upon something more than £100 a year with the gratification of indulging his imaginations to any worldly advantages. He has long been what He calls idle, *not writing*, finding that it affected His nerves; but He is now engaged on a more considerable work than any of his former ones which He calls '*The Recluse*' ... Sir George said He was infinitely indebted to Wordsworth for the good He had recd. from His poetry which had benefitted Him more, Had more purified His mind, than any Sermons had done."

12. Mid- or late Jan

W writes to John Thelwall: Answers questions concerning a review of *Thalaba* [by Jeffrey] containing a covert attack on W; Thelwall's pamphlet [*A Letter to Francis Jeffrey*, published in Edinburgh on 7 Jan]; urges Thelwall to follow up attack; W reads no periodical publication except *MP*; ignorance of a "school"; W's own metrics. (*EY* 431–35.)[7]

13. Jan 21, 26

RW's accounts charge W £10/15/– for a draft by James [Wood]. (RW accounts, DCP. See 1803:136; *CEY* 133.)[8]

14. Probably between late Jan and Feb 13

W writes to Francis Wrangham: Thanks Wrangham for letter and songs, a former letter, and a poem. *Prel.* W meditates a philosophical poem and a narrative poem. Johnny. Transcriptions of *To the Men of Kent, Sonnet. In the Pass of Killicranky, Anticipation.* STC. (*EY* 435–39.)[9]

---

[7] W gives Thelwall "joy of [his] reception at Glasgow," where he arrived on 17 Jan and began lecturing on 19 Jan. While it hardly seems sure that he is anticipating (see *EY* 431n), W probably wrote at a time near these dates.

[8] The charge is recorded under the different dates in different accounts.

[9] W states that STC is in London. STC arrived in London 24 Jan, was at Dunmow 7–17 Feb, and departed for Portsmouth 27 Mar (*STCL* II, 1037–38, 1058, 1060, 1066, 1109–10; Farington II, 207). W also speaks of STC's plan to go to Madeira (*EY* 437). STC was still, on 15 Jan, after leaving DC, speaking of Madeira as his destination (*STCL* II, 1034–35). W would probably have heard by 13 Feb, from STC's letter of 8 Feb (postmarked 10 Feb) of STC's decision to try to go to Malta instead. There is no reason to suppose that W knew the exact dates of STC's presence in London, or, on the other hand, that he would have regarded a visit to Dunmow as more than an incidental side trip (cf *EY* 435n). DW remarked on 13 Feb, however, that STC was in London and "tolerably well" (*EY* 441), a phrase which perhaps implies that STC's letter of 8 Feb had arrived. STC states plainly in that letter an intention of staying at Dunmow till "Tuesday Morning"—Feb 14th.

15. Feb–Apr

The Ws make a determined attempt at account-keeping, esp. concerning financial arrangements with the Cs. (DC MS 26.)[10]

[10] How far the accounts surviving in the Commonplace Book (see Appendix IX) are typical of those usually kept by the Ws about this time is uncertain. Apart from entries concerning butter and milk and the Montagu debt, the records seem to result from an effort to sort out matters between the DC and GH households in connection with STC's departure:

[p.1] February 1st. 1804. Mrs. C, the account being settled owes us. 1 £.9s.2d.½
    N.B. The London cotton not charged.
    Sent Mrs. C a Draft for £20 February.10th
    Received in return 5 £.5s
    Received. From Coleridge for [?cradle] 0 15
[p.2] February 18th paid for Butter 9d.
        April 30th. Began to get milk from F. Baty's—a 1d in the Evening
[p.3] account being settled. 1 £.9s.2½d
    By Draft—　　　　　　　　　　14 15-　-
[p. 4] April 15th. Received from Montagu. a Letter stating that he owed us (beside the Annuity) 160 £. namely. 100 £ lent, & 60 £ arrears.
    By this same letter received 5 £.
    A week before　　　　5.
    NB. 13 £ became due at Lady Day [25 Mar], and 8 £ was left yet unpaid of the sum Due at Christmas so 11 pounds yet due exclusive of the 160

It would appear that the 15s received from STC, apparently after 10 Feb, was not applicable to SFC's account, which was perhaps settled about Apr. The following notes in the hand of DW are found on a loose memorandum in the Commonplace Book:
[*on one side*:] I will set down the Sum Total again here to save you trouble
Mrs C's debt to us. 16 £.19s.2½d
[*beneath a line*:] [Received from Mr *cancelled*]
[*on other side*:] The Sums we have set down as having received from you are these . .
　　　　　　　　　　　　　　　　　5.　5.
　　　　　　　　　　　　　　　　　£5.　5
　　　　a note which you borrowed from
　　　　Mrs Southey when we were all
　　　　[*rest torn off except*:]　　　　　　1.　1

The total of 15s, £14/15, and £1/9/2½ is £16.19.2½. The loose memorandum was perhaps made out for STC at a time when the 15s was owed additionally, after 10 Feb. "The sum Due at Christmas" mentioned in the Montagu account (on which see esp. 1804:58; 1804:59) evidently refers to the regular quarterly payment (see *EY* 398) rather than the loan recorded by RW on 22 Oct 1803, which seems to have been ignored by all parties until the time of the final accounting between W, DW, and RW (see 1803:125).

16. Probably Feb 2, and perhaps a day or so following

DW resumes work on her *Recollections* [see 1803:107]; writes perhaps some part of the entries for 3–5 Sept. (*DWJ* I, ix, 439; *EY* 463; 1803:107.)[11]

17. Probably Feb 3

Derwent C departs DC, where he had arrived 20 Dec, with Sally Ashburner; returns to GH. (*EY* 441.)

18. Feb 10

On 10 Feb DW draws on RW for £20 by a bill in favor of Michael Dawson.

On the same day probably DW or W sends a draft for £20 to SFC, who shortly after returns £5.

On the same day DW writes to RW: W needs to draw, within a fortnight, for £20, due in one month to John Green; the £20 draft on Dawson. She has heard that one of her Uncle Cookson's girls is dead. W has no plan to build at Applethwaite. Her own health good. Henry Airey reported lost off the coast of Norway. (*EY* 438–39; 1804:15n.)[12]

---

[11] The probable imminence of the task of preparing MS M and its duplicate make it unlikely that DW worked long on the *Recollections* at this time. She was apparently writing again c 29 Mar, but had later advanced no further than the entry for 5 Sept 1803 when she resumed work "after a long pause" on 23 June. She had fairly certainly written through 2 Sept before 2 Feb (see 1803:107).

[12] RW's accounts charge payment of the Dawson bill to DW under 13 Mar, and the Green bill for £20 under 21 Mar (RW accounts, DCP; see *EY* 439n). RW's accounts record payment of the SFC draft under 14 Feb, as due at two months, in an account which generally seems to note charges under original date of draft rather than date due. In memoranda relating to an evident charge, under 13 Mar, of a £20 draft in favor of STC (another account records payment on 17 Apr, after STC's departure from England but of course about two months after 14 Feb) STC is said to have drawn for the sum but that it is to be regarded as coming from JW, as allowance to DW (see *EY* 337–38). Available information does not indicate whether this sum was identical with that sent to SFC. In a memorandum by DW covering sums drawn between late summer 1803 and early 1804 the only Coleridge drafts noted are that to Calvert of 6 Aug 1803 and "Mr. W. W. Mrs. Coleridge—20–."

19. Probably between but after Feb 10 and c Feb 28

W draws on RW for £20 by a bill in favor of John Green. (RW accounts, DCP. See 1804:18&n.)

20. Feb 13

DW writes to CCl: The mild winter; W composing rapidly [on *Prel*]; Johnny; Derwent; the Ss and Mrs. Lovell settled at Keswick, with the two families in the large house [see 1803:87]. (*EY* 440–41.)

21. Perhaps Feb 15

W draws on RW for £20 by bill in favor of Mr. Benson. (RW accounts, DCP.)[13]

22. Probably between mid-Feb and Mar 6, by perhaps Mar 13

Probably between mid-Feb and 6 Mar, DW, MW make a copy, as nearly complete as possible, of W's unpublished shorter poems for STC. This copy is now DC MS 44. (Appendix III; Appendix V.)[14]

23. Perhaps Feb 19–Feb 21

TCl visits at DC. He probably departs 21 Feb. (*EY* 443&n.)[15]

24. Probably Feb 20–Feb 24

DW is very ill. (*EY* 443.)

[13] RW's accounts charge the sum to W under the date of 15 Feb. In the account in question most bills seem to be recorded under date of draft rather than date due. The sum is elsewhere charged under 18 Mar, perhaps about the date due.

[14] On the MS M copy of *PB* see 1802:38.

[15] As noted *EY* 443n, which apparently draws on CCS II, 263, RS wrote on 19 Feb that TCl was "piping hot from Bristol" and that he left Keswick on the 19th. DW told STC on 6 Mar that TCl was "with us" on "this day fortnight"—presumably 21 Feb. It is probable, however, that RS stopped at DC on 21 Feb and took TCl on with him that day to the Lloyds': RS wrote to Thomas S on "Wednesday 1 Mar 1804" (BM Add MS 30, 928, fols. 41–42)—the Wednesday was in fact 29 Feb—that he had gone on Tuesday to Grasmere, found TCl, and proceeded with him to the Lloyds', "perambulated that neighborhood" on Wednesday, and proceeded to Ullswater on Thursday.

25. Probably Feb 21

RS probably calls at DC; takes TCl on with him to the Lloyds'. (See 1804:23n.)

26. Feb 22

DW writes to Samuel Ferguson: A local girl to carry the letter to America. She has written to Mr. Griffith; suggests that he obtain that letter. (*EY* 442–43.)

27. Feb 26, 27

DW writes to CCl: (26 Feb:) TCl's visit [see 1804:23]; CCl's health; Johnny; MW's and her health. The death of one of Uncle Cookson's children; symptoms of DW's recent illness. W writing down verses composed in his walk. (27 Feb:) The Thomas H household to remove to PH in five weeks. (*EY* 443–46.)[16]

28. Feb 29 or Mar 1; probably c early Mar

On 29 Feb or 1 Mar W finishes what he regards on 6 Mar as another book of *Prel*, 650 lines. (See Appendix V.) Probably c early Mar RC MS E$_2$ is written. (Appendix VI.)

29. Perhaps c Mar–Apr; possibly about this time

W writes a letter, perhaps to a friend, concerning the education of a daughter. (*MY* I, 284–88.)[17]

---

[16] The appearance of the letter (BM) implies that all of the postscript (*EY* 445–46) was written on the "Monday morning" of the last sentence.

[17] The paper of the MS of the letter, DCP MS Prose 3, watermarked with a crowned Britannia medallion dated 1802 and countermarked C HALE, is the paper of at least sixteen letters written by W or DW between 13 Nov 1803 and 27 Dec 1804 (*EY* nos. 196, 197, 198, 201, 202, 203, 207, 213, 223, 225, 226, 227, 235, 236, 237, 238) as well as of most of MS M.

W's abiding concern in the subject of formal education was no doubt intensified about 1804 by his preoccupation with *Prel* (his interest in William Betty, the "young Roscius," is a feature of his correspondence with Sir GB later in this and the following year), and perhaps by little Johnny's development (see 1804:36; 1804:57); but the phrasing of the conclusion of the letter appears markedly similar to that of the description of the prodigy in *Prel* V.294–349. Mrs. Moorman has suggested to me the likely possibility that the addressee is a fictional convenience.

He possibly about this time writes a psychological analysis of the daughter of a blind man (perhaps Idonea-Matilda). (See Appendix VI.)

30. Mar 4

W discovers an exciting stretch of brook scenery above Rydal. (*EY* 446–47.)

31. Mar 5

W writes to William Hazlitt: Comment and argument about Hazlitt's sketch of HC [see 1803:122]; will send it if Hazlitt thinks this will be of advantage. Hazlitt's clothes and box [apparently at Keswick]. Fawcett's death [see *CEY* 117n, 138]. *Prel.* Discovery of exciting stretch of scenery above Rydal. (*EY* 446–47.)

32. Possibly between c but by Mar 6 and c Mar 12; probably between Mar 6 and c Mar 12, Mar 18; perhaps between Mar 6 and June 13

Possibly between c but by 6 Mar and c 12 Mar MS M, *RC*, and *Prel* I–III.34 (1805), is prepared. Probably between 6 Mar and c 12 Mar W organizes *Prel* III–V in form of MS M. Probably by 18 Mar the Ws complete copies of *RC* and *Prel* I–V for STC (MS M) and a transcription of the poems in MS M for themselves.

Perhaps between 6 Mar and 13 June W writes *Prel* XIII.154–84 as MS W. (Appendix V.)

33. Mar 6, 7

On 6 Mar W, DW walk for four hours in the morning, see the stretch of scenery above Rydal that W had found on 4 Mar. DW, MW attend sale of Borwick's possessions. W reads *Hamlet*. (*EY* 448–49.)

On the same day W writes to DeQ: Apologies for delay in replying to DeQ's last letter, which arrived before the Ws' tour in Scotland. The tour; Oxford; his poetry; *The Recluse*. Has arranged the plan of a narrative poem; Peter Bayley. (*EY* 452–55.)

On 6, 7 Mar W, DW, MW write to STC: (DW commences the letter at 7:30 PM:) All of the smaller poems transcribed for STC; they have begun copying [*Prel*] and the *Pedlar*. *Prel.* (W:) DW; *Prel*;

anxiety to have STC's notes for *The Recluse*. (MW, probably writing on 7 Mar:) Is on way to look at the scenery above Rydal with W. (*EY* 448–52.)[18]

34. Probably c but by Mar 10

W writes to STC concerning his loan to STC of £100 [see 1803: 138] (letter not known to survive). (*STCL* II, 1086–87.)

35. Probably c Mar 12-late Mar, after Mar 24

W interrupts intensive efforts toward composition of *Prel*. He probably resumes in late Mar, after 24 Mar. (Appendix V.)

36. Mar 12

W writes to William Sotheby: Sends promissory note for £100 advanced to STC by Sotheby, payable with interest at ten months [see 1803:138n]. Thanks Sotheby for kindness shown him and DW on their way to France [see 1802:201]. *Prel*. (*EY* 455–57.)

DW this day makes an entry in the Commonplace Book concerning Johnny's speech since four months old. (DC MS 26. See Appendix IX.)[19]

37. Perhaps between Mar 13 and Mar 18

Portions of MS M possibly up to *Prel* III.34, or through IV, but not inclusive of V, are sent off to STC. (Appendix V. See Appendix III.)

---

[18] W cannot have had much time for letter-writing on the morning of 6 Mar. He likewise cannot have worked all evening to finish his letter to DeQ (*EY* 449–51, esp. 451); and his comments to STC are a postscript to the long letter begun by DW at 7:30 that evening. The remarks to STC thus almost certainly follow those to DeQ, and were possibly not even written that same evening. The letter, directed to STC at "No 16 Abingdon Street," is fairly certainly the one received by STC on 12 or 13 Mar (*STCL* II, 1087, 1094–95).

[19] Johnny's speech as recorded by DW apparently consisted on 12 Mar in sounds like "man man ma. Dad dad. da pap pap" that do not seem sufficiently remarkable for further quotation here.

38. Mar 17, 21

RW's accounts charge W £25, payment to Richard Cooke, under these dates. (RW accounts, DCP.)[20]

39. c but by Mar 18

The conclusion of MS M, probably including *Prel* V, is sent off to STC. (Appendix V. Cf Moorman II, 10n.)

40. Mar 19

W writes to DeQ: His earlier letter to DeQ [see 1804:33] possibly would have failed to reach DeQ. Thanks DeQ for his high opinions of his poetry. (*EY* 457–58.)

41. Probably c Mar 23

W walks to Rydal, receives letter from STC; is shocked to read of STC's recent severe illness [see *STCL* II, 1097–99] and disturbed that he does not have STC's notes for *Recluse*. (*EY* 462–65.)

42. Mar [25]

DW writes to CCl: MW and she have been making a copy of STC's poem for W [see Appendix V]; W's recent work on *Prel*; the difficulty of the MSS. STC; SFC and children to visit Grasmere. Johnny; DW's health; Dr. Beddoes. (*EY* 458–62.)

43. Probably between late Mar and 1807 early Apr; possibly by end of year 1804

W composes "I Wandered Lonely as a Cloud." (IF note; Appendix III; Appendix VIII.)[21]

44. Probably between late Mar and 1806 early Dec

W composes a first stanza for the *Ode to Duty* [see 1804:3]. (Appendix V; Appendix VII.)

[20] Payment is noted under the different dates in different accounts. The sum is a partial repayment of a debt of W to Cooke for £60 (see 1803:123).

[21] The IF note dates the poem, which does not appear in MS M, 1804.

45. Perhaps between late Mar and June 13; perhaps between late Mar and Apr 29; probably late Mar, by Mar 29

Perhaps between late Mar and 13 June W composes:
Prel VIII.75–740 as MS X [see GCL 1]
Prel VIII.736–38, 742–51 as MS X
Perhaps portions of *Prel* IX, X
Perhaps a large part of *Prel* XI, including lines toward XI in MS W [see GCL 1]
(Appendix V.)
Perhaps between late Mar and Apr 29 W organizes *Prel* VI. (Appendix V. See 1804:51.)
Probably late Mar, by Mar 29, W composes *Prel* VI.246–331. (Appendix V.)

46. Perhaps c, certainly by, Mar 24

A door is built from the stairway into the orchard at DC, perhaps following the advice, or even at the expense, of CCl and her sister. (*EY* 462.)

47. Probably c but by Mar 26

STC leaves [*Prel* I, II] at Grosvenor Square for Lady B to read. (*STCL* II, 1104. See *EY* 477, 592; 1804:10.)

48. Mar 27

STC departs London for Portsmouth. (*STCL* II, 1109–10.)

49. c Mar 29; Mar 29

DW probably briefly continues the writing of *Recollections* c 29 Mar, composing some part of the entries for 3–5 Sept and concluding Part II. (*EY* 463; *DWJ* ix, 439. See 1804:16n.)
On 29 Mar W, DW write to STC: (DW:) Warm thoughts of STC. *Prel* composition; W's health; Johnny. SH to visit next week; DW to go to PH. *Recollections*. (W:) Shock occasioned by STC's last letter but one; *Prel*; urgent desire for STC's notes for *Recluse*; lines possibly omitted from [MS M]. (*EY* 462–65.)

50. Perhaps c Mar 29 or 30, or early Apr

The Thomas H household moves to PH. (*EY* 462–63, 467.)

51. Probably between Apr 1 and 14

W composes *Prel* VI.61–62 and probably surrounding lines including 55–59. (Content; Appendix V.)

52. Early Apr, esp. c Apr 6–Apr 8

Probably SH visits DC in early Apr. W, probably c 6–8 Apr, visits PH, probably seeing Charles and Mrs. Luff on the way. He is in any case absent from DC for three days c 6–8 Apr. (*EY* 462–65, 467, 471.)[22]

53. Probably c Apr 7

W receives £5 from Montagu. (See 1804:15n.)

54. Apr 8

Johnny is weaned. (DC MS 26. See *EY* 472.)

55. Apr 9 (–1806 Aug 11)

STC sets sail for Malta from St. Helen's, Isle of Wight. (He arrives off Portsmouth on his return on 11 Aug 1806.) (*STCL* II, 1126.)

56. Apr 13

A cask of stout, a gift from the Bs, arrives at DC. (*EY* 465. See also *EY* 478.)

DW writes to Lady B: Thanks for cask of stout; for the Bs' recent attentions to STC. Her and MW's hopes for becoming acquainted with the Bs; invitation to DC. STC; Derwent; Johnny. Transcript of *At Applethwaite, Near Keswick*. (*EY* 465–68.)

A farewell letter from STC arrives as DW is writing to Lady B. (*EY* 468.)

---

[22] On 29 Mar DW states that they hope to see SH "for a couple of days next week," and on 3 May remarks that SH has been at DC for a visit, and that W has been at PH and seen the Luffs. It is not unlikely that W accompanied SH to or from PH. W was definitely at DC on 13 Apr (see *EY* 465–68).

57. Apr 14

Johnny stands on his feet by himself. W wagers a guinea with DW that he will walk in a fortnight. (DC MS 26.)

RW's accounts record a charge of £5/5/– to W for payment to Mr. Sanders for "gold-chain, seal, & key," under this date. (RW accounts, DCP.)[23]

58. Apr 15.

A letter arrives from Montagu stating that he owes [W] £160 besides the annuity (£100 loan and £60 arrears); probably stating his intention to arrange security for this sum with RW; and enclosing £5. (See 1804:15n; 1804:53.)

59. Probably c Apr 19

A letter dated 16 Apr arrives from Montagu proposing arrangements concerning Montagu's debt to W. (DCP. See 1803:21; 1804: 15n.)[24]

60. Probably Apr 28

W attends the field day of the Loyal Wedgwood Volunteers at and

[23] A note in W's autograph on another copy of the account (which records the amount as £5/5/6) states: "The article was a silver watch. . . . We never had a gold chain." In yet another account the date is recorded as May 1804; and in yet another as 17 Dec 1803. The present date is chosen in consideration of the time that the watch was sent to W (see 1804:69).

This record appears to mark the first stage of W's lengthy efforts to obtain a satisfactory watch.

[24] Montagu proposes that W authorize RW to destroy notes which he possesses for £100 and £26. RW possesses a bond for £200 given him for W's protection when Montagu had been dangerously ill. As W demands only his annuity and £160 (see 1804:58) RW should also be authorized to acknowledge £40 on the back of the £200 bond. Montagu will pay at least £40 annually in liquidation of the £160 debt, for which life insurance cover will be arranged. W's securities will then consist in the £300 bond for the annuity itself and the £160 bond just proposed, backed by the appropriate life insurance.

Available records do not appear to indicate whether Montagu's suggestion was implemented in this form. He appears to have paid off all arrears and the £100 loan by 12 Aug 1812.

near Gowbarrow Park, Ullswater. He dines with Charles Luff (the captain); expresses an enthusiastic response to the day's events. (Litch-field 152; letter, Luff to Tom Wedgwood, 20 Apr 1804, UKL.)[25]

61. Apr 29

W writes to Richard Sharp: Thanks for letter and Scott's *Border Minstrelsy*; a parcel containing books and other items, and in which he had some hopes of finding a MS poem by Sharp, has not yet arrived. Thanks for Sharp's kindnesses to STC; indebtedness to Sharp for pleasure on Scotch tour [see 1803:62n]. The estate occupied by Ibbetson is for sale. *Prel*, which is becoming much longer than he had ever dreamed of [see Appendix V]. (*EY* 468–70. See *STCL* II, 1064.)

62. May 3; probably May 3

On 3 May DW writes to CCl: Regrets not seeing TCl on a recent trip of his to the Lakes. DW to visit PH; Aggy Fisher dead; Molly now her brother's housekeeper. STC has sailed. Birth of [Edith May S]. (*EY* 471–72.)

Probably on 3 May DW writes to RW: Requests him to keep a parcel for Peggy Marsh. DW's pleasure in hearing of JW's safe arrival in China. (*EY* 472.)[26]

63. Probably May 5 (–May 8, –c May 20)

W, DW depart DC, walk over Grisedale Hause to the Luffs', where they pass the night. (W probably returns to DC on 8 May, DW c 20 May.) (*EY* 473, 475–76.)

64. Probably May 6–May 8

On 6 May W, DW ride together to Lyulph's Tower, leave the

[25] Luff apparently did not describe the day's events to Wedgwood until 21 May; but on 20 Apr he stated that the "Grand Field day" would be held at Patterdale on "Saturday the 28th," and described the preparations in progress.

[26] The letter is endorsed "1802 or 1804." JW reached the China coast at Macao on 25 Jan 1802, and news of his arrival can hardly have reached London by the beginning of May of that year. He next arrived in China in early Sept 1803. (*JWL* 32, 38.)

horse, walk to Airey Force, where they part. W walks via Matterdale to Keswick, and DW on to visit at PH. She arrives as SH and Thomas H return from Dacre Church. (*EY* 473. See 1804:67.)

W remains at Keswick and with RS probably until 8 May. He sees SC for the first time since [11 Aug 1803]. Probably on 8 May W returns to Grasmere from Keswick, and probably with RS. RS dines at DC, departing at 6:30. W walks with him halfway to Lowwood. (*EY* 473–76; Curry I, 358.)[27]

Before parting from RS W asks him to make investigations in Liverpool concerning a book of his there. (Letter, RS to Mrs. S, 11 May [1804], BM Add. MS 47, 888.)[28]

On 8 May DW, SH visit Eusemere; are entertained by Ellen Bewsher; return to PH. (*EY* 473–74.)

65. May 9

DW, SH write to CCl from PH: (DW:) W's and her recent travels; her trip to PH; visit to Eusemere [see 1804:64]. (SH:) Kind wishes. (*EY* 473–75.)

66. Probably c May 20

DW returns to Grasmere from PH. She sees the Luffs on her way home via Grisedale Hause. (*EY* 480. See 1804:64.)

67. May 25, 29

DW writes to Lady B: (25 May:) Visit to PH. SH. Hopes for visit from the Bs. *Prel.* W's health. (29 May:) News of STC's safe arrival at Gibraltar; appropriate kind of English residence for STC. Plans of W,

[27] RS wrote on 7 May that he was to depart Keswick the next day "to sleep at Grasmere" in his way south. W said that he stayed "three days" at Keswick (see *EY* 473, 475–76), and was therefore probably including both 6 and 8 May in his count.

[28] RS sent this message to Mrs. S on 11 May from Liverpool for conveyance to W through SFC: "[T]he Merchant well remembered having his book, but could not remember what was become of it. I have desired him, if he finds it, to send it to Koster, where it will be safe, if it comes too late for me, and will travel to Keswick when K himself visits the Lakes." The book is unidentified.

MW, Johnny to visit PH. The stout [see 1804: 56]. Hopes for visit from Bs. (*EY* 475–78. Cf *EY* 475n.)[29]

On 25 May W composes outdoors for at least two hours. (*EY* 477.)

RW's accounts charge W £35, payment of bill at six weeks to Richard Cooke, under 29 May. This payment, which possibly occurred earlier,[30] completes repayment of £60 owed to Cooke by W. (RW accounts, DCP. Cf *EY* 416n. See 1804:39.)

68. Probably c but by June 1

DW writes to CCl: CCl's health; Dr. Beddoes; Eusemere; Molly; the new servant; Johnny; plans of W, DW, MW to visit PH; STC's safe arrival at Gibraltar; *Prel.* (*EY* 478–81.)

69. June 2

On this date CL writes to DW that he has this day booked [to Grasmere] W's watch and books, obtained from RW, together with *Purchas His Pilgrimage*, Browne's *Religio Medici*, pens. (*LL* I, 370. See 1804:1.)

70. Perhaps c June 6, or June 11; probably June 10, perhaps June 11

Perhaps c 6 June two drawings, the gift of Sir GB, arrive at DC from Keswick, one depicting Conway Castle, the other Applethwaite Dell.

W visits GH, probably arriving 10 June and perhaps departing next day. Probably on 11 June he chats with HC. W possibly brings the two drawings by Sir GB with him on his return home. (*EY* 483, 517; *CCS* II, 294–96; 1803:59n.)

---

[29] DW's statement "I wrote so far several days ago" (*EY* 477) would appear to mark the division between the part of the letter written on 25 May and the portion written on "May 29th," the date with DW's signature. There is no indication of the letter's having been written at more than two sittings.

[30] The bill is also noted in another account as paid "at 6 weeks" under, and, presumably, from, 21 Mar.

71. Probably between c June 11 and early Aug

Richard Sharp visits the Lake District. His visit includes a stay in Keswick, which he reaches by 27 June, and meetings with W, who reads large amounts of poetry to him, including, probably, portions of *RC* and *Prel*. (*CCS* II, 294–96; *EY* 468–70; *Memoirs and Correspondence of Francis Horner*, ed. Leonard Horner, Boston, 1853, I, 272–73.)[31]

72. Probably June 13–June 14 (–June 23, possibly by July 8, probably by c July 13–July 14); between this time and early Oct

Probably on 13 June W, MW, DW, Johnny travel to Keswick in the jaunting car, arriving at 6 PM. They are met by SFC, Derwent, SC, Mrs. Lovell, Mrs. S. They pass the night at GH. (They depart next day, when DW returns to DC. W probably returns to DC 23 June. MW, Johnny possibly return by 8 July, probably by c 13–14 July.)

W probably composes little for *Prel* between this time and early Oct. (*EY* 482–85, 489, 500; *DWJ* I, 439; Appendix V.)[32]

[31] Horner comments ambivalently in a letter to Jeffrey of 13 Aug 1804:
Wordsworth's Poems, for he has two great ones, that is, long ones, will not be published so soon [as *Madoc*, which is to be published this winter]. One of these is to be called the Recluse, and the other is to be a history of himself and his thoughts; this philosophy of egotism and shadowy refinements really spoils a great genius for poetry. We shall have a few exquisite gleams of natural feeling, sunk in a dull ugly ground of trash and affectation. I cannot forgive your expression, "Wordsworth & Co.;" he merits criticism, but surely not contempt; to class him with his imitators is the greatest of all contempt. I thought our perusal of the Lyrical Ballads in the Temple would have prevented this; we found much to admire, but you will not admire. Sharp, however, is in the other extreme, I admit; but I insist it is the better of the two: he has been living at the Lakes, with these crazed poets; Wordsworth read him some thousand lines, and he repeated to me a few of these one day, which I could not worship as he wished me.
The firm distinction between the *Recluse* and the "history of himself and his thoughts" implies that the *Recluse* of which Sharp spoke was more probably *RC* (and perhaps associated fragmentary verse) than meditations in the author's own person organized along the lines of *HG*.
Charles Luff had seen Sharp by 7 July (letter, Luff to Tom Wedgwood, 7 July 1804, UKL).
[32] It appears likely that W's poetic leisure began with the definite break in the daily pattern of life that commenced with this excursion.
DW comments probably on 21 June (*EY* 484; see 1804:76) that MW and Johnny

73. June 14; probably July 14; between June 14 and June 23

On 14 June W writes to Walter Scott from Keswick: Repeats invitation to visit Lakes; STC; W would meet Scott anywhere in Border area. (*EY* 481.)

Probably on 14 June, W, MW, DW, Johnny depart from GH, travel to Threlkeld, whence DW returns to DC. W, MW, Johnny travel on to PH.

During this visit at PH W visits Eusemere but does not see TCl; MW visits there and does see him. (*EY* 482–88.)[33]

74. Probably June 17

W probably calls on Capt. and Mrs. W at Brougham Hall. (*EY* 485–86.)

75. Probably June 19

Capt. and Mrs. W call at PH. (*EY* 485–86.)

76. Probably June 21

DW writes to Lady B: Visits to GH [see 1804:72]. Regrets that Bs will not be visiting Grasmere this summer; thanks Sir GB for drawings [see 1804:70]; STC; family plans and expectations. (*EY* 482–84.)[34]

---

[33] That W almost surely visited Eusemere before MH did is clear from DW's statement to CCl that W failed to see TCl or learn whether he was expected. (Nor is any hint given that TCl has lately been present—information that DW would not have failed to report.)

[34] DW dates her letter "June 20th." While she says that she parted with W and MW "last Thursday morning" (which would have been the 14th) and that they had gone to GH "[y]esterday week" (which would have been the 12th), *EY* 486 makes plain that they passed only one night at GH. *DWJ* I, 439 confirms that the parting took place on a Thursday.

---

will stay three weeks longer at PH; and on 18 July she speaks, plainly from personal observation, of Johnny's "growth of a month" while absent from home (*EY* 488). In the earlier letter DW speaks of having parted with W and MW "last Thursday morning" (which would have been the 14th) and of having gone to GH "yesterday week."

77. Perhaps this summer

DW catches a cough that lasts for several months. (Letter, W to Richard Sharp, 30 Nov 1804, UTL. See F. G. Stoddard, "Two Autograph Letters of William Wordsworth," *MP* LXIX, 1971, 140–41.)

78. June 23

DW attempts composition for her *Recollections*, but cannot advance. (*DWJ* I, 439.) W returns to DC from PH. (*EY* 485.)

79. June 24

DW writes to CCl: W, MW, and their visit to PH; Eusemere and its reported sale to LdL. Dr. Beddoes; Johnny; visit to Keswick and PH; SC; Molly; Hs; George H; Joanna H; PH. (*EY* 485–87.)[35]

80. Perhaps c early July

Priscilla Lloyd calls at DC one night on her way to Keswick. (*EY* 489.)

81. July 7

RW's accounts record under this date receipt of payment of two notes from LdL of £2000 each, with one year's interest on both, total £4200. These notes conclude payment of the Lowther debt to the JW Sr. estate. (See 1803: 20; 1803: 52; 1804: 82; 1804: 90.)

The total paid by LdL in settlement of this debt, including interest, is £8700.

82. July 10

RW's accounts credit to W and DW purchase of 3200 3 percent consols for £1804 (including £4 commission) under this date. (RW accounts, DCP. See 1804: 81; 1804: 90.)

[35] Charles Luff wrote to Tom Wedgwood on 7 July that TCl "delivers possession" of Eusemere to LdL "this week" (UKL).

83. Perhaps c mid-July

W receives a set of Reynolds' Works, the gift of Sir GB, through RS. (*EY* 490–91, 494.)[36]

84. July 15
W draws on RW for £20 by a bill in favor of Thomas H, due in one month. (Copy of bill, DCP; RW accounts, DCP.)[37]

85. July 18; c July 18–July 19

DW writes to CCl: CCl's mother's death; MH's visit to Eusemere while staying at PH [see 1804:73]; Johnny; STC; JW; Mrs. Ibbetson; W; Johnny. (*EY* 487–90.)

Humphry Davy visits DC for a day and a half (probably two nights) c 18–19 July. W accompanies him to Patterdale on his departure. (*EY* 492, 494.)[38]

86. July 20

W writes to Sir GB: Thanks Sir GB for set of Reynolds' works [see 1804:83]; Reynolds. W regrets Bs not to visit the Lakes this summer. Davy. (*EY* 490–93.)

87. July 22–July 24 ff (–Aug 19)

On 22 July SFC, HC, Derwent, SC arrive at DC for a visit. SFC

---

[36] It seems a likely, though hardly certain, assumption that when DW speaks on 25 July of the books' not having been received at the time of her last letter, and of W's "not being at home" then, that she intends a reference to her letter to Lady B of 20 June. *EY* identifies the set as the Malone third edition (1801).

[37] RW's accounts charge the sum to W under 18 Aug.

[38] W states on 20 July that they had a day and a half of Davy's company, and DW states on 25 July that Davy was two days with her brother. W possibly omits, while DW includes, the time spent on the way to Patterdale. While Davy probably in any case departed by the 19th, it is singular that DW's letter to CCl of 18 July makes no mention of him, esp. in view of the mutual connection of Davy and CCl with Dr. Beddoes. RS wrote to Rickman on 6 Aug: "Davy has been here & appeared more Londonized than he did in London. He had the most coxcombical coat on that ever came from a Bondstreet taylor. . . . " (HEH.)

departs probably 24 July with Dr. and Mrs. Crompton of Liverpool, who are to visit Keswick, and probably returns within a few days. (The children probably depart together with SFC on 19 Aug.) (*EY* 493–96.)

88. July 23

DW attempts composition for her *Recollections* but cannot advance. (*DWJ* I, 439–40.)

89. July 25

DW writes to Lady B: Accepts Lady B's offer to stand godmother to the new child; DW will stand proxy [see 1804:103]. SFC's visit; the stout [see 1804:56); Davy's visit; the Ibbetsons; lack of news of STC. (*EY* 493–95.)

90. Aug 1

RW's accounts credit W and DW with £1845, nine-twentieths share of final payments on Lowther debt to the JW Sr estate, less £100 expenses, under this date. (RW accounts, DCP. See 1804:81; 1804:82.)

91. Aug 2

RS perhaps passes the night at DC. (Letter, RS to Thomas S, BM Add. MS 30,928, fol. 47.)[39]

92. Aug 6

The *Earl of Abergavenny* arrives off Portland on return from China. (It had sailed 7 May 1803.) (Log, East India Co.)[40]

93. Possibly c but by Aug 12, c but by Aug 19

Possibly c but by 12 Aug W sees Capt. W at Brougham Hall or

[39] RS writes: "Today I am going to Grasmere on my way to hear John Thelwall lecture at Kendal."

[40] On 8 Aug JW wrote to Capt. W that the *Earl of Abergavenny* had arrived safe in the Channel (*JWL* 140–42).

elsewhere, and writes to JW. He possibly writes again to JW c but by 19 Aug. (*JWL* 142–46.)[41]

94. Between c Aug 13 or Aug 14 and c Oct 13 or Oct 14, and shortly after

Probably between c 13 or 14 Aug and c 13 or 14 Oct RW visits for a few days at DC. Possibly he visits briefly again shortly after. (*EY* 511; 1804:93n.)

95. Aug 16; perhaps shortly after Aug 16

Dorothy Wordsworth (d. 9 July 1847), first daughter and second child of William and Mary Wordsworth, is born at DC at 5:50 PM. (*EY* 496; M-W Book of Common Prayer, DCP; *Mem* I, 367.)[42]

Perhaps shortly after 16 Aug TCl visits at DC, possibly a night, but only very briefly in any case. (*EY* 510.)

96. Probably Aug 17 (–Sept 23)

SH arrives for a visit at DC. (She remains until 23 Sept.) (*EY* 501–02, 510.)

97. Probably Aug 19

SFC, HC, Derwent, SC depart DC. (*EY* 496. See 1804:87.)[43]

[41] JW, who wrote to Capt. W at Brougham Hall on 8 Aug, wrote to him again on 15 Aug thanking him for his letter "written at the end of my Brothers." At the end of this letter he remarks, clearly about the same brother, "I have not written to my Brother for I do not know where a Letter will reach him—." The brother is probably not CW, and of RW, of whose absence from London JW appears to have heard on the evening of 14 Aug, he comments, "I have no doubt [that Richd] has been spending a pleasant time among his friends in Cumberland. . . " (*JWL* 144–46). Either W or RW might be the "Brother." It is unlikely, however, that the Ws' having had "no tidings of John ourselves" as of 22 Sept (*EY* 500) implies that they have received no communication from or concerning JW since his return.

[42] This Dorothy Wordsworth is regularly referred to below as "Dora" although that name was not commonly used by the family until some years later (see *Sara Coleridge and Henry Reed*, ed. L. N. Broughton, Ithaca, 1937, 103).

[43] DW states on 24 Aug only that SFC had departed the previous Sunday, but nothing is said to indicate that the children remained behind.

98. Aug 24

DW writes to Lady B: The baby. The recent visit of SFC and her children; SH; the health of the family. (*EY* 496–97.)

99. Aug 29; probably Aug 19–Aug 31; Aug 31

RW's accounts charge W £7/10/6, payment of premium on £300 policy on Montagu's life, under 29 Aug. (RW accounts, DCP.)

W probably visits Keswick on 29 Aug, returning home the same day or the day following. While he is there a letter to SFC dated 5 June arrives from STC. On 31 Aug SFC forwards the letter, which describes STC's voyage and his health, to DC. (*EY* 497–98.)

On 31 Aug W writes to Sir GB: His trip to Keswick. STC's letter. DW, MW, the baby; the Ws' friendship with the Bs. Reynolds. W is anxious to return to work after a two-month lapse. (*EY* 497–500.)

100. Sept and probably Sept, by Sept 23

During this month the Ws write to STC. (See *STCL* II, 1165.) Probably during this month, by 23 Sept, the Ws receive a letter from STC dated 4 Aug. (See *EY* 502.)

101. Sept 4

RW's accounts charge W £20, payment of a bill, under this date. (RW accounts, DCP.)

102. Perhaps shortly before, certainly by Sept 16 (–Sept 23)

Elizabeth M and MM arrive at DC for a visit. (They depart 23 Sept.) (*EY* 510; 1804:103.)

103. Sept 16 (–Sept 23)

Dorothy Wordsworth (Dora) is christened at Grasmere. Lady B is godmother; SH stands proxy. Elizabeth M and MM attend. (Grasmere PR; *EY* 501–03.)

Probably on this day W composes a basic version of *Address to My*

Infant Daughter, Dora, on Being Reminded That She Was a Month Old That Day, September 16. (See 1804:95.)[44]

104. Sept 22

    W writes to RW: A letter from RW of Branthwaite [concerning the debt of the W children to his family]. JW's good prospects. Suggested procedures regarding the claim of RW of Branthwaite. (*EY* 500–01.)[45]

105. Sept 23

    Elizabeth M, MM, and SH depart DC. (*EY* 501–02. See 1804:96; 1804:102.)

    DW writes to Lady B: Thanks for a gift of £10 for Dora from Lady B; their plan to lay it out in planting a small plot of ground near the house where they make their final settlement. Recent visitors. A letter from STC. (*EY* 501–03.)

106. Perhaps between Sept 23 and Oct 7 and about this time

    Perhaps between 23 Sept and 7 Oct Henry Edridge and Richard Duppa pay a call or visit at DC. Possibly at this time—if not, perhaps about this time—W agrees to translate some of Michaelangelo's poetry for Duppa's forthcoming *Life* of Michaelangelo. (*EY* 501, 503, 508, 517, 525. See 1805:1.)[46]

---

[44] The PR reads: [Baptism:] "September 1804 16th Dorothy Daugr of Mr William Wordsworth of Town End Grasm.—"

[45] On the settlement of the debt see esp. 1812:105.

[46] W implies when speaking of Edridge and Duppa in Dec (*EY* 517) that he saw the two men together. They must have come to DC, since Edridge saw Sir GB's drawing of Applethwaite (see *EY* 517; 1804:70). DW in early Jan 1805 (*EY* 525) mentions having seen Duppa "last summer," when he spoke of a tree planted by Klopstock on his wife's grave. In the absence of other evidence, the occasion was probably that of which W had spoken earlier. DW's manner of discussing Edridge on 7 Oct (*EY* 508) implies that he had visited there recently; but since Edridge talked with the Ws about Lady B, DW would no doubt have mentioned the artist's call in her letter of 23 Sept to Lady B had it taken place by then. Other contact between Duppa, Edridge, and W about this time is not precluded. Duppa was with RS on 11 Oct (Curry I, 359), and according to RS was "now gone" on 15 Oct (Curry I, 362).

107. Probably between Sept 23 and Oct 5, Oct 15, and a time shortly after (–c Mar 1806)

Probably between 23 Sept and 5 Oct W, DW make a five- or six-day tour, using the jaunting car, to Keswick, Ennerdale, Wastdale, and the Duddon Valley.

On the first day they travel to Keswick. On the same day or the next they visit Buttermere, and return to Keswick, with the Ss, SFC, and Mrs. Lovell.

On the following day W, DW proceed via Whinlatter Pass through Lorton Vale; view an ancient yew tree. This view probably gives W his primary suggestion for *Yew-trees*. Some portion of the poem, esp. perhaps lines 1–13, is possibly composed at this time or shortly after [see GCL 123]. They proceed past Loweswater to Ennerdale, where they pass the night.

On the following day they proceed to Wastdale; pass the night at the house of a "statesman," probably Thomas Tyson [see *CEY* 279].

On the following day, W, DW proceed to Seathwaite, in the Duddon Valley, where they pass the night at a public house of another Tyson, cousin of their host of the previous night. This visit to the Duddon Valley perhaps inspires "O Mountain Stream! the Shepherd and His Cot," which is possibly composed now or shortly after. (It is probably completed by c Mar 1806.)

Probably on the next day, which cannot be before 28 Sept, they return to DC. On their return they find Basil Montagu and George Dyer in Grasmere. Montagu and Dyer lodge at the inn; are still present on 15 Oct. (*EY* 505–09, 511; Appendix VII. See 1804:118.)[47]

[47] DW's remarks of Sunday 7 Oct make plain that she and W had returned by the preceding Friday; while she remarks on 15 Oct that the tour was made after SH's departure (see 1804:105). The tenses of the verbs in her letter of 15 Oct leave uncertain that Montagu and Dyer were present, but seem to tilt the balance in that direction: "At our return we found Mr Montagu and George Dyer. They lodged at the Inn, and we have not seen much of Dyer." (*EY* 511.)

No available evidence suggests that "O Mountain Stream" was composed before the writing of MS M; and while its absence from that MS is not firm ground for a date, earlier composition does not look likely for any other reason. It was perhaps complete by Mar 1806 (see Appendix VII). The head of the Duddon Valley is closer, in straight-line distance, to DC than Keswick, but hardly as convenient to reach. W

108. Probably between Sept 28 and Oct 15

Mrs. Lovell visits at DC for four days. (*EY* 511.)[48]

109. Perhaps between early Oct and early 1805; probably between early Oct and late autumn

Perhaps between early Oct and early 1805 W composes the bulk of *Prel* XII, and *Prel* XI.1–41 in MS Z form. (Appendix V.)

Probably between early Oct and late autumn W composes the bulk of *Prel* VIII, and portion of IX (including *Vaudracour and Julia*) and X [see GCL 1]; materials in MS Y [see GCL 1], including lines replaced by VIII.159–72 quoted PREL 571–78, *Prel* XIII.334–67, 374–85, and materials employed *Exc* II.1–26, *Exc* IV.402–12, 763–65, IX.437–48 (see PREL 581); possibly *Prel* X.445–66, 568–74, and the fragment "There Was a Spot" quoted *PW* V, 342, III (but on lines 1–11 see *CEY* 322) as DC MS 74. (Appendix V; Appendix VI.)

110. Oct 6

CW marries Priscilla Lloyd at Birmingham. (*EY* 511n; information from Mr. D. P. Sewell.)

111. Oct 7, 10

DW writes to Lady B: (7 Oct:) Lady B and her sister; a wishful thought of meeting STC in Switzerland and taking cottages there; STC; DC; tour to Ennerdale and Wastdale; Mary Ibbetson's mother-in-law; a poem of Cowper's which has perhaps set W on to writing sooner than he otherwise would have done [see GCL 123n]; Edridge. (10 Oct:) Jackson has (DW understands) sold GH. (*EY* 505–09.)

---

[48] She evidently arrived after W and DW had returned from their tour (see 1804: 107).

could have paid unrecorded visits thither, but this appears to be the one visit known to have occurred during the period in question, and appears the most likely choice for an occasion that might have evoked the sonnet.

112. Probably Oct 8 or Oct 15

W, DW write to RW: (W:) Necessity of seeing RW before he departs the country for London. (DW:) Disappointment at thought of not seeing RW again before his departure. (*EY* 503–05.)[49]

113. Perhaps early Oct, certainly by Oct 10

DW writes to CL, ML (letter not known to survive) informing them of the birth of Dora. (*LL* I, 377–79.)

114. Between Oct 15 and Dec 9

W, DW call at the public house in Grasmere. Robert Forster, a friend of CCl's, introduces himself. The next evening he calls at DC and stays until 11, pleasing the Ws. (*EY* 515. On Forster see esp. Moorman II, 133; CCS III, 29–30.)

115. Probably Oct 15

DW writes to CCl: TCl; the children; visitors; STC; Jackson's (presumed) sale of GH. RW; JW; W; recent activities. (*EY* 509–12.)

116. Oct 19

DW draws on RW for £20 by a bill in favor of Francis Bateman, due in one month. (Copy of bill, DCP; RW accounts, DCP.)[50]

117. c Oct 29

Thomas M visits Grasmere; probably calls at DC; promises to purchase some stockings for W in London. (*EY* 512.)

---

[49] The earliest possible date on which W and DW might have returned from their recent tour is 28 Sept, and while W wrote on a "Monday Morn," Monday 1 Oct would seem too soon for W to speak of conversing with a man who called "a few days ago" (*EY* 504). Montagu, who was present as W wrote, possibly departed by 15 Oct (see 1804:107); but while the evidence for that is not certain, DW's phrasing to CCl concerning RW on 15 Oct (*EY* 511) is so similar to the phrasing which she uses to RW himself in this letter, that both letters would seem likely to have been written on the same day.

[50] RW charges the sum to DW's account under 22 Nov.

118. Possibly c Nov, by Nov 26

Basil Montagu perhaps visits Grasmere or DC. (*EY* 515.)[51]

119. Nov 13

RW's accounts charge W £60/–/–, payment of bill on Thomas Cookson, under this date. (RW accounts, DCP.)

120. Probably c late Nov or Dec

W composes *Prel* X.690–728, later published separately as *French Revolution as It Appeared to Enthusiasts at Its Commencement.* (Appendix V. See 1804:127.)

121. Possibly c mid-Nov, by Nov 21

RS and possibly other members of his family perhaps call or visit at DC. (Letter, RS to Rickman, 21 Nov 1804, HEH; Warter I, 286; Robberds I, 522. See 1804:123.)[52]

122. Perhaps shortly before Nov 26

W receives a draft from Montagu, amount unknown. (*EY* 512. See 1804:118.)[53]

123. Probably Nov 26–perhaps Nov 30

Probably on 26 Nov Mrs. S calls at DC; persuades DW to come to GH that day for a visit. DW remains in Keswick until probably 30

[51] That a visit from Montagu entirely distinct from that paid with Dyer c late Sept–early Oct (see 1804:107) occurred now is quite uncertain. DW would probably, however, have mentioned Montagu's remarks about CCl's friend Miss Taylor in her letter to CCl of 15 Oct had Montagu made them by then.

[52] RS's letter to Rickman, dated "Wednesday" [21 Nov] states that "[w]e are at Lloyds." In a letter to Henry S of the same date RS remarks that they have been at Lloyd's "some days." On 23 Nov RS wrote to William Taylor, "William Wordsworth is very desirous of seeing you—" (cf *MY* I, 469).

[53] That the draft arrived before DW's departure from DC on 26 Nov is not certain but probable. Her phrasing on the 29th is, "We have received Montagu's draft—it is at home untouched" (*EY* 512).

Nov. While there she sees Mrs. [Bolton] at Mrs. Calvert's. (*EY* 512, 514–15.)

While she is gone, probably on 29 Nov, Johnny sprains his ankle. (*EY* 514.)[54]

124. Nov 29

DW signs and dates a bill, as from Grasmere, for £4/14/4, to Thomas M this morning, to buy stockings for W in London [see 1804:117]. DW draws on RW for £20 by a bill in favor of William Jackson, due in one month.

DW writes to RW from Keswick: Her draft in favor of Jackson; draft from Montagu [see 1804:122]; Thomas M. (*EY* 512; RW accounts, DCP; copy of bill to Jackson, DCP.)[55]

125. Perhaps Nov 30; Nov 30

Perhaps on 30 Nov DW returns to DC. (1804:123.)

On 30 Nov W writes to Richard Sharp from Grasmere: Thanks for help to JW. Send watch to [RW]; problems with his watch. His hopes for a visit from Sharp in the summer. (F. G. Stoddard, "Two Autograph Letters of William Wordsworth," *MP* LXIX, 1971, 140–41.)

126. Probably Dec 1 (–possibly Dec 2)

W, DW, Johnny visit Keswick to consult Mr. Edmondson about Johnny. They possibly call or pass the night at GH, returning home next day. (*EY* 512, 514, 521; 1804:123.)

127. Probably shortly after Dec 2

W composes *Prel* X.933–34 and probably surrounding lines, esp. 922–41. (Appendix V.)

---

[54] DW on 9 Dec says that she was "absent four days" but implies that she has helped to nurse Johnny for ten days.

[55] The bill to Jackson is also dated "Grasmere." RW charges payment of the M draft to DW's account under 18 Dec and payment of the Jackson draft under 1 Jan 1804 (see *EY* 512n).

128. Dec 9

DW writes to CCl: Health; DW's visit to Keswick [see 1804: 123]; Johnny's ankle; the Cs; Robert Forster; *Madoc*; weather; Montagu; DC; near-sale of GH. (*EY* 513–16.)

129. Dec 18, 28

RW's accounts charge W £20, payment of a bill by Tom H in favor of John M, under these dates. (RW accounts, DCP.)[56]

130. Probably mid- and late Dec, but by Dec 25; c but by Dec 25; 1805 between May 4 and early June

Probably in mid- and late Dec, by 25 Dec, W and other members of the family work at building a moss hut in the orchard at DC. Probably c but by 25 Dec W writes for it an inscription, "No Whimsey of the Purse." The hut is probably not completed until 6 June 1805. (*EY* 518, 521, 598; *DWJ* I, 439.)

131. Dec 25; probably between Dec 25 and 1805 Oct 17; probably between Dec 25 and 1805 Aug 24

W writes to Sir GB: Thanks him for invitation to Grosvenor Square; Reynolds and the *Discourses*; painting; art. Is to attempt translations of sonnets of Michaelangelo for Duppa's *Life*. Recent writing; plans for *Recluse* and *Prel*. DC; hopes for visit from Bs; the orchard hut and its inscription; the young Roscius; STC. (*EY* 516–19.)

DW writes to Lady B: Johnny's ankle [see 1804:123]; the young Roscius; Grasmere; the moss hut; SFC. (*EY* 519–22.)

132. Dec 27

W, DW write to JW and RW: (W to JW:) W's £100 promissory note to Sotheby for STC now due [see 1803:138]; asks JW to advance this sum. The moss hut; possible visits; composition since he last saw JW. Asks JW to have £10 ready for CL to use to buy books for him. (W to RW:) Tax gatherer just with them; taxes would be lessened by

---

[56] Payment is noted under the different dates in different accounts.

having his and DW's money parcelled between them. Has RW prepared papers for his aunt (widow of RW of Whitehaven) [see 1804: 104]? (DW to RW:) W has just asked her to remind RW to send *MC*. (*EY* 522–23.)

133. Probably shortly before Dec 31 (–1805 Jan 2)

George H arrives for a visit at DC. (He departs 2 Jan 1805.) (*EY* 524, 527.)

1805

[On writings of W possibly of this year see below and GCL 1–4, 27, 59, 72, 97–100, 106, 113, 115, 117–21, 123–26, 131–47.]

1. Probably early this year; probably this year, by Aug 24, by Oct 17; probably between this year and 1807 early May; possibly between 1805 and 1807 but not certainly before 1836–c 1840

Probably early this year W organizes *Prel* XII, XIII in basic final form. (Appendix V.)

Probably this year, by 24 Aug, W composes *From the Italian of Michael Angelo. I* ("Yes, Hope May with My Strong Desire Keep Pace").

By 17 Oct he has attempted translations of at least fifteen other of Michaelangelo's sonnets, but completed none. These efforts perhaps include work toward *At Florence* [ii], *From the Italian of Michaelangelo. II, III*; but see 1805:98. (*EY* 516–17, 628–29; *MY* I, 64–65, 79; Appendix VII; Curry *RES*.)

Probably between 1805 and early May 1807 W composes the four stanzas commencing "And Sweet It Is to See in Summer Time" (*PW* IV, 370–71), translation from the Italian of Michaelangelo. (Content.)

Possibly between 1805 and 1807 but not certainly before c 1836–c 1840 W composes:

"Grateful Is Sleep" (two versions; *PW* IV, 370–71), translation from the Italian of Michaelangelo

"Come, Gentle Sleep," translation from the Latin of Thomas Warton the Younger (*PW* IV, 372)

(Content.)[1]

2. Probably Jan 1

W, George H skate on Grasmere; push DW, MW, the children along on the ice on chairs. They resolve to travel to PH the next day if the weather is fine. (*EY* 524, 527. See 1805:4n.)

3. Probably Jan 2 (–perhaps Jan 10, fairly certainly by Jan 15) ff

W, DW, MW, the children, and George H, acting as charioteer,

[1] John Rickman wrote to RS on 14 Dec 1804, "I send certain Italian Poems from Duppa for you and Wordsworth" (HEH). Wordsworth received his copies, on proof sheets, by 25 Dec 1804, but does not seem to have been in a hurry to translate (*EY* 516–18), and it is safe to suppose 1805 the earliest likely year for any of W's translations from Michaelangelo. He had completed only one poem, "Yes, Hope," by 24 Aug, when RS sent the poem to Duppa, reporting that he was instructed "to add how mortified" W was "that he has not been able to translate any more" (*Bodleian Quarterly Record* I, 1914–1916, 29–31; see Curry *RES*). By 17 Oct W had attempted at least fifteen, but had still completed no more; and he had achieved no greater success by 7 Nov (*EY* 628–29, 640). Possibly the bulk of the work on the other sonnets known to have been completed by early 1807 had been done by 17 Oct. These sonnets include: "The Prayers I Make" (completed by 1 Aug 1806: *MY* I, 64–65), "No Mortal Object" (by 8 Sept 1806: *MY* I, 79), "Rid of a Vexing and a Heavy Load" (by early Apr 1807: Appendix VII). None of these can, of course, have been finished before 7 Nov 1805; and the last did not certainly reach its published form until 19 Jan 1840 (see *PW* III, 500).

The four stanzas commencing "And sweet it is" would presumably date between 1805 and the late stages of preparation of the second edition of Duppa's *Life of Michel Angelo*, which was published 29 May 1807. The same date appears at least possible for the "Grateful Is Sleep" translations, with which the translation from the Latin of Warton appears closely associated. The only surviving MS of these three efforts is, however, written in the first volume of a copy of *PW* 1836; and a date of 1836–c 1840 appears not improbable (*PW* III, 500; *PW* IV, 473). W's only other surviving translation from Michaelangelo, "Rapt above Earth," was written on 22 Aug 1839 (*HCRWC* I, 384–85). "Well-nigh the Voyage Now Is Overpast" (see *PW* III, 408, 573–74), although it is (as remarked *PW* IV, 573–74 from B. Ifor Evans, "Unacknowledged Sonnet by Wordsworth," *TLS* 1938, 172) copied and ascribed to W in the Coleorton NB, is probably not by W. It is ascribed to RS by Duppa himself, whom RS later called "somewhat less than a friend, [but] much more than an acquaintance" (CCS VI, 158), in both the 1807 and 1816 editions of the *Life*.

travel from DC over Kirkstone to PH. (They return to DC perhaps c 10 Jan, fairly certainly by 15 Jan.) The trip to PH probably gives MW a toothache and DW a cold, which DW while at PH attributes to W's hurrying them up Kirkstone and overheating them. W carries Johnny across Kirkstone. He suffers probably for some days following from an inflammation of the eyes. W later regards the present occasion as that on which he contracted the complaint in his eyes, probably trachoma, that recurred throughout the remainder of his life. (*EY* 524, 527–28; *LY* 68. See "A Little Onward" IF note; Moorman II, 255; Edith C. Batho, *The Later Wordsworth*, Cambridge, England, 1933, 318–36.)[2]

4. Probably Jan 4, 5

DW writes to Lady B from PH: STC; the trip to PH [see 1805:3]; Richardson's [*Correspondence*, ed. Anna Laetitia Barbauld]; Klopstock. GH not sold. They will wait to determine where to settle until they have seen STC and learned his intentions. Plans for return to DC; the children. (*EY* 524–27.)[3]

Probably on 5 Jan W takes a walk in the morning. (*EY* 525–26.)

5. Jan 6

W, DW walk in the morning up the Vale of Dacre to Hutton John. W, MW, DW, SH, George H, Joanna, Thomas H, HC sit around the fire in the evening.

[2] A memorandum by CW Jr. among the Rose papers (DCP) records of W that "His eyes suffered in the first instance by exertion and [?wind] heat in carrying his children over Kirkstone about 1805." The information is possibly first-hand, but could be derived from the IF note cited. The complaint is not known to have troubled W between this time and mid-1810 (see 1810:46).

[3] The appearance of the MS indicates that DW's date "January 5th" was probably not written at the time of the writing of the bulk of the letter. In the main part of the letter DW tells Lady B that the family came to PH the day before yesterday, and that they had been sliding on the ice the day before that. On Jan 6th, "Sunday" (*EY* 527), she tells CCl that they came to PH on "Wednesday," and that "the day before New Year's day" was the day when they went sliding. If the Ws came to PH on Wednesday, however, DW must have begun her letter to Lady B on 4 Jan; and the "day before New Year's day" (which DW might have been expected to call "the last day of the year," "New Year's Eve," or the like) would mean "the day before—i.e., New Year's day."

DW writes to CCl from PH: The trip to PH; Tommy Cl; earlier visits to Eusemere. Their own plans; STC. (*EY* 527–28.)

6. Perhaps c Jan 10, fairly certainly by Jan 15

The W family returns to DC, probably via Threlkeld and St. John's Vale. (*EY* 527–32.)[4]

7. Jan 16

W writes to Walter Scott: Thanks Scott for gift of *The Lay of the Last Minstrel* to DW (it has not yet arrived). Invites Scott to visit the Lakes and Grasmere. Scott's purchase of [Ashestiel]. Transcript [by DW] of *Yarrow Unvisited.* (*EY* 529–32.)[5]

8. Feb 5 ff

On 5 Feb the *Earl of Abergavenny*, JW Captain, rounding the eastern end of the Shambles on the Isle of Portland into Portland Roads under the guidance of a pilot, is becalmed, then swept onto the rocks shortly after 5 PM. At half past seven the ship beats its way clear of the Shambles and makes for shore at Weymouth. Shortly after 11, about two miles offshore, the ship sinks in 66 feet of water. JW, probably seized by a wave, is drowned. Of the 387 persons aboard 155 survive. (*JWL* 42–49; Moorman II, 33–37; E. L. McAdam, Jr., "Wordsworth's Shipwreck," *PMLA* LXXVII, 1962, 240–47.)[6]

The debt of JW's estate to W and DW includes, independent of interest, £277/10 to W, £180 to DW, and their combined share of £3000 of the Lowther inheritance. (RW accounts with JW, and accounts of JW estate, DCP. See *CEY* 142n; *MY* I, 546.)

---

[4] W states on 16 Jan that he had received a letter from Scott "yesterday." It is unlikely that Scott would have addressed his letter to W elsewhere than Grasmere. The family apparently had become determined soon after arrival at PH not to return home over Kirkstone (see *EY* 526).

[5] The *Lay* was apparently received by W only about early Mar (*EY* 553).

[6] Reflections in W's poetry, and in his future life generally, of his reactions to JW's death appear so numerous and complex as to preclude systematic listing or discussion in the present work.

9. Feb 7

RW writes to W, CW announcing the death of JW. (*EY* 540; DCP.)

10. Probably c but by Feb 8; Feb 8

Probably c but by 8 Feb W writes to Richard Sharp: W's watch, received some time ago with Sharp's aid, but inoperative on arrival, and now out for repair [see 1804:125]; apparent theft of money in box with watch. Seeks aid in finding a job for George H. STC; Crump's house [AB]. Composition. W is contemplating a voyage to Norway; JW's letter [of 24 Jan]. (*EY* 533–35.)[7]

On 8 Feb DW draws on RW for £10 by a bill due in one month. (*EY* 540.)

11. Feb 10

DW writes to CCl: Johnny, Dora. The moss hut. No word from STC, who is expected; W's composition; Sally and Peggy Ashburner; expected visit from SH; TCl; JW; Crump. (*EY* 536–39.)

12. Feb 11 (–probably c Feb 18); between Feb 11 and c late Apr

W, MW, out walking, are met at 2 PM by SH, who has come from Kendal to bring news of the death of JW, and who has brought from Rydal a letter from RW containing the same information, also a letter from Sir GB. (SH remains at DC for a week.) (*EY* 539–40, 544; *MWL* 3; letter, Joanna H to Thomas M, 27 Feb 1805, JFW Papers.)

W writes to RW about 9 PM: The arrival of the news of the death of JW; the household; W's wish for further news. (*EY* 539–40.)

W writes to Sir GB: JW's death; the household. W's fears concerning STC's reaction to news of JW's death. (*EY* 541–42.)

W's composition of *Prel*, and probably all composition of short

---

[7] Joanna writes to Thomas H on 27 Feb from PH that W has written to some of his friends in London to look for a place for George H (JFW Papers). JW had written to W on 24 Jan of the *Earl of Abergavenny's* narrow escape from damage in a collision with the *Warren Hastings*. See *JWL* 154–56.

poems, is interrupted between this time and c late Apr. (Appendix V; 1805:37; 1805:42.)[8]

RW's accounts charge W £10/-/-, payment of bill in favor of John Fletcher, under this date. (RW accounts, DCP.)

13. Probably between Feb 11 and Feb 27

Charles Lloyd and Mrs. Lloyd call at DC. (*EY* 550.)

14. Probably Feb 12

W writes to RS: Asks RS to come next day. (*EY* 542-43.)[9]

15. Probably Feb 13; Feb 13-Feb 15

On 13 Feb W writes to CW: The state of the household at DC; inquiries about CW and his wife. (*EY* 543-44.)

[8] On the immediate reaction of the family to the news of JW's death see esp. Moorman II, 42.

Joanna H wrote to Thomas M on 27 Feb: "[T]he last account I had of them was from Sara, who went to Grasmere as soon as she heard the news. & what a melancholy meeting it would be, for they had not heard the news when she got there. & she was obliged to be the bearer of it. She staid a week with them & then returned to Kendal, as they thought it was better she should leave them, & then they would be obliged to exert themselves more."

SFC wrote to Mrs. George C from Eaton-house, near Liverpool, in a letter endorsed 1 Mar and postmarked in Liverpool 2 Mar: "The family of the Wordsworths are in the greatest affliction! the loss of their best-beloved brother, attended with such shocking circumstances, has deeply wounded their poor hearts. he intended as soon as he had acquired enough to live on, to go into the North and live near his brother, or any where else, wherever his brother and sister should be settled.—he was a very amicable young man, only one and thirty, happily not married!" (UTL.) JW was actually thirty-two.

[9] Where proof transcriptions of the letters in the corrected proof copy of *Mem* (DCP) vary from the published versions, the proof versions normally correspond more exactly to the MSS of the letters. The conclusion of the last main paragraph of this letter (of which the MS is apparently lost) from "and human life, after all, what is it!" reads as follows in the proof copy: "and human life, after all what it is! Surely, this is not to be for ever, even on this perishable planet! Come tomorrow to me, if you can, at least to me; your conversation, I know, will do me good." The proof has been corrected to the readings of *Mem* ("for ever" became one word in Knight's edition of the *Letter*, 1907, and has remained so in later editions).

Probably 13–15 Feb RS visits DC to aid as he can in the consolation of the Ws. (*EY* 542–44; 1805:14. See also *EY* 577.)

16. c late Feb–c late May

Charles Luff visits the Ws, probably more than once. (Letters, Mrs. Luff to Tom Wedgwood, Apr 1805; Charles Luff to Tom Wedgwood, 1 May 1805, UKL.)[10]

17. Feb 16

W writes to TCl: The family's affliction. (*EY* 544–45.)[11]

18. Feb 17

Mrs. Harden and other friends call at DC; find DW near distraction. (Moorman II, 41.)

19. Probably shortly before Feb 18

W writes to CL about JW (letter not known to survive); probably requests CL to obtain information concerning the *Abergavenny* disaster. (*LL* I, 382–85.)

20. Probably c Feb 18

SH departs DC, returns to Kendal. (1805:12&n.)

[10] Mrs. Luff reports in Apr that the Ws have suffered severely, "but are now more composed—and more reconciled to the heavy loss they have sustained"; also that they have appreciated a kind remembrance from Wedgwood. Luff writes on 1 May that the Ws are more reconciled than he ever suspected they would be: "[T]hey are all gratitude to you, for your sympathy and kindness, they are your *sincere friends* and I sincerely think you can have [none] more trust worthy, the more I know of them, the more I love them, their eccentricities vanish on a nearer acquaintance, at least, their many excellent virtues completely sink them from observation. I have been a good deal with them lately, and poor Dorothy kindly said [?] that I gave them comfort. . . ."

[11] W's next-to-last sentence, "God grant us patience, for this life needs it above all other qualities," struck CCl forcibly. On 19 Mar her friend Jane Maling wrote to CCl: "Your letter affected me very much. . . . Wordsworth saying that patience is the quality we have more need of in this world than any other, gave me a sensation which resembled pleasure." (BM Add. MS 41, 267B, fols. 35–36.) CCl quoted the sentence to HCR from memory on 13 Mar 1842 (*HCRWC* I, 456).

21. Perhaps c Feb 20

RS returns to DC [see 1805:15] for a brief visit of consolation to the Ws. (*EY* 544; letter, RS to Rickman 17 Feb 1805, HEH; letter, RS to John May, 6 Mar 1805, UTL.)[12]

22. Probably Feb 27; Feb 27

Probably on 27 Feb DW writes to RW from Grasmere: Inquires after RW's health and feelings. The household at DC. (*EY* 549.)

On 27 Feb DW writes to CW: Inquires about CW's and his wife's health and feelings. A visit from the Lloyds [see 1805:13]. (*EY* 550–51.)

23. Probably c but by Feb 28

W writes to Sir GB: Thanks GB for his kindness. Brief summary, in response to Sir GB's queries, of major points in his financial history, esp. as affected by the Lowther debt, the Calvert legacy, and loans to JW. JW; STC. (*EY* 545–49.)[13]

24. Probably c Mar–Apr 11; probably c early May (perhaps after first few days)

Probably c Mar–11 Apr DW, perhaps MW, probably SH, during the period when SH is present [see 1805:30], make copies of some of W's MS poems. Some of these copies are possibly used later in the printer's copy of *P2V*. (*EY* 576; Appendix VII.)

Probably c early May (perhaps after first few days) W writes to CL (letter not known to survive) with questions for Gilpin about the *Abergavenny* disaster. (*LL* I, 387, 390.)

[12] In an unpublished portion, dated 17 Feb, of the letter to Rickman endorsed "Circ. 16 Feb 1805" printed in part CCS II, 313–15, as belonging to 16 Feb, RS remarks: "[P]oor Wordsworth & his sister are in a miserable state. & I have been over with them. & am going over again." On 9 Mar he wrote to William Taylor: "I have been twice over with him, & never witnessed such affliction as his and his sister's" (Robberds II, 77).

[13] The postmark of the letter, as noted *EY* 545, is 1 Mar, and W's date of 20 Feb would thus appear much too early. Some possibility may exist that W intended to write "26," but the MS in fact seems to read "20." The letter of Sir GB's to which W here replies was written on 17 Feb (DCP).

25. Mar 4

W, DW write to RW: (DW:) Inquiries about RW's health and feelings; seeks any comforting news about JW; wishes some keepsake, if any survives. (W:) Should not the clergyman at Weymouth be asked to see to the burial of JW if his body should be recovered? (*EY* 551–52.)

26. Mar 7

MW writes to CCl: Thanks for TCl's letter; CCl's health; the DC household; SH expected; Johnny; Dora. (*MWL* 2–3.)

W writes to Walter Scott from Grasmere: Thanks for copy of *The Lay of the Last Minstrel* [see 1805:7]; their pleasure in the poem; JW; renewal of invitation to visit Grasmere. (*EY* 553, 559.)

27. Probably c Mar 10–Mar 12; Mar 12

Probably c 10–12 Mar DW writes to Mrs. Rawson from Grasmere. (*EY* 558.)

On 12 Mar W writes to Sir GB: A letter and gift of money from Sir GB; W's feelings on the subject of the acceptance of pecuniary assistance by men of letters. W has heard that JW's death will probably not result in financial loss for the family; will keep Sir GB's note against the expenses of a possible trip and purchase of some books. Philosophical and religious implications of JW's death; JW; inaccuracy of newspaper reports of the disaster; further details. Quotation from Aristotle's Synopsis of the Virtues and Vices [see Appendix IX]. (*EY* 554–58.)

28. Probably Mar 15, 17, perhaps also Mar 16; Mar 16

Probably 15, 17 Mar, perhaps also 16 Mar, DW writes to JPM: The household at DC; JW's last visit there; the reports of the *Abergavenny* disaster. Thanks for letters from JPM and Mrs. Rawson. Possibility of changing residence, moving southward. Financial aspects of the disaster. (*EY* 558–62.)[14]

---

[14] As indicated *EY* 558n, DW's date of "Friday 16th March 1804" is plainly mistaken both in year and day of month. There seems no basis for certainty that the letter was written only on Friday and on the Sunday that it was sent off but not on the intervening Saturday (see *EY* 562).

On 16 Mar W writes to James Losh: JW and his hopes of assisting W and DW financially; the inaccuracy of newspaper accounts of the disaster; further details; his feelings. (*EY* 562–66.)[15]

29. Probably c but by Mar 18; probably Mar 18, 19

Probably c but by 18 Mar W writes to CL. (*LL* I, 390.)

Probably 18, 19 Mar DW writes to Lady B: (18 Mar:) JW; the household at DC; hopes for a meeting with the Bs; *Madoc*; receipt of half of a bill; MW. (19 Mar:) Receipt of letter from Lady B; Lady B's sister. (*EY* 566–69.)[16]

Probably on 18 Mar W, DW walk for two hours. (*EY* 567.)

On 18 Mar DW writes to CCl: CCl's health; JW and the household at DC. (*EY* 569–70.)

30. Possibly Mar 19, certainly before Mar 26–perhaps Apr 18; between this time and Apr 18; Mar 19

Possibly 19 Mar, certainly before 26 Mar, SH arrives at DC for a visit. (She departs perhaps 18 Apr.) (*EY* 570, 575; *SHL* 6–7; *MWL* 3.)

Probably during her visit she assists in copying some of W's MS poems. Some of these copies are possibly used later in the printer's copy of *P2V*. (*EY* 576; Appendix VII.)

Probably on 14 Mar MW brings a letter from Lady B to DW, who is sitting in a green field with Dora. (*EY* 568.)

W writes to RW from Grasmere: JW; the household at DC; the debt to Sotheby [see 1803:138; 1804:36; 1805:40]. The Ws would like any keepsake of JW; seek further information about the disaster. (*EY* 570–71.)

On 19 Mar W writes to Richard Sharp: JW. W seeks news concerning the disaster. Their feeling about JW; the household at DC. W requests Sharp to have his servant take W's watch, which W has broken by letting it fall, and has sent on to Sharp, to its maker [see 1805:10]; GH. (*EY* 572–73.)

---

[15] Losh's Diary notes receipt of the letter, with the comment "very affecting," under the date of 22 Mar.

[16] The half of a bill was probably the other half of the "note" received by W prior to writing his letter to Sir GB of 12 Mar.

31. Possibly between Mar 19 and Apr 2, esp. c Mar 26

W visits Capt. W at Brougham Hall. The exact length of the visit is unknown. (*EY* 570–73, 575, 583; *SHL* 6–7.)[17]

32. Mar 20, 21

On 20 Mar JW's body is recovered on the beach near Weymouth. On 21 Mar JW is buried in the churchyard at Wyke Regis. A relative of Priscilla Wordsworth, perhaps Mrs. T. H. Buxton, arranges the funeral. (*JWL* 50–51, 184; *SHL* 7; *EY* 574n; *Gentleman's Magazine* LXXV, 1805, 294.)

33. Probably Mar 26

A letter arrives from RW advising of the recovery and burial of W's body and perhaps providing other information of the *Abergavenny* disaster. A letter arrives for SH from STC concerning his health, plans, death of Major Adye, and possibly advising W of his intentions of repaying the Sotheby debt on his return [see 1803:138]. (*EY* 573–74, 583–84.)

SH writes to Mrs. Cookson of Kendal: Her box has arrived; the Ws well—physically; recovery and burial of JW's body; letter from STC; the Cooksons. (*SHL* 6–7.)

34. Probably Mar 27

DW writes to Lady B: News from STC [see 1805:33]. Recovery and burial of JW's body. (*EY* 573–74.)[18]

---

[17] W was fairly certainly absent from home on 26 Mar, and fairly certainly present on 19 Mar and 2 Apr. The letters received probably on 26 Mar from STC and RW are possibly those referred to by W in his letter to RW of 16 Apr. He remarks that the letter from RW came when W "had been over at Captain Wordsworth's." The visit would have followed W's letter to RW of 19 Mar.

[18] SH's letter of almost surely 26 Mar speaks of STC's letter as "just arrived," and mentions the news of the recovery of JW's body. DW refers to STC's letter and the news of JW as having arrived on the day preceding that of her letter, which she dates "28th March."

35. Perhaps very late Mar or early Apr

W writes to RS: His visit to Capt. W [see 1805:31]; burial of JW; RS would be welcome at DC. (*TLS* 1967, 673.)

36. Apr 2

DW writes to CCl: Robert Newton's house is to let for a three- or four-month period [see 1805:61]. They hope to make a trip at the end of the summer. CCl's health; SH; STC. (*EY* 574–75.)

37. Probably c Apr 11; Apr 11; between Apr 11 and May 31

Probably c 11 Apr W composes lines for *The Recluse* on the subject of JW. Composition is abundant, but W is able to remember few of the lines, becoming overpowered by his subject; and none are written down at this time, or perhaps ever. If any of this work survives, it remains unidentified. (*EY* 575–76, 586, 592.)

On 11 Apr DW writes to Lady B: JW. W has resumed composition, composing lines on JW for *The Recluse*. Johnny. They have been making transcriptions of some of W's MS poems; have definitely decided to leave Grasmere on STC's return. RS; Klopstock and his first wife. (*EY* 575–78.)

On the same day DW resumes the writing of her *Recollections* [see 1804:88]. Between this day and 31 May she writes Part III, covering, after a sentence concerning 5 Sept, the events of 6–25 Sept 1803, and concluding the work; and she makes a copy of the journal. (*DWJ* I, ix, 344, 439–40; EdS *DW* 405; *EY* 598.)[19]

38. Apr 14 (–probably Apr 16)

RS arrives for a visit at DC. (He remains probably until 16 Apr.) (*EY* 582.)

---

[19] What appears to be draft toward the description of Glenalmond in the entry for 9 Sept is written on the address portion of a letter from Sir GB to W of 29 Mar 1805 (DCP). In her letter to Lady B of 11 June 1805 DW seems to refer to her recent work on her journal as a task of copying only (*EY* 598); but *DWJ* I, 344 leaves little doubt that Part III of the journal was composed from 11 Apr. DW's original MS and transcript apparently do not survive.

39. c but by Apr 15; probably c Apr 15; Apr 15

Probably c but by 15 Apr a letter arrives from Thomas Evans with information about JW.

Probably c 15 Apr W writes to Thomas Evans (only a portion of the letter is known to survive): W thanks Evans for letter concerning JW; JW described. (*EY* 578–80.)[20]

On 15 Apr DW writes to Lady B: New information about the *Abergavenny* disaster from Evans; Capt. W; RS. (*EY* 580–83.)

40. Probably c but by Apr 16; probably Apr 16; Apr 16

Probably c but by 16 Apr DW writes to CCl: Robert Newton's house [see 1805:36]; CCl's projected visit to Grasmere. (*EY* 584–86.)

Probably on 16 Apr RS departs from DC. (*EY* 582.)

On 16 Apr W writes to RW: Thanks for RW's letter [see 1805: 30; 1805:33] and its information about JW. W wishes Sotheby debt paid immediately [see 1803:138; 1805:30]. (*EY* 583–84.)

41. Perhaps Apr 18

SH departs from DC. (*EY* 584–86. See 1805:30.)

42. c late Apr–early May, esp. c Apr 24–Apr 30, May 1

W organizes *Prel* XI, XII, perhaps composing many lines, in MS Z form, c late Apr–early May. Drafts toward *Prel.* XI.164–90 in the Windy Brow NB are probably written at this time.

W composes c 300 lines during the period c 24–30 Apr. On 1 May he expects that two books will complete the poem. (Appendix V; *EY* 586.)

43. May 1

W writes to Sir GB: His composition about JW [see 1805:37]; *Prel.* Dora has croup. Grace-Dieu [former seat of the Beaumont family]; John and Francis Beaumont; Sir GB's painting of The Thorn. W possesses, but has not read, *Madoc.* (*EY* 586–88.)

[20] The date is suggested on the basis of the tone of DW's comments about Evans's letter in her letter of 15 Apr.

44. May 4

DW writes to Lady B: Charges on the letters which they exchange. Interesting poetry, by a child, sent by Sir GB. *Madoc*; *Lay of the Last Minstrel*; STC; JW. W hard at work. (*EY* 588–92.)

45. Probably c May 20

W completes original version of *Prel.* (*EY* 594. See Appendix V.)

46. Perhaps between c May 20 and July 5, possibly shortly before July 5; probably between c May 20 and June 11

Perhaps between c 20 May and 5 July, possibly shortly before 5 July, W composes:
To the Daisy ("Sweet Flower!")
"Distressful Gift! This Book Receives" (*PW* IV, 372–73).
(*EY* 603, 598. See 1805:50.)[21]
Probably between c 20 May and 11 June W composes several short poems. These probably include *Glen Almain.* (*EY* 601–02. See 1805:48; 1805:50; Moorman II, 55–56.)

47. May 31

DW completes the copy that forms the basis of MS A of her *Recollections.* (*DWJ* I, viii–ix; EdS *DW* 405–06; Memorandum, MS Journal 12, DCP.)

---

[21] The similarity in tone and content and stanza form of *To the Daisy* and "Distressful Gift!" (see esp. lines 15–17) imply composition about the same time. DW on 11 June (*EY* 598) makes mention of only one set of verses in memory of JW in a context were she might well have mentioned any others extant; and that poem is probably *Elegiac Verses.* W speaks c but by 5 July of having composed "lately" two small poems in memory of his brother "too melancholy" for copying. *Elegiac Verses* might be one of the two, but the similarities already mentioned suggest that the two other poems have at least an equal claim. These three poems make up the contents of DC MS 57, described *PW* IV, 474 (see 1806:2), and appear the only surviving works fitting the comments in the two letters cited.

48. June 3

W, DW, Dora walk in the green field beside the Rothay. W composes *Stepping Westward*. (*PW* III, 444; EdS 405–06.)

W writes to Sir GB: The sunset scene, in which he writes; the news in the papers; a print of [Northcote's portrait of] STC; news of STC from Sarah Stoddart. *Prel* finished a fortnight ago; W's feelings about it; plans for *The Recluse* and a narrative poem. *Madoc*. (*EY* 593–95.)

49. June 6

W, MW, DW finish the Moss Hut at the orchard of DC. (*DWJ* I, 439.)

50. Probably June 8; June 8

Probably on 8 June W and a neighbor walk to Grisedale Tarn to fish. W is there overcome by his association of the spot with his last parting from JW [see 1800:145]. He quits his companion and, in tears, composes verses to the memory of JW—probably *Elegiac Verses in Memory of My Brother, John Wordsworth*. (*EY* 598; *Elegiac Verses*, note, and IF note. See Moorman II, 43; 1805:46.)

On 8 June DW writes to CCl from Grasmere at about 6:30 PM: Urges CCl to visit Grasmere. Letter from ML; garden; Tommy Cl. (*EY* 596–97.)

51. Probably June 10–June 14, and certainly by July 7

Probably on 10 June W, accompanied to a point near Grisedale Tarn by MW and DW, takes his fishing rod and walks to Patterdale. At Patterdale he is joined by Richard Sharp. He returns to DC on 14 June. Possibly at this time, certainly by 7 July, W gives Charles Luff verses in memory of JW—probably *Elegiac Verses*—to transmit to Tom Wedgwood. (*EY* 597–601; letter, Luff to Josiah Wedgwood, 7 July 1805, UKL.)[22]

---

[22] Luff wrote: "Wm Wordsworth had beg'd me to enclose to your brother [Tom] a few lines written to the memory of his late poor brother accompanied, by his kindest regards and warmest wishes for his happiness."

On 11 June DW writes to Lady B: Garden in order; hut complete. Has completed *Recollections*. W; STC. Daily life at DC. The print of STC [see 1805:48]. W has written some short poems. (*EY* 597–601.)

52. June 16

W, DW walk in the evening. W composes.

DW writes to Lady B: W's and her thoughts of Lady B; encloses copy of *Glen Almain*. W; Sharp; *DS, EW, SP.* (*EY* 601–03.)

53. Probably c but by June 18 (–probably c July 7)

SFC, SC arrive for a visit at DC. (They remain probably until 7 July.) (*EY* 608; letter, RS to Charles Danvers, 18 June 1805, BM Add. MS 30,928, fol. 59.)[23]

54. Perhaps July or Aug

Richard Sharp possibly visits DC. (*EY* 602, 615.)

55. July 3

The Longman records for *LB* 1805, commencing accounts for an edition of 500 copies, begin under this date. (See Owen CSP 94–95.)

56. Probably c but by July 5

W writes to Sir GB (only a fragment of the letter is known to survive): The Bs' letters; transcripts of *Prel* VIII.1–61, *Stepping Westward* with related entry from DW's *Recollections*. (*EY* 603–07.)[24]

---

[23] RS, advising Danvers about his route to Keswick, remarks: "At Grasmere if I can hit the time, & the weather be fair I will meet you: call at Wordsworth's to know if I be there, & do not feel aukward about it,—besides Mrs Coleridge is there, & you may ask for her if you like that better."

DW remarks on 14 July (*EY* 607) that SFC and SC departed "a week ago after having been here a fortnight."

[24] The letter was surely written between 3 June and 14 July (*PW* III, 444; *EY* 607); but chances seem good that this is the letter referred to by DW on 14 July as having been sent by W on the same day that DW received a letter from Lady B, which she also states to have been "a week [ago] Friday" (*EY* 608).

57. Probably c July 7

SFC, SC depart from DC. (*EY* 608. See 1805:53.)

58. Perhaps July 8, 9

RS possibly visits DC on 8 and 9 July or calls on 9 July. Charles Danvers possibly calls there to meet him. (1805:53; Curry I, 387; Danvers Journal, BM Add. MS 30,929.)

59. July 14; between July 14 and July 29

On 14 July DW writes to Lady B: Letter from STC; his plans; his notes of his ideas for *The Recluse* burnt; letters sunk; SC. (*EY* 607–09.)

Between 14 and 29 July DW is absent from DC for three days. (*EY* 607, 609, 611.)

60. Perhaps c July 23–July 24 ff

Perhaps c 23–24 July Mrs. Luff visits DC. Probably through a letter from Luff to Mrs. Luff written at Patterdale on 23 July and addressed to Mrs. Luff at Grasmere, W learns of the discovery of the body of Charles Gough by Willy Harrison at Red Tarn. (*EY* 611–12.)

The inferential history of Gough's death and his dog's faithful attendance inspires W's *Fidelity*. Probably the same circumstances also evoke W's *Incident Characteristic of a Favorite Dog* and *Tribute to the Memory of the Same Dog.* (*Fidelity*, *Tribute* IF notes; content. See 1805: 71.)[25]

25 The "incident" of the poem so titled probably occurred by 1800, prior to Thomas H's removal to Gallow Hill (see IF note), but the subject matter of the poem relates it closely to the other two mentioned. All three are dated 1805 *PW* 1836–*PW* 1850. The IF note to *Tribute*, omitted from *PW* but reproduced by Grosart (III, 164) and Knight (*PW* Knight, 1882–89 III, 41; *PW* Knight, 1896 III, 49–50), states that *Incident* and *Tribute* were written "at the same time, 1805," and that the dog described, Music, died by falling into a draw-well at Gallow Hill.

On Gough and the origins of *Fidelity*, see esp. "The Story of Gough and His Dog," in H. D. Rawnsley, *Past and Present in the English Lakes* (Glasgow, 1916), 153–208, 213; Kenneth Curry, "A Note on Wordsworth's 'Fidelity,'" *PQ* XXXII (1953), 212–14; *EY* 611–12; and Walter Scott's poem *Helvellyn*.

61. Perhaps c but by July 26; c late July, esp. c but by July 26 (–Aug 5, –probably c Aug 9, –probably c Oct 13)

Perhaps c but by 26 July Mrs. William Threlkeld and her daughter Elizabeth arrive for a visit at DC. (They depart probably c 9 Aug.) (*EY* 618–19nn.)

Probably c late July but by the same date CCl enters lodgings at Robert Newton's in Grasmere. She is perhaps accompanied thither, or in any case is by that date joined, by TCl, who remains here through 5 Aug and who probably does not depart the area finally until after 17 Sept. (CCl probably departs c 13 Oct.) (*EY* 609; H. D. Rawnsley, *Past and Present in the English Lakes*, Glasgow, 1916, 203–08; Danvers Journal, BM Add. MS 30,929. See 1805:64; 1805:66; *MY* II, 158; letter, Charles Luff to Josiah Wedgwood, 17 Sept 1805.)[26]

Probably between CCl's arrival and c 9 Aug Mrs. and Elizabeth Threlkeld, DW and probably the other Ws drink tea at Newton's with CCl. (*MY* II, 352–53.)

62. July 29

W writes to Sir GB: STC's duties at Malta. Is there room for him at Coleorton if he visits? W offers Houbraken and Vertue's *Heads of Illustrious Persons*, which he has purchased; *Madoc*; Francis and John B. MW transcribes a letter from Luff concerning the discovery of Gough's body [see 1805:60]. (*EY* 609–12.)

63. Probably c early Aug, by Aug 9

RW visits at DC for an unknown length of time, probably departing by 9 Aug. He informs DW of his intention of giving her a pony. W and RW probably discuss payment of the Sotheby debt [see 1803:138; 1805:40]. (*EY* 618–19, 631.)[27]

---

[26] Luff wrote from Patterdale on 17 Sept, "Mr Clarkson is shortly going to Town."

[27] DW's manner of referring, on 11 Aug, to the Threlkelds, RW's departure from DC, and her own trip to PH on 9 Aug suggest that RW's visit overlapped that of the Threlkelds, and that DW's departure from DC was not long delayed after RW's.

64. Aug 5

RS and Charles Danvers meet TCl on the road to Grasmere, dine with him, probably at Newton's, where they meet DW. W calls, takes RS and Danvers, and probably TCl, to tea at DC. TCl gives an account of the death of Gough. After tea RS and Danvers walk with W, find that the river has washed away the bridge at Rydal; see the falls; part with W to go on to the Lloyds'. (Danvers Journal, BM Add. MS 30,929. See Curry article cited 1805:60n.)

65. Aug 7

W, DW write to Lady B: (W:) Copy of *To the Daisy* ("Sweet Flower!"). (DW:) Lady B's mind should be at ease respecting a recent paragraph in the *Courier* about STC. CCl; James Satterthwaite. Possibility of the Ws' visiting the Bs. W anxious to get on with his great work. James Grahame's *The Sabbath*. (*EY* 613–18.)

66. Probably Aug 9–by Aug 15

Probably on 9 Aug DW, Mrs. Threlkeld, Elizabeth Threlkeld travel from DC to PH. DW returns to DC by 15 Aug. (*EY* 618–20.)[28]

67. Probably Aug 11–Aug 14; probably between Aug 11 and Aug 13, 15

Probably on 11 Aug DW writes to RW from PH: Asks for a side-saddle for the pony RW has promised her [see 1805:63]; her trip to PH [see 1805:66]; asks, for W, whether RW pays the tax on their property. (*EY* 618–19.)

Perhaps on this day W brings a pony to DW, who perhaps meets him on his way.

Possibly on this day W walks along the banks of the Eamont with Thomas Wilkinson; meets people going to and from church; meets two musicians by the bank playing the hautboy and clarinet.

---

[28] Since DW expresses a hope to RW, when writing from PH on 11 Aug, that he will visit her there before he leaves the country ("[H]ow glad I should be," she remarks, "if you were to chance to come in before I go away!"), she does not intend to depart within the next few days. But the actual date of her return to Grasmere remains uncertain.

Probably in any case W travels to Keswick by one route or another on this day. He visits at GH until 13 Aug. (He returns to DC 14 Aug.) (*EY* 619, 626; *DWJ* I, 420; 1805:68; 1805:70; Danvers Journal, BM Add. MS 30,929.)[29]

Probably while in company with W between 11 and 15 Aug, Walter Scott tells W that Lord Somerville regards himself as responsible for the sending of the spy to Somerset in 1797 [see *CEY* 204–05]. Possibly while both are with RS at GH, between 11 and 13 Aug, Scott reports that Lord Somerville has said that he still regards W and RS as Jacobins at heart. (Curry I, 392, 401.)

Probably between 11 and 15 Aug W reads a part of *The Recluse*, probably *RC*, to Davy. (*EY* 634; 1805:68–1805:72.)

68. Aug 12

W, Davy, RS, Harry S, Scott, Danvers walk after breakfast from GH to Watendlath and to the Bowder Stone, where probably the GH ladies and Mrs. Scott meet them for dinner, after which Scott, RS, Harry, Danvers climb Castle Crag. They reach GH by 9 PM. (Danvers Journal, BM Add. MS 30,929.)

69. Aug 13

W, Davy, Scott depart from GH for Patterdale and Grasmere. They pass the night at the inn at Patterdale. W and Scott are kept from their beds, which are to be spread on the floor, by a group of ladies who retain possession of their room until 12:30 AM, although W and Scott call out the half-hours like watchmen under their windows. Davy perhaps shares their discomforts. The ladies are Elizabeth and Catherine

---

[29] DW comments probably on 11 Aug (see 1805:66) that Mrs. Threlkeld and Elizabeth Threlkeld are to "set off for Newbiggin today after dinner, and William meets me with a pony." Danvers makes plain that Humphry Davy arrived at GH on 11 Aug, but he says nothing of the time of arrival of W, who is nonetheless reported with the group that walked to Watendlath "[a]fter breakfast" on the morning of 12 Aug. Sunday 11 Aug is the only Sunday during this summer when W is known to have been in the neighborhood of Lowther.

Smith of Coniston, Mary Dixon, who is on her way to Scotland, and the sister of Sir Alexander Tinlock, whom Miss Dixon is going to visit in the hope of being introduced to Scott. (Copy of letter, Thomas Wilkinson to Martha Frances Smith, 1 Jan 1806, Wilkinson Letters, Tullie House Library, IV; Mary Carr, *Thomas Wilkinson*, London, 1905, 83; Danvers Journal, BM Add. MS 30,929.)[30]

70. Aug 14

W, Davy, Scott climb Helvellyn. Davy goes on to Grasmere, where the others join him later. Mrs. Scott also joins the party at Grasmere. Probably all dine and pass the night at DC.

Musings near Aquapendente 55–65 refers to events of this day. (*EY* 621, 634; *MY* I, 96; *LY* I, 219; *Musings near Aquapendente* IF note; John Davy, *The Angler in the Lake District*, London, 1857, 195–96; *Moore Memoirs* IV, 334–35.)[31]

71. Probably between Aug 14 and Nov 10, 1806 Mar 2, Dec 23

Probably between 14 Aug and 10 Nov 1805, certainly by 2 Mar 1806 W composes *Fidelity*.

Probably between 14 Aug 1805 and 23 Dec 1806 W composes:
Incident Characteristic of a Favorite Dog

[30] Wilkinson's account of the incident at the inn makes no mention of Davy, who was almost certainly present at this stage of the journey. The Danvers Journal notes that on 13 Aug "Walter Scot, Davy, & Wordsworth left us for Grasmere"; and Davy accompanied W and Scott on the climb up Helvellyn next day. In *A Year in Europe* [1818–1819] (New York, 1823, 501) John Griscom records that a similar story was told at the Patterdale Inn in 1819, but of Scott, Davy, and RS.

On Elizabeth Smith, who was probably now already stricken with a fatal illness, see esp. *DNB*.

[31] Scott's *Helvellyn* probably draws esp. on the events of this day. John Davy records: "Scott, I know, once only, and for a day, visited Wordsworth whilst residing here [at Grasmere], and then in company with Davy; it was the day they ascended Helvellyn together." Moore records Scott's description of W's "manly endurance of poverty": "Scott has dined with him at that time in his kitchen; but though a kitchen, all was neatness in it."

Tribute to the Memory of the Same Dog
(1805:60n; 1805:70; 1806:14; 1806:115; *MY* I, 96.)[32]

72. Aug 15

W, DW, perhaps the other Ws, Davy, the Scotts go on Windermere. Davy parts from the others at Windermere. (*EY* 621. See 1805: 70.)

73. Aug 23

RW charges to W's account payment of £7/10/6, premium on £300 policy on Montagu's life, under this date. (RW accounts, DCP.)

74. Aug 24

RS sends to Richard Duppa, for his *Life of Michel Angelo*, W's "Yes, Hope May with My Strong Desire Keep Pace," translation from the Italian of Michaelangelo. (*Bodleian Library Quarterly* I, 1914–16, 29–31. See Curry *RES*; 1805:1.)

75. Aug 25–a time possibly by Sept 2, probably by c Oct 13, fairly certainly by Oct 27

SH arrives at DC for a visit on 25 Aug. She departs possibly by 2 Sept, probably by 13 Oct, fairly certainly by 27 Oct. (*EY* 620, 633–34. See 1804: 78; 1805:90.)

On 25 Aug W, DW write to RW: (W:) Interest is to be paid on Sotheby note [see 1805:40; 1805:63]. (DW:) Has written to Mrs. Crackanthorpe for their father's Bible; thanks for sidesaddle, which SH says has been ordered [see 1805:67]. (*EY* 619–20.)

76. Aug 26

DW writes to Lady B: Information about rooms and dimensions at DC, in response to Lady B's statement of her plans to prepare a cottage

---

[32] W's phrasing on 10 Nov 1806 (*MY* I, 96) indicates that W is unlikely to have mentioned *Fidelity* to Scott before that date, but that he is likely to have composed the poem by then. He would hardly have failed to mention *Fidelity* to Scott on 14 Aug if it were already written. It was certainly in existence by 2 Mar 1806. The *Incident* and *Tribute* seem unlikely to have been composed prior to *Fidelity*.

for them at Coleorton; visits from Scott and Davy [see 1805:69]. (*EY* 620–22.)

77. Between Aug 26 and Oct 24

Unidentified acquaintances of the Ws possibly visit DC for a week or fortnight. (*EY* 620, 622, 624, 630, 632.)[33]

78. c late Aug, by Sept 2; probably by c Oct 13, certainly by Oct 27

RS, Harry S dine at Grasmere with TCl and probably with W. Harry walks in the evening in shoes borrowed from W (his own being wet). RS probably stays the night at DC.

W, SH, and an unidentified lady visit GH. Possibly this visit is connected with SH's departure from DC [see 1805:75]. SH probably in any case departs by c 13 Oct and certainly by 27 Oct. (Curry I, 398; *EY* 634.)[34]

79. Perhaps late 1805 or early 1806

W composes *The Kitten and the Falling Leaves*. (Content; IF note.)[35]

[33] The visitors were present from the time of DW's receipt of Lady B's last letter but one as of 27 Oct. That letter probably arrived after 26 Aug (*EY* 620) but before Dora was weaned, some time before 24 Oct (*EY* 629). DW possibly refers only to CCl and SH (see 1805:61; 1805:75).

[34] RS remarks to Danvers that "Wordsworth, Sarah Hutchinson and a Lady of their acquaintance have been here." It is improbable that RS would have spoken of CCl as simply "a Lady of their acquaintance"; he had just spoken in the same letter of TCl (see also 1805:64).

RS mentions W only as the lender of the shoes on the occasion of his Grasmere visit, but it seems probable that W was RS's host.

[35] In editions from 1836 W dates the poem 1804, but in the IF note dates it 1805. The germ of the poem is probably *STCNB* 1813 (see *STCNB* 1813n), an entry which dates probably between 5 and 8 Jan 1804 (*STCNB* vol. I, part 2, 472). The poem is not in MS M (see Appendix III), and W is unlikely to have remembered wrongly when he states in the IF note that the child in the poem was Dora (see lines 103–04); so autumn 1804 would appear the earliest possible time. But Dora's apparently prolonged attention to the kitten, and her laughing, as described in the poem, would seem a response more likely in a child a year old than the recently born infant of 1804. (See Arnold Gesell and Frances L. Ilg, *Infant and Child in the Culture of Today*, New York, 1943, 123–40.)

80. Probably between early Sept and 1806 Feb 21

W composes:
Rob Roy's Grave
To the Sons of Burns, stanzas 2, 3, 4, 8
(*DWJ* I, viii; *PW* III, 443. Cf EdS *DW* 405–07.)[36]

81. Probably between early Sept and Nov 1

CCl makes a transcript, now MS A, of DW's *Recollections*. (*DWJ* I, viii.)

82. Perhaps c Sept 9

RS perhaps visits at Grasmere, dines with Lloyd, and returns to GH accompanied by W and Harry S. If so, W's visit at GH is probably very brief. (Curry I, 399.)

83. Sept 13

Five copies of *LB* [1805] are entered on W's Longman account, four without indication of recipient, and one for "W. Scott Esq," under this date. (Longman accounts, DCP.)

84. Sept 18

RW's accounts charge DW £45/–/–, payment of bill in favor Thomas H, under this date. (RW accounts, DCP.)

85. Oct 5

Probably MW inscribes a copy of vol. II of *LB* 1805 in W's name and that of STC to CCl at Grasmere. (J. E. Wells, note for item 23 in his catalogue of his W collection, Swarthmore College Library.)[37]

---

[36] Had these verses been composed by early Sept they would most probably have been included in MS A of *Recollections* (see 1805:81). They were certainly composed by the time that DW wrote MS B of the *Recollections* in early 1806, by 21 Feb. Possibly one or the other was the "other poem" that DW intended to send to CCl along with the introduction for *The Solitary Reaper* some time after 3 Mar 1806 (*MY* I, 11).

[37] At the BM is a copy of *LB* 1805 inscribed, probably by STC, to RS from W and STC without date.

86. Perhaps c Oct 6

DW, and perhaps W and MW, ride around Loughrigg Tarn; view a spot where Sir GB had once intended to build. (*EY* 631.)

87. Probably shortly after Oct 7

RW of Branthwaite sends to DC the books of JW Sr. in his keeping except for three small octavo volumes pertaining to law intended for RW. (Memorandum, RW of Branthwaite to W, 7 Oct 1805, DCP. See *EY* 620n.)[38]

88. Oct 9

LB 1805 is published in London. (*Times.*)

89. Perhaps c mid-Oct, certainly before Oct 27

DW visits GH; sees SFC, HC, SC. (*EY* 633–34.)

[38] Cousin RW's schedule of the books sent to W "at his request, Octr 1805," includes the following (semicolons and square-bracketed materials are editorial):

Parliamentary Debates, 14 vols; Cicero's orations [a volume containing *De Officiis, Cato Major,* and *Laelius,* London, 1754, is at DC; among inscriptions are "John Wordsworths Book 1770" and "Wm Wordsworth"]; Forsters [Michael Foster's] Crown Law; Horace (by Smart) 1 vol (2d) [presently at the Library of Pembroke College, Cambridge]; Cornelius Nepus [Nepos]; [John] Tillotson's Sermons, 5 vol (frm 4 to 8 inclve); a Book of Game Laws; Wynn's short Hand Minits, 6 Vol; Bishop of Carlisle's Border Laws; Compleat Solicitors or [?entire] Clerk's Tutor; Book of Help to Justices and their Clerks; Small Book (half bound *in Green*) entitled Systeme de la Nature [Holbach, probably the 1770 or 1780 octavo edition]; Christian Institutes by the Bishop of Chester [London, 1748; presently at DC, inscribed "William Wordsworth 1780"]; a Latin Book marked Wm Cookson; Mr John Wordsworth's Family Bible and Register (about the middle of the book) [presently at DC]; Mr John Wordsworth's History of England; Euclides Elements of Geometry; Florus's History of Rome; Law French Dictionary; [William] Shepherds Court keeper; an old Book of French Plays; Female Spectator 4 Vols; Gill Blas, 2 Vols; [Thomas] Seckers Lectures on ye Catechism; [Offspring] Blackall's practical discourses on the Lords Prayer; Shafloe's Estimate of the manners and Principles of the Times in Knowledge, Happyness, and Virtue; Family Instructor as to Children; Fieldings Works, 8 or 9 Vols; [James] Fosters Works on Natural Religion and Virtue. "Shafloe's Estimate" (seemingly thus, MS) is perhaps John Gordon's *New Estimate* [etc.] (London, 1761), dedicated to Robert Shaftoe.

90. Probably c Oct 13

CCl departs Grasmere. (*EY* 634.)

91. Oct 17, 24

W writes to Sir GB: (17 Oct:) Observations on landscape gardening, with special reference to Sir GB's new house; slowness of the workmen at Coleorton. Michaelangelo's poetry and W's attempts to translate it; transcript of "Yes, Hope May with My Strong Desire Keep Pace." (24 Oct:) Conveyance of game from Bs to DC. W will send Houbraken and Vertue's *Heads* [see 1805:62]. (*EY* 622–29.)

92. Oct 27

DW writes to Lady B: Lady B; prospect of visit to Coleorton; RW's gift of a pony [see 1805:67]; a ride to Loughrigg Tarn [see 1805: 86]; Grasmere; DW's health; Dora; resemblances between *Christabel* and *The Lay of the Last Minstrel*; the Cs; Davy. (*EY* 630–34.)

93. Probably Nov 1–Nov 3

W, MW depart on 1 Nov for a three-day trip to Patterdale and PH. They probably reach one of these destinations on this day. During this excursion they probably see Charles Luff and arrange for W and DW to visit the Luffs on 6 or 7 Nov.

They return over Kirkstone with the Cls on 3 Nov. W waits at Ambleside for the arrival of the newspapers, probably esp. for news of events at Ulm; receives by the same post a gift of game from the Bs [see 1805:91], which he brings home with him. (*EY* 635; *DWJ* I, 413.)[39]

94. Nov 4

DW writes to Lady B: The visit of W and MW to Patterdale and PH; news of the battle [Ulm; see 1805:93]; the Bs' gift of game; weather; Dora; W's shorter poems and plans for publication. (*EY* 635–36.)

[39] As remarked *EY* 637n, DW's journal throughout records the day of the month a day late in relation to the day of the week. On this excursion see also Moorman II, 59–60; *EY* 645.

95. Probably Nov 5

W composes *The Solitary Reaper*. (*EY* 636–39.)

96. Probably Nov 6 (–Nov 12)

W, DW travel from DC over Kirkstone to the cottage of the Luffs [see 1805:93], DW riding on her pony, W walking. They dine under the shelter of a sheepfold; reach the Luffs' two hours before tea. (They return to DC on 12 Nov.) (*EY* 536–37; *DWJ* I, 413–14. See 1805:102.)

97. Probably Nov 7; Nov 7

Probably on 7 Nov W, DW walk to Blowick. Charles Luff joins them on their way. After dinner they walk up the vale with Mrs. Luff. DW and Mrs. Luff leave W alone. He finds a spot which he prefers to all others that he has seen for building a house. Mrs. Luff walks out with him in the moonlight to view it. (*DWJ* I, 414–15; *EY* 636–37.)

Probably on this day DW writes to Lady B from Patterdale: Trip to Patterdale; Grasmere; Crump's house; other local changes. Transcript of *The Solitary Reaper*; W's difficulty with Michaelangelo's sonnets. Plans for return to Grasmere. (*EY* 636–40.)[40]

On 7 Nov W writes to Walter Scott from Patterdale: Hopes of meeting Scott next summer. Todd's edition of Spenser; Scott's edition of Dryden; comment on Dryden and editing him. (*EY* 640–44.)

98. Probably between Nov 7 and 1807 early Apr, 1806 Sept 8, 1806 Aug 1

Probably between 7 Nov 1805 and early Apr 1807 W completes "Rid of a Vexing and a Heavy Load," an early version of *At Florence* [ii].—*From Michael Angelo* ("Eternal Lord! Eased of a Cumbrous Load"). (1805:1; Appendix VII.)

---

[40] DW concludes her letter at "eight o'clock in the evening," having begun that morning. On 29 Nov DW says that she heard of the death of Nelson the morning after writing to Lady B, but she seems here to speak of Saturday as the day after next (*EY* 640), thus implying that she is writing on Thursday 7 Nov. Her statement that she and W intend to return to Grasmere the next day appears to reflect a plan soon afterward revised, perhaps as a result of W's discovery of the property which he so liked.

Probably between 7 Nov 1805 and 8 Sept 1806 W completes *From the Italian of Michael Angelo. II* ("No Mortal Object Did These Eyes Behold"). (1805:1; *MY* I, 79.)

Probably between 7 Nov 1805 and early 1806, certainly by 1 Aug 1806, W completes *From the Italian of Michael Angelo. III* ("The Prayers I Make Will Then Be Sweet Indeed"). (1805:1; *MY* I, 65.)

99. Nov 8

Probably W, DW, Charles Luff, and Luff's servant set off in a boat about 10; see some fishermen taking in their catch; land at Sandwick. They walk up Martindale; dine at the last house, at the head of Bannerdale, in a room built by Mr. Hazel. Walk up Place Fell. Luff shows them the ruins of a former chapel, probably at this time tells them the story that forms the basis of *Exc* II.730–895 [see *PW* V, 68–73; *Exc* IF note]. They descend to Patterdale. DW falls asleep after reaching the Luffs'. They sup upon some of the fish that they had earlier seen being taken in. (*DWJ* I, 415–19; *EY* 647.)

100. Nov 9–Nov 11 ff

At breakfast on the morning of 9 Nov W, DW hear the news of the Battle of Trafalgar and Nelson's death. They go to the inn to make inquiries. On returning they pass by the property that W had noticed as well suited for a home [see 1805:97]; W determines to buy it. They set off for PH so that W may ask Thomas Wilkinson's assistance in making the purchase. They proceed along the eastern side of the lake; call at Eusemere; cross the Eamont; reach PH. After tea W goes on to Wilkinson's and perhaps thence to Brougham to see Capt. W.

W's whereabouts until 11 Dec is not certain; but he probably calls on Capt. W, and examines a property, Waterside, recently purchased by RW. He perhaps spends one or possibly both nights with Wilkinson at Yanwath. W perhaps at this time, or if not now probably soon, authorizes Wilkinson to offer £800 for him for the Patterdale property.

Nelson later contributes to the character described in *The Character of the Happy Warrior*. (*DWJ* I, 419–20; *EY* 645–51; Wilkinson Letters,

Tullie House Library, IV, 83; Mary Carr, *Thomas Wilkinson*, London, 1905, 23, 83; *MY* I, 68, 104–05; 1805:101.)[41]

101. Nov 11

W, DW, SH, Miss Green [of Eusemere] go to Lowther. They cross the river [Eamont] at Yanwath; find Wilkinson at work with his spade. He walks with them to the quarry and to his new path. W hears from Wilkinson that a visitor from Coleorton is in the neighborhood; W sends a message inviting him to call at DC. They dine at Richard Bowman's; go with Miss Green to Penrith; drink tea at Mrs. Ellwood's; read Collingwood's dispatches; go to Mr. James's shop; call upon Miss [probably Elizabeth] M at Mrs. Coupland's. MM and SH mount at the George Inn; W, DW walk to Mrs. Ellwood's. SH, DW stop at Red Hill while W fords the river to Wilkinson's. They return to PH at 10. (*DWJ* I, 420–21; *EY* 647–51. See 1805:100n; 1806:71.)

102. Nov 12

W reads a book loaned him by Wilkinson; DW reads *Castle Rackrent*. They depart from PH shortly before 3; travel over Soulby Fell and along Ullswater to the Luffs' house at Patterdale, where they have tea. They travel over Kirkstone; reach DC at about 11. (*DWJ* I, 421–22.)

103. Perhaps shortly after Nov 12

DW writes, possibly for Lady B, an account of her excursion to Ullswater. DC MS Journal 13 is perhaps written at this time. (See *DWJ* I, xiv–xv.)

104. Probably Nov 13 or Nov 14

Capt. and Mrs. W call at DC. (*EY* 645.)

---

[41] On *The Character* see 1805:112; Moorman II, 44; W's note, *P2V*. On the Patterdale purchase see esp. 1806:12.

In a letter to Martha Frances Smith, d. "1st of 1st Month 1806," Wilkinson refers to "Wordsworth (whom I lately had for two days)."

105. Probably c but by Nov 15

W, DW write to RW: (W:) Inquiries concerning report of income for income tax. The visit to PH; RW's recent purchase of a property [Waterside] near there; a bad tenant on the property [see 1805:100]. (DW:) The pony recently given her by RW [see 1805:67] stumbles and will have to be exchanged. (*EY* 644–46.)

106. Probably Nov 18–Nov 22 or Nov 23

DW is ill: is bedridden probably 19–22 or –23 Nov. [William] Simpson attends her. The illness is diagnosed as peripneumony. (*EY* 646–47, 651.)

107. Nov 24–Nov 25; probably Nov 25–Dec 29, 30, or 31, or 1806 early Jan

John H of Stockton arrives at DC 24 Nov; passes the night there. (He departs next day.) (*EY* 646–47.)

On 24, 25 Nov DW writes to CCl: (24 Nov:) CCl's health. (25 Nov:) MW to visit PH; DW's recent illness [see 1805:106]; her recent visit at PH. (*EY* 646–47.)

Probably on the morning of 25 Nov MW and John H depart from DC to travel to PH. MW intends to remain a fortnight, but returns to DC probably on 29, 30, or 31 Dec, or in early Jan. During her absence Hannah Lewthwaite helps keep house at DC. (*EY* 646, 658; *MY* I, 10; 1805:119.)

108. Probably between late Nov and Dec 14, Dec 25, 1806 Mar 2

Probably between late Nov 1805 and 2 Mar 1806 DW copies *Prel* [MS A]. She completes the first five books of the copy by 14 Dec, eight books by 25 Dec, and the remainder by 2 Mar. (Appendix V; 1805:111.)

109. Probably Nov 28–c Dec 6; between Nov 28 and c Dec 6

Probably on 28 Nov W departs DC, travels to PH for a visit. He returns probably c 6 Dec.

During this period W and MW also visit Capt. and Mrs. W at Brougham Hall.

Probably during this period DW composes *Address to a Child during a Boisterous Winter Evening* and, probably after this, composes *The Cottager to Her Infant*. She copies some of W's poems. (*EY* 648–49, 652–54; *MY* I, 24–25. See Appendix VII.)[42]

110. Nov 29

DW writes to Lady B: The postal service at Grasmere. She is copying some of W's poems [see Appendix VII]. JW; the children; STC; death of Nelson. She is copying *Prel*. The Bs; Sir GB's mother; Lady B's sister. The recent visit to Lowther [see 1805:102]; DW's recent illness [see 1805:106]. Sir Michael le Fleming's white wall; Roscoe's *Leo the Tenth*. (*EY* 648–52.)

111. Probably between Nov 29 and Dec 14; c but by 1807 Jan 27

Probably between 29 Nov and 14 Dec the third part of DW's copy of *Recollections* and a copy of five books of *Prel* are lost while being

---

[42] DW explains (*EY* 654) that she was left alone for a week. I have assumed that she was not counting the day of W's departure or return.

The IF note dates DW's *Address to a Child* 1806, but the *MY* reference leaves little doubt of the time of composition. The *MY* comments suggest also that *The Cottager to Her Infant* was composed about the same time, after the other poem. W had added two stanzas to *The Cottager* (see *PW* II, 50 *app crit*) before it was copied into the back of *Recollections* MS A (see *DWJ* I, viii), along with the *Address*, *The Mother's Return*, *A Fragment* ("There Is a Cottage"), and *A Fragment* ("Peaceful Our Valley"). These same poems are copied into the Coleorton Commonplace Book (PML) following copies from W's letter to Lady B of 21 May 1807 and "From a Poem in M.S. by William Wordsworth" (*Exc* VII.395–481, with readings as the Essay upon Epitaphs printed third by Grosart) and preceding an "Extract from an essay on epitaphs by W. Wordsworth" (the opening paragraph of the Essay printed second by Grosart). *The Mother's Return* probably does not date before early May 1807, and neither set of copies can be supposed to precede that date. The poems were almost certainly copied in sequence with the materials from W's two Essays upon Epitaphs, which were perhaps sent to the Bs c early 1810, after 28 Feb (see *MY* I, 391). A copy of *The Cottager* in Miss Barker's album, probably made not before Oct 1814, contains only DW's three stanzas. That the *Address, The Mother's Return*, and *The Cottager* would all be copied in MS after publication of *P* 1815 seems somewhat doubtful. W's additional stanzas for *The Cottager* thus can be dated, hesitantly, after 1815; but they were in any case not published in his lifetime.

sent to MW by carrier. They are recovered probably c but by 27 Jan 1807. (*EY* 652; *MY* I, 3–4.)

112. Probably c Dec 6; probably between c Dec 6 and 1806 earlʸ Jan

Probably c 6 Dec W returns to DC from PH. (See 1805:109.)

Probably between c 6 Dec and early Jan 1806 W composes *The Character of the Happy Warrior.* (*MY* I, 6–7; letter, Sir GB to W, 25 Nov 1805; *Character* note, IF note. See also *PW* IV, 419–20.)[43]

113. Probably Dec 14

DW writes to CCl: Loss of MSS [see 1805:111]. STC; MW; W. DW requests that TCl's transcriber transcribe third part of *Recollections.* Transcript of *The Solitary Reaper.* (*EY* 652–55.)[44]

114. Probably Dec 15–by Dec 21

Probably on 15 Dec W departs DC and travels to PH. He perhaps meets SH at Threlkeld and accompanies her to PH. He probably returns from his visit there by 21 Dec. (*EY* 654, 656–57. See also 1805:100.)[45]

115. Dec 20

Molly Fisher comes at 6 to shake hands with DW at the hour of the sixth anniversary of her and W's commencement of residence at DC. (*EY* 661. See *CEY* 283–84.)

[43] Sir GB's letter to W of 25 Nov (DCP), which W would probably have found at DC on his return from PH, contains an encomium of Nelson including phrasing similar to, but clearly not in reminiscence of, W's poem (for example, "he was one of those characters with which mankind are rarely indulged in any line, sanguine, & rapid, without hurry, without rashness, bold, forward, & capable. . . "), and it seems likely that Sir GB's remarks prompted some part of the poem. W remarked to Sir GB on 11 Feb [1806] that the lines were written "several weeks ago" (*MY* I, 6–7). See also *CCS* III, 19.

[44] That DW's "Saturday December 11th" was a mistake for 14 Dec rather than 7 Dec is implied by her remark that MW has been at PH since last Monday fortnight (*EY* 564).

[45] DW's account of Molly Fisher's visit on 20 Dec (see *EY* 661) makes no mention of W, who seems nonetheless to have been present when Bragg called on the 21st.

116. Probably Dec 21, 22

On 21 Dec Joshua Bragg stops briefly in his carriage as he passes DC in his way to London. They send a book with him, probably Houbraken and Vertue's *Heads*, to RW's chambers for Sir GB. Bragg offers to convey parcels back from London for them. (*EY 656–57, 665.* See 1805:91.)

On 22 Dec DW writes to CCl: Repeats request [see 1805:113] that the Cls have the third part of *Recollections* copied. Asks that the task be completed soon, and the copy sent to RW forwarded to Grasmere by Bragg. (*EY 655–56.*)

117. Probably Dec 23

W walks to Ambleside; brings home a letter from CCl. (*EY 658.*)

118. Dec 25–Dec 26

On 25 Dec John and Molly Fisher are guests for Christmas dinner at DC. In the evening the fiddler comes and the neighborhood children gather to dance. (*EY 658–64.*)

W inscribes a set of *LB* 1802 for MM with this date. The volumes contain some draft and corrections for *Ruth, Remembrance of Collins,* "A Whirl-blast," *Song for the Wandering Jew*, and epigraphic lines for *Michael.* (St. John's College Library.)

On this day W, DW write to RW: (W:) A book for Sir GB being conveyed to RW by Bragg [see 1805:116]; a parcel with a valuable MS from CCl to be conveyed to RW for sending back with Bragg (probably *Recollections* MS A, or DW's original copy; see 1805: 81; 1806:17). W wants a copy of Bourne's poems that he had left [with CW] at Cambridge. Income tax; debt to Sotheby [1803:138; 1805:63]; W has owed £60 to Daniel Stuart for some time; STC is to call on RW for this. (DW:) Family. They will draw on RW for £40 or £50 soon [see 1806:6]. (*EY 657–58.*)

On this day DW writes to CCl: The copying of the lost portion of *Recollections* [see 1805:116]. Their years at Grasmere. JW, MW; the household and children at DC. A poor woman robbed. (*EY 658–62.*)

On 25, 26 Dec DW writes to Lady B: (25 Dec:) Thanks for letters. (26 Dec:) Christmas in her childhood; her father's house; STC;

MH's return expected; the household; the Christmas fiddler. Her hopes for the ministry of W's and STC's verses, [esp. *LB*]. She is copying *Prel.* W preparing self for work on *Recluse.* Nelson. (*EY* 662–65.)

119. Probably between Dec 29 and Dec 31, or 1806 early Jan–Feb 21, Mar 2 (–July 5, 6, or 7)

Probably between 29 and 31 Dec, or in early Jan, MW arrives home from PH. She is possibly accompanied by George and Joanna H; if so, however, the length of their visit is unknown. She is perhaps also accompanied by SH; if not, SH arrives for a visit at about this time. (She departs 5, 6, or 7 July 1806.)

While at DC but probably by 21 Feb 1806 SH makes a partial copy (Ci) and a full copy (Cii) of *Recollections* for STC [MS Cii follows revision by DW]. DW completes a copy of *Prel* [MS A], and makes a copy of her *Recollections* for Dora [MS B], completing it on 21 Feb. The copies of the third part are probably made after late Jan 1806. DW's copy is probably made after SH's. (*EY* 652–53, 659, 665; *MY* I, 10; *DWJ* I, ix–xii; Appendix V; PREL xx; MSS, DCP.)[46]

120. Perhaps very late 1805 or early 1806, by late May

W sends to Uvedale Price, or Price receives from another source (perhaps Sir GB), remarks by W on the subject of the Sublime. (*MY* I, 35.)

121. c late Dec; probably between c late Dec and 1806 mid-Jan

Probably c late Dec DW requests CL to obtain for her editions of Chaucer, Shakespeare, Spenser, Milton.

Probably by mid-Jan 1806 DW writes to RW: Requests RW

[46] Despite DW's statement of 25 Dec (*EY* 658) that MW was to return home that day, other remarks of hers on 25 and 26 Dec (*EY* 659, 662–63) make fairly clear that MW was expected on Friday 27 Dec. On 19 Jan DW states that MW returned two or three days "after the time [they] expected her" (*MY* I, 2). Also on Christmas Day DW did not expect SH until 5 Jan (*EY* 659–60). On 2 Mar, however, she says that SH came when MW was at PH. The various statements appear to allow the possibility that MW and SH came together (as supposed Moorman II, 69, and PREL xx), and to indicate that they both arrived during the period indicated.

to have books sent by Bragg [see 1805:116] and to reimburse CL. (*MY* I, 4–5.)[47]

1 8 0 6

[On writings of W possibly of this year see below and GCL 1–5, 34, 42, 72, 97, 99, 100, 106, 113, 117–21, 123–26, 131, 132, 137–40, 142–44, 146–61.]

1. Perhaps between c early Jan and Mar 2

MW copies *Prel* MS B. (Appendix V.)

2. Probably between Jan 1 and 14, and later Jan; probably between early Jan and Mar 29, and about this time

Between 1 and 14 Jan W composes a basic version of *The Waggoner*. Work on the poem probably continues for some days following. (*PW* II, 498; *MY* I, 1–3.)

Probably through much of Jan W is engaged in correction of his poems, perhaps esp. *Prel*. (CCS III, 19. See 1805:108.)[1]

---

[47] CL saw the books on the Kendal wagon on 1 Feb. The shipment also included books and pamphlets by George Dyer—gifts from the author to W and STC, which had been awaiting shipment for twelve months—as well as various items for STC and his family including Hazlitt's *On the Principles of Human Action*, and, for Johnny, CL's *King and Queen of Hearts*. The Ls were reimbursed by RW on 30 Jan (£6/–/6). (*MY* I, 4–5; *LL* I, 419–21; RW accounts, DCP.) On the editions requested and supplied see *LL* as cited.

[1] On the dates of *Waggoner* I.1–37 see 1802:165; on III.120–25 see 1802:163. An exhaustive examination of the chronology of *The Waggoner* will be provided by Professor Paul F. Betz in his forthcoming edition of *The Waggoner* (Cornell Wordsworth Series) and in his forthcoming article "The Dates of *Peter Bell* MSS. 5 and 6" (Betz *PB*). An outline, drawing heavily on the advice of Professor Betz, is here provided:

W consistently dated *The Waggoner* 1805 in editions from 1836 through 1850. The most specific indication of the time of composition, however, is W's note in MS [1] (BM Ashley 4637): "This poem was at first [writ *deleted*] thrown off [from *deleted*] under a lively impulse of feeling [in *deleted*] during the first fortnight of the month of Jan 180[6 *added in pencil*] and has since at several times been carefully revised and with the Author's best efforts, retouched and inspirited. W. Wordsworth." The writer of

Probably between early Jan and 29 Mar MW copies *The Waggoner*, MSS 1 and 2 (DC MS 56 and BM Ashley 4637). Probably about this

---

the "6" appears to have been the writer of the pencil numbering of the pages of the MS, perhaps T. J. Wise.

The paper of both MS [1] and MS [2] (DC MS 56)—laid, with a horn-in-shield watermark and a "1798" countermark—is like that of *PB* MS 5 (DC MS 60), DC MS 57, portions of *Prel* MSS A (from Book XI) and B, some leaves of BM Add. MS 47,864 (*P2V* printer's copy), and a memorandum leaf inserted in DC MS Journal 12 (*Recollections* MS D), booklet 1, concluding "Re transcribed & finished Febry 21st 1806," and various letters written between late 1805 and early 1808 or 1810 and later. Both *Waggoner* MSS appear to be in the autograph of MW (Professor Betz's recent studies of the autographs of MW and SH show that the traditional attribution to SH is incorrect). The state of the MSS suggests that DC MS 56 was probably fully transcribed before the MS of Ashley 4637 was made; hence DC MS 56 is properly termed MS 1. Ashley 4637, somewhat the neater of the two, is perhaps the one taken by W to London. The other MS contains notes by STC, of which the first would appear to have been written not long after STC's reunion with the Ws in late 1806: "From disuse of reading poetry, and thinking like a Poet, I am probably grown dull; but this X [*corresponding to an* X *beside the line*] line I did not discover the meaning or construction [of], for some minutes of endeavor. Might I propose the addition of

'will call,

     If he resist those casement Panes
     Which o'er his Leaders' Bells & Manes
     Will make th' old mossy High-way Wall
     Look at him with so bright a Lure:—
     For surely if—'"

The note, in which STC became virtually the author of the final reading of lines I.76–79, would appear to have been written between 25 and 29 Oct 1806 or 21 Dec 1806 (see 1806:114) and 17 Apr 1807, by which date STC departed Coleorton after his winter visit there. Both MSS may be regarded with reasonable certainty as dating from between 14 Jan and 29 Mar 1806.

MS 3, DC MS 72, a fair copy by SH, was probably copied in early 1812, c but by 29 Mar, in close association with but before the preparation of *PB* MS 6; and drafts in the autographs of W and SH, probably made shortly after the transcription of MS 3, appear on the recto of the first leaf of *PB* MS 5 (DC MS 60), which itself probably dates between 30 Oct 1806 and mid-Apr 1807. On the *PB* MSS see esp. Betz *PB*.

The draft for IV.99–108 noted in Appendix V as appearing in DC MS 47 probably belongs to the early stages of composition and dates between 1 Jan and 29 Mar; as do the drafts in DC MS 28 for II.145–48, 155–66, III.1–2.

DW's remark on 19 Jan 1806 that W "almost daily produces something," although not employed in his great work (*MY* I, 2) appears more likely to refer to *The Waggoner* than any other single poem; but RS writes to Walter Scott on 4 Feb that W, who

time she writes out what is now DC MS 57. (MSS.)[2]

3. Jan 19

DW writes to Lady B from Grasmere: STC's return; MW, SH. The lost MSS of *Prel* I–V and *Recollections* [see 1805:111]. W's opinion that Uvedale Price has had a favorable influence on taste in landscaping. (*MY* I, 1–3.)

4. Probably Jan 25 or Jan 26–Jan 27

Probably on 25 or 26 Jan W departs DC, travels to Keswick, where he visits at GH. (He returns on 27 Jan.) (*MY* I, 4; CCS III, 19.)

5. Probably c but by Jan 27; Jan 27

Probably c but by 27 Jan the lost MSS of *Prel* I–V and *Recollections* [see 1805:111] are recovered. (*MY* I, 3–4.)

On 27 Jan DW and probably other members of the W household attend the funeral of Mrs. Joseph Sympson at Grasmere. W returns from Keswick. (*MY* I, 4; Grasmere PR. See *DWJ* I, 437.)

On the same day DW writes to CCl: The recovery of the lost MSS. The Lloyds; MW; SH; Pitt; STC. Funeral of Mrs. Sympson.[3] (*MY* I, 3–4.)

---

[2] DC MS 57 contains copies of *Elegiac Verses*, *To the Daisy* ("Sweet Flower!"), and "Distressful Gift!" (*PW* IV, 372–73). The booklet is apparently dated by EdS in or not long after "spring of 1805" (see *PW* IV, 474); but the paper, with its horn-in-shield watermark and "1798" countermark, is one that appears elsewhere only in letters and MSS likely to date between late 1805 and early 1808 or else from 1810 (see 1806:2n). The general similarity of the pamphlet to *The Waggoner* MSS of early 1806, coupled with the broad chronological implications of the watermarks, suggests a date roughly of the same time as that of the *Waggoner* MSS. The content would likewise seem to make a much later date improbable.

[3] W apparently did not attend the funeral (see *MY* I, 4).

---

was with him last week, has "of late been more employed in correcting his poems than in writing others" (CCS III, 19). Work on *Prel* may have comprised a significant portion of this corrective effort (see 1805:108; 1806:1).

6. Jan 28

W draws on RW for £50, in favor of John Green, due in 40 days. (*MY* I, 5; RW accounts, DCP. See 1805:118.)[4]

7. Feb 5

DW writes to RW: Requests information about her and W's financial situation. The children; DW's pony [see 1805:105]. (*MY* I, 5–6.)

8. Feb 11

W writes to Sir GB: Sends transcription of *Character of the Happy Warrior*. Nelson; Pitt; landscape gardening; STC. (*MY* I, 6–8.)

9. Feb 15; perhaps c mid-Feb

The Longman accounts (DCP) charge W £1/19/0 for "1 Massingers Works boards"[5] under 15 Feb.

Perhaps c mid-Feb books sent to the Ws by CL arrive at DC. (1801:121.)

10. Feb 21

DW completes her transcript of her *Recollections* for Dora [MS B]. (*DWJ* I, ix; memorandum in DC MS Journal 12; 1805:119.)

11. Probably c but by Feb 23

W sees Robert [Forster], possibly accompanied by Thomas Wilkinson; sends him to see RS. (CCS III, 29–30.)

12. Probably c Mar–July 28; perhaps c Mar, by Mar 29

Probably c Mar W learns through Thomas Wilkinson that the price of the Patterdale property [see 1805:100] has been set at £1000. W perhaps at this time, certainly before 28 July, writes to the rector of

---

[4] RW's accounts charge payment under 12 Mar.

[5] Probably William Gifford's four-volume edition of the *Plays*, 1805 (see RM Sale Catalogue, lot 592; *MY* I, 21).

Patterdale, whose interest in the property has caused the price to be set so high, asking him to withdraw from competition. The rector does not cooperate. Despite W's letter of c 29 Mar [see 1806:17] Wilkinson mentions the affair to LdL, who offers to make up himself the £200 difference between W's offer and the price. Wilkinson and other parties concerned conclude an agreement on the evening of 28 July: £400 to be paid in cash; £600 to be paid on 5 percent mortgage, payment to be made and title given 25 Mar 1807. (Letter, Wilkinson to W, 29 July 1806, DCP; *MY* I, 68. See Moorman II, 60–62; 1807:20.)

Perhaps c Mar, by 29 Mar, SH, perhaps DW and MW, make copies of at least some of W's shorter poems. (Appendix VII.)

13. Probably Mar 1–Mar 2

Probably on 1 Mar the Ws hear indirectly from ML that STC had been in Naples 26 Dec. On 2 Mar they suppose him on the way home. (*MY* I, 9–12.)

14. Mar 2, 3; Mar 20

DW writes to CCl: (2 Mar:) STC; SH. Copying of poems. (3 Mar:) HCR; the family; the new administration. *Recollections* and a quotation from Stoddart therein. DW will send introduction to *The Solitary Reaper*[6] and [*Fidelity*]. Letter from Mrs. Luff; W has piles; Thomas H resolved to quit PH. (*MY* I, 9–12.)

On 2 Mar DW writes to Lady B from Grasmere: STC; W has thoughts of visiting London before the end of the month; transcription of *Fidelity*. (*MY* I, 12–15.)

On 20 Mar DW writes to Lady B from Grasmere: W's plans for visiting London, via Cambridge, leaving DC 30 Mar. Elizabeth Carter. (*MY* I, 16–17.)

15. Probably c but by Mar 24

W writes to Basil Montagu: Wants money for London trip. (*MY* I, 15–16.)

[6] As noted *MY* I, 11, no "introduction" is known for *The Solitary Reaper*. The reference is perhaps to an introductory note, possibly one including the passage from Wilkinson that inspired the poem.

16. Mar 28 (–Apr 8 or Apr 9)

DW writes to CCl from Grasmere: W's projected trip to London; the family; W's plans. (W finishes the letter in London on 8 or 9 Apr.) (*MY* I, 18–19.)

17. Probably Mar 29–Apr 4, –c May 20, –May 25 ff

Probably on 29 Mar W departs for London, arriving there probably on 4 Apr. He departs London on his return c 20 May; reaches DC 25 May. (*MY* I, 18–19, 31. See 1806:37.)

W probably visits Patterdale on his way, and perhaps the Misses M in Penrith, there forgetfully taking a trunk key of theirs in place of one of his. Perhaps while in the area of Patterdale or Penrith c 29 Mar W writes to Thomas Wilkinson: Thanks for Wilkinson's efforts on W's behalf in regard to the Patterdale property [see 1806:12]. The price is beyond reach. (*MY* I, 20; Curry I, 424.)

W probably travels much of the way to London with RS. They travel together at least as far as Lincoln, where they view the cathedral and the bell Great Tom. RS criticizes W's breeches. They possibly part at Alconbury Hill; if so, W probably travels directly on to London. If not, W has probably parted from RS earlier and gone on to Cambridge. (*MY* I, 16; Curry I, 419–23; Warter I, 368.)[7]

W brings with him various MSS of his poems, including *The Waggoner*, which he reads to CL. (*Waggoner* Dedication, IF note; *LL* II, 249. See esp. 1806:26; 1806:27.) He also brings a number of his unpublished shorter poems, of which the Bs read or hear some, probably not including *The Waggoner*, by 17 Apr. He probably also brings

[7] On 20 Mar W had some intention of visiting Cambridge, but nothing more is heard of the plan. On the other hand, if RS parted from W at 2 AM at Alconbury Hill (see Curry I, 419–23), the time would fit well with a report by DeQ—hardly soundly enough based for inclusion in the text—of W's having been overheard in Baldock (about 20 miles south of Alconbury Hill) complaining about the buttered toast that he had received for breakfast (Masson II, 314–15). DeQ records the incident as reported by one who recalled it as part of a journey to London with W and STC in 1805. That combination of date and companions would have been impossible; but a confusion of RS with STC, and 1806 with 1805, by DeQ or his informant would not.

The 29 Mar postmark on W's letter to Wilkinson recorded *MY* I, 20 is not apparent on the MS.

DW's *Address to a Child* and *The Cottager to Her Infant*, which he reads
to the Bs by 17 Apr, and SH's copy [MS C] of DW's *Recollections*. The
copy of *Recollections* is conveyed to a binder by J. F. Tuffin, and is to
be left with the Bs after binding; but the job is incomplete when W
departs, and the MS is left to be recovered by Sir GB, who probably
obtains it c early June. It reaches W by 23 June, apparently unread by
the Bs. (*MY* I, 21–25, 36, 45–46, 82; letter, Sir GB to W, 29 June 1806,
DCP; 1806:2.)[8]

In London W probably first visits CW [at Lambeth], staying at
least until 9 Apr. Possibly within a few days after 9 Apr CCl also visits
CW at Lambeth, and perhaps while W is still staying there suffers an
illness and retires to Purfleet. By 7 May W hears that she cannot return
to town. (*MY* I, 19, 22–23, 37.)

Probably a few days after 9 Apr he removes to a residence close by
the Bs', Grosvenor Square, and becomes in effect a household guest of
the Bs. Much or all of the remainder of his London visit is passed here.
(*MY* I, 23–24, 26.)

W possibly also visits with Basil Montagu, 36 Lower Thornhaugh
Street. If so, his residence there is likely to have concluded before mid-
May. (*MY* I, 19, 48, 137, 141.)[9]

Perhaps when at Sir GB's W sees one of Sir GB's paintings of Piel
Castle in a storm [see 1806:29n].

[8] Sir GB writes to W, in the letter cited: "I am glad the Tour is safe in your
possession. it made me very uneasy for the time, & I should have been much mortified
had any of the poems been prematurely & probably incorrectly given to the public.
it was this [sen]sation which made me feel a little provoked at the indiscretion (as it
appeared to me) of Mr T. in trusting a thing of such value into the hands of a German
bookbinder whom he had formerly discharged for some misbehavior, but who he
thought would be the more likely to perform this business with skill & dispatch, as
the price of restoration to his favor." *Recollections* was probably given to the Bs again
at Coleorton (see 1806:93). On Tuffin see also Curry I, 432.

[9] DW seems to have expected W to stay with the Bs upon leaving CW, but on 8 or
9 Apr W, in anticipation of the same departure, directs his mail to Montagu's (*MY* I,
19, 23–24). Mrs. Montagu was apparently very ill from about mid-May (*Gentleman's
Magazine* LXXVI, 1806, I, 590; *MY* I, 37). On his departure from London W left
clothes and a volume of TCl's *A Portraiture of Quakerism* at Montagu's, and other
articles at CL's (*MY* I, 48; *LL* II, 14). The articles at Montagu's were recovered between
16 Feb and 7 Mar 1807 (*MY* II, 137–141); those at CL's probably shortly after 25 June
(1806:53).

Probably during this visit, in company with CL, W sees, beside the Thames between Somerset House and Blackfriars Bridge, the spectacle that forms the subject of *Stray Pleasures*. In Leicester Square he sees the spectacle that forms the subject of *Star-gazers*. He probably also during this visit views the scene that forms the basis of *The Power of Music*. *The Power of Music* and *Stray Pleasures* are probably composed between 4 Apr and 10 Nov, *Star-gazers* probably between 4 Apr and 14 Nov. (*MY* I, 95, 100; IF notes; content.)[10]

Probably during this visit W dines in company with John Taylor, who finds W strongly disposed toward Republicanism. (Farington III, 249.) On this or his London visit of 1807, 1808, 1812, or 1815, W dines in company with Sir Egerton Brydges, but they have little conversation. (*MY* II, 300.)

Perhaps during this visit W visits the studio of Nollekins and there sees the monument of Mrs. Howard, later placed in Wetheral Church, that forms the subject of *Monument of Mrs. Howard*. He also sees there masks of Pitt and the Duchess of Devonshire. (*LY* II, 708; *Monument of Mrs. Howard* IF notes.)[11]

While in London W hears *The Lay of the Last Minstrel* spoken of frequently, and notes its popularity. (*MY* I, 41.)

W expects to be supplied by Harris the watchmaker with a new watch to replace his defective old one, but Harris does not complete the work before W's departure. (*MWL* 4–5. See *MY* I, 132, 141.)

On the pace of W's activities see esp. *MY* I, 89 (he is so much engaged that he does not read five minutes during the whole time). See also *MY* I, 80 (W is pleased with Lady Mulgrave's countenance); *MY* I, 242 (W infers the inutility and possible injury to the person concerned of standing advocate for the literary or moral reputation of a man of great powers [probably STC]).

18. Probably Apr 8 or Apr 9

W writes to CCl from London (this note concludes the letter

---

[10] Definite terminal dates are known for the composition of *Star-gazers* and *The Power of Music* (see *MY* I, 95). The close resemblance in style and content of *Stray Pleasures* to *The Power of Music* strongly implies in the absence of evidence to the contrary that the two poems are of much the same time.

[11] Pitt died on 23 Jan, and the Duchess of Devonshire on 30 Mar.

begun by DW at Grasmere on 28 May): His arrival in London; plans. (*MY* I, 18–19.)[12]

19. Perhaps c mid-Apr; probably between then and 1808 c end May

DW perhaps c mid-Apr makes some efforts toward composition of poetry. Possibly these include some portion or all of the *Fragments* "Peaceful Our Valley" and "There Is One Cottage." These are probably in any case composed by the end of May 1808. (*MY* I, 24–25.)[13]

20. c but by Apr 15; probably Apr 15

W writes to MW and/or DW. The letter is sent off probably on 15 Apr. (*MY* I, 25.)

21. c Apr 17–Apr 20; Apr 17

SFC, HC visit at DC c 17–20 Apr. (*MY* I, 21, 25.)

On 17 Apr W writes to CCl from London: SH has requested W to ask TCl about a farm which Montagu wishes to let (Sandleford). Because time is limited, W wishes to see CCl in London rather than Purfleet. W is to visit his Uncle Cookson. (*MY* I, 22–23.)[14]

22. Apr [19, 22]

DW writes to Lady B from Grasmere: (19 Apr:) Weather; health; W; her verse; the MS of *Recollections* [see 1806:17]. (22 Apr:) Health; weather. (*MY* I, 23–25.)[15]

[12] The date is indicated by the 9 Apr postmark.

[13] The content of the *Fragments* encourages the speculation that they were composed before the Ws' removal from DC at the end of May 1808. Except for *The Mother's Return*, DW is not known from external evidence to have made any poetic efforts in response to Lady B's request, other than the unidentified "several attempts" evidently just before her letter to Lady B of 19 Apr, between the time of *The Cottager to Her Infant* and 1810 (when copies of her verses, including the *Fragments*, were entered in the Coleorton Commonplace Book [see 1805:109]). The subjects and phrasing of these *Fragments* occasionally resemble those of *HG*.

[14] W's letter (Cornell 2299) is dated only "Thursday Morn," but the 17 Apr postmark fixes the Thursday.

[15] The MS suggests that all of the letter up to the second paragraph of the PS was written at once, on "Saturday afternoon," and the conclusion on "Tuesday morning." The Saturday which DW dates the 20th must have been Saturday 19 Apr (cf *MY* I, 23).

23. Perhaps c but by Apr 20

MW, DW write to W, adding their note to a letter of 6 Apr 1806 from DeQ to W which they are forwarding: The family; reading; a longer letter, to be sent by the same post, in preparation. (*MY* I, 20–22; Jordan 41–44.)[16]

24. Apr 21

RW's accounts charge W £20/–/–, payment of draft in favor of Mr. Wilcock, under this date. (RW accounts, DCP.)[17]

25. Apr 22

William Godwin calls on W, probably at Tuffin's; but W is probably not there. (Godwin Diary.)[18]

26. Apr 25

W dines at William Godwin's with James Northcote, CL, ML. Thomas Turner calls while the company is present. (Godwin Diary. See Farington III, 249.)[19]

27. Apr 26

W calls on CL; meets Godwin there. (Godwin Diary.) This evening W is in company with Joseph Farington and Sir GB. W confirms that Mrs. Sutton Sharpe has died. (Farington III, 206.)[20]

[16] The postmark, although faint except for the year, can be read as fairly certainly containing the date 23 Apr. W wrote to DeQ, plainly in reply to this letter, on 5 May (see 1806:31). The longer letter does not survive.

[17] The draft was probably made in anticipation of travelling expenses. See 1806:15.

[18] Godwin notes: "Call on Wordsworth (Tuffin)n. . . . " He had recorded a call on "Wordsworth" on 8 Apr, a date after W's arrival, but the presence of Joseph Godwin during the call indicates that Godwin called on RW, not W. Joseph Godwin, a man acquainted with legal grief (see esp. *Shelley and His Circle* I, ed. K. N. Cameron, Cambridge, Mass., 1961, 444–47), had been present in calls paid to RW on earlier occasions (such as 28 Feb and 7 Mar 1804).

[19] Godwin notes, "Wordsworth, Northcote, & Lambs dine; adv. TT. . . . " Northcote (on whom see also 1806:32) told Farington on 17 June (see Farington reference cited) that he had met W at Godwin's and that he preferred STC's conversation to W's, and W's poetry to STC's.

[20] Godwin notes, "Call on Lamb; adv. Wordworth. . . . "

28. Apr 29

W drinks tea at J. F. Tuffin's with William Godwin, R[ichard] Johnson, [John] Rickman, RS, [William?] Parsons. (Godwin Diary.)[21]

29. May 1

W is present at Sir GB's when Joseph Farington calls there at breakfast time. (Farington III, 209.) W dines at Godwin's with H[orne] Tooke, [Thomas] Manning, [J. B.] Trotter. CL calls while the company is present. (Godwin Diary.)[22]

30. May 2 ff

On 2 May W perhaps attends the Royal Academy exhibition. He probably there sees a painting of Piel Castle by Sir GB. He possibly thereafter sees another painting of the same scene by Sir GB. This picture forms the subject of W's *Elegiac Stanzas Suggested by a Picture of Peele Castle*. (Farington III, 210. Royal Academy Exhibition Catalogue, 1806. See 1806:17.)[23]

[21] Godwin notes, "[T]ea Tuffin's, w. Wordsworth, R. Johnson, Rickman, Southey, Parsons."

[22] Godwin notes: "H. Tooke, Wordsworth, Manning, & Trotter dine; adv. Lamb: invités Northcote & Hoare & Tuffin." Northcote, Hoare, and Tuffin, that is, were invited but did not come.

[23] The exhibition catalogue records that in addition to "A Storm: Peel Castle" (no. 78), Sir GB was exhibiting "The thorn.—See Lyrical Ballads, by W. Wordworth, vol i. the Thorn" (no. 96), and "Lake of Albano" (no. 85).

Farington records that he called on Westall on the same evening, 1 May, to have him sign cards in Dance's name for Sir GB and W for the private viewing of the Royal Academy exhibition next day, and that Farington met Sir GB there next day at 3. Thus, although W is not named in the second instance, he seems likely to have attended the exhibition. It was probably to this day that Sir GB was referring when he thanked W for his Peele Castle verses on 29 June 1806: "When you came to town you will recollect I did not show you Peele Castle tho it was in the room, because I thought it might raise painful sensations in your mind ..." (DCP). Presumably GB's remarks would not refer to a picture in a room which W frequented throughout his visit (see *MY* I, 63). W, however, apparently did see two pictures of Piel Castle. Sir GB painted two such pictures (see *Elegiac Stanzas* IF note); and he wrote to W on 6 Nov 1806 from London: "I have seen both the Peel Castles since I came here, & the foolish fondness of a parent having subsided, I agree with you the small one is on the whole

31. May 5

W writes to DeQ from London: His concern for DeQ; advice toward arrangement of a meeting. (*MY* I, 26; Jordan 41–44.)

32. May 7; perhaps between this date and c May 20

On 7 May William Godwin calls on W. They, together with [Richard] Duppa, call on [Henry] Edridge, [David] Wilkie, and North-cote. [Prince] Hoare joins the company at Northcote's. (Godwin Diary.) Perhaps between this date and c 20 May Edridge makes a drawing of W. (See Moorman II, 73; Blanshard 46–47.)[24]

Probably this evening W attends a *rout* given by the Marchioness of Stafford. He wears powder and carries a cocked hat. (Warter I, 386–87; *MP*. See also Simmons 117.)[25]

33. Probably c but by May 8; probably May 8

Probably c but by 8 May W consults [Anthony] Carlisle about Thomas H, who has suffered an accident.

Probably on 8 May W writes to Thomas H from London: Regrets Thomas H's accident; sends [Anthony] Carlisle's advice. The Cls; hopes for aid for the Cls concerning a new farm for Thomas H [see 1806:21]. (*MY* I, 22–23.)

34. May 10; probably between May 10 and May 20

RW's accounts charge W £120, probably for the purpose of

---

[24] Godwin notes: "Call on R. Johnson, Tuffin n, Wordsworth; & (w. Wordsworth & Duppa) on Edridge & Wilkie: do on Northcote; adv. Hoare. . . . " This is W's first known meeting with Wilkie (cf *MY* I, 79n). W afterward greeted Wilkie through Sir GB on 8 Sept 1806 (*MY* I, 79), and wrote of him again to Sir GB on 10 Nov 1806 (*MY* I, 95). Wilkie in turn sent "kind remembrances" to W through Sir GB on 11 Sept (letter, Sir GB to W, 11 Sept 1806, DCP), and his "respectful Compts" for conveyance by the same medium in a letter to Sir GB of 30 June 1807 (PML).

[25] Viscount Lowther is among the guests listed in *MP*. W's presence is not noted.

---

the best" (DCP). The first quotation from Sir GB might suggest in turn that W saw the other picture after having visited the Royal Academy exhibition.

repaying a loan from Sotheby to STC, under 10 May. (RW accounts, DCP; letter R. Nicol to RW [25 Sept 1813], DCP. See 1803:138; 1804:36; 1805:118; esp. *EY* 457n.)

Probably between 10 and 20 May W perhaps inquires about a seal that is being prepared for RS. (Letters, RS to John Rickman and Rickman to RS, 27 June and 2 July 1806, HEH; Warter I, 374.)[26]

35. May 16

William Godwin, [Mrs. Godwin] call on W, evidently in Pentonville. (Godwin Diary.)[27]

36. May 19

W calls on William Godwin. [John] Wolcot and Penwarne also call, perhaps while W is there. (Godwin Diary.)[28]

This evening W probably attends a ball given by Mrs. Charles James Fox, where he is introduced by Samuel Rogers to Fox, and possibly meets Lord and Lady Holland. (Rogers *Table-Talk* 161n; *MP* 19, 20, 21 May 1806; Mark L. Reed, "Wordsworth and Southey: New Letters, August, 1806," *Princeton University Library Chronicle* XXXII, 1971, 153–59.)

37. Probably c May 20–May 25; probably between c May 20 and June 27

Probably c 20 May W departs London. On his departure he leaves various belongings with Montagu and CL [see 1806:17n]. He stops one day at Windsor with his Uncle Cookson; sees Cookson's two elder boys for the first time; sees all children but one.

Possibly passing back through London on his way north, he comes down as far as Manchester with George Philips and Mrs. Philips.

---

[26] On 27 June RS wrote to Rickman that his seal had reached Grasmere; Rickman replied on 2 July that he did not know that W "had found it ready for export." The Warter reference indicates that RS departed London on 10 May. He arrived home on 12 May (letter, RS to Rickman, [12 May 1806], HEH).

[27] The Diary reads, "Call on Wordsworth, Pentonville, w. MJ."

[28] Godwin notes simply, "Wordsworth, Wolcot, & Penwarne call. . . ."

He probably visits the Thomas Cooksons in Kendal on his way. He arrives at DC 25 May, finding SH ill and in pain. (*MY* I, 24, 31, 42.)[29]

Probably between c 20 May and 27 June W composes *Elegiac Stanzas Suggested by a Picture of Peele Castle.* (Letter, Sir GB to W, 29 June 1806, DCP; *MY* I, 34–35. See 1806:17.)[30]

38. May 26

Richard Duppa's *The Life and Literary Works of Michel Angelo Buonarroti* is published in London. In it is first published W's *Translation from the Italian of Michael Angelo. I.* ("Yes, Hope May with My Strong Desire Keep Pace"). (*Times.*)

39. May 29–probably Aug 17 or Aug 18

Johnny departs for a visit to PH. (He returns probably 17 or 18 Aug.) (*MY* I, 31, 33.)

DW writes to RW: [Peggy Marsh's] house has burned down; a £5 gift from Sir GB and £2 from her and W. (*MY* I, 27–29.)

40. May 30

RW's accounts charge W £10/18/6, payment of a bill from Mr. Beck, tailor, under this date. (RW accounts, DCP.)

[29] On Philips see *MY* I, 210, 229, 233; *MY* II, 382. While W probably knew the Cooksons earlier (see 1804:119), this first direct evidence of a visit by W is an appropriate occasion for note of the remarks of William Pearson (Pearson 13): "When staying in Kendal with his friend Mr. Thomas Cookson, Mr. Wordsworth himself, was an occasional worshipper along with the family at [the Unitarian] chapel; and thus became acquainted with the minister, the Rev. John Harrison, and with one of his congregation, the well-known blind mathematician and botanist, Mr. John Gough. . . ."

[30] The poem was probably sent to Sir GB by 27 June: Sir GB thanks W for it on 29 June in a letter from Coleorton (DCP), quoted 1806:30n. Although Sir GB as remarked above would appear to be referring there to the picture exhibited at the Royal Academy as W's subject, this poem may well be, in view of the dates concerned, that to which W refers in a letter to Lady B of 3 June: "Since I reached home I have passed the chief part of my time out of doors, much of it in a wood by the Lake-side; a spot which you would love: The Muses without any wooing on my part came to me there one morning, and I murmured a few verses in which I did not forget Grosvenor Square, as you will know if I ever take up the strain again, for it is not finished." (*MY* I, 35. Cf *MY* I, 35n. See *MY* I, 63.)

On this day W writes to Mrs. Cookson: SH's health; health of others of family; Mrs. Watson. (*MY* I, 29.)

41. June 2

DW writes to JPM: Children's health; MW's approaching confinement; a new servant to come; W's visit to London; JPM's approaching confinement; the Fergusons. (*MY* I, 30–33.)

DW writes to RW: W; financial matters; requests information about accounts. RW's projected visit in the North; the pony sold [see 1806:7]; they have a cow. (*MY* I, 33–34.)

RW's accounts charge DW £10, payment of a bill in favor of John Smith, under this date. (RW accounts, DCP.)

42. June 3; probably June 3

On 3 June W writes to DeQ: General expression of concern for DeQ; invitation to visit. (*MY* I, 36.)

Probably on 3 June W, DW write to Lady B: (W:) Dora; recent composition; a summer house for the Bs at Grasmere; a letter and invitation from Uvedale Price [see 1806:93n]. (DW:) Thanks for the Bs' kindness to W. (*MY* I, 34–36.)

43. June 4 ff

Probably on 4 June Richard Sharp and two other gentlemen drink tea at DC. They perhaps spend the night in Grasmere this night or about this time. W perhaps sees Sharp hereafter as well. (*MY* I, 54, 82.)

44. Probably between June 8 and c June 10

W writes to Walter Scott: Congratulations on Scott's appointment as secretary to the Parliamentary Commission for the Improvement of Scots Jurisprudence. Time drawing near for proposed Border tour with Scott; W will meet him c beginning of next month. Possible obstacles. *The Lay of the Last Minstrel*. W has thoughts of publishing a little volume of poems. (*MY* I, 39–42.)[31]

[31] W discusses a letter from Montagu which had arrived at DC on 8 June as one which he had "just received" (*MY* I, 37, 40). MW's confinement was, according to

45. June 9

RS and his family drink tea at DC. (*MY* I, 38.)

DW writes to CCl: Lengthy delay in arrival of expected W baby; CCl's health; Montagu's wife; MW; the Ss; servants. SH to stay till MW recovers; the Bs expected in July; W family plans to visit Leicestershire at beginning of winter. Thomas H's lack of success in obtaining a new farm; marriage of John M and Isabella Addison; visit from Sharp; TCl's book not arrived [see 1806:17n]. (*MY* I, 37–39.)

46. June 14

Mrs. Lloyd and the Ss drink tea at DC. MW's labor pains begin before they depart. (*MY* I, 42–43.)

47. June 15 and at least two days following; June 15 or shortly after

Thomas Wordsworth, third child and second son of W and MW (d. 1 Dec 1812) is born at Grasmere on 15 June, probably between 8 and 8:30 AM. (*MY* I, 42–43; M-W Book of Common Prayer, DCP.)[32]

His name is not decided for at least two days. (*MY* I, 43.)

On 15 June W writes to CW: Birth of boy. Would like to be godfather to CW's next child. (*MY* I, 42.)

On this day or shortly after W walks out along Rydal Mere opposite Nab Scar and hears an echo from Nab Scar. The incident inspires "Yes, It Was the Mountain Echo," which he composes before returning from his walk. ("Yes, It Was the Mountain Echo" IF note.)

48. June 17

RS calls at DC in the morning; opposes name William for the new child. (*MY* I, 43.)

---

[32] The Prayer Book records the time as 8 AM.

W, expected "every hour" and the child was not born until 15 June; but the event had been supposed imminent since early in the month (*MY* I, 37).

MY I, 41n points out that W's reference to his proposed volume is his first indication of plans for what became *P2V*. This is true insofar as uninterrupted pursuit of the goal of a volume of smaller poems is concerned. DW had mentioned, doubtfully, to Lady B on 27 Oct 1805 that W "has talked of" publishing some smaller poems (*EY* 634); but the plan was authoritatively disclaimed in her next letter to Lady B (*EY* 636).

DW writes to Lady B: The new child; difficulty in naming him; Lady B's sister's ascent of Mont Denvers; house for the Bs at Grasmere. (*MY* I, 45–47.)

49. June 18

RW's accounts charge W, DW £7, cash remittance to Mrs. Marsh, under this date. (RW accounts, DCP.)

50. c June 19–Aug 18

Robert Grahame of Glasgow calls at DC c 19 June with Mrs. Grahame and their two daughters; W and Grahame, who pleases W, dine at the inn. (*MY* I, 50–51.)

Probably later in the summer but by 18 Aug, James Grahame, brother of Robert, and his wife call at DC, impressing W and DW. (*MY* I, 74, 103–04.)

51. Probably between c late June and early Sept

W, perhaps drawing on materials composed in 1800 or, in the case of the *Prospectus*, possibly as early as 1798, composes *The Recluse I. Home at Grasmere* in form of MSS A and B; possibly composes other lines now unidentified but perhaps used in *The Tuft of Primroses* or *Exc.* MS B (DC MS 59) from line 117 is unlikely to date before July. MS A includes *Water Fowl* as HG 203–29 with readings as *PW* V, 321 *app crit.* The drafts in MS R (DC MS 28) except for 75–77 and 597–607 probably also date from this time, before MS B. To this time belongs also a prose draft in MS R drawn on in *Prel*$_2$ IV.354–70. W possibly at this time also composes the *Prospectus* (but see Appendix VI). *Prospectus* MS 3 (EdS MS 2) is probably written at this time. (Appendix VI; 1806:56.)

52. June 24

DW writes to Lady B from Grasmere: Presents from Lady B; MW. (*MY* I, 45–46.)

The letter is taken to Rydal by W and SH. They arrive too late for the post, and bring the letter back. DW opens it and continues it with a long quotation from a letter from Stoddart concerning STC. (*MY* I, 45–47.)

DW probably also writes others letters. (*MY* I, 45.)

53. Possibly shortly after June 25

Boxes sent by CL containing chocolate, tea (25 pounds), and hats probably arrive at DC. (*LL* II, 14.)[33]

54. June 26

DW writes to RW: The £7 for Peggy Marsh [see 1806:39; 1806: 49]. £5 received from Sir GB. MW, Tommy, Johnny. (*MY* I, 47–48.)

55. Probably c but by June 27

DW writes to CCl: TCl's [*Portraiture of Quakerism*]; death of Mrs. Montagu; MW; visit from Grahames [see 1806:50]; Thomas H; others of family. (*MY* I, 48–51.)

56. Probably July

W composes 700 lines for *The Recluse*. Most of these are probably now found in *The Recluse I. Home at Grasmere.*

W composes the fragments published by Knight under the title *To the Evening Star over Grasmere Water, July 1806.* (*MY* I, 51; Appendix VI.)

57. Perhaps c July 1 or July 2

Thomas Wilkinson calls at DC; reports the Quakers surprised at the extent of TCl's knowledge of them as demonstrated in his book [*Portraiture of Quakerism*]. (*MY* I, 61.)

58. July 4

W writes to Walter Scott: Montagu, DeQ, the Bs; is obliged to defer proposed tour [see 1806:44]. Stoddart. STC. (*MY* I, 51–52.)

---

[33] CL had sent the boxes off the night before writing his letter to the Ws franked and postmarked 26 June.

59. Probably July 5, 6, or 7, and shortly after July 7 (–Oct 25)

Probably on 5, 6, or 7 July W, SH depart from DC. W accompanies SH to PH. (SH rejoins the Ws on 26 Oct.) W probably returns to DC shortly after 7 July. (*MY* I, 53, 60.)

60. July 7

DW writes to Lady B: The Bs' lodgings at Grasmere; plans for Coleorton visit; DW is reading R. P. Knight's *Analytical Inquiry*, recently sent by Lady B. (*MY* I, 53–55.)[34]

61. July 11

RW's accounts charge W £50, payment of draft by Thomas H in favor of J[ohn] M, under this date. (RW accounts, DCP.)

62. Perhaps July 12 or 13 and shortly after (–shortly after Aug 3)

Thomas H, MM, probably Joanna H arrive at DC for a visit. Thomas H probably departs on 13 July or shortly after. (Joanna H and MM probably depart shortly after 3 Aug.) (*MY* I, 60, 66; 1806:63.)

63. July 13

Thomas W is baptized at Grasmere. Thomas H is godfather, MM godmother. (*MY* I, 60; Grasmere PR.)[35]

64. Probably July 17–July 20, perhaps July 29 (–Aug 17 or Aug 18)

Probably on 17 July W, DW, Dora, Hannah Lewthwaite depart

---

[34] On W and Knight's *Analytical Inquiry* see esp. E. A. Shearer [and J. T. Lindsay], "Wordsworth and Coleridge Marginalia in a Copy of Richard Payne Knight's *Analytical Inquiry into the Principles of Taste*," *Huntington Library Quarterly* I (1937), 63–99; 1806:114. DW's date of "July 9th, Monday" is an impossibility for 1806, undoubtedly the year of the letter. The Monday in question would have been 7 July.

[35] DW states that the christening occurred a day after Tommy was a month old (*MY* I, 60). The description would fit neither the lunar nor the calendar month, and without further evidence it is more appropriate to doubt DW than the baptismal record of the PR, which reads: "[Baptism:] July 1806 13th Thomas Son of William Wordsworth of Town End Grasmere[.]"

DC at 10:30 AM, travel to PH. A letter from Lady B is sent after them, which they read along the way. W carries Dora on setting off. A young man carries Dora over Grisedale Hause; W carries her on to Patterdale, where they call at Luff's. They travel down Ullswater in a boat; arrive at the Soulby Fell boathouse at 8:30 PM; reach PH soon after the stars appear. (*MY* I, 55–59.)

Probably on 18 July W takes Johnny to Penrith, where he is expected to stay till 29 July, and where he visits for at least part of the time at John M's.

W, DW probably return to DC on 20 July. (Dora returns to DC on 17 or 18 Aug.) (*MY* I, 55–59. See 1806:71.)[36]

65. July 23

DW writes to Lady B: Disappointed hopes for the Bs' visit to Grasmere. The recent trip to PH. Peggy Marsh. (*MY* I, 55–58.)

DW writes to CCl: The trip to PH [see 1806:64]; MW; TCl's book; Montagu expected, with Basil. Illness of Dr. Beddoes. (*MY* I, 58–62.)

66. July 25

W, DW write to Montagu: (W:) Can accommodate Montagu with a bed, not a sitting room; urges Montagu to visit soon. (DW:) A letter from Mrs. Skepper concerning Montagu. (*MY* I, 63.)

67. Aug 1; probably between Aug 1 and Aug 5

On 1 Aug W writes to Sir GB: Sir GB's picture of Piel Castle and W's *Elegiac Stanzas*, suggested by the picture; STC; *The Recluse*; tourists; two strange summer neighbors. Transcription of "The Prayers I Make Will Then Be Sweet Indeed." (*MY* I, 63–65.)

Probably between 1 and 5 Aug W receives Thomas Wilkinson's letter explaining the arrangement made to conclude the purchase of the Patterdale property that W has wished to buy. (See 1806:12; 1806:70.)

---

[36] The moving about of the children was an attempt to keep them from contracting whooping cough (see *MY* reference cited). DW writes on Wednesday 23 July that "last Monday" was the day after their return, and that they had previously departed on "Thursday."

68. Aug 3

MW writes to Mrs. Cookson: Books sent by Mrs. Cookson. MW's health. Plans for visiting Coleorton during the winter. (*MY* I, 65–67.)

69. Perhaps shortly after Aug 3, or perhaps between c Aug 8 and Aug 15

Joanna H, MM depart DC. (*MY* I, 66. See 1806:71.)[37]

70. Aug 5, [6]

W, DW write to Sir GB: (W, 5 Aug:) Requests advice regarding his response to the arrangements made by Wilkinson with LdL to enable W's acquisition of the Patterdale property [see 1806:12]. (DW, [6] Aug:) Proprietor of DC appears willing to give a lease. (*MY* I, 67–71.)

71. Perhaps between c Aug 8 and Aug 15–probably Aug 17 or Aug 18

W, MW, Tommy, [possibly Joanna H, MM] depart DC, travel to PH.

During his visit at PH W, accompanied by Thomas Wilkinson, calls at Lowther Castle, but finds LdL not at home. He accompanies the Misses Lowther on their ride as far as Yanwath. It is probable that W and Wilkinson then work together on a walk. This incident inspires W's *To the Spade of a Friend.*

On 17 Aug Wilkinson meets W at Patterdale. They inspect the Broad How property. W, MW, the children probably return to DC this day or on 18 Aug. W perhaps takes away with him Wilkinson's Journal of his tours of the British mountains. (*MY* I, 70–71, 73–75, 104; Mary Carr, *Thomas Wilkinson*, London, 1805, 23. See Appendix IX.)[38]

[37] The visitors were expected to depart over Kirkstone on the "first fine day" after 3 Aug; but in view of the visit paid shortly by W, MW, and TW to PH, it seems not unlikely that the Ws and their visitors made the trip together. There seems no reason to doubt that the "Miss Monkhouse" referred to in DW's letter of 3 Aug as then visiting with Joanna H is the same who was at Grasmere with Joanna when DW was writing on 23 July (cf *MY* I, 66n).

[38] W wrote to Walter Scott from Grasmere on 18 Aug, and stated on 19 and 21 Aug that he visited the Patterdale property the previous Sunday (*MY* I, 73–77). On 5

72. Aug 11–Oct 30

STC's ship, the *Gosport*, arrives in quarantine off Portsmouth on
11 Aug. STC disembarks at Lower Halstow on 17 Aug and proceeds to
London, where he stays with CL until 29 Aug. He meets the Ws at
Kendal on 26 Oct, and reaches Keswick 30 Oct. (*STCL* II, 1174, 1176,
1186, 1199; *STCNB* 2905; *LL* II, 20. See 1806:92; Moorman II, 83–87.)

73. Aug 15

On this day DW hears from SFC that STC's ship has arrived off
Portsmouth. She writes to CCl: STC's arrival; W, MW, children at
PH. (*MY* I, 71.)

DW writes to Lady B: STC's arrival. Kind wishes to Sir GB on
loss of young relative. (*MY* I, 72.)

74. Aug 18; probably between Aug 18 and Oct 26

On 18 Aug W writes to Walter Scott: STC; the Bs; an expected

Aug he was apparently to set off "in a few days" (*MY* I, 70). DW supposed the family
at PH on 15 Aug (*MY* I, 71). If W's copy of Lord Holland's biography of Lope de
Vega, which W said on 19 Aug had arrived in his absence, came about the same time
as RS's, a date of departure about 8 Aug is likely: RS had read the book before writing
to thank Lord Holland on 8 Aug (see Mark L. Reed, "Wordsworth and Southey:
New Letters, August, 1806," *Princeton University Library Chronicle* XXII, 1971, 153–
59).

While the distinct notice that *DWJ* takes of a new walk of Wilkinson's, and his
spade also, under [11] Nov 1805 (*DWJ* I, 420–21) might suggest that the labor that
inspired the poem took place on 10 Nov 1805 (see 1805:101) the present occasion
appears a much more likely choice: Wilkinson in writing to W on 29 July remarks of
LdL, "He said he was personally unknown to [W]: but he wished to be acquainted
with him, and desired me to bring him to Lowther when he came again to see me..."
(DCP). In response to a letter from Mary Leadbeater concerning W's *Address* Wilkinson wrote (Carr as cited): "I had promised Lord Lonsdale to take [W] to Lowther
when he came to see me, but when we arrived at the Castle he was gone to shoot
moor-game with Judge Sutton. William and I then returned and wrought together at
a walk I was then forming; this gave birth to his verses." The tone and content of W's
letter to LdL of 19 Aug (*MY* I, 74–75) fit very exactly the circumstances described by
Wilkinson. The poem of course was only to be "supposed" to have been composed
that afternoon (*MY* I, 105).

visit from Montagu. A song sent by Scott ("materiam superabat opus"); death of Mungo Park. [Robert, James] Grahame. (*MY* I, 73–74.)

Probably between 18 Aug and 26 Oct W composes *To the Spade of a Friend*. During this period W probably visits Mr. and Mrs. Archibald Fletcher at Belmount, near Hawkshead. The visit is perhaps in inquiry concerning Belmount as a possible residence. W there recites *To the Spade of a Friend*. This is probably W's first meeting with the Fletchers. (*MY* I, 87; *Autobiography of Mrs. Fletcher*, Carlisle, 1874, 80–81. Cf *W of RM* 145.)[39]

75. Aug 19

W writes to LdL: Unsuccessful call at Lowther Castle [see 1806: 71]; thanks for LdL's assistance toward W's purchase of Patterdale property. (*MY* I, 74–75.)

W writes to Lord Holland: Thanks for gift of Lord Holland's biography of Lope de Vega. Good wishes for [Charles James Fox]. (Mark L. Reed, "Wordsworth and Southey: New Letters, August, 1806," *Princeton University Library Chronicle* XXII, 1971, 153–59.)

76. Aug 21

W writes to Sir GB: STC's arrival, dangerous illness. Patterdale, Applethwaite properties. Sir GB's intention of publishing [Sir John Beaumont's] poems; W offers his assistance. The strange summer neighbors [see 1806:67] have departed. (*MY* I, 75–77.)

77. Probably c late Aug

W takes a rest from composition of *The Recluse*. (*MY* I, 79. See 1806:56.)

---

[39] Had W composed the poem to Wilkinson before 18 Aug he would hardly have needed to send the poem to Wilkinson in a letter in Nov (*MY* I, 104–05). The *Autobiography* reports W's recitation as having been so impressive to the Fletchers' son Angus that he begged his mother to ask the poet to repeat it.

On Belmount see esp. T. W. Thomson, *Wordsworth's Hawkshead*, ed. R. S. Woof (Oxford, 1970), 52–53.

78. Probably c 25 Aug

W visits Keswick, [GH]. (Letter, Sophia Lloyd to CW, 27 Aug 1806, DCP.)[40]

79. Aug 28

RW's accounts charge W £7/10/6, payment of premium on £300 policy on Montagu's life, under this date. (RW accounts, DCP.)[41]

80. Perhaps Aug 29, probably between Aug 29 and late 1810

Perhaps on 29 Aug Sir GB's picture of [W's] *Thorn* arrives at DC. (*MY* I, 78.)

Probably between 29 Aug and late 1810 the Ws receive another picture, of a landscape near Coleorton, from Sir GB. (*MY* I, 507.)[42]

81. Possibly c Sept but probably between c Dec 1809 and 11 May 1810

W composes *Exc* II.1–763 in the form of the basic copy of DC MS 47, and most or all of the tale of the Old Man (c 730–825, and 881–85); but the composition more probably takes place between c Dec 1809 and c late May 1810. (See Appendix VI.)

82. Probably c early Sept

W writes the fragment "The Rains at Length Have Ceased" (*PW* Knight, 1882–89 IX, 389; *PW* Knight, 1896 VIII, 233; *PW* IV, 456), then writes *Lines. Composed at Grasmere* ("Loud Is the Vale!"). (Content.)[43]

[40] Sophia Lloyd writes: "I heard from Grasmere a day or two ago the children were thought to have hooping cough, your brother was gone to Keswick, & your sisters were well."

[41] Another record of the bill gives the date as 21 Aug; but 28 Aug corresponds more closely with the usual time of payment.

[42] The Coleorton landscape evidently hung at AB for some time; but it seems unlikely on present evidence to have been given to W before the painting illustrating *The Thorn*.

[43] Fox died on 13 Sept after a long illness. "The Rains at Length," an elegiac quatrain, so closely resembles the opening of *Lines* that it may be speculatively regarded as a rejected alternate beginning for a similar poem.

83. Probably between c Sept 1 and Sept 8

W writes 300 lines of verse which he regards as belonging to *The Recluse*. (See Appendix VI; 1806:56.)

84. Sept

W writes to Josiah Wedgwood (only a fragment of the letter is known to survive): Tom Wedgwood's striking appearance when he visited DC [24 Dec 1802]. (Litchfield 127.)[44]

85. Sept 8

W writes to Sir GB: Sir GB's picture *The Thorn*; STC's reluctance to return home because of domestic problems; plans for visiting Coleorton. Work on *The Recluse*. Transcription of "No Mortal Object Did These Eyes Behold." Whitby, which W has visited several times. (*MY* I, 77–80.)

86. Perhaps between c but by Sept 8 and mid-Sept, by Sept 18

W meets John Constable, evidently in the presence of Mrs. Lloyd, probably at the Hardens' or the Lloyds' at Brathay. W perhaps speaks of the depths of abstraction into which he was rapt as a schoolboy, and perhaps asks Mrs. Lloyd to examine the shape of his skull. (*John Constable's Correspondence*, ed. R. B. Beckett, V, Suffolk Records Society XI, 1967, 2–4, 74–75; Farington IV, 239; Moorman II, 232; J. R. Watson, "Wordsworth and Constable," *RES* N.S. XIII, 1962, 361–67.)

87. Sept 18

W writes to STC: Urgent concern to see STC. (*MY* I, 80.)

88. Probably Sept 19 or shortly after

DW writes to Lady B (only a fragment of the letter is known to survive): STC expected home 29 Sept; his plans to lecture; his domestic affairs. (*MY* I, 83–85.)

[44] Tom Wedgwood had died on 10 July.

89. Sept 28

W writes to J. F. Tuffin: Reassures Tuffin concerning worries expressed in his letter of some time since [see 1806:17]; invites him to visit Coleorton. Sharp's affection for, complaints about Tuffin. (*MY* I, 82–83.)

W writes to Josiah Wade from Grasmere: Thanks Wade for MSS deposited with him and for newspapers. *P2V*; will send Wade some poems shortly before publication for him to publish [in the *Mercantile Gazette*]. (*MY* I, 80–82.)

90. Probably Oct–Dec

The W family is much afflicted with colds during this period. W probably has a severe cold through much of Oct and early Nov. (See *MY* I, 88, 92, 104; Curry I, 435.)

91. Oct 4

RW's accounts charge W £30, payment of bill in favor of John Green, under this date. (RW accounts, DCP.)

92. Probably Oct 26–Oct 28, 29 ff

Probably on 26 Oct the W family, including Molly Fisher, departs for Coleorton. They travel to Kendal, where they are joined by SH, from whom they learn that STC is in Penrith. They send a messenger to Keswick to ask him to come to Kendal; but on the same evening at 7 STC arrives at an inn in Kendal and sends for W. Probably all the adults go to the inn. They are shocked by STC's appearance.

All stay in Kendal with STC till 28 Oct, and W and SH till 29 Oct. (*MY* I, 86–87, 92.)

W's *A Complaint* perhaps expresses a reaction to this meeting and STC's manner. (See esp. Moorman II, 94–95.)

Probably during this period W draws on RW for £60 by a bill in favor of Thomas Cookson due at 14 days. (RW accounts, DCP; *MY* I, 91.)[45] Probably all see the Cooksons. (Appendix X.)

---

[45] RW's accounts charge the sum to W under 13 Nov.

93. Probably Oct 28–Oct 30–1807 June 10

On 28 Oct at 9 AM DW, MW, Johnny, Tommy, Dora, Molly depart from Kendal for Coleorton in a chaise. They arrive at Coleorton on 30 Oct at about 9 PM.

W, SH depart Kendal on the morning of 29 Oct, perhaps at 10:30. They arrive at Coleorton on 30 Oct within twenty minutes of the other group.

On 30 Oct the two parties meet by chance at the inn at Derby at about noon. They come on to Coleorton via Buxton. (They reside at the Farm House at Coleorton till 10 June 1807.) (*MY* I, 86–87, 91, 139; Appendix II.)

W refers to this visit to Coleorton and that of 1810 in the Dedicatory Letter of the 1815 Poems. On this period generally see esp. Moorman II, 86–108.

Perhaps during this winter the family become regular churchgoers for the first period of such length. (*MY* I, 136.)[46]

During this winter SH is afflicted with toothache, perhaps to the detriment of her future health. (*SHL* 26.)

By 30 Nov, probably between 10 and 30 Nov, W is entrusted by the Bs with the planning and supervision of the planting of the winter garden at Coleorton. W consults Mr. Craig about the planting of thickets. By c 19 Dec W has evolved a formal plan. Further planning and the work of planting continues throughout W's residence at Coleorton. (*MY* I, 107–08, 112, 138. See below through winter months *passim*.)[47]

---

[46] DW writes on 16 Feb 1807 that "we are become regular churchgoers, that is, we take it by turns, two at a time, and always go two every Sunday when the weather will permit" (*MY* I, 136).

[47] On 1 May [1808] Lady B wrote to DW from London: "Mr Price is just arrived, and speaks with great pleasure of meeting your brother at Coleorton we agree very much in our opinion of his genius, tho' his heart may be less deeply affected than mine, the last volumes he had never seen I believe. . . . The plan of the winter garden pleased Mr Price much, but he wishes the strait walk were *not* there he thinks it interferes with the whole by dividing it, and the strait walk under the [walk *for* wall] he thinks sufficient." (DCP.) W and Price had already established an epistolary acquaintance (see *MY* I, 35), but the meeting at Coleorton appears to have been one projected rather than previously effected. On the winter garden generally see esp. Russell Noyes, *Wordsworth and Landscape Gardening* (Bloomington, 1968), 111–26.

Probably between 30 Oct and mid-Apr 1807, SH makes the fair copy *PB* MS 5. (Betz *PB*.)

Probably between 30 Oct and early Apr 1807 W composes:

Song at the Feast of Brougham Castle (IF note; *Thought of a Briton* IF note; Appendix VII.)

"Though Narrow Be That Old Man's Cares" (IF note; Appendix VII.)[48]

Between 30 Oct 1806 and early Apr 1807 W supervises preparation of the printer's copy of *P2V*. On the contents of the various surviving lots of copy, which do not in all instances correspond to the actual content of *P2V*, see Appendix VII.

Vol. I, lot 1 is probably prepared by 13 Nov and sent off to Longman and Rees c but by 13 Nov.

Vol. I, lot 2 is probably prepared by c 13 Nov but not completed before 10 Nov, and sent off c 13 Nov.

Vol. I, lot 3 is possibly prepared and sent off c mid-Nov, more certainly basically prepared by c early Dec, and sent off by c early Jan.

Vol. I, lot 4 is perhaps basically prepared by early Dec, but corrections are not completed before 21 Dec; and it is probably sent off between 21 Dec and mid-Jan.

Vol. I, lot 5 is perhaps basically prepared except for the first page by early Dec, and is probably completed by early Feb 1807. It is probably sent off between 21 Dec and early Feb 1807.

Vol. I, lots 6 and 7 are probably prepared by early Feb and sent off between Dec and early Feb 1807.

Vol. I, lots 8 [and 9, if such existed], including MS materials perhaps dating from c Mar 1806, are probably prepared by late Feb 1807, and sent off between 21 Dec and late Feb 1807. These materials conclude Vol. I.

Vol. II, lots 1 and 2 (lot 2 including MS materials perhaps dating between c 28 Nov 1805 and c Mar 1806) are perhaps basically prepared by early Dec, and sent off between Jan and early Apr.

Vol. II, lots 3 to 8, all except 8 including MS materials perhaps

---

[48] The IF note of "Though Narrow Be That Old Man's Cares" tends to suggest that composition did not occur immediately after arrival at Coleorton. On the folklore of the poem see *PW* Knight, 1882–89 IV, 74–76; *PW* Knight, 1896 IV, 69–73.

dating between c 28 Nov 1805 and c Mar 1806, are probably basically prepared between mid-Feb and early Apr 1807. Lot 3 is completed and sent off between early Feb and early Apr; the others are completed and sent off in very late Mar and early Apr. These materials conclude Vol. II. (Appendix VII; 1806:94.)

94. Between Oct 30 and early Dec; by Dec 7, 1807 late Feb, early Apr

Between 30 Oct and early Dec W is heavily engaged in composition (*MY* I, 110). Much of this work is probably in preparation of *P2V* [see 1806:93]. By 7 Dec W certainly composes two new poems. One is perhaps *November, 1806*, which is probably in any case composed before late Feb 1807. (Content; *MY* I, 104–05, 108–09; 1806:113; Appendix VII.)[49] Another possibility is *A Complaint*, which is in any case composed by early Apr 1807. (Content; *MY* I, 108n; 1806:113; Appendix VII.) Another possibility is *The Horn of Egremont Castle*, which, if in fact composed at Coleorton, is probably completed by early Dec. (Moorman II, 271n; *MY* I, 108n; 1806:113; Appendix VII.)[50]

Probably by late Feb W composes *Thought of a Briton on the Subjugation of Switzerland*. (IF note; *Song at the Feast of Brougham Castle* IF note. See Moorman II, 99.)

95. Between Oct 30 and Nov 2–some time after 1808 Jan 3

Between 30 Oct and 2 Nov the Ws and Bs spend a pleasant evening together. W reads from Milton. His readings probably include *PL* I and IV.768–84. Possibly this evening, or more certainly during this

---

[49] Acland 108–09 points out as the primary inspiration of the poem the "deadly blow" of the defeat of Prussia at Jena, 14 Oct 1806. *PW* Knight, 1882–89 IV, 44; *PW* Knight, 1896 IV, 50 list a series of "blows" concluding with the Napoleonic decree of a blockade of England (21 Nov).

[50] W dated the poem 1806 in editions 1836–1850. Mrs. Moorman points out its similarity, as a development of an old Cumberland story, to *Song at the Feast of Brougham Castle*, certainly composed at Coleorton. It seems possible that W's obviously confused statement in *Thought of a Briton* IF note that "the Song on the Restoration of Lord Clifford, as well as that on the feast of Brougham Castle, were produced on the same ground" as that on which he paced while he composed *Thought*—the walk to the Hall—was intended to refer to the *Song at the Feast* and *The Horn of Egremont Castle*.

period, W probably talks with Sir GB about, perhaps reads from, *Prel.* (*MY* I, 133; letter, Sir GB to W, 6 Nov 1806, DCP; Farington IV, 42.)

Probably during this period the Ws turn over to the Bs a copy of DW's *Recollections* which is probably not returned before 3 Jan 1808. (*MY* I, 36, 44, 111, 189. See 1806:17.)[51]

96. [Nov 1]

MW writes to Mrs. Cookson from Coleorton: Their journey from Kendal to Coleorton. (See Appendix X.)

97. [Nov 3] (–1807 June 3)

The Bs depart Coleorton early in the morning. (They return 3 June 1807.) (Letter, Sir GB to W, 6 Nov 1806, DCP. See 1806:95.)

98. Probably between Nov 3 and Nov 10; probably Nov 3, 4

Probably between 3 and 10 Nov W visits the fir-wood with SH; visits the pool with MW; takes a long walk with DW. (*MY* I, 93.)

Probably on 3 Nov, DW, MW, as a consequence of a hint from Lady B, walk to the hospital; on the next day Johnny begins attending school. (*MY* I, 98–99.)[52]

99. Nov 5, 6

DW writes to CCl from Coleorton: (5 Nov:) Distress on account of STC; their meeting with him. (6 Nov:) STC's family; resolution

[51] Sir GB wrote to W on 6 Nov about his departure early Monday [3 Nov]: "[A]t last the sun rose in full glory" and the lovely day "brought to my mind that sublime passage in Milton you read the other night . . . where he describes the Messiah's coming as shining afar off." W quotes from the same passage in his 1815 Preface (*P* 1815 I, xxviii). Farington records dining with Sir GB on 7 Nov, when Sir GB reported W "employed on a poem—*the progress* of *His own Mind*, viz: How He was affected by objects & circumstances as He advanced in life.—This work He proposes to delay publishing till He shall have made Himself more important & [of] course what respects Him more interesting, by some production of a different kind."

[52] The trip to the hospital was possibly in order to consult with the schoolmistress (*MY* I, 99). DW says that they went there "next day"—presumably after the hint from Lady B, who probably would have known of the excursion had she not left Coleorton already.

to separate from SFC; his appearance; the trip to Coleorton. (*MY* I, 85–88.)

100. Nov 7

W writes to Francis Wrangham from Coleorton: Will not write personal satire; wishes *Juvenal* destroyed; plans to publish a volume of small pieces; seeks two drawings of Brompton Church. (*MY* I, 88–90.)

W writes to STC [from Coleorton]: Urges STC against lecturing; encourages him to visit Coleorton. (*MY* I, 90–91.)

DW writes to RW from Coleorton: The trip to Coleorton; the family; financial information. (*MY* I, 91–92.)

101. Probably Nov 9

W, SH attend church. W notices a man of whom W has seen, probably with the Bs, a drawing by Mr. Davie. (*MY* I, 94.)

102. Nov 10

W writes to Sir GB [from Coleorton]: Coleorton; landscape gardening there. Plans for publication of a volume of small poems. (*MY* I, 92–95.)

W writes to Walter Scott from Coleorton: Visit at Coleorton; STC's projected lectures; preference for pocket-sized books; plans for a volume of small pieces. *Fidelity, The Seven Sisters*. W requests copy of *The Seven Sisters* for his book, supposing Scott to have a better copy than he himself possesses. Mungo Park. (*MY* I, 95–97.)

103. Probably between Nov 10 and Nov 30

W decides, or accepts decision, to publish his forthcoming collection of poems in two volumes rather than one. (*MY* I, 95–97, 104; Appendix VII.)

W writes to Thomas Wilkinson from Coleorton: Wilkinson's Journal is at Grasmere; transcription of *To the Spade of a Friend*, which W intends to publish in a collection of his poems to appear in two small volumes. (*MY* I, 104–05.)[53]

[53] As the decision to publish his collection of poems in two volumes was not made before 10 Nov (see Appendix VII), this letter must date from later in that month.

104. Probably Nov 12

W, DW walk in the evening, enjoy views near the Hall. (*MY* I, 98–99.)

105. Probably c but by Nov 13

The first lot of copy for *P2V* is sent off to Longman and Rees. (Appendix VII.)

106. [Nov 14]

DW writes to Lady B from Coleorton: Coleorton, landscaping and gardening. Copies *Star-gazers*. (*MY* I, 97–101.)
DW and others perhaps call on the schoolmistress this afternoon. (*MY* I, 99.)[54]

107. Nov 18

RW's accounts charge W £11/10/–, payment to John M, under this date. (RW accounts, DCP.)

108. Nov 23

W, DW walk to the post office at Ashby. Find there a letter from STC announcing his intention to separate from SFC but to keep Hartley and Derwent, and indicating that he is on his way to Coleorton.
Probably at the same time they find a letter from [Robert] Grahame. (*MY* I, 101–04.)

109. Probably between Nov 23 and Dec 7

W, DW visit Grace Dieu. The ass on which DW is riding lies down after two miles, perhaps in company with W's. Probably both W and DW walk the remaining distance. (*MY* I, 108–09.)[55]

[54] DW's date is "Friday 15th November," but the Friday in question was 14 Nov.
[55] DW says on Sunday 7 Dec that the excursion to Grace Dieu was made "last week," a phrase that might look back as much as a fortnight or only a few days.

110. Nov 24

DW writes to CCl from Coleorton: STC and his domestic plans; SFC has agreed to a separation; Coleorton; health of family. W is to publish two small volumes. (*MY* I, 101–04.)

111. Dec 6

MW writes to Thomas M from Coleorton: Thanks for a habit. RW; Henry H. W's watch not yet in his possession [see 1806:17]. (*MWL* 4–5.)

112. Dec 7

DW writes to Lady B [from Coleorton]: The family; STC. SFC has agreed to a separation. W's invitation to STC to bring the boys to Coleorton. Landscaping. W has written two poems [see 1806:94]. (*MY* I, 105–09. See *STCL* II, 1200.)

113. Probably c but by Dec 19 (–Dec 23); probably Dec 19, 20

W writes to Lady B [from Coleorton]: The family. W's plan for the winter garden at Coleorton. (DW completes this letter on 23 Dec.) (*MY* I, 112–20.)

Probably on 19, 20 Dec DW writes to Lady B [from Coleorton]: (19 Dec:) STC's expected arrival; Coleorton; W's poetical labors at a stand for more than a week. DW's *Recollections*. (20 Dec:) STC not yet arrived. (*MY* I, 109–11.)[56]

114. Dec 21 (–probably 1807 mid-Apr, but by Apr 17) and about this time; possibly between this time and early 1808

STC, HC arrive at Coleorton at 1:30 PM. (They depart probably mid-Apr, but by 17 Apr.) About this time the W children probably have whooping cough. (*STCL* II, 1204; *MY* I, 121; Curry I, 433.)

On the conversations of this visit see esp. *STCL* II, 1204.

---

[56] The letter is dated "Friday Evening," and is postmarked 22 Dec (cf *MY* I, 109), which was a Monday. The MS clearly states that W's "poetical," not "practical," labors have been at a stand for more than a week (cf *MY* I, 110).

Possibly between this time and early 1808 W and STC read, perhaps together, and annotate, a copy of R. P. Knight's *Analytical Inquiry into the Principles of Taste*. (See E. A. Shearer [and J. T. Lindsay], "Wordsworth and Coleridge Marginalia in a copy of Richard Payne Knight's *Analytical Inquiry into the Principles of Taste*," *Huntington Library Quarterly* I, 1937, 63–97; 1806:60.)

115. Probably c Dec 23; Dec 23

Probably c 23 Dec SH writes to Joanna H from Coleorton (only a fragment of the letter is known to survive): W's pleasure in Joanna's interest in his poems; sends copies of *Incident Characteristic of a Favorite Dog* and *On Burying the Above Dog Several Years After* (*Tribute to the Memory of the Same Dog*). (DCP.)[57]

On 23 Dec DW completes the letter to Lady B begun by W c but by 19 Dec: Arrival of STC and HC; the family. (*MY* I, 121–22.)

116. Late this year, esp. c Dec 23

W perhaps plans an anthology of poetry, for which he enlists the aid of CL. (*LL* II, 33.)[58]

117. Dec 25 and perhaps about this time

On 25 Dec W, STC perhaps discuss plans for STC's London lectures. (*STCL* II, 1205.)

About this time W and his family probably urge STC not to go to London. (See *STCL* III, 18.)

118. Dec 26

RW's accounts charge DW £16/16/–, payment of bill in favor of William Rawson, under this date. (RW accounts, DCP.)

[57] The date is inferred from SH's remark that MW is setting down a list of spices for their Christmas Day pudding to send to Ashby with the letter.

[58] ML writes to CCl on 23 Dec, "My brother sometimes threatens to pass his hollidays in town hunting over old plays at the Museum to extract passages for a work (a collection of poetry) Mr. Wordsworth intends to publish." Lucas (*LL* II, 34) suggests that W's name may be a slip, but this possibility seems not strong. Nothing further is known of the plan, although it possibly played a part in inspiring CL's own *Specimens of the English Dramatic Poets*, 1808.

119. Dec 27 ff

On 27 Dec STC forms a suspicion, which he later admits to have been a fantasy, of the existence of a sexual intimacy between W and SH. The incident responsible for the fantasy, if any incident properly termed real is concerned, takes place at the Queen's Head, [Thring]ton, at 10:50 AM. (*STCNB* 2975&n, 3148 f45.)

1807

[On writings of W possibly of this year see below and GCL 2–4, 34, 72, 97, 99, 100, 113, 117, 118, 123, 125, 131, 132, 142, 146, 148, 153, 159, 160, 162–73.]

1. Probably between Jan and early Apr; mid–Feb and early Apr; very late Mar and early Apr; perhaps early this year, by June 10

Probably between Jan and early Apr Vol. II, lots 1–2, of printer's copy for *P2V*, are completed and sent off. Between mid–Feb and early Apr Vol. II, lots 3–8, are prepared. Lot 3 is probably completed and sent off between mid–Mar and early Apr; lots 4–8 are probably completed and sent off in very late Mar or early Apr. (Appendix VII.)

Perhaps early this year, by 10 June W purchases a copy of Donne's *LXXX Sermons*, 1640. (RM Sale Catalogue, lot 224; *STCNB* 4291n.)

2. Probably early Jan, and Jan 7

On a series of evenings concluding 7 Jan W reads *Prel* aloud in the presence of DW, MW, SH, STC. This occasion forms the subject of STC's *To William Wordsworth*. (See *To William Wordsworth*, *STCPW* I, 403–08 and *app crit*.)

3. Jan 17

RW's accounts charge W £11/17/6, cash payment to Messrs. Wilkinson and Crosthwaite for balance of their bill for wine and interest, probably from a bill of 1790, under this date. (RW accounts, DCP; *CEY* 115.)[1]

---

[1] An accompanying note comments, "This is the Bal: of the same Bill on which £5/5 appears to have been paid on Account the 6th Nov 1790." See *CEY* 115.

4. Jan 20

W writes to Walter Scott from Coleorton: Thanks for copy of *The Seven Sisters* [see 1806:102]. Montagu was to visit at Christmas and bring a copy of Scott's [*Ballads and Lyrical Pieces*] from Longman, but has not come yet. Delays in publication of *P2V*. Scott invited to visit Coleorton. W seeks advice about an English equivalent of "Lega!" [for *The Blind Highland Boy*]. STC. A murder. (*MY* I, 122–24.)

DW, MW write to CCl from Coleorton: (DW:) STC, HC. W intends taking SH to London; uncertainty about own future residence. Johnny. (MW:) Greetings. (*MY* I, 127.)

5. Probably Jan 24

DW writes to Lady B [from Coleorton]: The winter garden; W visits the workmen twice a day. STC; Cowper's Homer; the last edition of Bruce's *Travels*. (*MY* I, 127–29.)

6. Probably c early Feb, by 15 Feb

W receives as a gift from the Ls a copy of their *Tales from Shakespeare*. (*LL* II, 35.)

W composes *To Lady Beaumont* ("Lady! the Songs of Spring Were in the Grove").

On a ramble DW and others discover a favorite cottage of Lady B's, which members of the family visit several times by 15 Feb. DW and others sit by the fireside of the old couple who live there. (*MY* I, 133–34.)

7. Probably Feb

W composes *A Prophecy. February, 1807.* (Title, content. See Appendix VII.)[2]

8. Probably between early Feb and early Apr, very late Mar or early Apr

---

[2] The date appears in the title of all editions from 1807 through 1850. The content is sufficiently appropriate for a poem of that month. See esp. *PW* Knight, 1882–89 IV, 63–64; *PW* Knight, 1896 IV, 59–60.

Probably between early Feb and early Apr, Vol. II, lots 3–8, of *P2V* are prepared. Lot 3 is probably prepared, completed, and sent off between early Feb and early Apr; lots 4–8 are probably completed and sent off in very late Mar or early Apr. (Appendix VII.)

Probably between early Feb and early Apr W composes "O Nightingale! Thou Surely Art." (IF note MS; *MY* I, 133–34; Moorman II, 97.)[3]

9. Probably c but by Feb 2

W writes to Lady B [from Coleorton]: Lady B's sister. Lord Redesdale's comments on landscape gardening as related to W's plan for the winter garden at Coleorton. (*MY* I, 129–31.)

10. Feb 5

W writes to RW from Coleorton: Settlement of debt to Uncle RW's estate: if delay in settlement originates in us, interest should be added to the £200 originally proposed for settlement; otherwise, interest should not be added [see 1812:105]. Asks RW to send attorney's letter to Harris, who retains W's watch [see 1806: 111]. (*MY* I, 132.)

11. Probably c Feb 7, and shortly after

Books arrive at Coleorton, including the *Memoirs of Colonel Hutchinson*, which W and MW read at once; Sir John Barrow's *Travels in China*; and Thiebault's *Anecdotes of Frederick II*, which DW reads probably within a few days. (*MY* I, 133.)

12. Probably between Feb 12 and Aug 25, esp. between mid-Mar and mid-Apr, or May 8 and June 10

W copies Blake's *Holy Thursday* (*Innocence*), *Laughing Song*, *The Tyger* (stanza 1), MW copies *The Tyger* (remaining stanzas), "I Love

---

[3] The MS of the IF note, which dates the poem "Town-End, 1806" (the year assigned *PW* 1836–*PW* 1850) has been corrected in pencil by MW to "at Coleorton" (see *PW* II, 506). The stockdove, if W did hear it on "very day" of composition as the poem states, may have been cooing somewhat earlier than usual (cf Moorman as cited), but a date before early Feb seems unlikely. DW notes the bursting into song of many birds about the second week of Feb (*MY* I, 134).

the Jocund Dance," into the Commonplace Book (DC MS 26), probably from Malkin's *Father's Memoir of His Child*. This appears the earliest surviving evidence of W's awareness of Blake's work. (Betz *BN*.)

13. Probably Feb 15

W, DW, STC, SH go on a ramble, discover an attractive cottage. (*MY* I, 134.)

DW writes to Lady B from Coleorton: Books sent by the Bs. The countryside. The winter garden. W and Craig to visit nursery at Nottingham next week or the week after [see 1807:15]. (*MY* I, 133–35.)

14. Probably Feb 16

DW writes to CCl from Coleorton: CCl's health. The Cls. Silhouettes of the Cls desired. STC: his family problems and plans; he has determined to make his home with the Ws. Possible residences for the Ws and STC. (*MY* I, 136–38.)

15. Probably c Feb 26

Probably on a day c 26 Feb W makes an excursion to Nottingham with Craig (gardener at Coleorton) to obtain plants for the winter garden at Coleorton. He probably passes Castle Donington on his way, both going and returning, and there observes gipsies who inspire his poem *Gipsies*. The poem is probably composed this day or shortly after. (*MY* I, 135, 139–40; *Gipsies* IF note; Appendix VII.)[4]

[4] W's IF note to *Gipsies* dates the poem "Coleorton, 1807"—the year assigned *PW* 1836–*PW* 1850—and remarks that the poet saw the gipsies "near Castle Donnington, on [his] way to and from Derby." W told Scott probably c 28 Feb that he had made an excursion of 20 miles from Coleorton, as far as Nottingham, on "the day before yesterday" (*MY* I, 139). Possibly the trip included Derby also, but Castle Donington would have stood along a more direct route to Nottingham, and ordinarily have been out of the way to Derby. Probably this is the occasion that W is remembering in the IF note.

A charge of £10/2/6 to W appears in RW's accounts under this date, for payment of a draft at two months to Montagu, drawn in Grasmere and endorsed to John Fisher; and is discussed in memorandum among the accounts. DW suggests that "the affair was between [Montagu] and [RW]," and RW appears to agree: "I think this would be on my account." The bill, dated 23 Dec, is also among RW's accounts.

16. Probably c Feb 28

W writes to Walter Scott [from Coleorton]: Thanks Scott for advice [see 1807:4]. They expect visit from Scott; directions. Scott's [*Marmion*]. W recommends [*Memoirs of*] *Colonel Hutchinson*. He awaits Scott's [*Ballads and Lyrical Pieces*]. Slow pace of printing of *P2V*. (*MY* I, 139–140.)

17. Mar 7; c but not before Mar 7

On 7 Mar W writes to RW from Coleorton: Has drawn on RW this day for £30, in favor of Mr. Farnell of Ashby, due in one month. Urges RW to visit. £200 for purchase of Patterdale property will be due 25 Mar. Thomas H may supply the money from sale of PH stock, but RW will have to supply if Thomas H cannot. W desires full statement of accounts from RW. Has received a box from Montagu with a coat of RW's in it; thanks RW. Montagu reports Harris the watchmaker bankrupt; can RW obtain anything from him [see 1807:10]? (*MY* I, 140–141.)

W draws c but not before 7 Mar on William Bailey for £30, probably by a bill due in one month. (*MY* I, 141.)[5]

18. Mar 18

DW writes to RW from Coleorton: RW will have to supply the £200 toward purchase of Patterdale estate; Thomas H or Thomas Wilkinson will draw on him for the sum [see 1807:17]. Difficulties in search for a new residence; possibility of staying for another winter at Coleorton. Please send statement of accounts. (*MY* I, 141–42.)

19. Perhaps between Mar 18 and Apr 27

W reaches an understanding with J. G. Crump that the Ws will occupy AB. (*MY* I, 141–42, 144.)

[5] RW's accounts charge W for a bill in favor of Bailey under the date of 10 Apr (RW accounts, DCP). Bailey had married the daughter of J. C. Ibbetson (see 1802:64) in Aug 1806 (M. R. Clay, *Julius Caesar Ibbetson*, London, 1948, 149). See also 1807:45.

20. Mar 25 and probably about this time

W's purchase of the Patterdale property is concluded on 25 Mar. W pays £200, and £600 is taken on 5 percent mortgage.[6] The deed and mortgage are probably arranged through the Penrith solicitor R. Ellwood. Probably about this time the deed is sent to Coleorton for W to execute. W makes an error in the execution—probably a failure to sign his name in a required place—about which Ellwood does not inform him. (*MWL* 5–6; *MY* I, 435; *Jollie's Cumberland Guide*, 1811. See 1806:12; 1807:17; 1807:18.)[7]

21. Probably Mar 26 or shortly after

Probably on 26 Mar or shortly after W writes *To Thomas Clarkson*. (*PW* III, 457; Appendix VII.)

22. Probably very late Mar and early Apr

Vol. II, lots 4–8 of printer's copy for *P2V* are probably completed and sent off. (Appendix VII.)

23. Apr 2

DW writes to RW from Coleorton: Requests RW to pay premium on STC's insurance policy; W has draft for £50 from STC due in June. Please send statement of accounts. (*MY* I, 142–43.)[8]

24. Apr 7

William Lowther, Viscount and Baron Lowther of Whitehaven, is

---

[6] RW charges the £200 to W's account for a bill by Thomas H on John M under the date of 27 Apr (RW accounts, DCP).

[7] The improperly executed deed caused annoyance when the mortgage was being paid off in the spring of 1811. See esp. 1811:19.

[8] RW's accounts charge W £27/5/6 for payment of premium on STC's life insurance under the date of 6 Apr (RW accounts, DCP). By 1 July STC had required the draft himself (*MY* I, 153; *STCL* III, 39), and STC appears eventually to have repaid RW directly. In response to a query by RW in the accounts, DW writes: "The sum of 27/5/6 was repaid by Mr. Coleridge to you. This I have an assured though general recollection of . . . but I have no doubt Miss Hutchinson will remember the circumstances." See also Curry II, 94.

created Earl of Lonsdale. (*The Complete Peerage* VIII, ed. H. A. Double-day and Lord Howard de Walden, London, 1932, 134–35.)

25. Apr 14

The Longman accounts (DCP) charge W £–/15/– for "1 Decame-ron 40 used calf" under this date.

26. Probably mid-Apr, by April 17 (–May 5, 6)

W, MW, SH, STC, HC depart Coleorton, travel to London. (SH departs London probably 5 May. W, MW return to Coleorton prob-ably 6 May.)

W, MW, perhaps the others stay at the residence of Basil Montagu, 36 Lower Thornhaugh Street. W and MW probably move to CW's residence, at Lambeth, c 1 or 2 May.

During this visit W and Walter Scott accompany MW, SH, HC to the Tower. W possibly sees and converses with John Constable. (*STCL* III, 9–11, 15; *MY* I, 142–44; *The Mother's Return* IF note; *The Poems of Hartley Coleridge*, ed. Derwent Coleridge, London, 1851, I, xxii–xxxv, cxcix–cciii; *John Constable's Correspondence*, ed. R. B. Beckett, V, Suffolk Records Society XI, 1967, 74–75.)[9]

27. Apr 17

W at some time during this day is present in a company before which STC reads c 150 lines of Sotheby's *Saul*. (*STCL* III, 11.)

28. Apr 19

William Godwin calls on W, but finds him not at home. (Godwin Diary.)[10]

29. Apr 21

W breakfasts with Walter Scott. (*Letters of Sir Walter Scott*. ed. H. J. C. Grierson, London, 1932–37, XI, 111.)

[9] DW's letter of 2 Apr to RW gives no hint of an approaching journey to London, although STC's letter of 3 Apr to HC implies that his departure toward Devonshire is imminent.

[10] Godwin notes, "Call on W Wordsworth n. . . . "

W writes a letter dated "Tuesday noon" to William Godwin from 36 Lower Thornhaugh Street: Thanks Godwin for call [see 1807:28]; regrets that he, MW, SH unable to accept dinner invitation from him for Thursday, but will call soon and hope to arrange a mutually satisfactory date. (Information from Mr. Alan Hill.)

30. Apr 23, 24

The Longman accounts for W record delivery of two copies of *P2V* to or for Walter Scott under 23 Apr, and delivery of eight copies (recipients not recorded) under 24 Apr. (Longman Joint Commission and Divide Ledger, 1803–07, opening 7.)[11]

31. Apr 25

W writes to DeQ from London: Thanks for a letter. STC. Will be happy to see DeQ in London, where W will be for ten days or a fortnight. (*MY* I, 143.)

32. Apr 27

W writes to [J. G. Crump] from London: Will be glad to help with garden [at AB]. Wishes workmen there to be hastened. (*MY* I, 144.)[12]

33. Apr 28

W writes to DeQ from London: Expects to leave London next Tuesday [5 May]. Expects to move from Thornhaugh Street to CW's, Lambeth, by [3 May]. STC. (*MY* I, 144.)

W calls on Joseph Farington with the Bs. All proceed to Grosvenor

[11] The notations for these and later copies delivered to various recipients in Apr and May include no evident charge to the author. Distribution of a few other copies is noted against W's account shortly hereafter; under 5 May, one copy each for [Richard] Duppa and Mr. [Thomas or William] Cookson, and three copies for STC; under 23 May, one copy for W, and 14 copies "as [per] Credit Book 29 Apr," an account apparently not surviving. See also 1808:31. The *Rosenbach Catalogue of Rare Books, Manuscripts, and Autograph Letters*, 1947, describes (item 634) a copy of *P2V* inscribed by RS, "Robert Southey from the author. June 6, 1807."

[12] W's tone suggests that he at this time expected to move into AB not long after his return to Grasmere, although the move was not actually made until c late May 1808.

Square, where they see a picture, [*The Hermitage*] by [Richard] Wilson sent by [Oldfield] Bowles to be disposed of. W gives a critique of it, theorizing on proper pictorial relations between landscape and historical subjects. (Farington IV, 129.)[13]

34. Apr 29

W, STC, Thomas Turner sup with Godwin. (Godwin Diary.)[14]

35. May; c May

The Longman Impression Book accounts for *P2V* commence with this date. These record that W was paid £105, probably about this time, and that 1000 copies were printed. (Owen CSP 95.)

36. Perhaps early May; about this time

W discusses with Daniel Stuart his debt for money loaned at the time of W's 1803 Scotch tour, probably £60; possibly repays the money about this time. (*STCL* III, 13. See 103:55; *EY* 657.)[15]

37. Perhaps c May 1 or May 2

W, MW, perhaps SH move to the residence of CW, Lambeth. (*MY* I, 143–44.)

38. May 2

The Longman accounts (DCP) charge W £1/11/6 "To paid coach hire" and £–/3/– for "Crusoes Life-Sheep" under this date.

[13] W thought the picture excellent "but objected to foreground dark trees on the left hand which seemed to him like a *skreen*, put before the more distant parts." Samuel Rogers purchased the picture by 8 May (W. G. Constable, *Richard Wilson*, London, 1953, 202–03). On Bowles see also *EY* 406.

[14] Godwin notes, "Coleridge, Wordsworth, TT sup. . . ."

[15] RW's accounts contain no record of W's repayment of Stuart. W possibly paid from money received from Longman, or arranged a direct transfer from Longman to Stuart. If so, he might later have remembered himself as having received much less than £105 for his book. This recollection might in turn have contributed to the discrepancy pointed out by Owen between W's statement of 1812 that he had received under £140 for his writings and the net total of over £180 seemingly indicated by other evidence. (See Owen CSP 95n.)

39. May 4

W, [MW or SH] attend the Royal Academy exhibition, just opened. They meet Joseph Farington, to whom they express their disappointment in the exhibition. (Farington IV, 132.)

40. Probably May 5

Probably on 5 May, SH departs London for a visit to CCl at Bury. (*STCL* III, 15; 1807:41.)

Perhaps on this day STC meets with W as W is packing for his departure from London. (*STCL* III, 13.)[16]

Perhaps on this day DW composes *The Mother's Return*. (Content. See 1807:41.)

41. Probably May 6–May 8

Probably W, MW, Walter Scott set off at 4:30 AM on 6 May for Coleorton, where they perhaps arrive late in the day. Scott probably departs Coleorton on 8 May. On his departure, W and DW accompany him to Lichfield, where they probably remain only a quarter of an hour, taking a brief look in at the west door of the Cathedral before returning (as they had probably come) by Tamworth. (*MY* I, 144, 165; *LY* I, 205, 216–19; Moorman II, 107–08; *Mem* I, 358; *Letters of Sir Walter Scott*, ed. H. J. C. Grierson, London, 1932–37, IX, 115–16; *Letters of Anna Seward*, Edinburgh, 1811, 337.)[17]

42. May 8

P2V is published in London. (*Times.*)

---

[16] STC states that his interview with W took place while W was "in the hurry of packing up." STC's phrasing seems more likely to refer to W's final departure from London than to his visit at Lambeth (cf *STCL* III, 13n).

SH next rejoined the Ws at Halifax between 12 June and 3 July. STC rejoined the Ws 1 Sept 1808.

[17] Scott on 4 May expected to set off from London with W at the time stated, and to visit W for a day (cf Edgar Johnson, *Sir Walter Scott*, New York, 1971, I, 271). He almost certainly visited Anna Seward, on his departure from Coleorton, on Friday 8 Apr.

43. May 16

The second edition of Richard Duppa's *The Life and Literary Works of Michel Angelo Buonarotti* is published in London. In it are first published W's four stanzas of translation from the Italian of Michelangelo "And Sweet It Is to See in Summer Time." (*MP*.)[18]

44. Probably May 19, possibly also a day or two after

W writes to Lady B from Coleorton: Lady B's concern about reception of *P2V*. Popularity; classes of readers; objects of his poetry. Discussion of "With Ships the Sea Was Sprinkled." W's confidence that his poetry will live. (*MY* I, 145–51.)[19]

45. May 21

RW's accounts charge DW £25/–/–, payment of bill on W. Bailey, under this date. (RW accounts, DCP.)

46. June 3; probably between June 3 and June 10

On 3 June the Bs arrive at Coleorton. (*MY* I, 152.)
Probably between 3 and 10 June W and Sir GB plant a cedar in the winter garden. ("The Embowering Rose," lines 3–4.)

47. June 5

W writes to RW [from Coleorton]: Montagu has applied to W for a £100 loan for a month, to be repaid from a sum to be loaned to him by RW on 24 [June]. This arrangement satisfactory from W's standpoint. Plans for departure from Coleorton. (*MY* I, 151.)

---

[18] The second edition of Duppa's work also contains W's translation *From the Italian of Michael Angelo. II* ("No Mortal Object Did These Eyes Behold"), first published on 8 May in *P2V*. In this edition of the *Life* Duppa acknowledges his indebtedness to his "friends Southey and Wordsworth . . . for the translations that enrich [his] work" (p. 238).

[19] W's date is "Tuesday May 21st 1807," and the postmark is 22 May (PML). The Tuesday in question must have been Tuesday 19 May. Since delivery of the letter need not have required more than one day, W's writing need not have been concluded on the day it began. A partial copy of the letter in the autograph of Lady B is in DCP.

48. June 7

DW writes to CCl [from Coleorton]: Plans to stay two days longer at Coleorton, then two days at Leeds, and to reach Halifax on [14 June]. SH. Family's health. TCl's *History . . . of the Abolition of the . . . African Slave Trade.* (*MY* I, 151–53.)

49. June 10

The Ws depart Coleorton. They travel by two post chaises to Nottingham, where they view the town and Castle and pass the night. (*MY* I, 157.)

50. June 11

The Ws depart from Nottingham by coach at 6 AM; travel to Sheffield. Molly is sent forward toward Grasmere by coach from Sheffield. The family travels to Huddersfield, where they pass the night. (*MY* I, 157.)

51. June 12–probably July 3

The Ws proceed to Halifax where they breakfast. They remain in Halifax until probably 3 July. They are joined at Halifax by SH. The children and DW or SH perhaps stay with Mrs. Threlkeld; the others probably stay with the Rawsons.ʼ(*MY* I, 152, 157. See 1807:53.) On their activities at Halifax see esp. *MY* I, 153, 157.[20]

52. June 27, July 2

The Rev. Joseph Sympson, curate of Wythburn, dies on 27 June; is buried at Grasmere on 2 July. (See *DWJ* I, 437; *MY* I, 158.)

53. July 1; probably July 1

On 1 July DW writes to RW from Halifax: STC cannot just now pay the £50 for which he gave W a draft [see 1807:23]; DW will draw on RW for £20 this day. The family's plans. (*MY* I, 153.)

[20] DW says that they remained at Halifax for "a fortnight" (*MY* I, 157); but they were plainly still there on 1 July, and then intending to leave on Friday 3 July (*MY* I, 153)—a plan apparently carried out (*MY* I, 157).

DW probably this day draws on RW for £20 by a bill in favor of William Rawson. (*MY* I, 153. RW accounts, DCP.)[21]

54. Probably July 3–July 6

The Ws proceed to New Grange with Mrs. Rawson. They remain there visiting John Marshall and JPM until, probably, 6 July. (*MY* I, 153, 157–58.)[22]

Perhaps on departing Halifax, W presents a copy of *P2V* to Elizabeth Threlkeld. (Catherine M. MacLean, *Dorothy Wordsworth, The Early Years*, London, 1932, 259.)

55. Probably July 6 (–July 10)

MW, SH, and the children depart from New Grange for Grasmere on 6 July; reach Kendal (where they remain until 10 July).

About an hour after their departure W and John Marshall, on horse, and DW, JPM, Mrs. Rawson, and a sister of JPM, in a carriage, set out from New Grange, proceed to Otley, thence along the Wharf to Bolton Abbey. W, DW take leave of the others six miles from Burnsall; walk to Burnsall, where they pass the night. (*MY* I, 157–58.)

Perhaps while in the area of Bolton Abbey W learns of the tradition of which he writes in *The Force of Prayer*. (See S. C. Wilcox, "The Source of Wordsworth's 'The Force of Prayer,'" *MLN* LII, 1937, 165–66.)

This visit probably serves as a principal incitement toward the composition of *WD*. (See W's note to *WD*, *P* 1820–*PW* 1850.)

Probably W at this time meets the Rev. W. Carr at Bolton Abbey. (Letter, RS to Mrs. Ann Montagu, 9 Oct 1812, Cornell Collection, Cornell 3118.)[23]

[21] RW's accounts record payment of the bill under 4 Aug.

[22] New Grange, formerly a residence of CCl (see *MY* I, 157–58), was apparently owned by her father William Buck at this time. It is described as the property of "———— Buck, Esq." in Cary's *Roads* from as early as 1798 through 1821. Paterson's *Roads*, 1822, names the owner as "T. Benyon, Esq."

[23] RS's letter explains that during the previous summer W had given him a letter of introduction to Carr for use in case of his visiting Bolton Abbey in the course of a planned tour. RS did not, however, reach Bolton Abbey. In the unpublished draft of his advertisement to *WD* (DC MS 61) W praises the appearance of Bolton Abbey as arranged "by the Rev Mr Carr, who has here wrought with an invisible hand of art, in the very spirit of Nature."

56. July 7

W, DW walk with a guide over the bare hills to Gordale. They climb up by the side of the waterfall and make their way to Malham Cove; drink tea at the inn; return in the late afternoon to Gordale, where they pass the night. (*MY* I, 158.)

The sights of this day perhaps contribute to, although they are not immediate stimulus of, "Pure Element of Waters!," *Malham Cove*, and *Gordale*.

57. July 8

W, DW walk to Settle; proceed to Ingleton, riding in a cart from Giggleswick Scar. They drink tea at Ingleton; ride on a coach to Kendal, where they join MW, SH, and the children, and pass the night. (*MY* I, 158.)

58. July 9

Probably the Ws pass the day at Levens Hall, and the night at Kendal. (*MY* I, 158.)[24]

59. July 10; perhaps July 10 and shortly after

On 10 July the W family travels to Grasmere in a post chaise. W, DW, and perhaps others probably walk in the evening. Perhaps at that time they learn, if they have not already learned, of various deaths that have occurred in their absence, including that of Mr. Sympson and George Dawson, who later becomes the subject of *Exc* VII.695–890, and of other changes in the neighborhood.

SH perhaps remains in Kendal visiting Mrs. Cookson; if not, she returns thither shortly. (*MY* I, 158–59; *Exc* IF note.)[25]

[24] W was probably drawn to Levens, a seat of the Viscountess Andover, by its gardens.

[25] DW states on Sunday 19 July that they arrived "Friday"; but they have been home, plainly, over a week, and her account of their tour does not leave much doubt that 10 July is the Friday in question. DW on the same date expected that SH would stay in Kendal at least six weeks longer.

W states in IF note to *Exc* that he attended the funeral of Dawson, but his memory and the description of the funeral in *Exc* must have drawn on secondhand report or some other occasion: as implied *MY* I, 168, Dawson died during the Ws' absence from Grasmere. The Grasmere PR unambiguously records that he was buried on 24 June.

60. Possibly 1807 after July 10; fairly certainly by late Oct 1814

W composes *Composed by the Side of Grasmere Lake*. (W's date, *PW* 1836–*PW* 1850; content; 1807:59; 1814:94.)[26]

61. Probably between July 10 and Sept 1

John Marshall visits W at Grasmere. W tells him of plans for a composition, probably a guide for travellers in the Lake District. They discuss planting and landscaping. (Letter, Marshall to W, 1 Sept 1807, DCP.)[27]

62. July 12

W writes to Francis Wrangham from Grasmere: *P2V*; Le Grice and his attacks on STC in *The Critical Review*; asks Wrangham to keep Le Grice from reviewing *P2V* in the *Critical*, either by writing the review himself, or by any other means. (*MY* I, 154–55. See Moorman II, 100n; 1807:74.)

63. July 13–July 16

On 13 July W goes to Keswick to visit with the Bs. He returns on 16 July. (*MY* I, 159.)

64. July 17

Thomas H calls or visits at DC. (*MY* I, 159.)[28]

[26] The earliest surviving MS, MS 80, appears to be a copy probably not written until 1814, although probably by the time of completion of the MS of *P* 1815 (GCL 224), and the poem was not published until 1819. W's own date is so much earlier that it commands respect.

[27] Marshall, writing from Edinburgh, states, "I hope you have made progress in your proposed work which was the subject of our conversation at Grasmere." He sends information about "the present mode of planting in Scotland," he says, "just as I found it, without attempting to make it square with our favourite ideas." On this letter, which probably eventually contributed to W's remarks on trees, esp. the Scotch fir and larch, in *G*, see also *MY* I, 164–65, 169. On Marshall's concern with landscaping see also *SHL* 93.

[28] DW remarks on Sunday 19 July that "T. Hutchinson has been with us on Friday."

65. July 19

DW writes to CCl: The Cls. The Ws' travels from Coleorton to Grasmere. Family news. (*MY* I, 157–59.)

66. Perhaps c July 29–c Aug 9

DW spends twelve days with the Bs at Keswick. They visit Buttermere twice. On one of those occasions she learns from some Quakers that TCl is in the neighborhood. (*MY* I, 159–62.)[29]

67. Perhaps c early Aug

The Ws receive and read eagerly a MS copy of TCl's *History . . . of the Abolition of the . . . African Slave Trade.* (*MY* I, 157–59.)

68. Probably c Aug 1

A review, by Byron, of *P2V* appears in *Monthly Literary Recreations* (III, July 1807). (See Ward; Hayden.)

69. Aug 22

TCl is expected. The Ws walk out in the evening to AB. TCl stops at DC and departs in their absence. DW writes a note to him to be delivered by Charles Lloyd. (*MY* I, 160.)

70. Aug 23

A note arrives at DC from TCl saying that he will spend next day with them. (*MY* I, 160.)

71. Aug 24 (–Aug 25)

TCl arrives at DC; passes the night there. (*MY* I, 160–61.)

72. Aug 25 (–Aug 27–Aug 29, Sept 5 or Sept 6); between Aug 25 and c Sept 5

On 25 Aug TCl departs from DC. W, MW depart for Eusemere.

[29] On 19 July DW states that she is to go in "about ten days" to spend a week with the Bs; on 30 Aug she indicates that she spent twelve days with them, but is unclear about the dates of the visit.

(They return together c 5 Sept; W returns briefly probably during the days 27–29 Aug.) W perhaps takes with him Thomas Wilkinson's Journal [see *MY* I, 104] to return to Wilkinson. W passes most or all the period of the visit with the Bs, as does MW also, except for a probable visit to Appleby. During this time W visits at Lowther, accompanied by the Bs; meets LdL; discusses landscape planting with him. (*MY* I, 161, 164–65, 166–67. See Moorman II, 109n; Betz *BN*.)

73. Aug 26 (–Aug 29)

John Crump arrives at DC seeking W's advice about the laying out of the grounds at AB [see 1807:32]. DW sends a messenger to Eusemere for him.

W probably arrives back at DC today. (He returns to Eusemere 29 Aug.) He receives an invitation from Lord and Lady Holland to dine or visit with them in the evening at the Low Wood Hotel. He goes thither in the evening. He impresses Lady Holland as a man perhaps putting his major energies into conversation. He maintains that the white houses in the Lakes area conflict with the scenery; says that he is preparing a guide for Lakes tourists. They perhaps also discuss the Bishop of Llandaff and his late prospects for obtaining the bishopric of York. The party perhaps includes also Charles Richard Fox, John Allen, Matthew Marsh, Mr. Knapp. (Lady Holland, *Journals*, ed. Earl of Ilchester, London, 1908, II, 230–32; BM Add. MS 51,937; *MY* I, 161; Masson II, 198–99. See also 1807:61.)[30]

74. Probably Aug 29 (–c Sept 5 or 6)

W returns to Eusemere [see 1807:72]. (He remains there until c 5 Sept.) (*MY* I, 161.)

[30] Lady Holland's journal of her tour commences on the "22d of August," and her visit with W took place on the following "Wednesday." W's day would have included much travel; but the Holland party proceeded to Keswick on Thursday, and no other day appears a possible one for the visit.

DeQ reports that the conversation about the Bishop of Llandaff took place as W rode by the bishop's grounds. No record survives that W went riding; but the bishop's grounds, Calgarth Park, lay only a short distance down the shore of Windermere from Lowwood, sufficiently close to make the bishop a likely subject of conversation.

W expresses his dislike of white houses for the Lake area in *G* 1810.

75. Aug 30

DW writes to CCl: A visit from TCl [see 1807:71]; TCl's book [see 1807:67]; AB. (*MY* I, 156–62.)

76. Aug 31

RW's accounts charge W £7/10/6, payment of premium of £300 policy on Montagu's life, under this date. (RW accounts, DCP.)

77. Probably c Sept 1

A review of *P2V* appears in *The Critical Review* (3rd ser. XI, Aug 1807). (See Ward; Hayden.)

78. Probably c but not before Sept 5 or 6 (–probably Sept 13); between Sept 5 and Sept 12; perhaps shortly after

Probably c but not before 5 Sept W, MW, the Bs travel probably from Eusemere to Grasmere. On their way up Kirkstone above Hartsop Hall they have a remarkable view of clouds, light, and mountains that later contributes to *Exc* II.826–81. (The Bs depart Grasmere 12 Sept.) (*MY* I, 161, 164, 170; *Exc* IF note. See *PW* V, 417.)[31]

During the visit W probably reads *PB* to the Bs. Lady B perhaps now urges W to omit the "Is it a party" passage [see *PW* II, 354 *app crit*]. (*MY* I, 188; *Blake, Etc.* 55. See Betz *PB*.)

79. Possibly shortly after Sept 5, or c summer 1808

W composes *Exc* II.c725–895. (See Appendix VI.)

80. Sept 10

DW presents a copy of Burns's *Poems* (Dundee, 1802) to Lady B. (See Cornell 2224; 1803:94.)

---

[31] On Sunday 30 Aug DW states that she is expecting the Ws and Bs on "Wednesday"; but on 19 Sept she states that W and MW had "12 days at Ulswater." In a letter to W of 30 Nov 1814 (DCP) Sir GB recalls that the view above Hartsop left W "struck dumb for an hour at least."

81. Probably Sept 13

The Bs depart Grasmere, probably early in the day. (Letter, Sir GB to W, n.d., DCP.)[32]

82. Probably Sept 15–Sept 18 and shortly after; perhaps c Sept 18

On 15–18 Sept W, MW make a tour including Wastdale, Ennerdale, Whitehaven, and Cockermouth. They possibly visit Catgill and see Jane Wordsworth, daughter of RW of Branthwaite [see 1808:96]. (*MY* I, 164–65, 169–70, 323.)[33]

Probably shortly after his return W attempts to write a description of the tour but is prevented, by what he later termed "an insuperable dullness," from proceeding. (*MY* I, 271.)

Perhaps c 18 Sept W composes *The Force of Prayer*. (*MY* I, 168.)[34]

83. Probably Sept 18, 19

DW writes to JPM from Grasmere: (18 Sept:) JPM's tour in Scotland. W, MW. Marshall's letter to W [see 1807:61]. (19 Sept:) W and MW's return from their tour. (*MY* I, 163–65.)[35]

[32] Sir GB writes to W, probably not long after departing, of his unhappiness at having to leave the mountains on the "13th." The Bs breakfasted with "Mr Green"— certainly William Green—in Ambleside on their way.

[33] DW states on 19 Sept that W and MW set out "two days" after the Bs' departure. This statement would appear more likely to be accurate than one of 18 Oct that the Bs departed the "very day before" W and MW set off. *MY* I, 165 makes clear that they returned on 18 Sept (despite DW's statement on 4 Nov that they were absent "a week").

DW writes probably c but by 29 Apr 1809 that W and MW saw Jane W at Catgill "last Summer." W was perhaps in that area in Sept of 1808, but MW and her newly born babe can hardly have been with him. DW was possibly thinking back to late summer of the previous year, or, alternatively, possibly thinking of W and SH (see 1808:96).

In a letter of 7 Oct 1805 RW of Branthwaite informs W of his approaching removal to reside at Catgill and invites W, DW, and MW to visit "at any time" (DCP).

[34] W's IF note to *The Force of Prayer* states, as remarked Moorman II, 110n, that the poem was "an appendage" to *WD*; but although it was published as an appendage to the *WD*, it was certainly written earlier. W dated the poem 1808 *P* 1815–*P* 1820, *PW* 1836–*PW* 1850.

[35] The letter is dated simply "September 19th"; but the concluding portion is separately dated "Saturday," which would have been the 19th.

84. Sept 27

W writes to Walter Scott: Delivery of a work for Scott concerning Flodden Field; advice about Dryden's *MacFlecknoe*. (*MY* I, 165–66.)

85. Perhaps late this year

W meets John Wilson. (Mrs. Gordon I, 125–26.)[36]

86. Oct 2

DW writes to RW from Grasmere: W will draw on RW c 18 Oct for £50, due in one month, favor of Mr. Sympson, Kendal, grocer [see 1807:89]. (*MY* I, 166–67.)

87. Probably between Oct 5 and Nov 15

W writes to CW (letter not known to survive) supporting Richard Duppa's candidacy for the situation at the BM vacated by the death of Horace Bedford. (Warter II, 21; Curry I, 462.)

88. Oct 16 and shortly after; probably between Oct 16 and 1808 late Jan

Copies of Dr. Whitaker's *History of . . . Whalley* and *History of . . . Craven*, on loan from the Marshalls or obtained through their aid, arrive at DC. W reads the *History of Craven* eagerly, probably for information for *WD*. (*MY* I, 167–68; note to *WD*, *P 1820–PW* 1850.)

Probably between 16 Oct and 8 Nov W writes an introduction to *WD*; between 16 Oct and 1 Dec he writes 500 lines toward the poem. About half the poem, c850–950 lines, is probably written by c 19 Dec. Over 1200 lines are written by 3 Jan, and the poem is finished, in a version of about 1700 lines, on 16 Jan. MSS 1, 2 are probably written,

[36] Mrs. Gordon confusingly states that Wilson's first meeting with W "did not take place till the year 1807, the poet and his family having lived the greater part of that year at Colerton [*sic*], returning to Grasmere in the spring of 1808. At his house there, toward the latter end of that year, Wilson met De Quincy. . . . "

DeQ's account of his own meeting with Wilson leaves no doubt that that event occurred at AB, and hence not before 1808; but the Ws were certainly acquainted with Wilson before they removed thither. The latter part of the year 1807 would appear by default the most likely time for the meeting.

including an advertisement, between 16 Oct 1807 and late Jan 1808. (Appendix VIII. See 1807:95; 1807:101; 1807:102.)

89. Perhaps c Oct 18; Oct 18

Perhaps c 18 Oct Mr. Sympson, the Ws' grocer, of Kendal, calls or visits at DC. Probably DW draws on RW for £50 through Sympson by a bill due in one month. (*MY* I, 166–67; RW accounts, DCP.)[37]

On 18 Oct DW writes to JPM: Thanks for Dr. Whitaker's books. W is at work on a poem. Transcription of *The Force of Prayer*. The Marshall and W families. (*MY* I, 167–69.)

90. Perhaps c Oct 25–Oct 30

Perhaps c 25 Oct W travels to Penrith, probably mainly to see RW. He remains probably at Sockbridge until 30 Oct, when he probably returns to DC. (*MY* I, 169, 171.)[38]

91. Probably c Nov 1

A review of *P2V* appears in *Le Beau Monde* (II, Oct 1807). Another review appears in *The Literary Annual Register* (I, Oct 1807). (See Ward; Hayden.)

92. Nov 4–probably Nov 5; probably Nov 4 (–Nov 5, –Nov 7, –Nov 12)

On 4 Nov W writes to Francis Wrangham: *The Critical Review's* response to *P2V* as he has heard it described. Errata in *P2V*. (*MY* I, 173–75.)

On 4 and probably 5 Nov DW writes to CCl: (4 Nov:) Recent family events; Uncle Henry H; SH to go to Appleby and to come to DC after Christmas; Miss Weir, Bessy and Jane H [daughters of John H] to pass Christmas at DC; others of family. (Probably 5 Nov:)

---

[37] RW charges the £50 to DW's account under 19 Nov.

[38] DW states on Sunday 18 Oct that W "is going to Penrith next week to see Richard"; and she states probably on 4 or 5 Nov (Wednesday or Thursday) that W spent "the whole of last week at Penrith" and left RW "on Friday."

Arrival of Cs and DeQ [see below]. They want first volume of TCl's *Portraiture of Quakerism. (MY* I, 169–73.)[39]

On 4 Nov SFC, SC, Derwent, HC, and Thomas DeQ, whom W now meets for the first time, arrive for a visit at DC, perhaps at about 4 PM. All pass the night at DC (two sleeping at Peggy Ashburner's). (The Cs depart for Keswick after dinner on 5 Nov. DeQ departs DC probably 7 Nov; parts company with W probably 12 Nov.) (*MY* I, 169–73; *Minnow* 7–8; Masson II, 235–52, 303–12; *RLP* 111–32, 185–94.)

On DeQ's visit see references just cited; *RLP* 111–32, 185–94; Eaton 136–40; Jordan 26–27, 47–51; Moorman II, 116.[40]

Probably on 5 Nov, a rainy day, W, DW, DeQ walk in Easedale, and around Grasmere and Rydal Water. The Cs depart for Keswick after dinner. (Masson II, 307; *MY* I, 173; *Minnow* 7–8. See Eaton 140.)

93. Probably Nov 6

W proposes a journey to Keswick via Ullswater. DW, DeQ perhaps walk to Esthwaite Water; on their return they call on the Lloyds at Brathay. (Masson II, 307, 382. See Eaton 140; 1807:92.)[41]

94. Probably Nov 7 (–probably Nov 11, Dec 23)

Probably W, MW, DeQ travel to Eusemere over Kirkstone in a cart driven by a young woman. DW perhaps accompanies them as far as Ambleside, passes the day with the Lloyds. (W and DeQ return to DC probably 11 Nov; MW returns 23 Dec.) (Masson II, 307; *RLP*

[39] The MS shows that the date at the head of the letter was corrected from 4 Nov to 5 Nov: DW opened it after the arrival of the visitors, and plainly concluded it the day after the arrival. Probably the entire second paragraph of the postscript was written and the date corrected on 5 Nov.

[40] DeQ later implies that he arrived on 5 Nov, but his circumstantial account of the visit makes it clear that he had passed four nights with the Ws before "the Sunday next," which would have been 8 Nov (see Jordan 48, 369).

[41] DeQ's description appears to leave no doubt that this meeting with the Lloyds occurred during his 1807 visit to DC; and 6 Nov appears the only possible day when there would have been time for a walk as far as Esthwaite Water.

189–90; Eaton 140; *MY* I, 170; letter, Sophia Lloyd to Priscilla W, 8 Nov 1807, JFW Papers. See 1807:92.)[42]

95. Probably Nov 8

W, DeQ probably leave MW at Eusemere; spend the morning roaming through the woods of Lowther. W reads to DeQ the introduction to *WD*. They dine at Eamont Bridge; walk to Penrith. DeQ passes the night at Capt. W's, Brougham Hall. Possibly W returns to Eusemere. (Masson II, 311; *RLP* 193; Jordan 48, 89; DeQ, *Selections Grave and Gay*, Edinburgh, 1854, II, 322. See 1807:92.)[43]

96. Probably Nov 9

W is perhaps with MW at Eusemere, Penrith or both places. DeQ walks to Keswick from Penrith; is received at GH by RS. (Masson II, 311; *RLP* 193. See 1807:92.)

97. Probably Nov 10 and shortly after –probably c Dec 19

Probably on 10 Nov W proceeds from Penrith to GH, probably

[42] DeQ states (Masson II, 307; *RLP* 189) that "the whole family, except the two children" were prepared for the journey, and implies that this party made the trip across Kirkstone. The W children numbered three; MW did not return till 23 Dec; there is no other evidence that any of the children made such a trip (DW was certainly looking after them in MW's absence on 2 Dec; see *MY* I, 179); and while DW may have started off from DC with W, MW, and DeQ, she is unlikely, despite DeQ's description of her banter with passers-by, to have accompanied the party far beyond Ambleside. Sophia Lloyd writes to Priscilla W, in her letter dated (although on the address panel, fairly certainly by the writer) 8 Nov (postmark 12 Nov): "Miss Wordsworth spent the day with us yesterday, & expressed a great wish to hear further of you. Mr & Mrs W were gone toward Durham." The plan entertained on 4 Nov was for W and MW to go alone (*MY* I, 170). It was perhaps during this excursion that Joanna H saw DeQ (see *SHL* 12).

[43] As noted Jordan 369, DeQ's letter to W of 25 Mar 1808 makes plain that DeQ heard the introduction on this day, and heard the remainder of the poem in London, although DeQ's 1854 phrasing concerning this day, while noting that the day was a Sunday, does not itself limit the content of the reading so narrowly. As remarked Moorman II, 116, no "introduction" to the poem now survives. (It seems doubtful that DeQ's phrasing refers to the preface—now surviving, if at all, only in fragmentary drafts [see Appendix VIII]—mentioned *STCL* III, 111; IV, 603.)

leaving MW at Eusemere or Penrith with Joanna H and Miss Elizabeth Green, with whom she travels, probably starting today or shortly after, to Stockton. She departs Stockton probably c 19 Dec. She sees her sister Elizabeth there. (On her visit see also 1807:104.)

W, DeQ dine, pass the evening and night with RS. (Masson II, 311–12, 322; *RLP* 193–94, 203–04; *MY* I, 170, 182. See 1807:92.)

98. Probably Nov 11

W and RS discuss public affairs after breakfast. Their sentiments strike DeQ as hostile to the royal family and monarchical government generally.

DeQ and W walk to Grasmere, accompanied by RS on their way as far as Shoulthwaite Moss. (Masson II, 322–23; *RLP* 203–04.)

99. Probably Nov 12

W, DW, DeQ dine perhaps at Mrs. Green's, with a pretty, timid young woman and a stranger. During the meal a single pheasant is offered to the entire company (the young woman excepted), and then, the others having declined to partake, eaten entire by the hostess. W is indignant. DeQ parts from W, DW at about 10 at an inn, probably the Salutation, in Ambleside, to take the coach and start his journey to Oxford. (Masson II, 348–59; *RLP* 226–37; Cary's *Roads*, 1806.)[44]

100. Probably c Dec 1

A review of *P2V* appears in the *Satirist* (I, Nov 1807); another appears in the *Literary Panorama* (III, Nov 1807). (See Ward; Haydon.)

101. Dec 1 (–Dec 23); between Dec 1 and Dec 23

---

[44] The identity of the hostess, DeQ's "Saracen's Head," remains uncertain; but DeQ's account of her accords sufficiently with descriptions of Mrs. Green in the Wordsworth correspondence, particularly as regards her parsimony and blue-stocking proclivities (see esp. *MY* II, 109–10, 184, 203; *MWL* 20), to justify an unchivalrous conjecture.

On 1 Dec W departs from DC on foot between 10 and 11 AM on his way to join MW at Stockton; drinks ale at Threlkeld; makes his way, partly on foot, partly by horse, to Penrith, where he arrives between 5 and 6 PM. He writes a description of his trip for DW (only a fragment survives, quoted *MY* I, 180–81). (He returns to DC with MW on 23 Dec.)

Perhaps during W's absence DW sees at the Lloyds' a copy of *ER* with Jeffrey's reviews of *P2V*. (*MY* I, 179–82, 185.)[45]

102. Dec 2

W writes to RW from Penrith: Mrs. RW of Whitehaven should receive £9 a year until settlement of the debt to her husband's estate [see 1804:104], including arrears for two years. (*MY* I, 176.)

W perhaps this day joins Thomas H; possibly they travel to and pass the night at Appleby, visiting with SH. (*MY* I, 170, 179–81, 185.)

DW writes to CCl: First volume of TCl's *Portraiture* still sought [see 1807:92]. Letters from STC; SFC's reluctance to have separation known publicly; STC. W's, MW's travels. W has written 500 lines of a new poem [see 1807:88]. They plan not to move till spring or summer. (*MY* I, 176–79.)

103. Dec 3

A review [by Francis Jeffrey] of *P2V* appear in *ER* (XI, Oct 1807). (*MC*. See Ward; Haydon.)

104. Probably c Dec 3 or Dec 4–perhaps c Dec 19

W, perhaps with Thomas H, reaches Stockton, where he remains visiting the Hs until perhaps c 19 Dec. Perhaps while at Stockton W composes much of the present first half of *WD*. On his methods of

---

[45] DW on 2 Dec was of the opinion that W "*must* stay at least a fortnight with M's friends," and opinion that she repeated on 6 Dec; so he may be supposed in any case to have spent fewer than nine days on the road. He probably passed a night at Penrith each way (*MY* I, 185), and possibly a night at Appleby each way as well.

composition see *WD* IF note. He writes to Dr. Beddoes for advice for John H.

He sees Daniel Stuart at Stockton. W and MW are in good favor with Uncle Henry H. (*MY* I, 170, 179, 185, 188; *WD* IF note. See 1807:88; 1807:102; Appendix VIII.)[46]

105. Dec 6

DW writes to Lady B: STC; DeQ; W's departure for Stockton; a gift of game from the Bs; Davy's, Wilkie's illnesses. (*MY* I, 180–83.)

106. Perhaps c Dec 19–Dec 23

Perhaps c 19 Dec W, MW depart from Stockton; proceed to Appleby, where they perhaps visit for one night or more with SH. The three probably proceed to Penrith; SH goes on to Eusemere. At Penrith W, MW see Jeffrey's review of *P2V* in *ER* [see 1807:100]. W, MW arrive home at DC on 23 Dec just before Johnny and Dora are put to bed. (*MY* I, 170, 185–188, 193.)[47]

107. Probably between 23 Dec and 1808 c Jan

W writes to RS: Reasoned comment on Jeffrey's complaints about W in Oct *ER*. (*MY* I, 162. See 1807:106; *MY* I, 191–92.)

108. Dec 28

DW writes to CCl: Possible visit by CCl at AB; the original plan was for STC and his sons to reside there with the Ws; but the idea no longer seems sound; no decision will be made till Mar, when (STC states) STC will rejoin them. W, MW, and their recent trip. A lecturer who, apparently, attended the funeral of JW Sr. Jeffrey's review of *P2V*. HCR. (*MY* I, 183–86.)

[46] Farington IV, 238 records under 12 Dec a report by Constable that David Wilkie was offended at W for offering to propose to him subjects for painting.

[47] The plan spoken of by DW on 4 Nov (*MY* I, 170) that Bessy and Jane H and Miss Weir would pass their Christmas with the Ws apparently did not materialize.

1808

[On writings of W possibly of this year see below and GCL 42, 97, 123, 146, 148, 153, 167–69, 171, 173–80.]

1. Possibly c 1808

W probably reads Philip Beaver's *African Memoranda* (London, 1805), borrowed from DeQ. W comes to regard Beaver as one of the most enlightened men any nation ever produced. (*MY* I, 297, 486; Musgrove 9.)[1]

2. Perhaps early this year

W, or possibly DW, writes the fragmentary sonnet *On Milton* ("Amid the Dark Control of Lawless Sway"). (*PW* III, 409, 574; *MY* I, 213.)[2]

3. Jan 3

A copy of Walton's *Compleat Angler* arrives as a gift to DW from Sir GB, with a note from Lady B. W reads in the book. (*MY* I, 187.)

DW writes to Lady B: Thanks for the gift of the *Compleat Angler*. W has written above 1200 lines of [*WD*]. When he has finished the poem W will write to Sir GB. Davy; *ER*; comment on extract from letter of Lady Susan Bathurst sent by Lady B; dangers of overindulgence of children; Elizabeth Carter's *Memoirs*. (*MY* I, 186–190.)

---

[1] W's high opinion of Beaver as expressed in Mar 1809 was almost certainly formed on the basis of *African Memoranda*, which DeQ stated on 29 May 1811 had been returned to him some time since. DW, however, read the book not long before 12 May 1811.

[2] At the end of the MS (DC MS 63) is written "The subject from Symonds' Life" (cf *PW* III, 574). W had not yet read Symmons's *Life of Milton* on 4 Nov 1807 (*MY* I, 175), but had done so—seemingly recently—by 17 Apr 1808 (*MY* I, 213). The MS is in DW's autograph, and very rough; and the quality of the verse is low. DW was possibly the author, or transcribed little-considered dictation.

4. Probably mid- or late Jan (–probably July 18)

SH arrives at DC for a visit. (She departs probably 18 July; and is perhaps absent c 10 Feb.) (*MY* I, 193; Penrith.)[3]

5. Jan 16, and shortly after

W finishes *WD* in a version of about 1700 lines on 16 Jan. A fair copy is probably written shortly afterward. (*MY* I, 191. See Appendix VIII.)

6. Jan 18

W writes to Walter Scott: *Marmion*; Scott's edition of Dryden; *Annus Mirabilis*; John Ogilby; other advice and comment about Dryden; Pope and Dryden. *WD*. Jeffrey has shown a gross want of the common feeling of a British gentleman. (*MY* I, 190–92.)

7. Perhaps late Jan, or Feb 1 or Feb 2

RS, with Thomas S, perhaps sees W and receives a MS of *WD*. RS certainly reads *WD* by 2 Feb. (Letter, RS to Mary Barker, 2 Feb 1808 [pub. in part *Atlantic Monthly* LXXXIX, 1902, 39]. See Appendix VIII.)[4]

---

[3] SH, according to DW, came to DC after the death of "Miss Green" at Eusemere on a Tuesday (*MY* I, 193 misreads "Tuesday" as "Thursday"). The Miss Green concerned appears unlikely to be Elizabeth Green (cf *MY* I, 193). A gravestone in the Penrith churchyard records the day of death of "Mary Green" as 11 Jan 1808, and that of her sister Elizabeth as 26 June 1830. This 11 Jan was, however, a Monday. The Penrith PR states that "Mrs Mary Green" was buried on 18 Jan. The combined weight of DW's remarks and the record of the PR would appear to fix the day of Miss Green's death as probably by Tuesday 12 Jan. (The style "Mrs" would not of course at this time have distinguished a married woman: see *OED s.v.* "mistress.")

[4] "Wordsworth has written a masterly poem called The White Doe of Rilston Hall, or the Fate of the Nortons. —a father & eight sons who were executed after the great Rising in the North, in Elizabeths days. The poem is 1700 lines, & is incomparably fine. It would amuse you to hear how he talks of his own productions,— his entire & intense selfishness exceeds anything you could have conceived;—I am more amused at it than offended, not being sufficiently attached to him to feel pain at perceiving his faults, & yet respecting him far too much on the average of his qualities to be disgusted. But Tom is absolutely provoked, as well as astonished.—It

8. Perhaps c early or mid-Feb, by Feb 22

William Havell visits DC; is pleased by Sir GB's paintings and sketches there. W purchases a view of the cottage at Glencoyne, by Ullswater, by William Green. (*MY* I, 195; 1808:14.)

9. Probably c Feb 1

A review of *P2V* [by James Montgomery] appears in *The Eclectic Review* (IV, Jan 1808). (Ward; Haydon.)

10. Feb 5

DW writes to CCl: STC; MW. *WD*; W intends to ask 100 guineas for 1000 copies. Luff's estate; SH, and death of Miss Green [see 1808:4n]; other local news. Wants a volume of TCl's *Portraiture of Quakerism*. (*MY* I, 192–93.)

11. c Feb 10

SH or DW is possibly absent from DC nursing a sick cousin. (*STCL* III, 62.)[5]

12. Probably between Feb 12 and Feb 22, 23

Probably between 12 and 22 Feb W decides to go to London to see STC. He is delayed for a time by an inflamation in his face from a cold and a decayed tooth. W writes to STC, and DW to ML, to obtain information about STC's health. (*MY* I, 196–98.)

W perhaps sees SFC about this time; if so, certainly by 23 Feb. (*STCL* VI, 1018–19; 1808:15.)

Probably between 12 and 16, esp. probably on 15 or 16 Feb, RS

---

[5] STC, in London, wrote to Mrs. J. J. Morgan on 10 Feb that MW was unwell and her sister "absent, nursing a sick Cousin in a house of sickness." He likewise wrote on 18 Feb (*STCL* III, 77) of MW's "alarming" state of health. Neither SH nor DW is otherwise known to have been absent from DC in Feb. Family letters indicate that MW, while not strong, was not seriously ill.

---

is so pure & unmixed a passion in him that Ben Johnson would have had him in a play had he been his contemporary." (I am indebted to Professor Robert Kirkpatrick for a transcription of this passage.)

sees W, and if he has not earlier received a MS of *WD*, does so now. He reports STC in poor health. The Ws evidently suppose that RS will take the MS to Leeds and deliver it to the Marshalls, who will in turn arrange its conveyance to Dr. Whitaker. RS does not go to Leeds. He perhaps carries the MS with him directly to London. W probably recovers it c late Feb. (*MY* I, 197–200. See 1808:7; Appendix VIII.)[6]

13. Probably c mid- or late Feb; perhaps c mid-Feb, certainly by Feb 23

Probably c mid- or late Feb Piranesi folios, perhaps sent by STC, probably arrive for W at DC, accompanied by a New Testament, a Chapman's Homer, and Francois Huber's *Natural History of Bees* sent to SH by STC. (*STCL* III, 67–68; MS of letter, George W. Meissner Collection, Washington University Library, St. Louis.)[7]

Perhaps c mid-Feb, certainly by 23 Feb W writes, probably, to CL (letter not known to survive) advising of his intention to visit London and commenting on Shakespeare. (*LL* II, 51. See 1808:15n.)

14. Probably c but by Feb 22

W, DW write, respectively, to Sir GB and Lady B: (W to Sir GB:) Sir GB's picture for *PB*; "the people" distinguished from "the public" as an audience for *PB*. A friend of the Bs' misreads poems of W's, esp. "I Wandered Lonely." W a teacher or nothing. GB's paintings; Havell; a pencil sketch by William Green which he has purchased [see 1808:8]; a pictorial subject in *WD*; STC; Davy. (DW to Lady B:) The MS of *WD*; Sir GB's picture of *PB*; Davy; STC; Davy. (*MY* I, 194–98.)[8]

6 The Ws received c but by 12 Feb a distressing account of STC's health "from Keswick." The news fairly certainly came to RS in STC's letter to him of 9 Feb (*STCL* III, 56–59), to which RS replied on 12 Feb (*CCS* III, 133–35). That RS spoke to W on the subject in person is uncertain but not unlikely (see *MY* I, 197). DW states on Wednesday 24 Feb that RS had left from Ambleside for Leeds "last Tuesday but one," taking a MS of *WD* with him.

7 For use of information in the MS of STC's letter I am indebted to Washington University Library and to Professor George Whalley, who will publish the full text of the letter in his forthcoming edition of STC's *Marginalia*.

8 As remarked *MY* I, 194n, Sir GB's reply from Dunmow (DCP) is dated 25 Feb. And W's letter is unlikely to have been written on the day of his departure for London (see *MY* I, 196).

15. Probably Feb 23; probably Feb 23–Feb 25 (–Apr 6)

Probably on 23 Feb W or DW writes to Dr. Whitaker (letter not known to survive), asks him to send *WD* MS to London. (*MY* I, 199–200.)

Probably on the same day DW writes to JPM: STC; W will go to London tomorrow to see him; STC has given up his lecturing after two lectures. The MS of *WD*. (*MY* I, 198–99.)[9]

W, MW depart DC in a cart driven by Molly Fisher. DW accompanies them as far as Lowwood. W, MW proceed to Kendal, where MW probably remains two nights before returning home and where W perhaps passes this night. (W returns to DC 6 Apr.) (*MY* I, 199–200.)

16. Between perhaps Feb 24 and probably Feb 27; between Feb 27 and Apr 3; and about this time

Between perhaps 24 Feb and probably 27 Feb W travels to London from Kendal, arriving probably 27 Feb. (He departs 3 Apr.) (*MY* I, 199–200; *STCL* VI, 1018; *LL* II, 51.)[10]

While in London W sees Basil Montagu, Richard Sharp; probably sees Samuel Rogers. Possibly in company with Rogers W passes an evening at CL's during which he reads and terms "abominable" Brougham's attack on Byron's *Hours of Idleness* in the Jan *ER*. (*MY* I, 211–12, 269; Rogers *Table-Talk* 234.) W probably passes most evenings not otherwise described with STC. (See *MY* I, 495; *LL* II, 55.)[11]

---

[9] On the fortunes of the MS see esp. Appendix VIII. DW states that W leaves "tomorrow"; in her letter to JPM of 24 Feb she states that W left "yesterday." That letter also makes plain, however, that the present letter was written the previous "night." The problem would be eased if DW had begun the letter on the 24th but not finished it till the day after (thus W would have departed DC on the 24th), but neither the appearance of the MS (DCP) nor its content supports such a conjecture.

[10] CL wrote sarcastically on 26 Feb: "Wordsworth, the great poet, is coming to town; he is to have apartments in the Mansion House. He says he does not see much difficulty in writing like Shakespeare. . . ."

STC wrote to Morgan on "Tuesday Morning" that "Wordsworth arrived here on Saturday."

[11] W's tone in his letter to Rogers of late Sept (see 1808:98) is suggestive of their having seen each other recently; but direct evidence is wanting. Rogers's report of W's comment about the review does not seem to claim first-handedness. STC stated on 9 Mar that W had been "a comforter" to him.

One evening W takes the MS of *WD* to CL's to read; finds Hazlitt and Sarah Stoddart there. After first refusing to read at all, he reads one book of *WD*; briefly discusses the passage commencing "Now doth a delicate shadow fall" (87 ff). Probably during this evening also occurs conversation concerning STC's possible indebtedness to Stoddart in his views concerning Shakespeare's sonnets. (*MY* I, 221–22, 241–43.)

During a visit to CL's in company with STC W criticizes Mrs. Barbauld's [*Hymn*] *to Content.* (*HCRBW* I, 61–62.)[12]

W reads *WD*, except for the "Introduction" [see 1807:95], in DeQ's presence, possibly at STC's. DeQ hears or sees W's translation from Ariosto. W states that he wishes to keep the translation for revision on account of some harshness in the versification. (Jordan 89–90.)

W, STC, using a letter of Sir GB to Thomas Lawrence, on a gloomy day see Angerstein's pictures, noting esp. "the great picture of Michael Angelo's Sebastian" (Sebastiano Del Piombo's "The Raising of Lazarus," after Michaelangelo) and a new Rembrandt ("The Woman Taken in Adultery") in which W most admires "the light in the depth of the Temple." (*MY* I, 208.)

STC perhaps writes to W suggesting the curse of Wallace's chaplain as a good subject for a poem. W does not reply. (*MY* I, 242.)

W dines once at Longman's, with Richard Heber, Sharon Turner, STC, probably also the Rev. Herbert Hill, Owen Rees, and Thomas Hill, about the last of whom W, probably later, seeks further information. (*MY* I, 237–38; *STCL* III, 80.)

W is possibly about this time contemplating publication also of *PB*. (See 1814:38n.)

W makes inquiries of Daniel Stuart and J. F. Tuffin concerning the possibility of a situation in Brazil for John M. (Letter, John M to Thomas M, 27 Apr 1808, JFW Papers.)[13] At Tuffin's W sees a collection of cabinet pictures which he finds pleasing. (*MY* I, 209.)

[12] STC stated in 1812 that W's criticisms were made at CL's "two years ago"; but the present visit was W's last to London before 1812. W apparently made similar criticisms of Mrs. Barbauld to HCR (see 1808:23). On W's unwillingness to be in company with Hazlitt see *HCRBW* I, 169–70.

[13] John M wrote to Thomas M from Penrith: "I had my wishes stated to W Wordsworth when in London who approved highly of the plan & spoke of it to Mr Stuart & a Mr Tuffin . . . who have acquaintance amongst the Merchants."

17. Feb 24

A note arrives from SFC advising that RS is proceeding to London via Liverpool.

DW writes to JPM: The MS of *WD* [see 1808:12; 1808:15]; STC. (*MY* I, 199–200.)

18. Probably Feb 27 or very shortly after

W sees STC. Among W's communications are probably that SFC is unwilling to send Derwent to live with his father, and perhaps that SFC's "unimpressability is almost a moral miracle." (*STCL* VI, 1019–20. See 1808:16.)[14]

19. Probably between Feb 27 and Mar 28

W offers *WD* to Longman, but will not allow inspection of the poem, and no agreement is reached. By 28 Mar W decides not to publish. (*MY* I, 207; *STCL* VI, 1021–22.)

20. Mar 3

W probably this day attends a debate at the House of Commons. STC or Daniel Stuart probably has a tea party at the *Courier* office, attended by W, CL, DeQ, Godwin, RS, as well as STC and Stuart, and a few others. Among CL's remarks is perhaps a speculation that everyone at the party will, on leaving, make up to the first pretty girl he sees. W questions the speculation. CL replies, laughing, that "sad Josephs are some of us in this very room." (Masson III, 25, 52–53; Godwin Diary.)[15]

[14] STC's letter of 1 Mar also advises that he has written, during the last week or more, "at least a Quire of letter paper in letters & replies to great & little men in order to procure the Discharge of Mrs Wordsworth's Brother, impressed from a merchant Ship—& have succeeded, as far as the Admiralty have any power. . . ."

[15] Godwin records simply that he drank tea at STC's with W, CL, and DeQ, adding, after a colon: "meet Hutchins. Talk of Greeks & Latins, Spenser, Milton." The note on the conversation almost certainly refers to the party, and the meeting with Hutchins probably occurred later.

This occasion appears the only one likely for DeQ's single meeting with RS in a distinctly small company (see Masson references), when CL's conversation moved at least part of the time upon a less than lofty plane.

The major items of business in Commons on 3 Mar were an attack on the Admiralty in the form of a motion from Calcraft for an inquiry into the circumstances of the

21. Mar 4

RW's accounts charge W £30/–/–, payment of bill in favor of John Green, under this date. (RW accounts, DCP.)

22. Mar 6

W calls on CW and his family at Lambeth; spends the afternoon. He gives a favorable account of Charles and Sophia Lloyd; perhaps now speaks highly of TCl's *History of the . . . Slave Trade*. (BM Add. MS 46,138, fols. 10–13, 16.)[16]

23. Mar 15–perhaps Mar 16 or Mar 17

On 15 Mar W breakfasts at CL's with HCR, whom he meets for the first time.

HCR walks afterwards with W to Hatcham House, New Cross, Deptford, where CCl is staying with her uncle Joseph Hardcastle. W perhaps stays one or two nights. He asks HCR to come for him. HCR dines at Hardcastle's, and he and W return to town together.

On W's conversations with HCR see *HCRWC* I, 52–54; *HCRBW* I, 10–11: W discusses his own poetry and that of others, including Mrs. Barbauld; speaks of an intention to write an essay on why bad poetry pleases. (*HCRWC* I, 52–54, 456; *HCRBW* I, 10–11; *LL* II, 55; Cary's *Roads* 1806; *Friend* R, II, 432. Cf Moorman II, 118).[17]

16 Priscilla Lloyd W wrote on 7 Mar, continuing a letter to Charles Lloyd Sr. dated 6 Mar: "Thus far I wrote yesterday, but was prevented finishing my letter by the arrival of my Brother W Wordsworth who came very unexpectedly and spent the afternoon with us. He is come to Town on Coleridge's account, who has been at the point of death. but is now I believe on the recovery. He gives a very favourable account of Charles and Sophia." In a letter postmarked 21 Mar she told Charles Lloyd Sr.: "My Brother William is coming to spend a few days with us, & with thy leave I shall present the third copy [of Charles Lloyd Sr.'s *Iliad*] to him. . . . Hast thou seen Mr Clarkson's [*History*]? W Wordsworth speaks highly of it." On 6 Apr she wrote to her father that her "Brother William has been our visitor." On 18 Apr she inscribed a copy of *P2V* "to her dear friend Emma Chapman" (Dobell's Antiquarian Bookstore, Cat. 14, Dec 1935, item 100).

17 STC wrote to HCR on 3 May that W had taught him "to desire your acquaintance & to esteem you" (*STCL* III, 97).

escape of the French squadron from Rochfort, and a motion from Lord Henry Petty for revelation to the House of any comment from "Foreign Powers" concerning the Orders in Council then in effect.

24. Perhaps c Mar 18–c Mar 25

Perhaps c 18 Mar W travels from London to Dunmow, where he visits Sir GB's mother for about a week, then returns to London. (*MY* I, 202, 208; *MY* II, 659. Cf Moorman II, 118.)[18]

25. Mar 19, 23, 25 ff

On the night of 19 Mar George and Sarah Green of Blintarn die in a storm. They are buried on 25 Mar. DW and MW visit the Green home on 23 Mar. Two elder daughters accompany them home; four other children come in during the day. (*MY* I, 200–01, 219; Grasmere PR.)

On 23 Mar DW writes to W: She expects to meet W at Kendal. George and Sarah Green. Sally Green is to stay with them. Molly; DeQ; STC. Discovery of the bodies of the Greens. (*MY* I, 200–03.)

The Greens' deaths and the consequences thereof form the subject of DW's narrative [*George and Sarah Green*] and W's "Who Weeps for Strangers?" and also the cause of a fund-raising campaign on behalf of the children [see below, esp. 1808:37–1808:76 *passim*].[19]

26. Perhaps between c Mar 25 and Apr 2

W resides much or all this time with CW and his family at Lambeth. Priscilla W perhaps presents to W a copy of Charles Lloyd Sr.'s translation of the *Iliad*, Book 24 (1807). (See 1808:22n.)[20]

W perhaps while visiting here sees St. Basil's *Letters* and reads Basil's letter to Gregory Nazianzen, a translation of which W includes in *TofP* as lines 346–420. (See Moorman II, 132–33; 1808:36.)

Perhaps during this period W calls on Lord and Lady Holland in Pall Mall, but does not see them. (*MY* II, 659.)

---

[18] DW wrote to W on Wednesday 23 Mar of a letter received from STC on "Monday, written just after you set off for Dunmow." W wrote to Lady Holland on 11 Apr that while on his trip he had had "several visits to pay, one of a week's length, to friends in the neighborhood of London."

[19] On the fund-raising generally see esp. Moorman II, 127–30. Final distribution of funds collected for the Greens took place 25 May 1829. (Minute Book, Green accounts, DCP. See *Some Letters* 17–18.)

[20] Lloyd's translation was in any case in W's possession later (RM Sale Catalogue, lot 580).

Probably during this period he hears STC lecture twice. (*MY* I, 208.)

27. Probably c but by Mar 28

W writes to MW and/or DW (letter not known to survive) advising of his decision not to publish *WD*. (*MY* I, 207. See Appendix VIII.)

28. Mar 28

DW writes to CCl: W's travels; *WD*; SH's illness; Joanna H's illness; Uncle Henry H; George and Sarah Green and their children. Sally Green is to stay with the Ws. DW hopes that W will bring TCl's *History* and first volume of *Portraiture of Quakerism* [see 1808:10]. (*MY* I, 203–06.)

29. Probably between c Mar 28 and Apr 3

STC is led to understand that he is authorized to negotiate with Longman for the publication of *WD*, and to correct the MS as needed. (*STCL* III, 110–16; VI, 1021–22. See 1808:27; Appendix VIII.)

30. Mar 29

W sups with William Godwin. (Godwin Diary.)[21]

31. Mar 30

The Longman accounts record on W's account the delivery of a copy of *P2V* to W (as "presented") under this date. (Longman Comission Ledger I, fol. 137.)

32. Mar 31

DW writes to W and STC (only the portion to W is known to survive): DW is much disappointed to hear that W has dropped his plan to publish *WD*. The family's need for money. (*MY* I, 207; *STCL* III, 113–14, VI, 1021.)

[21] Godwin notes, "Wordsworth sups: C Heath & H Corbould call." The callers probably came after W's departure.

33. Apr 2

W probably passes the night at STC's lodgings at the *Courier* offices in the Strand. (*MY* I, 209. See Moorman I, 125.)[22]

34. Apr 3; Apr 3–probably Apr 6; Apr 6–Apr 15 ff

On 3 Apr W parts from STC at 7 AM, walks toward the City; has the view of St. Paul's which he afterwards describes in the lines quoted *PW* IV, 374–75. He departs London for home. His departure has been hastened by the arrival of alarming news of SH's health.

At Lancaster, on the way, a fellow coach passenger speaks well of W's poems. W perhaps passes a night at Kendal, where he writes to STC. He probably arrives at DC on 6 Apr. (*MY* I, 208–11, 217.)[23]

On 6 Apr Johnny becomes very ill, with symptoms resembling [meningitis]. He is convalescent from 15 Apr. (*MY* I, 217–18. See 1808:46; 1808:47.)

35. Probably between Apr 3 and Apr 17, May 21

Probably between 3 and 17 Apr Longman agrees to publish *WD* at W's demanded figure of 100 guineas for 1000 copies.

Probably between 3 Apr and 21 May STC makes some alterations on *WD*; also recopies the last 200 lines of Canto III; also omits the advertisement. (*MY* I, 225; *STCL* III, 110–13. See Appendix VIII).

36. Probably between Apr 6 and early autumn

W composes:

The bulk of *TofP*, as part of *The Recluse*, including the lines developed to *Exc* III.367–405, VII.242–91, *Prel*₂ VI.420–88 as described PREL 556–570.

"Press'd with Conflicting Thoughts of Love and Fear" (View of St. Paul's [*PW* IV, 374–75]; probably also for *Recluse*)

---

[22] W's early morning parting from STC and his walk toward St. Paul's make the place where he passed the night fairly certain.

[23] SH "had burst a small blood vessel," probably about the end of Mar; she was "better though far from well" on 13 Apr (*MY* I, 211). Her health remained indifferent through late 1809.

To the Clouds ("Army of Clouds")
(*PW* V, 482–85; PREL 556–57; *MY* I, 207–10, 269.)[24]

37. Probably between Apr 6 and Apr 11

W writes a paper on the subject of George and Sarah Green; makes copies of an abridgement with a multiplying writer. (*MY* I, 218, 228–29; II, 659. See 1808:44; *G&SG* 13–19.)

38. Perhaps Apr 7 or Apr 8 or shortly after

W stops in the Grasmere churchyard; composes part of "Who Weeps for Strangers?" there; finishes the poem soon after. (*MY* I, 219, 225. See *PW* IV, 375n.)

39. Apr 7

MW attends a meeting of the committee formed for the Green

---

[24] Among the earliest lines of *TofP* are ones (37–48) fairly certainly referring to the illness of SH's which brought W home from London. The loose structure of *TofP* hardly precludes lines that are placed later from having been written earlier; but when W remarks to Rogers at the end of Sept that he has written "about 500 lines" of his long poem, "which is all that [he has] done" since returning (*MY* I, 269), he leaves no obvious alternative (esp. in view of the allusions to recent events cited *PW* V, 482–83) to the conclusion that these lines were composed following his return from London in 1808. W's estimate of "about 500 lines" hardly accounts for all of the 594 lines of *TofP*, the lines on St. Paul's, and *To the Clouds*, the last two of which appear with *TofP* in MS 65, and the first of which was almost surely written following W's epistolary account of the inspiring incident in his letter to GB of 8 Apr. Moorman II, 133 also reasonably suggests that W's adaptation, the first in English, of St. Basil's letter to Gregory Nazianzen (lines 346–420), was the consequence of a sight of the Latin original while visiting CW in London. A draft of sixteen lines of this, from "Come O Friend," including *TofP* lines 346–54, 368–70, 415–18, is found on the back of Wrangham's letter to W of 7 Mar 1808 (DCP). (On Gregory Nazianzen see also RM Sale Catalogue, lot 240.)

Moorman II, 131–32 suggests that the lines on St. Paul's and those published in 1842 as *To the Clouds* were intended for the *Recluse* as well as those now entitled *The Tuft of Primroses*. *To the Clouds* seemingly stands both in MS and in content as an independent poem, but the MS would suggest strongly that composition took place at about the same time as the St. Paul's lines. The total number of lines is beyond the number mentioned to Rogers on 29 Sept; but these verses may nonetheless be supposed largely composed between the time of his return to DC and that date.

children. The committee decides on the placement of the children. (See *G & SG* 24–28; Minute Book, Green accounts, DCP.)

40. Probably c but by Apr 8; Apr 8

Probably c but by 8 Apr W writes, and on 8 Apr sends, a letter to STC. (*MY* I, 217.)

On 8 Apr W writes to Sir GB: His return to Grasmere [see 1808: 34]; Dunmow; STC; Angerstein's pictures [see 1808:16]; AB; view of St. Paul's. (*MY* I, 207–210.)

41. Apr 9 (–between Apr 22 and July 3)

Dora goes to stay with the Lloyds at Brathay. (She returns between 22 Apr and 3 July.) (*MY* I, 226–27, 256.)

42. c but by Apr 10

DW and W write to STC. (*MY* I, 217.)

43. Apr 11

W writes to Lady Holland: Solicits aid for Green family; encloses an abridged version of his paper on the Greens. (*MY* II, 659; *MY* I, 218.)

44. Probably c Apr 13–Apr 17 and shortly after

W sends his abridged narrative of the Greens [see 1807:37] to Montagu, and shortly after to Rogers and STC. (*MY* I, 218.)[25]

45. Probably Apr 13; Apr 13

Probably on 13 Apr Mr. Scambler of Ambleside prescribes calomel for Johnny. (*MY* I, 215.)

On 13 Apr W writes to Richard Sharp: Sends abridged version of his paper on George and Sarah Green; Sharp should seek contributions

---

[25] Lady B wrote to DW on 1 May [1808] that she had met Rogers "the other evening," and that he had expressed "great interest for the poor orphans, from the history he had received from your brother of their parents' fate."

from Boddington, Philips, and any other friends. W's abrupt departure from London; STC; MW. (*MY* I, 210–11, 218.)

W perhaps writes to another correspondent on this day. (*MY* I, 211.)

46. Apr 14

RS stops at DC on his way to Keswick; is alarmed at Johnny's symptoms, which indicate [meningitis]. He warns W. W later goes to Scambler, who prescribes more calomel for Johnny. W later returns to Scambler, and at 11 PM the family sends to Keswick for Mr. Edmondson. Probably at the same time W sends to RS for a letter of Dr. King's concerning an operation of bleeding of which RS has spoken to W. Scambler comes and is unable to confirm that the disease is not [meningitis]. He bleeds Johnny in the neck. (*MY* I, 215; Warter II, 54–55.)

47. Apr 15 ff

On 15 Apr Mr. Edmondson comes to DC, meets Scambler. By the time of their departure both are convinced that Johnny's disease is not [meningitis]. From this day Johnny is convalescent. (*MY* I, 215–16.)

48. Apr 16

W perhaps on this day writes, and on this day sends, a letter to STC. (*MY* I, 217.)

49. Apr 17

W writes to Francis Wrangham: Sends account of George and Sarah Green's death; seeks contributions. Declines Wrangham's offer to build cottage for W near sea. Montagu; *WD*; Johnny's illness; W's trip to London; Symmons's *Life of Milton*; Wrangham's translation from Milton. Abridgement of W's paper on the Greens. (*MY* I, 211–14.)

50. Probably c but by Apr 18

DW writes to CCl: SH evidently improving; Johnny's illness; sympathy for CCl's brother and sister. (*MY* I, 214.)

51. c Apr 18

A letter arrives from STC. (*MY* I, 230.)

52. Apr 18–Apr 19

W writes to STC: (18 Apr:) Johnny's recent illness; SH's illness; George and Sarah Green; transcript of "Who Weeps for Strangers?"; collections of contributions for Green children; *WD*, CL's opinion of which W deprecates. Motto for *WD* from Daniel's *Musophilus*. (19 Apr:) SH has had leeches; seems improved from yesterday. (*MY* I, 217–24.)[26]

53. Apr 20

A short letter arrives from STC. W seeks a poem in a locked MS box but cannot obtain it because Lady B has the key. (*MY* I, 225, 230.)[27]

DW writes to Lady B: Thanks Lady B for half of £5 note for Green children; the Greens; transcript of "Who Weeps for Strangers?" Key to the MS box. *WD*. (*MY* I, 224–25.)

54. Apr 22

DW writes to CCl; W adds a sentence of greeting: Her and the family's health; SH has decided to make her home with the Ws. Thomas H expected; Joanna H wants to live with him. The Greens. (*MY* I, 226–29.)

55. Between Apr 22 and May 4

DW writes her *Narrative* of George and Sarah Green, finishing on 4 May. (*MY* I, 228–29, 235–36; *G&SG* 87; BM Add. MS 41,267A, fols. 12–31; DC MS 64.)

---

[26] W's date at the head of the letter is "Monday Morning, April 19th"; but the Monday concerned was 18 Apr. The two postscripts so designated by W were written Tuesday morning. The actual first postscript, not so designated, is undated.

[27] The box was possibly given to W during his visit to Dunmow in Mar (see 1808:24).

56. Apr 25

W writes to Richard Sharp: Thanks for Green donation; also thanks Boddington and Philips; describes other donations. (*MY* I, 226–30.)

57. Probably c May 1; c and including May 1; May 1

Probably c 1 May a review of *P2V* appears in *The Cabinet* (III, Apr 1808). (See Hayden.)

Thomas H visits at DC c and including 1 May. (The length of his visit is unknown.) (Letter, MM to Thomas M, 1 May 1808, JFW Papers.)[28]

On 1 May DW writes to STC (only a fragment of the letter survives): The Ws', esp. the womens', desire that *WD* be published as soon as possible. (*MY* I, 230–31; *STCL* III, 114–16.)

58. May 3–May 6

Henry H visits at DC. (*MY* I, 231–32.)

59. May 10

DW writes to CCl: SH's health. Henry H. Charities; the Green subscription; the Green family; the committee in charge of the children; a meddling lady, Mrs. North. Henry H; *WD*. (*MY* I, 231–34.)

60. May 11

On 11 May DW writes to JPM: Thanks for donation for the Greens; the committee; meddlesome Mrs. North. JPM's reaction to *WD*; W's disinclination to publish the poem. (*MY* I, 234–36.)

W writes a prefatory note to DW's *Narrative* of George and Sarah Green. (See *G&SG* 4.)

61. May 14

W writes to Walter Scott: A letter of Scott's of c three months earlier; expected copy of *Marmion* not arrived; thanks for information

[28] MM comments, "Tom is at present at Grasmere."

from Scott about the Norton family; Johnny's illness; dinner at Longman's in London [see 1808:16]; the Green disaster. Spring weather just arrived. (*MY* I, 237–39.)

62. Perhaps c May 16

W receives from STC a letter of severe accusation regarding W's conduct to him. W replies on the day of receipt of this letter. Two incomplete drafts of the letter, which was possibly not sent, survive: SH; answer to STC's query as to why more ambitious efforts have not been made on behalf of the Green children; answers to STC's accusations about W's conduct toward him. (*MY* I, 239–45; EKC 212–13.)[29]

63. Probably c but by May 18

W writes to Longman to prevent publication of *WD* (letter not known to survive). His letter somehow implies that STC has proceeded without authority in making the arrangements. (*STCL* III, 107–116. See Appendix VIII.)

[29] The paper on which the drafts are written, watermarked "RUSE & TURNERS" over "1806" was used for other letters by W and DW in early 1808. The latest instance that I have noted is DW's letter to JPM of 11 May.

The NB of STC's presently BM Add. MS 47,521 contains an entry on fol. 5 possibly indicative of the time when STC wrote to W. It reads in part (cf *STCNB* 3304):

On Friday. Midnight, 12 May 1808 [*the Friday would have been the 13th*], I for the first time suffered murmurs, & more than murmurs, articulate Complaints, to escape from me relatively to [Wordsworth's *deleted*] conduct towards me and that of Bell & Miss Wordsworth then first summoned up courage and dared tell him how highly I disapproved of his cowardly mock-prudence . . . .

Below, for *STCNB*'s illegible word following "I did not mention the affair of" I read "Dr Bell."

On the affair of Dr. Bell, precipitated by STC's lecture on 2 May (*STCL* III, 98), see EKC 209. The nature of W's supposed failure is unclear; and STC's NB complaints do not otherwise appear very precisely related to the statements of W's letter. But the NB entry and the no longer surviving accusatory letter seem the only records of STC's accusation of W of unkindness about this time; and the evidence tends to suggest that STC's letter was the fashion in which he "summoned up courage and dared tell" W his reasons for complaint.

64. Perhaps c late May and June

W possibly corresponds with Dr. Beddoes concerning an illness of John M's. He recommends Beddoes to John M. (Letters, John M to Thomas M, 18 May, 30 June, JFW Papers.)[30]

65. May 21 (ff)

STC writes to W defending his actions in regard to publication arrangements for *WD* and offering detailed criticism of the poem [see 1808:63]. He announces a plan which will secure from £12 to £20 a week, and that a prospectus is to go to press as soon as read by RS and Sir GB. The plan is probably that which eventually produced *The Friend.* (*STCL* III, 110–11; Appendix VIII.)

66. Perhaps late May, probably by c May 24; perhaps c May 24 (–between June 5 and Aug 3, –1811 between c May 26 and early June)

Perhaps in late May, probably by c 24 May, Henry H returns to DC. (He departs between 5 June and 3 Aug.) Perhaps c 24 May the Ws remove to Allan Bank. Henry H probably assists. W is perhaps absent during the removal, possibly visiting Robert Forster. (The family resides at AB until between perhaps c 26 May and early June 1811.) On the residence at AB generally see esp. Moorman II, 117–201. (*MY* I, 232, 252.)[31]

67. Perhaps c late May, by May 28

W passes a day with Joanna Baillie and her sister at their inn at Ambleside. He takes them to see sights in the neighborhood. The

[30] John M writes on 18 May that he has written to SH with a statement of his case (of which a symptom was chronic headaches) "to read to Dr Beddoes or some other physician of eminence." On 30 June he writes that Beddoes "is a particular friend of Mr Wordsworth by whose recommendation I applied to him. . . ."

[31] On 10 May DW writes, "We hope to remove now in about a fortnight." On 5 June she speaks of how busy she has been "for this fortnight past" with chores imposed by the removal.

Various taxes and assessments paid during the AB residence as noted (mainly by MW) in the Green family account book under dates from 16 July 1808 through May 1811 apparently total slightly under £50. A memorandum dated 12 Apr 1810 records, "No charge has been made in my accts to Mr Crump for property tax."

visitors call briefly on the Ws at Grasmere; meet DW. (Wilfred Partington, *Sir Walter Scott's Post-bag*, London, 1932, 38; Curry I, 477.)[32]

68. Probably June

Probably during June DW writes twice to ML. ML, from unwillingness to complain of STC, does not answer. (*LL* II, 62; Moorman II, 123n.)

69. June 4

W and a neighbor walk beside a brook. The neighbor speaks of his fondness for the sound of a brook. (*MY* I, 247–48.)

70. June 5

DW writes to CCl: SH. Removal to AB, and Henry H's and DW's labors. MW. View from AB. *WD* not to be published till winter. The first volume of TCl's *Portraiture of Quakerism* [see 1808:28]. (*MY* I, 251–53.)

W writes to Francis Wrangham: Montagu's mishandling of solicitation of funds for the Greens. Extended comments on education as a national object, developed from consideration of Wrangham's [*Human Laws Best Supported by the Gospel*]. (*MY* I, 246–51. See Appendix IX.)

71. Probably between June 5 and Oct 2

W reads Dr. Andrew Bell's *An Experiment in Education Made at the Asylum of Madras.* (*MY* I, 246, 269.)

72. Probably c June 5, June 7

Mary Fisher ("Molly") of Town End dies probably c 5 June. She is buried 7 June. (Grasmere PR.)

---

[32] RS learned on 28 May that Joanna Baillie was in Keswick. She had evidently gone thither from Ambleside, and would have had a convenient opportunity to call on W on her way.

73. June 8

Probably W writes to Lady Holland concerning the subscription to the George and Sarah Green fund. (J. E. Wells note, Swarthmore College Library.)[33]

74. June 18

A review of *P2V* appears in *The New Annual Register* (XXVIII, 1807). (*MP*. See Ward.)

75. Perhaps c June 20

A review [by Lucy Aikin] of *P2V* appears in *The Annual Review* VI (1807). (*MP*. See Ward; Hayden.)[34]

76. June 20

W writes to Lady Holland: Thanks for her aid in obtaining subscriptions for the Green fund; instructions for transmission of the money. (*MY* I, 253–54. See *MY* I, 253n.)

W writes to Walter Scott thanking him for Green subscriptions. The letter (not known to survive) is mislaid and not sent. (*MY* I, 263.)

77. Perhaps late June, probably by June 30 (–perhaps shortly before Aug 16); possibly c late June, perhaps c early July

Perhaps late June, probably by 30 June, Joanna H and Elizabeth M arrive at AB for a visit. (They depart perhaps shortly before 16 Aug.) (*MY* I, 254–56; Pering Journal, DCP; 1808: 87.)

Possibly c late June, perhaps c early July W composes *Pelayo*. (Content.)[35]

---

[33] Professor Wells notes seeing at Charles F. Sawyer, London, on 28 August 1937, a letter "by W. W. in his own hand dated June 8th [n.y.] to Lady Holland about a subscription to the George & Sarah Green fund with signature 'W. Wordsworth' @ £2/1os."

[34] The volume was announced for publication on 20 June in the *MP* of 14 June, but not advertised on the 20th.

[35] The Rev. Mr. Pering (see 1808:78) recorded that W stated on 30 June that there were visitors in the house; and on that same day Pering met there two "friends" of

78. June 29, 30

On 29 June the Rev. J. Pering calls at AB with a letter of introduction to DW obtained two years earlier from Mrs. Froude of Dartington.[36] He is received by MW. W, DW are not at home.

On 30 June Mr. Pering returns to AB; converses with W, DW. W talks chiefly about politics, the duties of a great statesman, and the manner of a statesman's use of available talent, and about his disgust at lotteries. W invites Mr. and Miss Pering to tea. They come, see MW, one of the boys, and two of MW's friends. W shows them two views not mentioned by the travel writers; discusses poetry, Gray; describes *WD*. DW tells of George and Sarah Green. (Pering Journal, DCP.)

79. July 2

RW's accounts charge DW £50/–/–, payment of bill in favor of Thomas Cookson, under this date. (RW accounts, DCP.)

80. Probably July 3

DW writes to CCl: STC; SH; Joanna and Elizabeth M; the family. (*MY* I, 254–56.)

DW writes to DeQ: W's wish for all books that are valuable and very cheap; names of a number of older, esp. classic, writers and works. (*MY* I, 257–58.)[37]

---

[36] Mrs. Froude was formerly Margaret Spedding (see esp. *EY* 115n).

[37] DW's date is "Sunday night July 7th"; but as indicated *MY* I, 257, 7 July was not a Sunday, and the letter is postmarked 7 July. DW probably wrote on Sunday 3 July.

MW. It would appear likely that Pering met one or both of these guests. SH was of course also staying with the Ws.

W's statement in *Pelayo* that "A foreign Tyrant speaks his impious will/And Spain hath owned the monarch which he gave" seems to refer to Napoleon's installation of Joseph Bonaparte as King of Spain. After weeks of varied, more or less well founded, reports concerning the fate of the throne of Spain, the possible ascendancy of Lucien or Joseph Bonaparte, and Spanish resistance to Napoleon, the *Times* on 27 June made a definite announcement, on the basis of Parisian reports originating in the *Bayonne Gazette* of 13 June, of Joseph Bonaparte's reception at Bayonne of several Spanish delegations declaring loyalty to him. The *Times* notice reprints an obedient "Address from the City of Madrid."

Mr. Scambler calls; SH's pulse leads him to proscribe animal foods for her. (*MY* I, 256.)

81. Probably between July 3, possibly July 15, and July 29; probably c but not before July 4; July 15 (–July 18, Aug 1)

Probably between 3 and 29 July, possibly after 15 July, nineteen persons, among them the W household and visitors and the Wilsons, set out for a picnic on Grasmere island as guests of Mr. Crump. A shower comes on as the party is on the way to the lake side, and all are wet through. The party dines at the inn instead. (*MY* I, 262–63; letter, MM to Thomas M, 24 July 1808, JFW Papers.)

Probably c but not before 4 July the W family spends a day with the Wilsons at Elleray. (*MY* I, 260.)

MM arrives for a visit on 15 July with John M (who departs 18 July). (MM departs 1 Aug.) (*MY* I, 254–56; 1808:82.)[38]

82. Probably July 18; probably between July 18 and July 29; c July 24

Probably on 18 July SH, John M depart AB for Eusemere. W is busily engaged in composition c 24 July. (*MY* I, 259; letter, MM to Thomas M, 24 July 1808, JFW Papers.)[39]

Probably between 18 and 29 July DW, MM dine one day at the Lloyds'; drink tea with Mrs. Green of Ambleside. (*MY* I, 259–60.)[40]

83. July 29–July 31

DW, MM rise early on 29 July, breakfast at Ambleside with Mrs. Green. John Wilson meets them at the head of Windermere with a

---

[38] DW's chatty letter of 3 July to CCl would probably have mentioned, had it already occurred, the excursion which she later describes to CCl on 3 Aug as having taken place "about a month ago." The letter would probably also have mentioned the rained-out picnic. MM, writing of the picnic in her letter of 24 July, seems to imply that it took place since she and John M came to AB: see 1808:82n.

[39] MM's letter to Thomas M of 24 July states: "John and I came here [to AB] about a week ago, he stay'd two days, and Sara returned with him to spend a few weeks with Miss Green." She remarks also, "William is as busy writing as ever but I do not know what he is employed with." (JFW Papers.)

[40] This outing apparently took place after SH's departure.

boat. DW is ill this night, better next day. They visit at Wilson's till Sunday 31 July when Miss Wilson brings them home in her mother's carriage. On Sunday afternoon they prepare for a trip to Eusemere. (*MY* I, 260–61; letter MM to Thomas M, 24 July 1808, JFW Papers.)[41]

84. Aug 1 (–probably, perhaps shortly before Aug 16)

W, DW, MM, and a maid set off for Eusemere in the morning, DW on a pony. MM mounts a horse which they borrow at Rydal, where W takes DW's place on the pony. DW becomes ill. They stop at Ambleside. W goes to the inn, finds John Wilson, who obtains a chaise. They travel over Kirkstone; dine at the Luffs' in Patterdale. The women proceed to Eusemere in a boat; W returns homeward with the chaise. (DW returns, with SH, probably shortly before 16 Aug.) (*MY* I, 261.)

85. Aug 3

DW writes to CCl from Eusemere: SH; MM; John Wilson; family activities; Henry H; Joanna H to sink her property; SH to stay in Grasmere; Luff's house; Mr. Askew's house; MW expecting; the rained-out picnic [see 1808:81]. (*MY* I, 259–63.)

86. Aug 4

W writes to Walter Scott: W's mislaid letter to Scott of 20 June; thanks for Green donations. *Marmion*, which W has read; an error in a quotation from *Yarrow Unvisited*; defence of Heywood, esp. *A Woman Killed with Kindness*, against Scott's censure. (*MY* I, 263–65.)

87. Probably shortly before Aug 16 (–perhaps c 1810 Mar 14)

DW returns to DC, accompanied by SH. (SH departs perhaps c 14 Mar 1810.) Joanna H and Elizabeth M depart probably on that day

---

[41] MM writes to Thomas M on 24 July (JFW Papers), "Dorothy & I are going on tuesday to spend the day with a very nice scotch family that are come to live on the banks of windermere." She adds below that "Dorothy (the elder) will return with me to Penrith the beginning of next week to spend a few days and then Sara and she will return here together."

or next in the gig used by DW. (*MY* I, 259; letters, MM to Thomas M, 24 July 1808, Joanna H to Thomas M, 16 Aug [1808], JFW Papers; 1808:83n.)[42]

88. Perhaps c late Aug or early Sept

W and Richard Sharp pass a day together, probably in or near Grasmere. (*MY* I, 265–268.)

89. Probably Aug 26 or Aug 27 ff

W probably sets out for Leeds on 26 or 27 Aug to see STC, who is reported confined there by sickness on his way to Grasmere. He perhaps stops or passes a night at Elleray on his way, and probably passes a night at the Cooksons' in Kendal. Perhaps at Kendal he receives a message advising him of STC's improved health and progress toward Grasmere; and he perhaps then turns back to Grasmere to await STC. During W's absence MM and Mrs. Robison call or pay a brief visit at AB. (Letter, MM to Thomas M, 2 Sept 1808, JFW Papers; *Friend* R II, 471–72.)[43]

---

[42] MM's letter correctly announced plans and dates for the visit to the Wilsons, and for the journey to Eusemere ("Penrith"), and was probably accurate about DW's plans to "spend a few days" at Penrith and return thence to AB with SH.

Joanna wrote to Thomas M on 16 Aug:

Mary would tell you in her letter from Grasmere that my Aunt & I had been some time there, & did intend to have made our stay much longer, but on account of a visit we had to pay to our good friend Miss Weir at Appleby—from whom I had a letter intreating our company at Appleby next week being the Assizes, & on that account she has holiday. . . . We came from Grasmere in a Gig that carried Dorothy Wordsworth & my Sister Sara from Miss Greens where they had been spending some time. My poor Sister Sara looks very ill, Bless her! I doubt indeed she is in a very bad way, for the pain in her Side returns so frequently that I doubt it will get the better of her at last.—I am happy when I think that she has, & will continue to have the very best advice. & that all possible care will be taken to prevent a return of so many dangerous simptoms as she has had. We left my sister Wordsworth in very good health, & the Children all well. You would be quite in love with their little Dorothy she certainly is a beautiful creature but so wild & playful! Marys Godsone Thos. is my favorite. he is such a nice quiet good tempered Creature. & very like my brother Tom. . . .

[43] MM writes from Penrith of a recent visit to Grasmere, the date of which is not indicated, with Mrs. Robison: "[W]e were very much disappointed that we did not

90. Aug 30 ff

On 30 Aug the Convention of Cintra is signed on behalf of Sir Hew Dalrymple and General Andoche Junot. The terms of the Convention specify that Junot's army is to be conveyed from Portugal to the west coast of France with all equipment and munitions, and there set free. Among literary responses to this event is W's *CC*. [See esp. 1808:114.]

91. Sept 1 (–1810 Oct 18)

STC arrives at AB, entering for the first time at 11:30 PM. (His residence at AB ends 18 Oct 1810.) (*STCNB* 3357; *STCL* III, 120.)

On STC's visit generally see esp. Moorman II, 134–92; EKC 215–36.[44]

92. Sept 2, 3

RW's accounts charge W £7/10/6, payment of premium on £300 policy on Montagu's life, under these dates. (RW accounts, DCP.)[45]

93. Sept 5–Sept 7

W and STC travel to Keswick. They visit there till 7 Sept. Probably during this visit W declares that he will write an essay, if STC does not, on the pleasures produced by bad poetry. (Warter II, 16–17.)

---

[44] It was perhaps STC's surroundings at AB or possibly conversation about a plan of W's (in whose writings the subject had long played a part) which led STC to make an entry in his NB just following that cited in the text: "Essay + Influence of Property on the affections of Families—W.Ws." (Cf *STCNB* 3358.)

[45] Two copies of the accounts differ on the date.

---

see Wm he was gone to see poor Coleridge who has been confined by sickness at Leeds on his way to Grasmere." STC arrived at AB on 1 Sept. The message reassuring W about STC's health was forwarded to Grasmere from Kendal by Isaac Wilson on 27 Aug and sent on to W at Thomas Cookson's back in Kendal via Elleray. Nothing is known of a journey by W further toward Leeds.

94. Sept 6

Catharine Wordsworth (d. 4 June 1812), second daughter and fourth child of W and MW, is born at Grasmere at 12 noon. (*Mem* I, 367; M-W Book of Common Prayer, DCP.)

95. Sept 7 (–c mid-Oct)

W, STC, SC travel from Keswick to AB. (SC visits until c mid-Oct.) (Warter II, 16–17; *STCL* III, 120.)[46]

For SC's recollections of her visit see SC *Mem* I, 17–25. On the visit see also esp. *STCL* III, 120–22.

96. Probably Sept 18 or Sept 19–c Sept 26

W, STC, probably SH, perhaps others, make a short tour, commencing probably on 18 or 19 Sept, to the Duddon Valley, Eskdale, Wastdale, and perhaps elsewhere. STC perhaps visits GH, and perhaps brings Derwent C with him on his return to AB. Derwent probably in any case comes to AB by c 26 Sept.

Probably W and perhaps the others are with STC during his entire trip. Possibly on this tour W and SH see Jane W, daughter of RW of Branthwaite, at Catgill Hall, near Egremont [see 1807:82].

The party perhaps travels via Walna Scar to Seathwaite, where they perhaps pass the night, on 19 Sept. They probably pass the night of 21 Sept in Eskdale at the Woolpack Inn, and make their way to Wastdale on 22 Sept, becoming lost for a time on the way. They perhaps pass that night at Thomas Tyson's at Wastdale Head. (*STCL* III, 122–26; *MY* I, 265, 271, 510; *STCNB* 3376, 3384.)[47]

---

[46] SC's memory of seeing DeQ at AB during this visit (SC *Mem* I, 19) is probably a misplaced recollection of DeQ in a later visit to AB or a visit to GH (see esp. 1808:111). DeQ probably did not arrive before her departure (see 1808:108).

[47] STC wrote to SFC c 15 Sept, "I take a little tour on Saturday [17 Sept] by Mr Scambler's Advice" (*STCL* III, 122). He wrote to Eliza Nevins on 16 Sept that "a literary Engagement, involving a small Tour on the Duddon, compels me to be absent from Keswick till Friday next with my honored Friend, Mr Wordsworth." Afterward in the same letter he spoke of his "return to Keswick next Friday." (*STCL* III, 123–24.) He wrote a letter to T. G. Street dated from Grasmere, however, on

97. Sept 27

W writes to Richard Sharp: Thanks for advice of Mackintosh's favorable comments on his poems. Two subjects likely to be debated in Parliament in which W interested: lotteries, author's copyright. W urges extension of copyright beyond the twenty-eight years that he has heard rumored as the probable new extension of the present fourteen-year period. The bombardment of Copenhagen. Indignation at the Convention of Cintra. (*MY* I, 265–67.)

98. Probably Sept 27, possibly Sept 29

W writes to Samuel Rogers: Thanks for Green donations; total collected near £500; the Green children. Sharp; Crabbe. W has written 500 lines of his long poem. Local anger at the Convention of Cintra. (*MY* I, 267–69.)[48]

[48] W's letter to Rogers would appear to have been the item for Rogers that W enclosed in his letter to Sharp of 27 Sept and wished Sharp to send to the twopenny post; and hence would seem to have been written also on 27 Sept, but postdated, perhaps to allow for delay in forwarding. The postmark date of both letters, 6 Oct, is oddly late for letters written on 27 Sept. Possibly W delayed sending the letter to Sharp for two days or more, and wrote the letter to Rogers on 29 Sept.

19 Sept. The letter is shown by *STCNB* 3376 possibly to have been predated or written very early on the 19th.

STCNB 3384 implies that the travellers crossed Eskdale Fell from the Woolpack. The "Telegraph-pile" (as I read the MS) is unidentified: no local feature has been found that is called by that name presently or in early maps and guides. (The earliest examples of the use of the word "telegraph" cited in *OED* date from 1794.) STC would seem to be using his own name for a cairn or prominence. The view of Wastdale decribed *STCNB* was probably that seen in descending from Eskdale Fell along the Old Corpse Road. On STC's "Capel Crag" see *STCNB* 1214 f 12v, 1217n.

RS wrote to Thomas S from Keswick on 27 Sept that STC "is settled at Grasmere, & the boys going forthwith to school at Ambleside.—indeed Derwent is already gone" (BM Add. MS 30,927, fols. 139–40; see 1808:100). W wrote to Sharp on 27 Sept from Grasmere; and he began a letter to the Rev. Mr. Pering on 2 Oct with the remark, "Your letter reached me the day I was setting off on a Tour from which I have just returned" (*MY* I, 271). W is scarcely likely to have made another tour shortly before 2 Oct. He probably wrote to Rogers from Grasmere on 27 Sept (see 1808:98).

99. Oct 2

Catharine Wordsworth is baptized at Grasmere. CCl is godmother. (Grasmere PR; *MY* I, 373.)[49]

W writes to Francis Wrangham: Thanks for Green contribution; the Green fund. Has read Dr. Bell's [*Experiment in Education Made at the Asylum of Madras*]. STC; Montagu. Encourages Wrangham to write a topographical history of his neighborhood along the lines of White's *Selborne* or Whitaker's *Craven* and *Whalley*, and unlike [the Rev. J. Graves's *History of Cleveland*, Carlisle, 1808] which he has just read. (*MY* I, 269–70.)

W writes to the Rev. J. Pering: Information about the Green family. Cannot comply with Greens' request that he write a description of objects in the Lake area; is dull at such work. (*MY* I, 271–72. See Appendix VI.)

100. Probably between c but by Oct 7 and mid-Oct (–1814 June, –1817)

SFC probably spends a week at AB, probably bringing HC with her. She is present on 7 Oct.

Probably at this time HC and Derwent enter Mr. Dawes's school at Ambleside. While at school (which HC leaves June 1814, Derwent in 1817) they spend most Saturdays and Sundays at AB and the Ws' subsequent residences and most of their long holidays at Keswick. (*MY* I, 280; *STCL* III, 121–22, 133; *SHL* 10, 12; *Minnow* 31; *Poems of Hartley Coleridge*, ed. Derwent Coleridge, London, 1851, I, xlix–lxiii.)[50]

101. Oct 7

A severe storm strikes the Lakes area. The chimneys at AB do not permit a fire except in the study; and even that chimney smokes so badly that the family cannot see one another in the room. Some of the

[49] The PR reads: "[Baptisms:] October 1808 2d Catherine Daugr of William Wordsworth Gentleman Grassmere." CCl would have been represented by a proxy.

[50] SH states in a letter of c but by 29 Oct that "Mrs C[oleridge] was here last week— she came to settle the Boys at Ambleside School; and carry back little Sara" (*SHL* 9–10). DW states in Dec, however, that SFC was "more than a week" under the same roof with STC at AB, and that she was there, with SC, at the time of "the great storm," an event of 7 Oct. SC *Mem* I, 18 probably refers to this arrival of SFC.

family go to bed with the baby in the middle of the day in order to keep her warm. (*MY* I, 280–82; *SHL* 9.)[51]

102. Oct 8

RW's accounts charge W £9/10/–, payment of bill of Messrs. Twining, under this date. (RW accounts, DCP.)

103. Probably c but by Oct 11; Oct 11

Thomas H visits AB, probably departing on 11 Oct. The length of his visit is uncertain. (Letter, Thomas H to John M, 12 Oct 1808, JFW Papers.)[52]

104. Perhaps c mid-Oct

George H visits AB. (*SHL* 9.)[53]

105. Oct 19; between Oct 19 and Oct 30

On 19 Oct W and John Spedding call on RS to discuss the Convention of Cintra. They are possibly joined by William Calvert. They decide to propose a county address; W and Spedding request RS to ask Humphry Senhouse to sign the requisition, and to write to LdL about the meeting. W probably states that he or STC would speak at the meeting. (Curry I, 483–85.)

[51] This was the most trying of numerous calamities produced by the chimneys at AB, concerning which see esp. the *MY* reference cited. In an unpublished portion of RS's letter to Thomas S of 13 Oct, RS states that the Ws were so terribly smoked in last Friday's gale that "they talk of abandoning the house in utter despair." *SHL* 11–12 indicates that the women of the house still despaired on 23 Nov (see 1808:118) and that W was then agreed to move to Troutbeck if a "*scientific* Dr" from Kendal did not effect a cure of the chimneys. In the same letter of 13 Oct RS remarks that "about half" of STC's books at GH have been sent to AB.

[52] Thomas had spent the night previous to writing (from Penrith) at the Luffs' in Patterdale; and so would probably have left Grasmere, from which he says "I have just returned," that day.

[53] SH says that George "was here last week." Her letter was probably written c but by 29 Oct; but she makes a similar remark of SFC, who is unlikely to have remained beyond the middle of the month, and I have assumed that she is implying about the same distance in time for George's visit.

The length of W's absence from AB at this time is unknown.

Perhaps as a consequence of the conference of 19 Oct, and between 19 and 30 Oct, W, STC, and RS agree that they will put the issues concerning the Convention of Cintra in their true light in the county newspapers and frame resolutions to be brought forward at the meeting, and that W will speak at the meeting. They understand that they are to meet at Calvert's on 4 Nov with J. C. Curwen. (*Prose* 197; Warter II, 116–17.)

On the progress of plans for the meeting see esp. Moorman II, 136–38; *Prose* 197.

106. Perhaps Oct 24 or Oct 31

W writes to DeQ: The household has been too busy to send for letters for a week, and DeQ's letter has lain at the post office accordingly. They will be happy to see DeQ but cannot provide a bed. (*MY* I, 272.)[54]

107. Probably c but by Oct 29

SH writes to MM: John M's and Thomas H's plans; Joanna H and Miss Green; the AB household; the Cs; the Ws. (*SHL* 8–11.)[55]

108. Perhaps c Nov 2 (–perhaps 1809 Feb, by Feb 20)

DeQ arrives at, takes up residence at AB. (He remains until perhaps Feb 1809, departing by 20 Feb.) (*SHL* 12.)[56]

On the visit generally see esp. Jordan 55–60.

[54] The letter would appear to have been written shortly before DeQ came to AB. As DeQ came perhaps c 2 Nov, the letter, dated "Monday Morn." was perhaps written on Monday 24 Oct or 31 Oct. DeQ apparently did reside at AB despite W's warning about lack of space.

[55] The postmark of the letter (DCP) is 1 Nov.

[56] Probably on 23 Nov SH states that DeQ has been at AB "3 weeks" (*SHL* 12; see 1808:118); and STC writes probably on 8 Feb 1809 that DeQ has been visiting "for three months" (*STCL* III, 177). Other evidence points toward a time about early Nov (see Masson II, 339; Warter II, 108), but SH's remark would appear to offer the firmest ground for detailed conjecture.

Although it is described as an event of a "summer evening," an incident described Masson II, 242–43, apparently undatable, may be noted here: W, DW, DeQ, and the Rev. Thomas J[ackson], rector of Grasmere church, walk in Langdale. DW is reported by DeQ as struck by W's meanness of figure beside Jackson.

109. Probably between c Nov 2 and 1809 Feb 20; probably between c
Nov 2 and Nov 22

Probably at some time between c 2 Nov and 20 Feb W and Crump
argue about the rent at AB. W expresses strong dissatisfaction with the
smoking chimneys; Crump remains courteous. (Masson II, 359.)

Probably between c 2 Nov and 22 Nov John Wilson calls at AB.
During a conversation with W in his study he is introduced to DeQ.
(Masson II, 432, V, 262–63; *SHL* 11. See 1808:108; 1808:117.)

110. Perhaps shortly after c Nov 2

Perhaps shortly after c 2 Nov W, accompanied by DeQ, calls on
Mr. K[ing] at the Hollins to discuss some matter of local business. DeQ
notices King's apparent mistrust of W. He attributes this to King's
awareness of W's dislike of larches, of which King has planted many,
and of King's unsightly barn. (Masson II, 428–31.)

111. Nov 4; perhaps Nov 4; probably between Nov 4 and Nov 6

RW's accounts charge W £ 2/13/–, payment of bill of Mr. Beck
for clothes, under 4 Nov. (RW accounts, DCP.)

Perhaps on 4 Nov W, possibly STC, probably DeQ go to GH to
meet Calvert, J. C. Curwen, and possibly others, to discuss the plans for
a county meeting dealing with the Convention of Cintra. (1808:105;
Warter II, 108.)

Probably between 4 and 6 Nov the plan for a county meeting
concerning the Convention of Cintra is abandoned as a result of opposition from LdL. Probably during this period W determines to write a
pamphlet on the subject of the Convention of Cintra. W, and DeQ and
STC, if present, probably return to DC on 6 Nov. (Robberds II, 226;
CCS III, 180; *Prose* 197–98.)[57]

---

[57] RS also writes on 12 Nov (Warter II, 108): "Little Mr De Quincy . . . was here
last week and is coming again. . . . Wordsworth . . . is now writing a pamphlet about
the Convention. . . ." He adds that Curwen had called the day after the meeting at
Calvert's, pressing him to visit at Workington, but that if he goes it will be with W,
to trace the River Derwent the whole way.

112. Nov 7

DW draws on RW for £50, favor of Mr. Wilcock, probably due in one month. (*MY* I, 274; RW accounts, DCP.)[58]

RW's accounts charge DW £30/–/–, payment of bill in favor of Thomas Cookson, under this date. (RW accounts, DCP.)

113. Nov 12

Longmans records on W's account delivery of three copies of *LB* 1805 to W under this date. (Longman Commission Ledger I, fol. 137.)[59]

114. Probably between c mid-Nov and 1809 Mar 26; perhaps between c mid-Nov and Dec 31

W, probably with close aid from STC, writes *CC*. He probably originally plans to publish it both in newspaper installments and in pamphlet form. The work has probably reached considerable length, perhaps as a set of connected essays, by early Dec. (*MY* I, 278; *STCL* III, 131, 134, 136–37. See 1808:111.)

One installment, perhaps corresponding to the first *Courier* installment as published 27 Dec, is probably completed and sent off c but by 15 Dec, and a second either at the same time or within a day or so. Three more are probably prepared, the last, except for final corrections, by 28 Dec. (*STCL* III, 151; *Prose* 199.)[60]

---

[58] RW's accounts record payment under 10 Dec.

[59] The entry is annotated "presented."

[60] STC wrote c but by 14 Dec that W's "first Essay, I hope, the two first, will be sent" [to Stuart] by "this or the following Post" (*STCL* III, 141). See also *Prose* 199.

News probably reached W at 11 AM on 2 Jan of the loss of at least the second installment, if not more, probably in London, and at least that much was probably rewritten, with a considerable amount of revision and addition, on 2–3 Jan (*STCL* III, 160; cf Moorman II, 141). Some or all of this rewritten material was probably published as the second portion of W's essay in the *Courier* of 13 Jan. Of this STC said that the last two columns, except for a few sentences and the last paragraph, were his (*STCL* III, 164, 174).

The date "1808" was appended to the title of the first Cintra sonnet *P* 1815–*PW* 1850.

Probably during this period, perhaps in 1808, W composes:
Composed While the Author Was Engaged in Writing a Tract Occasioned by the Convention of Cintra. 1808
Composed at the Same Time and on the Same Occasion
(Titles and content.)

115. Nov 15

DW calls on or visits the Lloyds at Brathay. She writes to RW, at Penrith, from Brathay: Disappointment at not seeing RW at Grasmere; RW's health. Smoke at AB; DW needs an oilcloth for the long passage and cross passages at AB. Hears RW has bought a good part of John M's furniture. (*MY* I, 273–74.)

116. Probably c but not before Nov 15

W and DeQ read together the 27 Oct address of the deputies of the new departments of Italy to Bonaparte and Bonaparte's reply. (*MY* I, 299. See *CC* 198–99; *Courier*, 12 Nov 1808.)[61]

117. Probably Nov 22

W, DeQ dine at Elleray with the Wilsons; bring home a letter from MM on their return. (*SHL* 11. See 1808:118.)

118. Probably Nov 23

SH writes to MM: Her recent illness; smoke at AB; DeQ; STC; the family; Wilson. (*SHL* 11–14.)[62]

119. Nov 25

W writes perhaps to J. C. Curwen: Cannot comply with correspondent's kind invitation for a fortnight, as he is writing [*CC*]; but is

[61] The speeches are quoted in the issue of the *Courier* cited.

[62] The initial letter of the month in the postmark (MS, DCP) is certainly "N," as recorded *SHL* 14; and SH's date is "Novr [*blank*] Wednesday." The content of the letter implies a late Nov date (see, for one example, the information on SH's illness *MY* I, 281, 283–84); but the letter can hardly have received a Nov postmark if written on Wednesday 30 Nov (cf *SHL* 11).

glad that correspondent is at leisure till Christmas. STC will wait upon correspondent also if health permits. W will write to RS on the subject this evening; will write again to set date for waiting upon correspondent. (*MY* I, 274–75.)[63]

W probably today also writes RS on the subject of this visit. (*MY* I, 275.)

120. Probably c Nov 26–c Dec 3

W writes several letters other than those that survive of 26 Nov, 28 Nov, and 3 Dec requesting assistance in circulating the Prospectus for *The Friend* and advising about possible subscribers. (*MY* I, 275–79; *STCL* III, 135.)[64]

121. Nov 26

W writes to Robert Grahame: *The Friend*; seeks advice concerning subscribers. The *Friend* Prospectus. Compliments of DW, MW to Mrs. and Miss Grahame. (*MY* I, 275–76.)

122. Nov 28

W writes to Walter Scott: Disappointment that Scott has not visited Grasmere. Requests Scott to distribute *Friend* Prospectuses if he has received them. STC requests information about subscribers. (*MY* I, 276–77.)

123. Dec 1

RW's accounts charge DW £20/–/–, payment of bill in favor of Robert Newton, under this date. (RW accounts, DCP.)

[63] The identity of the correspondent is not certain, but W's courteous tone is appropriate for address to the M.P. for Carlisle, who had early this month probably met with him and RS to discuss county action on the Convention of Cintra (see 1808:111). RS had supposed as early as 10 Nov that he might be visiting Curwen at Workington Hall with W before Christmas (Curry I, 489); and STC, c 4 Dec, wrote to RS that he was sorry that RS could not go to Curwen's and that "*W*. has given up all thought of going" (*STCL* III, 129). See also *MY* I, 311–12n.

[64] On W's early offers of assistance to *The Friend* by prose writings see also *Mem* II, 466.

124. Dec 3

W writes to Francis Wrangham: *The Friend*; asks Wrangham to circulate Prospectuses. Wrangham's *The Gospel Best Promulgated by National Schools*. Takes exception to certain of Wrangham's views of the Spanish. *CC*. Dr. Bell's system and rival claims for its invention. (*MY* I, 277–79.)

125. Dec 4

DW writes to JPM: JPM's mother, lately dead. Smoke at AB. SFC, SC, STC; *The Friend*; *CC*; SH. (*MY* I, 279–81.)

126. Dec 8

W dictates some portion of *CC* to MW. (*MY* I, 282–83.)

DW writes to CCl: Smoke at AB. STC and *The Friend*, of which not one essay is prepared. *CC*; DeQ; W family; SH better; MW, DW well. (*MY* I, 281–84.)

127. Probably c but by Dec 15, and within a day or so after; probably between Dec 15 and Dec 28, Dec 31

Probably c but by 15 Dec an installment, perhaps the same as that published in the *Courier* 27 Dec, of *CC* is completed and forwarded to Stuart. A second installment, probably later lost, is perhaps sent off at the same time or within a day or so. (*STCL* III, 142. See *Friend* R II, 475.)

Probably between 15 and 28 Dec the third and fourth installments of *CC* are sent off to Stuart; and a fifth is prepared except for final corrections. The fifth is perhaps sent off on 31 Dec. (*STCL* III, 151.)

128. Dec 27

The first installment of *CC*, *Prose* text 1–209, corresponding to *CC* 1809, p. 1–p. 11, line 13 (*Prose* text 1–209) is published in the *Courier*, signed "G." (See esp. Wells *CC* 65–71.)

129. Dec 28

W is ill. (See *STCL* III, 151.)

1 8 0 9

[On writings of W possibly of this year see below and GCL 42, 123, 146, 148, 167–69, 171, 173, 179–94.]

1. Probably Jan, by Jan 23

W twice walks to the Post Carrier's house [at Rydal] after 2 AM in order to post letters concerning, or containing MSS of, *CC*. (*STCL* III, 169.)

2. Jan 2–Jan 3

Probably at 11 AM on 2 Jan W receives a letter from Daniel Stuart advising that the second installment of *CC*—and possibly the third and fourth—have been lost. W and STC rewrite till at least 3 AM next morning, probably with considerable revision and addition. (*STCL* III, 160–61, 164, 174. Cf Moorman II, 141. See 1809:3.)

Of that installment STC states on 3 Feb that the last two columns, except for a few sentences and the last paragraph (*CC* 1809, 18, lines 27–23), are his (*STCL* III, 164, 174).

3. Jan 8

SH is ill. (*STCL* III, 163–64.)

W probably sends off some portion of *CC*, perhaps that published on 13 Jan. (*STCL* III, 162–65. See 1809:1; 1809:2.)[1]

4. Between c Jan 10 and probably Jan 26, certainly by Feb 3

W decides to publish *CC* only in pamphlet form. (*Prose* 200; *STCL* III, 174. See 1809:2; *CC* Advertisement.)

5. Jan 13

The second installment of *CC*, corresponding to *CC* 1809, p. 11, line 14–p. 25, line 2 (*Prose* text 210–564), appears in the *Courier*, signed "G." (See esp. Wells *CC* 65–71.)

[1] On 9 Jan STC comments to Stuart, whose last letter had arrived at Rydal on 8 Jan, "The very post by [which] your Letter was received, Wordsworth sent the Essay & a[nswers to] your Questions—."

6. Probably mid-Jan

DW writes to SFC (only a fragment of the letter is known to survive): No more *Friend* Prospectuses printed; those remaining are being sent; STC sends the letters. DeQ to accompany STC to Keswick if well enough. (*MY* I, 291.)[2]

7. Probably between mid-Jan and mid-Feb, by Feb 25, c Feb 25

Probably between mid-Jan and mid-Feb W writes (or in part rewrites) and sends off *CC* materials including *CC* 1809, p. 25, line 3– p. 96, last line (*Prose* text 565–2443). W probably sees proof of these materials by 25 Feb. Materials certainly through *CC* 1809, p. 111, line 6 up, probably not beyond p. 130, line 11 (*Prose* text 2842, 3333) are sent off by c 25 Feb. (Content; 1808:127; 1809:21; Jordan 110, 136; *Prose* 201–02.)[3]

8. Jan 23 or Jan 24–probably Jan 25 or Jan 26

On 23 or 24 Jan STC departs DC, travels to Keswick. He probably returns to AB on 25 or 26 Jan. (*STCL* III, 169.)[4]

9. Probably c Feb 2 or Feb 3

W, STC go to Kendal to make arrangements for the printing of *The Friend*. They perhaps return the same day. (*MY* I, 289.)[5]

10. Probably Feb 5–perhaps Feb 6

Probably on 5 Feb W writes to Daniel Stuart: *CC*, his concern about the pamphlet's subject. *The Friend*. Considerations regarding a second edition [of *CC*]. (*MY* I, 288–90.)

Probably on this day STC goes to Kendal to make arrangements

---

[2] The London prospectus, dated 2 Feb, was plainly not yet printed; and STC was expected to go shortly to Keswick. He did so on 23 or 24 Jan.

[3] The sentence beginning "Saragossa!—She also . . ." (p. 120) is annotated by W "Written in February."

[4] He was possibly accompanied by DeQ (see 1809:6) but no direct evidence on the point survives.

[5] This, as the first short journey that W is recorded taking in 1809, and when DeQ was visiting AB, may serve as occasion for noting DeQ's recollection of W's telling him laughingly, "on returning from a short journey in 1809," that a man in a stage-coach had supposed him over sixty years old. (Masson II, 249).

for the printing of *The Friend*. He probably now finds that Pennington is retiring and will not print and publish the work. STC perhaps returns to AB on 6 Feb. (*STCL* III, 175–76.)

11. Probably Feb 8–Feb 9

Thomas H arrives at AB for a visit probably on 8 Feb. He departs 9 Feb. In Kendal he draws on RW, with W's authority, for £50. (*STCL* III, 189; *MY* I, 290; letter, John M to Thomas M, 7 Feb 1809, JFW Papers.)[6]

12. Feb 10

DW writes to RW: W has authorized Thomas H to draw on RW for £50. RW's recent visit in the North. Thomas H has taken a farm in Wales with John M. SH is to spend the summer at Grasmere. Joanna H and MM are to go to Wales. (*MY* I, 290.)

13. Probably Feb 12 (–probably Feb 17)

On 12 Feb STC walks, probably via Grisedale Hause, to Penrith, where he makes arrangements with John Brown for printing and publishing *The Friend*. (He returns to AB probably on 17 Feb.) (*STCL* III, 180.)

14. c Feb 14, before Feb 20

DeQ is probably at GH on 14 Feb. The length of his visit is uncertain; but he probably returns to AB before 20 Feb. (*Memorials* I, 284; 1809:16.)

15. Probably Feb 17

STC returns to AB. (*STCL* III, 180.)

16. Perhaps shortly before Feb 20

The Ws probably volunteer to lease and furnish DC for DeQ. (Masson II, 359–60; *MY* I, 293. See 1809:17.)

---

[6] RW records payment of the bill in different accounts under 11 and 12 Mar (RW's accounts, DCP). John M writes from Penrith: "T.H. sets off tomorrow to Grasmere from whence he will proceed in a day or two after the Horses."

17. Probably c but by Feb 20; between this time and Mar 26

Probably c but by 20 Feb DeQ departs Grasmere for London, where he sees *CC* through press. W probably accompanies him on his departure as far as Ambleside, DW as far as Rydal. At their parting W suggests alterations for *CC*. (Jordan 91, 116, 187; *MY* I, 299, 340–41.)

W probably receives no more proof for *CC* after DeQ's arrival in London on 25 Feb. The last proof that he reads—perhaps about this time —is for sheet M. (Jordan 95, 119; 1809:23.)

On DeQ and *CC* generally from this point see esp. Jordan 60–85, 91–202; *Prose* 201–17.

DeQ is charged with obtaining a poem, almost certainly *WD*, from MM, but the poem reaches W without DeQ's help by 26 Mar. (Jordan 96; *MY* I, 302. See Appendix VIII.) Probably shortly after DeQ's departure W leases DC for him for six years. (*MY* I, 293. See 1809:16.)[7]

18. Probably c but by Feb 20–Feb 23 ff (–Mar 17, –perhaps June 29)

John M calls or visits at AB. He departs with SH and Dora c but by 20 Feb. Dora probably enters school at Penrith on 23 Feb; lives in Penrith with her Aunt M. She enters Miss Weir's school at Appleby between 7 Apr and 6 May. (She returns home perhaps 29 June. SH returns to AB on 17 Mar.) (*MWL* 5–6; *SHL* 14–15; *MY* I, 317, 339, 357; letter, Joanna H to Thomas H, 22 Feb [1809], JFW Papers.)[8]

19. Probably c Feb 20 and several days following

W is chronically afflicted with severe headaches. (*MY* I, 292.)

[7] One of the alterations that W suggested was for the passage concerning the King's reproof to the City of London, *CC* 99–106 (see Jordan 113n); another concerned Charles the Second, *CC* 198 (*MY* I, 299).

Many of DeQ's drafts for *CC* are preserved in the Cornell Collection (see Cornell 2804).

[8] Joanna H wrote to Thomas H from Penrith on 22 Feb that Dora was there, having come with John M and SH in the gig; that Dora was to enter school the next day; and that SH looked ill, "far worse than when I left her at Grasmere" (see 1808:87). On 22 June Dora was expected home on 29 June (*MY* I, 360), and for all that is known returned according to expectation. Elizabeth M wrote to John M on [Saturday] 17 June, "Miss Weir & my Dear little Goddaughtor set of for Grasmere by way of Kendal on Friday next" (JFW Papers).

20. Probably c but not before Feb 25

W writes materials for *CC* inclusive of paragraph at foot of *CC* 1809 150 (*Prose* text 3874 ff). (Content.)[9]

21. Probably Feb 27 (–June 13)

STC goes to Brathay. (He returns to AB after various travels, including visits at Penrith and Keswick, on 13 June.) (*MY* I, 291–92.)[10]

22. Probably c but by Mar 1

W sends off two packets (four MS sheets) of copy for *CC* to DeQ. These supply copy probably inclusive of materials *CC* 1809, p. 130, line 11 (*Prose* text 3333) –p. 150. (Jordan 96–97, 104; 1809:17; 1809:21; *Prose* 207.)

23. Perhaps between c Mar 1809 and some time in 1810

W composes:
"Avaunt All Specious Pliancy of Mind"
The French and the Spanish Guerillas. 1811
"Say, What Is Honour? 'Tis the Finest Sense"
(*MY* I, 460.)[11]

24. Probably c but by Mar 4

W sends off a single letter to DeQ, probably containing corrections for *CC*. (Jordan 101, 104–05.)

[9] On *CC* 150 W writes: "This moment (while I am drawing towards a conclusion) I learn, from the newspaper reports, that the House of Commons has refused to declare that the Convention of Cintra *disappointed the hopes and expectations of the Nation.*" The *Times* of 22 Feb reported the presentation and defeat of Lord Henry Petty's motion of censure of 21 Feb.

[10] STC thus probably took no part in the composition of *CC* from this time (see Moorman II, 142).

[11] DW says on 30 Dec 1810 that W "has written 15 fine political sonnets, which Mary and I would fain have him send to the Courier. . . . The King of Sweden, Buonaparte, and the struggles of the Peninsula are the subjects of these sonnets." (*MY* I, 460.)

The identity of only a few of the works referred to by DW is clear, and the span of time within which their composition occurred is doubtful. The fourteen sonnets listed below are those which, along with those listed in the main text, (a) seem to fit DW's description of subjects, (b) were not published in *P2V*, (c) were not published in *The*

25. Probably Mar 5

W sends off to DeQ two single letters containing what W then supposed to be the conclusion of *CC*.

Friend, and (d) were "fine" enough for inclusion in *P* 1815. Of these, several may be assigned *termini a quo* within the period suggested on fairly specific grounds. If, as is not unlikely, DW was in fact thinking of recent composition, the last two poems listed would appear those least likely to belong among the poems in question; and, although the evidence is not very strong, the remaining fifteen may be placed by default before the end of 1810. (W's remark in his letter to Wrangham of c 30 Mar 1809 that "Verses have been out of my Head for some time" would also appear too vague for a basis of calculation.)

"Ah! Where Is Palafox? Nor Tongue nor Pen"
"Hail Zaragossa! If with Unwet Eye"
"Is There a Power That Can Sustain and Cheer"
(Perhaps c late Mar, after 14 Mar 1809; fairly certainly between 14 Mar 1809 and 1810. Firmly reliable news of the surrender of Saragossa and the capture of Palafox probably did not reach W before 18 Mar, but the fall of the city was reported in the *Courier* of 11 Mar. See Jordan 111–12, 116–17, 119.)

"Call Not the Royal Swede Unfortunate"
"Look Now on That Adventurer Who Hath Paid"
(Perhaps c early Apr 1809. These appear to be companion works and were probably written about the same time. Gustavus IV abdicated 29 Mar 1809. News of his overthrow reached London on the night of 26 Mar and probably reached W on Thursday 30 Mar. See Jordan 122–23.)

"Brave Schill! by Death Delivered, Take Thy Flight"
(Perhaps c but not before 19 June 1809. Schill was shot 31 May. News of his death was announced in the *Courier* of 16 June. See also *MY* I, 354.)

1810 ("O'erweening Statesmen")
Indignation of a High-minded Spaniard. 1810
"In Due Observance of an Ancient Rite"
Feelings of a Noble Biscayan . . . 1810
The Oak of Guernica . . . 1810
(All perhaps 1810. "In Due Observance" appears an introduction to *Feelings of a Noble Biscayan*, and was probably written about the same time.)

"The Martial Courage of a Day Is Vain"
(Perhaps c but not before 15 Mar 1810. The death of Hofer was first reported in the *Times* on 12 Mar.)

Composed While . . . Writing a Tract Occasioned by the Convention of Cintra
Composed at the Same Time
(Probably composed between c mid-Nov 1808 and 25 Mar 1809. See 1808:114.)

The *termini a quo* of the three sonnets cited in the main text are suggested on the basis of the earliest probable date for the sonnets just listed.

Probably this night DW writes to DeQ (letter not known to survive) about obtaining furnishings for DC [see 1809:16]. (Jordan 104–05; *MY* I, 294–95.)[12]

26. Probably Mar 6

W, DW write to DeQ: (W:) Two small corrections for *CC*. Encouragement of DeQ to put the pamphlet forward, working with Stuart. (DW:) Plans for the day. (*MY* I, 294–95; 1809:25n.)

[12] DW's letter to DeQ of 7 Mar was written the day after receipt of DeQ's letter, which would probably have occurred on the Monday morning walk described in prospect *MY* I, 295. That letter states that she is afraid that DeQ cannot have been able "to make out what I wrote last night about the Manchester Goods." DeQ replies in obvious reference to this remark on 11 Mar, "I had no difficulty at all in reading your letter about the furniture &c" (Jordan 105). This letter, *MY* I, 294–95, must hence date from Monday 6 Mar, and would be the letter "dated Monday morng. before you walk to Rydale," and also the "letter with two or three corrections" sent off "yesterday" mentioned by DW on 7 Mar (*MY* I, 294; Jordan 105n). The 6 Mar letter states that the concluding sheet was sent off "yesterday."

Surviving evidence appears too slight for firm surmise of the content of the essay as originally completed. Most of the basic text to the commencement of the paragraph on p. 156 must have been present (1809:28; Jordan 97). W's phrasing at that point, esp. that hope has accompanied him "to the end," suggests that the original conclusion followed within a few paragraphs; hence, although W later stated that the supplementary passage which he began sending on 8 Mar began at the start of the paragraph on p. 156 (*MY* I, 299), DeQ's earlier indication that the passage began two sentences later, with "In Madrid," is probably more accurate.

The conclusion apparently contained *CC* 1809, p. 184, lines 13–21 (*MY* I, 294–95), *CC* 1809, p. 187, lines 13–15 (*MY* I, 295), and *CC* 1809, p. 189, line 2 (*MY* I, 294); but the materials of the foot of p. 189 and the top of p. 190 (to the third line) probably do not date before 14 Mar and the arrival at Grasmere of news of the final fall of Saragossa (1809:23n). The last consideration applies also to the materials from the foot of p. 179 to the top of p. 181. There seems no reason to doubt, esp. in view of the character of W's subsequent corrections (see *Prose* 203–04), that most or all of the materials between p. 156 and the top of p. 181 were written after the original conclusion. One might, then, speculate that W's introduction of the subject of hope (on p. 156) at first led on to general concluding remarks—concerning the strength of the human spirit, Spanish resistance of tyranny, and the grounds of the writer's hope—including much or all of c foot of *CC* 1809 183 (perhaps *Prose* text 4557)– p. 189, line 2 (*Prose* text 4899), plus the final three paragraphs as published. For more detailed argument see *Prose* 201–20.

W, DW walk to Rydal. DW goes to Ann Nicholson's, finds a letter from DeQ which she brings to W, who has been waiting at the foot of the hill. DW reads the letter. W walks on to Brathay, to meet STC and proceed to Patterdale. STC has gone. W returns to AB. (*MY* I, 291–95; Jordan 104–05.)

27. Mar 7

W works on an addition to *CC* but does not complete it in time to post it with a letter which DW writes to DeQ.

DW writes to DeQ: DeQ's trip to London; W's work on *CC*; STC; DC; Johnny; *CC*; DeQ asked to stop press at the words "career in the fulness of [her joy]" (*CC* 1809, p. 189, line 2; *Prose* text 4898–99). (*MY* I, 291–94; Jordan 104–05.)

28. Mar 8–Mar 26

On 8 Mar W and/or DW sends off a letter to DeQ. The letter probably contains the supplementary passage received by DeQ on 11 Mar beginning perhaps "In Madrid, in Ferrol, in Corunna" (*CC* 1809, p. 156, line 18; *Prose* text 4026) and probably concluding "much to be avoided, little to be imitated" (*CC* 1809, p. 161, line 12 up; *Prose* text 4168) to be placed following "fulness of [her joy]" (*CC* 1809, p. 189, line 2; *Prose* text 4898–99). (*MY* I, 294; Jordan 106–07; 1809:25n; 1809:27; 1809:31. See *Prose* 202–03. Cf *MY* I, 299.)

This alteration probably commences a large number of alterations and additions, completed, with final MS sheets sent off, by 26 Mar. The bulk of these revisions (which perhaps include as much suppressed as used) commences as above and runs probably to *CC* 1809, c foot p. 183 (perhaps *Prose* text 4757), and from *CC* 1809, p. 189, line 2 (*Prose* text 4898) to p. 190, line 3 (*Prose* text 4925). (*MY* I, 294, 298–99; Jordan 106–07; *SHL* 14; 1809:25n; 1809:31&n; 1809:34; *Prose* 202–08; Moorman II, 143.)

On a day c but not before 8 Mar visitors are present at AB much of the day. (1809:31n.)

29. Probably c but not before Mar 9

W suffers from a severe headache. (1809:31n.)

30. Mar 10

DW writes to DeQ; perhaps walks; if so, perhaps walks with W to Ambleside. (Jordan 109.)

31. Probably c but not before Mar 10

W completes another folio sheet of MS for *CC* continuing the supplementary MS of which the first sheet was sent off 8 Mar. This sheet, in the autograph of MW, contains an early version of the passage beginning "There is yet . . . " (*CC* 1809, p. 161, line 11 up; *Prose* text 4169) and concluding "generalized that this position" (*CC* 1809, p. 166, line 8 up; *Prose* text 4302). W adds notes apologizing for two days' more delay, thanking DeQ for his letter (probably that of 5–7 Mar), and advising that DeQ has filled a gap in an earlier MS with the proper word. This sheet is probably not sent off, and its content, in final form, is probably not sent off till 26 Mar. (DCP; 1809:28; 1809: 37; *Prose* 204–05, 218–20. See Jordan 66, 161–62.)[13]

32. Probably between Mar 13 and Mar 26

W writes portions of *CC* including *CC* 1809 179 (foot, c *Prose* text 4655)–181 (top, c *Prose* text 4670) and 189 (foot, c *Prose* text 4912)–p. 190, line 3 (*Prose* text 4925). (Content; Jordan 116–17, 119; 1809:23n; 1809:25n.)

33. Perhaps c late Mar, after Mar 14; fairly certainly between Mar 14 and 1810

W composes:
"Ah! Where Is Palafox? Nor Tongue nor Pen"
"Hail Zaragossa! If with Unwet Eye"
"Is There a Power That Can Sustain and Cheer"
(1809:23n.)

---

[13] W remarks to DeQ, "You filled up the [lacu *deleted*] gap with the proper word . . . ." He is referring to DeQ's query about a "lacuna" in the letter that DeQ sent off on 7 Mar. (See Jordan 97, 104.) W also apologizes for having to draw on DeQ's patience for "two days more," explaining that he had a severe headache the previous day and visitors for a great part of the day before that.

34. Mar 16 (–Mar 17) ff

On 16 Mar MW writes to John M: Anxiety about SH's health, and STC's. A decision has been reached to pay off the mortgage on W's Patterdale estate immediately. Requests that John M discuss the time and forms required with Mr. Ellwood, give due notice, and advise the Ws so that the money may be made ready. Dora; the family. (The letter is completed next day by Joanna H.) (*MWL* 5–6. See 1809:69.)

John M probably carries out the tasks as requested.

35. Mar 17, and shortly after–Mar 22

SH, Joanna H arrive at AB from Penrith, whence they have been accompanied part way by Jane Addison, on 17 Mar. Joanna H this day finishes, at 5, the letter to John M begun on 16 Mar by MW: The journey to AB. (*MWL* 6–7; MS, DCP.)[14]

Joanna H departs on the evening of 22 Mar. She is perhaps taken away by John M. (*SHL* 14.)

On 17 Mar DW writes to DeQ (letter not known to survive), finishing after the arrival of SH: Inquiries about *Friend* subscribers. Probably instructions to relocate the "In Madrid" insertion [see 1809: 28], following the beginning of the second paragraph of *CC* 1809, p. 156, lines 14–17 (*Prose* text 4024–26), and to expect a bulky insertion to follow *CC* 1809, p. 188, line 2 (*Prose* text 4872–73).

36. Mar 25–Mar 26; perhaps Mar 25; probably between c Mar 25 and c Mar 30; shortly after Apr 5

On 25–26 Mar HC and Derwent visit AB. (*MY* I, 300, 303.)

Perhaps on 25 Mar sheets N, O, P of *CC*, including a note by DeQ on Saragossa, are struck off by the printer. (Jordan 117, 119, 133.)

Probably between c 25 Mar and c 30 Mar *CC* sheets Q, R, S, T, U are set in type but not struck off. R reaches a second proof by 28 Mar. All are probably struck off shortly after Apr 5. (Jordan 117, 119, 123, 132–33, 139.)

---

[14] The autograph of the postscript of MW's letter of 16 Mar is that of Joanna H, not DW (cf *MWL*). Joanna was on her way to Hindwell to join the household at the new farm of John M and Thomas H. After leaving AB on Wednesday 22 Mar, she wrote next day that John M, who had been at Penrith c 17 Mar (*MWL* 7), had departed Kendal on the day of her letter (*SHL* 14).

37. Probably Mar 26–Mar 27; probably between Mar 26 and May 28

On 26 Mar W employs SH, probably in work on *CC*. He probably this day finishes the primary MS of *CC*. (*SHL* 15; Jordan 132; 1808: 114; 1809:28.)

Probably on 26 Mar W writes to DeQ: Sends concluding parts of *CC*; cancellation of page with footnote about Saragossa by DeQ; sends alterations, including revision of title page, and insertions; advice for the long extension noted 1809:28, an appendix (which became *CC* 1809 198–99), next-to-last paragraph of Advertisement, two other small corrections. Discusses distribution of copies of *CC*; Richard Vaughan as a possible recipient, and Vaughan's *Narrative of the Siege of Saragossa*; George Carleton's *Military Memoirs*, which they have.

DW concludes the letter: Catharine's ill health; STC; SH. (*MY* I, 298–303.)

On W's corrections see Wells *CC* 43–47. W's revision of the title page indicates final abandonment of any plan to write a second part of *CC*. (See *Prose* 214.)

W sends off four letters, probably including the one just described, by the 26 Mar post. The other letters probably contain W's *CC* MS, which probably contains the basic MS for *CC* 1809, p. 161, line 12 up (*Prose* text 4169) and forward as described 1809:28. Possibly DW carries out the letters while accompanying HC and Derwent to or toward Brathay. (*MY* I, 303–04; Jordan 125, 132; *Prose* 203.)

Probably between 26 Mar and 28 May W writes to Thomas Poole. (*MY* I, 351. See 1809:87.)

38. Probably Mar 27

W writes to Daniel Stuart: *CC*; pessimism about its prospects of success in view of the country's moral state. Need for reform of parliament and new system of education; military leadership; the *Courier* and the Duke of York; invitation to visit; STC. (*MY* I, 295–96.)[15]

SH writes to MM: AB; Joanna H; the family; DeQ; MM's plans;

[15] The postmark, 31 Mar (cf *SHL* 18), and W's information that he sent off the last sheets of the pamphlet—an event of 26 Mar—"yesterday" establish the date of the letter (cf *MY* I, 295).

John Wilson; STC, and *The Friend*; *CC*. DC rented to DeQ; furnishings for DC. (*SHL* 14–18.)

39. Probably Mar 28

W writes to DeQ: A few further corrections for *CC*; family. (*MY* I, 303–03. See Jordan 132; Wells *CC* 47.)

40. Mar 29, c Mar 29

Mr. Crump calls at AB. W and he discuss the situation in Spain, Crump arguing for the benefits that Bonaparte would bring Spain. (*MY* I, 306.)

W writes to DeQ: Consideration of corrections and amendments for *CC*. Crump; DeQ encouraged to review the recently published letters of Sir John Moore, which have had a prejudicial effect on public opinion of the Spanish; outlines arguments and methods. (*MY* I, 305–09.)

Probably c 29 Mar W writes another letter (not known to survive) to DeQ concerning Sir John Moore. (Jordan 137.)

41. Mar 30; probably c Mar 30

On 30 Mar W writes to Thomas Poole: Publication of *CC* imminent. STC and *The Friend*. Poole encouraged to visit the Lakes; W wishes to visit the Alfoxden area again. (*MY* I, 310–11.)

Probably c 30 Mar W writes to Francis Wrangham: *CC*, and his hopes for it; has not composed verse for some time; local topographical history as subject for Wrangham [see 1808:99]. The Catholic question and his fears for the English church in the event of emancipation. (*MY* I, 311–13.)[16]

16 W says he sent off the last sheets for *CC* "only a day or two since"; but the sheets were in fact sent off on 26 Mar; and it is unlikely that W wrote as early as 27 or 28 Mar, as the date of the frank is 3 Apr. (The paper, watermarked "G R WARD" over "1807," is of a sort used in other unfranked Grasmere letters of late 1808 and early 1809 and thus is not unlikely to have belonged to W in the first place [see 1809:42n].) The date recorded *Mem* I, 388, "Workington, *April* 3. 1809.," is plainly based on the frank.

42. Probably Mar 31 and/or Apr 1 (–Apr 5)

W travels to Appleby, perhaps passing a night somewhere along the way, and probably seeing Dora in Penrith for about an hour. Having met RS and STC on the way, before reaching Penrith, or having joined them and probably John Brown the printer at Appleby, W takes part, probably on 1 Apr, in signing bonds and securities for *The Friend*. (He returns to AB on 5 Apr.) (*MY* I, 310, 315, 317; *STCL* III, 314–16; *Friend* R II, 483.)[17]

43. Probably c Apr, including Apr 19 and May 1; about this time, and by May 7

Probably c Apr W works on *WD*; by 19 Apr he has made additions to the poem and determined to add another canto to it. On 1 May he is probably still at work on the poem. The additions made now are unidentified. (*SHL* 20; *MY* I, 325; Appendix VIII.)

About this time W employs himself in the arrangement of his published poems with a view to blending the four volumes together when and if they are reprinted. By 7 May he has evolved the scheme that he describes to STC *MY* I, 334–36. (*MY* I, 325–26, 334–36.)

[17] W says on Friday 7 Apr that he returned home "last Wednesday after a very agreeable excursion of five days" (*MY* I, 317).

STC expected on 28 Mar that he would go with RS, W, and Brown the printer to Appleby to sign the bonds and securities for *The Friend* on Thursday 30 Mar (*STCL* III, 314–16); but W was still at Grasmere for at least part of the day of 30 Mar (*MY* I, 315). It is not unlikely, but is unknown, that he passed a night somewhere on his way to Appleby. DW implies also, however, that STC and RS as well as W saw Dora at Penrith; so W may have met the others at Penrith or prior to arrival there.

Despite the 3 Apr frank by J. C. Curwen, addressed as from Workington, on W's letter to Wrangham, W does not appear to have gone to Workington. RS and STC had made plans to go to Workington Hall on 6 Apr (*MY* I, 319–20).

DW expected that W would return via Kendal. This route suggests that she supposed he would continue thither from Appleby; but W was back in Penrith at the beginning of the week, c 3–4 Apr, and passed at least one night at Sockbridge. (*MY* I, 317.) DW sent letters to W at Kendal so that W could write to DeQ from there. While W's first letter to DeQ since leaving home was written from Grasmere on 7 Apr (*MY* I, 317–19; Jordan 142), chances are good that he went on to Kendal (see 1809:48).

44. Perhaps c early Apr

W composes:
"Call Not the Royal Swede Unfortunate"
"Look Now on that Adventurer Who Hath Paid"
(1809:23n.)

45. Probably c Apr 1

A review of *P2V* appears in *The British Critic* (XXXIII, Mar 1809). (See Ward; Hayden.)

46. Probably Apr 1

A letter, pamphlets from Stuart, and a gift of pictures for Johnny arrive from DeQ. (*MY* I, 314, 316; Jordan 121–22.)[18]

47. Between Apr 2 and Apr 9

DW and SH possibly visit Elleray at some time during this period. (*SHL* 16.)[19]

48. Probably just before or on Apr 3, and c Apr 3–Apr 4

W probably just before or on 3 Apr sees J. C. Curwen, who franks W's letter to Wrangham of probably c 30 Mar. W c 3–4 Apr passes a night at Sockbridge in RW's bed; brings away a stick. Perhaps while in this area he calls on Thomas Wilkinson, who is not at home. (*MY* I, 258, 311, 317; 1809:41n. See 1809:55.)

W perhaps travels on to Kendal. On his way home, draws on RW for £50 by a bill in favor of Isaac Braithwaite. (*MY* I, 315–17; *Friend* R II, 417; RW accounts, DCP.)[20]

---

[18] For the identity of the pamphlets see the Jordan reference cited.

[19] SH writes on Monday 27 Mar, "Dorothy and I are going to spend a while at Elleray next week," but DW was fairly certainly at Grasmere on 5, 6, and 9 Apr; and no record survives of such a visit, which was perhaps postponed till 21 Apr (see 1809:64).

[20] DW states on 6 Apr that W drew his £50, with a bill due in one month, through Braithwaite, who lived in Kendal, "four or five days ago." RW records payment of the bill under 4 May. Evidence for W's visiting Kendal is otherwise ambiguous; but he does not appear to have been there on 1 Apr (see 1809:42n).

49. Apr 4

A letter [Jordan 132–37] arrives from DeQ. (*MY* I, 314.)
DeQ gives the final part of the body of *CC* to the printer. (Jordan 155–56.)

50. Probably shortly after Apr 4

DeQ gives the *CC* notes, including perhaps a page and a half of DeQ's Postscript on Sir John Moore's letters, to the printer. (Jordan 156–57. See 1809:74.)

51. c but by Apr 5; Apr 5

HC and Derwent visit at AB, departing 5 Apr. (*MY* I, 316.)
On 5 Apr DW writes to DeQ: Communications from DeQ. The women regret cancellation of DeQ's note on Saragossa [see 1809:37]. Mrs. Kelsall; DW's reading, including Cevallos' *Exposition* (one of the pamphlets sent by DeQ [see 1809:46]); Miss Smith's translation, *Memoir of Frederick and Margaret Klopstock.* (*MY* I, 314–16.)
Probably after DW writes this letter W returns to AB. (*MY* I, 317. See 1809:42.)

52. Probably between shortly after Apr 5 and Apr 15

CC sheets V, W, and X are set up and X perhaps reaches second proof stage. (Jordan 139, 142.)

53. Apr 6

DW writes to RW: W has drawn for £50 [see 1809:48]; W's visit to Sockbridge. (*MY* I, 316–17.)

54. Probably Apr 7

W writes to DeQ: His recent excursion; his reasons for cancelling DeQ's note on Saragossa [see 1809:37]; General Baird's letters on peninsular affairs; considerations of the language of *CC*, esp. concerning the Battle of Alexandria and Corunna. (*MY* I, 317–19. See Jordan 142.)
W, MW visit the Lloyds; stay for the post; receive no letter. (*MY* I, 320.)

55. Probably Apr 8; perhaps Apr 8 (–Apr 9)

Probably on 8 Apr W walks to the carrier's at Rydal, finds a letter from DeQ [Jordan 137–41]. (*MY* I, 320–21.)

Perhaps on 8 Apr HC and Derwent come to visit at AB. (They depart 9 Apr.) (*MY* I, 320–21. See 1808:100.)

56. Probably Apr 9

DW writes to DeQ: Instructions concerning *CC*; thanks for DeQ's help; STC is at Keswick; STC and DW's pessimism about him. (*MY* I, 320–21.)

HC and Derwent depart AB. (*MY* I, 320–21. See 1809:55.)

W perhaps goes to Ambleside, possibly accompanying HC and Derwent. Possibly today he sees William Green there and writes for him a letter of introduction to Thomas Wilkinson: Requests him to show Green the most interesting trees and scenes around Lowther. (*MY* I, 258.)[21]

57. Probably c Apr 14

The Ws are shocked to learn of the death of Jane W, daughter of RW of Branthwaite and Cockermouth. (*MY* I, 323.)[22]

58. Probably Apr 14 or Apr 15 (–c but by Apr 18)

STC arrives at AB. (He departs c but by 18 Apr.) (*STCL* III, 192–94.)

[21] W dates only "Ambleside[,] Sunday Even." *MY* conjectures "[?31 July 1808]" on the basis of the facts that the Ws stopped in Ambleside on their way to Patterdale on "Sunday (31 July)," and that Green's *Twenty-eight Studies from Nature*, 1809, includes a view of the River Lowther at Askham.

MY I, 261 makes clear, however, that the Ws stopped in Ambleside, on that excursion, on a Monday; and W's letter also expresses regret at not having found Wilkinson at home on a call "lately" at Yanwath. W is not known to have been in that area in late July 1808, but was certainly so in early Apr 1809. The publication date on Green's print of Askham Bridge, over the Lowther, in his *Seventy-eight Studies from Nature*, 1809, is 1 Aug 1809.

[22] DW writes to RW probably c but by 28 Apr that they had heard this news "about a fortnight ago." Jane W died at Catgill Hall on 10 Apr, and was buried on 12 Apr at Whitehaven (information from Mr. D. P. Sewell).

59. Possibly c mid-Apr

W probably sees Charles Luff, who perhaps calls at AB. (Letter, Luff to Josiah Wedgwood, 6 May 1809, UKL.)[23]

60. Probably between c Apr 15 and c Apr 25

CC half-sheets Y and Z are set up. (Jordan 139, 132, 145, 156.)

61. Apr 16 (possibly ff)

John Wilson calls (or possibly arrives for a short visit) at AB. He arrives wet; lets his clothes dry on him. (*SHL* 18, 21.)

62. c but by Apr 18

STC departs AB. (*STCL* III, 192–94.)

63. Apr 19

SH writes to MM: The Cooksons; Hindwell, and her plans to come there; TCl's old mare; household equipment for Hindwell, esp. churns; *WD*; *CC*; family news; W's concern that MM be married. (*SHL* 18–21.)

64. Perhaps Apr 21–probably c but by Apr 28

DW, probably SH, visit the Wilsons at Elleray. There DW reads, with indignation, the conclusion of the *ER* review of Burns's poems. (*SHL* 21; *MY* I, 323, 326. See: 1809:65n; 1809:68.)[24]

---

[23] Luff wrote to Josiah Wedgwood on 6 May, somewhat obscurely, that he had received 4s "of Mr Mounsey and Mr Wordsworth has desired me to transmit to you also for his Crate which I shall take the first opportunity of doing. . . ." He continues more plainly: "[W] is now busy in a pamphlet on the Cintra Convention, and from what I have seen of the manuscript, I think it will be a work of considerable Merit. I suppose you know that Mr. Coleridge is engaged in a weekly publication called the friend. whether his health will permit him to proceed in it is with me a doubt as he appears to be very ill and absolutely unfit for the conducting of such work." That Luff saw STC at Grasmere is quite uncertain, as is the time of Luff's visit.

[24] SH wrote on Wednesday 19 Apr that DW and she were going to Elleray on Friday. DW reported c but by 28 Apr that she had been at Mrs. Wilson's for "about a week." On 13 May CCl remarked to SH, "The Edinburgh Review has outdone all

65. Apr 24

W is probably out late this evening. (1809:67n.)[25]

66. Apr 25

A letter arrives from Daniel Stuart. (*MY* I, 321.)

67. Probably c Apr 26

MW forwards to STC a letter to him from Robert Grahame. She adds a note: *Friend* affairs; the family. (DCP.)[26]

68. Apr 26

W writes to Daniel Stuart: Seeks Stuart's help in completing *CC*; urges him to encourage pro-Spanish feeling through the *Courier*. W denies that he has stated as a general position that freedom of discussion could exist under arbitrary governments; explains his position. Books avail nothing without institutions of civil liberty. Thanks for pamphlets [see 1809:46]. (*MY* I, 321–22. See Jordan 155.)

69. Probably c but by Apr 28

John H probably calls or visits at AB.

W pays off the mortgage on his Patterdale estate with MW's monies from the Funds and £200 for which he draws on RW through John H, with a bill due at ten days. (*MY* I, 323, 339; 1809:34.)[27]

[25] It appears possible that W paid a weekend visit at Elleray; evidence is too slight for further speculation.

[26] MW writes (n.d.): "The Hull paper came addressed to you. I guess sent by your Malton Friend for the sake of your Advertisement—The letters came by Sunday's Post but W. was too late on Monday night to allow my sending them on Tuesday—Dorothy & Sara will not be at home till the end of the week—We rejoice to hear you have been so busy I hope the Paper will come in time to prevent any further delay. God bless you. M.W."

[27] Legal arrangements concluding the transactions were probably not completed till spring 1811. RW's accounts charge payment of the bill to W under the date of 9 May.

its former doings in regard to William in a paragraph wch for insolence & malice exceeds all that I ever read" (BM Add. MS 41,267A, fol. 34). The offensive paragraph appears *ER* XIII (1809), 276.

DW writes to RW: Advises of W's paying off the mortgage on the Patterdale estate; of W's drawing on RW for £200. Death of Jane W; DW is to visit the Wilsons. (*MY* I, 323.)[28]

70. Apr 28

A letter arrives from DeQ. DW writes to DeQ. (*MY* I, 324.)[29]

71. Apr 29; between Apr 29 and May 5; probably Apr 29–Apr 30

CC sheet AA is set up on 29 Apr. Between that date and 5 May *CC* sheet BB, through the notes (*CC* 1809 199), is set up. (Jordan 155–58.)

Probably on the morning of 29 Apr John Wilson arrives for a visit at AB. He remains till the afternoon of 30 Apr. W reads *WD* and *Christabel* to him. (*MY* I, 326.)

72. Probably c early May

DW writes to Mrs. Kelsall (letter not known to survive) probably about furnishings for DC for DeQ. (*Memorials* II, 1–2; *MY* I, 315, 326–27.)[30]

73. May 1

DW writes to DeQ: Johnny and his reaction to *Christabel*; the family; probability that they will have to move from AB in two years. W has resolved to write on public affairs for the *Courier*. W much employed in arranging his poems. The *ER* review of Burns's poems [see 1809:64]; someone should answer Jeffrey for W. Wilson and W possibly will visit Wales. Furnishings for DC. (*MY* I, 323–27.)

74. Probably May 3; perhaps May 3; May 3

Probably on 3 May W reads in an old magazine of Benjamin

[28] The letter is postmarked 1 May.

[29] This letter was probably received by DeQ on 2 May (see Jordan 155).

[30] Jane DeQ wrote to DeQ on 17 May that she had heard of DeQ from Miss W through Mrs. Kelsall. "I should much like to know Miss Wordsworth," she remarks, "and to see what sort of a woman you admire."

Flower's imprisonment for libel (1799). He writes to Daniel Stuart: Asks Stuart to examine *CC* for possible libelous statements. His concern about the "what greater punishment" remark [see *CC* 1809 97]. The printers' reported accusations that delays in publication were caused by DeQ and himself; a comment of Bacon's about controversial writing [used as epigraph for *CC*]. (*MY* I, 327–28.)

Probably on this day also DeQ gives to the printer the copy for the Suspension of Arms and the Convention (*CC* 1809 199–206), and probably also his Postscript on the letters of Sir John Moore (*CC* 1809 206–16). (Jordan 156–57.)

Perhaps on 3 May John Wilson passes the night at AB. W perhaps reads *PB* to him. (*MY* I, 325.)

RW's accounts charge W £30/–/–, payment of bill in favor of J. Graves, under the date of 3 May. (RW accounts, DCP.)

75. Probably between May 5 and May 7

W writes to STC: STC's health; W's fears about the "what greater punishment" remark—seeks STC's advice. Proposed arrangement of W's poems: childhood; affections, friendship, and love; natural objects and their influence on the mind; naming of places; human life; social and civic duties; old age. There should be a scale in each class and in the whole, and each poem should be placed to direct the reader's attention by its position to its *primary* interest. (*MY* I, 331–36. See 1809:43.)[31]

76. May 5

W and SH write to DeQ: (W:) Has decided that the "what greater punishment" remark [see 1809:74] must be altered, if necessary by a cancel leaf: gives correction. (SH:) Dislikes delay caused by the cancel. Workers at DC; W contemplating visit to Ireland; W will

[31] W's letter was written when W had heard in his last letter from DeQ that *CC* might be published "the day before yesterday." The reference is probably to DeQ's letter of Saturday 29 Apr, which reports DeQ's hopes of publication "on Wednesday." So W's letter to STC dates probably from 5 May, that day being the "very day" (*MY* I, 333) on which W wrote the present letter to Stuart.

accompany her to Wales, Wilson and DeQ will join W there, and they will proceed together thence. Family news. (*MY* I, 329–31.)[32]

W, DW probably go to Ambleside. (*MY* I, 331.)

77. May 6

DW writes to DeQ: Regrets delay for correction of "what greater punishment" passage; *Friend* delayed by want of stamped paper; felling and lopping of trees on Nab Scar. Dora. (*MY* I, 336–39.)

78. Between May 9 and May 17; and by May 11

Setting up of *CC* sheet Bb is completed through *Suspension of Arms*. Cc, Dd, a sheet used for cancel N 1 and possibly the errata leaf, and one probably used for the title and Advertisement, are set up, corrected, and prepared for final printing. All but the title page and Advertisement are in first proof 11 May. (Jordan 154–58, 161; 1809:80.)[33]

79. Probably May 10

W writes to DeQ: Urges DeQ to confer with Stuart about *CC*; Stuart is requested to remove any potentially actionable statement. W's hopes and zeal for his country are abated. (*MY* I, 340–41; Jordan 162.)[34]

[32] MM wrote to Thomas M from Hindwell on 22 May that she had heard from DW in a letter (probably written about this time) that SH had not been well, but that prospects of her recovery were favorable; that W was to accompany her to Wales; and that Wilson and DeQ "talk of journeying from here and taking a jaunt into Ireland." "Poor William," she says, "has been sadly disappointed about his pamphalet, the printer has behaved shamefully by putting them off from time to time & it is now too late for the season, & I suppose will not be published at all, at least this year." (JFW Papers.)

[33] DeQ refers on 12 May (Jordan 161) to the "2 canceled pages": he may simply mean the two pages of leaf N1 or be referring to two leaves, in which case the errata leaf (on which see the same reference) appears the only one unaccounted for in his description. An earlier title page was apparently cancelled and replaced by the three leaves containing the new title, the Advertisement and the errata (see Cornell 12), but that page seems not to have been one of the "canceled pages" referred to on 12 May. Leaf N1 was cancelled before issue (cf Cornell 12).

[34] On subsequent events in London with respect to W's request see esp. Jordan 79–80, 162–69; *MY* 341–54.

80. May 17

DeQ this night sends off four specially struck-off unstitched copies of *CC* to W. (Jordan 166–70, 238. See 1809:82.)

81. May 18–May 24

The printing of *CC* is completed at 9 AM on 18 Apr. Sheets for fifty copies are sent to Longman at 6 PM. None of these copies is distributed before 24 May. (Jordan 170–74.)[35]

82. May 23

This night the Ws receive the four unstitched copies of *CC* sent off by DeQ on 17 May. (*MY* I, 341, 344.)

83. May 24

W, SH write to DeQ: (W:) Errata in *CC*; praises DeQ's note on Sir John Moore; thanks DeQ for his help. (SH:) Errata; a corrected copy of *CC* to be sent to LdL; death of RS's second youngest child (Emma, d. 3 May); a copy of *CC* to go to Curwen in London. (*MY* I, 341–43. See Jordan 191.) W goes for a walk. (*MY* I, 343.)

The Longman records for *CC* commence with this date. (See Owen CSP 96–97.)[36]

84. May 25

W writes to Daniel Stuart: DeQ the occasion, but not the necessary

[35] The date of W's Advertisement, 20 May, is presumably an anticipation.

[36] "50 copies recd qrs" (see 1809:81) was recorded under the general date "May," but evidently not until the other accounts were begun. One copy of *CC* is recorded delivered to Stuart on 24 May and twelve more on 27 May, when twelve were also delivered to DeQ. A copy delivered to LdL is recorded but not charged under 3 June. A copy is charged to "Mr Wordsworth" under 17 June; and a copy is recorded delivered to "the Author's brother" under 18 July. By 30 June 170 copies had been sold (Jordan 83). By 2 May 1810, 238 copies had been sold, and a further 28 had been sold by June 1811. Concerning binding and sale see also Owen CSP 96–97; J. E. Wells, "Printer's Bills for Coleridge's *Friend* and Wordsworth's *Cintra*," *Stud Phil* XXXVI (1939), 521–23. DeQ found the pamphlet "in a course of delivery" at Longman's on 26 May (Jordan 181).

cause, of delay in *CC*; the printer must have become recalcitrant; regrets that a passage deemed libelous by Stuart was not cancelled. STC and *The Friend*. W fears the *Courier* not sufficiently encouraging reform. Invitation to visit. (*MY* I, 344–45.)[37]

W writes to LdL: Delay in publication of *Friend*; presents copy of *CC*. (*MY* I, 346–47.)[38]

85. May 26

W, MW write to DeQ: (W:) Praise of DeQ's temperate treatment of Sir John Moore in his note on Moore's letters in *CC*; regrets errors, praises DeQ's plan of punctuation, in *CC*. (MW:) Congratulations on conclusion and quality of DeQ's labors for *CC*; Grasmere; the children, and Dora; fears delay in publication of *CC*. (*MY* I, 347–49. See Jordan 191.)

86. May 27

The *Convention of Cintra* is published in London. (*Courier*; Wells *CC* 59. See Moorman II, 140n.)[39]

Probably this night the Ws receive a letter from DeQ [Jordan 171–76]. (*MY* I, 349.)

87. Probably May 28

W writes to Daniel Stuart: *CC* lying at printer's ten days; the fault is really DeQ's for not making arrangements with Stuart with sufficient care. STC and *The Friend*. W requests Stuart to examine *CC* if it is not published. Errata. (*MY* I, 349–51.)[40]

[37] W's remarks about DeQ generally appear to be a late reply to comments by Stuart in his letter to STC of 26 Apr (*Friend* R II, 490).

[38] LdL perhaps received *CC* on 3 June (see 1809:83n). He reported his dissatisfaction with the work (based on a reading of a dozen pages) to Farington on 6 June (Farington V, 179; see also 1808:111). The same diarist also records the enthusiasm of Lady B on 7 June (V, 182–83; see also V, 190) and the later negative response of John Taylor (V, 207). CL records favorable reaction from "all who have seen it" on 7 June (*LL* II, 74; see *MY* I, 358).

[39] Further advertisements appeared in the *Courier* on 29 May and 1 June.

[40] The postmark of 31 May and the considerations noted *MY* I, 349n practically eliminate the possibility of a date other than 28 May for the letter. The letter to Poole

W writes to Thomas Poole: DeQ's mishandling of the printing of *CC*. It is impossible that STC will carry on *The Friend*; so publication should not begin. STC neither will nor can execute anything of important benefit either to himself, his family, or mankind. Urges Poole to visit and assist in making provision for STC's children and STC himself. (*MY* I, 351–53.)

88. June 1

The first issue of *The Friend* is published.

89. Probably c but not before June 2; between this time and June 4

Probably c but not before 2 June W receives a parcel containing ten copies of *CC*. Between receipt of the parcel and 4 June W sends off seven presentation copies, after which he discovers that in two of the remaining three, the "what greater punishment" passage [see 1809:74; 1809:76; 1809:77] stands uncancelled. (Jordan 181; *MY* I, 353–54.)[41]

90. Probably June 4, and June 4

On 4 June W writes to Daniel Stuart: Discovery of copies of *CC* without cancel leaf correcting the "what greater punishment" passage. W asks aid in remedying matters [see 1809:89]. Advice about second edition if one is called for. (*MY* I, 353–54.)

Probably on 4 June W writes to DeQ about his discovery of copies of *CC* with the "what greater punishment" passage not cancelled. (*MY* I, 354.)

91. June 10

W writes to John Brown: The following are to be added to *Friend* subscriber list: W. H. Pyne, Mr. Wells, Timothy Holmes, John Losh. A package of stamped paper has been forwarded from Kendal by Mr.

---

[41] DeQ probably received the ten copies for W on 27 May, and certainly sent them off that day; but the parcel probably did not leave London till 30 May (Jordan 181, 190–91).

speaks of the length of delay in publication of *CC* in terms just the same as those of the letter to Stuart, and is most reasonably assigned to the same date.

Cookson last Saturday se'enight. It was already somewhat damaged, on arrival at Kendal, by careless packing. (MS, YUL.)

92. June 13 (–June 22, –1810 probably c May 2 or May 3)

STC arrives at AB at 10 AM. (He resides there until probably c 2 or 3 May 1810.) He probably brings with him a poem on birds by Thomas Wilkinson, with whom he has been staying, which he shows to the Ws. (*MY* I, 355, 362; *STCL* III, 211; Mary Carr, *Thomas Wilkinson*, London, 1905, 75–77.)

Mrs. Thomas Cookson and her son are brought by Mr. Cookson to spend a week at AB. (They depart 22 June.) (*MY* I, 357, 360. See 1809:93; 1809:97.)[42]

93. Probably June 14

DW writes to CCl: STC and *The Friend*; their regret for certain remarks in the first two issues; *CC*; the Ls; family news; Stuart will probably help with supply of stamped paper for *The Friend*. (*MY* I, 355–58.)

W writes to Daniel Stuart: *CC*, and instructions about second edition; STC and *Friend*—W's hopes higher than formerly; STC probably needs money; STC opposed to reform; W's continuing concern about reactionary leaning visible in the *Courier*. (*MY* I, 358–59.)

94. Probably between mid-June and early Nov

W composes a General Introduction for Joseph Wilkinson's *Select Views*. (Appendix VI.)[43]

[42] DW writes in a letter dated "Wednesday, 15th June" that STC arrived at "ten o'clock yesterday morning." STC states in a letter dated "13 June, 1809" that he arrived "yestermorning" (*STCL* III, 211). DW's "Wednesday" is probably accurate, although the date was 14 June; so STC's dating is probably another mistake. Despite DW's statements on 22 June that STC has been there "nearly a fortnight" and that Mrs. Cookson has been "spending a week" there, it seems certain that these visitors arrived on the same day.

[43] The subject matter of the Introduction makes it likely that it was in this period that W, if he ever did so at all, refused DeQ's offer of an account of the origin and character of the language of the Lake District for G. See A. H. Japp, "Early Intercourse of the Wordsworths and DeQuincey," *Century Magazine* XLI (1891), 862. (See also 1809:124.)

95. Probably June 19

The Ws make an excursion to Coniston in a cart; eat dinner in a field near the lake. (*MY* I, 359–60.)

96. Perhaps c but not before 19 June

W composes "Brave Schill! by Death Delivered, Take Thy Flight." (1809:23n.)

97. Probably June 22–June 29; probably between June 22 and Nov 16, Dec 21

Probably on 22 June W sets off with John Wilson and a group of his friends for a fishing party among the lakes and tarns. Among the party, which possibly numbers thirty-three (including as many as ten or as few as three servants) are the two Messrs. Astley [see *MY* I, 376], Humphries, and Alexander Blair. W probably returns home by 29 June, but possibly not until that day.

The party probably starts off from Grasmere and reaches Wastwater via Eskdale and Burnmoor Tarn by Sunday 25 June; camps at Wastwater. (*MY* I, 360. Wilson, *The Angler's Tent* and Advertisement [see esp. Wilson's *Isle of Palms*, Edinburgh, 1812, 200]; Mrs. Gordon I, 129–30.)[44]

Probably on 22 June DW writes to DeQ: Mrs. Cookson; request for DeQ to write; W's excursion with Wilson; DC to be ready soon; Johnny; STC; CC. (*MY* I, 360–62.)

Probably between 22 June and 16 Nov, certainly by 16 Nov, possibly between 22 and 29 June, W composes "Alas! What Boots the Long Laborious Quest?"

Possibly between 22 June and 21 Dec, certainly by 21 Dec, possibly between 22 and 29 June, W composes:

"And Is It among Rude Untutored Vales"

Feelings of the Tyrolese ("The Land We from Our Fathers Had in Trust")

---

[44] Mrs. Gordon states that the party included DeQ, but it cannot have done so (see Jordan 237). The poem, which indicates that only three servants came, implies also that the party reached Wastwater seven days after it started—impossible if the progress of the excursion conformed at all to DW's expectations.

"O'er the Wide Earth, on Mountain and on Plain"
(Mrs. Gordon I, 130–31; *The Friend* 16 Nov, 21 Dec 1809.)[45]

98. Probably late June (–perhaps c early or mid-Aug, after Aug 1)

George H arrives at AB for a visit. (He departs perhaps c early or mid-Aug, after 1 Aug.) (*MY* I, 362, 364.)

99. Perhaps c but not before June 28

A letter arrived for STC from Stuart. STC is unwell, and parts of the letter are omitted when it is read to him out of fear of agitating him. Perhaps about this time W, MW, DW mistakenly indicate to him that Stuart has expressed an intention to advance *The Friend* as far as the twentieth issue. (*STCL* III, 228, 238. See *Friend* R I, l–li.)

100. Perhaps June 29 (–perhaps c early or mid-Aug); possibly c June 29 or shortly after

Perhaps on 29 June the Ws boat on Windermere; meet Dora, the Cooksons, Miss Weir, and her niece at Bowness. At least Miss Weir and her niece accompany Dora and the Ws back to AB for a visit. (They depart perhaps c early or mid-Aug.) W possibly rejoins his family today after his excursion with Wilson [see 1809:97] if he has not done so already. Possibly c 29 June or shortly after, or possibly between 8 and 13 Sept, W assists Wilson in writing the four lines of Wilson's *The Angler's Tent* commencing "The placid lake that rested far below" (*Isle of Palms*, 1812, 187), esp. in the second of the lines, "Softly embo-

---

[45] Blair wrote ambiguously, of this time, or of the party, that W "[was] making, and reading to us as he made them, the 'Sonnets to the Tyrolese,' first given in 'The Friend.'" Of the seven sonnets presented in *The Friend* 26 Oct, 16 Nov, and 21 Dec as a set "on the same subject"—certainly that of the liberty of the Tyrol—*The Final Submission of the Tyrolese* was written perhaps after 24 Oct; and *Hofer* and "Advance—Come Forth" were probably composed on 10 Oct (1809:123). Blair's report is not sufficiently exact to encourage speculation about the others. All the poems cited may have been composed on the expedition, but the evidence is weak. "And Is It among Rude Untutored Vales" might refer to Peninsular affairs as well as, or rather than, Tyrolese.

soming another sky." (*MY* I, 360, 364; Mrs. Gordon I, 130. See 1809:18, 1809:97.)[46]

101. Perhaps c late June or early July

W possibly receives about £25 from Montagu. (Letter, Montagu to STC, 26 June 1809, DCP.)[47]

102. Probably between very late June and early Aug

AB receives numerous visitors, including perhaps Richard Sharp, possibly with RS; perhaps also with RS, Charles Danvers, his cousin Lewis, and David Jardine. If the Danvers group comes with RS, the visit probably takes place between 2 and 9 July. RS and Danvers themselves probably visit between 18 and 22 July, probably with James Rickards. (Warter II, 147, 152–53; Curry I, 510; fragmentary MS Journal of Lake Tour, Sharpe Papers, University College, London.)

TCl, his son Tom, and Samuel Tilbrooke visit AB for several days. The visit possibly extends into early Aug. (*MY* I, 360, 368–69.)

Probably during this period W composes little. (*MY* I, 364.)[48]

[46] The boating on Windermere and meeting at Bowness as described were the plan as of 22 June (*MY* I, 360). On 14 June Mrs. Cookson was to return from AB to Kendal in a week to meet Dora, Miss Weir, and Miss Weir's niece. After a week in Kendal Dora was to come home (*MY* I, 357). See 1809:17.

Mrs. Gordon's report about *The Angler's Tent* is, as published, confused. She records: "[Wilson's poem was written] soon after [the angling expedition] at Elleray, where Wordsworth was then living. One morning a great discussion took place between the poets about a verse Wilson had some difficulty in arranging. At last, after much trying and questioning, it was made out between them [*here follow the four lines as described*]. The troublesome line was—

'Softly embosoming another sky.'"

W could not be said to have "lived" at Elleray before 8 Nov 1810, but he visited there between 8 and 12 Sept 1809.

[47] Montagu wrote to STC on 26 June: "It is my intention to write to Wordsworth in the course of this week.—I am to send him about £25—Can he spare it for you?— & I will pay it to Foudinier [*sic*], & you may settle with W. Wordsworth."

[48] On Thursday 6 July RS writes to Thomas S that Danvers and his companions arrived on "Monday night" (Warter II, 147), and the companions were expected to depart the following Monday, when Miss Betham would be expected; and about the same time, TCl was to visit for a day and a half. On 29 July he writes to Rickman,

103. July 7

W writes to Thomas Wilkinson: Having heard that the overseer of husbandry proceedings at Lowther is leaving his place, W writes on behalf of George H as replacement. (*MY* I, 362.)

"I have been walking over the mountains with Danvers (who has now left me) . . ." (HEH). And on 30 July (a Sunday) he writes that Danvers left him on Monday last (Warter II, 152). Sharp was at Keswick on 6 July (CCS III, 240; Warter III, 148).

DW remarks on 1 Aug that "Mr. Clarkson, and his Son, and a Friend of his, have spent several days with us"—phrasing that leaves uncertain whether they have yet departed. Recent company is said also to have included "Southey and some friends of his" (*MY* I, 364).

A fragmentary journal among the Sharpe Papers, University College, London, records its not securely identified author as having met and dined with TCl at GH on successive days. "Miss Beetham" was then an expected visitor. The journal reports that RS determined to accompany its author and Danvers "in our expedition to Ulswater & the Lakes adjoining" fixed for that "Thursday," a trip which was to take them via Helvellyn to Grasmere, thence back to GH via Langdale and Borrowdale. An expedition much of this sort did take place (see Warter II, 153). The "Thursday" planned upon must have been 13 or 20 July, as TCl was yet to come on 6 July, and Danvers departed on 24 July. RS, however, wrote to John May on 15 July from Keswick, "I am suffering under my summer catarrh, which almost incapacitates me from doing anything" (MS, UTL; see Charles Ramos, "Letters of Robert Southey to John May, 1797–1838," Diss. University of Texas, 1965); he is unlikely to have departed on his expedition before that day, whatever the original plan.

RS's own account of the outing (Warter II, 152–53) indicates that it lasted three days, and the group must have arrived back at GH by 23 July. They probably visited Grasmere on the next-to-last day of the excursion (although the last day is a remote possibility if the travellers had transportation other than their legs for part of the journey). The journal noticed above breaks off before the commencement of the trip. The expedition may have begun as late as 20 July, but cannot have begun later, nor can the party have arrived at Grasmere before 18 July. Danvers became ill at Patterdale, where the party drank tea in Charles Luff's garden on the first day, probably, of the outing. (Warter II, 152–53.) Luff wrote to Josiah Wedgwood from Patterdale on 26 July with a prolonged and pessimistic report of STC's health and work (for example, "[H]e is positively killing himself by the *worst possible means*"), urging Wedgwood to write to STC: "[I]t would be a great satisfaction I know to Wordsworth, and others." The tone of Luff's comments suggests that he had received his news about STC quite lately.

During Danvers' illness at Patterdale RS and one of the party, James Rickards, walked to Angle Tarn and Haweswater (Warter II, 152–53); and Rickards was still in Danvers' company when he reached Liverpool on 26 July (Liverpool Journal of

104. Perhaps July 15–perhaps July 27; July 17; July 22

DW travels to Kendal, where she visits, probably at the Thomas Cooksons', till perhaps 27 July, when she returns to DC. She makes purchases there for DC; looks at the last reviews at the Book Club, seeking reviews of *CC*. (*MY* I, 362–64.)

On 17 July she draws on RW for £50 in W's name, by a bill in favor of John Simpson, due at two months. (*MY* I, 363; RW accounts, DCP.)[49]

On 22 July DW writes to RW from Kendal: Her draft on RW; plans for another [see 1809:109]. Please pay Twining £13/14/– owed for tea. (*MY* I, 362–63.)

105. Aug 1

DW writes to DeQ: DC almost ready; visitors [see esp. 1809:102]; STC busy. The reviews. W depressed by Austrian defeat [at Wagram]. The children. The Crumps will probably occupy DC for a week or ten days. Plans for the expedition to Wales and Ireland [see 1809:76]. (*MY* I, 363–66.)

---

[49] Despite DW's statement that the bill became due in two months, RW accounts record payment under 19 Aug.

Rebecca Reid, 1809, Sharpe Papers, University of London). Rickards (a confirmed example of whose autograph I have failed to discover) is perhaps the diarist. (I am much indebted to Mrs. J. Percival for assistance and advice concerning the Sharpe Papers.) RS tells his brother Thomas to look for further particulars of the "noble expedition" in "Don Manuel's next volumes." Further volumes of the *Letters from England* of "Don Manuel Alvarez" (pub. 1807) were not forthcoming, however; and no records of the outing appear among the fragments intended for the additional volumes published in RS's *Commonplace Book. Fourth Series*, ed. J. W. Warter (London, 1851), 352–426.

It was perhaps during this period, possibly when RS called at Grasmere in late July, that the Ws told RS that they would be glad to show Miss Betham the country around Grasmere. No meeting took place, however. SFC wrote to Miss Betham on 19 Dec (HEH): "[I]t seems you fully expected to pass some days there, [and] when I asked why they had not sent you an invitation, they said they had expressly told Southey they hoped they should see you, and they would show you the country around Grasmere."

106. Perhaps c early or mid-Aug

George H, Miss Weir and her niece depart AB. (*MY* I, 364. See 1809:100.)[50]

107. Perhaps second week of Aug–early Dec

Perhaps in the second week of Aug workmen come to AB to improve the chimneys and make other alterations. CCl's Uncle and Aunt Joseph and Mrs. Hardcastle and Miss Hardcastle visit AB. The length of their visit is uncertain. STC and Hardcastle discuss the fulfillment of the prophecies. The chimney workmen are about the house until early Dec. (*MY* I, 365, 367, 369, 380.)[51]

108. Probably c mid-Aug

SH visits Eusemere and Penrith. She calls at Sockbridge, but RW is in the fields and she does not see him. (*MY* I, 366, 370.)

109. Aug 17

DW draws on RW for £20 in W's name, in a bill in favor of John Robinson, due at one month. (*MY* I, 367; RW accounts, DCP.)[52]

110. Aug 20

DW writes to RW: SH's visit to Sockbridge [see 1809:108]; death of Mr. Strickland; recent financial transactions; payment of Twining [see 1809:104]; smoking chimneys at AB; illness among the children. (*MY* I, 366–67.)

[50] Evidence for the time of the departure appears entirely negative. All had been at DC "more than a month" on 1 Aug, and nothing more is heard of them in the correspondence. It is possible that SH's absence probably c mid-Aug, when she visited Penrith, may mark the time of the return of her friend Miss Weir to Appleby; and her brother George might have been one of the party.

[51] In her letter to DeQ of 1 Aug DW states that a workman is coming from Liverpool to try his skill upon the chimneys "next week" (*MY* I, 365). On 27 Aug she reports the Hardcastles' arrival on a day when the house was much confused, "the workmen having begun their operations" (*MY* I, 369). She remarks on the same day, "It was very unlucky that the Luffs came to Grasmere on the very day when the party went to Patterdale": her reference appears to be to the Hardcastle party. The Luffs probably stayed a week at Mr. King's, departing not before 27 Aug.

[52] RW's accounts record payment of the bill under 20 Sept.

111. Probably Aug 27

DW writes to CCl: Work on the chimneys and other alterations of the house. TCl, Tom, Tilbrooke [see 1809:102]. Malkin, and his *Father's Memoir*; Hardcastle [see 1809:107]; STC. Much admiration, few purchases, of *CC*. The children. (*MY* I, 367–71.)

112. Probably c Sept 1

A review of *CC* [by James Montgomery] appears in *The Eclectic Review* (V, Aug 1809). (See Ward; Hayden.)

113. Probably Sept 8–probably Sept 13

Probably on 8 Sept MW, SH, Johnny go to Elleray for a visit. DW probably accompanies them as far as Ambleside. W is part of the company some or all of the time. He possibly now assists Wilson in composing *The Angler's Tent* [see 1809:100]. He is probably present on 12 Sept, by which time he has urged Wilson to write to DeQ about the possibility of making a trip to Spain. MW, SH, Johnny, possibly W probably return to AB on 13 Sept. (*MY* I, 371–72, 378; 1809:114.)

114. Probably Sept 12

MW writes to DeQ from Elleray, adding her letter to one from Wilson to DeQ, 12 Sept: Thanks for letter [quoted Jordan 243–48]. W well; he will not go to Wales [see 1809:76; 1809:105]. STC very busy. *Friend* [esp. no. 4, of 7 Sept]. Family news. (*MY* I, 371–72; Japp 122.)

115. Sept 14

RW's accounts charge W £7/10/6, payment of premium on £300 policy on Montagu's life, under this date. (RW accounts, DCP.)

116. Probably late this year, and during the winter

Alexander Blair probably visits and passes the night at AB on a number of unrecorded occasions. (*SHL* 23.)

117. Probably late this year or early 1810, by c late Feb; possibly at this time

W composes "Torquato Tasso Rests within This Tomb," translation of Chiabrera's Italian epitaph on Tasso. (See 1809:118–1809:121.)

Possibly at this time W composes some portion of "Weep Not, Belovèd Friends! Nor Let the Air" and "True It Is That Ambrosio Salinero," translations from the Italian of Chiabrera. (1809:118–1809:121.)[53]

118. Probably late this year or early 1810, certainly by Feb 28

W composes "O Lelius, Beauteous Flower of Gentleness," early version of "O Flower of All that Springs from Gentle Blood," translation from the Italian of Chiabrera. (*Epitaphs and Elegiac Pieces* IF note; 1809:136; *PW* IV, 499.)

119. Probably late this year or early 1810, certainly by Feb 22

W composes "Perhaps Some Needful Service of the State" and "O Thou Who Movest Onward with a Mind," translations from the Italian of Chiabrera. (1810:13; *Epitaphs and Elegiac Pieces* IF note.)

120. Probably late this year, by Dec 22

W composes "There Never Breathed a Man Who, When His Life Was Done" and "Destined to War from Very Infancy," translations from the Italian of Chiabrera. (*Friend* R II, 383–86; *Epitaphs and Elegiac Pieces* IF note.)

121. Probably late this year, by Dec 11

W composes "Not without Heavy Grief of Heart" and "Pause, Courteous Spirit!—Balbi Supplicates," translations from the Italian of Chiabrera. (*Friend* R II, 383–86; *Epitaphs and Elegiac Pieces* IF note; 1809:129n; 1809:139.)

[53] The Tasso epitaph, which is copied in Essays upon Epitaphs (c), was probably composed about the same time as the bulk of W's other translations from the Italian of Chiabrera (see immediately below). It is reasonable to suppose that some work on the other epitaphs cited may have gone on at this time, although they were not published until 1837. "O Lelius" (1809:118) was also not published until 1837, and then only in revised form. The IF note to *Epitaphs and Elegiac Pieces* states that the epitaphs from Chiabrera "were chiefly translated when Mr. Coleridge was writing his 'Friend.'"

122. Probably c Oct 1

A review of *CC* appears in *The British Critic* (XXIV, Sept 1809). (See Ward; Hayden.)

123. Oct 10

Probably on 10 Oct W composes:
"Advance—Come Forth from Thy Tyrolean Ground"
Hofer
(*STCL* III, 243; MS, Library of the University of California, Davis. See 1809:97n; 1809:126.)[54]

124. Probably c Oct 20 and perhaps c early Nov–c Nov 20

Probably c 20 Oct DeQ returns to Grasmere; moves into DC; dislikes not having a housekeeper, and perhaps c early Nov moves to AB. He visits at AB probably till c 20 Nov. (*MY* I, 374, 376; Jordan 204, 255–56.)[55]

125. Probably between Oct 24 and Dec 21

W composes *On the Final Submission of the Tyrolese*. (Content; *The Friend*, 21 Dec.)[56]

126. Oct 26

Hofer and "Advance—Come Forth from Thy Tyrolean Ground" are published without titles under the heading "SONNETS" in *The Friend*, each signed "W.W." *Prel* X.690–728 (*The French Revolution*) is published also, signed "WORDSWORTH."

[54] STC states in a postscript to his letter to Sharp of 10 Oct, "I have not room or I would transcribe a sonnet, he has composed this morning—but I will inclose it under cover." The address wrapper, at the Library of the University of California, Davis, contains copies of both these poems in STC's autograph, headed by a note, "I transcribe two Sonnets both the work of this morning; but it is the second, which I [admire *underlined twice*]."

[55] DeQ expected to set off for Grasmere from Bristol via Birmingham on the night of 18 Oct, perhaps reaching his destination before a letter he had sent to Johnny that day. DW says on 18 Nov that DeQ has "lately" been "wholly with us."

[56] News of the treaty of Schönbrunn, signed 14 Oct, was published in the *Times* on 21 Oct.

127. Probably c late Oct–mid-Nov

Members of the AB household spend several evenings at DC, probably in part to escape smoke at AB. (*MY* I, 376.)

128. Probably c early Nov; probably by Nov 17; probably between c early Nov and 1810 May 10

Probably c early Nov W completes his General Introduction for G 1810. SH copies it probably by 17 Nov. (*MY* I, 372; Appendix VI. See 1809:131.)

The Introduction is probably published between c early Nov and 10 May 1810, esp. probably c early 1810. (*MY* I, 404.)

129. Probably between early Nov and Dec 11

W writes a basic version of the Reply to Mathetes. (*Friend* R II, 384–86. See 1809:139.)[57]

[57] Wilson and Blair wrote the Letter from Mathetes when in company with DeQ; it was probably completed, thus, after c 20 Oct (see 1809:124; Mrs. Gordon I, 131). When STC received the Letter, W was "at leisure, and disposed at that time to write something for the Friend" (*MY* I, 379). He was probably still occupied with G, however, into early Nov.

The portion of MS headed "X," Forster MS 112, fols. 88–89 (see *Friend* R II, 385) is a letter of corrections for the later portions of the Reply with directions indicating that these were for the essay marked "No. 18." The MS concerned is that commencing in Forster MS 112, fol. 81, headed "[The Friend *underlined twice*] No. 18." To the left of the heading is a large "B." No indication is given in the corrections marked "X" that a decision had yet been reached to postpone publication of the second part of the Reply. The first part appeared in *The Friend* No. 17, published 14 Dec. "X" contains also transcripts of "Not without Heavy Grief of Heart" and "Pause, Courteous Spirit." These leaves conclude with a note from SH quoted *Friend* R II, 386, in which SH states that she (or the AB circle) has concluded from the nonarrival of the *Friend* that the printer has not received [MSS] forwarded by [Thomas] Cookson "a fortnight this day . . . from Kendal—*Monday Dec.* 11." While her phrasing itself leaves unclear whether she is writing on 25 Dec or 11 Dec, the decision to print the second part of the Reply in an issue after No. 18 must have been reached by c 18 Dec, for No. 18 was published on 21 Dec: thus, 11 Dec is probably the date of SH's note, and the still-expected *Friend* probably that of 7 Dec, No. 16, containing *Satyrane's Letters* II.

Fols. 81–87 all appear to have been written basically about the same time, as part of an entire essay "sent off in a great hurry." Fol. 8, however, which is a letter to the printer, commences:

130. Nov 16

Exc I.626–34 are published in *The Friend* with attribution "WORDSWORTH. MSS."

"Alas! What Boots the Long Laborious Quest" is published in *The Friend* under the title *Suggested by the Efforts of the Tyrolese, Contrasted with the Present State of Germany*, signed "W.W."

> Mr Brown,   (Y)
>   Sir,
>   The Sheet marked B has been
> received, and the Manuscript is in the
> following manner to be resumed. [The
> Friend *underlined twice*] No 20[.]

Corrections used in No. 20 follow. The "Sheet marked B" is clearly that beginning with Forster MS 112, fol. 81, and reference is made below in fol. 8 to the content of this same MS as being in "the old MSS." Fol. 8 and corrections in fols. 81–87 were written in conjunction: for example, the cancellation described *Friend* R II, 385 is preceded by the inserted remark, "(Here let Mr Brown refer to this days Letter Marked (Y)." Plainly the *Friend* MS intended originally to be No. 18 was returned to W. W's corrections include also a reference to "X," mentioned above, as an "old Letter." Hence the original MS, including base readings of Forster MS 112, fols. 81–87 (see [W. J. B. Owen,] "Manuscript Variants of Wordsworth's Poems," *N&Q* N.S. V, 1958, 308–10) probably went off shortly before 11 Dec; and "X," with its translations from Chiabrera, was finished 11 Dec. The later portions of the MS were received back sometime after 11 Dec. The date by which corrections for the second part, including "(Y)" were sent off, remains uncertain, but was probably c but not before 27 Dec. STC on 24 Dec expected the copy for *Friend* No. 20 to go off on 26 Dec (*STCL* III, 267).

DW remarks in a letter of 28 Dec that the continuation of the Reply would appear in *The Friend* No. 19 (for 28 Dec)—a supposition one might imagine based on knowledge that the MS had gone off some days earlier; but DW learned before she concluded her letter that the essay would be concluded in No. 20. "(Y)" indicates an assumption that the continuation was to appear in No. 20. "(Y)" is partly in the autograph of W and partly in that of STC (cf *Friend* R II, 379); so W either had not gone to Kendal (see 1809:140), or had returned by the time "(Y)" was written. He had certainly gone there by 16 Dec; so that the decision to postpone publication of the conclusion of the Reply specifically to issue No. 20 would have had to be made, the MS returned, and the corrections including "(Y)" made between 11 Dec and 16 Dec; or else at least the last of these steps would probably have had to wait till W's return to AB on 27 Dec.

131. Perhaps Nov 17–Nov 21 or Nov 28 (–perhaps c Dec 1)

Perhaps 17–21 or 28 Nov DW writes to CCl: SH has been transcribing *Friend* and Introduction of G. CCl; SC and SFC; the family.
MY I, 372–75.)[58]

Perhaps on 17 Nov SFC, Mrs. Lloyd call at AB with SC, whom
they probably leave there. (SC departs perhaps c 1 Dec.) (*MY* I, 373.
See 1809:133n.)

132. Nov 19

DW writes to JPM: Fears that the family will have to leave Grasmere from want of a place to live; DeQ and his books; the children;
JPM's family. (*MY* I, 375–78.)

133. Perhaps Nov 20 (–perhaps c Dec 1)

SFC arrives at AB for a visit. (She departs perhaps c 1 Dec.) (*MY*
I, 373; letter, SFC to Matilda Betham, 19 Dec 1809, HEH. See 1809:
131.)[59]

134. Probably c Nov 20

DeQ resumes residence at DC. (*MY* I, 374, 376.)

135. Probably between c Dec and 1814 c late May

W composes the bulk of *Exc* III–IX. All *Exc* MSS from DC MS 47
not accounted for elsewhere probably date from this period. For
detailed information see esp. GCL and Appendix VI. "The Shepherd
of Bield Crag" [see *PW* V, 461–62] and other portions of Books V–VII
are possibly basically composed by 11 May 1810. (See Appendix VI.)

[58] The reasoning of *MY* I, 375n concerning the date of the letter is cogent. The
letter was possibly actually concluded, however, on 28 Nov, as it states, although
only the postscript may have been written after 21 Nov.

[59] DW writes perhaps on Friday 17 Nov that SFC is to come on Monday and spend
three or four days before taking SC to Keswick. SFC writes to Miss Betham on 19
Dec, however, that SC came home with her after staying a fortnight at AB.

136. Probably between c Dec and 1810 Feb 22, Feb 28

W composes three "Essays upon Epitaphs," at least one—the first published, of which STC probably writes the first paragraph—by 22 Feb 1810, and the others by 28 Feb. The essay commencing "I vindicate the rights" contains a version of *Exc* VII.395–481. (See *Mem* I, 434; Grosart II, 25–75, esp. 55; 1810:13; W. J. B. Owen, "The Text of Wordsworth's Essay upon Epitaphs," *N&Q* CCI, 1956, 214–15.)[60]

137. Perhaps c Dec 1

SFC, SC depart AB. (1809:133n.)

138. Dec 1

A review of *CC* by HCR appears in *The London Review* (II, Nov 1809). (*Times*; *MY* I, 374–75. See Ward; Hayden.)

139. Probably Dec 11; between Dec 11 and c late Dec

Probably on 11 Dec corrections for the second installment of the Reply to Mathetes, and copies of "Not without Heavy Grief of Heart" and "Pause, Courteous Spirit!" go off to the printer with a note by SH. Between 11 Dec and c late Dec the MS for this installment is returned, and W makes further corrections. (1809:129n. See *Friend* R II, 383–86.)

---

[60] The first essay to be published appeared in *The Friend* 22 Feb 1810. DW remarked on 28 Feb that W had "written two more Essays on the same subject, which will appear when there is need." The surviving Essay MSS of the second and third essays, in the order of Grosart's publication, are in the autograph of SH. They are headed respectively "The Friend No 1" and "[The Friend *underlined twice*] No. 2." Both have at some time been folded to large octavo-sized packets and labelled on the outside respectively "1 Essay on Epitaphs" and "2." The numbers possibly represent only prospective order of publication following an already printed essay (STC refers to the "two finishing Essays on Epitaphs" 24 Apr 1812—*STCL* III, 392); but they may cast some doubt on the definitiveness of the order in which they were printed by Grosart—who, however, conservatively headed them only (*a*), (*b*), and (*c*)—as an expression of W's own intentions. While no evidence precludes some composition earlier than c Dec 1809, contribution to *The Friend* was probably a chief object in W's writing, and nothing is known of earlier work. In the essay published second by Grosart, W remarks that the Chiabrera epitaphs "occasioned this dissertation."

140. Perhaps c Dec 14–Dec 27; probably Dec 16

Perhaps c 14 Dec workmen who have been making alterations at AB depart. DW and SH reorder the house and arrange books.

W probably accompanies MW to Kendal or joins her there by 16 Dec. Both come to Elleray with the Cooksons (probably all together) by 25 Dec. Probably either arriving or departing 16 Dec, John M visits AB for a day; helps DW, SH arrange books. DW, SH and the children go to Elleray on Christmas Day and join W, MW, the Cooksons, and John Wilson there. They are perhaps accompanied to and from Elleray by DeQ, who is a member of the Christmas party, as is Alexander Blair. The Ws stay at Wilson's cottage; Wilson, Blair, DeQ sleep at Bowness.

The W family returns to AB on 27 Dec. (*MY* I, 378–80; *SHL* 22–23; JFW Papers.)[61]

141. Dec 14 (–1810 Jan 4)

The beginning of W's Reply to Mathetes, through "direct as that of the Roman road with which we began the comparison," is published, unsigned, in *The Friend*. (The remainder is published 4 Jan 1810.) (1809:129n.)

142. Dec 21

Thought of a Briton on the Subjugation of Switzerland (previously

[61] SFC remarks on 19 Dec to Miss Betham that when she departed from Grasmere, evidently c 1 Dec, "Mrs Wordsworth was going to Kendal for a month" (MS, HEH). One cannot, of course, be certain that a plan for her to return on 27 Dec had already been set, but she probably intended to rejoin the family at Christmas.

DW writes on 28 Dec that she has been much engaged with the housekeeping chores "during the last fortnight." SH makes clear that "John" came while W was with MW at Kendal. That the "John" was John M (cf *SHL* 23, 453) is indicated from an inscription in a copy of Humphry Davy's *Syllabus of a Lecture* inscribed originally from Davy to STC in "1802" (JFW Papers):

S. T. Coleridge
to
Mr J. Monkhouse
Allan Bank, Grasmere
16 December, 1809

On the party at Elleray see esp. *MY* I, 379; *SHL* 22.

published in *P2V*); *Feelings of the Tyrolese* ("The Land We from Our Fathers Had in Trust"); "And Is It among Rude Untutor'd Vales"; "O'er the Wide Earth, on Mountain and on Plain"; *On the Final Submission of the Tyrolese* ("It Was a *Moral* End for Which They Fought," here titled *On the Report of the Submission of the Tyrolese*) are published in *The Friend*, the last signed "W.W."

143. Dec 22

STC probably this day sends off DW's copy of "There Never Breathed a Man Who, When His Life Was Done" and "Destined to War from Very Infancy" for *The Friend*. (MS, V&A; *STCL* III, 264. Cf *Friend* R II, 383.)

144. Perhaps Dec 27, or between Dec 27 and 1810 Jan 1; Dec 27

Perhaps on 27 Dec, otherwise between that day and 1 Jan 1810, the group composing the Christmas party at Elleray, possibly excepting the Cooksons, dines [at the Lloyds'] at Brathay. (*SHL* 22–23.)[62]
On 27 Dec the W family returns to AB. (1809:140.)

145. Probably c but not before Dec 27

W after returning to AB [see 1809:140] completes and sends off final corrections for the second installment of the Reply to Mathetes. (1809:129n.)

146. Dec 28

"There Never Breathed a Man Who, When His Life Was Done," "Destined to War from Very Infancy," and *The Influence of Natural Objects* (*Prel* I.428–89, here titled *Growth of Genius from the Influences of Natural Objects, on the Imagination in Boyhood, and Early Youth*) are published, unsigned, in *The Friend*.
DW writes to Lady B: John Wilson; letter from Mathetes, and W's reply; family news; STC and *The Friend*; *WD*; narrative of an English hermit, sent by Lady B; AB; STC's *Courier* articles on Spain. (*EY* 378–81.)

[62] The "99" of the last line of *SHL* 22 is a typographical slip mis-transcribing a dash.

1810

[On writings of W possibly of this year see below and GCL 42, 100, 101, 123, 132, 146, 148, 167–69, 171, 181, 182, 184, 188, 191, 193–95.]

1. Probably c 1810

Montagu probably proposes repayment of the £300 which he owes W. Because of his straitened income W expresses a preference for continuance of the 10 percent annuity arrangement between them. (*HCRBW* I, 210–11.)[1]

2. Perhaps this year

W composes:
1810 ("O'erweening Statesmen Have Full Long Relied")
Indignation of a High-minded Spaniard. 1810
"In Due Observance of an Ancient Rite"
Feelings of a Noble Biscayan . . . 1810
The Oak of Guernica . . . 1810
(See 1809:23n.)

3. Jan 1, 2–Jan 3, 4ff

On 1 Jan the Ws probably dine at DC with DeQ at 4, along with the Lloyds, perhaps John Wilson and Alexander Blair, and possibly the Cooksons of Kendal. (*SHL* 22–23; letter, DeQ to Lloyd, 31 Dec 1809, JFW Papers.)

On 1 and 2 Jan DW writes to JPM: (1 Jan:) Description of Ormathwaite estate: W will make further inquiries. Brathay Hall. (2 Jan:) Further information about Brathay Hall. (*MY* I, 381–83.)

On 2 Jan the W family, with SH, the Lloyds, probably Wilson and Blair, attend a fireworks exhibition given by DeQ at DC. DW finishes her letter to JPM at DC. Wilson and Blair pass the night at AB. Wilson departs next day. Blair probably visits at AB till 4 Jan or after. (*SHL* 22–23; *MY* I, 382–83.)

---

1 Available evidence does not fix the time of Montagu's offer. The present suggestion is made on the basis of W's apparent confidence in Montagu's financial prospects as expressed 27 Mar 1811 (*MY* I, 473).

4. Jan 3

SH writes to MM: Recent family activities, and the children; the Hs. (*SHL* 22–24.)

5. Jan 4

W writes to John Miller: Comments on a sonnet addressed to W and a poem called *The Vision of the Brothers* by a friend of Miller's, sent to him by Miller. W claims indifference to most praise or blame of his work. (*MY* I, 383–84.)[2]

The conclusion of W's Reply to Mathetes, from "The remarks, which were called forth" [see 1809:141], is published in *The Friend*, signed "M.M." with "Not without Heavy Grief of Heart" and "Pause, Courteous Spirit!—Balbi Supplicates," unsigned.

6. Jan 9

DW writes to RW: Disappointment at not having seen RW when he was in the North. RW should pay Twining's bill of £31/16 for tea sent to Ws and Cooksons last July or Aug [see 1809:104; 1809:110]. Urgent request for a statement of accounts between W, DW, and RW; fears that AB household is outrunning income; economies planned. (*MY* I, 385–86.)

7. Probably between Jan 9 and Mar 23

W passes a night at Sockbridge. (*MY* I, 385, 395.)[3]

8. Jan 25

Exc I.500–02 are published in *The Friend*, attributed to "the Poet."

---

[2] For the conclusion of the postscript of this letter see Reed *N&Q*.

[3] DW seems to have thought RW probably in London but possibly still at Sockbridge on 9 Jan; she seems hardly likely to have remarked to RW on 23 Mar that W "slept there [at Sockbridge] one night" since RW put his house in repair unless she is referring to a time when RW was not there himself. RW had been "some weeks" at Sockbridge on 26 Aug 1809 (*MY* I, 371), but not in early 1809; and he apparently remained there through the autumn. So DW would seem on present evidence to be referring either to W's first visit, of c 3–4 Apr 1809, or a visit between her 9 Jan and 23 Mar letters. The second possibility looks more likely.

MW inspects and signs the Green family accounts from April 1808 with Dorothy Watson, Elizabeth King, Sophia Lloyd, and Susannah Knott. (Green family accounts, DCP.)

9. Feb 9

DW writes to RW: Her extreme concern at RW's failure to forward accounts [see 1810:6]. She has this day written an order on RW for £34/16/- favor Messrs. Fourdinier [*sic*] due on demand, to repay a like sum received from STC. (*MY* I, 386.)[4]

10. Probably c Feb 14–perhaps c Mar 14

John M arrives at AB. He has been struck by his horse about a mile from AB. He remains a visitor at AB, probably under the surgeon's care most of the time, until perhaps c 14 Mar. (*MY* I, 390, 395.)

11. Probably Feb 21

DW writes to JPM (only a fragment of the letter is known to survive): Freedom from smoke at AB; primary need to be satisfied by new house is proximity to a grammar school; *Friend*; CW's [*Ecclesiastical Biography*]. (*MY* I, 387–88.)[5]

12. c late Feb, including Feb 28; c early or mid-Mar

Henry Addison visits AB probably for a week including 28 Feb; if not then, c early or mid-Mar for a week.

---

[4] RW's accounts record payment to "Messrs Fournier [*sic*] & Co Stationers" on W's account "for Mr Coleridge." Fourdrinier had supplied paper for *The Friend*. See esp. *STCL* III, 268, 270, 282. Richard Sharp had written to STC on 6 Feb enclosing an account which STC had spoken of repaying (amount not specified) and advising that the repayment "may be either from Mr Ward or Mr Wordsworth as best suits yourself" (DCP).

[5] Almost none of DW's surviving letters to JPM up to 1820 are endorsed with notation of both day and month. *MY* I, 30, 400 imply that where such endorsements have been made they record DW's own date. (In the case of *MY* I, 400, in fact, the endorsement records "13 April" for a letter that DW, although she must have written it on Sunday 15 Apr, dates "Sunday night, 13th Apr.") This letter was endorsed 21 Feb.

John Wilson visits AB for an undetermined length of time in late Feb. (*MY* I, 390, 395; *SHL* 23, 24, 27–28.)[6]

13. Feb 22

Essay upon Epitaphs (*a*) is published this day in *The Friend*, with "Perhaps Some Needful Service of the State" and "O Thou Who Movest Onward with a Mind," unsigned [see 1809:136; 1809:119].

14. Feb 28

DW writes to Lady B: The W children; John M and other visitors [see 1810:10; 1810:12]; STC and *The Friend*; W's Essay upon Epitaphs as printed there; expectations that the two other essays he has written on the same subject will appear there. W's composition on *Recluse* and hopes for completing *WD*; CW's *Ecclesiastical Biography*. (*MY* I, 388–92.)

W draws on RW for £50 by bill in favor of John Green, due in one month. (*MY* I, 392; RW accounts, DCP.)[7]

15. Mar 2

DW writes to Josiah Wedgwood: Sends order [£7/12/–] in payment for goods sent for DeQ during last summer. Invitation to visit Grasmere. (*MY* I, 393.)[8]

DW writes to RW: Her continued disappointment in not hearing from RW [see 1810:6; 1810:9]. She has this day sent an order for £7/12 due on demand to Messrs. Wedgwood and Byerly; and drew on 28 Feb for £50 by bill in favor of John Green due at one month. Extreme uneasiness at not having full accounts from RW. (*MY* I, 392–93.)

16. Probably between Mar 11 and Mar 18, and shortly after, at least until Mar 23

[6] Addison would appear the person whom DW calls "another gentleman from Wales" present at AB along with John M on 28 Feb.

[7] RW's accounts record payment under 31 Mar.

[8] RW's accounts charge DW's account payment to Messrs. Wedgwood and Byerly under 16 Mar. (Another account is dated with the date of the bill, 2 Mar.)

W, DW go to view a house near Bouth as a possible residence. They are favorably impressed and plan at least until 23 Mar to move there in the autumn if a suitable agreement can be reached with the owner. (*MY* I, 394–95.)[9]

17. Perhaps c Mar 14

John M departs AB, probably accompanied by SH, possibly also by Henry Addison, for Hindwell. (*MY* I, 389–90, 395. See esp. Moorman II, 189; 1810:12.)

18. Mar 15; perhaps c but not before Mar 15

The last issue of *The Friend* is published on 15 Mar. Perhaps c but not before this date W composes "The Martial Courage of a Day is Vain." (1809:22n.)

19. Mar 17, 18, or 19

DW draws on RW for £30 by bill in favor of John Robinson, due at one month. (*MY* I, 394; RW accounts, DCP.)[10]

20. Mar 23; between Mar 23 and May 10

On 23 Mar DW writes to RW: RW's continued failure to acknowledge her recent requests for accounts [see 1810:6; 1810:9; 1810:15]; search for new house [see 1810:16]; recent drafts on RW. (*MY* I, 394–95.)

Between 23 Mar and 10 May the Ws arrange to take the Rectory at Grasmere for their residence. (1810:16; *MY* I, 406.)

21. Probably Apr 7

Catharine W, probably in part through negligence of Sally Green, becomes very ill; is in convulsions for seven hours. Mr. Scambler calls. A letter arrives from CCl. (*MY* I, 395–96, 401–02.)

---

[9] DW writes on Friday 23 Mar that she and W visited the house at Bouth "last week." They expected to have advice from the owner on 23 Mar that would enable them to reach a decision.

[10] RW records payment of the bill under 19 Apr.

22. Probably Apr 8

Catharine is discovered to be partly paralyzed. Scambler calls. (*MY* I, 396–97; 402. See 1810:21.)

23. Apr 11

A letter arrives from SH. (*MY* I, 398.)
Catharine probably shows signs of recovery. (*MY* I, 396.)

24. Apr 12, Apr 13

Catharine continues to improve.
DW writes to CCl: (12 Apr:) Catharine's illness; concern for MW. Sally Green's stupidity. Servants; the difficulty of attending STC. Plans for summer; advantages of SH's departure; STC's habits; the Ws have no hope of him. (13 Apr:) STC is in good spirits. (*MY* I, 395–400.)

25. Probably between mid-Apr and May 12; and between this time and 1811 May 12 ff

Probably between mid-Apr and 12 May W writes to RW: Algernon Montagu; wishes that RW, now at Sockbridge, would come to see them; Catharine's illness. (*MY* I, 402–03.)
Algernon Montagu when at Dawes's school probably visits at AB on occasional weekends until 12 May 1811, and probably at the Rectory and RM thereafter. (See *MY* I, 402–03, 410–11, 486.)[11]

26. Probably Apr 15

DW writes to JPM: DW's fears upon learning of the Marshalls' taking a lease upon a home at Watermillock on the basis of Mrs.

[11] Various accounts dating between 1 May 1810 and apparently Dec 1811, with others undated, confirm the indications of the letters that the Ws were heavily responsible for superintendence of Algernon during the next three years, and had charge of many of the financial arrangements for his schooling and expenses at Mrs. Ross's, where he resided much of that time. The accounts appear to indicate expenses of £104/7/9 during the period against receipts on account of £119/5/6, but do not appear to provide useful information concerning W's activities. Disposal of the surplus is not accounted for. The same account book contains information noted 1811:3 and 1811:46.
Visits by Algernon have been noted only where directly documented.

Rawson's recollections. Prepares JPM for the worst, but describes attractions of the place. Catharine's illness. (*MY* I, 400–02.)

27. Probably c May 2 or May 3

STC departs AB for Keswick. (*MY* I, 407; Curry I, 537.)

28. May 9

DW writes to RW: W will come to Sockbridge [after MW's baby is born and MW doing well]. A bill from Twining's, for which DW has this day forwarded a draft in payment for £45/10/-. (*MY* I, 403.)[12]

29. May 10, 12; May 11, 12

On 10, 12 May, W, DW write to Lady B: (W, 10 May:) Thanks for Lady B's kind remarks on G. Plans for visiting Coleorton. Disgust at Wilkinson's engravings. Lady B's report that Canning has acknowledged W's truth in *CC*. (DW, 10 May:) Catharine's convalescence. The Rectory to be their new residence. (DW, 12 May:) Birth of [Willy]. (*MY* I, 404–06.)

On 11, 12 May DW writes to CCl: (11 May:) MW's baby not yet come; Catharine's convalescence. STC; the children. The Rectory to be their new residence. (12 May:) Birth of [Willy]. (*MY* I, 407–08.)

30. May 12

William Wordsworth [d. 7 Feb 1883], third son and fifth child of W and MW, is born at AB c 2:15 AM. (*MY* I, 408–09; M–W Book of Common Prayer, DCP.)

31. Probably May 20 and a few days thereafter

Probably 20 May DW writes to RW: Asks for 5 guineas; is glad RW did not comply with her request for oilcloth for AB [see 1808:115], as their time of need for it is drawing to a close. The children. (*MY* I, 409–10.)[13]

---

[12] RW's accounts record payment variously under 9 May and 16 May.

[13] The letter is dated only "Sundy mng." DW mentions Willy, does not dwell on the subject as might be expected had the birth taken place only three days earlier; so Sunday 13 May seems a less probable date for the letter than Sunday 20 May.

W probably journeys to Sockbridge on the same day carrying DW's letter. He probably returns to AB within a few days, having seen RW and perhaps called on Capt. and Mrs. Wordsworth at Brougham Hall. (If so, they are not at home.) (*MY* I, 410–11.)

32. Probably a few days after May 20; May 26

After returning from Sockbridge [see 1810:31] W calls at Brathay to see Priscilla W, who has come there for a visit. He finds that she has gone to Kendal to escape the distress of the funeral of Arthur Lloyd, who had died on 18 May two hours before her arrival. Arthur is buried at Colthouse 26 May. (*MY* I, 410–11; E. J. Satterthwaite, *Records of the Friends Burial Ground at Colthouse*, Ambleside, 1914; information from the Rev. Canon J. P. S. Morton and Miss Joan H. Whitworth.)

33. Perhaps c June

W composes portions of the letterpress for Joseph Wilkinson's prints, as part of *G* 1810. These materials as now written are not used in the published volume. (See Appendix VI.)

34. June 1, possibly June 2

DW writes to RW: W's hopes of visiting Sockbridge again [see 1810:31] before RW's departure abandoned. Request for money. (*MY* I, 410–11.)[14]

35. Probably June 2–June 3; probably June 3

Probably 2–3 June HC, Derwent visit at AB.

Probably on 3 June DW writes to CCl: Catharine's convalescence; birth of Willy; W's and her plans to visit Coleorton. DW's hopes to visit CCl and W's plans to visit Wales; STC; Lloyds. (*MY* I, 411–13.)[15]

36. Between June 3 and June 11

Priscilla W calls several times at AB. (*MY* I, 411–14.)[16]

[14] As DW's date on her letter of about the same time to CCl is "Sunday June 2nd," a mistake for Sunday 3 June, it is possible that her 1 June dating is also a day early.

[15] DW dates "Sunday June 2nd." The Sunday in question was 3 June.

[16] DW had "not yet seen" Priscilla on 3 June; but Priscilla had been "several times at Grasmere" by 11 June.

37. June 11

DW writes to RW: Begs RW to send the £5 previously requested [see 1810:31; 1810:34]. DW is to go to Coleorton with W. Other travel plans; Priscilla W. (*MY* I, 413–14.)

38. June 15

Charles Luff probably calls or visits at AB. (*MY* I, 414.)
DW writes to RW: Earnestly asks RW for the £5 or 5 guineas earlier requested [see 1810:31; 1810:34; 1810:37]. (*MY* I, 414.)
Luff takes the letter for delivery. (*MY* I, 414.)

39. June 19

DW writes to RW: Uncertain whether Luff has delivered [her letter of 15 June], DW writes to renew her urgent request for £5 or 5 guineas [see 1810:31; 1810:34; 1810:37; 1810:38]. (*MY* I, 415.)

40. June 22

DeQ inscribes a three-volume set of Political Disquisitions (probably *Political Disquisitions; or an Enquiry into Public Errors, Defects, and Abuses*, 1774) to W at Grasmere with this date. (RM Sale Catalogue, lot 59.)

41. June 24

William Wordsworth, Jr., is baptized at Grasmere. John Wilson and DeQ are godfathers. (Grasmere PR; letter, W Jr. to Mrs. Gordon, 18 Dec 1860, BM Add MS 30,262, fols. 96–97.)[17]

42. Probably c June 29–July 2 or July 3, July 4 (–possibly by c Sept 3, –Oct 25)

Probably c 29 June W, DW depart AB for a trip to Coleorton, then, separately, to Wales and Bury respectively. (W returns to AB possibly by c 3 Sept; DW 25 Oct.) They probably spend at least three

[17] The PR records: "[Baptism:] June 1810. 24th William Son of William Wordsworth Esqre Grasmere."

nights at Kendal with the Cooksons. At least three days after their departure, they receive a letter from MW advising of Catharine's improved health. They depart Kendal on 4 July. W draws on RW probably on 2 or 3 July for £45 by a bill in favor of Cookson due in one month. (*MY* I, 416–18.)[18]

43. Perhaps July 1

A note for 5 guineas for DW arrives from RW. (*MY* I, 418. See 1810:31; 1810:34; 1810:37; 1810:38; 1810:39.)[19]

44. Probably July 4

W, DW travel by coach—both probably on top—to Preston and Manchester. They reach Manchester at 9:30 PM and pass the night there. (*MY* I, 431. See 1810:42.)[20]

45. Probably July 5

W, DW proceed to Ashbourne; meet Alexander Blair; walk with him to Dovedale; pass the night at Ashbourne. (*MY* I, 431–32. See 1810:44n.)[21]

[18] DW implies in her remarks to CCl, probably of 9 July, that she left home by a week ago; but below she indicates that while she was at home ten days before, she had been away, probably at Kendal, not less than three or four days, before receiving MW's letter and leaving the area entirely. W and DW fairly surely left Kendal on 3 July.

RW's accounts record payment of the bill under 6 Aug.

[19] It is remotely possible that this is the sum recorded in the 1816 accounts between RW and W and DW under the date of 12 Oct as "Cash lent Miss DW at Sockbridge." More probably, however, DW drew on RW in London, perhaps through his partner Addison, on 12 Oct, when RW was likewise at Sockbridge. Another account records 5 guineas "Cash remitted" to DW under the date of July 1810. In another account DW notes by the 12 Oct charge: "(This sum was lent to me by you at Sockbridge) DW." But see 1810:72.

[20] Although DW's letter to Mrs. Cookson, from which the basic information about the trip to Coleorton is obtained, does not assign dates to the several days of the journey, the fair certainty of the arrival at Coleorton on 7 July leaves little doubt of the probable dates of specific events reported below.

[21] DW wrote "Ashby" for Ashbourne.

46. Probably July 6 and probably about this time

W, DW, Blair proceed to Derby in a chaise, visiting Lord Scarsdale's estate Keddlestone on the way. At Derby they meet John Edwards, with whom W converses. The party or W perhaps now meets Joseph Strutt. They send their luggage on to Coleorton by wagon; walk to, pass the night at an inn a few miles beyond Derby. (*MY* I, 432, 471. On Edwards see esp. *Friend* R II, 426; Reed *N&Q*. On Strutt see esp. *Friend* R II, 461.)

Probably about this time W is attacked by an inflammation in his eyelids. This is perhaps the first of many recurrences of a disease—almost certainly trachoma—from which W first suffered in Jan 1805. (*MY* I, 470. See 1805:3.)

47. Probably July 7 (–July 11, –Aug 6, –Aug 10); between July 7 and Aug 6

W, DW, Blair walk by the Trent, converse about literary and aesthetic matters; visit Sir Francis Burdett's estate Foremark, walk on to Coleorton, arriving at 10 PM. They are at first mistaken for wandering troopers, then joyfully received by the Bs. (Blair departs probably 11 July, W probably 6 Aug, DW 10 Aug.) (*MY* I, 417, 432; *LY* I, 283–84.)

While at Coleorton the Ws see no company and pay no visits except a morning call at Lord Moira's to see [Donington] Park. (*MY* I, 432.)[22]

48. July 9

DW writes to CCl from Coleorton: Catharine W; DW intends to leave Coleorton in the first week of Aug if she does not visit CCl at Bury; W's plans for visiting Wales. (*MY* I, 416–17.)

49. July 11

Alexander Blair departs Coleorton. (*MY* I, 432.)

---

[22] On the visit generally see *MY* I, 432.

50. Probably c but by July 15

DW writes to RW from Coleorton: Thanks for 5 guineas; W's draft on RW of 2 or 3 July [see 1810:42]. (*MY* I, 417–18.)[23]

51. Aug 3

DW, perhaps W and the Bs, go to see the Wonder of Tutbury. (*MY* I, 419.)

52. Aug 4

DW writes to CCl from Coleorton: Good news of the health of the W children; DW thus feels free to visit CCl. Her plans for travelling to Bury; W's for visiting Wales. The Wonder of Tutbury. (*MY* I, 418–19.)

53. Probably Aug 6–Aug 10, –late Aug, –c but by Sept 3

W and Sir GB depart from Coleorton together on 6 Aug. They make a tour in the area of Birmingham. In Birmingham they attend a performance of *Venice Preserved*. They also visit the Leasowes and Hagley. Sir GB returns to Coleorton on 8 Aug.

W proceeds to Hindwell, arriving at 10 AM on 10 Aug. Probably on that day he and SH write to DW (letter not known to survive): All well, including SH, at Hindwell.

W's activities until c late Aug are not known, except that before his return to AB, which occurs possibly c but by 3 Sept, he visits Uvedale Price for a day and a half at Foxley, Mansell Lacey. W is annoyed by Price's daughter and Mr. (probably Richard) Fitzpatrick.

On the afternoon of 6 Aug DW goes to Ashby; looks, probably with the other ladies at Coleorton, at drawings illustrating Chaucer; reads half of Chaucer's *General Prologue*. (Letter, Sir GB to W, 11 Nov

---

[23] The postmark is 16 July; she would have had to write very early in the day on the 15th for her letter to reach London next day. The mail departed Loughborough, twelve miles away, at 1 PM. (Cary's *Roads*, 1810.)

1810, DCP, and Sir GB to J. Bannister, 20 Nov 1820, Folger Library; *MY* I, 422–23, 430, 505–06.)²⁴

54. Aug 7

DW looks at Chaucer illustrations; reads *The Knight's Tale*. (*MY* I, 423.)

55. Aug 10–Aug 12 (–Oct 9)

DW travels from Coleorton to Bury on 10–12 Aug. On her activities on 10 Aug see *MY* I, 424–25. She departs Coleorton at 8 PM that day; goes to the inn at Ashby, writes a note to Lady B; rests till 12.

On 11 Aug she leaves Ashby shortly after midnight, travels to Leicester on top of the coach; rests from between 3:30 and 4 till 6 at

---

²⁴ Sir GB states in the DC letter that he reckons the three days of his tour with W "amongst the *whitest* of [his] life." He also comments:

I again & again make myself glad with the favorable character we received from the old farmer at the Leasowes of poor Shenstone, & again sympathize with the sorrows of the starved actors at Birmingham when the empty walls of their extensive pit & boxes echoed back the dispairing rants of the poor forsaken Belvidera. . . .

The Folger Library letter contains further recollections of the performance:

Some years since, I made a little tour to the Leasowes, Hagley &cet with my friend Wordsworth the poet—& we visited amongst other places Birmingham, & of course we went to the Theatre, to see Venice preserved, I can assure that literally were but five persons in the boxes, & seven in the pit—I thought the house would be discharged, but the boxkeeper told me that it was a very tolerable one—then thought I, my friend you must have lenten entertainment here. However on they went, & exerted themselves so vociferously, that the bare walls returned dismal echoes, which together with the doleful nature of the play was indeed melancholy. Of the performers I only recollect the person who performed Pier, who I think was just come from America, & who appeared so stupified with porter, ale, & malt liquor of all kinds, that *Beer* would have been a far more appropriate appellation. A Lady also of my own name performed Belvidera a very little creature with a voice so [?perseant] it pierced the ear like a canary birds. she exerted her shrill organ with such astonishing power in the mad scene, I thought she would have broken a blood vessel, & I began to think her mad in real earnest—However, I believe she survived, & *I* have entirely recovered my hearing. . . .

Foxley, though out of W's probable way for what appears to have been an expeditious journey from Birmingham to Hindwell, lies only some twenty miles southeast of Hindwell and would have been easily accessible any time after his arrival there.

Leicester; travels, again on top, to Huntingdon via Stamford, where she changes coaches again. From Huntingdon she takes an inside place to Cambridge, which she reaches at 9:30 PM. At St. John's College the coach stops to let out John Palmer, Professor of Arabic. She is met by TCl at the inn, where she has supper. Samuel Tilbrooke [see 1809:102] comes in to invite her and TCl to breakfast; they decline the invitation.

On 12 Aug DW and TCl visit Trinity Chapel and St. John's, where DW sees the ash tree described *Prel* VI.90–100; dine with Tilbrooke; visit King's College Chapel; depart Cambridge about 4:15; drink tea at Newmarket; reach Bury at 9. DW departs Bury 9 Oct. (*MY* I, 420–27.)

On DW's activities at Bury, see esp. *MY* I, 427, 434–35, 442, 445–46, 450–51, 466, 491.)

56. Probably between Aug 11 and Aug 18

Mrs. and the Misses Wilson, John Wilson, Jane Penny visit, pass a night at AB and DC. (*MY* I, 429–30.)[25]

57. Aug 14

A letter from W, SH [see 1810:53] to DW arrives at the Cls' as DW is writing to W. DW's letter: CCl; her journey from Coleorton to Bury. (*MY* I, 423–27.)

DW also writes to Lady B from Bury: The journey from Coleorton to Bury; the letter just received from W and SH. (*MY* I, 420–23.)

58. Aug 19, 20

DW writes to W from Bury: (19 Aug:) Yesterday attended court, hopes to visit the ruins again tomorrow; the ruins; plans for further travel and return home about the beginning of second week of Oct. Reports of bad management of the housekeeping at CW's; Bocking. Lady B's failure to recollect a £1/14/6 indebtedness to her and W. Is to dine with Capell Loffts this evening. (20 Aug:) The dinner was pleasant enough. She likes Lofft, finds Mrs. Lofft too theatrical. A letter from MW received [18 Aug] with good accounts of her health. She is reading

[25] MW states on Monday 20 Aug that the overnight visit occurred "last week."

Malkin's translation of *Gil Blas*, which she finds vulgar, although the book is beautifully printed. (DCP.)

59. Aug 20

MW writes to DeQ: Bills for DeQ's household at DC; she intends to draw on Kelsall on DeQ's account for about £30 at end of month. HC has returned to school without Derwent, who has a broken arm. Catharine; a visit from the Wilsons and Miss Penny [see 1810:56]; the Astleys; W expected in less than a fortnight; the Ss. (*MY* I, 427–30.)

60. Aug 29

DW writes to Mrs. Cookson from Bury: Her journey to Coleorton, visit there, and journey to Cambridge and Bury. Plans not to be home in less than eight weeks. (*MY* I, 431–35.)[26]

61. Possibly c but by Sept 3; perhaps this time and c mid-Nov

Possibly c but by 3 Sept W returns to AB from Hindwell. (*MY* I, 430.)[27]

Perhaps between the time of this return and c mid-Nov, W composes "Section I" and "Section II" of *G* 1810. (Appendix VI.)

62. Sept 12

RW's accounts charge W £7/10/6, payment of premium on £300 policy on Montagu's life, under this date. (RW accounts, DCP.)

63. Sept 23 (–probably Oct 18)

Basil Montagu and his wife arrive at AB possibly with Algernon Montagu and Anne Skepper. (They probably depart finally on 18 Oct.) (See Moorman II, 191–92; 1810:77n.)[28]

[26] The letter was in fact first published *Some Letters* 52–56 (cf *MY* I, 431).

[27] Evidence for the time of W's return appears confined to MW's remark of 20 Aug that W was expected in "less than a fortnight" (*MY* I, 430).

[28] Montagu reports on 29 Sept (a Saturday) that they arrived last Sunday. While the Montagus would not have brought Algernon in order to enter him in Dawes's School—he was already in attendance there the preceding spring (*MY* I, 402, 410; cf Moorman II, 191)—it is not improbable that he accompanied them and reentered the school after holidays.

64. Sept 28

HCR probably calls on CCl, DW at Bury. (HCRNB.)[29]

65. Perhaps between Sept 29 and c Oct 6

The Ws and Montagu perhaps tour near Grasmere. (Letter, Montagu to Josiah Wedgwood, 29 Sept 1810, UKL. Cf Moorman II, 191–92.)[30]

66. Sept 29

Charles Luff calls at AB; sees Montagu and W. (1810:65n.)

67. Oct 3, 5, 7

On 3 Oct HCR drinks tea with Miss Kitchener, the Cls, probably DW. On 5 Oct, he walks with DW in the morning on Hardwick Heath, and on 7 Oct he drinks tea at CCl's, probably with DW. (HCRNB.)[31]

68. Perhaps late 1810

W perhaps now receives and reads RS's *History of Brazil*, I, and *The Curse of Kehama*. (*STCL* III, 296; *MY* I, 458.)

DeQ perhaps loans three MSS of STC's on logic to W; borrows from W Fichte's *Das System der Sittenlehre* (perhaps STC's copy). (Musgrove 9. See 1811:20.)

[29] HCR notes: "Mrs Clarkson, Miss Wordsworth kurzer Besuch." HCR had come to Bury the day before.

[30] Montagu wrote from Grasmere on 29 Sept of his plan to visit Keswick the following Tuesday to Saturday and to tour lakes of the area, then to depart on 18 Oct. The final departure took place as thus scheduled; but Mrs. Montagu added in the same letter that immediate plans had changed since Basil wrote his part: "We shall remain at Grasmere the next week for the purpose of seeing what is most beautiful in the neighborhood, and shall then go to Keswick. . . ." W does not seem to have gone to Keswick, and was fairly certainly at home on 10 Oct (see 1810:77). Montagu's letter also states that Charles Luff had come into the same room where he and W were sitting on the morning of the day on which Montagu was writing. Luff wrote to Josiah Wedgwood in a letter endorsed with the general date of Oct 1810: "I the other day saw Mr and Mrs Montague, at Mr Wordsworths[.]"

[31] HCR notes: (3 Oct:) "Thee bei Mrs Kitchener—[d]ie Clarksons da"; (5 Oct:) "Vormittag mit Miss Wordsworth spazieren gegangen in Hardwick heath geschwäg uber Poesie &c"; (7 Oct:) "Thee bey Mrs Clarkson."

69. Oct 9 (–Oct 13, 22)

DW, in company with HCR, travels to London from Bury. She visits at the Ls'. (She departs 13 Oct and again on 22 Oct.) They perhaps travel with or meet John T[?rost], Miss North. (HCRNB.)

This evening DW probably drinks tea and dines with CL and ML in the company of Godwin and Mrs. Godwin, Dawe, Hazlitt; HCR probably calls briefly. Mrs. Godwin's staying late and DW's arrival produce an adverse effect on ML which lasts beyond the time of DW's visit. (HCRNB; Godwin Diary; *LL* II, 103, 112.)[32]

70. Oct 10

W, Louis Simond, Mrs. John Millar, Miss Wilkes (grandniece of John Wilkes), DeQ, and perhaps others walk to Blintarn. W informs Simond of the high cost of local real estate; probably tells the story of George and Sarah Green, also that of Gough [see 1805:60]. (Louis Simond, *Journal of a Tour and Residence in Great Britain, 1810–1811*, New York, 1815, I, 338–40; Masson II, 374–79.)[33]

[32] CL describes ML's indisposition as commencing on a night when Hazlitt left town and Miss W came. On DW's London visit see also *MY* I, 467.

HCR records: "Journey to London Miss Wordsworth. seh[r] interessant Unterredung die ganze Zeit John T[?rost] u. Miss North

"Ab: Thee bey Lamb—Die Godwins, W. Hazlitt, Dawe [?kurze] zeit."

The Godwin Diary records: "[S]up at Lamb's, w. Miss Wordsworth, Dawe, Hazlit & MJ; adv. HRn."

In a letter dated 8 Oct but evidently not finished before 10 Oct John Rickman wrote to RS: "I hear Miss Wordsworth is in Town,—& for a Hermit, enjoys herself prodigiously well in the Croud." (HEH.)

[33] W's account of the Greens as reported by Simond apparently differs from other accounts in stating that it was after the eldest girl had gone twice for milk to a neighboring farm that suspicions of the disaster arose; also in stating that Sarah Green had been warned of her own danger by her husband's fall, had reached safely the base of the rock from which he fell, lost her shoes while groping about for him, and sunk simply from cold. Cf *G&SG*, esp. 14–15; *MY* I, 201–06, 213–14, 219–20.

DeQ records of W and Simond, "They met, they saw, they inter-despised." He recalls also, incorrectly, that Simond did not mention W in his book. On the reactions of the two men to each other see also James Hogg, *De Quincy and His Friends* (London, 1896), 152 (from J. R. Findlay's *Personal Recollections*). DeQ dates the meeting "about the May or June of 1810," and states that DeQ told the story of the Greens to Simond. Simond's earlier memoir is probably the more accurate record.

On this day DW walks with HCR outside [Westminster Abbey], visits West-Hall, sees a panorama of Malta. (HCRNB.)[34]

71. Oct 11

HCR probably walks with DW. They probably call on Mrs. Collier; perhaps go to BM but find it closed; possibly visit Liverpool Museum. (HCRNB.)[35]

72. c Oct 12 (–Oct 29); Oct 12

Dora and Thomas are sent c 12 Oct on a visit to Hackett, in Little Langdale. (They return to AB 29 Oct.) (*MY* I, 441.)[36]

On 12 Oct HCR probably accompanies DW to the BM. ML possibly also comes. They perhaps together visit Mr. and Miss Betham. This evening probably HCR, DW, ML go to Covent Garden Theatre. (HCRNB; *MY* I, 436–37.)

DW draws on RW for 5 guineas through Richard Addison. (RW accounts, DCP. See 1810:43n.)[37]

73. Oct 13–probably Oct 19

On 13 Oct DW travels to Binfield, where she visits her Uncle Cookson and his family till probably 19 Oct. (*MY* I, 436–39.) On the visit see esp. *MY* I, 437–38.

74. Probably c but by Oct 15

Catharine is ill. W writes to DW on the subject. (*MY* I, 439.)

[34] HCR records: "Spazierg: mit Miss W. Outside Abbey. West-Hall Panorama Malta."

[35] HCRNB records: "ffruh zuruck. Spatz Miss W. bey Mrs. C. Brit Mus: nicht geöffnet. Liverpool Museum." HCR had apparently parted from DW before he read, that afternoon, her narrative of George and Sarah Green.

[36] On Hackett, the home of John and Betty Youdell or Yewdale, parents of the W's servant Sarah, see esp. *MY* I, 441; *PW* V, 442–43 (*Exc* IF note); *Epistle to George Howland Beaumont, Bart.* IF note.

[37] HCRNB notes: "Vorm: Brit Mus: Miss W. Bey Mr & Miss Beetham."

75. Oct 15

DW writes to CCl from Binfield: Illness at Grasmere; her plans; her visit to London; the Cooksons. (*MY* I, 436–38.)

76. Shortly before or on Oct 18; Oct 18–Oct 26

Shortly before or on 18 Oct W advises Montagu against domestication with STC. On the terms of the warning see esp. *STCL* III, 403–08.

On 18 Oct STC departs Keswick at 5 AM; travels to Grasmere, where he joins the Montagus and Anne Skepper, with whom he proceeds toward London, where they arrive on 26 Oct. Although W and STC have no opportunity for prolonged conversation, W reminds STC of a story about the condition of Schiller's entrails and brains after his death. (*STCNB* 3995; *HCRBW* I, 77.)[38]

77. Oct 18, Oct 19–Oct 22

On 18 Oct DW, at Binfield, receives a letter from W advising that Catharine is ill. On 19 Oct she returns to London, where she remains till 22 Oct. She probably stays with CL and ML.

During her visit she sees MM three times; goes with her to Dr. [Henry] Ainslie. HCR calls on her at CL's probably on 20 and 21 Oct. (*MY* I, 436–37, 439; *LL* II, 103–04; *HCRNB*.)[39]

78. Oct 21

James Losh and Mrs. Losh call on the Ws at AB. They find the Ws not at home, but meet W on the road and have a long conversation with him. W is still sanguine in his hopes about Spain and Portugal. (Losh Diary. Cf Moorman II, 134n.)

[38] On STC's appearance see *MY* I, 454.

[39] DW received W's letter via CL and apparently first replied that she intended to remain at Binfield till [22 or 23 Oct].

HCRNB records under 20 Oct: "Wollte mit [Madam Lavaggi] in das Theater gehen Miss Wordsworth aber kam unerwarteter [?Wege] zuruck & wolte Morgenfort, desswegen entschuldigte ich [?mich ?und ?so] bey C. Lamb." The same NB notes under 21 Oct: "Ab bey Captn Burney. Kurze zeit. Miss W da dann bey C.L."

79. Probably Oct 22–Oct 25

On 22 Oct John M, CL, ML, probably HCR accompany DW to the Mail. She departs for Grasmere from Lombard Street at 8:10 PM. She travels via Manchester, Preston, Kendal. At Kendal she passes the night of 24 Oct with the Cooksons. On 25 Oct she proceeds to Grasmere in a gig, perhaps driven by Mr. Cookson; stops at Elleray on the way; reaches AB at 3, where she is met by the family and stunned by Catharine's appearance. (*MY* I, 439–41; HCRNB.)[40]

80. Oct 26–Oct 27, –Oct 29

On 26 Oct W, MW, DW, Catharine, Sarah the maid join Dora and Tommy at Hackett [see 1810:72]. W departs, probably returns to AB, next day; the rest of the family returns on 29 Oct.

On 27 Oct W and the family sit on a ledge in the sun. W reads the Morning Hymn from *PL* V. This evening W departs; DW accompanies him for a part of his way, becomes lost in returning; makes her way to a cottage; is guided back to Hackett, where the household is much disturbed about her. (*MY* I, 447–49.)

81. Oct 28 and perhaps shortly after

Montagu reports to STC comments of W's made to Montagu before their departure from Grasmere about STC's habits and prospects. Montagu perhaps states that W had commissioned or authorized him to report the comments.

Perhaps shortly after, Montagu writes to W that he has repeated W's remarks to STC and that STC had been very angry. (*STCL* III, 387, 389; *MY* I, 488–89; *STCNB* 3991, 3995, 3997, 4006. See 1810:76.)[41]

---

[40] HCR records under 22 Oct: "Vorm: . . . Abschied v. Miss Wordsworth."
[41] On the initiation of the rupture see Moorman II, 193–95; *STCL* III, 296–99; *HCRBW* I, 70–84.

82. Oct 30

MW and DW go out with Catharine and the baby. (*MY* I, 441.)

DW writes six letters. The only known addressee is CCl, DW's letter to whom is the only surviving: Her trip northward from Binfield and London; the family. (*MY* I, 438–42.)

83. Nov 6

DW writes to HCR: Thanks for attention in London; invitation to the Lakes; concern about the Ls; the family; request for Spanish, Portuguese, French papers for RS. (*MY* I, 442–45.)

84. Nov 8, 9 (–Dec 18); between Nov 8 and Dec 18, esp. Nov 8, 9, 10, 12

On 8 Nov the family determines to go to Elleray, esp. in order to escape the danger of scarlet fever in the neighborhood. W probably departs this morning to prepare the way. MW, the children, Fanny follow in the afternoon. DW follows next morning on foot. (The family returns to AB on 18 Dec.) (*MY* I, 448–49. See 1809:100.)

John Wilson probably passes the night at Elleray on 8 and 9 or 10 Nov, probably 12 Nov, and probably some other nights between 8 and 18 Dec. (*MY* I, 449.)

85. Probably Nov 10

DW writes to DeQ from Elleray: Instructions for Sarah at AB. (*MY* I, 451. See 1810:72.)[42]

86. Nov 11; Nov 11, 12; probably c mid-Nov

On 11 Nov DW composes the passages of *G* 1810 "Section II" corresponding to *G* 1810, p. 42, lines 28–20 up and p. 43, lines 24–9 up. W probably concludes composition of "Section II" c mid-Nov. (Appendix VI; *MY* I, 449. See Moorman II, 160.)

On 11, 12 Nov DW writes to CCl from Elleray: (11 Nov:) The family; friends at Bury, esp. the Gowers; presents for the children from

---

[42] *MY* dates "Saturday [17 Nov. 1810]." The directions to Sarah about butter in her letter of 18 Nov appear to supersede, unhurriedly, directions subsequent to those of this letter. DW's remarks about the family's plans to stay "at least a fortnight longer" resemble those that she made on 11 Nov.

CCl; recent visits from home by the Ws. (12 Nov:) Catharine; STC. (*MY* I, 445–51.)

87. Nov 18; perhaps between Nov 18 and Dec 18

On 18 Nov DW writes to DeQ from Elleray: Aggy Black and Mr. Crump; the new Ministry; fever; plans to stay at Elleray; instruction for Sarah. (*MY* I, 452–53.)

Perhaps between this day and 18 Dec MW, Willy, and Tommy, who is very ill, stay in lodgings at Ambleside for four days to be under Scambler's care. (*MY* I, 464.)

88. Probably Dec 6–perhaps Dec 15; probably Dec 9

Probably on 6 Dec DW travels to Kendal, where she visits with the Cooksons till perhaps 15 Dec, when she walks back to Elleray.[43]

Probably on 9 Dec she writes to CCl from Kendal: Recent activities. She does not wish publication of her *Narrative* of George and Sarah Green for three or four decades. The W children; STC; SH. (*MY* I, 453–55.)[44]

89. Dec 18

The W family returns to AB from Elleray. (*MY* I, 455.)

90. Probably between Dec 19 and Dec 21

The Ws see HC and probably RS, who spend two nights at DC. (*MY* I, 457–58; Curry I, 547.)[45]

91. Dec 21

The Ws dine with DeQ. Possibly HC, RS are present. (*MY* I, 456; Curry I, 547. See 1810:90n.)

[43] The date is conjectured on the assumption that such an absence would have been mentioned by DW in her letter to DeQ of 10 Nov or 18 Nov had it occurred by then.

[44] DW states that she stayed ten days at Kendal; and she came on the Thursday preceding Sunday 9 Dec. DW's concluding date appears to be "Kendal Sunday [?] Decr."

[45] DW states on Sunday 30 Dec that "the Boys went to Keswick last Friday but one" but that HC "walked with his Uncle Southey who spent two nights at Mr de Quincey's." The meeting possibly occurred when the Ws dined with DeQ on 21 Dec.

92. Dec 23

W, DW walk to Brathay and Ambleside. DW writes to SH. (*MY* I, 456.)

93. Dec 24 (–perhaps early Jan)

The family prepares for Christmas. Jane and Mary H, daughters of MW's brother John H, arrive to pass their holidays at AB. (They depart perhaps early Jan.) (*MY* I, 456.)

94. Dec 25 or Dec 26 and perhaps shortly after

The children and probably the servants, including three servants of John Wilson's, dine in the kitchen at AB. Wilson himself probably visits at AB now. He departs perhaps shortly after. (*MY* I, 456.)

95. Dec 30

DW writes to CCl: Return to AB; plans to move to Rectory in May; Elleray; SH; MM; old Henry H; STC, HC, Derwent; RS; *The Lady of the Lake*, DeQ's and STC's comments on it; the children; Johnny scalded [on 26 Dec]. W has written fifteen political sonnets [see 1809:23n]. W's political feelings. (*MY* I, 455–60.)

96. Probably during the week commencing Dec 30(–mid-Jan)

Miss Weir perhaps visits at AB; if so she probably arrives during the week commencing 30 Dec and departs by mid-Jan. (*MY* I, 456.)[46]

1811

[On writings of W possibly of this year see below and GCL 14, 42, 123, 146, 148, 167–69, 171, 184, 196–204.]

1. Possibly this year; probably between 1813 Jan 3 and c late May 1814

W composes *Characteristics of a Child Three Years Old*. (IF note.)[1]

---

[46] DW remarks on Sunday 30 Dec that Miss Weir is expected "in the beginning of next week to finish *her* holidays with us."

[1] EdS notes that if W's IF comment that the poem was composed at AB is correct, it must have been written before June, when the move to the Rectory took place

2. Perhaps this year; perhaps between this year and Nov 1813

Perhaps in 1811 W composes:
Conclusion. 1811 ("Here Pause: the Poet Claims at Least This Praise")
1811 ("The Power of Armies Is a Visible Thing")
Spanish Guerillas. 1811 ("They Seek, Are Sought; to Daily Battle Led")
Perhaps between 1811 and Nov 1813 W arranges his *Sonnets. Dedicated to Liberty. Second Part* in much or exactly the order of *P* 1815, except for Part II, xxxii ("Now That All Hearts Are Glad"). (Titles of poems. Cf Moorman II, 173n. See also 1811:4; 1813:104n.)

3. During this year

W perhaps draws on Montagu for £50. (RW accounts, DCP.)[2]

4. Probably early 1811, by Feb 10; probably early this year, until May 11–May 12; probably early 1811, by Mar 27

Probably early 1811, by 10 Feb, W experiences an attack of trachoma. (*MY* I, 461. See 1810:46.)
Probably early 1811, until 11–12 May, HC and Derwent visit at AB every, or virtually every, school weekend through 11–12 May. Algernon Montagu comes occasionally, and also visits during the short [Easter] holiday. (*MY* I, 486. See 1808:100.)
The Ws attend church so consistently that DW by 12 May regards the family (taking it by turns) as regular churchgoers. They are attracted to church in part by the qualities of the curate, William Johnson. (*MY* I, 487. Cf 1806:93.)[3]

---

[2] The draft was apparently one of two by Montagu during this year, the other perhaps drawn on 6 Sept, more probably due on that date. Accounts apparently dealing with Montagu note:

[debit]	[credit]
Wordsworth Dr 257/1/1	229/15/2
Draft Septr 6.1811 29/19	Sept 1811 Annty 26/–/–
Do 1811 50	March 1812 26/–/–

[3] On Johnson see esp. *DNB*.

(*PW* I, 359). Surviving MS evidence, however (see Appendix VI), points to a later date. W's note perhaps looks back to the year that Catharine became three.

Probably early 1811, by 27 Mar, W works on corrections of his poems, probably begins planning a new arrangement of them designed to make more clear his intentions in writing them. (*MY* I, 471. See 1809:75; 1811:72.)

5. Jan 1

RW's accounts charge W £30, payment of bill in favor of Thomas Cookson, under this date. (RW accounts, DCP.)

6. Jan 25

A review of *P2V* appears in *The Poetical Register for 1806–07.* (*Times.* See Ward; Hayden.)

7. Jan 28

Old Henry H of Stockton dies. His will leaves to MH a farm estate near Stockton currently letting for £100 per annum. (*MY* I, 463; genealogical charts, *SHL, MWL.*)

8. Feb 10

DW writes to RW: Regrets missing RW in London [see 1810:72]; illness in the family; old Henry H's death and bequests. Plans to move to the Rectory; W will draw next week for £49/19/–, due at one month; request for statement of accounts [see 1810:6; 1810:9; 1810: 15]. (*MY* I, 461–62.)

9. Perhaps c Feb 17

W draws on RW for £49/19/– though bill in favor of John Robinson. (*MY* I, 461–62. See 1811:8.)[4]

10. Feb 22–Feb 27, 28, Mar 1, perhaps Mar 2

On 22 Feb DW begins a letter to CCl (she finishes it 27, 28 Feb, and 1 Mar): Death of old Henry H; his bequests; his injustice to Henry and George H. (*MY* I, 462–64.)

Catharine is very ill; Miss Knott calls and urges DW and probably others to come with Catharine to visit at Ambleside. (*MY* I, 464–65.)

[4] RW records payment under 17 Mar.

Miss Knott sends her car. DW and Catharine ride in it to visit Miss Knott at Ambleside. They remain there until perhaps 2 Mar.

Probably on 25 Feb W calls at Miss Knott's.

On 27 Feb DW continues her letter to CCl begun 22 Feb: Family illness; visit at Miss Knott's. John and Thomas H are expected soon; Joanna to come in a few weeks; [MM] also expected.

On 28 Feb she continues the letter: Distresses at Miss Knott's home; Catharine; old Mrs. Knott.

On 28 Feb HC and Derwent, possibly SFC and SC, call on DW.

On 1 Mar DW concludes the letter: HC and Derwent; Scott's poetry, and Campbell's; clothes. (*MY* I, 462–67.)[5]

11. Probably early Mar, by Mar 9

ML writes to W or DW mentioning the coolness which she knows to exist between W and STC, and perhaps urging W to come to town immediately. DW writes to ML denying that the coolness exists. W perhaps writes to ML, or someone else makes remarks to her, to the effect that STC's wearing powder shows that he cannot be deeply affected by W's alleged unkindness to him [see also 1811:20, possibly containing a reference to the same letter]. (*STCL* III, 309, 376; *MY* I, 457, 489.)[6]

12. Mar 9

W writes to William Godwin: Declines to write a verse account of the tale of Beauty and the Beast; suggests William Taylor of Norwich for the job; asks for a copy of Godwin's *Essay on Sepulchres*. (*MY* I, 467–70.)

13. Probably c Mar 20; probably between that date and Mar 30

W probably c 20 Mar receives the loan of a copy of C. W. Pasley's *The Military Policy and Institutions of the British Empire* and reads it twice.

---

[5] DW states on 1 Mar that the "Coleridges came to see me yesterday morng," but subsequently discusses only the two boys.

[6] ML's letter was written, according to DW, "a few days before her last confinement" (*MY* I, 489).

He composes, probably between that date and 30 Mar, *On a Celebrated Event in Ancient History* and *Upon the Same Event*. (*MY* I, 473–82; *MY* II, 660–61; Musgrove 3.)

14. Mar 27

W writes to John Edwards : Apologies for his excessive delay in replying to Edwards' letter (probably of early 1811, by 10 Feb); STC is in London, but neither he nor RS has heard from him; thanks for verses. Their meeting last summer [see 1810:46]. W's complex feelings about his own poetry; transcript of *Composed While the Author Was . . . Writing a Tract Occasioned by . . . The Convention of Cintra*. (*MY* I, 470–72.)[7]

W writes to Francis Wrangham: STC; the Catholic question; the Bible Society; the Montagus. (*MY* I, 472–73.)

15. Mar 28, and perhaps Mar 29 and Mar 30

W writes to C. W. Pasley: Apologies for delay in writing. Pasley's [*Military Policy and Institutions of the British Empire*]: comment. DeQ makes a copy of the letter, to which W appends an informal note and transcription of *On a Celebrated Event in Ancient History* and *Upon the Same Event*. (*MY* I, 473–82; *MY* II, 660–61.)[8]

W writes to [Richard Sharp]: Encloses letter to Pasley, which he invites Sharp to read; adds comment about the Whig position on European affairs. (*MY* I, 482–85.)

16. Perhaps c Mar 31 or early Apr (–perhaps c Apr 24, May 11)

Probably Thomas H and perhaps John H arrive at AB for a visit of undetermined length.

---

[7] The missing twelve lines of the transcript and the address are on a fragment in the Berg Collection, NYPL.

[8] While W's letter would appear fairly certainly to have been begun on 28 Mar (*MY* I, 473), its length makes it improbable that both copies can have been completed on the same day. The 2 Apr postmark on the DeQ copy, however, makes fairly certain that this letter and the covering letter to Sharp were sent off by 30 Mar. The copy retained by W is in DCP.

Possibly about this same time Elizabeth M arrives for a visit at AB. She perhaps departs c 24 Apr. (*MY* I, 465; letter, Thomas H to John M, 29 Mar, endorsed 1811, JFW Papers; 1811:19.)

Possibly about the same time Joanna H arrives for a visit at AB. (She departs 11 May.) (*MY* I, 465, 487; letter, Thomas H to John M, 29 Mar [1811], JFW Papers; letter, MM to Thomas M, p.m. 30 May 1811, JFW Papers.)[9]

17. Perhaps c Apr 17, probably by c Apr 24

W visits Penrith; probably visits or sees RW at Sockbridge. He goes on to Patterdale, where he fishes, unsuccessfully, for a day. (*MY* I, 436. See 1811:19; Musgrove 3.)

18. Probably c Apr 23

W draws on RW for £49/19/– by a bill in favor of William Wilcock. (*MY* I, 436; 1811:19.)

19. Probably c Apr 24 and perhaps later spring 1811

Probably c 24 Apr W writes to RW: The deed for the Patterdale estate originally erroneously executed. Ellwood, with whom RW has agreed to make final settlements in paying off the mortgage, not justified in charging W for the expense of a trip to Grasmere to correct matters. W regrets necessity of a reconveyance. He fished at Patterdale for a day; drew on RW for £49/19/– yesterday. [Elizabeth] M is to carry the letter. (*MY* I, 435–36; RW accounts, DCP. See 1809:34; 1809:69.)[10]

[9] Thomas H writes, "Here I am at the lively town of [?Sedgwick] on my road to Grasmere." "[?Sedgwick]" is a highly speculative suggestion.

MM writes from Hindwell of having received a letter from Joanna "this morning": "She was to leave Stockton yesterday and will be at Grasmere some time next week. my Aunt is at present there, and quite in the fidgets least Joanna should detain her a day longer than the time she has fixed for setting off to London, which is the first week in May, and I should think they will not be willing to part with Joanna so soon." (JFW Papers.)

[10] *MY* I, 435 dates the letter "probably early Sept. 1810." The RW accounts appear to mention only three drafts of £49/19/–; these are recorded under the dates of 17 Mar (Robinson), 23 May (Wilcock), and 12 July (Simpson) of this year. Letters

Legal arrangements concluding the paying off of the mortgage on W's Patterdale estate are perhaps completed by RW later this spring. (See references just cited.)

20. Probably between c early May and possibly c early July; probably c early May

Probably between c early May and possibly c early July W is engaged in composition of *Exc.* (Appendix VI.)

Probably c early May W learns by a letter from SFC that STC has lately complained to her of having been much injured by W's conduct toward him, and that STC wishes the MSS of his that W retains. The Ws probably send these MSS shortly, perhaps with Fichte's *Sittenlehre* [see 1810:81; 1811:11]. W writes to SFC (letter not known to survive) probably denying intention to do injury and asking her to transcribe his letter or parts of it for STC. SFC declines. (W's letter is possibly, nonetheless, that referred to 1811:11.) (*MY* I, 488–90, 495. See Moorman II, 197; Musgrove 9; *STCL* III, 324, 327.)[11]

21. May 11; May 11, 12

On 11 May Joanna H departs AB. Charles and Mrs. Lloyd call at AB. (*MY* I, 487, 490.)

On 11, 12 May HC, Derwent, Algernon Montagu come to AB; pass the night there; return to Ambleside next day. This is probably

---

[11] DeQ wrote on 29 May to SFC, who had also apparently made a request for such MSS of STC's as DeQ had, that he had had no other such MSS when SFC's note arrived than the three "logical ones" which he had loaned to W some months before. The *Sittenlehre* of Fichte, then at his house, he had returned to W at once.

The "logical" MSS remain unidentified, but see Alice D. Snyder, *Coleridge on Logic and Learning* (New Haven, 1929), xi–xii, 50–138; Musgrove 10; *MY* I, 362.

---

survive advising of the first and last: a letter of 10 Feb advises that the draft will be made in a week, due in one month; and a letter of 11 June advises that the draft was made 9 June, due at one month (*MY* I, 461, 491). The draft here mentioned was probably the one of £49/19/– not otherwise noticed among the letters, and was probably due in one month also. On Elizabeth M's visit see 1811:16. The present letter is endorsed "1811."

their last visit for the summer. (*MY* I, 486–87, 493. See 1808:100; 1811:4.)

On 12 May at c 6:30 PM occurs a fierce storm with a fine rainbow.

On 12 May DW writes to CCl: CCl's family; bustle at AB; [Philip] Beaver's *African Memoranda*; HC, Derwent, Algernon Montagu, other visitors; plans for moving; CL; STC and his offense at W [see esp. 1811:11]; background and comment; W has begun to work at his great poem. Family and other acquaintance. (*MY* I, 485–91.)

22. Probably between May 12 and July 30, possibly c early July

W visits Watermillock. The visit marks the commencement of a rest from work on *Exc.* (*MY* I, 490, 502.)[12]

23. Between perhaps May 26 and June 11 (–perhaps c June 30, –1813 May 12); probably late May, by May 29

Between perhaps 26 May and 11 June the Ws move into the Rectory at Grasmere. (They reside at the Rectory until probably 12 May 1813.) The family possibly is obliged to disperse to various lodgings as the removal is in progress. (*MY* I, 487, 492.)

Tommy W probably late May, by 29 May, goes to GH to visit. (He perhaps returns c 30 June.) (*MY* I, 491, 493, 497; Musgrove 9.)

24. May 30

W receives and is, according to DeQ, greatly mortified by news in the *Gazette* of the repulse of Masséna. News arrives while W and DeQ are together of Beresford's defeat of Soult [at Badajoz] and Masséna's loss of a battle. W resolves to meet the post at Ambleside next evening. (Rain probably spoils W's plan.) (Musgrove 12.)

[12] DW remarks on 14 Aug: "William's poem has been at a stand ever since he made a visit to Water-Millock. It is very unfortunate that any interruption stops him. Perhaps he may be inspired by the murmuring ocean." Her tone does not imply that the lapse in composition has been very lengthy. W might easily have visited the Marshalls' home in late Apr; but DW's remark in Aug would not make sense, in view of her comments about W's work in this letter of 12 May, if she were referring to a visit at that time.

25. Perhaps c early June

After removal to the Rectory W, beside Grasmere brook, composes *Upon the Sight of a Beautiful Picture.* (*MY* I, 507.)

26. June 8

The Ws attend the funeral of Sarah ("Sally") Ashburner Stuart. (*MY* I, 495; Grasmere PR.)

27. June 9

DW draws on RW in W's name for £49/19/– by a bill in favor of John Simpson due in one month. (*MY* I, 491–92; RW accounts, DCP.)[13]

28. June 11

DW writes to RW from Grasmere: W's draft of 9 June, and a problem about the stamp. The removal to the Rectory. (*MY* I, 491–92.)

29. June 16 (–June 18)

DW writes to CCl: Sunday school, and her and MW's plans to attend as often as possible. The new house; plans and comments; STC and her feelings about him. (DW finishes the letter on 18 June.)

HC visits at the Rectory. W, DW walk to Ambleside, perhaps taking HC back to school. (*MY* I, 493–96. See 1808:100.)

30. June 17

The Ws carry in books from the barn and arrange them. (*MY* I, 496.)

31. June 18

DW completes her letter to CCl begun 16 June: Weather; Catharine and the other children; plans for Dora to go to school at Miss Weir's; SH to come to Grasmere in Sept. (*MY* I, 496–98.)

[13] RW records payment of the bill under 12 July. On the negotiation of the bill see also the *MY* I reference cited.

32. Probably late June and early July

The normal routine of W household is upset by hay-making. (*MY* I, 499.)

33. Possibly c early July

W visits Watermillock. (1811:22.)

34. Probably mid-July–c July 27

Mrs. [Thomas] Cookson and her daughter visit the Rectory. (*MY* I, 499.)

35. Possibly July 27 (–perhaps c mid-Dec)

Dora departs with Miss Jameson by coach for Miss Weir's school at Appleby. DW sees her off at Ambleside. (She perhaps returns c mid-Dec for Christmas holidays.) (*MY* I, 501. See Moorman II, 224.)[14]

36. Perhaps July 30–perhaps Aug 4 or Aug 5 (–probably Sept 8)

W, MW, Tommy, Catharine, and Fanny Turner the maid depart before dawn, probably travel to Duddon Bridge, where they intend a visit to the sea. They remain at Duddon Bridge till perhaps 4 or 5 Aug; W while there goes bathing at Broughton. (They reach the Rectory on their return probably on 8 Sept.) The party probably meets the dog of Mr. Rowlandson the curate soon after starting. They proceed via Red Bank and past Hackett, greeting Betty Yewdale from a distance, to a

---

[14] DW's phrasing indicating the times of the departure of Mrs. Cookson and her daughter, of Dora, and of W's party for the seaside is ambiguous: "Mrs Cookson & her Daughter also stayed with us a fortnight, which altogether kept us so busy that we could not get Dorothy's cloaths all prepared against her departure the last day of this month; & in three days after she was gone. i.e. on this day fortnight, William [and the others], left me to go to the sea-side." (BM Add. MS 36,997, fol. 108. See *MY* I, 499.) DW was probably writing on Tuesday 14 Aug (see 1811:41). DW's phrasing as it stands produces the contradiction that Dora and W's party left both on the same day and three days apart. DW's account of her activities between the time of W's departure and her own trip to Hackett on Sunday 4 Aug seems to leave no doubt that four full days passed between those two events. By an unsatisfactory default it must be supposed that Dora departed 27 July, and Mrs. Cookson about the same time. Dora's clothes were sent off after 8 Aug.

house, Waterhead, owned by Mr. Knott, at the head of Yewdale, where they breakfast. The trip thither forms the main subject of the *Epistle to Sir George Howland Beaumont, Bart.*, lines 101–269, and *Departure from the Vale of Grasmere. August 1803*, which is originally a part of the same poem [see 1811:38].

Possibly today on their way to Duddon Bridge W discovers a well near Ulpha. (*MY* I, 499–500, 509; *Epistle*, content and IF note; *Mem* II, 450.)[15]

37. Aug 4

DW, Johnny, Willy, and Sarah the maid travel to Hackett for a visit. (DW, perhaps all, return on 8 Aug.) (*MY* I, 500–01.)

38. Perhaps c Aug 5 (–probably Aug 30); between c Aug 5 and probably Aug 30

W and his party travel from Duddon Bridge to a cottage near Bootle (Cumberland). (They depart probably 30 Aug.) (*MY* I, 499–500, 503.)

On their surroundings and activities at Bootle see esp. *MY* I, 499–500, 503–08, and *Epistle to Sir George Howland Beaumont, Bart.*, lines 1–100. While there they see a remarkable view, one afternoon, of clouds above the Isle of Man; and, one evening, of a sloop-rigged vessel. They see what they can of Muncaster Castle from the public road. W converses with James Satterthwaite, rector of Bootle, whose house is a short walk distant, who probably at this time tells W the story that forms the basis of *Written with a Slate Pencil . . . Black Comb*, lines 20–29, and discusses a fine painting at Hagley. (*Written with a Slate Pencil . . . Black Comb*, IF note; *MY* I, 500, 504, 507–08.)[16]

39. Aug 8

DW, perhaps Johnny, Willy, and Sarah the maid return to the Rectory from Hackett. (*MY* I, 500. See 1811:38.)[17]

---

[15] A main object of the trip was probably sea-baths for Catharine (see *MY* 507, 509).

[16] DW states that the tide at Duddon Bridge "only served them for 4 or 5 days."

[17] DW says, probably on Wednesday 14 Aug, that she "came home with him" on "last Thursday." The identity of the "him" is obscure. He may have been one of the

40. Aug 11

DW is with Richard Sharp at some time during this day. He perhaps calls at the Rectory. Perhaps at this time she obtains one or more franks from him. (*MY* I, 498, 502–03. See 1811:41.)

41. Aug 14 and perhaps Aug 15

DW writes to CCl, commencing her letter on 14 Aug and perhaps concluding it next day: CCl's health; possibility of a visit to Bury; household activities for past two months; the Ss gone to Bristol. (*MY* I, 498–503.)[18]

42. Probably c Aug 26–c Aug 28

W writes probably the bulk of *Epistle to Sir George Howland Beaumont, Bart.*, also *Departure . . . 1803* as part of the same poem. (*Epistle*, content, esp. line 26, and IF note; *Departure* IF note; *MY* I, 503–08; 1811:38.)[19]

43. Aug 26

RW's accounts charge W £7/10/6, payment of premium on £300 policy on Montagu's life, under this date. (RW accounts, DCP.)

44. Aug 28

W writes to Sir GB from Bootle: Apologies for not having written for twelve months. The Leasowes and Hagley [see 1810:53]; a remark-

---

[18] The letter is franked "Keswick Augt fifteen 1811/Mrs Clarkson/Bury St Edmunds/f Rd Sharp" and stamped KESWICK. DW clearly began the letter on 14 Aug, but remarks near the conclusion "I must give over or I shall lose my Frank" (*MY* I, 498, 503). A point of division is not obvious in the MS.

[19] The *Epistle* is unlikely to have been completely finished until 1842 (see IF note). W's date in the IF note, 1804, perhaps looks slightly erroneously back to the year of W's first meeting with Sir GB (1803). The date 1811 is assigned in editions 1842–1850. In line 26 W remarks that he has been "more than three weeks' space" a prisoner in his dwelling. He wrote a prose letter to Sir GB on 28 Aug. The IF note states that the poem was never seen by Sir GB.

---

boys, but DW would probably not have left either behind, and nothing is known of the return of the party at another time. The "him" would seem on balance likely to be her host Jonathan Yewdale.

able painting at Hagley, and its owner; Uvedale Price and his estate, Foxley; transcription of "Praised Be the Art." The seaside, and the Ws' activities there. (*MY* I, 503–08.)

45. Probably between late Aug and 1812 late Mar; probably between late Aug and c Nov 1812, c 1813

Probably between late Aug 1811 and late Mar 1812 W is engaged in composition of *Exc.* (See esp. GCL 42 and Appendix VI.)

Probably between late Aug 1811 and c 1813 W composes:

Written with a Slate Pencil on a Stone, on the Side of the Mountain of Black Comb

View from the Top of Black Comb

At least one of these poems is probably composed by c Nov 1812. (1811:38; *Epistle to Sir George Howland Beaumont* 276–77; Appendix VI.)[20]

46. Perhaps Sept 6; probably by Sept 6

Perhaps on 6 Sept W, MW, Tommy, Catharine, Fanny the maid depart Bootle, proceed to Duddon Bridge, whence the children and Fanny proceed to Coniston, probably to Tamar Turner's (sister of Fanny the maid). W, MW set off at 9 up the Duddon to Ulpha, where they dine in the Porch of the Kirk; they pass two hours there and in the churchyard. At 4:30 they reach Newfield, at Seathwaite, where they pass the night. W perhaps now makes notes concerning Ulpha church-yard and collects information about the Rev. Robert Walker. (*MY* I, 509–10; Appendix VI.)[21]

Probably by 6 Sept W draws on Montagu for £29/19/–. (1811: 3&n.)

---

[20] While both poems would appear to have had their inspiration in the visit to Bootle (see 1811:38), the last two lines of the *Epistle* suggest that W cannot have written either of these poems or anything but the *Epistle* during the visit. W dated both works 1813 *PW* 1836–*PW* 1850; and in the absence of other evidence a date about that year must be regarded as a possibility for at least one of the poems.

[21] W indicates (*MY* I, 509) that the family enjoyed good weather for their last four days at the seaside. Settled weather had not obviously begun when W wrote to Sir GB on 28 Aug (see *MY* I, 507–08). While DW wrote on 14 Aug that she expected them home in "about a fortnight" (*MY* I, 503), on 28 Aug W expected to return to

47. Perhaps Sept 7

W, MW walk across Walna Scar and into Yewdale, where they probably join the children and pass the night at the home of Tamar Turner. (*MY* I, 509–10.)

48. Perhaps Sept 8; perhaps between Sept 8 and late Sept

Perhaps on 8 Sept W, MW, Tommy, Catharine, Fanny the maid proceed home to the Rectory, arriving in the morning. (*MY* I, 509–10.)

Perhaps between 8 Sept and late Sept W, MW, Tommy and perhaps other of the Ws drink tea at DC with DeQ's mother and sister. Probably the W and DeQ families meet often during this time.

W advises the women about landscaping. (*Memorials* II, 79–81, 102–03; 1811:49n.)

49. Perhaps Sept 12

W, MW write to SH: (W:) The children; their return from the coast; plans for W to meet SH on her way to Grasmere. (MW:) Wishes that she could accompany W to meet SH; news and information of the Hs.

As W is writing his letter the Misses DeQ call; he breaks off writing and probably takes them to the waterfall at Ghyll-side. Thomas Cookson calls; W confers with him about his projected trip to meet SH. MW and DW accompany the DeQs to Hackett. (*MY* I, 509–11.)[22]

50. Probably c late Sept (–1813 Aug 31)

SH arrives at the Rectory for a visit. (Her next lengthy absence from the Ws commences probably 31 Aug 1813.) W probably travels

---

[22] DeQ's sisters Mary and Jane probably came for a visit to DeQ at DC some time in August or early Sept (*Memorials* II, 160–61; Eaton 195–96). They departed perhaps 22 Oct. It was perhaps in the course of this expedition to Hackett that Mary DeQ and DW walked in Tilberthwaite Vale (see *Memorials* II, 79–81; Eaton 195–96); an excursion probably of 19 Oct (see 1811:56) is another possibility. The letter appears to have been written six days after W and MW's departure from Bootle, to judge from the comments on weather (*MY* I, 509).

Grasmere "in a few days" (*MY* I, 507). Evidence is not strong either way, but it appears unlikely that W would speak of his return to Grasmere so indefinitely if he were leaving Bootle in less than forty-eight hours.

to the George Inn, Warrington (Lancs) to meet her, and accompanies her home.

W probably sees Basil and Mrs. Montagu in Grasmere or the neighborhood. (*MY* I, 510–11; *SHL* 26–33; letter, Montagu to Josiah Wedgwood, 4 Oct 1811, UKL.)[23]

51. Possibly c Oct

Henry H possibly visits Grasmere. (Letter, MM to SH, 10 Oct [1811], JFW papers.)[24]

52. Oct 9

RW's accounts charge DW £29/7/–, payment of a bill of Messrs. Twining, under this date. (RW accounts, DCP.)

53. Perhaps c mid-Oct, probably by Oct 26

W composes:

In the Grounds of Coleorton ("The Embowering Rose, the Acacia, and the Pine") in a form preceding that described *MY* I, 513.

Written at the Request of Sir George Beaumont, Bart. ("Ye Lime-trees, Ranged before This Hallowed Urn," with lines 4–7 and perhaps other lines possibly in a form not surviving.) (*MY* I, 513–14; letter, Sir GB to W, 28 Oct 1811, DCP.)[25]

[23] Montagu writes from Ambleside: "Wordsworth is at Grasmere but, if he were here, I am sure he would unite with us in every kind wish to you."

[24] MM writes to SH at Grasmere on "Thursday Octr 10th": "I suppose you will have seen Henry and heard of all Mr Curwens elegant behaviour as he said he would go to Grasmere as soon as he heard you were arrived" (JFW Papers). The nature of Mr. Curwen's behavior in this instance is unknown.

[25] DW's letter of c but by 30 Oct contains transcriptions of "altered" versions of the poems. The original versions were probably sent off by 26 Oct, since Sir GB writes to W from Coleorton on 28 Oct thanking him for lines referring to Reynolds ("Ye Lime-trees") and requesting alterations. Sir GB's reference to a single poem suggests that "The Embowering Rose" was sent off earlier. W dates "The Embowering Rose" 1808 in editions 1836–1850; but the correspondence under discussion strongly implies a date about this time. Farington quotes 37 lines of "Ye Lime-trees," including two sets of alterations, in his diary under 23 Oct 1812, on which day Lady B read the poem to him (Farington VII, 122–23). It is probably to one of these poems that W refers *MY* II, 289, where he recalls having taken a year to compose an inscription for a monument in a friend's garden.

54. Probably Oct 14–Oct 17 and c but by this time; probably Oct 17 (–Oct 18, –Oct 20)

Probably on 14–17 Oct W attends the Grasmere school regularly two or three hours every morning and evening, probably teaching and observing instruction according to the Madras System of Dr. Bell, which W has lately introduced at Grasmere.

Probably on 17 Oct SH commences a letter to MM: MM's teeth; the W children; visitors; household activities; W's teaching. (The letter is continued and completed 18, 20 Oct.) (*SHL* 26–33; *MY* I, 514–15.)[26]

W probably walks by SH's side as she rides the pony to Ambleside. This afternoon the Ws probably join the Crumps and the Kings at DC for a party. (*SHL* 28.)

55. Probably Oct 18

W, DW walk by SH's side as she rides the pony to Town Head. They join her after she sets off.

SH continues her letter to MM begun probably 17 Oct: Excursion to Town Head; MW; W. Bingley's *North Wales*. W's and DW's teaching, Dr. Bell's system, and the Grasmere school. The Lloyds.

[26] The dating of *SHL*, "Thursday, Octr [27, 1811]," for SH's "Thursday, Octr [ ]," seems unlikely, 27 Oct having been a Sunday. DW wrote on 3 Nov (*MY* I, 512), a Sunday, that SH "was at Patterdale last week" and that Henry H was visiting at the Rectory. SH's letter indicates that she had yet to visit Patterdale, having "half promised Mrs Luff" that she would go there (*SHL* 27), and that Henry had yet to come. SH's description of the exodus of Lakers *SHL* 27 suggests more exactly that the letter must have been begun on the Thursday before the Tuesday preceding the last Monday of the month. The last Monday was the 28th. SH had plainly been at the Rectory for some while, but is unlikely to have arrived before late Sept. So, on balance, the letter seems most likely to have been begun Thursday 17 Oct and concluded Sunday 21 Oct. Dr. Bell called before W wrote his letter of c but by 20 Oct, and Bell was at GH on Wednesday 23 Oct (Curry II, 11). Apparently on Sunday, SH states that she could not send off her letter on Saturday because of the visit from Bell and other interruptions. But she goes on to discuss activities of the preceding day, commencing with the phrase "then yesterday," as if "yesterday" were distinct from the day of Bell's visit. She then concludes her letter with what is fairly certainly a description of churchgoers as seen from the Rectory. The most probable explanation is that SH meant "Friday" when she wrote "Saturday."

SH also speaks of a plan for DW and her to visit Keswick shortly; but the visit is not known to have taken place.

RS, Mrs. S, SC, Edith and Herbert S, in a chaise, and Dr. Bell and a servant, on horse, call for a half-hour at the Rectory. W rushes Bell off to the school, where Bell instructs W, the master, and the boys for about twenty minutes. Bell forms an immediate liking for the master, the Rev. William Johnson. Later a man brings a load of shrubs from Mrs. King. The DeQs perhaps come to tea at 5. (1811:54n; *SHL* 28–31; *Life of Bell* II, 398–99; *MY* I, 110–11. Cf Moorman II, 178.)[27]

56. Probably Oct 19; probably Oct 19 and Oct 20; probably Oct 20

Probably on 19 Oct Charles Luff probably calls at the Rectory; he and W discuss the Spaniards.

W, MW, Tommy call at Rydal Hall, at Miss Pritchard's, and at the Lloyds'.

DW, SH, Johnny, the DeQs, William Johnson make an excursion to Yewdale. The DeQs and Johnson visit Coniston also; and DW and SH visit a house at the head of Yewdale that SH had visited as a child. All drink tea at Tamar Turner's [see 1811:46; 1811:47].

Probably on 19 and 20 Oct HC and Derwent visit at the Rectory [see 1808:100; 1811:54n].

Probably on 20 Oct SH finishes her letter to MM begun 17 Oct: A visit from the Ss and Dr. Bell [see 1811:55]; an excursion to Yewdale [see 1811:56]; Henry H expected. (*SHL* 31–33.)

57. Probably between Oct 20 and Nov 3 (–possibly c Dec 20)

SH probably departs Grasmere, visits Mrs. Luff at Patterdale for a few days, and returns. Henry H arrives at the Rectory for a visit. (He departs possibly c 20 Dec.) (*SHL* 27; *MY* I, 512; 1811:54n.)

58. Perhaps Oct 22

DeQ's mother and sisters depart Grasmere. On the morning of the departure W gives them roots of *osmundia regalis*. Possibly at this time

---

[27] Johnson departed next year to assist Bell in London (see 1812:15n; *DNB*). The *Life of Bell* dates the visit in Sept.

MW gives them a commission to obtain print and cotton cloth through Mr. Kelsall. (*Memorials* II, 79–81; *SHL* 27.)[28]

59. Probably c but by Oct 29

W composes *In a Garden of the Same* [Coleorton] ("Oft Is the Medal Faithful to Its Trust") in form described *MY* I, 514. (*MY* I, 513–14.)

60. Probably c but by Oct 30

W writes to Sir GB: Transcriptions of altered versions of "The Embowering Rose" and "Ye Lime-trees"; transcription of "Oft Is the Medal." W's plan of publishing the poems of Sir John B perhaps with those of Frances B; suggests a finely printed limited edition. Bell and his system. (*MY* I, 513–15.)[29]

61. Probably c early Nov, certainly by Nov 16

W makes extensive revision toward *P* 1815 version of *ISHS*. (*MY* I, 518. See 1811:63.)

62. Nov 3

DW writes to RW: MW, DW intend to visit RW at Sockbridge for two or three days as soon as possible, perhaps accompanied by W. SH, Henry H are visiting. (*MY* I, 512.)

63. Nov 16; between Nov 16 and Nov 20

On 16 Nov W writes to Sir GB: Sir GB's agent Taylor; Allston arrived in London. Alterations of "Ye Lime-trees" in response to Sir GB's requests. Wilkie; Arnald. Revisions for *ISHS*. W has some intention of calling upon LdL shortly, partly to pay his respects,

---

[28] SH remarks probably on Thursday 17 Oct that "the DeQs go on Tuesday."

[29] W's letter, postmarked 2 Nov, probably crossed one of Sir GB's to W concerning "Ye Lime-trees" (see 1811:53). W replied to B's request for alterations in his letter of 16 Nov.

and partly because he must devote part of his time to making money. (*MY* I, 515–19.)[30]

Between 16 and 20 Nov W makes further revisions toward *P* 1815 version of *ISHS*. (*MY* I, 520. See 1811:65.)

64. Nov 19

W accompanies DW to Brathay. They possibly return separately. On his walk back W composes *For a Seat in the Groves of Coleorton* ("Beneath Yon Eastern Ridge, the Craggy Bound"). (*MY* I, 519.)[31]

65. Nov 20

W writes to Lady B: Transcription of *For a Seat in The Groves of Coleorton*[32]; transcription of re-revised *ISHS* [see 1811:63]; recommends Daniel's *Epistle to Lady Margaret*. The Coleorton winter garden; the *Courier*, and a poem on the comet, perhaps by STC, that he has read in it today. John Dyer. Transcription of *To the Poet, John Dyer.* (*MY* I, 519–22.)

66. Probably Nov 23–Dec 4; perhaps c Nov 23–Nov 25

Probably 23 Nov–4 Dec SH and Henry H visit Miss Weir at Appleby, spending a night with the Cooksons in Kendal on their way thither, and two nights at the house of the Luffs in Patterdale on their way home. (*SHL* 34–36.)

[30] *MY* letter no. 231, published as belonging to this date, more probably was written in Nov 1812 (see 1812:96). Sir GB evidently responded to this communication enclosing a bank note in a letter postmarked [23 Nov]; but W refused the proffered aid. Sir GB on 6 Dec expressed regret that W did not feel himself "justified in making use of what I sent."

[31] W dated the poem 1808 in *PW* 1845–*PW* 1850. As noted by Dowden (*PW* Dowden V, 337) W remarks in the letter in which he copies the poem as "composed yesterday morning," that the "thought of writing the inscription occurred to me many years ago."

[32] It is probable that in the lost original of the letter the full poem was copied. See *Mem* I, 363. The poem mentioned below which W suspected to be STC's was not.

Perhaps c 23–25 Nov the Luffs visit for two days at the Rectory. (*MY* I, 526; *SHL* 36.)

67. Perhaps Dec 4 and Dec 5

SH writes to MM: (Perhaps 4 Dec:) The Rectory; MM; SH, and Henry H; visit to Appleby. The Luffs to move. DeQ has polled the ash tree and cut down the hedge around the orchard at DC. (Perhaps 5 Dec:) MM; STC; William Johnson; the children; the Hs. Transcriptions of "Ye Lime-trees" and "The Embowering Rose." (*SHL* 33–42.)[33]

68. Perhaps c, certainly by Dec 15–perhaps c, certainly by Dec 25

Perhaps c, certainly by 15 Dec, W is seized by a sudden fancy to go to Keswick, and journeys thither accompanied by DW. Both return by Christmas Day. DW passes a week at GH and three days at William Calvert's. SFC reproaches DW for her inconveniently sudden arrival. (*MY* I, 522, 526; letter, RS to Thomas S, 16 Dec 1811, BM Add. MS 30,927, fol. 190.)[34]

69. Possibly c Dec 20

Henry H departs from the Rectory. (*SHL* 39.)

70. Perhaps c, certainly by Dec 23 (–perhaps c early Jan)

Dora arrives home from Miss Weir's school for the Christmas holidays. (She departs perhaps c early Jan.) (*MY* I, 524.)

---

[33] SH's date "Thursday Evening, Decr 3rd" is possibly a mistake for "Tuesday Evening, Decr 3rd," as 1 Dec was a Sunday; but SH goes on below to write the concluding section of her letter, on the day evidently following that on which all the preceding portion was written, under another date of "Thursday." I have assumed that her second "Thursday" was correct. The appearance of the MS makes remote the chance that the first two words of the first date were written after the conclusion of the letter. The transcriptions of "Ye Lime-trees" and "The Embowering Rose" follow, with inconsequential and probably unauthorized variants, the readings of W's 16 Nov letter for the former, and of W's letter of c but by 30 Oct for the latter.

[34] RS writes, "Wordsworth and his sister are here."

71. Dec 25

W, DW walk in the morning. The family dines on roast beef and plum pudding. In the evening W, MW walk by moonlight; DW plays cards with the children. (*MY* I, 525.)

72. c Dec 27; Dec 27

W is at work on *Exc*, works on new arrangement of his published poems, c 27 Dec. (*MY* I, 527.)[35]

DW writes to CCl: CCl's family. STC and his quarrel with W. The Rectory, its inconvenience. Dora; the family. Charles Lloyd; Mrs. Joseph Wilkinson; Wilkinson has not sent colored or other views. DW in robust health; W at work.

The fiddlers visit this evening. Dora and DW join in the dance. (*MY* I, 522–27.)

[35] Notes in a copy of *P2V* belonging to the Tinker Library, YUL (see *The Tinker Library*, comp. R. F. Metzdorf, New Haven, 1959, item 2335) survive from W's preliminary work toward the order of the poems in *P 1815*. These notes, to which attention has been called by a note by Gene W. Ruoff (*Essays in Criticism* XVI, 1966, 359–60), are occasionally illegible, but do not seem to mention any poem certainly composed between this time and late 1814, and might therefore represent work of this time. "Eughtrees in Borrowdale," which cannot, however, be dated confidently before late 1811, appears on the list, as does "Prospect from Black Comb"—certainly not written before c late Aug 1811. The lists do not include (except for notes of the general headings) the Sonnets, the Inscriptions, or the Epitaphs and Elegiac Poems, among which most of the poems written after *P2V* appeared in 1815. The only poems definitely composed after 1811, but published in groups here listed and not mentioned on these lists, appear to be *Laodamia* and *Yarrow Visited*. W would certainly have completed his 1815 classifications before the composition of *Laodamia* (see 1814:94; 1814:112); and as *Yarrow Visited* was probably not composed until between 1 Sept and 16 Sept 1814, the classification could easily have been made up about this time, but before the poem's completion. The classifications and groupings, if not always the order of the poems, so generally approximate those of the 1815 edition that a date near the time of final preparation of those volumes is probable.

Other notes on the same subject evidently postdating the letter to STC of 5 May 1809 but preceding the *P2V* lists are found in DC MS 24 (see Appendix VI). These too might record work of Dec 1811, but cannot be dated with confidence more precisely than between 5 May 1809 and late Oct 1814.

1812

[On writings of W possibly of this year see below and GCL 34, 42, 123, 146, 148–50, 167, 168, 171, 191, 201, 205–08.]

1. Possibly this year, if not 1806

W composes *Song for the Spinning Wheel*. (W's date, editions 1836–1850.)[1]

2. Perhaps early this year

Perhaps early this year W indirectly indicates to William Pearson that he wishes to buy his Town End estate. (Letters, Pearson to W, 10 Aug 1812, 29 Mar 1813, DCP. See Moorman II, 228n; T. W. Thompson, *Wordsworth's Hawkshead*, ed. R. S. Woof (Oxford, 1970), 360; 1812:76.)[2]

3. Probably early this year by Apr 12; perhaps by Apr 12

Probably early this year by 12 Apr W writes to Francis Wrangham: W's delay in writing; his family. The only modern books W cares for are travels or such as related to matters of fact; he spends any spare money for old books. (*MY* II, 8–9.)[3]

Perhaps early this year by 12 Apr W receives a letter from Eustace Baudouin, held prisoner at Oswestry. W perhaps replies offering money and other assistance. (*MY* II, 18–19. See 1812: 20.)

---

[1] W dates the poem 1812 in editions 1836–1850, but 1806 in its IF note. As it was first published only in *P* 1820, however, it perhaps was not completed before 1815.

[2] Pearson's letter of 10 Aug states that W's wish was conveyed by George Mackereth "some months earlier."

[3] Content indicates that the letter can hardly have been written after W's departure for London, probably on 12 Apr, since one of the five children of whom he speaks had died before his return. The dedication of Wrangham's *Sufferings of the Primitive Martyrs* —the earliest separately published work of Wrangham's that W is likely to be referring to when he says that Wrangham's "Poem" has not reached him—is dated 25 Dec 1811.

4. Probably early this year, perhaps c, certainly by Mar 29; probably early this year by Mar 29

Probably early this year, perhaps c, certainly by 29 Mar, SH makes a fair copy of *The Waggoner*, MS 3. (1806:2n.)
Probably early this year W works busily on *Exc*, but stops by 29 Mar. (*SHL* 46–47.)

5. Probably Jan

W writes to Dr. Andrew Bell: William Johnson has agreed to offer himself as a candidate for office or offices about to be instituted [by or in association with Bell]. W received letter with proposals and showed it to Johnson earlier in the day. Johnson's present income and advantages; Bell's work. (*MY* II, 661–62.)

6. Perhaps c early Jan (–June 17)

Dora returns to school at Miss Weir's. (She returns home on 17 June.) (*MY* I, 525.)

7. Jan 14

The Longman accounts record presentation of three copies of *CC* to Mr. Jameson under this date (without charge). (Longman accounts, Commission Ledger C1, fol. 359.) The Longman accounts (DCP) also charge W £–/5/10 for "2 Goldsmiths England [per] Mr Jameson" under this date.

8. Probably late Jan–perhaps c Feb 6

DW visits Kendal; probably stays with the Thomas Cooksons. (*MY* II, 1. See 1812:12.)

9. Jan 30 or Jan 31

W draws on RW for £50 by bill in favor of J. G. Crump. (*MY* II, 1; RW accounts, DCP.)[4]

[4] RW's accounts record payment under 3 Mar.

10. Perhaps c Feb; perhaps between c Feb and Mar 29

Perhaps c Feb SH makes a copy of *G* 1810 for Charles Luff. (*SHL* 46.)

Perhaps between c Feb and 29 Mar W makes corrections and additions to *PB* in MS 5. (Betz *PB*. See 1812:16.)

11. Feb 2

DW writes to RW from Kendal: A draft by W [see 1812:9] and one to be made by her [see 1812:12]; W plans to visit London about mid-Apr; MW is to visit Wales. (*MY* II, 1.)

12. Perhaps c Feb 3–Feb 6

DW draws on RW for £50 by bill in favor of Thomas Cookson, due at one month. (*MY* II, 1; RW accounts, DCP.)[5]

13. Feb 6

W writes to LdL: Statement of basis and history of W's commitment to literature; his independence and his financial need. Emboldened by the long connection of his family and that of LdL, he requests an office. (*MY* II, 2–4.)[6]

14. Probably Feb 19

STC travels from Kendal to Keswick, bringing HC and Derwent with him from Ambleside. He drives past W's house without stopping. (*STCL* III, 370–76; *Minnow* 16.)[7]

---

[5] RW's accounts record payment of the draft, which DW on 2 Feb intended to make in "a day or two," under 6 Mar.

[6] LdL's reply to this first step toward W's appointment to a Stamp Distributorship in 1813 was written on 25 Feb 1812 from Cottesmere, and expresses regret that LdL is unable to help W. See 1812:19; 1812:77.

[7] STC remarks on Sunday 23 Feb that he reached Keswick on "Tuesday last before dinner." He had, however, written a long letter to Morgan from Kendal (where he arrived at midnight Monday) on Tuesday; and in it he stated that he intended to "arrange some affairs," then to depart Kendal Wednesday morning at 5. Probably he could not have reached Keswick before dinner on Tuesday, but made the trip there on Wednesday. STC's description of the progress of his "violent cold" (*STCL* III, 376) also seems to point to a Wednesday arrival.

15. Perhaps Mar 4

W writes to Dr. Andrew Bell (only a fragment of the letter is known to survive): Praise of William Johnson. Everything will be done to enable Johnson to depart [to become headmaster of the National Schools] as soon as he receives the bishop's permission. (*MY* II, 662.)[8]

16. Mar 28–Mar 29

On the morning of 28 Mar SH rides to Ambleside and returns.
On 29 Mar a letter arrives from Joanna.
SH writes to John M: (28 Mar:) The farm at Hindwell and its prospects. MW's approaching visit there; the National Schools and William Johnson, whom Joanna ought to be happy to have if she can get him; the health and plans of various members of the family; the discomforts of the Rectory. (29 Mar:) MW's trip [see 1812:19]; STC has returned to London[9]; his offense at W; the Luffs have departed; ML; SH has been transcribing; W's composition. (*SHL* 42–47.)

17. Probably c but by Mar 29 ff

SH transcribes for W. After her copy of *The Waggoner* [see 1812:4], and probably c but by 29 Mar she makes a copy of *PB*, probably MS 6, DC MS 72. She perhaps begins another copy on 29 Mar and completes it within a day or so. (Betz *PB*; *SHL* 46; 1806:2.)

18. Perhaps c Apr 12

W suffers from some sort of gastrointestinal illness. (*MY* II, 4; 1812:19.) Willy has chickenpox. (*MY* II, 6.)

---

[8] *Life of Bell* II, 402 states: "'Every thing,' writes Mr Wordsworth in reply to this letter [of Bell's, apparently from London], dated the 1st of March, 'will be done here to enable Mr. Johnson to depart as soon as he receives [&c].'" Probably it was Bell's letter that was dated 1 Mar. Johnson evidently departed Grasmere within a few days (see *SHL* 44).

[9] STC departed Keswick to return to London via Penrith on 26 Mar. He reached London on 14 Apr (*STCL* III, 381, 383).

19. Probably Apr 12–perhaps c July 5

W, MW, Tommy depart Grasmere on 12 Apr, travel together probably to Chester. They perhaps spend a day at Kendal, two days at Liverpool, and arrive at Chester on 17 Apr. MW, Tommy are probably met there by Thomas H and taken on to Hindwell. (*SHL* 45; *MY* II, 4, 10–11. Cf *MY* II, 4n.)[10]

W perhaps proceeds to London via Binfield, or proceeds to Binfield immediately upon arrival in London, visiting perhaps for a few days c 20 Apr with the William Cooksons. In London W stays at the Bs'. (All probably reach the Rectory on their return perhaps c 5 July.) (*MY* I, 4, 6, 16–17; *HCRBW* I, 70.) W's main motive for visiting London is to clarify the problems between him, STC, and Montagu.

Probably W reaches London for his long visit between 24 Apr and 1 May. Between these dates W probably sees Richard Sharp, and he is certainly shown a letter from STC to Sharp of 24 Apr complaining of W's conduct toward him. (*STCL* III, 388–90; *MY* II, 14–16; letter, Rickman to RS, 24 Apr 1812, HEH.)

Probably in very late Apr W calls on Montagu. (*HCRBW* I, 78. See 1812:27.)

Probably between 12 and 25 Apr a request reaches DW through SFC from STC for the two unpublished Essays upon Epitaphs to complete this part of *The Friend*, and probably for some books at the Rectory. DW sends word, with some memoranda about the books and the books themselves, that STC should ask W for the Essays directly; that transcripts would be prepared pending the conclusion of arrangements. (*STCL* III, 392; *MY* II, 13–14.)[11]

[10] DW writes to W on 23 Apr that the family had hoped to receive a letter "from you or Mary from Chester," and looked for one from him from Binfield on Friday 24 Apr. DW says that W and MW departed "three weeks yesterday," and on Sunday 29 Mar SH says that the travellers are to depart "this day fortnight." DeQ wrote to W at Kendal from London on 16 Apr (postmark 18 Apr) with advice concerning coaches from Liverpool to London. The letter was sent back to London on 23 Apr cross-written with DW's letter of that date.

Rickman wrote on 24 Apr, "Coleridge is in Town & Wordsworth they say is coming" (HEH).

[11] STC's inquiries about the essays in his letter to SFC of 24 Apr are evidently not his first, since the family at Grasmere was looking over German books to decide which were to be sent by coach and which were to be sent to RS, and packed two chests, on

On W's activities apart from those immediately connected with the quarrel with STC see esp. Moorman II, 209–10. Probably during this visit W dines more than once in company with Uvedale Price, on at least one occasion at Samuel Rogers'. (*LY* I, 175.) W probably sees and converses with John Constable. W gives him a copy of [*For a Seat in the Groves of Coleorton*] ("Beneath Yon Eastern Ridge, the Craggy Bound"). (*John Constable's Correspondence*, ed. R. B. Beckett, V, Suffolk Records Society xi, 1967, 75–76.) W possibly meets Washington Allston (the meeting appears somewhat more likely to have taken place between 31 May and 19 June 1815). (1815:82.)

While in London W probably sees Mr. Twining to pay a bill; probably sees or inquires about William Johnson. (*MY* II, 7.) He probably calls on LdL to explain some circumstances connected with the application in his letter of 6 Feb. (Letter, Sir GB to W, 31 Aug 1812, DCP.)[12]

On the reconciliation of the quarrel with STC generally see esp. *STCL* III, 375–408; Curry II, 32–34; *Blake Etc.* 48–50; *HCRWC* I, 69–70; *HCRBW* I, 70–81; Moorman II, 202–209; *Minnow* 16.

20. Between Apr 12 and Apr 22 and perhaps shortly after

DW writes two letters to W. The second is written across a letter to W probably from Eustace Baudouin. (*MY* II, 18–19.)[13]

Perhaps shortly after receipt of the second letter W applies to Daniel Stuart for assistance in obtaining the release of the French prisoners among whom Baudouin is numbered. (*MY* II, 47–48.)

---

[12] Sir GB writes that he has received a letter from LdL: "[H]e says when you called upon him in London it was to explain some circumstance connected with the application you made to him in the winter on a subject in which you thought he might be of use to you but in fact he could not be of any." Sir GB goes on to advise W of LdL's offer of £100 per year until he can do more.

[13] Concerning Baudouin, whose letter advised W that he needed no money, and that he wished for W to assist him in his release, see *MY* II, 18n, Moorman II, 330.

Sunday 26 Apr. They packed and sent off a third chest, probably to Keswick, on Friday 1 May.

21. Apr 16, 18

RW's accounts charge W £29/12/–, payment of a bill in favor of John Green, under these dates. (RW accounts, DCP.)[14]

22. Apr 23

DW writes to W across a letter to him from DeQ [see 1812:19n]: Illness in the house, esp. of Sarah Yewdale and Fanny Turner, and in the neighborhood. Sarah's grandmother a recent visitor, and her mother Betty, who will come again at end of week. The new schoolmaster [and curate, Bamford]; the weather; the household; acquaintances in London and elsewhere. They read novels; Mrs. Opie's *Adeline Mowbray*. (*MY* II, 4–7.)[15]

23. Between Apr 24 and May 17

DW writes to W, MW. (*MY* II, 18–19.)

24. Probably c but by Apr 29

MW adds a cheerful postscript (not known to survive) to a letter from MM to DW and/or SH. (*MY* II, 10.)[16]

25. Probably c but by Apr 30

W writes to DW and/or SH from London. This letter is not known to survive, but for a possible portion of its contents see *MY* II, 16. (*MY* II, 10.)

26. Apr 30

W probably this day calls on J. F. Tuffin, who is not at home. He attends a play, possibly *Julius Caesar*.[17] (*MY* II, 9–10.)

[14] Payment is noted under the different dates in different accounts.

[15] *MY* II, 5, implies that Bamford commenced work on 20 Apr. He relinquished his duties c mid-Sept. See *Life of Bell* II, 424; 1812:69.

[16] The letter was received at Grasmere on 1 May.

[17] *Julius Caesar* was the play presented at Covent Garden on this day (*Times*).

W writes to Tuffin from Grosvenor Square after receiving a note from Tuffin upon his return from the play: Regrets having missed Tuffin; invites him to call at Grosvenor Square. (*MY* II, 9–10.)

On this day DW, probably SH and others visit Hackett. Sarah Yewdale is very weak. (*MY* II, 11.)

27. Probably very late Apr or May 1 or 2; May 2

Probably in very late Apr or on 1 or 2 May W proposes, through CL, to meet with STC in Montagu's presence. On 2 May STC agrees, with reservations; asks CL to transmit to W a letter, begun by STC to SH long ago, on the affair. W refuses to read it. W also asks STC through CL to stop talking about the affair. (*STCL* III, 394–98. See Moorman II, 204.)

Perhaps at this time STC communicates to W his intention of drawing up a statement of Montagu's assertions. W replies via CL that he wishes nothing more than a dry account of Montagu's remarks. (*HCRBW* I, 70–76. See 1812:28.)

28. May 3

Derwent and Algernon Montagu visit the Rectory. (*MY* II, 12. See 1812:29.)

HCR leaves a card for W at Sir GB's, Grosvenor Square. He calls on STC. STC states to him that he will see W alone, or with friends; but will not meet with him and Montagu in order to confront Montagu. They discuss other aspects of the quarrel. STC states that he will write a detailed statement of Montagu's assertions. STC gives HCR permission to repeat his remarks to W. (*HCRBW* I, 70–76. See 1812:27.)

29. Probably May 4

W receives a letter from STC, probably written 4 May [see 1812: 28]. W refuses to read it, as he has no assurance that it contains only a dry account of Montagu's remarks. He writes to CL asking for this assurance. STC does not provide it. The letter remains unopened. (*MY* II, 17; *STCL* III, 397–402; *HCRBW* I, 76. See 1812:30.)

DW writes to W, MW: A short letter from W and a long one from Luff, who says that he will want the whole of the £100; W will settle this with Woodruffe. Recent household affairs; Sarah Yewdale; Johnny, Willy; STC's books and his request for the unpublished Essays upon Epitaphs [see 1812:19]; comments and advice about STC; husbandry at the Rectory. (*MY* II, 10–16.)[18]

30. Probably May 5

W writes to CCl from Grosvenor Square (only a fragment of the letter survives): The STC affair; plan of meeting with referee abandoned; STC. A letter from STC which W has not opened [see 1812:29]. W's belief that foul play and atrocious falsehood have played a part in the quarrel. (*MY* II, 16–17.)[19]

31. May 7 (–May 17); between May 7 and May 17

On 7 May SH goes to Keswick for a visit at GH. (She remains until 17 May.) Between 7 May and 17 May DW writes to W. (*MY* II, 19.)

32. May 8

W calls on HCR, who delivers to him STC's message of 3 May. W sends HCR to STC with an oral denial of some expressions allegedly used by Montagu, and a statement indicating that he is not determined to pursue his plan of meeting with STC and Montagu. W accompanies HCR as far as Newman Street. STC agrees to have ready on the morning of Sunday [10 May] a statement of the sort requested by W [see 1812:28]. HCR writes to W making an appointment for Sunday. (*HCRBW* I, 75–81; *HCRNB*; *STCL* III, 397, 403–04.)[20]

33. May 10

HCR calls on STC, who gives him the promised statement [see 1812:32]. HCR takes it to W. W and HCR converse at length about

[18] DW's letter is dated "Monday May 3rd," but 1 May was a Friday. The £100 remains unexplained, but probably represents a proffered loan toward expenses of the Luffs' removal to Mauritius (see *MY* II, 5).

[19] W evidently dated his letter "Tuesday, May 6," but 1 May was a Friday. Moorman II, 205 states that HCR saw W on 6 May.

[20] HCRNB notes that HCR left a card for W at Sir GB's on 2, 3, and 5 May. For 8 May HCRNB reports: "M[orning]. Wordsworth at Chambers. a long chat with him A call on Coleridge. from W."

STC; walk toward the City; call on Sgt. Rough and the Colliers. (*HCRBW* I, 79; HCRNB.)[21]

34. May 11

HCR calls on W by appointment at 10:30. They work on a letter to STC; W writes a draft dealing with STC's charges, explaining, affirming, denying. He absolves himself of blame except for mistaken judgment in speaking on such a delicate subject to a man whose conduct is so little governed as Montagu's by the laws of friendship and regulations of society in such cases. HCR draws up a second draft.[22] Probably W writes a final copy, which does not survive. HCR is probably primarily responsible for the final phrasing of the statement. CW joins them. They walk into Oxford Street, where HCR leaves [them] after 2. HCR tries to deliver W's letter but STC is not at home; he probably leaves the letter. HCR returns again after dinner and tea, finds STC and the Ls. STC is conciliated by W's letter and writes to W to this effect. The affair is thus settled. (*HCRBW* I, 79–81; HCRNB; *STCL* III, 403–08.)[23]

Probably this evening W, perhaps with Sir GB, dines with Samuel Rogers. W is probably met at the door by Byron, who informs him of the assassination of Perceval. This is perhaps the occasion referred to *LY* III, 1306, when Byron disarms W by laughing at his own review of W's *P2V* [see 1807:68]. Later this evening Tom Moore probably also calls with the news about Perceval, and finds W and Sir GB present. (Letter, W to unidentified addressee, 2 Jan 1847, McGill University Library; Charles W's memoranda of W's conversation, Aug 1844; *Moore Memoirs* V, 228.)[24]

[21] HCRNB records: "Vorm: Coleridge. . . . Several Hours with Wordsworth. Calls with him at C's & Rough's [.]"

[22] The drafts are quoted *STCL* III, 403–06.

[23] HCRNB records simply: "Vorm mit Wordsworth v½ p 10 bis 2 Ab: bey Coleridge[.] *Perceval Shot.*"

[24] In a letter of 2 Jan 1847 to an unidentified recipient (McGill University Library) W says, "I never saw [Byron] but twice, both times in the house of Mr. Rogers, and in one instance only for a few minutes." This occasion would appear to be the meeting that lasted a few minutes. On 18 June 1815 the two dined together. In a pencil memo-

35. Between May 11 and May 19, June 4

Between 11 and 19 May and STC meet frequently; do not discuss their recent correspondence. (*HCRBW* I, 84.) Between 11 May and 4 June W and STC meet several times but are not alone much. One morning they walk to Hampstead. (*MY* II, 22.)

36. May 13

W dines at William Rough's with CW, HCR, and Mrs. Rough. W converses on Landor, Kirke White, RS, Scott, Wilson; reads from Jeremy Taylor.

W accompanies HCR to join a company at Dr. Charles Aikin's. The company includes Charles, Mrs., Miss, and Arthur Aikin; the Misses Jane Porter, Benger, Clarke, Smirke; Messrs. Cullen, Roscoe (son of William Roscoe), Yates of Liverpool, and James Montgomery; and Mrs. Barbauld. W asserts that Francis Burdett's speech of ten days past might have encouraged the assassin of Perceval. Roscoe and Yates contradict W. W is pleased with Mrs. Aikin. (*HCRBW* I, 82–84; *HCRWC* I, 69, 93n; Mrs. Herbert Martin, ed., *Memories of Seventy Years*, London, 1884, 78; letter, Rough to W, 12 May 1812, DCP; HCRNB.)[25]

---

[25] Rough's letter, addressed to W at Sir GB's, invites the poet "to take a chop" with the company named. HCRNB records: "Mit Ess: Rough, with the Wordsworth[s] ab: Mrs Chas Aiken with Wordsworth ((a party) [.]"

---

randum by Charles W in my possession appears the following record of W's conversation in Aug 1844:

> My uncle met Ld Byron twice—both times at Mr Rogers
> 1 On one occasion he Ld B met my uncle at the door & announced to him Mr Perceval's death.
> 2 on the other, Rogers, Ld B, My U & a 4th (think Charles Lamb) [*sic*] dined together. on the Sunday of the Battle of Waterloo. Ld B. [?argued] & seemed to wish that Buonaparte wd be victorious. My Uncle on the Contrary maintained He had no chance whatever if the allies kept together.

This account appears a more accurate record of the means of W's learning the news of Perceval's death than Tom Moore's claim that he was the bearer of the report to Rogers, W, and Sir GB. Moore, however, also acknowledges Rogers' recollection that the messenger was Byron, concluding, "I rather think both stories are true."

37. Probably c but by May 14

Probably c but by 14 May W writes to DW (the letter is not known to survive, but probably reports the conclusion of the reconciliation between W and STC). (*MY* II, 19.)

38. May 15

W writes to HCR from Grosvenor Square: W is obliged to break his engagement with HCR for Sunday [19 May, probably with the Aikins] because of prior arrangements which he had forgotten and of which he has just been reminded by Lady B. Mrs. Charles Aikin. (*HCRWC* I, 69; *MY* II, 17–18. See Mrs. Herbert Martin, ed., *Memories of Seventy Years*, London, 1884, 78.)

39. May 17 (–perhaps c May 27)

W probably dines with a party of friends, perhaps at the Bs', but fairly certainly including the Bs. (*MY* II, 17–18.)

SFC, SC, Edith S arrive with SH at the Rectory for a visit. (SFC, SC, Edith S depart perhaps c May 27.)

DW writes to W: Letters that she has written to W since his departure; SH; STC. (*MY* II, 18–20.)

40. May 19

W calls on HCR at noon. They walk to Rough's chambers. W agrees to meet [Elton] Hamond and [Joanna] Baillie [see 1812:42]. After a cold luncheon [all] proceed to Willis's rooms for STC's first lecture; hear STC for about a quarter of an hour. W talks with STC, Mrs. [William] Pattison. Thomas Madge possibly pushes himself into W's company. (*HCRBW* I, 84, 87–88; HCRNB.)[26]

[26] HCRNB records, "Chamb bis 12 Wordsworth called[.]"
HCR states that on the occasion of STC's third lecture, on 26 May, "Madge came and *pushed* himself again into the society of Coleridge and Wordsworth." No record appears to survive of W's having attended the second lecture, and HCR's "again" hardly implies that the present occasion was the time, or the only time, of an earlier meeting. It may be noted, however, as the possible reference of William James, *Memoir of the Revd Thomas Madge* (London, 1871), 108, where Madge is said to have "had the pleasure," after moving in 1811 to Norwich, of "an introduction" while

41. Possibly c May 21

W dines with John Stoddart, evidently hoping to meet Capt. Pasley [see 1811:15]; but he is disappointed, the more because he learns that Pasley is out of town and that they are unlikely to meet during W's London visit. (*MY* II, 20.)[27]

42. May 24

W meets HCR in Oxford Road at 10:30. They walk to Hampstead; talk of Byron. HCR reads some of Blake's poems to W, who is pleased with some of them and expresses an opinion that Blake possesses the elements of poetry a thousand times more than Byron or Scott. They meet Joanna Baillie, accompany her home, where they meet W's old acquaintance [T. W.] Carr, Solicitor to the Excise. They discuss politics, Mrs. Barbauld's new poem [*Eighteen Hundred and Eleven*], TCl, Malkin. W and HCR accept an invitation to dine with Carr, whom they accompany home, on Sunday 30 May.

W and HCR dine with [Elton] Hamond, Mrs. Deacon of Milk Street, [J. F.] Pollock, [Charles] and Miss Hamond. W, HCR, Pollock walk home at 8. W and Pollock carry on a dispute on the subjects of property tax and annuity assessment. W, alone with HCR, speaks of RS and Unitarianism. (*HCRBW* I, 85–87; *HCRNB*.)[28]

43. Probably May 25

W writes to Capt. Pasley from Grosvenor Square: Has heard from Stoddart that Pasley has cause for complaint against a person high in office in his profession. An intimate friend of W's is an intimate friend of that person. W offers assistance if Pasley desires it. (*MY* II, 20.)

[27] W's letter to Pasley, probably of 25 May 1812, speaks of this dinner as having taken place "the other day."

[28] On W's remarks on Blake, and the poetry of Blake's which HCR could have read to W, see esp. Mark Reed, "Blake, Wordsworth, Lamb, Etc.: Further Information from Henry Crabb Robinson," *Blake Newsletter* III (1970), 76–84. On W's first acquaintance with Blake's verse see 1807:12; Betz *BN*.

HCRNB records under 24 May: "Day with Wordsworth at Hampstead."

there to W, with whom Madge was to enjoy "frequent and friendly" contact in visits to the Lakes thereafter. W can hardly have visited Norwich on his way to London; but he was certainly sought out by Madge "again" on 26 May. See also 1813:61.

44. May 26

W attends STC's third lecture; probably converses with STC. The two are intruded upon by [Thomas] Madge. W possibly also converses with HCR and Mrs. Collier. (*HCRBW* I, 87–88. See 1812:40n.)

45. Perhaps c May 27

SFC, SC, Edith S depart from the Rectory. (*MY* II, 19, 35.)[29]

46. May 29; May 30

On 29 May W probably attends STC's fourth lecture. He is later with STC and HCR at the J. J. Morgans'. W praises Burns; concurs with STC in a low opinion of Goethe. (*HCRBW* I, 88–89; *Blake, Etc.* 56.)

On 30 May W perhaps dines at T. W. Carr's with HCR. (1812:42.)

47. May 31

W visits [Elton] Hamond at Hampstead; discusses his philosophic and poetical theories with Hamond, [?John] Miller, and with HCR, who arrives as the conversation is in progress. W speaks of his poems as a new power; he plans to reprint his published works arranged according to the fancy, imagination, reflection, or mere feeling contained in them; discusses imaginative creation as demonstrated in his poems; Campbell, Gray; his fears of class war; the manufacturing system as an evil; defends church establishment. W and HCR dine at Mr. and Mrs. Carr's with Sir Humphry and Lady Davy, Joanna Baillie and her sister, Richard Duppa, Mr. and Miss Stable, J. F. Pollock, Mr. Burrell. W and Davy deprecate Mrs. Scott; Lady Davy and Joanna Baillie defend her. Other visitors arrive after dinner, including Samuel Hoare. W, Burrell, HCR walk home. W and Burrell express displeasure in Pollock. (*HCRBW* I, 89–92; *Blake, Etc.* 53–55; HCRNB.)[30]

[29] DW remarks on the day of the visitors' arrival, 17 May, that they would stay, she supposed, "about 10 days." On 23 June she remarks contradictorily that they stayed a fortnight but left ten days before the death of Catharine (4 June).

[30] HCRNB records: "Hampstead day Walk with Hamond round by Mrs Becher's Mit: Ess: Mr Carr's. Sir Humphry: & Lady Davy. &sw Return with Burrell & Wordsworth[.]"

48. June 3; probably June 3

On 3 June W calls on TCl, finds him at dinner; departs after a brief greeting. (*MY* II, 21.)

Probably on 3 June W calls on, or is called on by, HCR. They discuss Joanna Baillie. At 4 W and HCR dine at Rough's with CW and Richard Cargill. W talks of fancy and imagination; reads *The Waggoner* (probably from MS 3) after dinner. W, CW, HCR walk to Lambeth Palace, and W and HCR on to the end of Oxford Road. W discusses RS, Shakespeare, Byron, his own poems. W perhaps today lends a copy (probably MS 6) of *PB*, and of *The Waggoner*, to HCR.(*HCRBW* I, 92–94; *HCRNB*; 1806:2.)[31]

At about 9:30 Catharine W is seized by convulsions.(*MY* II, 23–24.)

49. June 4 and about this time

W writes to Thomas M from Grosvenor Square: Asks whether M could carry W to Hampstead for tea with Miss Baillie this afternoon. If M could provide him a bed, would return with him to town next morning, or would dine with M and his friends today.

W perhaps drinks tea with Miss Baillie and passes time in company with Thomas M in one or more of the fashions suggested above. (*MY* II, 22–23.)

W writes to CCl from Grosvenor Square: He intends to depart for Bocking with CW on Monday and proceed to Bury on Saturday or Sunday. His call on TCl [see 1812:48]. Public affairs; MW, Joanna H, Thomas H are making a tour in South Wales. STC. (*MY* II, 21–22.)

HCR reads *PB*, and under this date makes a résumé, with extended quotation, of the poem; also comments, with quotations, on *The Waggoner*. About this time probably HCR advises W to leave out the "Is it a party" passage from *PB* (*PW* II, 354 *app crit*). (*HCRBW* I, 94–102; *Blake, Etc.* 55–56. See 1812:48.)

Catharine W dies probably between 5 and 5:15 AM. (*MY* II, 23–24;

---

[31] *HCRNB* contains almost identical entries for 2 and 3 June: (2 June:) "Mit Es Rough (The Wordsworths & Cargill ab: walk with Wordsworth[).]" (3 June:) "Mit: Ess: Roughs. The Wordsworths & Cargil ab: spaz Wordsworth[.]" It would seem probable that both entries refer to the same day. Deference is here given to the date of the diary entry, presumably based on careful recollection.

M-W Book of Common Prayer, DCP.)[32] On W's reaction see esp. *HCRBW* I, 103; *Blake, Etc.* 57; Aubrey De Vere, *Essays* (London, 1887) II, 280.

DW probably this morning writes to W. Probably after a few days SH writes to Thomas H at Radnor; she expects that her letter will arrive there after W. But it arrives before W, and MW learns of the event then. (*MY* II, 24; 28–29.)

W later writes of MW's and Tommy's reaction to Catharine's death in *Maternal Grief* [see Appendix VI].

50. June 5

DW writes to DeQ: Catharine's death. (*MY* II, 23–24. See Masson II, 443.)

51. June 6

HCR lends *PB* [see 1812:48], perhaps also *The Waggoner*, to CL. W joins the Colliers, the Ls, and HCR at Anthony Robinson's for tea and supper. W speaks of Fox, STC's political views, Johnson. (*HCRBW* I, 103; *Blake, Etc.* 55–56; HCRNB.)[33]

52. June 8 (–June 11)

Catharine W is buried at Grasmere. DW, SH, Johnny attend. (Grasmere PR; *MY* II, 33.)[34]

W, CW travel to Bocking from London. (W visits until 11 June.) (*MY* II, 24–25.)

53. Probably June 10

W, CW take a long walk. On their return W finds DW's letter advising him of Catharine's death.

---

[32] The Prayer Book gives the hour as 5.

[33] HCRNB records: "Vorm: Breakfd Parkin. Peter Bell, Benj the Waggoner Ab: at A Robinson with Wordsworth the Lambs Colliers &[c.]"

[34] The PR reads: "[Burial] June 1812 8th Catherine Wordsworth Daughtr of William Wordsworth Esqre Grass."

W writes to CCl from Bocking: Catharine's death; his plans. (*MY* II, 24–25.)[35]

54. Probably June 11

W comes to London from Bocking. He leaves at Bocking a copy of DW's *Narrative* of George and Sarah Green for transmission to CCl.

W probably today writes to Thomas H instructing him to break the news of Catharine's death to MW [see 1812:49]. W calls on HCR. The two walk to see STC, and then to see DeQ. DeQ bursts into tears on seeing W, having heard of Catharine's death from DW [see 1812: 50]. W speaks kindly and respectfully of Anthony Robinson. He passes the night in London. (*MY* II, 24–26, 46; *HCRBW* I, 103; *Blake, Etc.* 57; HCRNB. See also Masson II, 440–45.)[36]

55. Probably June 12–June 14

W departs from London on the Hereford coach at 2 probably on 12 June. DeQ sees him off. (Jordan 263–64.) W reaches Hindwell on 14 June. On his way he travels forty miles with Gilbert Malcolm[37], with whom he discusses CW's chances of an upcoming professorship at Cambridge. Perhaps while on his journey he writes to CW mentioning this meeting. (*MY* II, 25–27, 662–63.) RW's accounts charge DW £30, payment of bill in favor of James Graves, under 14 June. (RW accounts, DCP.)

56. Probably c mid-June

DW, at DC, sees JW (nephew) with Mr. Saltmarsh. He is at this time attending school at Ambleside. (*MY* II, 30.)

---

[35] The letter, although first published in full in *MY*, is quoted *in extenso* in Maggs Catalogue no. 352 (Christmas 1916), item 2157.

[36] HCRNB records simply: "A walk with Wordsworth from Chambers[.]"

[37] Malcolm was a friend of CW's, cousin of Capt. Pasley, and brother of the Ws' later friends, the Misses Malcolm (see esp. 1814:47). W speaks to CW on 18 June of "Mr Malcolm, with whom as I said, I was greatly interested." His phrasing seems to leave little doubt that he wrote to CW after this meeting with Malcolm but before his letter of 18 June. W apparently wrote no letters between the time of his arrival and 18 June.

57. June 17

Dora returns home from Miss Weir's school. (*MY* II, 33.)

58. Probably June 18 or June 19, and about this time; June 18

Probably on 18 or 19 June W or perhaps MW writes to DW and/or SH from Hindwell (letter not known to survive): W, MW cannot return before 30 June.

About this time MW writes to DW and/or SH. (*MY* II, 30, 34.)

On 18 June W writes to CCl from Hindwell: Arrival at Hindwell; MW and her dejection; his stopover in London; improbability that MW can be diverted from her grief by an excursion in Wales. (*MY* II, 25–26.)

On this day W also writes to CW: Arrival at Hindwell; MW and her dejection; Malcolm [see 1812:55]; urges CW to seek professorship; address will be Hindwell for at least ten days. (*MY* II, 26–27.) On this day W also writes to Capt. Pasley: His sudden departure from London on account of Catharine's death; Malcolm [see 1812:55]. (*MY* II, 662–63.)

On this day W also writes to DeQ: Arrival at Hindwell; MW and her dejection; address will be Hindwell for at least ten days. (*MY* II, 27–28.)[38]

59. June 19–June 21

On 19 June DW goes to Ambleside to seek a letter from W and MW (but finds none), and to consult Scambler about Willy, who is quite ill. Between 19 and 21 June Willy improves. (*MY* II, 28–29.)

On 21 June DW writes to JPM: W, MW and their reactions to Catharine's death; an expected visit from Mrs. Rawson[39] and Elizabeth Threlkeld, whom she hopes the Marshalls will accompany. Expectations concerning the return of W, MW. Johnny attending school at Ambleside. (*MY* II, 28–31.)

DW or SH writes to W and MW on 21 June (letter not known to survive) urging them to return home at once. (*MY* II, 30.)

[38] The similarity of content and phrasing between this letter and the other three letters of the same day, and the postmark of 20 June which it shares with the letters to Pasley and CW (cf *MY* II, 26), leave little doubt that the letter was written on 18 June.

[39] DW apparently saw Mrs. Rawson only in July, at the Marshalls'. See 1812:63.

60. June 23

DW writes to CCl: Catharine's death; the family; Dora, John, Willy, SH. W, MW expected home next week; MM expected in a few weeks. (*MY* II, 31–36.)

61. Perhaps c July 2 or July 3–probably c July 5

W, MW, Tommy set off from Hindwell perhaps c 2 or 3 July. They arrive at the Rectory perhaps c 5 July. (*MY* II, 26, 28, 30, 35, 39.)[40]

62. Possibly between c July 5 and the end of the year

W sees and admires a large painting of George Dawe's, of a mother rescuing her child from an eagle's nest. (Pearson 27; letter, RS to Mrs. Montagu, 19 Oct 1812, Cornell Collection, Cornell 3118.)[41]

63. Probably c July 7–probably July 24; shortly before but by July 24; perhaps c mid-July

DW departs c 7 July for a visit to Ullswater, at the Marshalls', Watermillock, and for four days at Eusemere with Capt. and Mrs. W. She is possibly accompanied thither, probably to the Marshalls', by W. Her main purpose in the visit is to see Mrs. Rawson, who is probably staying at Watermillock. The first morning of her visit at Eusemere she spends alone wandering in the grounds and in the neighborhood. During her Ullswater visit she calls twice at Sockbridge (RW is not there) and visits Penrith at least once. DW visits Haweswater and Rawson Bay with JPM.

W probably comes shortly before but by 24 July to fetch DW

[40] DW writes on 31 July that she departed for a visit at Ullswater two days after MW's return, and stayed there "a fortnight and three days" (*MY* II, 39). She apparently returned home on 24 July.

[41] W is said by a Mr. Preston (see Pearson reference) to "admire" the painting "much." Dawe was expected at Keswick in May (*MY* II, 11) and RS writes from Keswick on 19 Oct that Dawe "is painting a huge picture here. . . . " Preston also states, however, that STC "is quite warm upon it." STC must have seen the painting elsewhere than in the Lake area if he saw it at all about this time, and the place may have been London, where W might also have seen it. The present suggestion seems the more probable. Dawe is said by Preston to be "intimate" with W. SH probably saw the picture in early Nov at Ambleside (*SHL* 47–48).

home. He sees Capt. and Mrs. W; learns that RW has been in poor health. W or DW probably now receives a gift pig for the family from Capt. & Mrs. W.

Probably on 24 July W and DW return home. They are accompanied probably to the neighborhood of Brothers Water by John Marshall and JPM's sister, with whom they eat a picnic dinner. They probably proceed up Dovedale and Dove Crag, across Fairfield and so home, probably bringing the pig with them. They arrive a little after 6. The pig delights the children. (*MY* II, 36–41, 43.)

Perhaps c mid-July RS calls or visits at the Rectory. W gives RS a letter of introduction to the Rev. Mr. Carr at Bolton Abbey [see 1807: 55]. (Letter, RS to Mrs. Montagu, 19 Oct 1812, Cornell Collection, Cornell 3118.)[42]

64. July 26; perhaps July 26 (–Nov 2)

On 26 July DW writes to JPM: Her return to Grasmere from Watermillock; the children; Tilbrooke; C. J. Blomfield. She will send Wilkinson's prints by carrier next Thursday, with *The Curse of Kehama*. The pig [see 1812:63]. Plans for visits and visitors. (*MY* II, 36–38.)

This afternoon the Ws probably drink tea with Tilbrooke and Blomfield. (*MY* II, 37.)

Perhaps today MM arrives for a visit at the Rectory. (She departs 2 Nov.) (*MY* II, 38.)

65. July 28; probably July 28 or shortly after, but possibly early Sept, by Sept 8

On 28 July the family, except for MW, visits Hackett, in company with Richard Sharp and Tilbrooke. Tilbrooke plays the flute. The incident prompts W to compose, probably today or shortly after, but possibly in early Sept, by 8 Sept. "The Fairest, Brightest Hues of Ether Fade." (*MY* II, 39–40; "The Fairest, Brightest Hues" IF note. See 1812:66n; 1812:80.)

---

[42] RS mentions having received such a letter "last summer." He was at Settle on his way for the tour concerned on 23 July (CCS III, 344).

66. July 31

DW writes to CCl: Her recent visits to Watermillock and Euse-mere [see 1812:63]. Blomfield and Tilbrooke. The children. (*MY* I, 39–40.)[43]

DW writes to RW: W will draw for £50 at one month in a few days [see 1812:81]. Her wish to see RW, and to have a statement of their accounts. (*MY* II, 40–41.)

67. c early Aug, by Aug 6

Richard Sharp and Samuel Rogers are often in company with the Ws about this time. W is fairly surely in company with Rogers, per-haps at Lowwood, and perhaps also with Sir James Mackintosh, by 6 Aug, possibly at Ullswater. (*MY* II, 45; *R&C* I, 91; *Moore Memoirs* VIII, 114. See 1812:76.)[44]

68. Probably Aug 2

The W family attends church. Blomfield preaches, and Tilbrooke reads prayers. (*MY* II, 41–42.)

69. Probably c 5 Aug–possibly Sept 28 or Sept 29

Dr. Bell arrives for a visit in Grasmere. He probably stays a few days at the Rectory; takes lodgings in a farmhouse next door by 10 Aug. (He possibly departs Grasmere 28 or 29 Sept.) During his visit DW virtually rewrites the portion of Bell's *Experiment* published in 1814 as *Elements of Tuition, Part II. The English School.* (Few or none of DW's revisions are adopted for publication.)

During Bell's visit Mr. Bamford spends an evening at W's house with him. Bell soon gives him a letter of recommendation to William Johnson in London. Bamford departs Grasmere, and is succeeded c late

---

[43] DW's letter to CCl of 31 July is written on a frank by Sharp, "Kendal July thirty one 1812 Mrs Clarkson Bury St Edmunds f R Sharp" (cf *MY* II, 39).

[44] Rogers writes to Moore perhaps from Ullswater, on 6 Aug, "Here are Sharp, and Wordsworth, and Macintosh, who desire to be remembered to you." He and Sharp went to Lowwood, probably, on 9 Aug. (*R&C* I, 91.) On the comings and goings of the Mackintoshes, Sharp, and Rogers see *ibid* 91–104.

Sept by the Rev. Robert Powley. (*Life of Bell* II, 418–19, 428; *MY* II, 79.)

70. Probably Aug 8, –possibly Aug 9 (–possibly Aug 27)

Probably on 8 Aug W, MW, DW, Johnny, Dora, Dr. Bell travel together to Keswick, where Miss Fricker and Miss Barker are visiting. They return the same day, or possibly next, leaving Dora and bringing back with them Herbert S (who visits at the Rectory till possibly 27 Aug). (*MY* II, 42. See 1812:78.)

71. Aug 10

DW writes to CCl: Sends greetings by Blomfield, who is departing with Tilbrooke. Blomfield and Tilbrooke. The family's activities. (*MY* II, 41–43.)[45]
The family, perhaps without W, eats a parting dinner with Tilbrooke at DC. W probably today goes to Lowwood, and in company with Sharp, Rogers, and probably John Wilson, attends a wrestling match between the young men of Cumberland, Westmorland, and Lancashire, at Ambleside. Mr. Preston is present but probably does not join the company. W perhaps sees the Mackintoshes. (*MY* II, 42; Pearson 27; *R &C* I, 91.)

72. Aug 12

Rogers arrives at the Rectory at 4:30; goes with the Ws to drink tea with Dr. Bell. (*R &C* I, 91. See *MY* II, 69.)
W writes to RW: Asks RW to give up to Montagu every security except the Annuity Bond and Insurance Policy.[46] RW's health; the family at the Rectory. (*MY* II, 43.)

73. Aug 13; probably c Aug 13 (–perhaps c Aug 27)

MW walks to Brathay. On her return she finds [W and] the

---

[45] Blomfield's and Tilbrooke's lodgings were taken by Dr. Bell (*MY* II, 45).
[46] W's request is a fairly clear indication that Montagu's debts to W exclusive of the annuity were fully paid. On subsequent financial arrangements between W and Montagu see esp. 1813:15.

family at tea with Sharp, Rogers, Sir James and Lady Mackintosh, and Miss Knott of Ambleside.[47] (*MY* II, 45; *R &C* I, 91–93.)

Probably c 13 Aug SH and MM travel to Appleby to spend a fortnight with Miss Weir. (They return perhaps c 27 Aug.) (*MY* II 43–44.)

74. Aug 14

W, MW ride to Lowwood; drink tea with Rogers; walk with him up the Troutbeck road; watch the sunset. (*MY* II, 45; *R &C* I, 94.)

75. Aug 15

Sharp breakfasts with W. (*MY* II, 45; *R &C* I, 94.)

DW writes to CCl: A proposed tour of Wales by CCl. The marriage of CCl's sister; approaching marriage of MM and Thomas H; MM; MW; Dr. Bell, Rogers, Sharp, other visitors. (*MY* II, 43–46.)[48]

76. Perhaps c mid-Aug

W receives from William Pearson a letter of 10 Aug offering to sell his Town End estate to W. W probably replies with an offer. (Letters, Pearson to W, 10 Aug 1812, 29 Mar 1813, DCP. See Moorman II, 228n; 1812:2.)

77. Perhaps Aug 20 or shortly after

Rogers, at Lowther Castle, speaks to LdL of W's straitened circumstances. LdL writes to Sir GB asking advice about W's needs, remarking on his possible inability to provide a suitable office or similar arrangement for some time, but offering £100 per annum to W in the meantime. (*R &C* I, 92, 103; Rogers *Table-Talk* 206–07.)

[47] DW's statement that such a party took place "Sunday" [9 Aug] is clearly a slip.

[48] Rogers' description of the events of 13–15 Aug and DW's of the same events leave no doubt that DW's letter was written on 15 Aug, although dated *MY* II, 43, "16 August 1812." The only date on the letter appears to be that of Sharp's frank, "Augt sixteen 1812."

78. Between Aug 24 and Aug 27, fairly certainly Aug 26–Aug 27

RS passes at least one, perhaps as many as three days, in Grasmere, perhaps with DeQ at DC. Herbert S possibly accompanies RS home. (Curry II, 40; Masson II, 173. See 1812:70.)[49]

79. Perhaps c Aug 27

SH, MM return from Appleby to the Rectory. (*MY* II, 43–44.)

80. Probably early Sept, including probably Sept 7 or Sept 8

W, DW make a tour including probably Wastwater and Loweswater; spend three days in Borrowdale; return home probably 7 or 8 Sept. W and perhaps DW probably now make notes at Loweswater and Nether Wastdale from which W draws information on Henry Forest included in W's Memoir of the Rev. Robert Walker. W spends a night at Rosthwaite sharing a bed with a Scotch pedlar. W, DW call, wet and dirty, at GH on their way home, probably on 7 Sept. They perhaps pass a night there. (Moorman II, 222; "A Visit to Southey," *The Countryman* XXXVII, 1948, 55–56; DCP. See Appendix VI.)[50]

W perhaps on this excursion composes:
"Even as a Dragon's Eye That Feels the Stress"
"Hail, Twilight, Sovereign of One Peaceful Hour!"
He possibly also now composes "The Fairest, Brightest Hues of Ether Fade."[51] On his return home W finds a letter from Sir GB

---

[49] RS writes on 28 Aug, "Yesterday I returned from Grasmere after a three days absence."

[50] Harriet Green records in an undated journal entry that the Ws called at GH "last Monday night." It appears improbable that W could have reached home and written to Sir GB and LdL on the same Monday night: see his letter of Monday 14 Sept, *MY* II, 46.

[51] The three sonnets have been copied by Lady B into the Coleorton Commonplace Book successively as *Sonnet 1812 in Borrowdale* ("The Fairest, Brightest Hues"), *Do in Borrowdale 1812* ("Even as a Dragon's Eye"), and *1812—To Twilight in Borrowdale* ("Hail, Twilight"). The year has possibly been added late to the last two titles, but seems to have been part of the original writing of the first. These titles appear to be otherwise unknown, and the factual accuracy of the first just quoted seems subject to some doubt, at least in respect to location (see 1812:65). But they are unlikely to have been invented by Lady B; and in the absence of other evidence of so specific a nature they must be regarded as grounds for a conjectural dating. All three were published in *P* 1815. No other visit to Borrowdale by W during this year is known.

explaining LdL's intention of helping W [see 1812:77]. (*MY* II, 46; letter, Sir GB to W, 31 Aug 1812, DCP. See Appendix VI.)

81. Sept 4

R W's accounts charge W £50/–/– payment of bill in favor of John Simpson, under this date. (RW accounts, DCP.)

82. Probably c but by Sept 14; Sept 14

Probably c but by 14 Sept W writes to Sir GB declining LdL's offer of a temporary £100 annuity; requests B to forward his letter to LdL. (*MY* II, 46; letter, Sir GB to W, 2 Oct 1812, DCP.)

On 14 Sept W writes to LdL: Sir GB's letter [of 31 Aug; see 1812: 80]. W has replied to Sir GB, who has been requested to forward his letter. W intends to wait upon LdL to express his thanks personally. (*MY* II, 46.)

83. Possibly Sept 28 or Sept 29

Dr. Bell departs Grasmere. (*Life of Bell* II, 423.)[52]

84. Sept 30

R W's accounts charge W £7/10/–, payment of premium on £300 policy on Montagu's life under this date. (RW accounts, DCP.)

85. Perhaps early Oct (–Oct 10)

Probably Thomas M, Thomas H, and Joanna H come to Grasmere. (They depart 10 Oct.) (*MY* II, 47.)[53]

---

[52] *The Life of Bell* states that Bell departed at the "end of September" and that he wrote to [William] Johnson a few days before his departure that he was to leave on "Monday or Tuesday." The days concerned were perhaps Monday and Tuesday 28 and 29 Sept. Bell had delayed his departure to assist the new curate, Powley, to begin his duties at the Grasmere School, a task in which he was helped by "the ladies (of Mr Wordsworth's family)." See 1812:69.

[53] That the M brother was Thomas, not John, is not quite certain. But MM writes to Thomas from Grasmere in a letter postmarked 3 Nov that she "was sorry when [he] left us," but that she feels better now (JFW Papers); and see 1812:91.

86. Probably c Oct 4

W receives a letter from Sir GB indicating that LdL seems hurt by W's refusal of financial assistance. (Letter, Sir GB to W, 2 Oct 1812, DCP.)

87. Oct 10

Probably Thomas M, Thomas H, MM, SH, and Joanna H depart Grasmere. (*MY* II, 47. See 1812:91.)

88. Oct 12

DW draws on RW for £30, by bill in favor of SH, due at one month.

DW writes to Richard Addison: The bill for £30. M and H visitors and plans. (*MY* II, 47. RW accounts, DCP.)[54]

89. Oct 13

W writes to Daniel Stuart: Thanks Stuart for his trouble about the French prisoners [see 1812:2; 1812:20]; because of his action, W did not interfere further. Asks Stuart's aid in finding him a place of the kind for which W has already applied to LdL; he does not object to leaving the Lakes. (*MY* II, 47–48.)

90. Probably Oct 21

DW draws on RW for £30 by a bill in favour of James [Graves], due at one month. (*MY* II, 49; RW accounts, DCP.)[55]

91. Oct 26, and c but by Oct 26

On 26 Oct DW writes to Richard Addison: The bill for £30 [see 1812:90]. (*MY* II, 49.)

The letter is probably delivered by Thomas M; so that he and perhaps Thomas H, MM, SH, Joanna H have perhaps returned to Grasmere c but by this time. Thomas M, however, probably also departs about this time. (*MY* II, 49; 1812:85.)

---

[54] RW's accounts record payment under 15 Nov.
[55] RW's accounts record payment under 24 Nov.

92. Oct 29

W draws on RW for £60 by bill in favor of Edward Partridge, due at one month. (RW accounts, DCP.)[56]

DW writes to Richard Addison: W's draft; her letter to Addison of 26 Oct. (*MY* II, 49.)

93. Perhaps Nov 1

W composes *Composed on the Eve of the Marriage of a Friend in the Vale of Grasmere, 1812*. (Title and content. See 1812:94.)[57]

94. Nov 2; perhaps Nov 2

On 2 Nov W attends, and with John Wilson is a witness for, the wedding of Thomas Hutchinson to Mary Monkhouse at Grasmere. W writes out two copies of "What Need of Clamorous Bells, or Ribands Gay" (*Composed on the Eve of the Marriage of a Friend in the Vale of Grasmere*), with title *To Mary Monkhouse*. (Grasmere PR; JFW Papers. Cf *PW* III, 423.)

Thomas H, MMH, Joanna H perhaps depart Grasmere this day. (Letters, MMH to Thomas M [31 Oct 1812], 7 Nov 1812, JFW Papers.)[58]

---

56 RW's accounts record payment under 2 Dec.
57 The date was first added to the title in the 1838 *Sonnets*.
58 W's copies of the poem are dated "Grasmere, 2 Novbr 1812."
The PR reads:

"Thomas Hutchinson of Hindwell in the County of Rednor [*sic*] and Mary Monkhouse of this Parish were Married by Licence in the Parish Church of Grassmere, 2d Day of November 1812

Robt Powley Curate

This marriage was solemnized between us $\{$ Thos Hutchinson / Mary Monkhouse

In the Presence of $\{$ William Wordsworth / John Wilson"

In a letter dated "Saturday morg" and postmarked 3 Nov MM remarks that "Monday [2 Nov] is the day fixed upon for our departure"; and on 7 Nov she writes from Shrewsbury that "[w]e left them all well at Grasmere." The letter of 31 Oct adds: "[W] presses me to say that he has availed himself of your kind offer and will thank you to forward the letters as soon as possible." The "letters" are unidentified.

95. Probably between Nov 2 and Nov 17; Nov 17

Probably between 2 and 17 Nov W, MW, Dora visit at Keswick, W also at Lowther. They go to parties. At Lowther W discusses with LdL the contents of two letters that LdL has lately received concerning W's need for a place, one from Daniel Stuart [see 1812:89], the other perhaps from Sir GB. LdL expresses a wish to be of service to W [see 1812:77–1812:89 *passim*]. The ladies at Lowther perhaps take W to Penrith in a carriage on his departure. He escorts them back as far as Thomas Wilkinson's; goes to Sockbridge, where he probably sees RW and receives from him records of W's and DW's debits in account with RW through June 1812.[59] He calls upon Miss Green, who is ill in bed.

On 17 Nov W, MW, Dora return to Grasmere from Keswick. MW throws herself on Catharine's grave before coming to the house. (*SHL* 48, 51; *MY* II, 77; RW accounts, DCP.)

96. Perhaps Nov 17 or Nov 18

W draws on Basil Montagu for £20 by bill in favor of John Green, due at two months.

W writes to Basil Montagu: The bill; Robert Jameson; Algernon Montagu; Montagu should send money to Mrs. Ross; an earlier request for advice on behalf of a friend who wishes to lay out some money in an annuity: please send advice. (*MY* I, 515.)[60]

97. Nov 18 (–Dec 2)

DW departs over Grisedale Hause for a visit to JPM at Watermillock. W walks with her probably as far as Grisedale Tarn. (She returns 2 Dec.) (*MY* II, 62–63, 77; *SHL* 47–48.)

[59] One copy of RW's accounts with W, DW contains a note following a debit account through 14 June: "Novr. 1812. Delivered copy of the above Account to Mr Wm Wordsworth at Sockbridge. (R.W.)"

[60] *MY* dates the letter, headed only "Grasmere 16th Nobember" [MS], 1811. But the immediate connection of the content with the content of W's letter to Montagu of c but by 19 Jan 1813 leaves little doubt that the year is 1812. A difficulty nonetheless remains with this date in that W's letter is definitely dated 16 Nov but appears from content to have been written, as W states, at Grasmere, although W was almost certainly not at Grasmere on 16 Nov. The balance of evidence suggests that W misdated his letter by a day or so.

98. Nov 19

SH writes to MMH: Good wishes; the family's recent activities. Dr. Bell; Willy; Grasmere Church and School. A Madras School is to be established at Keswick; W has suggested that DW assist in its early operations, but MW has prevented her. CCl; MW; DeQ is at Ilfracombe, says he will come to Grasmere in two weeks. (*SHL* 47–51.)

The Charles Lloyds possibly come to tea. (*SHL* 47, 49–50.)

99. Probably c late Nov; perhaps about this time

W probably c late Nov pursues plans to publish a prose work for profit. The work is probably an expanded version of *G*. W writes to Samuel Rogers (letter not known to survive) asking his aid in publication procedures. He perhaps about this time writes the prose toward a descriptive guide in DC MS 69, including "Borrowdale" and "From Ambleside to Keswick . . ." and the bulk of the surviving *G* MSS. (For detailed descriptions see Appendix VI.) (*MY* II, 69; letter, Rogers to W, 9 Jan 1812, DCP; Moorman II, 159, 242–44; Appendix VI.)[61]

100. Nov 26–Dec 1; Dec 2

Thomas W is attacked by measles on 26 Nov. The disease takes its course unalarmingly until 1 Dec. Perhaps on 30 Nov SH writes to DW at Watermillock (letter not known to survive) advising that Tommy has been ill. DW receives the letter on 1 Dec. On that day Scambler, probably in the late morning, calls, finds Tommy progressing well. W and he walk out. W returns, finds Tommy worse; goes without alarm to fetch Scambler again. On his return he is met at the door by SH, who informs him that no hope remains. Tommy dies before 6 PM.

W is possibly preoccupied with poetic composition at this time, but the chance of this is not strong. (*MY* II, 52–53, 55–56, 62–64; M-W

[61] Rogers reports that W's letter was accidentally burned as Rogers was replying to W on 9 Jan after having returned from Scotland on 8 Jan. Rogers also alludes to the fact that the book was in prose: it hence could not have been a poetic and almost equally surely not a dramatic anthology, and thus was probably not an anthology at all (cf Moorman II, 242–44). He adds, "I hope it is that which relates to your own Lakes and mountains."

Book of Common Prayer, DCP; Aubrey de Vere, *Essays*, London, 1887, II, 280–81.)[62]

On 1 Dec W writes to DeQ: Death of Tommy. (*MY* I, 50–51.)

Perhaps on 1 Dec, probably on 2 Dec W writes to Basil Montagu: Death of Tommy. Mrs. Ross's wish to know if Algernon has had measles. (*MY* II, 50.)[63]

On 2 Dec W writes to RS: Death of Tommy; asks RS to come visit the Ws, and to inform the GH household, Miss Barker, and the Calverts. (*MY* II, 52–53.)

On this day W meets DW, who is on her way toward Keswick on the outside of the Penrith coach, at Threlkeld. He tells her of Tommy's death. DW rides home in a Grasmere cart. W rides in beside her part of the way and walks part of the way. (*MY* II, 51, 62–64, 71, 77.)

101. Dec 5

Thomas W is buried at Grasmere. Probably all the family except SH attend. (Grasmere PR; *MY* II, 63, 77.)[64]

102. Probably c Dec 7 ff (–Dec 24, –1813 Jan 2)

W, MW, DW, SH, Johnny, Dora, Willy travel to Ambleside.

---

[62] W's earliest letters concerning Tommy's death all say that Tommy died before 6; DW on 5 Jan recalls that the time was 5 o'clock, which is the time recorded in the Prayer Book.

De Vere reports that at the time of the fatal illness of one of his children W was under the spell "of one of these fits of poetic inspiration which descended on him like a cloud." If the story possesses any truth at all, it can hardly refer to the time of Catharine's death (see 1812:49). But hard work, of the sort that did occur, on a poem in Jan would have sufficed to generate such a memory in a mind of De Quinceyan turn; and as noted elsewhere, W probably had lately been at work on a prose Guide.

[63] Although W's letter is dated 1 Dec, which was a Tuesday, his reference to "Tuesday" suggests that he is writing on some other day. He also implies that DW has returned home, as she did not do until 2 Dec. W is probably not more than a day off in any case.

[64] The PR reads: "[Burial] December 1812 5th Thomas Son of William Wordsworth Esqre Grassmere[.]"

W's epitaph "Six Months to Six Years Added" was probably not written until several years later (see *MWL* 88).

Among the JFW Papers is an epitaph for Tommy in the autograph of DW. This was not used on the gravestone but may be conjecturally assigned to c Dec 1812.

(DW, SH, Dora, Johnny return on 24 Dec; W, MW, Willy, 2 Jan.) The purpose of the visit is to be close to Mr. Scambler, all three children having the measles. Johnny and Dora are probably convalescent by 17 Dec, when, probably, Willy is still very ill. (*MY* II, 52–53, 56, 58, 60, 72.)

Perhaps about this time W removes Algernon Montagu from his lodgings at Mrs. Ross's and places him at Mrs. Steele's with Robert [Jameson] for his protection. (*MY* II, 56.)

103. Probably between Dec 7 and Dec 24

DW writes to CCl. (*MY* II, 60.)

104. Probably c mid-Dec but by Dec 17; Dec 17

Probably c mid-Dec but by 17 Dec, W receives from LdL a letter advising that he has applied to [Charles] Long and Lord Liverpool on W's behalf. The outlook for a place is not hopeful, and a pension appears the only solution, though this cannot be immediate. (*MY* II, 52–53; letter, LdL to W, 12 Dec 1812, DCP. See 1812:95.)

On 17 Dec W writes to LdL from Ambleside: Thanks LdL for friendly exertions on his behalf. Because of distractions caused by Tommy's death and the children's illness, asks for a few days for further consideration. (*MY* II, 52–53.)

105. Perhaps c late Dec

RW pays £412 to the heirs of RW of Whitehaven, settling the accounts between the estate of RW of Whitehaven and the heirs of JW Sr. W and DW are debited a 2/5 share, of £164/16/–, in the 1816 accounts for this settlement. (*MY* II, 68, 271; RW accounts, DCP.)

106. Dec 22

W writes to Daniel Stuart as from Grasmere (probably from Ambleside): Thanks Stuart for advice [see 1812:95]; LdL's efforts. A stamp distributorship that may become vacant; but the efficacy of LdL's patronage may not extend to the job. Seeks Stuart's opinion of the propriety of acceptance of a pension. (*MY* II, 53–55.)

107. Probably Dec 24

DW, SH, Dora, Johnny return to Grasmere. (*MY* II, 58.)

108. Dec 27, and probably soon after

On 27 Dec W writes to LdL as from Grasmere (probably from Ambleside): W accepts LdL's offer of a £100 annual gift [see 1812:77; 1812:82] until a place become available. English vs German and French policy concerning the award of pensions. (*MY* II, 56–58.) W probably soon drops his plan to publish a prose work for money [see 1812:99]. (*MY* II, 69.)[65]

On 27 Dec W writes to Basil Montagu from Ambleside: Anxiety about Willy's health; Algernon; residence at Ambleside. (*MY* II, 56.)

109. Dec 31

On 31 Dec DW writes to Mrs. Thomas Cookson: Invites Strickland and James Cookson to visit at Grasmere for a few days starting Saturday [2 Jan]. The family is determined to quit Grasmere. MW's distress; Henry H. (*MY* II, 58–59.)

1813

[On writings of W possibly of this year see below and GCL 42, 123, 146, 148, 167, 168, 171, 196, 201, 208–10.]

1. Probably between some time in this year and c mid-Oct 1814

W composes "Surprised by Joy." (IF note; *P* 1815. See 1814:112.)[1]

---

[65] A partial draft of W's letter to LdL is in DCP, as is a draft of W's subsequent letter to LdL of 8 Jan (see *MY* II, 66n).

The reason given by W to Rogers on 12 Jan 1813 for deferring work on the proposed publication is the death of Tommy; but the project does not appear to have been resumed thereafter. See 1813:9.

[1] W comments in his IF note that the poem was composed "long after [Catharine's] death" (4 June 1812); but it was published in *P* 1815.

2. Perhaps c early this year

Algernon Montagu and Miss Jameson arrive on a visit to the Ws. The length of the visit is undetermined. (*MY* II, 74.)

3. Perhaps during this year, by May, or Aug or later

W, DeQ visit Legburthwaite together. They ask for food at a house and are fed sumptuously. They are prevented by a servant girl from making the blunder of offering payment. (Masson II, 324–25; Eaton 198n.)[2]

4. Probably Jan 2, and possibly a few days following

W, MW, Willy return to Grasmere from Ambleside. Possibly today, and accompanying the Ws, Strickland and James Cookson come to Grasmere for a few days' visit at the Rectory. (*MY* II, 58, 60.)

5. Probably between 3 Jan and 1814 c late May

W completes composition of *Exc*, bringing Books II–IX to published form and organizing the entire poem as published. This composition includes the materials drawn on by W for *Characteristics of a Child Three Years Old* and *Maternal Grief*. (GCL 42, 196; Appendix VI.)

6. Jan 5, perhaps Jan 6

DW writes to CCl: Family events of last five weeks. MW's dejection. Their determination to quit Grasmere [see 1812:109]; they expect to obtain RM as residence. Tommy and his death; STC. She encloses a few lines to Thomas M, which CCl is to keep until she receives another cover from DW which will contain a letter from France to be enclosed in that to Thomas M. (*MY* II, 59–66.)

Perhaps on 6 Jan DW and Dora go to Ambleside, where Dora has two teeth pulled. Perhaps on this day W looks over DW's letter. (*MY* II, 64–65.)[3]

---

[2] DeQ dates the incident in this year. He was apparently absent from the area, however, between May and Aug.

[3] DW states near the end of the letter (*MY* II, 64) that she has written at three sittings. The appearance of the MS does not allow confident conjecture regarding the

7. Perhaps between Jan 5 and Jan 8

W arranges for the lease of RM from Lady le Fleming, with expectation of removal thither on May Day. (*MY* II, 61, 66, 68, 79.)

8. Probably c Jan 6 or Jan 7

W receives a draft for £100 from LdL. (*MY* II, 66; letter, LdL to W, 2 Jan 1813, DCP.)

9. Jan 8

W writes to LdL: Thanks for £100, which will relieve the financial burden of removal to RM, and allow him to put aside his plan to publish a work for profit [see 1812:99] and return to serious poetic work. (*MY* II, 66–67. See 1812:108.)

10. c but not before Jan 8

W composes *Exc* III.584–98 and *PW V app crit* lines 2–6 as draft following his letter to LdL of 8 Jan. (DCP.)

11. Jan 11

DW writes to RW: Advises of death of Tommy; thanks for accounts of her and W's drafts on RW; would like accounts of assets. Urges RW to visit them. (*MY* II, 67–69.)

12. Jan 12

W writes to Samuel Rogers: Has deferred intended publication for profit [see 1812:99]. Death of Tommy. Expected removal to RM; Sharp; a derogatory epigram about Scott. (*MY* II, 69–70.)

13. c but by Jan 19

W writes to Montagu: It is Miss Weir of Appleby who wishes to

---

points of division. Her remark "Mary is better this morning than when I began this letter" (*MY* II, 63), however, implies that this and succeeding parts of the letter were written at least one day after its commencement; and the last paragraph of the letter was plainly written with a different pen from that used for the preceding portions.

invest money [see 1812:96]; W seeks detailed advice about possible income and securities. Algernon and Miss Jameson staying at the Rectory. Montagu's wish to assist the education of Robert Jameson. A verbatim reprint of the 1616 translation of *Don Quixote* for which W wants to trade Algernon a modern translation. Prospective removal to RM. (*MY* II, 73–75.)

14. Jan 19

DW writes to Elizabeth Threlkeld and JPM: (to Miss Threlkeld:) Tommy's death; the health of the family; removal to RM; JPM's family, and hers. (to JPM:) Her spirits; good wishes. (*MY* II, 70–73.)

15. Jan 20 (–1814 May 17)

Basil Montagu writes to RW asking him to call and bring all securities held by RW for W respecting the annuity bond, also his bond with Mr. Newley; advises that he will accept the bills when he sees RW. (By 17 May 1814 Montagu has liquidated the capital sum of his annuity to W.) (Letter, Montagu to RW, 20 Jan [1813], DCP. See 1812:72; 1813:51; 1814:19; 1814:31.)

16. Jan 24

DW writes to JPM: A letter just arrived from JPM, and one from Mrs. Rawson. Tommy. W has grown very thin. The prospective move to RM. (*MY* II, 75–77.)

17. Perhaps c Jan 27

W draws on RW for £19/–/– by a bill in favor of Edward Partridge. (*MY* II, 68; RW accounts, DCP.)[4]

18. Feb 1

DW writes to MMH: Tommy's death; MW; desirability of removal to RM; need for a carpet there; Miss Green will probably

---

[4] It is not certain but is probable that the bill, of which RW's accounts record payment under 27 Feb, became due at one month, the usual case with W's and DW's drafts of this time.

move to Rydal; departure of Mrs. King; local news. Johnny is now studying Latin under DeQ by a plan of DeQ's for teaching Latin in six weeks. William Johnson. Plans for RM. [*Remorse*] successful, to SFC's delight. (*MY* II, 77–82.)

19. Feb 15

W draws on RW for £50 by a bill in favor of Henry Thompson due at one month. (*MY* II, 82; RW accounts, DCP.)[5]

20. Feb 16

W sends an order for £16/3/6 to Messrs. Twining.[6]
DW writes to RW: Hopes that RW has seen William Crackanthorpe and brought matters to a conclusion with him [see 1813:65]. Requests account of assets [see 1813:11]. Draft of [15 Feb] and order to Twining today; future accounts with Twining. MW. (*MY* II, 82–83.)

21. Probably c early Mar

The Ws receive word that STC, although he has repeatedly expressed an anxious desire to come to comfort the Ws, is going to the seaside. (*HCRWC* I, 71. See also *HCRBW* I, 123–24.)

22. Probably c but by Mar 6

MW writes a copy of *Exc* V.922–43 as *PW* V, 182–83 and *app crit* to line 15 of page 183 *app crit*. W continues with copy or draft to page 183 *app crit* line 21. W writes draft toward *Exc* VII.c529. (DC MS 75. See Appendix VI.)

23. Mar 6

W receives a letter from LdL, dated 28 Feb, advising that LdL will recommend W as successor to Mr. Wilkin in the office of Distributor of Stamps for Westmorland and the Penrith district of Cumberland.
W writes to LdL: He will be happy to succeed Wilkin. He will

---

[5] RW's accounts record payment under 18 Mar.
[6] RW's accounts record payment under 20 Feb.

need to hire an assistant to manage accounts. Thanks LdL. (*MY* II, 83–84; letters, LdL to W, 28 Feb 1813, 18 Mar 1813, DCP.)

W goes to Ambleside; inquires reason for delay in receipt of LdL's letter. Upon his return he adds a postscript on the subject. (*MY* II, 83–84.)

24. Mar 9

SH writes to Thomas M: Parcels, including two pots of char, and commissions, including the purchase of carpets [see 1813:18]. (*SHL* 51–52.)

25. Mar 11

DW writes to Robert Forster: Inquires on behalf of a friend with a sixteen-year-old son (perhaps John Marshall) whether Mr. Peacock continues to take pupils. Deaths of Catharine and Tommy. Plans to remove to RM. (*MY* II, 84–85.)

26. Probably c but by Mar 12

DW writes to RW: Is sending an order on RW for £14/12/6 in discharge of an enclosed order for tea for Thomas Cookson of Kendal to Messrs. Twining. (*MY* II, 85.)[7]

27. Mar 14

W receives a letter from LdL dated 10 Mar with enclosure from Wilkin advising of Wilkin's readiness to resign the stamp distributorship for a payment of £100 per annum.

W writes to LdL: agrees to Wilkin's terms. (*MY* II, 86.)

28. Perhaps c mid-Mar (–Apr 11)

SH goes to Appleby to assist Miss Weir in nursing one of her nieces. (She perhaps returns to the Rectory on 11 Apr.) (*MY* II, 88; 1813:34.)

[7] On the fate of this letter and the details of the order for tea see *MY* II, 94 and 1813: 39. RW's accounts record payment of £14/12/6 under 10 Apr.

29. Probably c Mar 19

W receives a letter from LdL dated 15 Mar enclosing an account of the income of the stamp distributorship for Westmorland. (Letter, LdL to W, 15 Mar 1813, DCP.)

30. Mar 28

W inscribes a copy of TCl's *History of the Abolition* (London, 1808) to the Rev. Robert Powley at Grasmere with this date. (Copy of TCl's *History* in the possession of Mr. Richard Wordsworth, on display RM.)

31. Mar 30

DW writes to Josiah Wedgwood: Requests articles [of pottery for RM]; recent deaths in family; greetings. (*MY* II, 86–87.)

32. Probably c early Apr ff

W receives a letter from William Pearson suggesting that arbitrators agree upon a compromise figure as a basis for W's purchase of Pearson's Town End estate. (Letter, Pearson to W, 29 Mar 1813, DCP. See Moorman II, 228n; T. W. Thompson, *Wordsworth's Hawkshead*, ed. R. S. Woof, Oxford, 1970, 360; 1812:76.)

33. Probably c Apr 7; Apr 7

Probably c 7 Apr W draws on Montagu for £20. (*MY* II, 97–98.)[8]
Probably on 7 Apr W receives through LdL a letter advising that directions have been given for his appointment to the office of Distributor of Stamps for the County of Westmorland.
On the same day W writes to LdL: He has received LdL's letter; thanks him. (*MY* II, 91.)

34. Apr 8 –Apr 11

On 8 Apr W departs for Appleby, which he perhaps reaches today. MW, DW accompany W as far as Rydal, on their way to which they

[8] The bill is said to have been drawn at two months and to become due on 7 June.

meet Miss Knott, who informs them that her grandfather was Distributor of Stamps for Westmorland while living at RM.

On this day DW writes to CCl: Tommy W; W's new appointment; MW's health. The Norths removed from RM three weeks or more ago, but will not allow the Ws access to the house. STC; HC; Derwent. W will be able to assist HC to college. (*MY* II, 86–91.)[9]

At Appleby W probably receives instructions from his predecessor about the conduct of the stamp business; sees SH. On his return home he is probably accompanied by SH. He or they probably see RW on their way home; pass the night at RW's at Sockbridge on 10 Oct. He or they reach home c 9:30 on 11 Apr.

On his return home he receives a letter from William Kapper, Secretary to the Stamp Officer, dated 9 Apr, requesting W to provide two sureties to join with him a bond of £8,000, and to execute a separate bond of £15,000. (*MY* II, 88, 92–93; MS of letter quoted *MY* II, 92–93; 1813:35.)[10]

35. Probably Apr 12–Apr 13

W sets off to Wigton to obtain RW's advice concerning the procurement of sureties for the bond for the distributorship [see 1813:34]; travels to Keswick, where he passes the night [at GH]. But at Keswick he determines to ask LdL and Sir GB to be his sureties, and probably on on 12 or 13 Apr writes with that request.

Probably on Tuesday 13 Apr W writes to RW from Keswick: His trip to find RW; his decision concerning sureties; immediate travel plans. (*MY* II, 92–93. See 1813:36.)[11]

W returns home this day. (*MY* II, 92.)

[9] *MY* II, 87 gives the date "Thursday April 6th," but the MS seems to me to read "8th." In any case, 8 Apr 1813 was a Thursday.

[10] In W's letter probably of Tuesday 13 Apr he states, in my reading of the MS, that he reached home on "Sunday morning." *MY* II, 92 reads "Tuesday morning."

[11] *MY* II, x (although not *MY* II, 92) dates W's letter 7 Apr. The contents of W's letter to LdL from Penrith, 19 Apr, and of this letter of "Tuesday" together make clear that the "Tuesday" concerned was the last before Monday 19 Apr. This letter is written on the double sheet containing the letter from Kapper received the previous Sunday night.

36. Perhaps c Apr 18–perhaps c Apr 20

Perhaps c 18 Apr W travels to Sockbridge, probably to consult with RW on business related to the stamp distributorship. He and RW discuss settlement of the Montagu debt. Probably while visiting there, on 19 Apr, he receives a letter from Sir GB, dated 15 Apr, and a letter from LdL dated 16 Apr, in which the writers agree to stand surety for W's bond [see 1813:35].

On 19 Apr he writes to LdL from Penrith: Thanks LdL for his agreement to stand surety.

He probably writes to Sir GB to the same effect on the same day.

He returns home perhaps c 20 Apr. (*MY* II, 92–93, 97; letters, LdL and Sir GB to W as cited, DCP; 1813:35.)[12]

37. Perhaps c late Apr or May (–1814 Apr 15)

W contracts [with John Fleming of Applethwaite] to purchase a property at Applethwaite. (The transaction is probably completed 15 Apr 1814.) (*MY* II, 97; 1814:21; information from Mr. B. C. Jones.)[13]

38. Apr 26, and probably shortly after; probably c Apr 26

On 26 Apr W, probably at Ambleside, signs a Distributor's Bond, penalty £15,000, to manage stamp duties "in the County of Westmoreland and part of the County of Cumberland"; and another bond for the same duties, penalty £8,000. His signature is witnessed by William Green and Richard Scambler. The second bond is probably shortly after signed also by LdL and Sir GB. Two copies are made at once and

[12] Sir GB replied on 22 Apr expressing his pleasure that the bonding arrangements had been settled (MS, DCP).

[13] Mr. B. C. Jones has kindly supplied information from the Tithe Award of the manor of Brundholme of 1 Apr 1815 identifying the property purchased by W as a parcel surrounding one of the two pieces near Applethwaite Gill which he already owned, and largely surrounding, also, an enclosure of Fleming's. The lot was probably made up partly of "Commons and Waste grounds" and partly of a piece of the ancient enclosure occupied by Fleming himself (portions designated no. 36 and no. 37 in the Award).

certified together by C. Morris and Thomas France. (Bonds and copies, DCP.)[14]

Probably c 26 Apr Mary W Peake visits for a few days at the Rectory. (*SHL* 53.)

39. Apr 27

DW writes to Richard Addison: An order and bill for Messrs. Twining sent some time ago in a box from SH to Joanna H [see 1813: 26]; order to Twinings for 40 lbs of Souchong tea, 1 lb Pekoe; 1 lb of the best black to be sent to Mr. Cookson [of Kendal]. Please pay former debt to Twinings of £14/12/6 for Cookson [see 1813:26n]. Hopes that Thomas M has purchased carpets [see 1813:24]. (*MY* II, 94.)

40. c May–June ff

W is absent from home a large part of the time on distributorship business c May–June. It is probable that from this time forward W is absent frequently on unrecorded trips required by stamp business. (*MY* II, 117. See 1813:53.)

41. May 1

W draws on RW for £7/7/– by a bill in favor of John Hanson.
W writes to Richard Addison: W's draft on RW. (*MY* II, 95.)[15]

42. Probably May 12

The W family removes to RM, where W, MW, and DW reside for the remainder of their lives. (*MY* II, 94–96.)

On the family's residence at RM generally see esp. Moorman II, 229–612; Frederika Beatty, *William Wordsworth of Rydal Mount* (London, 1939).[16]

[14] A family account memorandum notes, some time not before Feb 1813, "Wm for Bonds [£] 7."

[15] RW's accounts record payment of the sum under 20 Aug.

[16] The commonly accepted date of removal to RM, May Day (see, for example, Moorman II, 229; *MY* II, 95; and *CEY* 283) can hardly be correct. DW's letter to JPM, written the day after the removal, is clearly dated "Thursday," and May Day was a Saturday. DW wrote on 27 Apr that they expected to move on about 12 May—which was in fact a Wednesday. See Reed *N&Q* 94n.

43. Perhaps between May 12 and late 1815

On a Sunday evening DW writes to DeQ: Suggests that DeQ bring dry slippers and stockings if he comes next day. (Reed *N&Q* 94.)

44. Probably May 13

DW writes to JPM: Removal from RM yesterday; wants Miss Watson's novel. (*MY* II, 95–96. See 1813:42n.)

45. c May 14–c but by May 16; May 16

W visits, near Cockermouth, Mary W Peake and her family, who have heard that Mary W Peake's husband had been killed in the West Indies and her brother perhaps also. He returns c but by 16 May. (*MY* II, 96–97; *SHL* 52–53.)[17]

On his return he decides that a Turkey carpet must be obtained for the dining room at RM. SH writes to Thomas M and Mary Addison on 16 May: (to Thomas M:) Turkey carpet 19′ 4″ by 13′ 4″ required; grey and drab pantaloons needed for W. The stamp distributorship. Mrs. Peake. (to Mary Addison:) Commission to purchase drab rug worsted and canvas. (*SHL* 52–54.)[18]

46. Perhaps c late May

W engages John Carter as clerk for his stamp business and to work in the garden. (*MY* II, 117.)

47. Probably May 17

DW, perhaps W walk to Brathay. They are accompanied part way by MW. They meet the post, which brings a letter from Mrs. Cookson of Kendal perhaps inviting Johnny and the C boys for a visit, probably very shortly, to the Cooksons. MW turns back with the letter. DW, perhaps at Brathay, makes arrangements with the Cs for the trip.

This evening DW writes to Mrs. Cookson from Ambleside: The

[17] Capt. Peake died on 24 Feb (information from D. P. Sewell).

[18] RW records payment to Thomas M of £53/–/6 for "what he had paid for carpets etc for you" under date of 6 Aug.

visit of Johnny and the Cs to Mrs. Cookson; Mary W Peake and her family. (*MY* II, 96–97.)[19]

48. Probably May 18–possibly c but perhaps not before May 22, and soon after; May 18

Probably on 18 May W sets off for, and perhaps reaches, Appleby, where he assumes the duties of his new office. He is perhaps in Penrith with Mr. Robison, formerly Wilkin's subdistributor, and now his, on 22 May. On that day he receives from Robison an acknowledgment for stamped paper and parchment received by him to the amount of £2,246/2/8. He returns home possibly c but perhaps not before 22 May.

Perhaps during this trip he sees RW; discusses with him procedures for Montagu's settlement of his debt to W. He possibly travels with John Carter, and while on this trip—or if not, then some time in late May—visits Whitehaven with Carter. There they probably lodge at the home of Robert Blakeney and are probably attended by and conduct business with Joseph White, Whitehaven subdistributor of stamps.[20]

Soon after 22 May, W is informed by Robison that Robison has six additional [parchment] skins to the value of £13/1/–; W credits Wilkin for these accordingly. (*MY* II, 97–100.)

On 18 May DW draws on RW for £50 by a bill in favor of Thomas Cookson.

She on the same day writes to Richard Addison: The draft. (*The Letters of William and Dorothy Wordsworth. The Middle Years*, ed. EdS, Oxford, 1937, 560; RW accounts, DCP.)[21]

49. Perhaps May 19 (–probably c but not before June 5)

Perhaps 19 May SH probably departs to visit Miss Barker [at Keswick]. (She returns probably c but not before 5 June.) (*SHL* 54.)

---

[19] DW writes on "Monday Night." Portions of the content of SH's letter of 16 May (see 1813:46) coincide closely with DW's remarks.

[20] White is identified by Jollie's *Cumberland Guide*, 1811 (II, 92) as a clerk in the Whitehaven Custom House, of which Blakeney is described as "customer."

[21] RW's accounts record payment under 21 June. *MY* II omits this letter.

50. c May 23–c June 23, and later summer

The W family is unengaged scarcely a day during this month. The number of visitors later in the summer is heavy. (*SHL* 55–58.)

51. May 30; between May 30 and 1814 Apr 1

On 30 May W writes to Montagu: W has discussed with RW the procedures for Montagu's payment of his indebtedness to W [see 1814: 19]. RW has probably instructed Addison to give up whatever [securities] may be in his hands. Montagu's new child. Books received, and not received, including the 1740 reprint of Shelton's translation of *Don Quixote*, from Algernon Montagu [see 1813:13]. (*MY* II, 97–98.)

By 1 Apr 1814 Montagu has paid W £100 in liquidation of the annuity. (*MY* II, 136. See 1814:19. Cf Moorman II, 241.)

52. Probably c very early June, before June 6

W and RS meet at Brathay, where Owen Lloyd shows them two worm-like objects produced by immersion of horse-hairs in water. (CCS IV, 34–35.)[22]

53. Probably c early June; probably c but not before June 4

Probably c early June W visits Penrith on stamp business.
Probably c but not before 4 June DW writes to CCl: Carpets for RM; the removal to RM; invitation to CCl; the Curate bill; the Bonar (*MY* "Brown") murders; TCl's [*Life of Penn*]; the Luffs; W's stamp business. (*MY* II, 113–17.)[23]

[22] RS's letter describing the phenomenon of the horse-hairs was written on Sunday 9 June, and indicates that the demonstration took place while "we were there [at Brathay] last week."
[23] *MY* II dates DW's letter "[about 14 Sept. 1813]." Its contents, however, indicate that it was written very shortly after the family's removal to RM. The letter remarks that Miss Barker is expected "tomorrow," SH having been with her at Keswick. SH probably went to Keswick for a fortnight commencing 19 May, expecting to return to RM (see 1813:49). The carpeting being awaited at the time of this letter had arrived by 1 Aug (*SHL* 60). The first *Times* report of the Bonar murders appeared on 1 June.

54. Probably c but not before June 5 ff; c early or mid-June; c early June, by June 6

SH returns from Keswick. She is perhaps accompanied by Mary Barker, who pays a visit of unknown length at RM. Miss Barker is any case probably visits c early or mid-June. (*MY* II, 117; 1813:53.)

55. Probably c but by June 9; June 9–June 13

Probably c but by 9 June W departs RM for Penrith and Appleby. W probably visits Penrith on 9 June. On this day W takes account of Robison's stamp stock: Robison pays him £87/14/4, which with poundage (£1/2/2½) makes up the total of £2,246/2/8 accounted on 22 May [see 1813:48] and represents stamps sold since. W forgets to apply the £13/1/– for the six [parchment] skins of which he was informed late [see 1813:48] to the Government account. On 9–13 June W is engaged both in Penrith and Appleby with private business and settlements with subdistributors. At Penrith he also sees Henry Addison. He returns to RM probably 13 June. (*MY* II, 100; *SHL* 55–56. See 1813:48; 1813:56; 1813:60.)

56. Probably June 14

W writes to Robert Blakeney: Regrets missing Blakeney in Whitehaven [see 1813:48]; hopes to visit Blakeney with MW. Thanks for attending to business in Kendal with Mr. Fell. Compliments to White. Stamps for W should be at RM tomorrow and Mr. White's order at Whitehaven the next day. (*MY* II, 98–99.)

57. June 22

W writes to Joseph White (only a fragment of the letter is known to survive): Sends regards to Blakeney. (MS, Cornell Collection, Cornell 2308.)

58. June 23

SH writes to Thomas M: The carpeting not yet arrived; Joanna H; Bonaparte; the Luffs. (*SHL* 55–57.)

59. Probably June 25 or June 26

W writes to Joseph White: Has received White's bill for £442/13/11 [payment for stamps], and has forwarded legacy receipts to the Board; these receipts must be forwarded on the first Tuesday of the month hereafter. Conditions required for visit to Whitehaven. (*MY* II, 101.)[24]

60. June 28 and thereabouts

W visits Penrith on 28 June; calls on Robison; discusses the matter of the forgotten [parchment] skins [see 1813:55].

On this day W writes to George Thompson from Penrith: Accounts with Robison; Thompson to advise if Wilkin is agreeable to being charged £13/1/– for the [parchment] skins. (*MY* II, 100.)

The length of W's absence from RM on this trip is not known.

61. c July; by Aug 1

Richard Sharp visits in the Ws' neighborhood, perhaps at RM, c July. He departs by 1 Aug.

Probably c July the Ws are visited by John Stoddart and Mrs. Stoddart and an unidentified poetess accompanying them; [Thomas Cookson]; Mr. [? Kinneson] and his son; JPM's two eldest sons; Thomas Madge. Mr. and Mrs. Chippendale and their two eldest girls and their little boys call. (*SHL* 58–61; *HCRBW* I, 130.)

62. Probably early July

W writes to George Thompson from Ambleside: Requests advice respecting an affadavit about a certain number of issues of the *Westmorland Advertiser* printed on unstamped paper. Asks about final arrangements concerning Wilkin's six [parchment] skins [see 1813:60]. (*MY* II, 102.)

63. Perhaps c, more certainly on, July 10

Probably W and DW visit RW at Sockbridge. RW advances £5

---

[24] W speaks of having just received White's letter of "the 24th" [from Whitehaven]; so his letter is unlikely to have been written more than a day or two after.

to W and £10 to DW. (RW accounts, DCP.)[25] RW's accounts charge DW £9/6/–, payment of bill in favor of John Rawson, under this date. (RW accounts, DCP.)

64. July 13

W writes to [a subdistributor of stamps, possibly White or Robison] (only a fragment of the letter is known to survive): Advice concerning rectification of a small mistake in stamp business; W will supply all needed materials. (MS, Cornell Collection, Cornell 2309.)

65. Probably c late July

Probably c late July William Crackanthorpe, the Misses Crackanthorpe, and Mrs. Crackanthorpe visit RM. (Crackanthorpe, who is to go abroad soon, wants the family accounts settled.) The Misses Crackanthorpe pay at least two visits, during the second of which they stay at Ambleside at night. Mrs. Crackanthorpe probably stays at RM the entire time. A party of Miss Green's including DW, SH, and possibly W and MW attends the regatta with Crackanthorpe. Miss Green, Miss Ellwood, Willy attend the ball, the Misses Crackanthorpe going with Mrs. Fleming. Mr. Thorpe is frequently of their parties. (*SHL* 58–61; *MY* II, 103; *HCRBW* I, 130.)

66. Probably July 31–early Aug, after Aug 3

W, MW depart for, probably travel to, Whitehaven on 31 July. They probably stay at the home of Robert Blakeney. They probably pay their respects to LdL—or W does so alone—while there. This meeting is probably the main purpose of the trip. They probably return home in early Aug, after 3 Aug. (*MY* II, 98–99, 101–04, 124; *SHL* 58.)[26]

67. Aug; probably early Aug

The Ws are perhaps visited in Aug by the Marshalls, the Calverts,

---

[25] RW charges a £5 cash advance to W "at Sockbridge" under 10 July, and a £10 advance to DW "at Do" under the same date.

[26] DW, when mentioning in her letter of 3 Aug that W and MW are in Whitehaven, gives no indication that they are expected home immediately. On 4 Oct she describes the visit as having been "a few days" long.

Mary Barker, and the Lloyds' new governess, Miss Fletcher (who is to teach other children, including Dora, and adults, in various subjects, on a year's trial). The visits of the Calverts, Miss Barker, and Miss Fletcher probably take place in early Aug. (*SHL* 58.)

68. Probably Aug 1

SH writes to MMH: Visitors and activities at RM. The RM carpets; living arrangements at RM; her plans; her pony. (*SHL* 57–62.)

69. Aug 2; perhaps Aug 2; perhaps Aug 2 or Aug 3 ff

On 2 Aug W writes to RW from Whitehaven: Mr. Burrow, of the neighborhood of Ravenglass, has advised that RW's Ravenglass property is without a tenant. Requests RW to procure a copy of the bond required of W by the government [for his subdistributors] and advise him about stamps for his securities. (*MY* II, 102–03.)

Perhaps on 2 Aug the Crackanthorpes return to RM, the younger Crackenthorpes perhaps rejoining Mrs. Crackanthorpe there [see 1813: 65]. Perhaps on 2 or 3 Aug SFC, SC, and Elizabeth Fricker arrive for a visit of undetermined length at RM. (*SHL* 58, 63.)

70. Aug 3

DW writes to RW: Please send accounts for William Crackanthorpe, who has been at RM and with whom they have spent some pleasant days. Requests statement of her and W's assets [see 1813:11; 1813:20]. (*MY* II, 103–04.)

71. Probably early Aug but not before Aug 3

The Cls possibly but not probably visit at RM for an undetermined period. (*SHL* 58; *MY* II, 124.)

72. Aug 13

RW's accounts charge W £–/5/–, fee for calculating the value of [the] policy on Montagu's life at the Equitable Insurance Office, under this date. (RW accounts, DCP. See 1813:15; 1814:19; 1814:31.)[27]

[27] A note of calculation, dated 11 Aug, is among RW's accounts. The surrender value of the policy before 1 Sept was calculated at £95/1/–.

73. Perhaps c mid–Aug

W is absent from RM on stamp business. (*MY* II, 108.)

74. Perhaps Aug 17; between Aug 17 and Aug 27

Perhaps on 17 Aug RM is full of company [see 1813:67]. Daniel Stuart and his bride perhaps spend that day and night at RM. Between 17 and 27 Aug they probably stay another night. (*SHL* 63.)

75. Aug 19

W writes to RW: W believes that Montagu is entitled to the benefit of the insurance policy held as security for the annuity [see 1813:15; 1813:51; 1813:72]; RW is to settle the matter with Montagu. Family accounts [for the Crackanthorpes]; W's anxiety to have the forms for sureties [for subdistributors; see 1813:69]; money due Thomas M [see 1813:45n]. (*MY* II, 104–05.)

76. Probably Aug 20 (–perhaps Aug 31); Aug 20

Probably on 20 Aug Henry H arrives at RM for a visit. (He departs perhaps 31 Aug.) (*SHL* 62–63.)

On 20 Aug W writes to Robert Blakeney: Advice concerning Humphrey (evidently a tenant of Blakeney's by whom Blakeney is being misused). Has paid Clark and Hartley £12/8/–. (*MY* II, 106–07.)

RW's accounts charge W £7/7/–, payment of bill in favor of John Hanson, under this date. (RW accounts, DCP.)

77. c late Aug

W is heavily engaged in composition, stamp business, and attendance on visitors to RM. (*SHL* 64.)[28]

78. Aug 27; perhaps later this year; Aug 27, 28

On 27 Aug W writes to RW: The accounts have arrived; W

[28] SH remarks on Friday 27 Aug that RS "set out for London on Wednesday"; but he probably did not travel via RM (see *SHL* 63).

hopes to meet Crackanthorpe and settle their business soon [see 1813: 65; 1813:75]; wants forms for subdistributors' bonds. (*MY* II, 107.)[29]

Perhaps later this year Crackanthorpe pays £318/9/2½ to the estate of JW Sr in settlement of the debt of his father's estate. Of this sum RW's 1816 accounts credit a ⅖ share (£127/7/8) to W and DW under the general date of 1813. (RW accounts, DCP; *MY* II, 271.)

On 27, 28 Aug SH writes to John M: (27 Aug:) Plans for visiting Stockton; delays in setting off as a consequence of injury to Henry H's pony Lily. Visitors at RM. (28 Aug:) Lily's failure to respond to treatment. (*MY* II, 62–65.)

On 28 Aug W writes to Francis Wrangham: The deaths of Catharine and Tommy. W supports the Ministry, esp. because of its commitment to military opposition to Napoleon and its opposition to Catholic emancipation. (*MY* II, 108.)

RW's accounts charge W £7/10/–, payment of premium on £300 policy on Montagu's life, under this date. (RW accounts, DCP.)

79. Probably Aug 31 (–late Nov)

SH, Henry H depart RM for Stockton.[30] (SH next returns late Nov.) DW perhaps now asks SH to obtain money of hers in Thomas H's hands.

The Ws attend a sale, perhaps at Dove's Nest. They purchase some chairs. W purchases drawing room curtains with a cornice. (*MY* II, 109–13.)

---

[29] The accounts, which show William Crackanthorpe, representing his grandfather William Cookson and his father Christopher Crackanthorpe, owing £984/4/5 to RW as administrator of and representing JW Sr and also in RW's own right (respecting receipts and payments of the Sockbridge estate), accompanied a letter from RW to W dated 20 Aug which included a copy of a letter to Crackanthorpe of the same date.

On the rationale of the distribution of the sum to W and DW see *MY* II, 271, 278–79. The amount owing to the JW Sr estate was that noted immediately below in the text.

[30] Their departure evidently occurred on the Tuesday preceding Grasmere Fair, which always took place on the first Tuesday in Sept. This year 7 Sept was the first Tuesday of the month. See *MY* II, 111n; *DWJ* M 37.

80. Sept, probably by Sept 26

Numerous visitors come to RM in Sept, including, probably by 26 Sept, Samuel Tilbrooke, whom DW meets on the street in Ambleside, Mrs. Peake, her mother and two sisters, and John W, returned from [enemy] prison [see 1813:89]. (*SHL* 53, 67–68; *MY* II, 124.)

81. Probably Sept 1; perhaps Sept 1

Peggy, Mary, Jane Ashburner and three Ashburner children visit RM. Mrs. Fleming, Mrs. Green, Jenny Mackereth join them for tea. Miss Malcolm and her nephew call with Mrs. Richardson of Kendal. Perhaps today W attends the second day's sale at Dove's Nest; obtains a meat safe and a writing desk. (*MY* II, 110–11.)

82. Probably Sept 2 (–Sept 6)

W dines with Bishop Watson [at Calgarth]. At Ambleside he meets Miss Malcolm, who probably today comes to RM with her nephew for a visit. (They probably depart 6 Sept.) (*MY* II, 110.)[31]

83. Probably Sept 3

A rainy day. The family apparently stays close indoors. (*MY* II, 110.)

84. Probably Sept 4

The Ws and their visitors dine, probably picnic style, at Grasmere. They walk around the lake to Butterlip How, which is perhaps the site of the picnic. (*MY* II, 110.)

85. Probably Sept 5

Bishop Watson, John Wilson, Miss Green dine at RM. (*MY* II, 110.)

---

[31] DW is not explicit that these events took place on 2 Sept; but her account of events of other days at this time appears to offer no alternative.

86. Probably Sept 6

Miss Malcolm and her nephew depart RM. W, DW call on Mrs. Green at Ambleside. Mrs. Royds, her niece, and Mrs. Barlow are present. W is chatty. (*MY* II, 110.)

87. Probably Sept 7–probably Sept 9

W, MW, DW, Miss Green go to a sale at Coniston. W, MW, Miss Green lodge at the Black Bull; DW walks home, arriving at 9:30 PM. DW stays home next day. Probably Fanny brings orders to return to Coniston with a cart, and DW and she go thither on the morning of 9 Sept. W, MW, DW walk home at night, DW carrying a decanter and glass, W and MW bearing a mirror. The Ws' purchases include the decanter, glass, and mirror; a bed; tubs, and chairs for Fanny; a cupboard table for SH; glasses, knives, pillows, baskets, stocks, probably a sofa for W's room. Fanny brings a cartload of purchases home. (*MY* II, 110–13.)

88. Sept 10–Sept 20

W makes a trip to Penrith; Lowther Castle; Kirkby Steven, where he perhaps dismisses the subdistributor Mr. Winter. DW accompanies W on his way as far as The Swan.

Probably during his visit to Lowther W meets the Duchess of Richmond and other persons of rank or consequence.

W perhaps visits RW at Sockbridge c 19 Sept; he certainly sees RW on 20 Sept, and parts from him then, perhaps on his way home. (*MY* II, 112, 118, 125.)[32]

John Carter goes to Coniston with a cart to fetch home furniture from the sale [see 1813:87]. (*MY* II, 111.)

Carpeting arrives from London. Miss Green calls, chatters, dines at RM. (*MY* II, 112.)

89. Sept 10, 11–Sept 28 (–possibly 1814 c mid-June)

On 10, 11 Sept DW writes to SH: (10 Sept:) Visitors at RM;

[32] DW on 10 Sept expected that W would be gone "8 or 9 days."

attendance and purchases at sales; Miss Green. (11 Sept:) Expected visitors; carpeting; Miss Green; errands. (*MY* II, 109–13.)

Perhaps on 11 Sept, more surely between 11 Sept and 14 Sept Elizabeth W (wife of RW of Branthwaite), her daughter DW, her daughter Mrs. Peake, another daughter, and son John visit RM. Elizabeth W remains for a few days. The others probably remain about a fortnight, leaving DW of Branthwaite at RM on their departure on 28 Sept. (DW of Branthwaite lives at RM regularly until possibly c mid-June 1814.) (*MY* II, 112, 123, 130–31.)[33]

90. Possibly Sept 20

W arrives at RM. (1813:88.)

91. Sept 24–Sept 27

W visits Kendal on this day. He writes to [Richard Addison] from Kendal: Please call on Mr. Kapper, Secretary to the Commissioner of Stamps, and pay to him £24/4/– on W's account. (*MY* II, 117–18.)

This request is carried out on 27 Sept. (Note on back of W's letter, and RW accounts, DCP.)

92. Sept 28 (–probably Oct 11)

DW accompanies Mrs. Peake and Mrs. Peake's sister and brother to Kendal on their way from RM. (DW remains at Kendal until probably 11 Oct.) (*MY* II, 123–25.)

93. Probably c but not before Sept 28; probably c Sept 28–c Sept 29, –perhaps shortly after Oct 4

Probably c but not before 28 Sept RW, at Sockbridge, receives from Robert Nicol the RW accounts with W, DW as best Nicol has

---

[33] DW remarks on 4 Oct that DW of Branthwaite has been "with us" for "the last three weeks," and Mrs. Peake for a fortnight, having left, apparently, last Tuesday —that is, 28 Sept—with her sister and brother. The mother had visited "for several days." At least the mother and two daughters were expected, on the basis of word received at RM the previous night, on 11 Sept.

The exact time of this DW's departure remains uncertain. DW comments on 23 Jan 1814, that she is to stay at RM "till the midsummer holidays."

been able to determine them. (Letter, Nicol to RW, [25 Sept 1813], DCP.)

Probably c 28 Sept Henry Lowther and his bride dine at RM. W, MW dine with them at Ambleside probably next day. Probably c 29 Sept Robert Blakeney arrives at RM for a visit. He departs perhaps shortly after 4 Oct.[34] (*MWL* 8–9; *MY* II, 121, 124, 126.)

94. Oct 3

A letter arrives from SH. (*MY* II, 118.)

95. Oct 4, 5

On 4 Oct DW writes to CCl from Kendal: Lack of time for reading; family occupations. A lady [Miss Fletcher] is to begin a school at Ambleside where Dora will go, with DW of Branthwaite. Mrs. Peake and her family. Tilbrooke, [John] Gough as possible tutor for Tommy Cl; Blakeney; RS and the Laureatship; SH expected c 20 Oct. (*MY* II, 121–25.)

On 4 Oct SH's letter [see 1813:94] is forwarded to DW.

On 4, 5 Oct W, MW write to SH: (W, 4 Oct:) Declines invitation to Stockton from John H[35]; proposes meeting SH at Appleby, Penrith, or Hawes. Expressions of affection for SH. A local murder; the Flemings. (MW, 4 Oct:) Blakeney; reluctance to write to Joanna; Miss Fletcher not come; Miss Green and her sofa. (MW, 5 Oct:) Visitors. Charles Lloyd says he will quit Brathay immediately. (*MY* II, 118–21; *MWL* 8–9.)

---

[34] DW states on 4 Oct that Blakeney has been at RM ever since she left (on 28 Sept); but *MWL* 9 indicates that Blakeney arrived on the day on which the Lowthers departed, and implies also that the Lowthers came at or after the time of DW's departure.

[35] The farm at Stockton of which W says that John H will take care of it "for us" is, as remarked *MY* I, 463n, perhaps the land left to MW by her uncle Henry H in 1811. W here speaks of "300 acres," while MW's inheritance was only 50 acres; but since in context his primary object appears to be to describe his pleasure in a friend's conversation, his statement that he prefers half an hour of such conversation to views of his own land may use the phrase "300 Acres of land of my own" primarily as hyperbole for "a property of my own even much larger than MW's 50 acres."

96. Probably Oct 5–Oct 6; c Oct 6 or Oct 7; between Oct 7 and early 1814

Dr. Henry Parry, the Inspector of the Stamp Office, arrives for a visit probably 5 Oct. W probably takes Parry to visit an interesting cool nook. On 6 Oct W, Parry, perhaps MW, dine at DeQ's with the John Wilsons. Parry perhaps departs 6 or 7 Oct, and Robert Blakeney about the same time.

Between 7 Oct and early 1814, Parry sends a collection of books to W including the poems of [Thomas Heywood]; and W writes to Parry, and perhaps sends him a book and prints of Cardinal Richelieu and others. (*MY* II, 119, 126; letter, Parry to W, 9 Feb 1814, DCP.)[36]

97. Probably Oct 9

DW writes to SH from Kendal: Her visit to Kendal prolonged [see 1813:92]. The family; W's unexpectedly low income from the stamp distributorship; social life at Kendal; STC and the Morgans reported coming to Keswick: this will prevent DW from visiting Miss Barker at Keswick. Parson Harrison. Impatience to be home. DW is to call on Gough. DW brought measure for tombstone (probably for Tommy); W has not sent copies of texts for it. (*MY* II, 125–28.)[37]

98. Probably Oct 11

DW returns to RM from Kendal. (*MY* II, 127.)

99. Probably Oct 18–probably Oct 23

W, DW depart RM; probably travel to Watermillock. DW remains there, and W probably either this day or next goes to Lowther,

---

[36] W apparently thanked Parry mistakenly for "Hayward's" poems while describing the author as his "favorite Dramatist." W's letter evidently also described in ironic terms a spouse-hunting pensioner whose best hope would lie in "persuading some middle aged lady . . . rich enough to bring her own comforts along with her." Parry remarks that he has often thought of the "charming winter *retreat* you took *me* . . . to view, where, e'en the Dog Days' Sun beams are frozen, and surly Winter must be colder than Charity itself."

[37] DW dates the letter "Saturday 10th August." August, in view of content, is clearly a slip for Oct; and 10 Oct 1813 was a Sunday.

where he visits LdL until 21 Oct, leaving with a promise to return during the week of 24 Oct. He probably returns to Watermillock.

A purpose of this excursion is to meet SH and escort her to RM. They hear nothing of her by 23 Oct, when, probably, W and DW return home. MW, on discovering that no one has received word from SH, writes to Miss Weir and John H. (*MWL* 10–11. See 1813:102.)[38]

100. Perhaps c late Oct–c early Jan 1814

Young Basil Montagu comes to reside for a time, perhaps until c early Jan, at Ambleside, probably at Mrs. Ross's. Perhaps c late Oct he visits, perhaps dines at, RM every day.

One purpose of his visit is to apologize for having told slanderous stories about W. (*MWL* 12; Moorman II, 237–38; *MY* II, 129. See 1813:107–1814:3.)[39]

101. Probably Oct 24

Letters arrive bringing word that SH has had an accident or illness and has not left Stockton at the time expected. (*MWL* 9–10. See 1813: 99; 1813:102.)

102. c Oct 25; probably Oct 25

Alexander Blair possibly visits at RM c 25 Oct. (*MWL* 11.)[40]

Probably on 25 Oct MW writes to SH: SH's letters received; another must have miscarried. Ws and DW's trip to meet SH [see 1813:99]; advice about SH's journey; errands. Local illness; the Lloyds, Blair, Wilsons, other local news. (*MWL* 9–12.)[41]

---

[38] W possibly visited RW at Sockbridge, but no direct evidence appears to bear on this speculation.

[39] Basil's letter (Montagu Autobiography, DCP) indicate that his health and the opportunity for at least informal study in the proximity of Mr. Dawes's school were other considerations.

[40] MW's phrasing is that "Mr. Blair is here—the Wilsons depart this week." It is not unlikely that Blair stayed with his close friend Wilson, and that "here" means simply "in the neighborhood"; but the matter remains uncertain.

[41] MW wrote on a Monday. As SH was expected c 20 Oct (*MY* II, 125), and the confusions attendant on her failure to appear as expected at Penrith had occurred during the previous week, MW probably wrote on Monday 25 Oct.

103. Nov 4

Robert Southey takes the oath of Poet Laureate. (Letter, RS to Thomas S, 13 Nov 1813, BM Add. MS 30,927, fol. 214; CCS IV, 48.)[42]

104. Perhaps c mid-Nov, not before 6 Nov

W composes *November, 1813* ("Now That All Hearts Are Glad, All Faces Bright"). (Title and content.)[43]

105. Nov 22

W writes to the Commissioners of Stamps: Explanation and apologies for a mistake by the newly appointed subdistributor at Appleby. (*MY* II, 128–29.)

106. Perhaps Nov 28

W, MW attend church at Grasmere; converse with young Basil Montagu there. (Copy of letter of Basil to his stepmother, "Sunday Eve," Montagu Autobiography, DCP.)[44]

107. Probably c late Nov, certainly by Dec 5

SH resumes residence at RM. (She stays at Miss Green's for a time. She next departs from RM for a lengthy absence probably 16 Sept 1814.) (Copy of letter of Basil to his stepmother, 5 Dec 1813, Montagu Autobiography, DCP. See 1814:99.)[45]

[42] RS's letter remarks that his appointment dates from 12 Aug. This was the date of the death of the previous Poet Laureate, Pye.

[43] The title in 1815 is *Added, November, 1813*. The first word was dropped *P* 1820 and thereafter. The official government statement concerning the outcome of the Battle of Leipzig was circulated 3 Nov, and a report appeared in the *Times* on 4 Nov.

[44] The letter is shown by its contents to have been written on a Sunday in late Nov or Dec, and includes accounts to 1 Dec. Algernon Montagu's Christmas holidays have not yet begun, however, and copies of letters from Basil to his stepmother survive from the first three Sundays of Dec (5, 12, and 19) and from Saturday–Sunday 25–26 Dec.

[45] Basil's letter of Sunday 5 Dec reports that SH returned "last week," but that having come from a house that had had scarlet fever, and having a sore throat, she has been made to perform quarantine at Miss Green's. SH is not mentioned in Basil's letter of perhaps 28 Nov. (See 1813:106.)

108. Perhaps c Dec and Jan 1814

W has influenza. (*MY* II, 141.)

109. Dec 2; probably between Dec 2 and Dec 7 (–between Dec 19 and Dec 25)

On 2 Dec young Basil Montagu visits at RM. (Copy of letter of Basil to his stepmother, 5 Dec 1813, Montagu Autobiography, DCP.)[46]
Probably between 2 and 7 Dec Miss Barker arrives for a visit at RM. (She departs between 19 and 25 Dec.) During her visit she and SH probably make extracts from *ER* for notes for RS's *Carmen Triumphale*. (1814:110; Kirkpatrick.)[47]

110. Dec 7

Young Basil Montagu probably drinks tea at RM with the W family, Miss Barker, the Ladies Fleming, Mrs. and the Misses Watson. (Copy of letter of Basil to his stepmother, 12 Dec 1813, Montagu Autobiography.)[48]

111. Dec 13

The W family, including Miss Barker, probably dines at the Lloyds' with young Basil Montagu. (1813:110n.)

112. Between 19 Dec and 25 Dec; probably between Dec 19 and Dec 22

Between 19 and 25 Dec Miss Barker departs RM and returns to Keswick. (Copies of letters of Basil to his stepmother, 19 and 25–26 Dec 1813, Montagu Autobiography, DCP.)[49]

---

[46] Basil writes on Sunday 5 Dec that he was at Rydal on Thursday and saw the W family, who were well except for colds and other disorders.

[47] Young Basil would probably have mentioned Miss Barker, his reactions to whom tended to bear an emphasis, had she been present at RM on 2 Dec.

[48] Basil's letter of Sunday, 12 Dec dates this event "on Tuesday." He notes in the same letter that he is to dine at the Lloyds' "tomorrow to meet the Rydal family and shall endeavour to think more justly of Miss Barker," of whom he had by then plainly formed an unfavorable impression.

[49] Basil writes on 19 Dec that "Miss Barker is still at Rydal," and that the family

Probably between 19 and 22 Dec the young Ws and DW attend a wild beast and Punch-and-Judy show [at Ambleside]. They probably pass the night at Mrs. Ross's. (Copies of letters of Basil to his stepmother, 19 and 25–26 1813, Montagu Autobiography, DCP.)[50]

113. Dec 26

Basil and others probably walk to RM. (Copy of letter of Basil to his stepmother, 25–26 Dec 1813, Montagu Autobiography, DCP.)[51]

114. Perhaps c late Dec–early Jan 1814

The W children perhaps visit at GH. (Copy of letter of Basil to his stepmother, 25–26 Dec 1813, Montagu Autobiography, DCP.)[52]

1 8 1 4

[On writings of W possibly of this year see below and GCL 27, 42, 77, 123, 146, 148, 167, 168, 171, 173, 184, 196, 208, 209, 211–20.]

1. Early this year, until c late May; perhaps c early this year

W and the family are heavily preoccupied until c late May with preparation and printing of *Exc.* Perhaps c early this year *Exc* V is written as DC MS 74A and *Exc* VII.30–58, 201–36, 252–85 as MS 75. (See Appendix VI.)

---

[50] Basil states on Sunday, 19 Dec that Algernon is to depart "Wednesday next." On 25 Dec he indicates that Algernon was still present when the Ws came to the show, which is not mentioned in earlier letters.

[51] Basil writes on "Sunday" (26 Dec): "We intend walking up [*sic*] Rydall this afternoon to see Mr Wordsworth but I do not think he will say anything about Robert Jameson. It is a very delicate thing he says for him to interfere in as he knows nothing about his attainments." On Jameson, to whom the elder Basil Montagu gave instruction and the use of his chambers, see esp. *MY* II, 74; *MY* I, 331n; *HCRBW* I, 171.

[52] Basil writes: "Miss Barker is gone she begged I would go and spend a week with her at Keswick which I must do if not unwell. . . . I shall probably go in a week or ten days as she particularly mentioned she wished to see me when Mr Wordsworth's children returned which will be in that time." On Basil's visit to Miss Barker see esp. 1814:3.

---

there is quite well. He writes on 25 Dec that she is gone, and that he is invited to spend a week with her at Keswick, a plan that suggests that Miss Barker had just departed.

2. Jan 1

November, 1813 ("Now That All Hearts Are Glad, All Faces Bright") is published in the *Courier* without title, initialled "W.W." (See Woof *SB* 189.)

3. Jan 19 (–perhaps Apr 25)

DW travels to Keswick with Mrs. Lloyd to assist Mary Barker in caring for young Basil Montagu, who has become ill while visiting Miss Barker. Mrs. Lloyd returns the same day. (DW concludes her visit perhaps 25 Apr, although she returns to RM for a week perhaps 17–24 Mar.) (*MY* II, 129–30, 140. See also *Minnow* 24–26.)

During DW's absence *Exc* is copied and great alterations are made in the poem. (See Appendix VI.)

4. c late Jan

W, Johnny skate on Rydal Water every day. (*MY* II, 130.)

5. Jan 20

W writes to Basil Montagu: Young Basil's illness [see 1814:3]; Basil needs money. Other advice concerning Basil. (*MY* II, 129–30.)

W draws on RW for probably £30/15/8 by a bill in favor of Isaac Dickinson, due at one month. (*MY* II, 130; RW accounts, DCP.)[1]

6. Jan 23

DW writes to RW from Keswick: W's draft of 20 Jan [see 1814:5]; DW, Miss Barker, young Basil; cousin DW. (*MY* II, 130–31.)

7. Feb 2

DW draws on RW for £50 by a bill in favor of Miss Mary Crosthwaite, due at two months. This money is perhaps for Miss Barker.

---

[1] DW, reporting the draft, calls it £40/15/8; but RW's accounts record payment of what is clearly the same bill under the date 26 Feb in the amount £30/15/8. A loose memorandum of MW's notes the sum as £30/16/11.

DW writes to RW from Keswick: Her draft; she is to order tea from Messrs. Twining; will ask them to draw on RW for their last year's bill on W; young Basil. (*MY* II, 131; RW accounts, DCP.)[2]

8. Feb 9

Richard Wordsworth and Jane Westmorland are married at Addingham, Cumberland. (Addingham PR: information from Mr. D. P. Sewell.)[3]

9. Perhaps c Feb 12 ff

W probably receives a letter from Dr. Parry [see 1813:96] advising, in a postscript, that he has found certain verses copied at Greta Bridge, and asking whether they are W's. W's reply is unknown. (Letter, Parry to W, 9 Feb 1814, DCP.)[4]

[2] A memorandum by MW for 1814 notes "[Drawn by DW] for Miss B 50." No other draft of £50 is recorded under this year.

RW records payment of the £50 draft under the date of 5 Apr. The next notation in RW's accounts of payment of a Twining's bill is dated 6 Apr 1815.

[3] The letter published by Knight as having been written this day (see *The Letters of William and Dorothy Wordsworth, The Middle Years*, ed. EdS, Oxford, 1937, II, 585) was written 9 Feb 1821 (information from Mr. Alan Hill).

[4] The lines as copied by Parry are:

> Oh Rokeby woods are tall & strong
> And Greta's stream is fair
> And often has that Son of Song
> Fam'd *Walter* rambled there !!!
> Wordsworth
> Oh where in Southern Clime is found
> A stream like dear romantic Tees
> Which with a sweet & murmuring sound
> Runs roaring o'er the stones at ease !!!

The first quatrain possibly parodies *Yarrow Unvisited*, esp. the third and fifth stanzas. W of course knew the rivers mentioned; but a facetious acquaintance or reader of W, possibly Parry himself, would seem the likely author. The verses were probably written recently in any case: Scott visited Rokeby and the Greta in late 1812, and *Rokeby* was published 10 Jan 1813 (Edgar Johnson, *Sir Walter Scott*, New York, 1971, I, 400–06).

10. Perhaps c mid-Feb

W sends verses, evidently concerning the power of ties of local affections over the mind, to the Bs. (Letter, Sir GB to W, 20 Feb 1814, DCP.)[5]

11. Feb 21

W writes to Richard Sharp: Seeks Sharp's aid in obtaining admission to Christ's Hospital for a nephew of Mrs. William M. (*MY* II, 131–32.)

12. Mar 13

A memorandum of MW's notes the cashing of a draft for £14 under this date. The draft appears not to be recorded in RW's accounts, and is possibly an inaccurate recollection of a draft of c 25 Apr [see 1814:25].

13. Probably c mid-Mar

W makes inquiries of Longman & Co. about publication of *Exc.* (Owen LLW 25–26.)

14. Perhaps Mar 17–perhaps Mar 24

DW returns to RM from Keswick for a week's visit. She goes back to Keswick perhaps on 24 Mar. (*MY* II, 138.)[6]

15. Probably c late Mar

Edward Stanley of Ponsonby visits more than a fortnight at Rydal Hall. W sees much of him. (*MY* II, 135–36.)[7]

---

[5] Sir GB, thanking W, remarks: "[the verses are] in a strain with which I can perfectly sympathize it is surprising the hold local affections have upon my mind [.]" The generality of Sir GB's phrasing (his remarks might apply to large numbers of W's verses) prevents conjecture of the identity of the lines concerned.

[6] DW says on 24 Apr that she returned to Keswick "a month [ago] today." Probably she is remembering the day of the week rather than the day of the month.

[7] W remarks that he liked Stanley "better than I had done before, though he is no conjurer." The time of the earlier meeting is uncertain.

16. Mar 26

W writes to RW: In view of approaching peace, W and DW wish power to sell out of stocks when an apparent high is reached. RW is asked to advise what W and DW are entitled to, and give all necessary powers at once. (MS, DCP.)

17. Probably Mar 27; possibly Mar 29

DW writes to Josiah Wade from Keswick: Writes at SFC's request seeking information about STC and his plans; young Basil; the W and C families. (*MY* II, 133–34.)[8]

18. Mar 31

W and the ladies of the family visit Fox Ghyll. (*MY* II, 135.)

19. Apr 1

W writes to Robert Blakeney from RM: Advice about windows and other parts of the house at Fox Ghyll, under construction for Blakeney. Humphrey [see 1813:76]. Blakeney's marriage. (*MY* II, 135–36.)

W writes to RW: RW asked to receive £200 on W's account from Montagu; deliver up securities relating to the annuity. After this Montagu will owe W only about a year's interest and what is due on account of the life insurance policy. Will draw for £250 in a short time [see 1814:21]. (*MY* II, 136. See 1813:51.)

20. Possibly 1814 Apr 10

(Easter.) W composes a basic version of *Composed in One of the Valleys of Westmoreland, on Easter Sunday*. (GCL 223n; title. See *PW* III, 422.)[9]

---

[8] DW's date resembles perhaps a "29" more than a "27"; but Wade's endorsement "ansd Apl 1. J. W." suggests that DW ought to have intended "27."

[9] The year and Easter on which the poem was composed remain quite conjectural. This Easter is suggested only because it is closest to the apparent date of the earliest surviving MS.

21. Apr 15

DW signs a draft on RW, on W's account, for £250 in favor of John Fleming, due in one month. This draft probably completes W's purchase of property at Applethwaite, in the vale of Keswick [see 1813:37]. (*MY* II, 136–37. RW accounts, DCP.)[10]

22. Apr 16

DW writes to Richard Addison: Her draft of 15 Apr; Montagu has £200 ready to pay into W's account. Expects to draw for £10 on her own account in a day or two. (*MY* II, 137.)[11]

23. Apr 20

RW's accounts charge W £6/6/8, payment to Miss L. Monkhouse, under this date. (RW accounts, DCP.)

24. Apr 24

DW writes to CCl from Keswick: Miss Barker, and her quarrel with the Ss; young Basil. *Exc* printing, will probably be published next winter; a new edition of W's poems will be published at the same time; and shortly after will be published *PB*, *WD*, *Waggoner*. MW and her health; Johnny; Tommy; the armistice with Napoleon. (*MY* II, 137–43.)

25. Probably c Apr 25

DW draws on RW for £14 by a bill in favor of Mary Barker. (RW accounts, DCP; *MY* II, 137. See 1814:12.)[12]

[10] RW's accounts record payment under the date of 18 May.

[11] A note on the RW accounts dated 14 May and probably written by Addison or Nicol perhaps records the sense of instructions from RW: "Rd Wordsworth is to give WW credit for £200 recd from Mr Montagu on Redemption of annuity & Mr W.W. drew on Rd W. for £250 in favor of John Fleming as charged to him above."

[12] DW expected to draw in favor of Miss Barker for £10 a day or so after 16 Apr (*MY* II, 137); but RW's accounts record payment of £14 under 25 May—probably a month after the draft, although a bill due at six weeks is a possibility. See also 1814:42.

26. Perhaps Apr 25

DW returns to RM. (*MY* II, 137–38.)

27. Apr 26

W writes to Francis Wrangham: Seeks to interest Wrangham on behalf of [Thomas] Jameson, who is entering on a curacy at Sherburn. W busy with printing [of *Exc*]; planning a trip to Scotland. (*MY* II, 143–44.)

28. Apr 28

W writes to Thomas Poole: Solicits Poole's assistance for HC, esp. in measures to send him to a university. A fund needed. Employment, family, poetry. (*MY* II, 145–46.)

29. May 5

W writes to Samuel Rogers: Sharp has referred W to Rogers regarding assistance in obtaining admission to a charity school for the child of a close connection of MW's. Gifts from Rogers of his *Poems* and *Columbus*. W about to print *Exc*. Plans for trip to Scotland. (*MY* II, 147–48.)

30. Perhaps c May 8 (–perhaps c late May)

Mary Barker perhaps arrives for a visit at RM. (She departs perhaps c late May.) (*MY* II, 139.)

31. May 17–1817 Dec 27

RW's accounts credit W with £200 cash, received in redemption of Basil Montagu's annuity to W under the date of 17 May. W having already received £100 from Montagu [see 1813:51], this completes repayment of the capital sum of the Montagu annuity. Final settlement of Montagu's debt does not take place until 27 Dec 1817, when Montagu pays a balance of £7/13/1 and W agrees to turn over the insurance policy on Montagu's life. (Memoranda, 27 Dec 1817, DCP;

Moorman II, 241n; *HCRBW* I, 210–11. See also 1803:21; 1803:51; 1803:125.)[13]

32. Perhaps c late May

Mary Barker perhaps departs RM. (*MY* II, 139; 1814:30.)

33. Probably c June, possibly 29 June

W completes the dedicatory sonnet for *Exc*, "Oft, through Thy Fair Domains, Illustrious Peer!" (Date with published poem; Moorman II, 260; *LL* II, 129; *MY* II, 151n. See 1814:35.)[14]

34. June

Probably during this month HC leaves Dawes's school at Ambleside to reside at home. (*Minnow* 31.)

35. June 4

W writes to LdL: Asks permission to dedicate *Exc* to him. (*MY* II, 148–49.)

36. Perhaps between June 5 and June 12, and about that period

A French officer, probably Eustace Baudouin, probably visits RM some time about the period 5–12 June. Perhaps between 5 and 12 June W accompanies him to Keswick and GH. SH possibly visits GH at or about this time. (CCS IV, 79; Curry II, 102; Moorman II, 330–31.)[15]

---

[13] W's letter to RW of 19 Aug 1813 makes clear that the bad feeling which later developed over the assignment of the policy was a result of RW's dilatoriness in explaining affairs to Montagu. RW's 1816 accounts with W and DW add £20/1/1 interest credit from RW to W (cf *MY* I, 398n).

[14] The date accompanying the first publication of the poem is "Rydal Mount, Westmorland, July 29, 1814." Moorman II, 260 suggests that the month is a slip for "June." *MY* II, 151n offers the alternate suggestion that W may have instructed Longman to append the date on which the poem was published. See 1814:75.

[15] RS remarks on 16 June (CCS) or 15 June (as the MS appears to read) that W brought his young visitor, "apparently one of the best of these Frenchmen," last week. He complains to Thomas S on 10 July of delays to his work on *Roderick* till 15 June caused in part by "the interruption of Miss Hutchinson and the Frenchman."

37. Possibly c June 21–June 24

DW of Branthwaite departs RM. (1813:89.)[16]

38. Probably c late June

W probably offers to Sir GB his choice of the Dedication of the new collected edition of his poems, or *WD*, or *PB*. (Letter, Sir GB to W, 4 July 1814, DCP.)[17]

39. Probably July

W writes to RW: Urgent request for accounts; worries about falling stock market. (*MY* II, 149. See 1814:16.)

40. Perhaps c early July; probably c early July

Perhaps c early July MW writes, and W probably now sends, a MS of *WD*, probably that presently at King's College Library, Cambridge, to Longman & Co. (Owen LLW 26–27. See Appendix VIII.)

41. Probably between July 7 and July 16

W writes to Sir GB asking him to accept the Dedication of his Collected Poems rather than of *PB*. (Letter, Sir GB to W, 19 July 1814, DCP. See 1814:38.)[18]

42. July 9

RW's accounts charge DW £10/–/–, payment of bill in favor of Benjamin Hunter, under this date. (RW accounts, DCP.)

---

[16] DW in Jan had expected DW of Branthwaite to remain until the following "midsummer Holidays" (*MY* II, 131). Whether DW was thinking of the astronomical midsummer or the legal quarter-day (24 June), or simply a time roughly about either, is unknown.

[17] Sir GB chose *PB* because he had painted a picture that would make "a good tailpiece"; and he requested W to let him know the size of the print at once. He had written to W on 25 Feb 1808 of a "very small" picture of which he wished to bear the expense of engraving, should an engraving be made for *PB* (DCP).

[18] Sir GB wrote on 19 July agreeing to this arrangement and asking various questions concerning the engraving for *PB* (see 1814:38). Between this time and 20 Nov 1814 an engraving was made, evidently of the "tailpiece" picture, by Alexander. On that date Sir GB had also almost finished "a picture from the White Doe."

43. July 16–July 17

W writes to Francis Wrangham on 16 July: A copy of *Exc* to be sent to Wrangham when published. W is to begin a tour in Scotland next day. (*MY* II, 149–50.)

The Ws do not, however, depart next day, when RM is perhaps visited by the Marshall family, or at least John Marshall, from whom W receives a copy of the third edition of *The Traveller's Guide through Scotland* (Edinburgh, 1806). (DCP.)[19]

44. July 18 (–Sept 9)

W writes to LdL: Has ordered a copy of *Exc* to be sent to LdL previous to publication. Is departing this day for a tour in Scotland. (*MY* II, 151.)

W, MW, Johnny, SH, Miss Alms travel with the jaunting car to Keswick, on their way towards Scotland. They pass the night at Keswick. (W, MW, Johnny, SH reach RM on their return perhaps 9 Sept.) (*SHL* 71–72; SMJ.)[20]

---

[19] The book bears the signature "J. Marshall" (in John Marshall's autograph). Below is an inscription by DW:

> given to Wm Wordsworth
> Rydale Mount. July 17
> 1814.

MW adds the note, "Previous to setting out with Mary and Sarah on their Tour through Scotland."

[20] Overlapping journals of the tour survive as DC MS 77. The longer and later one, covering 20 July–1 Sept, is in the autograph of MW. The other, covering 18 July–30 July, is in the autograph of SH. Each, where it overlaps with the other, contains some unique details; but MW's copy is plainly reworked from SH's. MW's regularly refers to MW in the third person. Portions of the entries from 31 July may draw on records by SH no longer surviving. Where reports below draw on the journals, information from the overlapping portions is a consensus. Spelling of place-names has been silently modernized and corrected to accord with the authorities cited 1803:62n. As the journals frequently omit specification of companions, I have regularly assumed that all three travellers participated in the events recorded unless specific reason appears for supposing otherwise.

45. Probably between July 18 and late Aug; perhaps between July 18 and late July ff

Probably between 18 July and late Aug DW sees Henry and Mary Addison, Mrs. Buchanan, someone whom SH terms the "bold Capt[ain]," and a party. Perhaps between 18 July and late July DW determines to visit France [for the wedding of Caroline W to J. B. Baudouin]. (*SHL* 77, 79; *MY* II, 158.)

46. July 19

W, MW, Johnny, SH, Miss Alms travel through [Mun]grisdale, Mosedale, Sebergham. At Sebergham they dine. SH and probably others walk to Warnell Hall while dinner is preparing; walk also in the Town-head orchard and garden. They pass Rose Castle. At Carlisle they drink tea with James Losh; sup with Anthony Harrison at Mrs. Pearson's (the sister of Miss Alms) where they have left Miss Alms. They pass the night at the coffee house. (*SHL* 72; *SHJ*; Losh Diary.)[21]

47. July 20

W, MW, SH, Johnny breakfast at Brampton. While the horses rest, they take a post chaise to visit Naworth and Lanercost Priory. At Naworth they drink wine and eat cake with Mr. Ramshay (a stamp distributor) and his bride, D. Maunsly. At Lanercost they look at tombstones, including that of James Dacre. They return to Brampton; proceed to Longtown; look at the view from the moss hut of the Duchess of Buccleugh between crossings of the river. They dine at Longtown. They proceed past Langholm to the Malcolm farm, Burnfoot, where they are hospitably received at 9. Present besides the four Malcolm sisters [see 1813:82] are Miss Milward of Parton and two friends of Thomas H's acquaintants Mrs. Spencer and Lady Maxwell,

---

[21] Losh notes: "My old Friend W Wordsworth, his Wife & Sister. Wordsworth seemed cheerful and less affected than formerly." SH states that the route was past "Grisedale," an early alternate name for Mungrisdale (see John Speed's Map of Cumberland, 1610).

and perhaps also a friend of Francis H. Swain. (*SHL* 72–73; SMJ; Moorman II, 258.)[22]

48. July 21

Probably W, MW, SH pass this day and night at the Malcolms'. In the morning they visit Miss Wilhelmina Malcolm's museum. The company is joined for dinner by Lady Johnstone, her daughter and her daughter's governess, a sea captain, and his aunt. At night the dancing master comes; all dance except W, SH, and the sea captain's aunt. (*SHL* 73–74; SMJ.)[23]

49. July 22 (–probably Sept 4)

W, MW, SH depart Burnfoot, where they leave Johnny. (They return probably 4 Sept.) They travel past Westerhall, Westerkirk, cross the Esk, Eskdalemuir; see a disorderly burial ground and two druid circles. They dine at Boreland; walk to the church. They proceed across the Wamphray, thence, with the Annan on their left, along the valley to Moffat, which they reach at 6, and where they pass the night. They walk up to the well. (*SHL* 74; SMJ.)

50. July 23

W, MW, SH proceed along Evan Water to the Clyde, past Evanfoot and Crawford. Near Crawford they pass a deserted church; W goes in and finds the ground strewn with fragments of coffins. They cross [Duneaton Water]; proceed to Douglas Mill, where they dine and pass the night. They walk to and look inside Douglas Castle; see a portrait of Lord Douglas when a young man, Justice treading Envy under foot, and medallions with the heads of Camden and Mansfield. (*SHL* 74; SMJ.)[24]

[22] SMJ records: "found an English acquaintance there Miss Milward of Parton—and a friend of coz. Fannys." It is remotely possible that the friend of cousin Fanny was identical with one of the friends of Thomas H's acquaintances.

[23] SMJ records: "Dancing Master at night. all the family with the addition of Lady Johnson her Daughter & Governess stood up to dance. . . . "

[24] SMJ states that the party crossed "the Neeta," which, in the phrasing of SH's copy, "fall[s] into the Clyde near the point where the road turns to the left to Glasgow." The description suggests that SH misunderstood the name of Duneaton Water.

51. July 24

W, MW, SH proceed to Lanark, crossing the Clyde at Hyndford Bridge, and passing Smyllum Park. They breakfast at Lanark; attend the kirk, where they hear a vehement preacher, see two infants baptized. They walk to the Cartland Crags. SH sleeps all afternoon. W, MW visit the New Town, enjoy the sight of the mill workers in their holiday clothes amusing themselves by the river. They pass the night at Lanark. (*SHL* 74; SMJ.)

52. July 25 (–July 28), and shortly after

On 25 July W, MW, SH view the Falls of Clyde (Corra Linn) in Lady Perth's grounds before breakfast; they depart Lanark, probably after breakfast; see [Chatelherault]; visit Barncluith; dine at Hamilton; view the pictures at Hamilton House; visit Bothwell Castle, view it from a moss hut up the river; proceed to Glasgow, which they reach at dusk. The horse is frightened and the travellers annoyed by children rolling in the street. (They remain at Glasgow until 28 July.) They pass the night at an inn.

Their visit to Corra Linn probably prompts W to write *Composed at Cora Linn*. W possibly composes some part of the poem now or shortly after. (The poem is not completed until c but by 1820.) (*SHL* 74–75; SMJ.)[25]

53. July 26

SH, perhaps W, MW, visit Glasgow Cathedral. They pass the night at the country house of Robert Grahame. (*SHL* 74–75; SMJ.)

54. July 27

W, MW, SH go sightseeing in a hired landau with Robert Grahame. They see steam weaving and a cooperage with circular saws operated by steam. They dine and pass the night at Grahame's. (*SHL* 75; SMJ.)

[25] *Composed at Cora Linn* was not published until 1820, and no probable occasion of completion of the work in the near future is evident.

55. July 28

W, MW, SH travel along the Firth of Clyde to Dumbarton and thence to Ardencaple, where they pass the night at the inn. They obtain water from an old man at Gileston Burn. (*SHL* 75; SMJ.)[26]

56. July 29

W, MW, SH cross Gare Loch at 6 AM, visit Rosneath Castle. Walk across the peninsula to the Stables. W, MW ascend the Stables to look at the country; all return to Ardencaple for breakfast. They travel by Garelochhead and along Loch Long to Arrochar. At the toll bar at Garelochhead they are rained indoors, where they are kindly attended by Mrs. Turner. Having resumed their journey, they are later rained in at a house occupied by the family of Provost Dixon of Dumbarton (according to SH's copy of SMJ) or (according to MW's version) a lady, the wife of Captain Smith, with her family, from Dumbarton, who has seen RM. They dine at Arrochar. W loses his whip. They proceed past Tarbet and southward along Loch Lomond to Luss, where they pass the night in the most disagreeable inn they have visited. (*SHL* 75; SMJ.)

The dedicatory sonnet for *Exc* is dated 29 July. (See 1814:33.)

57. July 30

W, MW, SH, after a breakfast without bread, visit Inchtavannach and Castle Galbraith; sail around Inchcruin. They land on the Deer Island, Inchlonaig, where they are entertained by the forester's wife; see an old woman from Paisley lodging there in hope of improving a sprained ankle or rheumatism. They eat black currants; see an indolent servant; see a large goat brought in and gutted by the forester and the fowler. They gather bilberries on the Jail of Luss; walk in the evening to a hill behind the inn and to the churchyard. (*SHL* 75; SMJ.)

58. July 31

W, MW, SH travel beside Loch Lomond; see Cameron House,

[26] The early copy of SMJ drops a day for the period 28–31 July, describing events under a calendar date one day late. (Sunday the 31st is thus called the 30th.)

Tullichewan Castle, and Bellvidere, built by Mr. Buchannan. W, MW ascend Mt. Misery. They visit Kilmaronock Church and manse, and a ruined castle. They cross Endrick Water; breakfast at Drymen; attend the kirk there, hear a gentlemanly preacher, a recent widower with a young family. They proceed over Gartmore to Aberfoyle, where they pass the night in the inn parlor. On their way they meet a woman who points directions to Buchlyvie and Campsie, names made familiar to SH by James Patrick in her youth. (*SHL* 75–76; SMJ.)

59. Aug 1

W, MW, SH in the morning view Loch Ard and Loch Chon; meet and are accompanied for a time by a Highland gentleman, Mr. Graham; see Graham's wife and little boy. They proceed from Aberfoyle by Loch Monteith to Callander, where they pass the night. They see Stirling Castle gleaming in the setting sun at a distance. (*SHL* 76; SMJ.)[27]

60. Aug 2

W, MW, SH cross the Leny; travel beside Loch Venachar, Loch Achray to the Trossachs, where they are drenched by rain. They shelter at the house of a Highlander, Duncan Stuart, where they have already left their car. MW tastes whiskey for the first time. They pass the night back at Callander. (*SHL* 76; SMJ.)

61. Aug 3

SH begins a letter to MMH at Callander (*SHL* 71–76). The rain abating, W, MW, SH travel by Loch Lubnaig to Lochearnhead, where SH continues her letter (*SHL* 76–77) and W and MW go to see the castle, falls, and mausoleum. On their way they see Bruce's house [Ardchullarie], probably see or stop at Miss Campbell's house. They proceed to Killin, crossing the River Lochay at dusk. They probably view Dochart Falls. (*SHL* 76; SMJ.)

[27] *SHL* calls the first lake "Loch Earn," which was, however, too distant for a morning's visit from Aberfoyle. The later journal clearly says "Ard."

62. Aug 4

SH finishes her letter to MMH. W, MW, SH view the Earl of Bredalbane's burial ground and the MacNab burying ground. They travel up the Dochart, dine at Tynluib on whiskey pudding and chicken; proceed down Glen Falloch. They pass the night at an inn near or at the head of Loch Lomond, where they are treated hospitably but obtain only oatmeal scones to eat. (*SHL* 77; SMJ.)[28]

The Longman accounts for *Exc* commence under this date. On this day Longman forwards five copies of *Exc* to W.(Longman accounts. See Owen CSP 97; Owen LLW 26–27.)[29]

63. Aug 5; Aug 5 or shortly after (–c but by 1820)

On 5 Aug SH buys a slice of bread from some itinerant potters for MW's breakfast. W, MW, SH travel along Loch Lomond to Tarbet, where they pass the night. Probably on this day W meets the last of the MacFarlanes; hears from him, in front of Pulpit Rock, or Clach-nan-Fairbh, the legend of the Brownie's cell. The story forms the basis of *The Brownie's Cell*. W possibly composes part of the poem now or shortly after. (The poem is probably not completed until c but by 1820.)

[28] MW's copy of SMJ remarks: "M. sick of *chacken*." Cf *DWJ* I, 258: "[T]here are always plenty of fowls at the doors of a Scotch inn."

[29] Charges are made (usually 1/6 per copy for what are probably usually delivery costs; see Owen CSP 97n) for eighteen copies charged to "Sundries" and one to author under this date. Similar charges are made for the following, through 1815, in Divide Ledger 1, op. 102.

1814	Aug	10	1	Mr Hutchinson
		27	1	S. hall [Stationers Hall]
		30	3	Reviews
	Sep	6	1	Sir E Brydges
	Nov	11	3	Reviews
1815	Jan	18	9	Statrs Hall Sd
	Mar	18	1	Augustan Rev
	June	6	1	do returned Aug 7

On the credit side of the ledger is recorded "1 from Mo Rev Nov 2 1815." CL had received and read his copy "before the rest of the world" by 9 Aug (*LL* II, 126–29). HCR saw a copy at the apartments of Thomas Madge on 13 Aug (*HCRBW* I, 147). The first announcement of publication discovered appeared on 17 Aug; see 1814:75. The first installment of Hazlitt's review appeared in the *Examiner* of 21 Aug.

(SMJ; *The Brownie's Cell* n; *PW* Knight, 1882–89 VI, 28–32; *PW* Knight, 1896 VI, 21–25; *Memorials of a Tour in Scotland 1814* IF note.)[30]

64. Aug 6 (–Aug 8)

W, MW, SH travel around the head of Loch Long and into Glen Croe, thence into Glen Kinglas and to Cairndow Inn, where they dine. They have a fine view of The Cobbler. They purchase fruit at a gentleman's house. They continue around Loch Fyne to Inverary, where they pass this and the next night. They walk to the castle. W walks up Duniquoich hill. (*SHL* 77; SMJ.)

65. Aug 7

W walks into a neighboring vale, probably Glen Shira. MW, SH attend the kirk. After dinner, W, MW walk to the valley that W visited earlier. They pass a second night at Inverary. (SMJ.)

66. Aug 8

W, MW, SH travel [up Glen Aray] to Loch Awe and Dalmally, where they pass the night. They are wet by rain a mile and a half from Dalmally. (SMJ.)[31]

67. Aug 9

W, MW, SH travel [through the Pass of Brander] to Taynuilt. They visit Bonawe; row on Loch Etive; land at Glen Kinglass; walk to the farmhouse at Mr. MacIntire's sheep farm. They probably pass the night at Taynuilt. (SMJ.)[32]

68. Aug 10

W, MW, SH probably breakfast at Connel Ferry in the room of

[30] Concerning the travellers' route from 5 through 21 Aug, cf Moorman II, 259. *The Brownie's Cell* was not published until 1820.

[31] SMJ does not specifically state that the night was passed at Dalmally; but its report that the party travelled sixteen miles this day leaves little doubt about the matter.

[32] SMJ reports that the party travelled twelve miles this day; Taynuilt is thus probably where they passed the night, although SH does not say so specifically.

Charles Long, a young man travelling with numerous maps and copies of Ossian and Thomson's *Seasons*. They travel via Connel Ferry, Shian Ferry, Appin Church, and Portnacroish to Ballachulish, where, probably, they pass the night. (SMJ; *LY* I, 194.)

69. Aug 11

W, MW, SH visit Glen Coe in the rain. They set out from Balla-chulish at 6 PM; probably proceed along Loch Linnhe to Fort William. They enter Fort William, where they pass the night, followed by a rabble; Miss Bell McLaughlin and her maids at first refuse them admittance at the [inn], supposing them mountebanks or show folk because of their odd travelling carriage. MW talks her over. (SMJ. See *LY* I, 194.)[33]

70. Aug 12

W, MW, SH proceed across the Nevis and on to Loch Lochy; see unusually poor huts. Gentlemen pass in a gig, promise to order them a fire at Leitir Finlay. On arriving there, they find that the peats are wet and a fire impractical. They warm themselves in the kitchen; dine on eggs and bacon. W drinks whiskey punch possibly prepared for MW and SH. They continue by Loch Lochy, Loch Oich, Invergarry, the Oich, to Fort Augustus, where, probably, they pass the night. (SMJ.)[34]

71. Aug 13

W, MW, SH travel toward Inverness on the east side of Loch Ness; view or visit the House of Knockie; cross the Fechline; reach the General's Hut, where they pass the night. (SMJ.)

[33] The later copy of SMJ states that they travelled two miles by Loch Linnhe, and from the "5th mile stone" by Loch Eil. The description appears to confuse Upper Loch Linnhe with Loch Eil.

[34] SMJ gives the distance of their day's journey as 29½ miles. The journal mischie-viously reports that at Leitir Finlay "Ladies agreed to comfort themselves with Whiskey Punch, but W. seized it & drank it off.—"

72. Aug 14

W, MW, SH visit the Falls of Foyers and the House of Foyers. They dine in their room at the General's Hut with Mr. and Mrs. Bristo. Departing the hut at 3, they proceed along Loch Ness, seeing a castle on the opposite shore (probably Urquhart Castle), to Inverness, where they pass the night. (SMJ. See *LY* I, 194.)

73. Aug 15

W, MW, SH, in a landaulet, visit Beauly, where they breakfast, Beauly Falls, Kilmorack Church, on their way toward Strath Glass. They fail to reach Strath Glass; return to Inverness. They proceed southward past Loch Moy; view Port George; pass the night at an unpleasant inn (perhaps Freeburn Inn), probably in the neighborhood of Tomatin. (SMJ. See *LY* I, 194.)[35]

74. Aug 16

W, MW, SH set off at 6:30 AM. They stop for two hours at Aviemore; walk to see the Duchess of Gordon's Lodge, Kinrara, but are unsuccessful; see Kirk o' Alvie and Loch Alvie. They notice a kirk at Kingussie; notice the ruins of Ruthven [Barracks] on the opposite bank; reach the Pitmain Inn, where they pass the night. They share a room and form a friendly acquaintance with Mr. and Mrs. Dunbar. (SMJ.)

75. Aug 17; probably on Aug 17

W, MW, SH set off at 5:30 AM; cross the Spey; proceed southward down Glen Truim; breakfast at Dalwhinnie Inn. W probably makes inquiries concerning the ways to Loch Rannoch and Loch Laggan. Mr. and Mrs. Dunbar [see 1814:74] arrive, give them a brace of grouse. They travel down Glen Garry to Blair Atholl, where they pass the night. They dine at Dalnachardoch on the way. (SMJ.)

---

[35] SMJ records that they progressed 45 miles today and 29 miles next day before stopping at Pitmain Inn. Their resting place is conjectured on the basis of these distances.

Probably on this day *The Excursion* is published in London (*MC*. See esp. 1814:62.)[36]

76. Aug 18

W, MW, SH travel through the Pass of Killiecrankie; stop for two hours at the Falls of the Tummel; notice Lady Bath's castle and garden; dine at the half-way house; have a fine view of the Tay. At dusk they reach Dunkeld, where they pass the night. They drink tea there with Mr. and Mrs. Dunbar [see 1814:74; 1814:75]. (SMJ.)

77. Aug 19; Aug 19 or shortly after

W, MW, SH perhaps visit the Duke of Atholl's pleasure-ground this morning. They travel up Strathbraan to Amulree, where they pass the night. (SMJ.)

W possibly today or shortly after composes, prompted by this and his earlier visit to the Duke's pleasure-ground, some part of *Effusion. In the Pleasure-ground on the Banks of the Bran, near Dunkeld.* (Title and content. See GCL 215.)[37]

78. Aug 20; perhaps Aug 20 or Aug 21

On 20 Aug W, MW, SH travel through the Sma' Glen of Glen-almond; wish to visit Monzie but are misdirected; probably cross the bridge at Buchanty, where they rest at a miller's house; proceed along the Almond; probably visit the grave of Bessie Bell and Mary Gray, Lynedoch Cottage, Methven Castle. They proceed to Perth, where they pass the night. Perhaps today or next day W purchases a duo-decimo copy of the *Poetical Works* of Burns (London, 1813), a Perth

[36] The *Courier* of 18 Aug speaks of the poem as "just published" and quotes the dedicatory sonnet.

[37] The *Effusion* was first published in 1827, and was probably finished after *PW* 1820; but it seems unlikely that no attempt at composition was made before 1820. W's 1803 visit probably contributed to the *Effusion*, however, and the poem was placed among the *Memorials of a Tour in Scotland, 1814* upon publication.

Guide, and perhaps a small edition of Ossian. (SMJ; copy of Burns's *Poetical Works*, London, 1813, DCP.)[38]

79. Aug 21

W, MW, SH climb Kinnoull Hill. They attend the kirk; hear a sermon from Dr. [Jeremiah] Romeyn, an American, whom they consider the best preacher they have ever heard. They hear him again at the middle kirk in the afternoon but do not like him so well. This evening they walk to Scone [and back]. They fall in along the way with a bookseller from whom W had bought books [see 1814:78]. They probably pass the night at Perth. (SMJ; *MY* II, 161.)

The first part of Hazlitt's review of *Exc* appears in *The Examiner*. (See also 1814:86; 1814:106.)

80. Aug 22

W, MW, SH depart Perth at 6 AM; climb Moncrieff Hill; cross the Earn; proceed through Glenfarg to Kinross. At Kinross they probably visit Kinross House and churchyard; dine. The waiter touches W for sixpence. They proceed past Crook of Devon to Alloa, where they pass the night. (SMJ.)

81. Aug 23

W, MW, SH visit Alloa Tower. W, MW visit Clackmannan Tower. They probably pass a second night at Alloa. (SMJ.)

[38] The Burns volume contains two inscriptions:

> Wm Wordsworth
> bought
> at
> Perth   Augst 1814

> Wm Wordsworth
> from
> his
> affectionate Father
> 20th Octr 1831

SMJ remarks only: "fell in with a bookseller of whom W had bought a small Ed. of Ossian & the Perth Guide. . . ." An 1813 two-volume edition of Ossian was part of lot 628 in the 1859 Rydal Mount Sale (RM Sale Catalogue).

82. Aug 24

W, MW, SH proceed to Stirling, where they are turned away from two inns because of crowds. They look at the view from the castle. They continue through Falkirk, where they visit the churchyard, past the pleasure-grounds of Callendar House, and to Linlithgow, where they pass the night. They view the Palace, church, and fountain. (SMJ.)

83. Aug 25–Aug 30; possibly at this time, probably between Aug 25 and late Oct, possibly c early Oct

On 25 Aug W, MW, SH proceed along byroads to Abercorn; visit Hopetoun House; perhaps breakfast at the Society Inn; proceed through Queensferry to Edinburgh, where they arrive at 3:30. They dine at the Black Bull Hotel; go shopping.

They remain in Edinburgh until 30 Aug. They pass much of their time at Mrs. Wilson's residence. Probably esp. at dinner on these days the travellers meet what SH later calls "all the *wits*" who are in town [see 1814:84–1814:87]; but they probably also meet other Edinburgh residents, perhaps including the sea captain and his aunt with whom they had dined at Burnfoot on 21 July.

W probably here meets J. M. Lappenberg, possibly in company with R. P. Gillies [see 1814:87].

W perhaps here composes "From the Dark Chambers of Dejection Freed," and possibly now copies the poem into an album of Elizabeth Wilson's. He fairly certainly composes and so copies the poem by late Oct, and possibly c early Oct. (SMJ; *SHL* 79; *MWL* 18–19; *MY* II, 167–68; "From the Dark Chambers" IF note; Mary Barker Album, Bodleian Library; 1814:103.)

Perhaps during this visit W meets "Sir" Peter Nimmo, who obtains access to W by using John Wilson's name. (Mrs. Gordon II, 25; David Masson, *Edinburgh Sketches and Memoirs*, Edinburgh, 1892, 285–88.) He perhaps here meets Dr. James Gray. (See *Letter to a Friend of Robert Burns*; Moorman II, 295.)

84. Aug 26

On 26 Aug W, MW, SH walk to Calton Hill; probably walk to Queen Street, the Castle, and Arthur's Seat. They dine at Mrs. Wilson's, perhaps with R. P. Gillies, C. K. Sharpe, and an unidentified "brother advocate." (SMJ; Gillies II, 140–41.)[39]

85. Aug 27

W, MW, SH visit Bridewill, Heriot's Hospital; dine at Miss Taylor's; see Holyrood House. (SMJ.)

86. Aug 28; Aug 28 or Aug 29

On 28 Aug W, MW, SH attend church. W, MW walk to and probably up Corstorphine Hill, probably with Gillies and James Wilson. They dine with Mrs. Wilson, perhaps with James Hogg. Perhaps on this day or next W makes some calls with Hogg. (SMJ; Gillies II, 140–45; 1814:83; 1814:84n.)[40]

The second part of Hazlitt's review of *Exc* appears in *The Examiner* on 28 Aug. (See also 1814:79; 1814:106.)

87. Aug 29; between Aug 29 and Nov 23

On 29 Aug W, MW, SH visit Roslin Castle and Chapel, perhaps also Dryden; return to Edinburgh. They dine at Gillies'. (SMJ. See 1814:84n.)

Between 29 Aug and 23 Nov W reads Hogg's *The Queen's Wake.* (SMJ; *MY* II, 167–69.)

[39] The reports of SMJ and Gillies conflict. Gillies records, many years later, that he dined with—and evidently at—the Wilsons', with C. K. Sharpe and "a brother advocate" to meet W "on the day of his arrival," and walked with W, MW, SH, and James Wilson up Corstorphine Hill next day. SMJ records dining at the Black Bull on the day of arrival, at Mrs. Wilson's next day, at Miss Taylor's next day, at Mrs. Wilson's next day after W and MW had walked up "Kirkstophan's" hill, and at Gillies' next day. SMJ seems the more reliable basic report, and I have reconciled Gillies' recollections with it speculatively 1814:84–1814:87. Gillies would probably have recalled Hogg's presence at the dinner he attended had the Ettrick Shepherd been present.

[40] Hogg records that some time after meeting W at dinner, to which he had been invited by James Wilson, he and W "called on several noblemen and gentlemen in company."

88. Aug 30

W, MW, SH travel through Peebles, where they dine, to Traquair, where they pass the night, perhaps at Traquair Knowe. (SMJ. See *MY* II, 193.)

89. Aug 31–Sept 1; certainly between Sept 1, probably Sept 2, and Sept 16

On 31 Aug W, MW, SH probably visit Traquair House; dine at the Manse, where Dr. Robert Anderson and his daughter are visiting. Perhaps all walk to the Bush above Traquair, [41] which appears to MW and/or SH no bush at all. The pastor and his wife promise to call at RM next summer. (SMJ; *MY* II, 193; *Yarrow Visited* IF note.)

On 31 Aug or 1 Sept or both W and Dr. Anderson probably discuss the possibility of additions to Anderson's *British Poets*. Probably W offers to supply Anderson with a list of suggestions for making the *Poets* complete, which Anderson may use for approaching a publisher. (*MY* II, 151–55; 1814:101.)

On 1 Sept W, MW, SH, Dr. Anderson, James Hogg meet at Traquair; walk till they come in view of the Yarrow, where Dr. Anderson turns back. The others visit St. Mary's Loch, pass the day along the Yarrow, where they take refreshment at Hogg's father's cottage. Hogg perhaps accompanies them as far as Selkirk, where they pass the night. They drink tea at a farmhouse on the way. (SMJ. See *MY* II, 193; *HCRBW* I, 269; Hogg Autobiography, 463.)[42]

Certainly between 1 Sept, probably 2 Sept, and 16 Sept W composes most of *Yarrow Visited*. (*Yarrow Visited* IF note; *SHL* 79; 1814:99; *MY* II, 170.)[43]

[41] See Robert Crawford's "The Bush above Traquair."

[42] Hogg records: "In tracing the windings of the pastoral Yarrow from its source to its confluence with the sister stream [Ettrick], the poet was in great good humour, delightful and most eloquent. . . . From Selkirk we were obliged to take different routes, as Wordsworth had business in Teviotdale and I in Eskdale . . . ."

[43] W's alterations would probably not have had to be sent to SH had they been composed before 16 Sept, when she departed RM; but some version of the poem would appear to have been in her possession before she left.

90. Sept 2

On 2 Sept W, MW, SH breakfast with Mrs. Scott [at Abbotsford]. Scott's daughter shows them around the grounds at Abbotsford. All visit Melrose Abbey; lunch with Lord Buchan at Dryburgh Abbey. W, MW, SH proceed along the Tweed to Kelso, where they pass the night.

At Kelso SH writes to MMH: Joanna's health; their recent travels; possibility that letter from MMH has been lost; inquiry about *Exc.* (*SHL* 78–80; *LY* I, 929.)[44]

91. Sept 3

W, MW, SH probably travel to Hawick; pass the night there. (*SHL* 79.)

92. Probably Sept 4–probably c Sept 6

W, MW, SH probably travel to Burnfoot on 4 Sept. They probably visit there until c 6 Sept. (*SHL* 79.)

93. Probably c Sept 6–Sept 9; Sept 7 ff

W, MW, SH, Johnny travel from Burnfoot to RM, arriving home on 9 Sept. Their route probably does not include Penrith. (*SHL* 79; *MY* II, 160.)[45]

Probably on 7 Sept James Hogg visits RM and is entertained by DW. He remains an actual or virtual visitor at RM until W's return. Perhaps about this time Hogg lets become known to John Wilson, possibly to W, and probably to the family circle at GH, remarks of Byron's, in a letter to Hogg, concerning the Lake Poets. Among Byron's comments is that the Lake Poets are "such fools as not to fish in their own waters." The supposition of Byron's sneers probably provokes W's and Mary Barker's *Lines Addressed to a Noble Lord.* (Hogg

---

[44] Scott himself was absent on a voyage to the Shetlands (see Edgar Johnson, *Sir Walter Scott*, New York, 1971, I, 440–53). On Lord Buchan's attitude toward W see *MWL* 19.

[45] DW states that they arrived on the Friday preceding her departure for Hindwell, which occurred on Friday 16 Sept. Cf *SHL* 79.

Autobiography 463–64, 466; Thomas Medwin, *Journal of the Conversations of Lord Byron at Pisa*, ed. E. J. Lovell, Princeton, 1966, 196–97; *The Works of Lord Byron, The Letters and Journals*, ed. R. E. Prothero, London, 1898–1901, IV, 494, VI, 398. See 1814:97; 1814:99; Kirkpatrick.)

94. Probably between Sept 9 and late Oct

Probably between 9 Sept and late Oct W prepares poems for *P* 1815. It is perhaps at this time that most copying in DC MS 80 toward *P* 1815 takes place. Probably c Sept, after 9 Sept, W determines the final arrangement of the poems for *P* 1815. (See 1811:72n; 1814:112.)

Perhaps c late summer, after 9 Sept, W gives a copy of *Exc* to Charles Lloyd or Mrs. Lloyd with an injunction against lending the book to anyone able to afford to buy it. (*MY* II, 184; *MWL* 20.)

95. Probably c mid-Sept, after Sept 9

W probably shows Hogg around the neighborhood of RM. Perhaps one day Hogg becomes tired, expresses a wish not to see "ony mair dubs" and to have some whiskey. (*N&Q* 5th Series II, 1874, 157–58.)

96. Sept 10

A review of *Exc* appears in *Variety*. (See Ward; Hayden.)

97. Perhaps Sept 11

John Wilson, DeQ, Lloyd, Hogg dine at RM. The party sees an unusually bright meteor from the upper terrace. Hogg suggests that the meteor is a triumphal arch, raised in honor of the meeting of the poets. W's reaction, as reported to Hogg by DeQ, is insulting to Hogg. (Hogg Autobiography 463–64; Moorman II, 276; *LY* II, 617–18; A. L. Strout, *The Life and Letters of James Hogg*, Lubbock, Texas, 1946, 81–83.)

98. Probably c mid-Sept; probably between c mid-Sept and c early Oct

Probably c mid-Sept W converses with RS on the subject of

additions to Anderson's *British Poets*. They draw up a list of authors and works. (See 1814:89; 1814:101.)

Probably between c mid-Sept and c early Oct [Robert] Tyrwhitt calls at RM. W and he enjoy reminiscing about Cambridge. (*MWL* 26–27; MS of MW letter, DCP.)[46]

99. Probably Sept 16–Sept 27 (–probably between Dec 10 and Dec 15), and possibly about this time

Probably on 16 Sept John Wilson, Hogg, and others, probably including DeQ, dine at RM. They walk down the hill to see DW and SH off in the jaunting car. DW, SH travel to Kendal, where they probably visit with the Cooksons till 18 Sept.

On 18 Sept DW, SH depart at 5 AM on top of the coach with J. G. Crump. Another companion is an American friend of Romeyn [see 1814:79], Mr. Warner, whom the ladies find attractive. They reach Liverpool on 19 Sept at 7 PM; visit with the Crumps till 22 Sept.

On 21 Sept DW draws on RW for £30 by a bill in favor of J. G. Crump.[47]

On 22 Sept they travel to Chester, where they visit Nancy W Ireland (daughter of RW of Whitehaven) until 24 Sept, when they travel to Shrewsbury.

On 25 Sept DW writes to Richard Addison from Shrewsbury: Advises of draft on RW of 21 Sept.

They depart Shrewsbury on 26 Sept, when Thomas H meets them with a gig. They travel to Ludlow on 26 Sept, and on 27 Sept proceed to Hindwell. (DW returns to RM probably between 10 and 15 Dec. SH returns probably Sept 1815.) (*MY* II, 155, 160–61, 241; *SHL* 84.)

Possibly about this time W gives to Hogg a MS of *Yarrow Visited* for a miscellany that he is compiling. (A. L. Strout, *The Life and Letters of James Hogg*, Lubbock, Texas, 1946, 76–78; *MY* II, 168. See 1814:132.)

100. Probably between Sept 16 and c early Oct, c mid-Oct, late Oct

Probably between 16 Sept and c early Oct, but after giving *Yarrow*

---

[46] The surname of the caller that *MWL* 26 records as "T." is unmistakable in the MS. MW recalls that Tyrwhitt's call took place "long" before a visit by W to Troutbeck. See 1814:111.

[47] RW's accounts record payment of the bill under 24 Oct.

Visited to Hogg [see 1814:99] W revises *Yarrow Visited*; copies revised version into Elizabeth Wilson's Album or collection of MS poems; and by late Oct returns the album to her. Possibly now W also copies there "From the Dark Chambers of Dejection Freed." (*MWL* 18–19; 1814:83; *MY* II, 167–68; 1814:106; Mary Barker Album, Bodleian Library.)

Possibly between 16 Sept and c mid-Oct W and the family prepare a preliminary MS for *P* 1815. DC MSS 78, 79 of *EW* are perhaps prepared at this time. (They are drawn on only for excerpts in *P* 1815.) (*MY* II, 151–55; DCP. See 1814:112; 1814:113.)

101. Sept 17

W writes to Dr. Robert Anderson: Advises of his and RS's recommendations of authors and works for additional volumes of Anderson's *British Poets*: the object is to complete Anderson's edition of the British poets; the list includes materials in Chalmers not in Anderson. W gives list. (*MY* II, 151–55. See 1814:89.)[48]

102. Probably Sept 25–Sept 29; between Sept 29 and Oct 1

Probably on 25 Sept W departs RM at 5 AM, travels to Patterdale, where he breakfasts with Mr. Askew. He travels on to Lowther, where he visits LdL. John Marshall's servant accompanies him, perhaps from Watermillock, to carry W's portmanteau and to bring his pony back to Sockbridge.

Probably during this visit to Lowther W calls at Sockbridge but finds RW and Mrs. W gone to Allonby. He talks with Barbara Wilkin-

---

[48] Anderson had perhaps agreed to push forward with his addition upon receipt of a letter of this sort. The project was apparently dropped in the following Feb [see 1815: 12; 1815:15]. James Irving later wrote to W on 21 Nov 1816 asking views regarding an anthology of selections from the British poets from Chaucer, and seeking advice on authors not in Chalmers and the most worthy selections. W apparently referred him to Anderson, for Irving writes on 1 Feb 1817: "Accept my sincere thanks for your attention respecting the Poets, the list of whom I got from my good old friend Dr Anderson, who with Miss Anderson beg their respects to you and family. At present no bookseller of my acquaintance seems fond of the Extract you mention, but I think Blackwood here, will in the end wish such a work." (DCP.)

son. At Lowther W probably meets Prince Frederic of Orange. He probably converses with Henry Brougham, who tells him that Leigh Hunt values his poems.

W probably departs Lowther on 29 Sept, possibly stopping for a day or two at Watermillock, but reaching RM by 1 Oct. (*MWL* 13, 17; *MY* II, 163, 195.)

On 27 Sept JPM, Miss Marshall, Catherine Pollard, two Misses Smith and John [Marshall] call at RM for tea. The visitors make MW uneasy by not asking to stay at RM. MW and Dora go to Ambleside next day, 28 Sept, to join the Marshall party for an excursion to Windermere, but JPM has too bad a cold to go. MW sits with her till the rest of the party proceeds homeward over Kirkstone. MW and Dora return to RM. Probably on her way home MW meets [Richard] Sharp, Lord Calthorpe, and some unidentified men, who have just called at RM. Mr. Powley sups at RM with MW; hears Dora recite Latin.

On 29 Sept the tax man calls; takes £8. Sharp, Lord Calthorpe, perhaps with companions including Lady Olivia Sparrow, probably call at RM; MW perhaps now obtains some franks from Calthorpe.[49]

On 29 Sept MW writes to DW, SH: The trip of DW, SH to Hindwell; W, Lowther, and the Marshalls; possibilities of assisting HC to college; Miss Barker; CL, Hazlitt, and *Exc.* One of the Hs' volumes of *LB* said to be lost. Miss Pollard had expected a visit from DW. (*MWL* 12–16, 18.)

103. Probably c early Oct, by Oct 17; possibly at the same time, or between this time and c Mar 1815

The Ss visit at RM for a week. RS leaves a copy of *Roderick* in sheets. Possibly at the same time Mary Barker visits RM. W possibly at this time contributes to Miss Barker's *Lines Addressed to a Noble Lord* [see 1814:111; 1814:124]. Between this time and c Mar 1815, she obtains a copy, or copies, of "From the Dark Chambers of Dejection Freed," Gillies' *To Mr Wordsworth*, and other poems of W's and DW's including *Yarrow Visited* (this copy was perhaps obtained not before early Nov),

---

[49] Lady B wrote to W on 17 Jan 1815 that CW had told her that Lord Calthorpe and Lady Olivia Sparrow, "who visited you, belong to the powerful evangelical Sect, and his ardour will not rest in silence" (DCP). W almost certainly did not return to RM in time to meet these visitors. See *R&C* II, 166.

To Dorothy Wordsworth (*The Cottager to Her Infant*), *Address to a Child in a High Wind*, *The Mother's Return*, *A Fragment* ("Peaceful Our Valley").

RS and W probably discuss arrangements for sending HC to college. (*MWL* 14, 20–21; *MY* II, 162; Curry II, 107, CCS IV, 82; 1814:83; Mary Barker Album, Bodleian Library; 1815:44; letter, RS to John May, 9 Nov 1814, UTL.) [50]

104. Probably c Oct 1

A review of *Exc* appears in the *New Monthly Magazine* (II, Sept 1814). (See Ward; Hayden.)

105. Oct 1

W writes to LdL: W encloses an extract from a letter from CCl concerning TCl's inquiries about the possibility of the abolition of the slave trade in France. (*MY* II, 155–57.)

106. Oct 2

The third part of Hazlitt's review of *Exc* appears in *The Examiner*. (See also 1814:79; 1814:86.)

[50] Miss Barker had not visited RM any time as recently as 29 Sept (*MWL* 14), but MW's phrasing *MWL* 21 strongly suggests that the women had met and conversed between 29 Sept and 22 Oct. MW on 29 Sept thought that Miss Barker would like to visit RM with the Ss. What lines of Miss Barker's poem W wrote at this time remain uncertain. The contribution that he had made by 10 Dec is much more readily identifiable. See 1814:111; 1814:124; 1815:21.

The poems noted, the first dated "Rydale Mt., Oct. 1814," are copied by Miss Barker together with "The Year 1814," signed "Anthony Harrison" (between *Yarrow Visited* and *To Dorothy Wordsworth*), preceding *Lines Addressed to a Noble Lord*. *Lines* is dated "November 1814," and while this date is probably not that of the copy, the copy can hardly date after c Mar 1815. The copy of *Yarrow Visited* generally corresponds to that transcribed by DW from Stow on 11 Nov. Apparently the only variant with chronological significance is that in line 6, where the Barker MS has "notes," as in the printed text, for the "words" of DW's MS. The Barker copy is hence possibly later than DW's, which DW apparently received shortly before 11 Nov (*MY* II, 164); but the evidence is not strong.

RS writes on 9 Nov that he had recently visited W for a week. (See Charles Ramos, "Letters of Robert Southey to John May 1797–1838," Diss. University of Texas, 1965.) He does not appear, despite W's indication, probably on 4 Dec, that the Ss were there "not above a month ago," to have visited c early Nov (see 1814:125; Warter II, 377; CCS IV, 83; Curry II, 106–09).

107. Oct 8

W writes to LdL: Approves of LdL's mode of proceeding in regard to TCl [see 1814:105]. W hopes to visit Lowther toward the beginning of next month. (*MY* II, 157.)

108. Oct 9

DW writes to CCl from Hindwell: The planned marriage between Baudouin and Caroline. Annette's and Caroline's and DW's wish that DW attend; necessity that she wait till spring or summer; seeks advice about travel arrangements. Hazlitt's review of *Exc.* The trip to Hindwell; Hindwell and the family there. (*MY* II, 157–62.)

109. Oct 13; probably Oct 13

On 13 Oct W writes to RW: Urgent pleas to supply an accounting of his and DW's affairs. They wish to have their money at their command. (*MY* II, 163. See 1814:39.)

Probably on 13 Oct W, MW dine at Rydal Hall with the Dalbys and Pennys. (*MWL* 16.)

110. Perhaps shortly before Oct 14

W or MW writes to DW. (See 1814:113n.)

111. Probably Oct 14

W, MW, with MW mounted, set off for Elleray via Troutbeck Chapel; Mr. Scambler lends his horse to W at Ambleside. They dine at Elleray. W, John Wilson walk to Bowness. W, MW come home to tea.

Possibly at this time Wilson expresses [to W] his belief that W is the author of the first stanza and of part of the description of the rural feast (lines 134–65) in Miss Barker's *Lines.* (*MWL* 16; *MY* II, 176.)[51]

---

[51] On the Ws' relationship with the Wilsons between late Sept 1814 and 14 Feb 1815 see *MY* II, 197. On W and Miss Barker's poem see Kirkpatrick; 1814:103; 1814:124.

112. Between c mid-Oct and c early Feb; by Oct 27, 29, c early Nov

Probably c mid-Oct, certainly by 27 Oct, W composes *Laodamia* in a basic form of c 130 lines. The poem is possibly sent off to the printer by 27 Oct, but W is still thinking about it on that day and continues to do so thereafter. W probably completes the poem in *P* 1815 form by c early Feb. (*MWL* 23–24; *MY* I, 194–95.)[52]

Probably a preliminary MS for *P* 1815 is completed by c mid-Oct. During late Oct W is troubled by night sweats. Copying of the main portion of the printer's MS is completed to the middle of *Idiot Boy* (*P* 1815 I, c 190) by 29 Oct 1814, and perhaps largely concluded by c early Nov. (*MWL* 25–27. See 1814:130.)[53]

113. Perhaps Oct 15 and shortly after; probably Oct 15

Perhaps on 15 Oct W or MW finds a copy of *DS* belonging to SH. Probably shortly afterward excerpts from *DS* are sent off for inclusion in *P* 1815.

Probably on 15 Oct W writes to DeQ: DeQ does not need to search for a copy of *DS*, since a copy has been found this morning.

Probably on 15 Oct a party of the Crumps comes to tea at RM with Scottish friends, strangers to the Ws. (*MY* II, 163–64; *MWL* 16, 18.)[54]

---

[52] MW writes on 27 Oct that she had spoken of the poem in her last letter (almost certainly that of 22 Oct) but that W made her remove her remarks because "it would never be done if it was promised."

[53] *MWL* readings of MW's remarks indicating that the "MS" had been finished well before MW's letter of 27–29 Oct seem substantially correct, despite other remarks of MW's implying that the MS is to go off about the "12 or 14th of next Month" and her concluding comment that they "have got to the 19th page, about the middle of the Idiot Boy." W's nocturnal nervousness (*MWL* 25) apparently followed the preparation of a MS for *P* 1815 that formed the basis of the printer's copy, readied between perhaps c mid-Oct and c mid-Nov.

[54] W's letter is apparently dated only "Sat: Morn." News of the discovery of the copy of *DS* was seemingly not immediate but recent on Saturday 22 Oct. MW's letter of that date to DW suggests that she or W must have last written not long before 14 Oct and that a copy of *DS* had not been found at that time. See esp. *MWL* 16, 18.

114. Oct 16

Johnny, Derwent dine at Rydal Hall as a reward for protecting a kitten. (*MWL* 16.)

115. Oct 21

Lady le Fleming and Miss Penny call at RM as MW is conducting business with George Mackereth (the Misses Penny are to depart next day). (*MWL* 20–21.)

Tonight a letter (not known to survive) arrives from DW, written from Stow. (*MWL* 22.)

116. c but including Oct 22; Oct 22

Mary Bell visits at RM for a few days c but including 22 Oct. She perhaps now promises to return three weeks after Martinmas. Basil Montagu possibly arrives at RM this day for a brief visit. (*MWL* 17, 19–20, 24, 26.)[55]

On 22 Oct MW, Dora write to DW: (MW:) Recent visitors and activities at RM; the Montagus; Gillies and news from Scotland; Elizabeth Wilson's book [see 1814:83; 1814:100]; message from Willy. (Dora:) Family events; Algernon Montagu. (MW:) Mrs. Green's refusal to purchase *Exc*; Mary Barker; Thomas M; Sally Green; RS's [*Roderick*]. (*MWL* 15–21.)

On 22 Oct MW writes to Thomas M: Her regrets that he (now at Penrith) is not to visit RM. (*MWL* 21–22.)

Perhaps about this time MW writes also to MMH. (Letter, MMH to Thomas M, 27 Oct [1814], JFW Papers.)[56]

[55] MW expected Montagu on the 22nd, and trusted that RM was "clear of him" on the 29th; that he did in fact visit remains uncertain. A plan to call on Crump on 23 Oct was not carried out (*MWL* 19, 27).

[56] MMH writes from Hindwell: "We had a letter from M Wordsworth yesterday lamenting much that they did not see you at Rydal. . . . D. W. is delighted with this country it is a thousand times more beautiful than she expected & as she has become a *compleat* horsewoman since she came I hope she will see every thing that is worth seeing before she leaves us."

117. Perhaps between Oct 23 and Oct 29

W perhaps attends a sale of furniture at the Moggs'. (*MWL* 16.)

118. Probably Oct 23, 24

Robert Blakeney calls unexpectedly at teatime on 23 Oct; remains till bedtime; passes the night at the inn; returns for dinner next day. (*MWL* 23.)[57]

119. Oct 26

W, MW call on DeQ, who is ill. While they are absent Miss Alms and Priscilla Lloyd call at RM. Willy makes himself ill by gorging elderberries. Perhaps this evening W and Dora walk to Brathay, hear from Mrs. Lloyd that Dr. Parr has described *Exc* as "all but Milton." A note arrives postponing a visit to the Bests. (*MWL* 24–25. See 1814: 120n.)

120. Probably Oct 27 (–Oct 29)

Anthony Harrison and Mrs. Harrison call in the morning. W, with the children, makes a bonfire of dead leaves.

MW probably today begins a letter to DW (she completes it on 29 Oct): A boil on W's hand. *Laodamia*, concerning which W is still reading and hunting more although the poem is finished; Blakeney [see 1814:118]; Montagu; Hazlitt's review of *Exc*; Dora's studies, which have seemingly not flourished under Miss Fletcher; DeQ; STC. (*MWL* 23–25. See 1814:122.)[58]

121. Oct 28

Tonight a letter arrives from DW. (*MWL* 25.)

[57] MW leaves unclear whether the night that Blakeney sat late was that of the first of the two days that he visited. The context generally suggests that he passed only a single night in the neighborhood.

[58] MW's letter, headed "Thursday Octr 2[?]," was possibly continued on 28 Oct, but the first clear change in appearance of autograph occurs with the new date "Saturday" (*MWL* 25).

122. Oct 29

MW finishes her letter to DW begun 27 Oct: DW's proposed journey to France; W's plans to go to Lowther; Tyrwhitt [see 1814: 98] and his matrimonial intentions respecting Miss Parker. W very much wishes SH to come home with DW, evidently to help with preparation of *P* 1815. The MS has now reached a point about the middle of *The Idiot Boy*. (*MWL* 25–27. See 1814:112; 1814:120.)[59]

Johnny and perhaps Dora and Willy go to Ambleside Fair. (*MWL* 27.)

123. Perhaps between c Nov and late Jan 1815

W organizes *WD* in final form. (Appendix VIII.)

124. Perhaps c Nov, probably by Dec 10

W revises Miss Barker's *Lines Addressed to a Noble Lord*, adding numerous lines. A copy of this version is made and sent to DW by 10 Dec. This version is most closely represented, among surviving versions, by MS W. W probably revises the entire poem. W's contribution by 10 Dec probably includes at least composition of lines 124–61, 182–89, correction and composition for 162–75, possibly heavy correction or composition of 90–123 [see 1814:103; 1814:111; 1815:21]. (Kirkpatrick; information from Professor Kirkpatrick; *MY* II, 174–76, 204–05.)

125. Perhaps Nov 2–perhaps Nov 7; Nov 4

Perhaps on 2 Nov W travels to Lowther.

He writes to DW from Lowther Castle on 4 Nov (letter not

[59] Miss Parker's attractions had preoccupied Henry Addison during the previous year (*SHL* 56). John M writes to Thomas M from Stow on 2 Nov:

> I have had a good deal of conversation with D Wordsworth about the Excursion & her Brother and am glad to learn that he is rising fast in reputation to the eminence where I doubt not his genius will some day place him. he is surely the first of modern Poets and this I hope will make his enemies regard him at last with more respect. I should like much to see it review'd. Coleridge has promised to do it in the Quarterly but as there is so little dependence to be placed upon him, Chas Lam[b] will have a review ready in Case, as he expects, the former breaks his word.

See 1815:3.

known to survive): He has just missed meeting the Duke of Devon-shire, who has been greatly pleased by *Exc.*

W perhaps returns to RM on 7 Nov. Probably during this trip W sees RW and Mrs. RW at Sockbridge. This visit perhaps occurs as W is on his way home. W perhaps borrows a greatcoat from RW for his journey as far as Patterdale, whence he sends the coat back. (*MWL* 26; *MY* II, 164, 171, 178.)[60]

126. Nov 11

DW writes to CCl from Stow: W's poems are now in press; he intends publishing *WD* in the spring. W's letter to her of 4 Nov; Hazlitt's review of *Exc.* Plans for returning to RM, for visiting France. Transcription of *Yarrow Visited.* (*MY* II, 164–67.)

127. Nov 12 ff

W writes to R. P. Gillies: Thanks for his appreciation of *Yarrow Visited* [see 1814:99]; wishes Hogg to use revised version as copied in Miss Wilson's MSS [for his miscellany]; advice concerning Gillies' melancholia. (*MY* II, 167–68. See 1814:100.)

W perhaps soon withdraws *Yarrow Visited* from Hogg's projected miscellany. (Hogg Autobiography 453.)

128. Probably c but not before 12 Nov

W receives a letter from John Hamilton Reynolds thanking him for the pleasure that W's poems have given him. (Letter, Reynolds to W, 9 Nov 1814, DCP.)

129. Nov 13

W writes *Lines Written November 13, 1814, on a Blank Leaf in a Copy of the Author's Poem, "The Excursion," upon Hearing of the Death of the Late Vicar of Kendal.* (Title, *P* 1815–*PW* 1849.)[61]

---

[60] *MY* II, 172 seems to suggest that the Ss visited at RM c early Nov; but such a visit is doubtful (see 1814:103).

[61] The Rev. Matthew Murfitt, Vicar of Kendal, died on 7 Nov (Venn; *PW* IV, 457).

130. Perhaps c mid-Nov

The MS for *P* 1815 is sent off to the printer's. (*MWL* 25, 27, 29. See 1814:112.)[62]

131. Possibly c mid-Nov, certainly by 26 Nov

W sees Mrs. Lloyd, who tells him that CW has received *Exc.* (*MY* II, 171.)

132. Nov 23

W writes to R. P. Gillies: Thanks him for parcel [of books], including Gillies' *Egbert, Ruminator,* and Hogg's *Queen's Wake.* Comments on these and other works. Hogg's, Gillies' style. Comments on revised *Yarrow Visited.* (*MY* II, 169–70.)

133. Nov 25

A letter arrives from Sir GB informing W that the Bishop of London is enchanted with *Exc.* (*MY* II, 171.)

134. Nov 26

W writes to CW: Curiosity as to why CW has not written him about *Exc.* Printers have just begun vol. II of *P* 1815; W's hopes that his poems will be published about the beginning of Jan. W owes CW for set of CW's *Ecclesiastical Biography* presented to [William] Johnson. DW; the Lloyds; Willy, who has a cold; Dora. Bishop Watson is declining more in mind than in body; inquiry regarding CW's chances of succeeding him [as Professor of Divinity at Cambridge]. (*MY* II, 170–72.)

135. Perhaps between Nov 26 and Dec 3; probably by late Dec

A sheet or sheets of *P* 1815 arrives at RM. The last sheet that arrives by 3 Dec is probably sheet F of vol. II. Probably by c late Dec

---

[62] MW wrote on [28] Oct that the completed MS was to be taken to the post "about the 12 or 14th of next Month" along with "*circulars.*" "*Circulars*" was probably MW's facetious description of letters of advice to interested friends about *P* 1815.

a large portion of the printed sheets have arrived. (*MY* II, 177; *MWL* 28.)[63]

136. Probably c early Dec–perhaps 1815 Jan 2; c early Dec; probably c Dec 1–5

HC visits Mr. Dawes in Ambleside probably c early Dec–perhaps 2 Jan. He probably visits RM occasionally during this period. (*Minnow* 31.)

Probably c 1–5 Dec Willy has a severe cold; c early Dec Dora also has a cold. (*MY* II, 172–75.)

137. Probably c but not before Dec 2

W receives a letter from Sir GB advising that [S.W.] Reynolds and Longman want to know the pages to which the pictures for *Lucy Gray* and *Elegiac Stanzas . . . Peele Castle* are to be referred. (Letter, Sir GB to W, 30 Nov 1814, DCP.)[64]

138. Probably Dec 4

W writes to DW: Willy's cold. W wishes that DW would return home to assist MW. (*MY* II, 172–73.)

W takes this letter to the post office. Mr. Scambler visits RM; pronounces Willy's cold a dangerous case of inflammatory croup. (*MY* II, 173.)[65]

DW writes to the Ws at RM from Hindwell. (*MY* II, 175.)

[63] Sheet F, concluding with the last lines of *TA*, extends only through page 80 (see *MY* II, 177n). Whether W was mistaken in his statement probably of 10 Dec that "the last [sheet] was the 82nd page of the 2nd Vol. Tintern Abbey," or a change in pagination occurred later, remains uncertain. W's comment that no sheets arrived "this week" seemingly implies that a sheet or sheets had arrived during the previous week, which began 27 Nov. His remarks on 26 Nov about the commencement of the printing of *P* 1815 may indicate very recent arrival of the sheets in question.

[64] Lady B writes to W on 17 Jan 1815: "[W]e expect an engraving from the Snow cottage every post, Sir George could not approve of the scraping and has had it redone by Bromley Mr Alexander took the picture of the White Doe (I think a successful effort) to be engraved by him larger than the Peel Castle, which since Reynholds has retouched is much improved. The Peter Bell Sir George is pretty well satisfied with."

[65] MW afterward doubted that the disease was inflammatory (see *MY* II, 175).

139. Probably Dec 5

Mr. Scambler calls, probably passes the night at RM. Mrs. Lloyd calls, pronounces Willy mending. (*MY* II, 173–74.)

140. Probably Dec 6; Dec 6

Probably on 6 Dec W writes to SH: Willy is much better. (*MY* II, 173–74.)

On 6 Dec a review of *Exc* [by Francis Jeffrey] appears in *ER* (XXIV, Nov 1814). (*Times*. See Ward; Hayden.)

141. Probably Dec 9 (–Dec 10)

Miss Alms and Priscilla Lloyd (daughter of Charles) visit, pass the night at RM. (*MY* II, 177.)

DW's letter of 4 Dec arrives at RM. (*MY* II, 175.)

142. Probably Dec 10; probably Dec 10 or Dec 11

Probably on 10 Dec Miss Alms and Priscilla Lloyd depart RM.

Probably on that day W writes to SH: Willy; land purchased by Thomas H; W's contributions to Mary Barker's *Lines … to a Noble Lord* [see 1814:124]; Mrs. Mogg. Printers have sent no sheets for *PW* 1815 this week. (*MY* II, 174–77.)

Probably on 10 or 11 Dec Mary Bell (servant) arrives at RM. (*MY* II, 177. See 1814:116.)

143. Probably between Dec 10 and Dec 15

DW arrives back at RM from Wales. (*MY* II, 177. See 1814:99; 1814:138.)[66]

144. Dec 15

W writes to RW: Asks Addison to pay £325 into the Stamp

---

[66] DW's arrival would certainly have been mentioned in W's letter to SH of 10 Dec had it occurred before W finished writing.

John M wrote to Thomas M on 17 Dec from Stow that SH had been staying with him for the last week (JFW Papers). Possibly she came to visit him about the time of DW's departure from Hindwell.

Office on or before 31 Dec [see 1814:148]. DW has been brought home by Willy's illness. Requests RW to see to settlement of their accounts [see 1814:109]. (*MY* II, 177–78.)

145. Dec 19

RW's accounts charge DW £20, payment of a bill in favor of Thomas M, under this date. (RW accounts, DCP.)

146. Probably late Dec, including Dec 31; and about this time

Miss Weir and Miss Jameson visit at RM. The exact time of their arrival and departure is uncertain; but they are certainly present on 31 Dec. About this time, W, DW walk daily, sometimes with MW, sometimes with Dora. (*MY* II, 183, 186.)

147. Dec 22

W writes to R. P. Gillies: Concern for Gillies' well-being; invitation to visit. Discussion of principles of composition laid down by Gillies, whose *Exile* W has lately been reading. The *Ruminator*; Hogg's *Badlewe*, and Hogg; *Exc* and Jeffrey's review [see 1814:140]; Scott. (*MY* II, 178–80.)

148. Probably c but by Dec 27; Dec 27

Probably c but by 27 Dec W receives, completes, and forwards to the Kendal bankers RW's draft for £325 [see 1814:144].

On 27 Dec DW writes to RW: RW's draft. The bankers will remit bills due at end of month to the Stamp Office. Willy back in good health. DW's visit to Hindwell. (*MY* II, 180–81.)[67]

Probably c but by 27 Dec DW writes to Joanna H (letter not known to survive), advising of MW's improved health and spirits. (Letter, Joanna H to Thomas H, 30 Dec [1814], JFW Papers.)[68]

---

[67] RW's accounts record payment of the draft, due at two months, under the date of 20 Feb.

[68] Joanna wrote on a "Friday" that was also "30 Dec" that she had "had a letter from dear Dorothy, & she tells me Marys health & spirits are wonderfully improved."

149. Dec 30, 31

Late on 30 Dec W receives a letter from CL, perhaps that quoted *LL* II, 145–47. (See letter of J. M. Turnbull, *TLS* 1929, 846.)[69]

W, DW write to CCl: (W, 30 Dec:) *Exc* and W's hopes and wishes for it; urges TCl or CCl to assist its fortunes as best they can; Jeffrey's review of *Exc*; the favorable opinion of various influential persons.[70] (DW, 31 Dec:) Urges TCl, CCl to help sales of *Exc*, esp. among the Quakers; sales and loans of *Exc*; problems and doubts regarding DW's proposed trip to France; activities at RM. (*MY* II, 181–86.)[71]

1 8 1 5

[On writings of W possibly of this year see below and GCL 35, 77, 146, 173, 218, 219, 221–23.]

1. Probably c Jan, certainly by c early Feb

W writes the 1815 *Preface*; probably writes in its final form the *Essay, Supplementary to the Preface*. (*MY* II, 180, 195–96, 199–200, 204; Appendix IV. See 1815:16; 1800:74n; *HCRBW* I, 161; Moorman II, 276n.)

2. Perhaps Jan

W writes to Daniel Stuart: Recommends DeQ, who will call; asks Stuart to find space in the *Courier* for a short series of letters by

---

[69] Turnbull suggests that CL had forwarded to W a copy of the *Champion* of 4 Dec 1814 containing CL's *On the Melancholy of Tailors*; that W had replied with a story of a tailor who had fallen from a precipice; and that Hogg's knowledge of W's story helped to suggest one of his parodies of W, *The Flying Taylor*, in *The Poetical Mirror*.

[70] W's phrasing does not confirm a direct acquaintance at this time with Jeffrey's review (cf Moorman II, 261). DW states on 25 Feb 1815 (*MY* II, 206), "We have seen none of the Reviews."

[71] The date is written by DW, and only once, at the end of her portion of the letter (BM Add. MS 36,997, fols. 132–33): "New Years Eve—Decr."

DeQ intended to discredit *ER*, esp. as it relates to W. Thanks Stuart for notice of *Exc* in the *Courier*. (*MY* II, 198–99.)[1]

3. Jan 8

A review of *Exc* by CL, extensively altered by Francis Gifford, appears in the *Quarterly Review* (XII, Oct 1814). (*LL* II, 148–50 and MS, UTL; *Courier*; *MC*.)[2]

4. Jan 8

MW writes to Thomas M: Congratulates him on purchase of Sebergham Hall; she regrets Thomas H's late purchase [see *MY* II, 175]. Asks help in arranging for conveyance of items including remaining sheets of *P* 1815, of which they have a large portion, with Algernon Montagu. (*MWL* 27–29.)

5. Probably c but not before Jan 10

W receives the letter from CL quoted *LL* II, 148–50. He writes to RS: Encloses CL's letter; asks RS's aid in recovering the MS of CL's review of *Exc*. Walter Scott; thanks RS for copy of *Roderick* [see also 1814:106]. (*MY* II, 186–87. See 1815:3.)[3]

6. Probably early 1815 after Jan 10, possibly Jan 14–Jan 16 or Jan 21–Jan 23

W writes to CCl: (Possibly 14–15 or 21–22 Jan:) Answers to criticism of *Exc* by Patty Smith; the reviews of *Exc* in the *Quarterly* and the *ER*. (MW adds a brief conclusion, possibly on 16 or 23 Jan:) W and she are going to Bowness. (*MY* II, 187–92.)[4]

---

[1] The letter seems to have been written before DeQ departed for London—that is, by 5 Feb (*MY* II, 194). Notices of *Exc* had appeared in the *Courier* on 18 Aug (see 1814:75n), 21 Oct (with quotation of IV.575–98), and 17 Dec (with quotation of II.546–92).

[2] The postmark of the explanatory letter from CL to W, obviously written soon after CL had seen the printed version of his review, is 7 Jan. The *Courier* advertises publication on 6 Jan.

[3] RS wrote to Grosvenor Bedford on 14 Jan to seek his help in pursuing CL's MS (Warter II, 393–94).

[4] The letter appears written not long after W's receipt of the news of Gifford's

7. Probably c late Jan

Some haddock and a letter arrive from John H. (*MY* II, 203.)

8. Jan 30

A review of *Exc* appears in *The Monthly Magazine* (Supplement to XXXVIII, 30 Jan 1815). (See Ward; Hayden.)

9. Possibly Feb

W receives and answers a letter from Mary Hawkins. (*MY* II, 208.)

10. Perhaps c early Feb

DW writes to SH. (*MY* II, 199–200.)
Mrs. Lloyd and Miss Alms call at RM. Mrs. Lloyd brings the story that [Tommy] Cl is dead. (*MY* II, 201.)

11. Perhaps c early Feb, by Feb 19, probably before Feb 13, certainly by Feb 5

Perhaps c early Feb, by 19 Feb, one sheet of W's 1815 *Preface* arrives from the printers. (*MY* II, 200.)[5]
Perhaps c early Feb, probably before 13 Feb, Derwent C visits at RM. (*MY* II, 201.)
Perhaps c early Feb, certainly by 5 Feb, W composes lines 115–20 of *Laodamia*. (*MY* II, 194–95.)

12. Possibly c early Feb, by Feb 4, ff

Possibly c early Feb, by 4 Feb, Mr. Knox calls at RM bringing a

---

[5] HCR saw a proof sheet from *P* 1815 on 6 Feb, but his notes do not identify it more closely (*HCRBW* III, 850).

mistreatment of CL's review of *Exc* (see 1815:5). It seems to have been commenced on a Saturday, and was certainly finished on a Sunday and Monday.

MW states that she and W are going to Bowness to "take the Quarterly bath"; but I am unfamiliar with other documentation of this custom. The word "bath" is badly written in MS. "Back" is a possible reading suggesting that "Quarterly" (so capitalized) might refer to the *Quarterly Review*, but W states previously in the same letter that he has not seen the *Quarterly* containing CL's review of *Exc* (see 1815:3).

letter from Dr. Anderson. W is absent. W probably shortly afterward discusses with RS the contents of the letter, which relate to their plans for an expansion of Anderson's *British Poets*. (*MY* II, 193. See 1814:101; 1815:15.)

13. Probably c Feb 1

A review of *Exc* [by James Montgomery] appears in the *Eclectic Review* (2nd Series III, Jan 1815). (See Ward; Hayden.)

14. Feb 1

W so dates, and probably on this day writes, the letter of dedication to Sir GB of *P* 1815. (*P* 1815; *MY* II, 192.)

15. Perhaps Feb 4

W writes to Dr. Anderson: RS and W doubt that their plans concerning Anderson's *British Poets* are feasible at this time. W is glad that Anderson and his daughter like *Exc*. (*MY* II, 193. See 1814:101; 1815:12.)[6]

16. Probably c but by Feb 5, and about this time

Probably c but by 5 Feb W writes to DeQ: Transcript of passage from Reply to Mathetes; transcript of stanza to be added to *Laodamia* [see 1815:11]. Comment on a request from DeQ that W's rough copies of the *Preface* be kept. (*MY* II, 194–95.)

(DeQ is thus probably now supervising the printing of *P* 1815. The extent of his labor is unknown.)

17. c Feb 12–Feb 18; Feb 12

W composes little or nothing c 12 Feb–18 Feb. He perhaps now considers plans for *The Recluse*. (*MY* II, 200.)

On 12 Feb W writes to Leigh Hunt (in third person): Presents a copy of *P* 1815 to Hunt. (*MY* II, 195.)

---

[6] W's date is "Janry 4th 1815" which *MY* II, 193 conjectures, in view of the 25 Feb postmark, to be a slip for 4 Feb. The gap between date and postmark is hardly less curious, however, in the second case than in the first. The letter was probably temporarily mislaid, either before sending it or in transit.

18. Feb 13

Derwent C departs RM. (*MY* II, 201.)

19. Probably c but by Feb 16

W writes to R. P. Gillies: Thanks for letter and copy of Gillies' *Albert*. Recent composition; *Albert*; Hogg and Scott; Wilson; Jeffrey. (*MY* II, 195–98.)[7]

20. Feb 16

W, MW walk to Brathay. MW sees Mrs. Harden; sees Derwent C at the Lloyds'. (*MY* II, 200.)

21. Feb 18, 19; c Feb 19

On 18 Feb W, MW, Willy call on Mrs. Knott. W takes *Exc*, attempts to read to her [c *Exc* VII.923–75, the story of Sir Alfred Irthing, ancestor of the Knott family]. She is unable to hear him, but understands the story when it is read by her niece. She returns the book next day, 19 Feb, writing that she has ordered a copy. (*MY* II, 202–03.)

On 19 Feb a letter arrives from Mary Barker. W works for three hours over the opening (lines 1–11) of *Lines Addressed to a Noble Lord*. He has by now probably composed lines 88–89. Probably c this time he also revises other portions of the poem.

W, DW go for a walk around the lake; view Grasmere from Loughrigg. W reads in *FQ*. DW writes to Mrs. Rawson, Miss Pollard, Mary Barker.

DW writes to SH (W adds a postscript): (DW:) Plans for trip to France; DW would prefer the project abandoned. W occasionally talks as if he wished to visit London. W's composition, recent period of rest. *Preface, Essay*. Their occasional callers the Bests; Mrs. Harden; the Lloyds; Tommy Cl. HC going to Oxford; SFC; the Crumps. Presentation copies of *Exc*, and sales; DeQ. The visit to Mrs. Knott [see 1815: 21]; review [of *Exc*] in the *Eclectic Review* by James Montgomery [see

---

[7] The date of "Feb 14. 1815" (*The Letters of William and Dorothy Wordsworth. The Middle Years*, ed. EdS, Oxford, 1937, II, 631; repeated *MY* II, 195) does not appear to be part of the original letter.

1814:13]; MW reading A. M. Porter's *Recluse of Norway*; DW's opinions of *Waverley*. John H; Joanna H; the pony. Mary Barker, and W's work on [*Lines Addressed to a Noble Lord*]. (W:) Readers' opinions of *Exc, Yarrow Visited*. (*MY* II, 199–205; Kirkpatrick.)[8]

22. Perhaps between Feb 19 and early Mar

The concluding sheets for *P* 1815 [see 1815:11] arrive at RM and are returned to the printer after correction. (*MY* II, 200; *MWL* 29.)

23. Probably Feb 23; between Feb 23 and Feb 25

On 23 Feb Miss Alms dines at RM. She informs the Ws that CW's *Sermons* have arrived at Brathay. W walks there with her, borrows the second volume. By 25 Feb W and MW read several of the sermons and are delighted by them. DW reads a part of the sermon on national education. (*MY* II, 206. See 1815:25.)

24. Probably Feb 24; between Feb 24 and Mar 16

Two sheets of proof of *WD* [arrive]. (DC MS 80; *MY* II, 207.) A letter from Priscilla W arrives in the same post. (*MY* II, 205.)

Between 24 Feb and 16 Mar a third sheet of *WD* arrives. (*MY* II, 222.)[9]

25. Probably Feb 25

DW writes to Priscilla W (W adds a postscript): (DW:) William Jackson; CW's *Sermons*. W has directed that *P* 1815 be sent to the CWs. Reviews of *Exc*. The William Cooksons; Johnny; Dora; Willy. A letter from Mary Hawkins; Thomas Jameson. (W:) Compliments on CW's *Sermons*. (*MY* II, 205–08.)[10]

[8] DW's letter is dated at its commencement "Sunday night. 18th February." The Sunday probably being referred to was 19 Feb.

[9] A note in DC MS 80 reads

Postage of Proofs for White Doe

Feb 24   2 Proofs   [?11½] 1-1

[10] The letter is dated "[27 Feb. 1815]" *MY* II, 205, but does not appear to have been dated by DW or W. An endorsement of "Feby 27 1815" appears to have been written much later. The postmark is C /28 FE 28/ 1815. This, together with the external information available concerning the time of arrival of the *WD* sheets mentioned *MY* II, 207, fixes the date as 25 Feb.

26. Possibly c 1815 but not before c Mar 1815

W composes basic version of *Artegal and Elidure*; does some work on *Dion*. (DC MS 80; *Laodamia* IF note; GCL 222n.)

27. Perhaps c early Mar–Mar 10

Miss Alms visits RM, departing 10 Mar. (*MY* II, 218.)

28. Probably c Mar 1

T. N. Talfourd's "An Attempt to Estimate the Poetical Talent of the Present Age," containing extensive and appreciative comment on Wordsworth, appears in *The Pamphleteer* (V, Feb 1815), 413–71.
A review of *Exc* [by J. H. Merivale] appears in *The Monthly Review* (LXXVI, Feb 1815). (See Ward; Hayden.)

29. Probably Mar 9

DW writes to Annette advising of plans for a journey to France (letter not known to survive). (*MY* II, 217, 227.)

30. Possibly c Mar 10

W probably visits GH; he learns that HC is to go to Oxford about Easter (26 Mar). SFC asks him to ask Thomas Poole for the £10 he has promised for HC. (*MY* II, 209.)

31. Mar 13

W writes to Thomas Poole: HC to go to Oxford about Easter [see 1815:30]; conveys SFC's request for promised money. Has urged HC to pursue a steady course of study. Possibilities of maintenance for Derwent, SC, STC. The Madras system of education. *Exc*. His wish to present a copy of *P* 1815 to Poole. (*MY* II, 209–11.)
Mr. Scambler calls, bringing news of Napoleon's escape from Elba. W goes to Ambleside to see the papers. (*MY* II, 217.)

32. Probably c mid-Mar

W writes to Miss M. Malcolm and Col. Pasley: (to Miss Malcolm:)

W would be happy to welcome Col. Pasley at RM. Directions and advice for the trip. (to Col. Pasley:) Urges a visit. (*MY* II, 215–17.)[11]

33. Mar 16

DW, W write to SH: (DW:) Distress at the news of Napoleon's progress; Miss Barker's determination to go to France with the Ws. Possible living arrangements if the trip is undertaken. The Corn Laws. (W:) The Corn Laws. Napoleon might redeem himself by unifying and freeing Italy. (DW:) Napoleon; the trip to France; health of the family; Miss Fletcher's school; Robert Jameson, and his failure to repay DW £3 as promised at Christmas; DeQ; Hannah More; John Edwards, whose letter arrived last night, and James Montgomery on *Exc*; *WD*. (*MY* II, 217–22.)

DW writes to CCl: The prospect of postponement of the French trip because of Napoleon's adventures. DeQ, just returned; Tommy Cl; ML; Hannah More; reception of *Exc*; John Edwards and James Montgomery on *Exc*; the health of the family; the Lloyds. (*MY* II, 211–14.)

W walks out with MW, Dora, Willy. (*MY* II, 221.)

34. Probably Mar 16 or shortly after

W writes to John Edwards (only a fragment of the letter is known to survive): Sends an order with which he may be able to obtain a copy of *P* 1815 without expense; thanks for conveying Montgomery's praise of *Exc*. (Reed *N&Q*.)

35. Perhaps shortly after Mar 16; certainly between Mar 16 and Apr 8; c early Apr

The fourth sheet of *WD* arrives at RM perhaps shortly after 16 Mar, certainly between 16 Mar and 8 Apr. During that period, perhaps c early Apr, the pace of printing of *WD* picks up rapidly. (*MY* II, 226. See 1815:24.)

---

[11] W's brief note to Pasley, although begun with a separate salutation, is appended to the letter to Miss Malcolm (cf *MY*).

36. Probably Mar 17–probably Mar 23 ff

Probably on 17 Mar W writes to RS: Please send by the bearer, Mary Bell, who returns to RM on Thursday (probably 23 Mar), Humboldt's books on South America and Montgomery's *World before the Flood*. Napoleon. (*MY* II, 216.)[12]
The books are probably conveyed as requested.

37. Probably c late Mar

A long letter from Annette and Caroline arrives at RM. Caroline describes accommodations awaiting DW and the visitors; Annette describes political events. Another letter written the day after also arrives. (*MY* II, 227.)

38. Mar 27 (–Mar 29)

W attends the funeral of Mr. Robinson, Overseer of Quarries. During his absence Col. Charles Pasley arrives at RM for a visit. (He remains till 29 Mar.) W returns three hours after his arrival. (*MY* II, 226.)

39. Mar 28

MW writes to Thomas M: Thomas M's health; *P* 1815; the sheets [see 1815:4] have been sent by coach long since. Presentation copies for John M and Joanna H; asks Thomas M to call at Longman's for his presentation copy. Napoleon, and his disruption of the Ws' plans. An order of tea to come from Twinings; perhaps the carpeting that Thomas M has for them may be sent with it. (*MWL* 29–30.)

40. Mar 29

Col. Pasley departs RM in the afternoon or evening. (*MY* II, 226; *MWL* 29–30.)

[12] The rough similarity of the comment on Napoleon in this letter with his remarks in the letters of 16 Mar together with W's date of "Friday evening" appear to justify a conjectural date of Friday 17 Mar.

41. Mar 30

The Longman accounts for *P* 1815 commence under this date. (See Owen CSP 98.)[13]

42. Perhaps c Apr–May

DW is ill. (*MY* II, 240–41.)

43. Between early Apr and May 2

The printing and correction of the verse portion of *WD* is completed. (1815:35; *MY* II, 236. See 1815:65.)

44. Perhaps c early Apr

Printing of Mary Barker's *Lines Addressed to a Noble Lord* is com-

---

[13] On publication date see 1815:57.

Longman's Divide Ledger 2 and Impression Book 5 supply a record, here presented in conflated form, of specially sold or delivered copies (the only charges are small sums, usually £–/1/2 per copy, probably ordinarily for delivery):

Ap 3	2 Copies bds Mo Rev & B Crit	
5	25 ,, ,, Author	
15	1 ,, ,, Sir E Brydges	
19	1 ,, ,, Mr Alexander	
May 2	Entering at S. hall 2/	
June 12	1 copy bds Stationers hall	
15	1 Mr Lappenburgh	
Aug 22	10 S[old] Stationers Hall	

The Impression Book also contains this item, cancelled:

June 7	1 Copy to Augustan Review returned Aug 7. [Cf 1814:62n.]

The private account (DCP) charges

1815 April 6	2 Poems 2 Vols 80 Russia Mr Munkhouse		3.18.0
18	6 do—bds Sir G. Beaumont	6.–.–	
July 18	1 Poems 2 Vols 80 bds Miss Burnfoot		1.–[.]–

"Miss Burnfoot," otherwise unknown, is possibly a defective record of a copy to Miss Malcolm at Burnfoot (see 1814:47). HCR received a copy from W before 16 Apr (*HCRBW* III, 850).

pleted, and copies are distributed. (Letter, John M to Thomas M, 4 Apr 1815, JFW Papers.)[14]

45. Apr 1

DW writes to Messrs. Twining, forwarding an order on W for £26/10/-.

DW writes to Richard Addison: DW's order on Twining. She supposes RW still in the country. (*MY* II, 223; RW accounts, DCP.)[15]

46. Apr 3–perhaps Apr 8

W, MW set off at 2 on 3 Apr toward Kendal; probably walk to Stavely, which they reach at 6. After tea they walk on to Kendal, which they reach at 8. They perhaps reach home on 8 Apr.

At Kendal they probably stay with the Cooksons. W's business is the appointment of a new subdistributor to replace Mr. Pennington; W perhaps now appoints Mr. Dawson. (*MY* II, 223–24.)

47. Possibly c Apr 5, and shortly after

A number of readers probably receive copies of *P* 1815. (1815:41n; 1815:57.)

48. Apr 5

Dora, Mary Bell attend the funeral of Dinah Black. (*MY* II, 226.)

49. Probably Apr 6

W, probably MW dine with Dr. Harrison. Afterward, probably in part as the result of wine, company, and verses, W is awake till 6 AM. (*MY* II, 224.)

---

[14] John M wrote from Stow on 4 Apr that SH expected that a parcel would be sent to him for her from Longman containing copies of *Lines*. Thomas H is allowed to take a copy of the work, which is "not to be published but is printed to distribute among [Miss Barker's] friends."

[15] RW's accounts record payment of £46/14/6 under 10 Apr. A memorandum by MW notes that the sum included this bill and another of £20/4/6—perhaps the bill referred to by DW in her letter to RW of 1814 Feb 2 (see 1814:7).

50. Apr 7

Mrs. Harden calls at RM. (*MY* II, 224.)

51. Apr 8

DW writes to SH: W's trip with MW to Kendal [see 1814:46]. Johnny's stupidity; W's unbridled spoiling of Willy; Miss Barker is to have her money. Young Basil Montagu; printing of *P* 1815 completed, but book not published; printing of *WD* advancing rapidly. Col. Pasley's visit [see 1814:38]. Napoleon; letter from Annette and Caroline; DW intends to visit Miss Barker for not longer than a week, probably commencing the latter end of week after next. The garden. *Roderick*. (*MY* II, 223–28.)

Dora and Willy go to Brathay Hall for Jane Harden's birthday celebration. Johnny dines with the Lloyds. (*MY* II, 224–25.)

52. Apr 11

DW writes to CCl: Bonaparte; her projected trip to France. *WD* printing; W will order copy sent to CCl; *P* 1815 published. Urges CCl to review [*Exc*] for *The Philanthropist*. Tommy Cl and the affairs of the Cls. (*MY* II, 229–31.)[16]

53. Perhaps c and probably on Apr 20

Perhaps c and probably concluding on 20 Apr W writes "In Trellis'd Shed with Clustering Roses Gay," Dedicatory Verses for *WD*. W probably completes the poem on 20 Apr. (Date with published poem.)

54. Perhaps c late Apr and early May, including May 2

Henry H visits at RM. (*MY* II, 234.)

55. Possibly late Apr, commencing c Apr 21 or 22; perhaps late Apr, shortly before Apr 25

Possibly late Apr, commencing c 21 or 22 Apr, DW possibly visits Miss Barker for not more than a week. (*MY* II, 228.)

[16] On the *Philanthropist*'s review of *Exc* see *MY* II, 230n.

Perhaps late Apr, shortly before 25 Apr, W decides to visit London with MW. (*MY* II, 231.)[17]

56. Apr 25

W writes to R. P. Gillies: Plans for visiting London. Has ordered *P 1815* sent to Gillies and Scott. Comment on *Guy Mannering* and *Waverley*. W has heard that [Henry] Mackenzie is to spend part of the summer at the Lakes; offers him assistance. (*MY* II, 231–33.)

57. Perhaps Apr 27

Poems by William Wordsworth is published in London. (*MC*.)[18]

58. Apr 30

DW writes to SH. (*MY* II, 234.)

59. Probably c but not before May 1

A letter arrives from LdL offering to W the Collectorship of Customs at Whitehaven. (*MY* II, 235. See 1815:55n.)

60. May 2–May 4 or May 5; May 6–probably July 1, c early Aug

On 2 May, W, MW, DW write to SH: (MW:) SH should set off for London immediately. They are to accompany HC to Oxford; hope to reach London before Sunday. (W:) Repeats MW's urgings.

[17] SH (*SHL* 81) later indicated that the main purpose of the London trip was W's wish to speak to LdL personally when declining LdL's offer of the office of the Collector of Customs at Whitehaven; but LdL's letter with this offer apparently did not reach W before 1 May (*MY* II, 235). The offer was surrounded by much rumor, however (see *SHL* 81–82), and it is possible that W had informal advice concerning it prior to 25 Apr. See also *Mem* II, 4.

[18] The *MC* advertisement of this day is the earliest notice found, but copies had been given out as early as 3 Apr (see 1815:41n). CL thanks W for "successive book presents" probably on 17 Apr (the postmark date, MS, UTL—recorded as 7 Apr *LL* II, 153). DW thought the book published by 11 Apr, and 27 copies were distributed to reviews and author by 5 Apr (see 1815:41n). A number of readers probably had access to copies, thus, by shortly after 5 Apr.

Henry H. (DW:) Hopes that Thomas H will accompany SH. Willy. (*MY* II, 233–34.)

On 2 May DW writes to CCl. (*MY* II, 234.)

On 2 May SFC, SC, HC possibly come to RM. Today also, probably late, W, MW set off by coach with HC for Oxford and London. (W, MW reach home probably c early Aug.) They perhaps reach Oxford on 4 or 5 May, and certainly leave HC there, under the protection of his tutor William Hart, on 6 May, on which day they arrive in London and take up lodgings at 24 Edward Street, Cavendish Square. (They depart London finally probably on 1 July.) Late on 6 May W writes to LdL from his lodgings: W will, unless otherwise instructed, call on LdL next day at 10 to speak to him on the subject of his letter of 28 Apr. (*MY* II, 233–35; Minnow 34; *Letters of Hartley Coleridge*, ed. G. E. and E. L. Griggs, Oxford, 1941, 11.)[19]

On W's London visit generally see esp. Moorman II, 278–85. On W's relations with Hazlitt at this time see esp. *HCRBW* I, 169.

61. Perhaps between May 6 and June 19; possibly between May 6 and June 4

Perhaps between 6 May and 19 June W is probably at some time in company with Amelia Opie. (M. E. MacGregor, *Amelia Alderson Opie: Wordling and Friend, Smith College Studies in English* XIV, no. 1, Northampton, 1932, 61.)

Possibly between 6 May and 4 June W meets William Taylor of Norwich, who likes W's conversation better than his poetry. (See *HCRBW* I, 169.)[20]

62. Perhaps shortly after May 6

SH joins the Ws in London. (*MY* II, 233–34.)

63. May 7

W perhaps today calls on LdL; declines the Collectorship of

---

[19] The cited letter of HC, although addressed to CL, is clearly for W.

[20] HCR's anecdote indicates that Taylor's acquaintance with W was slight at this time. They were both in London now, and no earlier meeting is known.

Customs at Whitehaven offered him by LdL. (1815:60; *MY* II, 235; *SHL* 81. See 1815:55n.)

W probably leaves a card at HCR's; calls, with MW, on CL. HCR calls at CL's; sits half an hour with the Ws; accompanies them to their lodgings. (*HCRBW* I, 165; HCRNB.)[21]

64. May 9

W writes to John Taylor C, probably from 24 Edward Street: Left HC at Oxford on Saturday; invites C to dine with Sir GB next day. (*MY* II, 235–36.)

W, MW drink tea at CL's with HCR. W discusses his poems, Hunt; gives HCR a copy of *Lines Addressed to a Noble Lord*. (*HCRBW* I, 166; HCRNB.)

RW's accounts charge payment of £20/–/– to W, in town, under this day. (RW accounts, DCP.)

65. May 10

W writes to Longman and Co. from 24 Edward Street: Having been called to town suddenly W has left proof correction of the prose portion of *WD* to Ballantyne. W has brought three misbound volumes (vol. I) of *P* 1815 for replacement [see 1815:41]. Inquiries about sales of *Exc*. (*MY* II, 236–37.)

W probably dines with Sir GB at 6. They are perhaps joined by John Taylor C, whom W now meets. (*MY* II, 235–36.)

66. Probably May 15

W writes to John Scott from 24 Edward Street: Thanks for copy of Scott's *Visit to Paris*; W's concurrence with Scott's unfavorable picture of the French. (*MY* II, 237. See also John D. Gordan, "William Wordsworth, 1770–1850. An Exhibition," *BNYPL* LIV, 1950, 347.)[22]

---

[21] HCRNB records: "Ab: called Lambs Walk with Wordsworth[.]"

[22] W's letter is dated "Monday May 14t[h] 1815." The Monday in question would have been that of 15 May.

67. May 15

The Longman accounts for *WD* commence under this date. (Longman accounts. See Owen CSP 98.)[23]

68. May 16

W perhaps sees *Romeo and Juliet* (Eliza O'Neill in the role of Juliet) at Covent Garden. (*LL* II, 163.)[24]

69. May 17

"In Trellis'd Shed with Clustering Roses Gay," Dedicatory Verses to *WD*, is published without authority in the *Courier*. (*Courier*; *MY* II, 238–39.)

[23] Distribution of copies between 30 May, when *WD* was entered at Stationers Hall, and 1820 is recorded as follows (no distribution of copies being recorded before 30 May):

[1815]	May 31	[?18]	Copies to Sundries ext bds
	June 1	3	do Reviews
	7	1	do Augustan Review— returned Aug 7 [*this item cancelled*; cf 1814:62n; 1815:67n]
	17	1	do Stat Hall
	Aug 22	10	do sewd do [*a marginal note by this entry appears to read* 2[?8]/. bds]

Here may be recollected the incident, probably of 1820, of W's informing Davy, at a large dinner gathering, of his publishing *WD* in quarto to show the world his opinion of it (*Moore Memoirs* III, 161).

[24] CL's note informs W that he [and ML] "have just returned from our expedition" and postpones a meeting until an evening after Thursday, when Hazlitt was to be present. W was with CL frequently in late May, from Monday 22 May. The "expedition" was to Mackery End, which CL and ML visited on Whitsun Eve (Sotheby Catalogue, Sale of 23 June 1969, lot 205); the church feast of Whitsuntide took place on Sunday 14 May and the legal Whitsuntide 15 May. This note would thus appear to have been written by Thursday 18 May. CL concludes: "I don't know whether you would not have form'd a correcter estimate of Miss O'Neill from Isabella than from Juliet. Shakespear bothers them all sadly." If CL and W were discussing specific performances, CL is most likely referring to Miss O'Neill's appearances at Covent Garden as Juliet on 16 May and as Isabella (in *The Fatal Marriage*) on 18 May (*Times*). His phrasing perhaps implies that W had seen and commented unfavorably on the O'Neill Juliet.

70. May 18

W possibly (the chance is small) sees *Isabella; or, the Fatal Marriage* (Eliza O'Neill in the role of Isabella) at Covent Garden. (1815:68n.)

71. Perhaps between May 19 and June 19

W possibly dines with Henry Herbert S. (Curry II, 122.)

72. May 21

W dines with Sir GB, John Taylor, LdL, Joseph Farington, and perhaps others. W discusses reviews; comments on Scott's poetry, on Goldsmith's. (Farington VIII, 1–2.)

73. May 22

W writes to STC from 24 Edward Street: Asks STC not to publish [*To William Wordsworth*]; seeks STC's comments on *P 1815*, *Exc*. Objectives in *Exc*. Hopes to send *WD* in a few days. (*MY* II, 238–39. See *STCL* IV, 570–76.)

W drinks tea at CL's. HCR joins the company. (*HCRBW* I, 167; HCRNB.)[25]

74. May 23

W breakfasts with B. R. Haydon. (Haydon *Diary* I, 446.)

W, SH, perhaps MW, take tea at the Ls'. They are joined by HCR, [Thomas Massa] Alsager, Barron Field, T. N. Talfourd, the Colliers, and probably others. W is chatty on the subject of poetry. This is perhaps W's first meeting with Talfourd and Field. W perhaps now sees Field's interleaved copy of *P 1815* containing MS copies of *EW*, *DS*, and *FV*. (*HCRBW* I, 167; letter, Barron Field to W, 18 Apr 1828, DCP.)[26]

[25] HCRNB records: "Walk to Town before dinner Wordsworth at Lambs."

[26] Field wrote to W in 1828: "I am he who formerly completed in MS. interleaved in my copy of your 2 octavos, your Epistles from the Lakes and from the Alps and your Female Vagrant, which you may remember to have seen at our friend Charles Lamb's 13 years ago." Field's volumes, later owned by James Dykes Campbell, were purchased by GGW in 1904 and are now at DC.

75. Probably May 24

W writes to Walter Scott: Invites Scott to join him and Richard Heber and the Bs next Friday morning, or any morning next week after Tuesday, for breakfast and a drive afterwards to look at the portrait of Milton [found by John Lamb]. (*MY* II, 239; *LL* II, 159–60. See 1815:77.)[27]

76. May 25

The Ws and perhaps SH, probably J. T. Coleridge, certainly [J. M.] Lappenberg, join HCR and ML in front-row seats to see *Richard II* at Drury Lane. (*HCRBW* I, 167; *HCRNB*; *The London Theatre, 1811–1866*, ed. Eluned Brown, London, 1966, 64.)[28]

77. Possibly May 26, or May 29 or shortly after

W perhaps breakfasts with Walter Scott and Richard Heber at the Bs'; goes with them to look at John L's portrait of Milton. (*MY* II, 239. See 1815:75.)

78. Perhaps between late May and June 19

W breakfasts with Walter Scott and Mrs. Opie at the residence of Sir George Phillips. (C. L. Brightwell, *Memorials of the Life of Mrs. Opie*, Norwich, 1854, 175–76; Edgar Johnson, *Sir Walter Scott*, New York, 1971, I, 493.)

79. May 27

W calls on Godwin. His call possibly coincides with one from Mary Godwin. (Godwin Diary.)[29]

[27] As the postmark of the letter is 24 May, that would appear the most likely date for the letter itself. The portrait of Milton is now the "Lenox portrait" of the New York Public Library.

[28] HCRNB records for 25 May: "Ab: Play Miss L Wordsworth's." An account entry opposite records "Play & oranges Richd 2d –/4/6."

[29] Godwin notes: "Wordsworth & M call...." Whether W and M[ary Godwin] met at this time remains uncertain.

80. May 28

W, MW, possibly SH, dine at the Colliers'. The company includes [C. M.] Young, [Thomas] Barnes, [T. M.] Alsager, HCR, and others. W discusses the work of Byron and Crabbe.

HCR departs; later goes to the Ls', where they are joined by the Ws. HCR probably walks with W. (*HCRBW* I, 167–68; HCRNB.)[30]

81. May 29

W breakfasts with William Wilberforce; walks in the garden with him; remains long. This is the first meeting of the two men. (Robert and Isaac Wilberforce, *The Life of Wilberforce*, London, 1838, III, 260.)[31]

82. Perhaps between May 31 and June 19

The Ws, perhaps SH also, call on Washington Allston; admire his pictures. W notices esp. "Jacob's Dream." (*STCL* IV, 576; *LY* III, 1184–86; transcript of *Composed upon an Evening of Extraordinary Splendour and Beauty*, Cornell Collection, Cornell 2276. See 1812:19.)

83. Probably c June 1

A review of *Exc* appears in *The British Critic* (2nd Series III, May 1815). Another appears in *La Belle Assemblée* (XI, May 1815). (See Ward; Hayden.)

84. June 1

W, MW, SH breakfast at HCR's. The company also includes [William] Rough, TCl (self-invited), [Richard] Cargill, [Barron] Field, J. P. Collier, [George] Long, and Anthony Robinson. W, MW, SH depart, after a short time, to visit St. Paul's. (*HCRBW* I, 168; HCRNB.)[32]

[30] HCRNB records: "Mit Ess. Colliers Wordsw. a party Ab: Lamb, Walk with Wordsw."

[31] Wilberforce, who found himself "much pleased" with W, had written to the poet on 23 May inviting him to breakfast the "first fine morning after tomorrow" (DCP). On DW's acquaintance with Wilberforce see esp. *EY* 26–28.

[32] HCRNB records: "Frühst: Wordsworth & party [.]"

85. June 2

WD is published in London. (*Courier*. See 1815:67n.)

86. June 9

W dines perhaps at Sir GB's, with Samuel Lysons, Wilberforce, Joseph Farington. W expresses fears concerning Bonaparte's strength. (Farington VIII, 8; Robert and Isaac Wilberforce, *The Life of Wilberforce*, London, 1838, III, 260; *HCRWC* I, 359.)[33]

87. June 11

A short attack on W by Hazlitt, suggesting W's political apostacy, appears in the *Examiner* as part of Hazlitt's review of a performance of *Comus*.

B. R. Haydon makes a plaster cast of W's face. W breakfasts afterwards with Haydon and John Scott, who has peeked in on W while the cast was on his face. W speaks of his plans for *The Recluse*. Perhaps all go afterwards to call on Hunt in Edgeware Road. Hunt disclaims the *Examiner* article and is profusely complimentary. Perhaps W and Haydon afterwards walk to Hampstead. (Haydon *Diary* I, 450–51; *HCRBW* I, 169; *Autobiography of Leigh Hunt*, ed. Roger Ingpen, Oxford, 1903, II, 19–21; letter, Haydon to W, 18 Nov 1816, DCP.)[34]

88. June 13; probably June 13

RW's accounts record payment to W, in town, of £40/-/- under 13 June. (RW accounts, DCP.)[35]

[33] Wilberforce now found W "very manly, sensible, and full of knowledge, but independent almost to rudeness" (cf 1815:81n).

[34] Haydon writes of W's comments on *The Recluse*: "I yet remember how I was affected at your powerful description and Scott and I have often talked of it with great delight."

While the Haydon *Diary* seems to place W's visit to Hunt on 12 June, W almost certainly visited Hunt only once about this time, and since HCR's notes appear to fix the day beyond question, Haydon is likely to have misdated his diary entry by one day.

[35] A memorandum of MW's notes the payment under the date of 30 June— probably in reference to the general time of final departure from town.

Probably on 13 June W, Rogers, Bowles, perhaps Sir GB, possibly MW, SH go by boat to Greenwich. Possibly Bowles asks, from timidity, to be put ashore at Greenwich. W, Rogers, Sir GB, possibly MW, SH walk. Bowles composes *The Two Sailors* (*The Greenwich Pensioners*). (Copy of Bowles poem, DCP; letter, Bowles to W, 15 Apr 1839, DCP; Rogers *Table-Talk* 258n; Charles W memorandum, 1844.)[36]

89. June 15

HCR calls on W; they walk; discuss the *Examiner* attack [see 1815: 87] and Hazlitt. W, HCR, perhaps MW, SH, call on Daniel Stuart, possibly lunch with the Colliers. W perhaps now speaks of *WD* as an imaginative poem. (*HCRBW* I, 169–70; HCRNB.)[37]

[36] A transcription by MW of W. L. Bowles' "The Two Sailors—written at Greenwich June 13th 1815" (published in revised form as *The Greenwich Pensioners*: see Bowles' *Poetical Works*, ed. George Gilfillan, Edinburgh, 1855) is in DCP. The MS describes as being among the party, apart from the author,

> He whose rich pencil, mid the silent strife
> Of colours, bids the Landscape beam with life;
> And He to whom sad Memory gave her shell,
> And bade him tones of sweetest cadence swell;
> And, He whose [muse *underlined twice*] in Vision
> *high and holy*,
> Marks all things with a quiet melancholy—

These persons are said to have gone, after landing, "to range the Hills" while the author remained near the Hospital.

Bowles wrote to W on 15 Apr [1839] (DCP) of "not having seen you, I think, since, you and I, Rogers, were in a boat together, on the *Thames*, & I *got out & run away*, & heard your pronounc'd—My the *boldest man*, in England!" The anecdote as recounted in Rogers *Table-Talk* (258n) states that the party consisted of W, MW, Dora, and Bowles, but no location is named. A memorandum of W's conversation made by Charles W in 1844 gives no description of the party but records W as saying that Bowles asked to be put ashore at Chelsea on the way to Richmond. W's 1844 recollection might confuse Chelsea with Greenwich because of the hospitals and pensioners at both places. Bowles's verses as copied by MW seem to refer fairly plainly to Rogers, author of *The Pleasure of Memory*, and (esp. in view of the copyist) to the author of *Exc*. The artist referred to is less certainly identifiable, but was most likely Sir GB. It seems possible that MW was of the party, and SH also.

[37] The callers on Stuart are described by HCR as, besides himself, "Wordsworth, etc." HCRNB records: "Vorm: The Wordsworths Call Stuart & Mit Ess Colliers[.]"

W probably this day calls at Longman & Co.; receives £105 for *WD*; initials the Longman account book (Impression Book 5, op. 201) in receipt. (Longman accounts. See Owen CSP 98; *MY* II, 236.)

90. June 16

W, probably also MW, SH, visit the BM. They are joined there by HCR. The group is conducted about the Museum by [William] Alexander. (*HCRBW* I, 170; HCRNB.)[38]

91. June 18

HCR breakfasts at W's. W is not at home and HCR is unexpected, but he remains, chatting with MW and SH until 2. John Scott and Haydon call, stay a considerable time. Daniel Stuart and [?Pamflay] perhaps also call. (*HCRBW* I, 170–71; HCR *Diary* I, 255–56; HCRNB.)[39]

W probably today dines with Samuel Rogers in company with Byron and perhaps CL. Byron displays pro-Bonapartist feelings; W argues that Bonaparte cannot win if the Allies keep together. (Charles W memorandum, 1844. See 1812:34n.)

92. Perhaps shortly before June 19, or June 19; probably June 19 (–perhaps June 28)

Perhaps shortly before or on 19 June, W takes leave of CL and ML in St. Giles [High Street]. (*LL* II, 168.)

Probably on 19 June W, MW, SH travel to Bury to visit the Cls. (They depart perhaps 28 June.) They travel part of the way, perhaps to Cambridge, by coach, and are taken the rest of the way by TCl. (*SHL* 80; *MY* II, 239–40.)[40]

93. June 25

A review of *WD* [by John Scott] appears in *The Champion*. (See Hayden; *TLS* 1944, 7, 31.)

[38] *HCRBW* remarks that he joined "Wordsworth, etc." at the Museum. HCRNB notes: "Vorm: Br Museum Wordsw."

[39] HCRNB records: "Vorm: ffrust: Wordsworth (Stuart, Scott, Haydon & [?Pamflay])"

[40] On a letter probably written by MW while at Bury see *MY* II, 241.

94. June 27

W almost gives £25 for a curricle and pair. Consideration of the unsuitability of this rig for the journey home restrains him.

Probably W, MW, SH, the Cls dine at the Capell Loffts'. (*SHL* 80, 82.)

95. June 28–probably July 1

On 28 June W, MW probably travel from Bury to Bocking, where they visit the CWs probably till 1 July. (*SHL* 80–81; *MY* II, 239–40.)

On 28 June (letter postmarked 29 June) SH writes to MMH from Bury: Journey from London to Bury; visit there; the Ws' departure. SH's plans. They suspect W's money to be invested in RW's land; W's refusal of the collectorship [see 1815:63]. Bonaparte; ladies' dress styles; SH's plans. (*SHL* 80–83.)

On the same day DW writes to CCl: W, MW, and their plans; sickness at RM; Tilbrooke; the Cls. News of Bonaparte's abdication arrived this morning. DW will probably visit France next year. The Lloyds; criticisms of W's poems in *The Champion, British Critic*. A poem from Thomas Wilkinson.

She adds a postscript on 29 June. (*MY* II, 239–43.)

96. Probably c July 1

A review of *WD* appears in *The Theatrical Inquisitor* (VI, June 1815). (See Ward; Hayden.)

97. Probably July 1; perhaps July 2–c late July

Probably on 1 July the Ws set off to Coleorton via Cambridge, perhaps arriving 2 July. They probably visit at Coleorton and return to RM c late July. (*MY* II, 243, 245; Warter II, 423.)[41]

---

[41] DW on 25 June did not expect the Ws home before 15 July. It is unlikely that they returned after the arrival of the Bs at Rydal, which occurred by 6 Aug. The decision, c 1 Aug, to send Willy and Dora to the seaside in the company of DW perhaps reflects parental judgment.

Appendices

APPENDIX I

DC MS 29

DC MS 29, containing copies of some of W's shorter poems, is a notebook of twenty-three leaves, measuring c 16.5 × 20 cm, of laid paper watermarked with a crowned circular Britannia-in-shield and countermarked "1798." A front leaf laid in contains the inscription "Manuscripts of *Wordsworth*" in the autograph of Thomas Poole. An accompanying note by GGW dated May 1931 records that the NB once contained a copy of W's *Somersetshire Tragedy* which GGW cut out and destroyed (see Jonathan Wordsworth, "A Wordsworth Tragedy," *TLS* 1966, 642). Copies of the following poems (listed in the order of the MS) were allowed to remain: *Hart-leap Well*; *The Two Thieves*; *The Idle Shepherd Boys*; "Strange Fits of Passion"; *Lucy Gray*; *The Reverie of Poor Susan*; "There Was a Boy"; *WDQR*; *The Waterfall and the Eglantine*; *ISHS*. The stubs of the leaves once containing the *Somersetshire Tragedy* are found between *The Idle Shepherd Boys* and "Strange Fits of Passion."

All of the copying is in the autograph of DW except the last stanza of *The Waterfall and the Eglantine*, written in by JW in pencil, and "Strange Fits of Passion," which is in W's autograph. Except for the stanzas just cited and the entire copy of *The Reverie of Poor Susan*, all the materials are copied on rectos. The *Reverie* (on which see *CEY* 29, 323–24) was possibly copied in as an afterthought; the content of the concluding stanza of *The Waterfall and the Eglantine* suggests that it was at first omitted only through oversight.

All these poems—except, of course, for the missing *Somersetshire Tragedy*, which like *The Reverie* would have held particular interest for Poole (see *CEY* 196n, 324)—were printed in *LB* 1800; and all variant readings appear to precede the readings of the printer's MS. *Hart-leap Well* and "There Was a Boy" were given to Davy c early June 1800 (see 1800:48) and a bare possibility exists that this MS, which fairly certainly belonged to Poole sometime thereafter, was what Davy received then; but the case is unlikely in view of W's statement on 29 July that he had not looked over the MS materials given to Davy. It is probable that *Hart-leap Well*, *The Two Thieves*, *The Idle Shepherd-boys*, "Strange Fits of Passion," and *Lucy Gray* were copied

613

in before 29 July, when "There Was a Boy" and *Hart-leap Well* were sent off for the printer. *The Waterfall and the Eglantine* was forwarded by 4 Aug (see 1800:94). The beginning of *WDQR*, which precedes *The Waterfall and the Eglantine* in this MS, reads, however, like the corrected version sent off in the fifth sheet by 13 Aug; not like the opening lines cancelled in the fourth sheet forwarded by the same date but almost certainly after 4 Aug; so that the *Waterfall* was possibly written in here after that date (one earlier reading is corrected by erasure). The last poem, *ISHS*, was sent off probably c but by 13 Aug; and the heading here, "Inscription for the remains of the Hermitage on St. Herbert's Island Derwentwater" ("remains of the" added over a caret), precedes the printer's MS. Unless, as is most improbable, this variant was a revision later than the printer's copy but not adopted in the printed text, the copying in this book is likely to have been completed by 13 Aug.

APPENDIX II

The Christabel NB

For a description of the main portion of the Christabel NB, DC MS 15, see *CEY* 322–25. Surviving material at the end of the NB containing the smaller portion of the entries commences with the last five lines of *WSIG*. A leaf that probably contained the rest of the poem has been cut out. Although position in the NB is hardly a firm indication of order of entry, these lines may be assumed, in default of evidence to the contrary, to have been entered before the rough drafts for *The Brothers* which follow (lines c 252–54, 92–96, and other lines apparently intended for the poem but not used). *The Brothers* drafts must date from between shortly before 24 Dec 1799 (see *CEY* 36) and 5 Apr 1800 (see 1800:41n). *WSIG* was in any case complete (and this draft thus written) by 13 Aug, when the poem was sent off for *LB* 1800.

Stubs of probably twenty-four leaves follow. Contents of the original pages as indicated by surviving traces of writing include *The Two Thieves* [?29]–36, 38–39, 42–48; *Hart-leap Well*, 20–24, [?41–55], 56–64; *WDQR* [?24]–27; and *Rural Architecture* [?1–13], 14–18. *Hart-leap Well* probably dates from early 1800: W later recalled composing the first eight stanzas "one winter evening at the cottage" in the midst of composition of *The Brothers* and then completing it in "a day or two" (IF note). The poem was sent to the printer on 29 July. *The Two Thieves* thus probably dates by that time; *WDQR* was probably composed as here by 4 Aug 1800; and *Rural Architecture* was forwarded to the printer on 10 Oct. The close connections in theme and content between *Rural Architecture*, *The Idle Shepherd-boys*, and other "pastorals" of 1800 strongly suggest composition in that year. Next appears draft associated with *Michael*, quoted and discussed Parrish *WBS* and *Ariel* discussion.

Two pages of copy by DW of *Christabel* I follow. Then appear, in turn: a version of *PW* V, 342, IV, i; *PW* V, 343, ii, iii, iv; eight descriptive lines perhaps concerning water droplets on moss and mentioning the "mighty Niger"; *PW* V, 342, IV, i (this version appears earlier than the one already cited); *PW* V, 343, v; *PW* V, 343–44, vi; *PW* V, 344, vii, viii. Following these the copying of *Christabel* I continues, first in the autograph of DW, then in that of MH (cf *STCPW* I, 213), to the end of Book II ("Led forth the Lady Geraldine"). The last seven leaves of *Christabel* belong to a gathering stitched into the NB. The position of the writing indicates that the copy was made before the gathering was stitched in. The autograph of MH, however, begins several pages before this gathering, probably at line 294. The general appearance of the MS suggests that all was written about the same time; and MH plainly took up her part of the copying soon after DW concluded hers. The copy of *Christabel* would appear unlikely, in view of the presence of the autograph of MH, to have reached completion prior to 6 Nov 1801, unless, as seems most improbable, STC carried W's NB along with him to Gallow Hill the previous summer.

The appearance of the materials quoted *PW* V, 342–44 is generally so similar to that of much of the rhymed draft related to *Michael* that it seems impossible to date these at a time much different from *Michael*. Their divergence in style and content from *Michael* as it was completed is considerable, but their difference from the meditative materials belonging to earlier stages of composition of *Michael* quoted *PW* II, 479–84 is much less pronounced. Indentations and pinholes in the paper indicate that the leaves between the first two pages of the *Christabel* copy and the later pages were joined to form a single leaf with *Christabel* copy on recto and verso. Hence these intermediate materials certainly preceded the *Christabel* copy. No other work in this end of the NB can be dated before 1800; and the imagery of i and vii, it may also be remarked, appears to reflect a fairly direct response of the poet to mountain scenery.

APPENDIX III

Lists and Copies of Poems in DC MS 38, DC MS 44, and in a Copy of Agostino Isola's Pieces Selected from the Italian Poets

The following notes detail the contents of two sets of copies of W's poems, one of sonnets only (lists 1 and 4), and two lists of sonnets (lists 2 and 3).

1. Copies of sonnets in MS 38, in autograph of DW. The reading of the first line of the sonnet commencing "Brook" in list 2 corresponds, as far as it goes, to that of the same line in the full copy of the poem in MS M (list 4), while the reading of the same line in the group of sonnet copies described immediately below appears to precede that reading. On the other hand, the reading "When I Have Borne in Memory" here looks later than the second corresponding reading in list 2, "When I have borne in mind." The copies noted in list 1 appear to have been written by DW in two groups of seven and six poems respectively; but the length of time that may have elapsed between the copying of the groups is not evident, and one may conclude by default that the second set followed the first into the NB without great delay. List 2 would seem not improbably associated with the collective and collecting effort that produced MS M. "It Is Not to Be Thought of" was published 16 Apr 1803, and "When I Have Borne in Memory" was probably also among copies of sonnets sent off to Stuart in early 1803. These copies may thus be conjectured to belong to c late 1802, possibly by 25 Dec. The seemingly earlier readings of "When I Have Borne" in list 2 are probably slips or experimental changes afterwards rejected. (1802:264; 1803:11; 1803:15.)

"Dear Fellow-traveller here we are once more" [*Composed in the Valley near Dover*]
"Are souls then nothing? Must at length they die"
"It is not to be thought of that the flood"
"Fond words have oft been spoken to thee, Sleep"

"Dear native Brooks your ways I have pursu'd" [a quinzaine; see *PW* III, 523]
"A flock of Sheep that leisurely pass by"
"'Tis six miles from our dwelling-place; no rill"
"Brook that has been my [joy for *corrected to* comfort] days & weeks"
"A plain Youth, Lady, & a simple Lover"
"When I have borne in memory what has tam'd"
"I thought I saw the footsteps of a throne"
"'Dear Vale'! I said 'when I shall look upon'"
"Nuns fret not at their Convents' narrow room"

2. Lists of sonnets in MS 38, in autograph of W. Pencil marks on a stub following the present conclusion of this list, although unidentifiable, suggest that W's notes may have continued for some part of another page.

Introduction [probably "Nuns Fret Not"]
Dear Vale
O gentle Sleep
A flock of Sheep
[How Sw *deleted*]
Where lies the land
How sweet it is when
Milton thou shouldst
Edward I know not which [way]
I griev'd for Buonaparte
Great Men have been among us
[Not for all India's wealth *deleted*]
Jones when from Calais
Fair Star of Evening
[Festivals have I seen *deleted*]
Are souls then nothing
It is not to be thought of
[Calling to mind *deleted*]
When I have borne in mind
Festivals have I seen
It is a beauteous evening
[Fond words have oft been spoken *deleted*]
[The world too much *inserted late then deleted*]
We had a Fellow passenger
Toussaint thou most unhappy
Dear Fellow Traveller

Is it a reed that's shaken

Ere we could reach the wish'd [*Composed after a Journey across the Hambleton
Hills*]

With ships the sea was

Not for all India's wealth

Translation from Milton [probably "A Plain Youth, Lady"]

Is that a Spirit who from

Fond words have oft [*This and next entry inserted late in pen.*]

The world is to a man

Brook that hast been my solace

3. List of sonnets, in autograph of W, in the copy of the second edition of
Agostino Isola's *Pieces Selected from the Italian Poets* (Cambridge, 1784; see
PW IV, 472, and Woof *SB*) at the Fitzwilliam Museum, Cambridge.
"Methought I saw" and "There is trickling" both indicate a later stage of
development of the poems concerned than that represented by list 1.

Ho[w s]weet it is

Methought I saw

With ships the sea

O gentle sleep

Ere we could reach

These words were utter'd

Brook that hast been [*This and the second short title below appear to have been
inserted late, but at the same sitting as the others.*]

Where lies the land

The world too much

Fond words

A flock of sheep

It is a beauteous evening

[Calvert it shall no(t) be *deleted*]

There is trickling

Calvert it shall

4. Copies of poems in MS 44, in autograph of DW and MW. The copies
may be supposed to have been made, except for the first and the last two
poems, between mid-Feb and 6 Mar 1804 (see 1804:22). List 4 corrects and
supplements the description given *STCNB* II, vol. 2, pp. 423–25.

RC [MS M; lines 1–58 missing]
Anticipation. October 1803 [*followed by note*] "End of Part 1st" [*Preceding the*

619

next short title, and on the verso of the same leaf, is the heading] "Sonnets. 2nd Part."

"How sweet it is when Mother Fancy rocks"

"Where lies the Land to which yon Ship would go?"

"Methought I saw the footsteps of a throne"

"The world is too much with us; late and soon"

"O gentle Sleep! do they belong to thee"

"A flock of sheep that leisurely pass by"

"Ere we had reach'd the wish'd-for place night fell"

"These words were utter'd in a pensive mood"

"'Beloved Vale,' I said, 'when I shall con'"

"England! the time has come when thou should'st wean"

To the Men of Kent. October 1803.

October 1803. ("Six thousand Veterans")

October. 1803. ("These times strike moneyed worldlings")

Written by the Sea-side, near Calais.

August 1802 ("Is it a reed")

To a Friend. Written near Calais, on the Road leading to Ardres. August 1st 1802

To Toussaint l'Ouverture

Calais. August 15th. 1802. ("Festivals have I seen")

"I griev'd for Buonapartè, with a vain"

September 1st 1802 ("We had a Fellow-passenger")

"Dear Fellow-traveller! here we are once more"

To a Friend. ("Coleridge! I know not which way I must look")

"Great Men have been among us, hands that penn'd"

"It is not to be thought of, that the flood"

"When I have borne in memory what has tam'd"

October. 1803. ("One might believe")

October. 1803. ("When, looking on the present face of things")

"How dolefully, O Moon, thou climb'st the sky!"

"Whom pure despite of heart could so far please" [pub. beginning "Degenerate Douglas!"]

"Nuns fret not at their convents' narrow room"

"There is a trickling water, neither rill"

"With ships the sea was sprinkled far and nigh"

"Brook, that hast been my solace days and weeks"

"It is a beauteous evening calm and free"

"Fond words have oft been spoken to thee, Sleep"

"Pelion and Ossa flourish side by side"

To the Memory of Raisley Calvert.

"Beaumont, it was thy wish that I should rear"
"I am not one who much or oft delight" [*The three following poems are copied with an indentation of the first line as the only division from the preceding poem.*]
"'Yet life,' you say, 'is life; we have seen & see'"
"Wings have we, & as far as we can go"
"Nor can I not believe but that hereby"
[*The Sailor's Mother*]
"It is no Spirit who from Heaven hath flown"
Motto intended for Poems on the naming of Places. ("Some minds have room alone for pageant stories")
To the lesser Celandine ("Pansies, lilies")
To the Same flower ("Pleasures")
"Up with me up with [me *omitted*] into the clouds" [A *leaf has been cut out before the next poem.*]
To H.C.
To a Butterfly ("I've watched you")
To the Cuckoo
"My heart leaps up when I behold"
To the Daisy ("In youth")
The Sparrow's Nest
[*Yarrow Unvisited*]
"Among all lovely things my Love had been"
To a Butterfly ("Stay near me")
"Once in a lonely hamlet I sojourn'd" (*The Emigrant Mother*)
Ode to Duty [*Space has been left at the beginning for an opening stanza not written in.*]
Travelling ("This is the spot")
[*Repentance*] ("O Fools that we were we had lands which we sold")
Alice Fell
"When first I journey'd hither, to a home" ["When to the attractions of the busy world"]
[*The Small Celandine*] ("There is a Flower")
"Dear native Brook your ways I have pursu'd"
"I travell'd among unknown men"
"I have been here in the Moon-light"
On seeing a Red-breast chacing a Butterfly
"The sun has long been set"
[*The Tinker*]
"These Chairs they have no words to utter"

Half an hour afterwards (" I have thoughts that are fed by the sun")
"The cock is crowing"
Stanzas written in my Pocket copy of the Castle of Indolence
Foresight
The Green Linnet
[*A Farewell*] (" Farewell thou little Nook of mountain ground")
"She was a phantom of delight"
[*Resolution and Independence*]
Beggars
"Sweet Highland Girl a very shower"
"The Owl as if he had learn'd his cheer"
[*Ode*]
PB [MS 4]
Prel I–V

The second item of list 4 implies that a large number of sonnets has possibly been lost from the MS. Among them were perhaps the following, certainly in existence by the time of this copying:

London. 1802 (" Milton!")
On the Extinction of the Venetian Republic
September 1802 (" Inland, within a Hollow Vale")
"There Is a Bondage Worse, Far Worse, to Bear"
"Are Souls Then Nothing?"
"A Plain Youth, Lady"
"Fly, Some Kind Harbinger"
Composed upon Westminster Bridge

STC read the last of these aloud, apparently from a MS, in London on 25 Mar 1804 (Farington II, 209–10). The couplets *Lines on the Expected Invasion, 1803*, closely associated by subject with some of the political sonnets, are also absent from the MS.

Leaves have been cut out among the sonnet copies, but whether the excisions were made before or after the MS was sent off cannot be determined. Numberings indicating sections of the MS include a "2" at the top of the page containing *Anticipation*, and "3" on that containing *Written by the Sea-side near Calais*. A "4" appears below on a page containing the beginning of *To the Lesser Celandine*. Section "2" now consists of seven leaves containing fourteen sonnets; and "3" consists of fifteen leaves containing twenty-nine sonnets in addition to other materials. The numbering is in the autograph of STC, and must have been made prior to and for reasons other than the binding of the volume as we have it, inasmuch as the *PB* MS is not numbered and STC has instructed the binder, in a note, to insert it "Fra [sections] 6 e 7." That the numbering indicates the packets of MSS as sent to STC in 1804 is hardly certain, but seems a possibility (see PREL xxx–xxxi).

The eight other MS sections in which numbers (through "11") remain consist, in any case, of between seven and seventeen leaves. All but three have ten leaves or fewer; and the two smallest have seven. If the MS section numbered "1" had been that containing *RC*, it would probably have consisted of not less than seventeen leaves (the *RC* MS is copied at the rate of twenty-nine to thirty lines per page, and fifty-eight lines, probably, are missing); other materials would have made this section longer than any other that survives. But more positive evidence supports supposition that the section numbered "1" contained short poems—in the form of DW's remark to STC on 6 Mar 1804 that "We have transcribed all William's smaller Poems for you, and have begun the Poem on his Life and the Pedlar . . . " (*EY* 448). A section containing smaller poems together with *RC* is thus an improbability; as would be a "Part 1st" (as referred to in the note "End of Part 1st" following *Anticipation*) consisting of *RC* and *Anticipation* only. Since the title "Sonnets. 2nd Part" heads the verso of the same leaf, there would not seem much doubt that the sonnet *Anticipation* concluded a group of copies of sonnets. A single leaf (now containing drafts for *RC* beyond the main copy), of paper different from that of the sections of the MS generally (which is laid, with a watermark of a medallion containing a seated Britannia with the date 1802 at her feet, and countermark of C HALE), has been bound in between the conclusion of *RC* and the leaf containing *Anticipation*, suggesting that the binder himself regarded these materials as standing in separate lots.

For a "Part 1st" of sonnets to have contained as many sonnets as the "2nd Part"—forty-two—over thirty sonnets must be supposed to have been present there that are either (a) now lost or (b) now unknown from surviving evidence to have been in existence when the MS was made up; and these, with the nine works already named above, would have required a section of about twenty-one leaves. If section "1" had been in fact as small as section "2," of course, fewer than ten sonnets would be left unaccounted for; but the number of poems in the group would have been disproportionate to that of "Sonnets. 2nd Part." Had it been intended, however, that "Sonnets. 2nd Part" itself be divided about equally in two, but the heading "Sonnets. 3rd Part" forgotten as copying proceeded, a proportionate section "1" would have contained ten or eleven leaves.

Such speculation can achieve few decisive results; but it must be noticed also that a large section "1," if the question of proportionate numbers of sonnets is left aside, might have contained poems other than sonnets. Such a supposal, for reasons noted elsewhere (see Appendix VI), would offer temptation to conjecture that a version of *HG* or at least the *Prospectus* had stood here. But an arrangement juxtaposing the *Prospectus* and the sonnets would appear anticlimactic—or, indeed, if W knew anything of STC's opinions about the relative importance of his sonnets and *The Recluse* (see *STCL* II, 1013), defiant of STC. And any at all coherent version of *HG*, with or without the *Prospectus*, seems a most doubtful possibility for one of the "smaller poems" mentioned in DW's remark of 6 Mar 1804 just quoted, which seems to indicate that *Prel* and *RC* are the only poems to be copied. No hint is given by the MS itself that any large loss of leaves has occurred except from section "1"; and the probable content of section "1" is sufficiently indicated by the facts that (a) sonnets certainly extant at the time of copying are missing from the MS as it now stands, and (b) while a proportionate "1st Part" of sonnets would probably not have contained fewer than fourteen sonnets by any calculation, only one sonnet remains from that "Part"; and it commences the MS section "2" (see also 1804:71). Likewise, neither the leaves containing *RC* nor DW's remarks appear to offer grounds for supposing that copies of any other poetic materials (such as the *Prospectus*, which, with *RC*, would have made that section at least two leaves longer than any other in MS M dating from this time) preceded *RC*; nor does evidence survive of the copying in early 1804 of any long poems besides *RC* and *Prel*.

APPENDIX IV

A Fragment of Critical Prose in DC MS 28

W was apparently preoccupied on 3 Oct 1800 by the subject of a Supplementary Essay for the second volume of the forthcoming edition of *LB* (*LY* II, 910; 1800:155). He announced on 18 Dec that he had "nearly finished" the essay, but that "so many quotations" were required for illustration of the argument that the resulting length would be unsuitable for the second volume. While portions of the argument in the 1802 *Appendix* differ considerably from that of the 1800 Preface—especially those portions dealing with figurative language and the interrelationship of poet, primitive poet, and rustic (see W. J. B. Owen, *Wordsworth as Critic*, Toronto and London, 1969, 60–63)—the large number of "quotations" that W mentions seems suitable, insofar as W's later critical prose provides any grounds for conjecture, only for some sort of examination of poetic language and readers' responses to it, hence not improbably to the subjects of fictitious or imitative versus real or effective poetic language and the audience's responses to these, dealt with in the 1802 *Appendix*. Evidence is shadowy, but suffices to justify the assumption that W at this time wrote some materials drawn on in the 1802 *Appendix*. The subject is intimately related to that of poetic popularity as such, and hence to the central concern of the 1815 *Essay, Supplementary* as well; but that work must have been shaped into its present form, with particular attention to Jeffrey, not very long before its publication—probably c Jan, by c early Feb 1815. The possibility remains that the 1815 *Essay, Supplementary* draws occasionally on these materials.[1]

[1] Owen shows that in the *Essay, Supplementary* W was almost certainly directly alluding to phrasing in Jeffrey's own reviews, esp. that of *The Lady of the Lake* (*ER* XVI, 1810, 263–93); and W was certainly intensely thoughtful about Jeffrey in late Dec 1814 (*MY* II, 182). As late as 22 Dec, however, W was stating that he was afraid that his indolence would prevent his prefixing any prose remarks to his poems. The only suffix then in contemplation appears to have been the "old preface."(Jordan 158, 216, 318; W. J. B. Owen, "Wordsworth and Jeffrey in Collaboration," *RES* XV, 1964, 161–67; *MY* II, 180. See also 1814: 149.)

Appendix IV

The following fragmentary draft found in DC MC 28, may offer a small clue to the character of the 1800 Supplementary Essay (the hand is DW's):

[. . .] frequently done in [composition *deleted*] any class of Composition which has taken deep hold of the affections of the People By imitating such transpositions a poet may sometimes [excite a recoll, call forth, excite *deleted in turn*] revive the pleasurable feelings attached to the recollection of these poems in the mind of his Reader, & by so doing may [give *deleted*] produce a pleasure which will more than counterbalance any [dislike of, aversion *deleted*] displeasure which such transposition wd otherwise [excite *deleted*] occasion. But this liberty must be used with great caution: Not wantonly & capriciously but under [certain *deleted*] the controul of certain fixed laws. What I have said upon metre to which this subject is nearly akin may be applied here.

From this review, [imperfect as it is, *added above a caret*] the Reader will be able to [perceive *deleted*] collect [what *deleted*] how small must be the stock of words & phrases, how few the peculiarities of language [to *added above caret*] which the Poet, [even when he *added above without caret*] [speaks *corrected without deletion from* speaking] in his own person can have any relational claim.

Various analogies between these comments and others among W's writings may be noticed against the general observation that the passage appears plainly to have been intended to follow some kind of review of the practices of earlier poets with respect to the subject of stock phrasing, although here W is apparently defending the practice of limited use of phrasing deliberately like that of earlier poets:

(1) The concept of the "People" is one that elsewhere receives marked notice in W's formal criticism only at the conclusion of the *Essay, Supplementary*, although he distinguishes "Public" and "People" in a letter to Sir GB written between 17 and 22 Feb 1808, and STC refers to W's distinction during the same year (*MY* I, 194–95; *STCL* III, 112).
(2) The concluding paragraph of the quoted draft appears to assert the smallness of the quantity of preestablished phrasing available to the poet, an emphasis of both the 1800 *Preface* (*PW* II, 390) and the conclusion of the 1802 *Appendix*.
(3) The use in this passage of the phrase "the Reader" for a third-person address recalls W's frequent use of that device in the 1800 *Preface*. The phrase is employed much less often in W's later critical writings.

(4) The reference to "the controul of certain fixed laws" is reminiscent in a general way of the comments of the 1800 *Preface* about "certain laws" of meter to which the poet and reader willingly submit.

It would thus seem a fair guess that the passage represents draft toward some portion of one of the 1800 essays—perhaps, taking into account the "review," which probably involved a number of quotations, the Supplementary Essay. Its direction in terms of future published writings appears to be toward the 1802 *Appendix* and the 1815 *Essay, Supplementary*, which develop the negative aspects of the subject of stock phrasing to an extent seemingly not envisioned here.

MS 28, consisting of pages 131–75, interleaved, of STC's *Poems on Various Subjects* (1796), with drafts on the interleaves, on printed versos, and on some rectos, otherwise contains draft materials unlikely to date before 1806. DC MS 30, the only matching MS, consists of interleaved pages 33–64 of the same book and almost certainly of the same copy. MS 30 contains draft material toward *Michael*. The prose draft just discussed was thus perhaps written in before the book was broken apart.

APPENDIX V

The Chronology of The Prelude

Much evidence about the chronology of *Prel* between 1800 and 1805 is conveniently summarized Prel xix–xxxii, xliii–liv; and duplication of all information there recorded is not required. Some repetition, correction, and supplementary description will, however, be necessary; circuitous argument will be unavoidable; and conclusions must often be speculative and imprecise. A warning made in the Preface may usefully be rephrased here: "*The Prelude*" is a term convenient for designation of a poem for which W himself never fixed upon a formal title; and W does not appear to have formed a conception of this work that he was able to realize as a poem that he regarded, even temporarily, as complete until 1804–05, although the poem finished in 1805 contained verses composed as early as 1798. "*Prel*" references below and elsewhere are normally based on the 1805 text, but I have assumed that the reader will not regularly require artificial indications that these refer to the version of those lines belonging to the stage of the poem's development, or the MS, under discussion.

The brief and well-known retrospective passage *Prel* VII.1–13, which surveys the progress of the composition of the poem from the time of the Preamble through the summer of 1804, makes a convenient starting point. Here the poet states that "five years"—the figure is changed by a correction in MS E, probably by CW Jr., possibly Dora (see *WBS* 5, 8n) to "six"— have vanished since the poet first poured out the "glad preamble" of his verse. Although that moment of inspiration was short-lived, the "interrupted stream" broke forth once more "not long" after, and

> flow'd awhile in strength, then stopp'd for years;
> Not heard again until a little space
> Before last primrose-time.

The statements are part of the poet's announcement that he is returning to work after a delay of a "whole summer."

Concerning the "glad preamble," *Prel* I.1–54, *Prel*₂ I.1–45, it will be

628

recalled that such MS work toward these lines as survives from a date before 1800 consists only of draft, used for lines 20–21 and 43–47, in MS JJ (see *CEY* 256–57); and Professor Finch has shown (Finch THE 8–9) that the passage, at any rate as we know it, is unlikely to have been completed before 18 Nov 1799. Without quarrelling with Professor Finch's general line of reasoning, one may observe that the content of the lines as presently known would also seem likely to draw on the experience of W's journey of removal to his home at Grasmere in Dec; so that a date not before the Grasmere residence would seem a safer suggestion for any finished version (see *CEY* 30n, 285–86). W does not, of course, explicitly assert that the Preamble was the first passage composed of all the *Prel*; and completion of the lines cannot be fixed certainly prior to completion of the entire introductory section of *Prel* I.1–271; and that date, in turn, can not be fixed certainly, for reasons adduced below, prior to early 1804. But the implication of W's phrasing in *Prel* VII remains fairly obviously that the passage was composed very early; and the content of the passage can leave little doubt that its composition was connected with events that brought with them a prospect of prolonged opportunity for uninterrupted poetic labor. A date of perhaps c Jan 1800 appears reasonable, on balance, for completion of a basic version of *Prel* I.1–54 (see *CEY* 30–31).[1]

The fragmentary state of MS JJ makes speculation uneasy about any larger intentions W might have had as he wrote this MS for a poem using these materials, but his plan even then seems to have been that some survey of the poet's early life unfold, out of an assertion of either poetic mission or self-doubt, from the pivotal phrase "Was it for this" (see PREL 633). This intention is in any case plainly established by the later MSS U and V, which commence with those words. The absence of preceding lines in both these MSS, which were intended as fair copies, clearly indicates that effective composition of the introductory lines I.1–271 did not take place till after the completion of base MSS U and V, hence not before 26 Nov 1799.[2] The two-

---

[1] That the autobiographical references of I.1–271 are synthetically allusive to more than one journey is hardly to be doubted (see esp. Finch THE *passim*). W's reflection that he is not to be a "settler on the soil" [I.36], for instance, would probably fit his feelings concerning his earlier journey to Racedown, or departure from Goslar and journey to Sockburn, better than even his earliest thoughts about residence at Grasmere.

[2] The *terminus a quo* of MSS U and V is Nov 1799, as implied but unfortunately not stated *CEY* 31, 276: *Prel* II.33–47, added late to MS RV, probably drew on events of 2 Nov 1799; and the concluding lines of RV probably allude to STC's return to London in late Nov (see *CEY* 281). The completion of Part II in MS RV, which precedes U and V, thus is unlikely to have preceded W's return to Sockburn, on 26

part stage of the poem represented by U and V (on which see especially GCL 1, note 2) contains verses that in revision were used as, or reworked to the following (1805 line numbers, with one designated exception, in U–V order): (Part I) (a) I.271–304, (b) I.310–509, (c) I.535–70, (d) I.509–24, (e) V.450–72, (f) XI.258–65, (g) XI.274–316, (h) XI.345–89, (i) I.571–663; (Part II) (a) II.1–144, (b) $Prel_2$ VIII.458–75, (c) II.145–484. The corresponding passages in the Wordsworth-Gill and Parrish texts are: (Part I) (a) 1–26, (b) 27–206, (c) 207–33, (d) 234–46, (e) 258–79, (f) 288–94, (g) 295–325, (h) 328–72, (i) 373–462; (Part II) (a) 1–139, (b) 140–78, (c) 179–514.

The larger chronological patterns of the early stages of composition of *Prel* likewise stand in somewhat uncertain relation to descriptions in Book VII.1–13. The traditional assumption (see PREL xlvii) that the account there of the stream's breaking forth "once more" not long after composition of the Preamble and flowing in strength before stopping for years refers to the period of composition and copying of 1798–1799 is complicated by the fact that W is likely to have composed most of what became Books I and II before the Preamble. He then, after a prolonged break during which *LB* 1800 was prepared, probably returned to work on the poem in early 1801 (see below). Professor Finch has suggested that the work following the Preamble that took place during the second period of composition referred to in Book VII was work in early 1800 toward *The Recluse*. W, however, seems to be referring quite specifically in VII.4 to the progress of composition of "this Verse," the verse in hand, not to the greater task of *The Recluse*; and W would in this interpretation be ignoring one, and possibly two, periods of work definitely on *Prel* itself. Possibly W is referring to some preliminary composition on the Preamble in late 1798 (see *WBS* 4–5) followed by the stream of composition of the first parts of the poem as represented by MSS U and V, and neglecting both the practical composition of the Preamble and such work as took place in 1801—or is connecting any work of 1801 with the earlier

---

Nov 1799, from his walking trip of Oct–Nov 1799. MS U, the NB of which concludes with a copy of *The Beggar*, most likely in the autograph of SH, and MS V most probably date between 26 Nov and 17 Dec 1799. (See Jonathan Wordsworth and Stephen Gill, "The Two-part *Prelude* of 1798–9," forthcoming *JEGP*; GCL 1, note 2.)

A possible source for the lines (I.185–89) identifying Mithridates with Odin, in addition to those cited by the edition of Basil Worsfold (*Prel*, London, 1928, 581–82) and PREL 513–14, 632, may have been Joseph Cottle's long note about Odin at the beginning of his *Alfred* (London, 1800, 2–3), of which W perhaps knew something by late 1799 (see *STCNB* 494; *CEY* 274). He had not seen the complete poem, however, as of 19 Dec 1800 (letter, W to Cottle, 19 Dec 1800, Rosenbach Foundation; information from Professor James Butler).

composition. The literal facts as presently known do not seem to fit W's own phrasing about the earliest stages of composition very precisely.

With regard to the development of the poem between the copying of MSS U and V and the occasion when the sound of the "stream" was heard again, a "little space/ Before last primrose-time" (VII.12–13), W's description again leaves much unclear. The resumption of composition mentioned is undoubtedly that of mid-Jan 1804, and the suggestions of W's stream metaphor are manifold, but the statement that the stream had "stopp'd for years" before the time of this resumption (VII.11) is undoubtedly a simplification. As already implied, composition certainly went forward between the writing of MSS U and V and Jan 1804. JW's remark to DW on 28 Mar 1801 that he is "glad to hear that Wm is *going on* with the recluse," if a reference to *Prel*, represents a confusion of the "recluse" and the poem on W's own life uncharacteristic of the family's usual terms for discussion of the works, although in late 1799 STC spoke of the "tail-piece" of *The Recluse* (cf *JWL* 110, 209).

But there is little doubt that W was at work on *Prel*, perhaps in the late winter, certainly in the spring (probably not, of course, before conclusion of preparation of *LB* 1800 in late Dec). On 9 Apr 1801 JW writes to DW that he wishes that she "could send [him] the first part of the poem." He had thanked DW two days earlier in the same letter for two letters that had enclosed two large and full sheets of W's unpublished verse copied by SH. Then on 22 Apr he expresses his gratitude to DW for the "poems [that she has] copied" and his pleasure in "the corrections in the [2d *deleted*] in the poem[s *deleted*] to Col:" and adds that "the beginning of what Sara copied is very much improved and I like the poem altogether much better than at Grasmere." On [5] May he remarks that he likes the "additions & corrections in the long [poem]." (*JWL* 114, 117–19, 124.)

Identification of the verses to which JW is referring in his various remarks seems impossible. It appears highly probable, however, that his remarks of 22 Apr and 5 May refer to materials that fulfilled his request of 9 Apr. The obvious significance of "the beginning of what Sara copied" is "the first portion of what Sara copied," whatever that may have been. His words might, by attenuated speculation, mean "the lines properly preceding what Sara copied"; and the "first part of the poem" might by this interpretation have been the opening of, or even, conceivably, the entire first part. "[T]he beginning of what Sara copied" and the "first part of the poem" would rather more probably be one and the same. (It is unlikely that JW's statement of 22 Apr refers to corrections that took place between the sending off of MSS that had reached JW by 7 Apr and the writing of the materials he

631

received later but by 22 Apr, as he seems uniformly to speak of basic MS copy.)

If the two phrases do mean the same thing, but not something equivalent to "the entire first part," they suggest that W had written new lines for the opening of the poem since JW left Grasmere—possibly even ones presenting some complete version of the passage now I.1–271. JW's deleted "2d" might, further, have had to do with corrections on the second part of the poem; if so, the cancellation could be supposed a reflection of JW's consciousness of having had pleasure in the corrections to both parts of the poem. JW would seem unlikely to use such warm expressions about correction consisting mostly of the excisions that constitute the primary difference (aside from I.1–271) between the U–V text and I and II as copied in MS M. Negative evidence of another sort will be noticed hereafter that perhaps further encourages speculation that I.55–271 were written now; but these lines cannot confidently be supposed to have been in existence until early 1804. Other conjectures not less tenuous might be offered about JW's meaning, but the only clear fact would appear to be that W made additions and corrections to the poem between 29 Sept and 1800 and mid-Apr 1801.

Corrections evidently continued energetically for over a month following the transcripts for JW in the spring of 1801. DW's remarks of [29] Apr 1801 (*EY* 332) indicate that W had been ill as a consequence of his efforts at altering at least one "old poem"; and extreme symptoms of this sort had by 22 May forced him to allow DW to bar him access to "all the manuscript poems" (*EY* 335). What the interdicted MS poems were is uncertain, but as W had plainly been at work in recent weeks on *Prel*, *Prel* remains a highly probable object of his concern. The nature of any progress on the poem at this time however, remains obscure.

No report survives that W was engaged in other such work during the summer or autumn. *DWJ* reports him once more engaged with the poem at the end of the year: On 26 Dec he "wrote part of the poem to Coleridge," and on 27 Dec MH "wrote some lines of the 3d part of Wm's poem which he brought to read to us when we came home." On 28 Dec he was again at work, perhaps on related materials (*DWJ* M 73–74). The last two references noted might be to *RC*, on which W had worked 21–23 Dec (see *DWJ* M 71–73), but as W apparently did not work on *RC* between now and 26 Jan, and definitely worked on *Prel* on 26 Dec, chances weigh on the side of *Prel*. Drafts toward the opening lines of III are found on both the front and rear outermost pages and inside covers of MS 16 (see *CEY* 325)—which contains description of the Pedlar drawn on *Prel* III.82, 122–27, 141–47, 156–67 (see *Mus Hum* 167)—and these appear to have been written there after the rest of the NB was filled. That the opening of III was the first part of III written deliberately for the autobiographical poem to STC, and that the *DWJ* references allude to the earliest such work seem to me assumptions too vulnerable for definite ascription of the lines just mentioned to 25 or 27, possibly 28, Dec 1801; but supposition that the work of those days was toward III as we know it is reasonable, and the MS materials cited may be regarded as belonging in any event to 1801. Messrs. Wordsworth and Gill ("The Two-Part *Prelude* of 1798–9," forthcoming *JEGP*) regard it as "virtually certain" that W's work in Dec reached and stopped at III.167 (see *Mus Hum* reference cited). But Book III was not completed, as will be seen, before 1804.

No ambitious composition appears to have gone forward in 1802, although some work may have taken place on 25 or 26 Jan (see Appendix VI). *DWJ* next records W at work on the poem to Coleridge on 11 Jan 1803 (*DWJ* M 166). This composition cannot be identified. Other work possibly followed later in the year, although the main items of relevant evidence yield little distinct information:

(1) STC's remark on 14 Oct 1803 that W "has made a Beginning to his Recluse" (*STCL* II, 1012), if taken to refer to the completion of I.1–271, offers a convenient escape (employed PREL xlviii) from a vexing problem of dating; but the conclusion is hardly supported by the vague and emotional character of the context of the statement—nor is STC known ever to have identified the *Recluse* proper with the autobiographical poem addressed to him (see also Appendix VI). Further, DW's comments of 13 and 21 Nov that "William has not done anything of importance at his great work" and that "two little poems" suggested by the tour in Scotland are "all that he has actually done lately" (*EY* 421, 423) may not, indeed, preclude all possibilities of work on *Prel* during the autumn of 1803 up to that point; but added to W's explicit indication on 14 Oct that he has written since early Aug "only" three sonnets and the three lines later used as the beginning of *Address to Kilchurn Castle* (*EY* 409–10), they leave little chance that any *Prel* work can have gone on after early Aug. (Cf also *STCNB* 1546.)

(2) A statement made by DW on 25 Mar 1804 seems to imply some composition in mid-1803: she remarks to CCl then that W has written 1500 lines of the poem since STC left them (14 Jan 1804), and "since we parted from you [i.e., CCl] a still greater" addition to the poem (*EY* 459). The parting would seem to be that of the Cls' permanent removal from the Lake District in early July 1803, although DW

might be recalling also her return from her spring visit to Eusemere in early June (see *EY* 391–96; 1803:36). Unless she is thinking merely of composition within the few days preceding STC's departure from DC in Jan—and her phrasing makes this unlikely (nor could much composition have taken place then anyhow)—she must be alluding to work done in 1803 about July or early Aug, by 9 Aug (see 1803:45).

On 4 Jan 1804 W read "the second Part" of the poem to STC (*STCNB* 1801). In mid- or late Jan he remarks to Thelwall that he is "now after a long sleep busily engaged in writing a Poem of considerable labour" (*EY* 432). Between late Jan and 13 Feb he remarks to Wrangham that three parts of a projected five-book poem on his own earlier life are nearly finished (*EY* 436). On 13 Feb DW remarks to CCl that W is "chearfully engaged in composition, and goes on with great rapidity. . . . He walks out every morning, generally alone, and brings us in a large treat almost every time he goes." (*EY* 440.) W's comments, with others in Mar to be quoted below, seem, although slightly inconsistent, to justify the assumption that W resumed work about the time of STC's departure and was heavily engaged with the poem by sometime in Jan. The statement to Wrangham just noted may be taken as a strong indication that W had written the first 271 lines of Book I (including of course the earlier Preamble) by 13 Feb.

To summarize: Neither the chronological relationship of the Preamble to what W describes at the opening of Book VII as the early flowing of composition "in strength," nor that of the progress of the poem thence till early 1804 to what W in the same place describes as a subsequent silence of "years," seems capable of firm explanation in terms of other surviving evidence. While drafts of a few lines employed in the Preamble appear in MS JJ, the Preamble as a whole seems unlikely to date before 18 Nov 1799, and was perhaps composed mostly c Jan 1800. Lines 1–271 as a whole cannot be assigned a date before 13 Feb 1804, although some chance may exist that a version was composed in early 1801, by 4 Apr. The early more or less continuously developing composition that commenced in Goslar probably resulted in MSS RV, U, and V, by 17 Dec 1799. The two Parts copied in U and V include, of course, versions of passages later used as V.450–72 (the drowned man), *Prel*$_2$ VIII.458–75 (blank verse development of "Dear Native Regions" theme); *Prel* XI.258–65, 274–316, 345–89 (spots of time, gibbet scene, death of father). A significant, although (in proportion to the final poem) not great, amount of composition took place between 1800 and early 1804, especially probably in the early months of 1801; probably 26 and 27, and possibly 28 Dec 1801; 11 Jan 1803; and possibly July or early Aug (by

9 Aug) 1803. Probably some part of the opening of III and possibly other portions of the book belong to 1801. Books I and II were probably virtually finished in 1805 form and Book III largely composed (although not finished) by 13 Feb 1804.[3] It does not appear possible to assign W's various corrections of MS V to any particular time between that of the base MS and early 1804, although early 1801 would appear to offer an attractive possibility.

The obscurities that interfere with determination of the development of *Prel* from this point are not less dense than those already encountered. In such circumstances it will be useful to bear in mind that despite the three and one-half months' interruption in 1804 and the delays caused by JW's death early

[3] An important impetus to critical discussion has been provided by studies by J. R. MacGillivray ("The Three Forms of *The Prelude* 1798–1805," *Essays in English Literature . . . Presented to A. S. P. Woodhouse*, ed. Millar Maclure and F. W. Watt, Toronto, 1964, 228–44), by John Finch ("Wordsworth, Coleridge, and 'The Recluse,' 1798–1814," Diss. Cornell University, 1964, esp. Ch. IV), and by Jonathan Wordsworth ("The Growth of a Poet's Mind," *Cornell Library Journal*, spring 1970, 3–24), who have argued that MSS U and V present, in Mr. Wordsworth's phrasing (perhaps stronger than Professor Finch's) "a short, self-contained . . . poem," or, in Professor MacGillivray's phrasing, a "proto-Prelude." (See also Jonathan Wordsworth and Stephen Gill, "The Two-part *Prelude* of 1798–9," forthcoming *JEGP*, and *Prel*, ed. J. C. Maxwell, Middlesex, England, and Baltimore, U.S.A., 1971, 17.)

One must remember that the "poem" of 1799 is different in kind from that of 1805 (or at least was so in the eyes of its author) and that conclusions about the works as revelations of W's conscious artistic objectives or judgments must be qualified appropriately—in that W probably did not regard the 1799 poem as a work complete in itself. No external evidence appears to exist in family documents of this period that W regarded the poem as finished before 1805, although he of course planned for a while in early 1804 to make a conclusion in five books. "Was it for this," the in-complete-line opening phrase of MSS U and V, plainly implies that W intended pre-ceding matter that would explain the dangling "this." The concluding notations of MSS V and RV, "End of the Second Part" ("second" in RV; U contains no notation) are especially significant: MSS with comparable notations surviving from 1798–1804 include *SP* MS 2, *RC* MSS B, D, and E, and *PB* MSS 1–4. In all six of the MSS in which concluding notation appears, it is "End" or "The End"; in no case is a phrase like "End of part [ ]" used at the end; and a phrase like "End of part [ ]" is used in four of the eight MSS at the conclusion of sections other than at the last. The existence of two fair copies of this stage of the poem indicates the poet's satisfaction with what he had completed of it thus far. The poem's history during the next few years gives strong indication that his plans for its development from this point can hardly have been conclusively drawn when the copies were made. Two fair copies of a portion of the still-incomplete work were again written out in Mar 1804 (see discussion below).

in 1805, some eleven books of *Prel* were completed in the sixteen months commencing Jan 1804. W evidently radically altered his intentions respecting the length of the poem in Mar 1804; but this portion of the composition may be regarded, in comparison with the earlier, as relatively unified, and, if hardly steady, yet not impeded by prolonged attention to other poetic tasks.

The unique character of *Prel* MS M as the only surviving virtually fair copy of a part of *Prel* between 1800 and MSS A and B makes the fixing of the date of DC MS 44, in which the MS is contained, a necessary preliminary to subsequent discussion. This MS is described generally PREL xxx–xxxi, *STCNB* II, Part 2, 423–25, and above, Appendix III. The question of whether this MS was the one sent to STC prior to his journey to Malta has evoked long controversy. Cogent evidence that M is the MS that accompanied STC includes these facts (W's inference of Aug 1806 that STC's MS was destroyed —see *MY* I, 64—may be disregarded):

(1) Two MSS were prepared containing the materials copied in M (*EY* 448), but nothing is known, on the one hand, of the existence at any time of a third, or, on the other, of STC's having ever lost such a MS and having accordingly needed a replacement; and M is easily proven not to be the MS retained by W in Mar 1804 when the other was sent to STC (see PREL xxx).

(2) Sections of the MS are numbered by STC as if in accordance with their receipt as mailed packets. (see PREL xxx–xxxi; Appendix III.)

(3) As I have noted elsewhere (see *JEGP* LXIX, 1970, 532–3), a set of leaves is present that is not so numbered, MS 4 of *PB*, which contains on its first page a pencil annotation in Italian in the autograph of STC: "Fra 6 e 7." The note is clearly a direction for a binder: the MS of *PB* is bound between the sets of leaves numbered respectively "6" and "7." The instruction was fairly certainly written while STC was on his travels.

One item of evidence with contrary implication has till lately remained incontrovertible: that portions of the MS seemed to have been written in the autograph of SH, who cannot have helped prepare the MS sent to STC (see Moorman II, 2n; *EY* 459). Professor Betz has resolved this problem, however, in a forthcoming article which demonstrates that the autograph hitherto supposed SH's is actually MW's. It is thus reasonable to assume that the work begun "a little before last primrose-time" completed the version of Books I–V represented specifically by M, and, in effect, MSS A and B.[4]

[4] Thus this MS of *PB* was probably the one read by DeQ in 1809 (see Jordan 326).

Appendix V

DW writes on Sunday 25 Mar (*EY* 459) that STC was to have departed London for Portsmouth on the preceding day, and that he would have received the "last pacquet we sent off" three days before his departure, which DW evidently considered the termination of possibilities for reliable correspondence with him; and W assumed, as remarked P<small>REL</small> xxx, that STC had Book V by him on 29 Mar (*EY* 464–65). The entire MS M, hence, must have been sent off by three days before 21 Mar. STC apparently received on 16 Mar what he next day called "all" of W's poems; but on 18 Mar he found reason, via a note from DW in one of the packets, to expect yet another packet (*STCL* II, 1094–97). On 29 Mar W refers to "those last 3 books"—the context suggests that he is referring to *Prel*—in a fashion that implies that he possibly supposed that they arrived separately from the rest.

Much of available information on the subject of W's and DW's references to the progress of *Prel* hereafter, and the relation of these comments to specific parts of the poem, is treated P<small>REL</small> xix–liv, to which the following remarks are frequently indebted.

W's composition seems to have gone on rapidly between late Jan and early Mar of 1804 (see, for example, *EY* 445), except possibly c 20–24 Feb, when DW was seriously ill (see *EY* 443–45; cf Moorman II, 19). On 5 Mar W remarks to Hazlitt that he has been "tolerably busy this last month having written about 1200 Lines of the Poem on [his] own life" (*EY* 447). On 6 Mar he makes two pertinent comments: To DeQ he writes that the poem "is better than half complete"—"4 Books" long, about 2500 lines—and that he has just finished the part in which he speaks of his "residence at the University" (*EY* 454). To STC, probably later that same day (see *EY* 448–49), he writes that he five or six days ago finished a book of 650 lines and that he is arrived at the subject that he spoke of in his "last." He states finally, "When this next book is done which I shall begin in two or three days time, I shall consider the work as finish'd" (*EY* 452). W was planning a five-book poem when he wrote to Wrangham in late Jan or Feb; and his remarks to DeQ on balance imply that he is still planning a poem of that length, although his comment to DeQ that the poem is better than half complete is a curiously understated characterization of a work actually about four-fifths finished, and "work" might by tenuous speculation be regarded as a possible allusion to the "work" of preparing a suitable but not necessarily complete version of the poem for the MS being prepared for STC. As DW regarded herself and MW as having begun copying *Prel* and *The Pedlar* by 6 Mar (*EY* 448), one may safely assume that Books I and II had reached the form of MS M by then. What W had been doing during the last "five or six days" after

637

finishing a book of 650 lines is not known; much time perhaps went to completion of shorter poems.

Other comments make times of *Prel* composition later in Mar fairly plain. On 12 Mar W tells William Sotheby that he is "advancing rapidly in a Poetical Work, which [he hopes] will not be destitute of Interest," and has been "very busy during the last six weeks" (*EY* 455–57). On 25 Mar DW writes, as remarked above, that W has composed 1500 lines since STC departed DC—that is, since 14 Jan (*EY* 459). On 29 Mar DW writes to STC that W has begun another part of the poem and has "written some very affecting lines" which [she] wishes that STC could have taken with him; and W writes in the same letter that he is "now after a halt of near three weeks, started again." He adds: "It was very fortunate th[at you] were so earnest about having the poem. [It wa]s an intricate and weary job; but I do believe that one half of those last 3 books [has b]een preserved by it . . ." (*EY* 463–65).

One or two general conclusions may be derived: W's "halt of near three weeks" before 29 Mar suggests that he cannot have worked on original composition or broad reorganization of extant materials for many days after 6 Mar; a maximal allowance would place the termination of extensive efforts c 12 Mar, the day on which he speaks of himself to Sotheby as "advancing rapidly" on the poem (a characterization which of course hardly precludes his having written to Sotheby during a temporary halt). PREL li properly calls attention also to the fact of W's "almost constant superintendence" of the copying for STC, necessitated by the "wretched condition" of W's MSS (*EY* 459; see also *EY* 465). Further, in view of his letter-writing, walking, and reading on 6 Mar (see *EY* 449–55) he cannot have worked intently on the poem for more than part of that day. The plan for a five-book poem was thus probably abandoned, and Books III–V organized in the form in which MS M presents them, between 6 and c 12 Mar. The MS itself seems certainly to have been completed by 18 Mar.

The exact state of advancement of Books III–V on about 6 Mar must remain a matter for speculation. One problem posed by W's remarks of 6 Mar is that the book which he then speaks of having recently finished is said to have 650 lines—a total that fits Book III of the completed poem (672 lines) nicely, but fits Book IV (504 lines) rather poorly. Books I–III as now known, on the other hand, do not contain "about 2500" lines, the total mentioned to DeQ, or anything like that number, while I–IV contain 2331 lines, a sum not greatly divergent from W's rough total. It may be assumed in any case, in view of the composition after 6 Mar, that virtually all of the lines used in Books I–IV had been completed by that date, although there can be no certainty that Books III and IV even then corresponded to the books so numbered as they appear in MS M.

MS M reveals that Book IV was probably altered after 6 Mar so extensively as to be unsuited for STC, from a version that ended, as do all texts of IV from MS M on, with the Discharged Soldier episode. The opening lines of Book V in MS M were written by DW on a leaf originally containing the last nineteen lines of IV. These concluding lines, cancelled with a large X, are in the autograph of MW, who was the copyist of I to III, and appear to have belonged to the same process of copying that produced I to III. Below the conclusion of the cancelled materials appears draft by W toward the readings of IV.464–65 contained in the full MS M copy, which like the copy of Book V is in the autograph of DW. (The correction, and corrected M readings of 491–93, have been recopied in pencil, apparently by STC.) The first twenty-four lines of DW's copy of Book V are written on the verso of this leaf, and transfer of ink from STC's section number " 11 " onto the verso of the last leaf of DW's Book IV indicates that the cancel page was originally bound as a recto. The rest of Books IV and V is written on leaves cut (or torn) and folded from only three folio sheets (or six half-sheets) from which the paper of this leaf was not taken. Although the appearance of the second page of Book V does not suggest that the first was written out of sequence with the rest of IV and V, there appears no reason for the presence of this leaf except as a device adopted to save time because a copy of the opening of Book V was already present on it, having been written there by DW before W decided to alter the preceding Book so that its conclusion needed rewriting. Had the preceding Book contained some 150 lines more than that of the final copy, W's figures on 6 Mar would of course be quite accurate. That it was the fourth book referred to by W, however, is far from certain: it ends, as does the present Book IV, with the Discharged Soldier, but the present Book IV, while it deals with W's college years, is not about his "residence" at the university, the subject mentioned to DeQ.

A few more circumstances, however, deserve attention. First may be noted the implications of W's remark of 29 Mar, already mentioned, that he believed that STC's insistence on having copies of the unpublished poems was responsible for the fact that half of "those last three books" had been "preserved" (*EY* 465). W's preceding remarks suggest that he was referring to *Prel* III–V. In literal terms one-half of these books would amount to slightly over 900 lines. Some verse used in these books but certainly composed much earlier would seem to have stood in no danger whatever of becoming lost— notably versions of III.122–67, IV.363–504, V.389–422, and V.450–72 (see especially *CEY* 29–31), possibly also some few other lines of III (see above)—

perhaps some 300 lines altogether. W's remark can hardly be presumed to state that some 600 or so lines had long since been organized, more or less, in written form, for the rescue of those older lines would have been no less possible—if no less difficult—some other time. STC's urgency to have copies of the poems probably was not felt by W as a strong pressure till elaborated in STC's letters of 8 and 15 Feb (*STCL* II, 1060, 1065), by which time a considerable quantity of verse must have been drafted within the early weeks of the year. W is on balance more likely to be speaking of lines composed early in 1804 but either not written or else written in scribbles that would be legible only to the writer, and even then only when the writer's eyes were sharpened by fresh acquaintance with their content.

Other more specific Mar references to quantities of recent composition seem incapable of perfect reconciliation or complete explanation, although they indicate the energy of W's activities. It might be reasonable to assume, for example, that W's statement to Hazlitt on 5 Mar that he had written 1200 lines within the last month was intended as a rough approximation of the total number of lines composed in 1804: the figure of 2500 lines mentioned to DeQ as the length of the first four books as of 6 Mar minus the total number of lines in Books I and II as they stand in MSS A–B is 1345, and minus the 217 lines I.55–271 (if they were composed early this year) would be the much closer 1128. But W's "month" concluding 5 Mar obviously omits a known period of intensive production in late Jan and early Feb. The "six weeks" of work mentioned to Sotheby on 12 Mar seem more in accord with the length of time that W had been at work, but still short measure. W may also not have been intending to include, in his descriptions to Hazlitt or DeQ on the following day, lines not yet written in neat copy. Nonetheless, if one assumes that only some 300 lines of III–V had been written before Jan, W would in fact have written, between Jan and a few days after his comments to Hazlitt, c 1500 lines that actually appear in neat copy in MS M. And if one assumes lines I.55–271 written in early 1804, the lines written since mid-Jan would number over 1700. W's description of his work to Hazlitt would in this case seem oddly modest.

DW's remark of 25 Mar (before W is likely to have resumed composition in significant quantity) that W had composed 1500 lines since STC departed —that is, between 14 Jan and c 12 Mar—might fit circumstances better: if one assumes that some 300 lines of III–V had been written before 1804 and 216 of I were written in 1804, the total number of verses written in 1804 and used in I–V would be almost exactly 1500. If one supposes, however, that I.55–271 had been written before 1804, and that some 150–200 MS lines not used in I–V were included both in W's estimate to Hazlitt and DW's of 25

Mar, the actual amount that W was thinking of when writing to Hazlitt would fall somewhere about 1100 lines, and DW's estimate would still remain reasonably close. Enough lines survive, especially in the form of MS WW, to allow the last assumption to remain a possibility, although the content of all the lines concerned seems to me, as will be plain from remarks below, to point to early 1804.

MS WW was employed, at least at times, closely in conjunction with MS W (DC MS 38), and the two MSS may be usefully discussed together. WW, not described PREL, consists of twenty-three card-like leaves cut from a pocket NB, measuring 10.5 to 11 by 8.45 cm. One leaf contains a water-mark "E & P" over "1801." A few pages have been used by DW for rough notes concerning the 1803 Scotch tour.[5] Most surviving pages have been used for pencil drafts of *Prel*. While some of these drafts are more complete and organized than others, their obvious hastiness and remarkable illegibility make it fairly certain that they are the first drafts written of the lines concerned. The contents, as far as I have read them, may be described in rough and highly conflated fashion as follows (many of the lines in fact represent only very early, and not closely correspondent, drafts toward the lines as listed; and rejected lines, except for those on PREL 623–24, are not noticed): III.297–307, c329–c45; IV.c183–92, 201, 204–c21; V.17–37, 44–60, 103, 113, 121–35, 149–65, 301–2, c313–18, 322–25, 329–33, 336–37, 349,[6] 473–500, 538–48, 551–57,[7] c588–c607; VI.220–30, c323–c27, 347–54, 426–27, 469–c86, 494–97, 500–19, 524–30; VIII.711–17, 720–24, 727; XIII.1–38, 66–89 (readings practically as PREL 482–83 *app crit* from 482, 6 lines up to foot, and 483, line 3), 78–85, 89–90, 93–94; PREL 623–24, lines 1–7, 31–47.

The order of entry appears most likely to have run, in the terms of the description here used: III.297–307, c329–c45; V.17–37, 44–60, 121–35 (including 103, 113), 149–65, 349, c313–18, 301–2, 322–25, 329–33, 336–37, 482–500, 473–81, c588–c607; XIII.1–38; V.538–48, 551–57; XIII.66–89 (see description above), 78–85, 89–90, 93–94; PREL 623–24, lines 1–7, 31–47; IV.c183–92, 201, 204–c21; VI.c323–c27, 494–97, 500–19, 524; VIII.711–17,

---

[5] The notes look as if they might have been made while the tour was in progress, but their appearance is somewhat less varied than would be expected were that the case. DW later said that she took no notes at the time. (See *EY* 421; *MY* I, 111; "A Visit to Southey," *The Countryman* XXXVIII, 1948, 55–56.) The notes are so telegraphic as hardly to contradict DW's claim in any case.

[6] On V.294–349 see also *PW* V, 345–46; PREL 545–46; *CEY* 326. Cf Moorman II, 11. On the date of Book V see also Paul D. Sheats, "Wordsworth's 'Retrogrades' and the Shaping of *The Prelude*," *JEGP* LXXI (1972), 488–90.

[7] On V.553 see also *STCNB* 1706&n.

720–24, 727; VI.524–30; ?XIII.c89; VI.220–30, 347–54, 426–27, 469–86. But the appearance of the entries leaves little doubt that all were written at about the same time, and worked up in close interconnection with each other. With reference to the question of the advancement of *Prel* III–V on about 6 Mar, it may be remarked that this NB contains over 180 lines used for Books VI–XIII. Not all of these need have been written before 6 Mar—the draft toward VI.c323–c27 seems not likely to have been (*EY* 463)—but much of the NB itself is probably lost. The materials toward III and IV, on the other hand, tend to confirm that this MS was in use before that date.

The complexity of MS W likewise makes exhaustive description imposs-ible here. The small notebook in which it is contained was apparently origin-ally the physical counterpart of DC MSS 47 and 48 (which contain *Prel* MSS X and Y), also of MS 70 (which contains mainly drafts toward *Exc* IV and V), and of MS 45 (the Green family account book, containing the earliest surviving MS of the *Prospectus*). While the Green family account book contains sixty-one leaves and one stub, MS W, as remarked by EdS, retains only forty-four. PREL xxix accurately describes the first portion of the NB as used "first by W.W. for a copy of Marvell's 'Horatian Ode,' then by D.W., who transcribed a *Tale, Imitated from Gower* [see 1802:207] and afterwards a number of W.W.'s sonnets." Both of these may be assigned (in view of the probable date of the sonnet copies) to perhaps c late 1802.[8] The sonnets are listed in Appendix III. The *Prel* draft which was entered following these includes at least the following lines, here described in a highly conflated fashion (and without full record of rejected lines) in the order of the finished

---

[8] W states on 7 Nov 1805 (*EY* 642) that he has not seen Marvell's poems "these many years." W's copy differs from what was probably the only available printed edition of the poem, that in Capt. Edward Thompson's *Poems of Marvell*, 1776, in numerous accidentals and one reflexive pronoun, and his source may have been else-where. CL seems likely to have been a professed admirer of Marvell, and probably of the poem, at this time (*LL* I, 234, 335; Howe VI, 54; Pierre Legouis, *Andrew Marvell*, Oxford, 1968, 232–33); and both the Marvell and Gower copies may derive from the Ws' contacts with the Ls in London. The Gower copy is a verse adaptation of the first Tale of the *Liber Secundus* of the *Confessio Amantis*. It is in the autograph of DW with corrections by her.

At DC is a five-volume set of the "Bibliothèque Portative du Voyageur," including La Fontaine's *Les Amours de Psyche et Cupidon, avec le Poëme d'Adonis* (Paris, 1801), the *Œuvres* of Boileau (Paris, 1801), and the *Œuvres* of Racine (3 vols., Paris, 1802), with bookseller's label "Se vend à Calais,/Chez BELLEGARDE, Librarie,/Rue Egalité No. 6." Three of the volumes bear signatures "W Wordsworth" very closely resembling the signatures in the NBs like MS W. These NBs are perhaps the "Calais" books of which DW speaks *DWJ* M 166.

poem: IV.270–345 (see PREL 535), 353–65; V.1–7, 10, 19–25, 28–48, 294–376, 445–515, 590–94, 630–37; VIII.860–70; XI.42–44, 121–64, c176–85, 199–257, 274–77, 316 (entire line)–45; XIII.1–184 (see PREL 619–22, and 482–92 *app crit*); MS W materials quoted PREL 620–29.

Comparative readings and the appearance of the contents allow a few other remarks: The materials finally used in Book V, which follow the sonnet copies, appear to have been very early, perhaps first, among *Prel* materials entered. These seem to have been followed by the "5th Book" materials commencing with the Climbing of Snowdon; and the draft (beginning with fair copy) toward what is now IV.270–365 was also entered early on versos left blank when the *Horatian Ode* was copied. Generally, the materials used in XIII and XI (including the drafts quoted PREL 620–28) seem to have been entered beginning after the heading "5th Book" and to have run on to the end of the NB, thence on to available space in the front of the NB, concluding with draft toward XI.224–57, 274–77. At the rear, drafts toward XI.c176–85, 199–223 possibly preceded drafts toward 121–61, c243–53. In the front, the materials toward XIII quoted PREL 620–22 were fairly surely entered before the XI drafts were concluded. But the appearance of the MS leaves no doubt that most or all the copies and drafts were entered within a short time of one another.

Inverting and reversing the NB, one finds at its other end first a pencilled list of sonnets (see Appendix III)—possibly preparation for MS M, but probably preceding the sonnet copies at the front of the NB. A stub follows showing traces of lines 7–10 of "She Was a Phantom of Delight," then a page retaining, at the top, lines 17–20 of the same poem. Below this appears a rough pencil draft, used *Prel* VIII.860–70, which tells how the poet's scale of love for his fellow man was filling fast but was yet "high" compared to that in which lay the mighty objects of nature. This page is overwritten by drafts in ink toward *Prel* XI.c243–53, which are drafted in later form among the materials in the preceding part of the NB. The "She Was a Phantom" copy certainly preceded the copy of the poem in MS M, and thus does not date after 6 Mar (*EY* 448). Where MS W and MS WW contain parallel passages, it may be remarked also, the readings of MS W are later than, and often plainly worked off from, WW.

The relation of the "5th Book" of this MS to W's plans for a five-book poem seems to me on present evidence to remain ambiguous, and full discussion would require a quantity of transcription and editorial analysis beyond the limits of the present study. Among apparent indications that this "5th Book"—or at least all the MS now appearing to belong in it—was intended for a longer work is draft concluding the section of the NB dealing with books, the subject of *Prel* V, in which the poet apologizes to STC for his lengthy discussion of books, the later gifts of which "do yet remain untold," by announcing as an impending subject "an abasement in my mind/ Not altogether wrought without the help/ of Books ill chosen": materials following in the "5th Book" that might be construed as relating to such abasement appear too brief to represent the sequel contemplated, and the drafts concerned do not seem noticeably different in time of entry from preceding drafts. Messrs. Wordsworth and Gill argue toward contrary conclusions in "The Five-book *Prelude* of Early Spring 1804," forthcoming *JEGP*. See also the forthcoming Norton edition of the 1805 *Prelude* edited by Wordsworth and Gill, and my forthcoming Cornell Wordsworth Series edition of the 1805 poem.

Speculation about the date of I.55–271 may be brought to a close here. Evidence noted above appears to allow a possibility that these lines were composed before 1804; if so, c early 1801 appears the most likely time. MSS WW and W, however, suggest that in returning to his work on the poem in early 1804 W was preoccupied with the object of exploring in his poem the complexities and ironies of the relations between the physical world, personal identity, intellectual construction, and vital or creative being, with particular reference to the nature of books and great writers. MS W contains various passages used in Book V dealing with the physical frailty and immortal essence of books—the complaint that the mind lacks an element to stamp its image on sufficiently like itself; the dream of the Arab; the paradoxical characterization of Shakespeare and Milton, "labourers divine," as "poor earthly caskets of immortal Verse." It contains some of the lines used in Book V exploring the defects of education exclusively in terms of fact and rule, and the powers of fanciful literature to fit the mind to reality. It contains passages used in Book XI describing the poet's seduction by false taste and the ability of the eye to impose upon reality. It contains the notice of the poet's failing powers used in Book XI (especially 334–39); also "The Climbing of Snowdon" and discussion of the scene as an analogue of imaginative power; the descriptions, quoted PREL 623–24, of the rainbow and the motionless horse, with the accompanying discussion of nature's power to act on the mind; the sunrise dedication scene near Hawkshead; and the lines used at the end of Book VIII about the relative importance of nature and man.

In addition to earlier drafts of several of the same passages, MS WW contains drafts (used in Book III) of the incident of the poet's drinking libations to Milton at Cambridge; the affectionate reminiscence (used in Book IV) of the poet's "household dame" at school, Ann Tyson (including her use of her

Bible as a pillow); and, among verses used for Book VI, a description of the French countryside as a "book" before his youthful eyes, his memories of roving near Penrith in sight of the castle where Sidney might have penned part of his *Arcadia*, and lines beginning with the exclamation "Imagination!" The foundation of *Prel* from I.271 in a lengthy discussion by the poet of his unsuccessful efforts to form and pursue poetic objects comparable to the greatest poetic achievements of the past would appear so obviously akin thematically to his concerns in early 1804 that, in the absence of evidence to the contrary more cogent than that already noted, this time must be supposed the most likely for I.55–271—more particularly, as remarked above, a time by 13 Feb, by which date W had told Wrangham that three parts of the poem were nearly finished. All materials in WW or W would appear in fact to date from the spring, but a broader view of the relations between the materials discussed above and the chronology of composition of later books of the poem, from mid-Mar, is obviously appropriate at this point. Descriptions of two other MSS containing basic composition of 1804–1805 will make a useful beginning.

MS X, DC MS 47, is written into a NB physically similar to those of MS W and MS Y, and retains fifty leaves or stubs of possibly an original sixty-two. It opens with stubs on which remain traces of draft probably for *Prel* VI. 1–54 and possibly for VII.c78–c80. Next appear drafts toward VIII.736–38 and VII.92–c125. Next come stubs on which appear traces of VII.c136–39, 237–76, and whole pages on which appear drafts toward VII.182–238. Next stand drafts, respectively on the recto and verso of a single leaf, toward *Waggoner* IV.99–108 and *Exc* II.741–63. Both of these last two drafts certainly date from a time later than that of the surrounding entries, but probably tell nothing about chronological breaks in composition of *Prel*: the VII and VIII materials before them seem immediately interconnected with the *Prel* copy that follows (cf PREL li–lii). Next appears fair copy of the lines now *Prel* VIII.742–51; this runs directly on to a copy of VII.75–740 (end of the book). The remainder of the NB is occupied by a copy of *Exc* II.1–c725 (see *PW* V MS X readings).

The NB of MS Y, MS 48, retains fifty-four leaves or stubs. Much of the front part, as noted PREL xxxi, has been obscured by heat and water damage. First appears draft toward VIII.629–31 (these and all other materials in MS Y are in W's autograph unless described otherwise). The next legible writing, after a stub, is a fragmentary description of a baby (see 1803:108). Hasty verse draft follows, all apparently toward the first 160 or so lines of the 240-line passage quoted PREL 571–78 ("Two feelings have we"; lines 1–5 contribute to *Exc* IV.763–65), which was probably originally intended to stand where *Prel* VIII.159–72 now stand (see below). This is followed by drafts forming the basis of VIII.68–73, but here including XII.117. Next appears a copy of IX.293–[c521], after which appear VII.43–c50 (see facsimile opposite Prel lii). These lines run on to XIII.334–67, which run on to lines which became *Exc* II.1–26 (a passage here definitely describing the poet of *Prel*), which in turn introduces VIII.75–158. These lines lead on to the passage quoted Prel 571–78, which leads on to a draft of VIII.173–221. Next follows an alternate version of VIII.157–82, now omitting the Prel 571–78 materials. Next follows a copy of VIII.222–311 ("The Matron's Tale"—see 1800:148) in MW's autograph, heavily corrected by W. W's autograph then recommences with VIII.312–405. After a stub containing cancelled draft including work toward VIII.362–63 and a gap some five lines long appear lines 7–19 of the second section of the lines quoted Prel 581; these are cancelled also. The lines quoted Prel 581 here were possibly a false start toward a continuation of VIII materials on the leaf that is now only a stub, although they are closed off by a line drawn across the page. Next follows, in the autograph of MW, Book VIII.436–97, then the rejected passage quoted Prel 581, drawn on for *Exc* IV.404–12 and IX.437–48; then, in the autographs of MW and W, VIII.498–661.

A line count by W commences with what is now VIII.312 and runs forward, generally by twenties, through what is presently line 623, where the number "333" has been written above another number, "722." The numbering skips from "80" to "140" under the present lines 390 and 449, which are among the materials surrounding the stub and deleted Prel 581 materials just mentioned. The almost exact correspondence between the jump in the numbering of the MS and the length of the corresponding materials in VIII justifies the assumption that the thirty lines missing, which must have stood on the page that is now a stub, closely resembled the present VIII.406–35.[9]

[9] The discrepancy between W's total of "333" lines and the actual 311 to which W's total corresponds is probably basically accounted for—although the heavy alterations to the MS allow no certainty—by exclusion of twenty-seven lines (now presented Prel 581) following line 497 and addition of three and deletion of six lines between 584 and 611.

The "722" is less easily explained. It may be considered in connection with another enigmatic line numbering, either "1500" or "5500," under VIII.152. A count backward from the "722" to the "1500" (if that is the figure) through the "333" lines and what preceded them—VIII.222–311, 173–221, the 240 lines of Prel 571–78, and VIII.153–82—produces a total of 800 lines. This might be the explanation of the "722" itself, in which case the significance of the "1500" remains uncertain. The "722"

Next follows draft of materials apparently related to VIII.802–15, and draft of VIII.824–59. Then comes, without definite indication of division from the preceding materials, lines which became XI.9–14; followed by a version of XII.112–26 at first joined integrally to, then disjoined by revision from, the XI lines; then, beneath a line, by a relatively fair copy of a version of XII.112–277. The NB concludes with more draft, for the most part rough, including the following, here arranged according to the order of the completed poem: VIII.c355–63, c375–90, c418–28, c450–52, c479–90, possibly c561; XI.c48–c56; XII.174–77, 300–04; XIII.374–85, the last written vertically with some effort at neatness. Where VIII draft corresponds with work standing before in the NB, however, this draft seems earlier and hence is not likely to have been added later (cf PREL xxxii). Although correspondent draft for XII work standing before seems later, this work appears generally likely to date from about the same time, and to have been written in close connection with the main *Prel* work in the NB.

Several other points may be made about these MSS:

(1) DW's remark to STC of 29 Mar about the "very affecting Lines" that she wishes STC could have taken with him and that W has written since resuming work—evidently within the past few days—after his mid-Mar halt (*EY* 463, 465) fairly certainly refers, as conjectured PREL li, to the lines that became VI.246–331; and W's reference in VI.61–62 to his turning thirty-four "this very week" assures that those lines were composed within a week of 7 Apr and that W was at work on some portions of Book VI at about that time. If so, MS X, which contained work toward at least the opening of VI, may well also have been in use in the spring. (It has already been observed that the drafts for *Waggoner* and *Exc* near the front of the MS are plainly of later date than the *Prel* material.) Hence this NB in itself presents no evidence

---

added to 800, however, is obviously 1522: the figure may be part of a more inclusive line count.

Not much more light seems to be shed by the facts that beside line 156 of the passage quoted PREL 571–78 appears the number "400" and under line 221 of the same passage, "525." W's immediate intentions respecting cancellations are uncertain; but the lines total sixty-six as they stand and seem written out consecutively. As far as the "400" is concerned: even if one supposes that all the materials after the IX drafts which from their subject matter cannot be connected with the present lines) are materials leading directly on to the passage, and adds a presumed further forty-two lines corresponding to the present opening of VII to VII.43–51, *Exc* II.1–26, *Prel* XIII.334–67, VIII.75–158, and 156 lines of the PREL 571–78 passage, the total comes to only 350 lines.

tending to indicate that the parts of VII drafted here were written in the autumn rather than the spring.

(2) The lines in MS Y corresponding to VII.43–c50 are, as suggested PREL, fairly certainly work of autumn: sufficient traces of the passage remain, despite washing out, to confirm that its glowworm is described here, as in MS A, as the "child/ Of summer, lingering, shining by itself"; and readings from line 43 through 47 appear to correspond with MS A. The succeeding lines, however, continue:

> Nor is that invitation thrown away
> The last nights genial feeling overflows
> Upon this morning efficaceous more
> By reason that my Song must now return,
> If she desert not her appointed path
> Back into Nature's bosom.
>   Since the time
> When with reluctance I withdrew from france
> The Story hath demanded less regard
> To time & place [?&] where I liv'd & how
> Hath been no longer scrupulously trac'd [.]
>   . . . . . .
>
> I led an Undomestic Wanderers life
> In London chiefly was my home & thence
> Excursively as personal friendships [. . .]
> Or inclination led or slender means
> Gave leave I roam'd about from place to place [.]

The lines, which from the sixth were drawn on for XIII.334–47, do not imply that the poet is here resuming work after a long holiday. PREL lii states that a few pages have been torn out between the draft for *Prel* IX.293–[c521] and the draft for VII.43–c50, and on this basis concludes that "anything entered in Y *before* [VII.43–c50] must be the work of the spring." But the general appearance of the IX and VII draft does not differ significantly: a break between lines 48 and 49 is rather more marked, indeed, than that between lines 43–48 and the lines used for Book IX preceding them. No stubs or other evidence of the amount of material removed now remains in the NB. There exists no strong reason for supposing that the materials in MS Y used in Book IX were written there in the spring, although the copy concerned is probably mainly from previous draft which no longer survives. W's phrasing in the lines quoted also indicates (a) not only the prior existence or firm conception of a description of the poet's long visit in France (see especially X.189–92) as does, of course, the presence in the NB of IX.293–[c521], but (b) also the prior existence or firm conception of materials describing (with lessened attention to matters of time and place, residence, and manner of living) the period following the poet's return from France.

The phrasing of the passage, further, shows no immediate concern with the subject of the present Book VII, the speaker's residence in London. This indifference might result either from the poet's having already written materials corresponding to VII or from his having no intention as yet to treat the London residence as a subject important in its own right. The balance of probabilities will be discussed further below. Lines 1–74 of Book VII may of course be reasonably supposed to be work of the autumn.

(3) The draft toward *Prel* VIII.860–70 (the conclusion of Book VIII) in MS W reads as follows:

> Thus, more & more my thoughts were turnd to [?man]
> Nature had led me on & now I seemd
> To travel as it were without her help
> As if I had forgotten her but [?but]
> Even [?then] my fellow beings were to me
> Far less than [?She] was though the [?scal] of Love
> Was filling fast twas high as yet compared
> To [wh *overwritten* in] [?which] her mighty objects [?lay]
> [?If ? ?is ?fruit] if life [?] when to her
> [?That ?might] obj that [?whenever ?ye]
> Receive, what [?thy ?fellow ?beings]

This draft, as already remarked, almost certainly preceded drafts, on the same page, of materials toward what became XI.c243–53; and these XI materials are finished more perfectly elsewhere in MS W. The draft is possibly connected, to judge from theme, with work which produced IV.222 ff, but it tends to confirm that the poet's concern with the subject of the development within himself of love of man relative to love of nature, the topic of Book VIII, was well defined in the spring.

(4) In broad view, which comment below will attempt to focus further, the evidence of the MSS appears to indicate or to allow the possibility that W had written or conceived during the spring materials dealing with the main subjects and themes of the later portions of *Prel*: his postcollegiate travels and personal history, residence in France, the relation in himself between love of nature and love of man, and the nature of imaginative power. More exact speculations follow.

Possibly the firmest external clue to W's later progress on the poem in the spring from mid-Mar on is provided by W's remarks to Richard Sharp of 29 Apr (*EY* 470):

> I have been very busy these last 10 weeks [?having] written between two and three thousand lines, accurately near three thousand, in that time, namely 4 books, and a third of another, of the Poem, which I believe I mentioned to you, on my own early life. I am at present in the seventh book of this work, which will turn out far longer than I ever dreamed of . . . .

Even these remarks pose obvious problems. One is whether W is consciously referring to his entire production in 1804: "10 weeks" would look back only to mid-Feb; W's remarks to Hazlitt of 5 Mar look back to 5 Feb and those to Sotheby of 12 Mar back perhaps to late Jan. This puzzle is not, however, excessively troublesome: W seems to have composed lines in a quantity loosely on the order of 1500 between c 14 Jan and c 12 Mar, and he resumed composition, as DW's comments of 29 Mar indicate, between 25 and 29 Mar. So his remark to Sharp would in any case imply the composition of between 1000 and 1500, "accurately" near 1500 lines, between late Mar and 29 Apr. A more complex difficulty lies in W's description of this work as comprising four books and a third of another. The one-third book might be I.55–271, but his statements also indicate that he is fractionally advanced in a seventh book, and a plain interpretation of his remark is accordingly that he is one-third on in what he regards as the Seventh Book.

To suppose that W composed nearly 1500 lines between late Mar and late Apr is difficult for one reason because Book VI, which would seem likely to be one of the four and one-third books mentioned, and toward which W was fairly certainly composing lines in late Mar, contains, in the form in which we know it, only 705 lines—a total leaving as many lines again to be described merely as one-third of another book. PREL l–liii solves the problem by leaving Book III out of consideration (apparently as dating before the commencement of W's ten-week period, taken to mean "since February") and suggesting that the books referred to are IV, V, VI, one-third of VII, and some book now appearing in the poem after VII. This book is identified as Book IX, since the lines toward IX.293–[c521] in MS Y precede W's summer holiday, as indicated by a gap in the MS between them and lines used for VII.43–51. But it has already been noted that the gap concerned provides no apparent evidence of a significant chronological break between the MSS toward IX and VII.

Another impediment to the argument of PREL l–liii is that W would hardly, when his immediate purpose was to impress upon Sharp the abundance of his recent production, have reported himself at work on the "seventh book" of the poem without mentioning that another book had also been written intended to stand after that one—in other words, that he would have neglected to refer to some eighth book (whether to be numbered VIII or a higher number) if it existed. If W's figure of "nearly 3000," however, was a loose calculation comprehending all the books that he had basically written in 1804 together with their total number of lines even where these lines included verses composed originally earlier than 1804—and it is reasonable to suppose that in a rapid calculation he would think of the line totals in the Mar fair copies of III–V—the total number of lines in these books, III–V plus VI as it now stands plus one-third of another (calculated on the basis of the average number of lines per book in Books I–V, 612), would come to 2722. If the one-third book were I.55–271, the total would be 2835. W may also have been including in his total a few lines already composed but not yet organized within books, despite his apparent equation of his "nearly 3000" lines with four and one-third then-extant books; his phrasing is in any case sufficiently explained by a minimum total of 2722 lines. There seem no firm grounds for guessing the content of a seventh book of which W may have thought that he had composed one-third. In view of what has been said, materials following the heading "5th Book" in MS W toward what became Book XIII, materials used in Book VIII or XI in MSS W and WW, or some portions of IX or X, all appear possibilities.

The evidence of MS Y implies that Book VIII was probably worked out mostly in the autumn. Surviving MS evidence, as indicated, neither confirms nor denies extensive composition concerning the visit to France before autumn, although some sort of work on the subject certainly had taken place by the time that W wrote the passage in Y quoted above. MS X, on the other hand, contains no work that appears necessarily to date from the autumn. Work on a book like the present VII in the spring is not a certainty, but as in the case of Y copy already discussed, a large portion, at least, of this copy is likely to be from earlier MSS. This MS itself may well date from the spring. The likelihood that the NB was used in the spring is increased by the presence there of work on the opening of Book VI. The general appearance of MS WW precludes the possibility of its having been used over a long period of time, and fairly well assures that none of its drafts dates later than spring. And the close connection of the MS WW drafts toward the opening of XIII with the related materials in MS W quoted Prel 620–29—together with the lack of any indication that the NB was used in the autumn (draft there used as VIII.860–70 has been shown above to be work of the spring)—

further encourages the assumption that the contents of MS W date from the spring.

Thus the materials that became Book XI, one may conclude with additional confidence, were accumulating rapidly at that time: with the passages of XI already composed by the time of MSS U and V taken into account, most of XI.121–389 (the book finally contained only 397 lines) would probably have been written (along, of course, with a substantial portion of XIII), although one cannot be sure of the time of organization as book, during the spring. Materials after "5th Book" in MS W probably date after 6 Mar. It may also be remarked that the neat copy XII.112–277 in MS Y commences with comment about the city but is concerned mainly with the subject of love of man; and the lines are plainly copied into MS Y because of their connection with the theme "Love of Nature Leading to Love of Man," a theme which, as noted, had perhaps begun to concern W in the spring. Thus the subject matter of the present Book VIII may have been at some time before the writing of MS Y intimately connected with the poet's considerations of what is now the main concern of Book VII, his residence in London. The organization of the bulk of Book VI may be supposed, on the basis of the small amount of evidence available, to belong to a time between late Mar and 29 Apr 1804. Work of autumn was probably in large part a process of sorting out and developing more discretely subjects well in mind in the spring, although evidence does not indicate as satisfactorily as one might wish the main subjects of W's work.

One may fairly conjecture that W wrote some 2750 lines, if not fully 3000, in 1804 by 29 Apr. With 1150 lines of Book I and II added, *Prel* would by late Apr already have contained some 3900 lines. W continued composing, however, and apparently at a good pace, till 13 June, when he stopped, as matters turned out, for some weeks (see *EY* 477, 481–85, 489, 500). In 1810 W was described by DW as "deeply engaged in composition" when producing fifty or more lines a day (*MY* I, 392); and DW notes that on 29 Mar 1804 W wrote twenty lines in three-quarters of an hour (*EY* 463). If an average rate of composition, minimal by such standards, of thirty lines a day is supposed for the period 29 Apr to 13 June, W would have composed about 5200 lines of *Prel* by 13 June.

W probably did not write much, if anything, between 13 June and early Oct 1804. The combination of what is known of his activities during the late summer (see esp. *EY* 511) with the statements at the opening of Book VII and with DW's remark to CCl on 15 Oct that W "goes on with his work again" (*EY* 511), also with his statement to Sir GB on 25 Dec that he has written "upwards of 2000 verses during the last ten weeks" (*EY* 518), appear to fix the time of resumption fairly certainly about early Oct and to indicate that composition went forward rapidly during the autumn. He remarks to Sharp on 30 Nov that "not long after my last letter to you, I fell again to work in earnest at the Poem on my own earlier life and have dispatch'd 1,600 or 1,700 lines of it since that time" (*EY* 513); but that particular statement does more to indicate the time of a lost letter to Sharp than to clarify *Prel* chronology.

On 9 Dec DW states that W "is well and works hard" (*EY* 514). PREL l apparently indicates that lines X.933–34 must have been written shortly after 2 Dec, when "a Pope/ [Was] summon'd in to crown an Emperor." As a date of composition this is reasonable: official confirmation that the Pope intended a journey to Paris appeared in the *Times* of 30 Nov. The suggestion of PREL liii that the reference shortly below (X.947–51) to STC's being in Syracuse implies a late Dec date of composition is, however, uneasy: on the one hand, DW on 23 Sept (*EY* 502) supposed that STC had been in Sicily since mid-Aug and "might probably" depart during the first week in Oct, and W is not likely to have written the passage by that date; on the other hand, the Ws probably did not have definite word of STC's departure from Syracuse before mid-Feb (see *STCL* II, 1156–57).

Even the slender evidence of X.933–34 serves to show unequivocally that W was at work on some portion of Book X in Dec. It has been noted already that beyond the point of the draft for VII.43–c50 MS Y is quite certainly work of autumn, but that there is nothing in the appearance of the preceding materials to suggest that they are not also of that time. The amount of fair copy and draft in MS Y alone is over 1100 lines, and if most of Book X had been composed by 25 Dec (for instance, through lines 933–34), W's "upwards of 2000 verses" would be accounted for at once. The fact is hardly likely to be quite so simple: no evidence, one may recall, precludes work on Book VII in the autumn. But the suggestion may help in a general way toward some conclusions concerning the late stages of composition in 1804–05. It may be added parenthetically before proceeding to these, that drafts, on a portion of a NB of mathematics instructions, of X.445–66, 568–74, and "There Was a Spot," survive as part of DC MS 74, and may reasonably be attributed possibly to autumn 1804 also (see Appendix VI).

In general, the completion of *Prel* from late Dec was probably a process of filling in, expanding, and arranging materials already in existence by 25 Dec. Substantial portions of all the books following V had almost certainly been written by that time. The 2000 lines composed in late 1804 by 25 Dec combined with the possibly 5250 lines in existence by 13 June would leave only about 1200 lines yet to be composed for completion of the 8484-line poem.

Composition apparently continued without serious interruption through Jan and early Feb of 1805: "My Poem advances quick or slow, as the fit comes," he writes c but by 8 Feb (*EY* 534); on 10 Feb he is said to be going on "almost regularly" (*EY* 538). Following receipt of the news of JW's death, however, he did not return to work till late Apr. He writes to Sir GB on 1 May that he has turned his thoughts again "to the Poem on [his] own life, [and has] added 300 lines to it in the course of last week." "Two more books," he adds, "will conclude it." (*EY* 586.) The "two books" were probably, as implied already, books that needed, for their completion, more organization and revision than actual basic writing. One may reasonably suppose that the final organization of XII and XIII took place in early 1805, and perhaps at this time. On 4 May DW writes that W's poem "is nearly finished" (*EY* 592). MS Z, DC MS 49, probably dates from this general time, not before late Apr.

MS Z is sufficiently described for present purposes Prel xxxii: it contains Books XI and XII in well-organized form, although the first forty-two lines of XI are written on the second of two stitched-on leaves that contain also X.690–711, and that hence (in view of the probable time of composition of X) possibly date as early as late 1804 or very early 1805. All readings with parallels in MS W are, where different, uniformly later in MS Z and probably from intervenient MSS. The Windy Brow NB, MS 10, it may be added, contains a draft of lines toward XI.164–90 intermediate between MSS W and Z, probably preparatory for Z and written near the same time. As noted by EdS, the headings of the two books copied in MS Z are "Book 12th" and "Book 13th," a fact which EdS reasonably interprets as indicating that Book X was then divided in two as subsequently published in 1850. At the top of the first page appears the number "366." This looks like a page number, but no similar numbers appear elsewhere in the MS. The direction "back again nine leaves" on the first page of the main MS, on the other hand, implies the earlier presence of preceding main MS materials, although the present first two leaves look as if they had been stitched on specially and by themselves to replace leaves cut out.

In all, the MS may be taken to indicate that the poem through the present Book X was by now organized into a form roughly similar to that of the present work. The paper from which Z is made up (the stitched-in leaves, as well as main MS) is the wove paper watermarked 1801, described Finch *HG*, of which other known uses are confined to the period between c 23 Feb 1805 and 28 Dec 1807: so from the standpoint of negative evidence, at least, this MS would certainly appear to date from 1805, and not before late Feb— hence, in fact probably not before late Apr.

One may safely assume that the presence of a "Book 13th" (the present twelfth book) in MS Z shows W within sight of his two-book goal. The surviving portion of Z may thus be supposed written by c early May. A further comment of W's to Sir GB on 3 June—"I finished my Poem about a fortnight ago" (*EY* 594)—establishes the probable time for completion of the poem as c 20 May.

Professor Betz's conclusions concerning the autographs of SH and MW establish that MW was the copyist of *Prel* MS B (as well as of *Waggoner* MSS 1 and 2 and DC MS 57). DW's phrasing on 2 Mar 1806 that SH "came when Mary was at Park House and we have kept her ever since, having been engaged in making two copies of William's poem" (*MY* I, 10) does not indicate who has been doing the copying, but the time when DW made the copy that is now MS A is fairly clear: she was "engaged in making a fair and final transcript" of the poem on 29 Nov 1805 (*EY* 650) and seems likely to have begun copying at about that time. By 14 Dec at least five books had been copied and the old copy of these books had been lost in transmission to MW (*EY* 653; *MY* I, 3–4). The lost MS was found by 27 Jan, but has since disappeared again. Eight books had been copied by 25 Dec (*EY* 660, 664), and the remainder of the copy was probably finished in early 1806, certainly by 2 Mar of that year (*MY* I, 10). Paper watermarked with a crowned horn-in-shield and countermarked "1798," not otherwise known to have been in use before 1806 (see Appendix VII), is found in this MS, one bifolium at the conclusion of Book VII, then frequently from the commencement of XI, and in MS B frequently from III onward. MW is unlikely to have done any copying before her return to DC—that is, 29 Dec at earliest.

The interchange of corrections between A and B is complex, and probably reflects more than one stage of very early revision. While it is probable that little of the basic copy of B was written before the corresponding part of A, the general similarity of appearance of the two leaves no doubt that they were prepared in close connection. MS B had been completed by 2 Mar (*MY* I, 10).[10] A note by MW at the conclusion of B, "June 1805," apparently represents a slightly inaccurate recollection of the date of the original completion of the poem. The word "Finis," probably in the autograph of STC, stands at the end of Book VI in MS B, but the entire poem was, as has been shown, already in existence when the note was made.

[10] DW's reference to "Sara's copy for Coleridge" on that day notes not a copy of *Prel* but of *Recollections*, presently DC MS 55 (cf *MY* I, 10n; Prel xx).

APPENDIX VI

The Chronology of Home at Grasmere, Prospectus, The Ruined Cottage, Guide to the Lakes, and The Excursion

The content of portions of *HG* of course strongly suggests composition in 1800. The following passages for example, seem especially likely to reflect conceptions from that year:

> 71–79 ("On Nature's Invitation")
>
> 170–92 (Arrival and early residence at Grasmere. Perhaps in form resembling *PW* V, 319–20, lines 170–71 *app crit*: perhaps c but after 10 Mar. See *PW* V, 475. Cf Vergil, *Æneid* III.645–48.)
>
> 238–68 (The two swans. Perhaps c but not before early Mar.)
>
> 471–90 (Prospects opening to the newcomer.)
>
> 502–44 (Dwellers in sight of the vale.)
>
> 648–63 (JW. Perhaps between late Jan and late Feb, as the lines suggest that JW is present and MH and STC are yet to come.)

And some work possibly proceeded in spring 1801 (see Appendix V).

The following considerations advanced by Finch *HG*, however, appear to establish beyond question that main composition took place in summer 1806:

> (1) When W speaks on 6 Mar 1804 of his contemplated "moral and Philosophical Poem" (*EY* 454), he mentions having written only "one Book and several scattered fragments" of the work; and the "one Book" can only be *RC*.
>
> (2) On 3 June 1805 W speaks to Sir GB of his conceptions of "the task of [his] life" as including a "narrative Poem of the Epic kind" (*EY* 594–95); but in *HG* he specifically renounces "All hope which once and long was mine, to fill/ The heroic trumpet with the Muse's breath" (see *PW* V, 337–38, lines 745–53, & *app crit*).
>
> (3) MS A, DC MS 58 (commencing as *PW* V, 318 "A" readings for

151/2—"We will be free" [the twenty-fifth line numbered 215], in W's autograph except for 190–237, which are in MW's), is written on paper watermarked 1801 of which no other known example among Wordsworthian MSS was certainly in use before early 1805.

(4) MS B, DC MS 59, a complete copy in the autographs of W, DW, and MW (Finch identifies MW's hand as SH's), is written on the same sort of paper.

(5) MS R, DC MS 28, which contains drafts for 75–77, 383/84–648 (see *PW* V, 326–34; the lines include *Exc* IV.332–72, VI.1080–1187), contains also early drafts toward *The Waggoner* probably dating from early 1806 (II.145–49, 155–56; III.1–2), which definitely precede portions of the draft for *HG* (corresponding to *Exc* VI.1116–25 and some later lines); and the *HG* draft precedes MS B.

(6) W is not reported as again engaged in composition toward his great work after completing *Prel* in May 1805 before July 1806 (see *EY* 617, 650, 664; *MY* I, 58, 61, 64).

(7) DW on 23 July 1806 reports W engaged in rapid composition on *The Recluse*; W announces on 1 Aug composition of 700 lines of the poem within the last month; and on 8 Sept W states that he has been busily employed lately: "I wrote one book of the Recluse nearly 1000 lines, then had a rest, last week began again and have written 300 more" (*MY* I, 61, 64, 79).

To these circumstances may be added the fact that although DW states on 25 Mar 1804 that she and MW have been engaged in making "a complete copy of William's Poems for poor Coleridge to be his companion in Italy" (*EY* 458), MS M, surely the MS which STC took with him to Malta, is not likely to have contained the poem (see Appendix III). While parts may have been in existence, DW's phrasing does not encourage the belief, otherwise hardly tenable, that well-developed portions would have been omitted from a MS collection being prepared for the deeply concerned adviser from whom W was then urgently seeking crucial aid in developing *The Recluse* itself (see, for example, *EY* 452, 464). The same consideration applies, perhaps even more decidedly, to the *Prospectus*, which W first published separately from *The Recluse* and which is seen joined with *HG* for the first time in *HG* MS B (see also Appendix III). Another fact bearing on the date of *HG* (and *Exc* as well) is that following 8 Sept 1806 nothing is heard of composition toward *The Recluse* till 29 Sept 1808, when W reports to Samuel Rogers that since he last saw him (in the spring of 1808) he has written 500 lines of his "long Poem" (*MY* I, 269). As the meditative *TofP* fairly certainly dates from about this time, and is itself almost 600 lines long, most or all of the verses that W is describing to Rogers probably belonged to *TofP*. (Moorman II, 131–32 suggests that the lines published as *To the Clouds* may also have figured in W's calculations.) After W's statement to Rogers, nothing more is heard of work for the great poem until 28 Feb 1810, when DW describes W as "deeply engaged in composition" and continues: "Before he turns to any other labour, I hope he will have finished 3 books of the Recluse. He seldom writes less than 50 lines every day." (*MY* I, 392.) As will be remarked again below, the work that DW is here referring to is almost certainly toward *Exc*, and no grounds appear to exist for speculation that basic composition of *HG* dates from that time or later. Yet another item of evidence for a date of 1806, finally, is the lesser fact of W's facetious but probably fairly accurate description to Sir GB, on 1 Aug 1806, of a ludicrous interruption by a pair of summer visitors to the Lakes one recent morning while he was "calling some lofty notes out of [his] harp, chaunting of Shepherds, and solitude, etc." (*MY* I, 64), phrasing obviously if loosely suggestive of the content of *HG*.

MS 28 contains also a prose draft, forming the basis of *Prel*$_2$ IV.354–70, on the subject of solitude. The prose draft is written over pencil draft of verse toward the beginning of the story of the Motherless Family, *Exc* VI.1116 ff, here for *HG*, and it thus dates not before the time of use of MS 28 for *HG* drafts. It is fairly certainly associated with the *HG* composition and thus probably dates between c late June and c Sept 1806.

Various details concerning the date of composition of *HG*, however, remain unresolved. Among the most obvious of these is the exact character of the development of *HG* in the summer of 1806. It appears impossible, for one thing, to be certain of the relative order of writing of MSS A and R, MSS 58 and 28. The drafts toward lines 75–77 and 597–607 in MS R, in the autograph of MW, appear to be toward the late MS D. The other drafts may be supposed to date, like MS B, between c late June and early Sept. Corresponding portions of MSS A and B are closely similar, although A precedes B, and it is reasonable to suppose that the presumably c 190 lines that stood before the materials surviving in MS A (the twenty-fifth line of which, as remarked above, is numbered "215") closely resembled the opening portions of MS B as well. Lines 117–28, which probably draw on the fragment entitled "To the Evening Star over Grasmere Water, July 1806," first published by Knight (*PW* Knight, 1882–89 IX, 389–90; *PW* Knight, 1896 VIII, 262)—whose title one has no choice but to accept—from leaves of DW's journal apparently no longer surviving, were by this evidence probably unwritten and not a part of MS B before July 1806, and they may have been present in some form in MS A. MS B is thus to be dated, from line 117 in any case, probably July 1806 or after. Professor Finch and, more lately, Professor James Butler, have advanced more detailed conjectures about the progress of the composition of *HG* as revealed by MS B. Professor Butler, in "'This Sublime Retirement': A Textual and Literary Study of Words-worth's *Home at Grasmere*," Diss. Cornell, 1971, conjectures particularly that the portion of the MS commencing after the line numbered by W "878" (664 in the final text) represents the portion composed after W's temporary rest from composition c late Aug. The appearance of the MS leaves little doubt that all the copying in it was intended to be fair, and that all the basic copy was done at about the same time, although at many different sittings; and the break at line "878" seems no more decisive than that following the line now numbered 702. I am not confident, thus, that the MS confirms the chronological division suggested.

Yet other problems remain, among them the fact that MS A, although it dates plainly from an early point in the development of the poem as a coherent unity, is generally too neat for first draft. Further, a small section of MS A, lines 290–305, is written on a slip of paper that has been stitched on to a space left blank, plainly to allow room for the stitch-on, on the larger sheet. A MS of not less than that portion of MS A was thus in existence already. The stitched-on slip contains part of a watermark of a horn-in-shield over an elaborate cursive monogram, perhaps GR. I have found only two identical examples of this watermark, these in letters to W from TCl and CCl written from Purfleet on 1 and 14 Mar 1805 respectively. The fact that a portion of the MS partially preceded MS A does not therefore constitute an indication that *HG* achieved coherent form before 1806. Possibly a blank space in a letter from CCl lying nearby may have been used before MSS A and B for fragmentary fair copy. CCl of course visited Grasmere for several weeks late in 1805 (see 1805:61).

To summarize briefly: Some work on *HG* may well have gone on as early as 1800, and various portions may have been composed, at least in W's mind, between that time and 1806. But no occasion can be fixed prior to mid-1806, on present evidence, when W can have composed the poem in its basic present form. The drafts in MS R are certainly very early and can hardly date before that time. These suggestions, although not without ambiguity, provide a basis for a proportionately limited examination of other problems connected with the chronology of the *Recluse*, especially the date of the *Prospectus*, the post-1800 *RC*, and *Exc*. Discussion of the date of *Recluse* MS D will be postponed until various relevant questions concerning the paper of the MS have been taken up in other contexts below.

A quick survey of the main items of external evidence will be a useful beginning. In describing his great poem to DeQ on 6 Mar 1804 W says that he has written "one Book and several scattered fragments" (*EY* 454). On 25 Dec of the same year he remarks to Sir GB that he has written about 2000 lines of *The Recluse*, including *The Pedlar* (*EY* 518). *The Pedlar* in the version of MS M (*RC*)—and it is surely this poem of which he is thinking when he speaks of "one Book" to DeQ—probably contained about 1000 lines (the surviving MS is not complete). To repeat information cited earlier, W in describing his recent composition to Sir GB on 1 Aug 1806 says that, having returned to *The Recluse*, he has written 700 additional lines for it within "this last month." On 8 Sept he talks of having lately written "one book . . . nearly 1000 lines," then, after a rest, "300 more" within the last week. His phrasing is not perfectly clear. The explanation offered by Professors Finch and Butler is that the first 878 lines (as above described)—so counted and numbered by W—were in Aug regarded by W as a full book which he in Sept described as "nearly 1000 lines," and that the "300 more" were the lines that brought the total to the "1047" lines—so numbered by W—of *Recluse* MS B. The "878" is the only unrounded line numbering in MS B apart from the "1047" at the conclusion, and indicates a full count of all preceding lines up to that point, as if to a stopping place. While W does seem to have been capable of overestimating quantity of composition, the succeeding copy, as already remarked, shows no special sign of having been written after a long break.[1] W's remarks to Sir GB of 8 Sept 1806, also, seem to suggest that he

---

[1] One example of overestimation appears in W's statement of 25 Dec 1804 to Sir GB about his *Recluse* work. The identity of the "scattered fragments" of *The Recluse* mentioned to DeQ by W when describing extant composition on 6 Mar 1804 is obscure, but no tally based on available information identifies 1000 more than RC of the "about 2000 lines" of *The Recluse* later spoken of in Dec. Among the materials in his mind when he made the earlier statement may have been some of the fragments copied in DC MS 16, including lines corresponding to *Exc* IX.1–26, 124–52 (see *PW* V, 286–91 and *app crit*; *CEY* 327) and VIII.276–334 (see *PW* V, 274–76 and *app crit*; *CEY* 327); *Redundance* (*PW* V, 346); the fragment "For Let the Impediment" (*PW* V, 344–45) eventually contributive to *Prel* XII.194–201; parts of other fragments quoted by *PW* V, 340–45; lines associated with *Nutting* (see *CEY* 331–32), esp. "I Would Not Strike a Flower," also in MS 16 (see PREL 612–14), or portions of the lines quoted *PW* II, 504–06 from the same source (see *CEY* 332); lines from the "Addendum" to RC MS B eventually used *Exc* I, IV (see *PW* V, 400–04); materials in DC MSS 38, 43, 47, and 48 used in Books V–XIII of *Prel*, including "Two feelings have we also from the first" (PREL 571–78) and portions of unused draft for *Michael*, among them "The Matron's Tale" (*Prel* VIII.222–311).

Not much of *Prel* MSS X and Y, DC MSS 47 and 48, is likely to have been written

had not only completed the "book" before he rested, but also that the additional 300 lines were distinct from that completed book. Since portions of *HG*, if not the *Prospectus*, had probably been conceived as early as 1800, W's phrase "nearly 1000 lines," unless intended to refer only to the actual process of copying out the lines, may well have been an extremely generous estimate of real composition even for the 1047 lines of the completed MS B, not to mention the "878" lines. No certainty exists, of course, that W was thinking of MS B at all. If, however, all remarks in 1806 do refer to the materials of MS B as divided from line 878, W would first have been making an exaggerated description of 878 lines (which he had surely totalled prior to his remarks) as 1000, then have been describing an additional 169 lines (which he seems likely to have totalled in the whole with his note "1047" upon completion of copying) as yet 300 more. The miscalculation seems of curiously large proportions. Another problem is posed by negative evidence: there is no reason to suppose that W abruptly stopped composing on 8 Sept. It seems entirely possible that a large number of verses were composed c Sept 1806 that are now unidentified. These must have been written, if they were written, elsewhere from MS B as it now survives.

Much further speculation about the identity of such lines would seem profitless. Some portion of *Exc* II may be, however, a remote possibility. The description of the vision of the cloud-city at the conclusion of the story of the Old Man Lost can not have been composed before 5 Sept 1807 (see *Exc* IF note—*PW* V, 417–18—and 1807:78); but the rest of the story need date only after 8 Nov 1805 (see 1805:99). While the story is not recounted in MS X (MS 47), pencil and pen drafts of II.741–63 are present there, and the preceding copy and draft for *Exc* II.1–c725 includes the description of the Old Man's funeral and the announcement by the Solitary that he will tell the Old Man's story: so the story would very likely have resembled the one

---

by early Mar 1804, however, when W wrote to DeQ; and by late Dec Book VIII of *Prel* is likely to have been near completion, including "The Matron's Tale" and excluding "Two Feelings Have We from the First" (which contains 240 lines). W is of course not likely to have worked much on blank verse except toward the poem on his own life between Mar and Dec. Even if some scores of lines possibly composed for *HG* as early as 1800 are added to those just noted the overall total of the lines mentioned seems, although not calculable precisely, well short of 1000. That W had by Mar 1804 composed many other lines eventually used for *Prel* but then thought of as for *The Recluse* is not a likelihood on the basis of present information. Overestimation is thus both a possible and obvious explanation of some part of W's Dec 1804 total, and it may affect his remarks about recent composition on *The Recluse* in 1806 as well. But the main text above explains why it more probably does not.

supplied in MS P. But it is to be remarked also that MS 47 was used by W early in 1806 for a draft of *The Waggoner* IV.99–108, which appears on the recto of a leaf on the verso of which appears the pen draft toward *Exc* II.741–63. The fundamental structural difference between the narrative method of *Exc* II and the discursive meditation of *HG* separates the works in an obvious way, and the apparent connection between the sort of tale told for the Old Man and the kind of composition probably going on c early 1810 makes a date about the latter time an attractive likelihood for those verses (see below); but *Exc* II also includes a considerable amount of philosophic comment within the dialogue, and W wrote a significant amount of narrative verse for *HG*—notably the stories of Wilfred Armathwaite and the Motherless Family (eventually used *Exc* VI.1080–1187)—between 1 July and early Sept 1806: so that composition of these *Exc* II materials of MS X c Sept 1806 remains a remote possibility.

Yet to be noticed, although they do not pose a large problem respecting the development of *The Recluse*, are three comments of STC written in 1803: one, made 10 June, that W has wished STC to "write to him at large on a poetic subject, which he has at present sub malleo ardentem et ignitum" (*STCL* II, 950); another, of 14 Oct, that W has "made a Beginning to his Recluse," doing so as a consequence of the entreaties of STC, who has "seen enough, positively to give [him] feelings of hostility toward the plan of several of the Poems in the L. Ballads," considering it "a misfortune that Wordsworth ever deserted his former mountain Track to wander in Lanes & allies [sic]" (*STCL* II, 1012–13); the third, probably written within a few days of the second, that W "has bidden farewell to all small Poems—& is devoting himself to his great work . . ." (*STCNB* 1546). W's wishes as characterized by STC in the first instance sound quite similar to ones that W himself was expressing a year later (see especially *EY* 452, 464) when still awaiting the advice requested from STC, and when he had still written very little indeed of the work concerned: he remarks on 6 Mar 1804, "I should reproach myself forever in writing the work if I had neglected to procure this help." With regard to the second and third instances, DW states to CCl on 13 Nov 1803 (*EY* 421) that "William has not yet done anything of importance at his great work," and eight days later remarks (*EY* 423) that "William has written two little poems on subjects suggested by our tour in Scotland [concluded 25 Sept]—that is all he has actually done lately . . ." (see also *EY* 409; Moorman I, 604–05). While W had almost certainly written more than two short poems since the tour (see 1803:105–1803:120), DW's comments appear a much more certain reflection of actuality concerning a long poem than STC's. W may well have been thinking about the poem through the year 1803, and he may have expressed an intention, c early Oct, to resume work on it; but if any composition toward a major poem occurred at all, the poem was probably *Prel* (see Appendix V), and the composition not in Oct.

Scattered comments of other dates pose a small difficulty—DW's record, for example, of W's reading "parts of his Recluse" to her on 13 Feb 1802 (*DWJ* M 90; see 1802:34); or the fact of W's reading "a part of the Recluse" to Davy between 11 and 15 Aug 1805 (*EY* 634; see 1805:67). No references by name to *RC* occur at a time near the latter statement, and W had spoken of *The Pedlar* on 25 Dec 1804 as part of *The Recluse* (*EY* 518); the allusion in that case may accordingly be to *RC*. But the earlier remark occurs as an apparent specific distinction of the lines mentioned from *The Pedlar*, and it is hardly possible that if a distinction between *The Pedlar* and *RC* were intended, the *RC* as a story of Margaret would thus suddenly and uniquely become *The Recluse*. Known fragments (see note 1 above) would supply an ample body of materials for recitation, however, and may have included short portions of *HG*.

The *Prospectus* now commands attention. As already suggested, the probable omission of these lines from MS M implies that they had not been composed by early Mar 1804 (see above, and Appendix III). Hence late Mar 1804 appears the probable *terminus a quo* (see Appendix V). MS 1, the earliest surviving copy of the *Prospectus*, appears in DC MS 45, a notebook otherwise used for family accounts (none before 1808), accounts concerning the Green family, and a fragment of prose in the autograph of DW, seemingly psychological speculation about the daughter of a blind man.[2] The NB is similar to those containing MSS 38, 47, 48 and 70 (see *CEY* 29n), with blue-green cardboard covers. MS 45, seemingly the most complete surviving example, contains sixty-two leaves. All the NBs are inscribed inside one cover, apparently with the same pen, "W Wordsworth," "Wm Wordsworth," or "William Wordsworth." MS 38, MS 47 (already mentioned as *Exc* MS X), and MS 48 contain, among other materials, *Prel* MSS W, X, and Y respec-

---

[2] The subject of the prose fragment suggests Idonea-Matilda in *The Borderers*. The gender of the person considered is indicated by a single hastily written word which I read without perfect confidence as "her." W is not known to have worked on *The Borderers* during the years shortly after 1800, and the appearance of the MS is not indicative of priority of entry. This sort of NB was apparently not used by W before c late 1802 (see Appendix V). The common concern which this fragment shares with the Letter on the Education of a Daughter suggests also a time about that of the Letter, possibly c Mar–Apr 1804.

tively; and MS 70 contains drafts of lines used in *Exc* II, IV, and V. MS 70 was in use as late as 1810 (see below), while the others, apart from MS 45, were probably used between possibly c late 1802 (see Appendix III; Appendix V) and 11 May 1810.

Paper provides even less clue to date in the case of EdS's MS 3, actually MS 2, which contains on one side *Prospectus* from "[must] hear humanity" to the conclusion, and on the other two quotations concerning Chaucer (see below) and the single phrase, used in *Prospectus* MS 1, "Innocent mighty spirit." Comparative readings show that this MS preceded and probably provided the copy text for EdS's MS 2 (MS 2 is thus actually MS 3), *HG* MS B, DC MS 59. The actual MS 2, in DC MS 24, is written on a leaf of laid grey paper measuring 14.5 × 22.3 cm. Ripping and other marks in the various leaves of MS 24 permit conjecture of the order in which the leaves formerly stood in relation to each other. But the poems copied upon them will indicate that this order, here described, implies little about relative dates: The *Nutting* fragment discussed *CEY* 331–32; leaves containing drafts for *Fidelity* (between late July 1805 and 2 Mar 1806); leaves containing very early drafts for *Address to My Infant Daughter, September 16, 1804*; leaves containing drafts for *Written with a Slate Pencil on a Stone on a Side of the Mountain of Black Comb* (probably between Aug 1811 and 1813), with, on the verso of one such leaf, the following brief draft of a classification of W's poems, which appears obviously later than W's letter to STC of 5–7 May 1809 (*MY* I, 331–36) and earlier than the classified listings in the Yale (Tinker Collection) copy of *P2V* (YUL; see 1811:72) and the final copy for *P* 1815:

These Poems are to be divided into th[ree] classes
1st according to their subjects as childhood proceeding through the Intermediate [?stages] till old age
2ndly accordingly to the mold in which the composition is cast. as Inscriptions Sonnets. Characters. Naming of Places &c
And 3rdly
According to the Powers. Of Fancy Imagination. Thought, or Observation put forth in the Composition of them.

The quotations concerning Chaucer on the *Prospectus* leaf are (1) the lines from *Il Penseroso* used from 1820 as the epigraph to *The Prioress's Tale* and (2) a quotation about Chaucer from Drayton's *Elegy to Henry Reynolds*, used as epigraph to the 1841 *Poems of Chaucer, Modernized* (see *PW* IV, 472). The quotations possibly date from as early as late 1801 or as late as the preparations for *P* 1820 (see 1801:117n). The last such leaf contains *Troilus and Cressida* and perhaps dates from c Dec 1801. The writing on the first three MSS noted is inverted in relation to that of the remainder (thus the writing runs forward in one direction from the first page of the *Infant Daughter* MS through *Nutting* and in the other from the first page of *Black Comb* through *Troilus and Cressida*). Only one page number remains on these leaves, a "69" on the first page of the *Nutting* fragment, which is on paper different from that of the other leaves. The content and complications of the leaves are preoccupying, but do not appear to fix a date for the *Prospectus* more exact than between c late Apr 1800 and 1820. But the priority of this MS to EdS's MS 2 of course limits the time more narrowly. Since EdS's MS 2 was probably written between late June and early Sept 1806, this MS may be supposed no later than early Sept 1806. The probable absence of the verses from MS M, as indicated, suggests that no approved text existed before late Mar 1804 (see Appendix III). No evidence, on the other hand, absolutely precludes composition—and such a speculation remains persistently appealing on the basis of content—between 1798 and 1800 (see *CEY* 29).

A main problem in tracing the progress of *RC* between 1800 and MS M is the ambiguity, perhaps incapable of resolution, that obscures the relations of the titles *The Pedlar* and *The Ruined Cottage* as used in *DWJ*. Some MSS possibly belonging to 1800 or after have been treated in *CEY*: *RC* MS D, as there stated, was probably written between possibly c 14–21 Mar, more certainly very late Apr 1799, and perhaps c 5 June 1800; the copy in the Alfoxden NB toward the description of the Pedlar quoted *PW* V, 405–08, lines 5–82, was there assigned a date between 6 Oct 1798 and early 1802 (*CEY* 28). The "addenda" to MS D (see *PW* V, 405–09) of course postdate the earliest probable date of D and are all likely, with two exceptions, to have been copied into MS 16 by Oct 1800 (see *CEY* 326–28). The exceptions are Addenda iv and v, which like the Alfoxden NB lines just cited may be dated between 6 Oct 1798 and early 1802, but are especially likely, as *PW* suggests, to have been written while work was going forward on *The Pedlar* in late 1801 or early 1802. In a forthcoming article Professor James Butler argues persuasively, on the basis of his researches into watermarks and related evidence, that MS E—despite the reasoning of *PW* V, 409–10—is unlikely to date as early as 1802, and more probably belongs to late 1803 or early 1804; and that MS E_2 almost surely belongs to the process of copying that produced MS M; and was thus written c early Mar 1804. (See also 1802:49.)

Jonathan Wordsworth notes omission of most lines descriptive of the Pedlar's background from *RC* MS D and their inclusion in DC MS 16 as surplus material following MS D; and he reasonably concludes that this treatment of the descriptive lines indicates that they have been rejected from the main body of *RC* (see especially *Mus Hum* 157–71). The use of the title *The Pedlar*, by STC from 9 Oct 1800 and by DW from 21 Dec 1801, in reference to a poem almost certainly containing description of the Pedlar and closely related to *RC*, but not definitely inclusive of the story of Margaret, opens the possibility that the rejected materials may for a time have been thought of as belonging to a separate poem called *The Pedlar*. While most of the references to *The Pedlar* might possibly be no more than uses of a new and preferred title for *RC*, the *DWJ* entry for 8 July 1802, noting that W was looking at *The Pedlar* when DW arose and that he "arranged it, and after tea [she] wrote it out—280 lines" seems a reference to a complete poem. *The Pedlar*, as a description of the growth of the Pedlar, might thus have existed for a while as a separate poem; and if it did, the likely time is the period between 21 Dec 1802 and the writing of MSS E-E$_2$. The materials of the composition may be largely represented by *The Pedlar* in the text of *Mus Hum* 172–83. Professor Butler, however, offers attractive arguments that the "280 lines" were a full copy of description of the Pedlar, of which only a single leaf, edited PW V, 405–08, now survives, at the rear of the Alfoxden NB. Addendum iv is shown by comparative readings to precede the Alfoxden fragment. Some possibility may remain that DW's phrasing in her Journal entry of 8 July 1802 does not intend to record that she copied an entire poem, but simply that she "wrote 280 lines" that put a revision of the poem into order. The trace disappears, anyhow, with the writing of MS E, where the poem as a union of the Pedlar's history and the story of Margaret becomes established, as far as surviving evidence goes, as W's definitive conception.

This description of the progress of *RC* and *HG* will have suggested that a great amount of continuous or methodical composition toward a poem similar to the present *Exc* cannot have taken place before late 1809 or early 1810, although many passages used for later books of the poem, and possibly some portion of Book II, were already in existence. The nearly 600 lines of *TofP* were probably, as already remarked, written for *The Recluse* in the summer of 1808. W seems fairly surely, however, to have been hard at work on what can properly be called *Exc* on 28 Feb 1810, when DW, as already noted, describes him "deeply engaged in composition" and expresses a hope that he will have finished "3 books of the Recluse" before he turns to any other labor (*MY* I, 391–92). On 11 May 1810 she adds that W has been "deep in poetry for a long time," and to the detriment of his health, but "has written most exquisitely" (*MY* I, 408). Following this statement, however, a year passes without indication that W is advancing in his work on the poem.

Such silence justifies the speculation that little composition went on from c late May 1810 until c early May 1811. W is next known to have been thus engaged only as of 12 May 1811, when DW states that "William has begun to work at his great poem" (*MY* I, 490). On 14 Aug 1811 she reports that his poem "has been at a stand ever since he made a visit to Water-Millock" (*MY* I, 502), possibly c early July. She describes him on 27 Dec 1811 "at work with his great poem" and arranging the published ones (*MY* I, 527). On 29 Mar 1812 SH states that he "has been busy with the *Recluse* but the smoke put him off" (*SHL* 46–47). He may therefore have composed a large number of lines during the ten months commencing May 1811—more exactly, between c early May and c early July 1811, and between late Aug 1811 and late Mar 1812. The next surviving reference to such work dates from 5 Jan 1813, when DW remarks—implying that not much work can have gone on recently (and see 1812:99–1813:4)—that W has begun to look into his poem "within the last two days" (*MY* II, 64). On 27 Aug 1813, however, SH states that W is "over head & ears in his verses" (*SHL* 64). And, finally, DW remarks on 24 Apr 1814 (*MY* II, 140) that W's long poem "has been copied in my absence" (that is, since 19 Jan). She adds: "[G]reat alterations have been made some of which indeed I had an opportunity of seeing during my week's visit [perhaps 17–24 Mar]. But the printing has since been going on briskly. . . ." W had apparently made inquiries of Longman about publication c mid-Mar (Owen LLW 25–26). He was busy with the printer's devils c 26 Apr (*MY* II, 144). Longman had not received all of the MS by 20 May (Owen LLW 26), but a date of c late May is probably likely for the completion of the poem as published. Copies were being distributed on 4 Aug (see 1814:62).

The content of *Exc* and the appearance of the MSS offer a few other clues; but the chronology of the poem remains, in all, highly speculative. More detailed conjecture should follow examination of the progress of W's efforts toward the work that probably claimed more of his attention during the period 1810–1812 than any other save *Exc* itself, the *Guide to the Lakes*, written as the letterpress for the Rev. Joseph Wilkinson's *Select Views in Cumberland, Westmoreland, and Lancashire*.

At least four kinds of materials are present in the main body of G MSS, DC MS 68: (a) draft toward G 1810, published there in much the form of this draft; (b) fair copy clearly preceding G 1810 but not published in this form; (c) draft for a guide but almost certainly, on the basis of content, written after G 1810; and (d) draft seemingly not definitely assignable on the basis of content to either before or after G 1810, and thus to be dated, if at all, by other means.

Highly abbreviated descriptions of the MSS follow. In the first category fall:

(1) A half-folio sheet without watermark, laid, containing draft concerning Borrowdale corresponding to G 1810 p. 42, lines 5–27.

(2) A quarto single and a double sheet containing draft concerning the Ullswater area, corresponding to G 1810 p. 44, line 28–p. 46 end. (1) and (2) were made by dividing a folio sheet.

(3) A quarto double sheet containing draft concerning Buttermere, Ennerdale, and Wastdale, corresponding to G 1810 p. 42, line 28–p. 43, line 9 up. The portions corresponding to p. 42, line 28–line 20 up and p. 43, line 24–line 9 up are written by DW, the rest by MW. The autograph thus confirms the astute suggestion of Moorman II, 160 that DW was the author of the portion of G describing Wastwater Screes. This MS thus probably dates from 11 Nov 1810, when DW states that she was employed by W "to compose a description or two for the finishing of his work for Wilkinson" (*MY* I, 449).

In the second category fall:

(4) A portion of a leaf of fair copy headed "Section 2," containing on the recto a cancelled beginning "On the best approach to the Lakes &c" and on the verso description of the area of Seathwaite. W has written a brief undated note, plainly to Joseph Wilkinson, at the head, advising that he is sending herewith "matter for two more numbers"; will send for two additional ones in a couple of days; and supposes that Wilkinson will judge best to print "matter for two numbers with each month," as Wilkinson has only six months before him and his numbers are twelve.

(5) Another portion of a leaf of fair copy also sent to Wilkinson (the address panel, with postal stamps, but none containing a date, remains) headed "Section 3d/ Donnerdale &c &c. continued," concerning (recto) Ulpha Kirk and (verso) Yewdale and Tilberthwaite. Also present is a note by W (undated) advising that CW has subscribed to Wilkinson's venture and requesting that "a copy of as good impressions as you can command" be sent to CW. This fragment is stitched on to a quarto double sheet to be discussed below. Items (4) and (5) were originally parts of a single folio sheet.

(6) A folio of fair copy containing "Section 4th/ Upon Windermere

&c" and "Section 5th/ Windermere &c in continuation." A panel with an address to Wilkinson remains. The folio is written on laid paper watermarked with a crowned horn-in-shield and counter-marked "1798," apparently the paper of (4) and (5) also. Items (4) to (6), although originally fair, contain extensive cancellation.

In the third category fall:

(7) At least portions of material on a folio double sheet, and all of a quarto double sheet commencing "The little inconvenience," concerning ways of approaching the Lake District and also dealing with Lancaster Castle. Copy on the folio at one point breaks off with the note "Here take up Wilkinson's Book." Fair copy on the quarto sheet starts with copy from this draft and continues with minor variants as part of p. 37 of G 1810.

(8) A quarto double sheet headed "Donnerdale" ("The head of Conistone Water....") which breaks off, after dealing with the approach to Seathwaite, with the note "See part of an old letter." The "old letter" is clearly (4) above, marked "X" at the point in the description of Seathwaite that would link it with this draft. The term "old letter" is used also in (9) to refer to a letter sent to Wilkinson.

(9) The quarto double sheet onto which (5) above is stitched. The recto of (5) breaks off with brief mention of "a pleasing Epitaph the only one in the place if I remem[ber]" at Ulpha Kirk and a reference to a druid circle. The quarto sheet commences with an actual quotation of the pleasing epitaph, as if it had been copied at Ulpha Kirk by W or an associate since the writing of (5). The same sheet contains a recommendation of an ascent of Black Combe, following which appears, centered on the page, the single word "Poem." W's reference must be to either *View from the Top of Black Comb* or *Written with a Slate Pencil . . . Black Comb*, neither of which is likely to have been written before late Aug 1811 (see 1811:45). W passed more than two hours at Ulpha Kirk perhaps on, certainly within a day or two of, 6 Sept 1811 (see 1811:46). The text of the quarto double sheet runs on to the verso of the stitched-on (5) with the note "see old letter stitched to this sheet."

(10) Two long quarto sheets containing, in the autograph of DW, materials related to G 1810 pp. vii–x, but clearly developed out of the printed version. These materials in effect constitute a basic draft of G 1820 p. 235, line 14–p. 239, line 12. The paper of (10) is laid, with a watermark of a cursive "P" and a countermark of "1810."

This is the only MS among these materials that clearly corresponds with a portion of the "Introduction" of G 1810 rather than with parts of "Section I" or "Section II."

Into the fourth category fall all other G materials among the MSS classified as DC MS 68. These include descriptive discussion of the area of the Duddon, Coniston, Hawkshead, Windermere, Ambleside, Grasmere, the road to Keswick, Borrowdale, and W's Essay on the Sublime. The last develops around description of the Langdale Pikes, and thus fills an important gap in the descriptive materials. Except as already described otherwise the paper of all these G MSS is laid and watermarked with a cursive "P" over "1806." Except for the folio sheets mentioned in (1) and (8) and the MS dealing with Grasmere and the road to Keswick, which is on a folio folded to a quarto, the paper has been divided into quarto single or double sheets. Paper, general character of autograph, and content leave little doubt that (1) to (3) were written at about the same time, and before G 1810. The bulk of the quarto MSS (including the Essay on the Sublime), which appear to be of slightly darker and often coarser paper, seems to have been written within a short time, mostly in the autographs of W and MW. The paper and autograph of the Essay on the Sublime so closely resemble those of most of the rest of these materials that it is reasonable to suppose that the essay grew out of the same considerations and was written within the same period as they. The MS dealing with Grasmere and the road to Keswick contains direct allusions to the etchings. The reasons for my not including this sheet in the first category above, where this obvious tie with Wilkinson's work would seem to place it, will be given below.

G MSS are also found in DC MS 69; these include draft entitled "Borrowdale," certainly later than the materials on the same subject described above, and brief drafts dealing with fashions in viewing and writing about scenery and with the journey from Ambleside to Keswick. These materials, the first and last in MW's hand, the other in W's, must be supposed of the same general date as the post-G 1810 materials mentioned already, a date to be discussed hereafter.

Evidence fixing the dates of several categories of MSS described is scant, but the following additional notes may be made: (a) W seems to have written some remarks on the Sublime c very late 1805 or early 1806 (see 1805:120). (b) W described himself to Lady Holland on 26 Aug 1807 (see 1807:73) as then preparing a guide for Lake tourists; and he seems to have spoken in similar terms to John Marshall at about the same time (see 1807:61). (c) A letter from W to the Rev. J. Pering, 2 Oct 1808, indicates that an attempt to write an account of a brief tour soon after in 1807 came to nothing (see 1807:82), and in that same letter W admits an incapacity for topographical description. (A desire to avoid further correspondence with Mr. Pering possibly contributed to W's self-deprecation in this instance.) (d) Nothing more is heard of any such project, apparently, till 1809. In that year, however, Joseph Wilkinson wrote to STC shortly after receiving the first issue of *The Friend* (1 June 1809): "I am just returned from Town, where I have been making arrangements for my publication, and as I have seen some of Mr. Greens numbers I will be obliged to you if you will tell our friend Wordsworth, that no two works, descriptive of the same country can be more different, or less likely to interfere with each other, than his and mine. but I shall write to Mr Wordsworth in a few days more fully upon the subject when I hope either Mr W- or yourself, or both, will afford me the assistance I shall explain to enable me to make my work more perfect and acceptable to the public than it otherwise would be[.]" W had evidently received word of Wilkinson's project, and perhaps an overture for assistance, already, but been concerned about the project's possible effect on the sale of his acquaintance William Green's *Seventy-Eight Studies from Nature* (1809). Equally clearly W had yet to arrive at a specific arrangement with Wilkinson. On perhaps 17 Nov 1809, however, DW records that SH has been busy transcribing "the introduction to a collection of prints to be published by Mr. Wilkinson" and that "he has only finished the general introduction, being unable to do the rest till he has seen the prints" (*MY* I, 372).

Nothing among surviving MSS suggests that he altered his "Introduction" significantly before its publication, which had evidently occurred by 10 May 1810 (*MY* I, 404); but his "Section I" and "Section II" appear to have undergone considerable revision before they appeared. W's note in (4) above seems best explained as an indication that W regarded himself as at work on installments for twelve monthly numbers of Wilkinson's, but that six of those numbers had already appeared, so that Wilkinson would therefore presumably wish to print two of W's installments for distribution each month with his remaining numbers. One interpretation of W's statement that he would "send for" two more numbers would be that he was drawing on a backlog of Wilkinson's prints and was writing, as DW had earlier supposed he would, materials closely related to the numbers. The prints were published four at a time on the first day of every month in 1810 except 1 Aug and 1 Sept, when three and five prints, respectively, were published; but the order of publication bears no conceivable relation to the progress of a tour of the Lakes, the concept underlying W's "Section I" and "Section II." W may thus have begun writing his descriptions only about June 1810.

It is difficult to imagine, on the other hand, that W can have seen even what is apparently the first of Wilkinson's installments (nos. 20, 22, 40, and 45 of the finished volume) and still have supposed it possible for him to write a description of a tour as a direct accompaniment to Wilkinson's numbers as they appeared. W may have seen proofs of the engravings, sent in a different order; or his "send for" may merely be a slip for "send." Had W, on the other hand, never intended to coordinate his letterpress with the order of the prints as issued but only with the prints as a group, it would have made sense for him to wait till the series was well advanced before he began writing. The engravings as bound correspond in general order with the content of the letterpress.

What is clear is that if any plan for publication of portions of W's letterpress in installments ever existed, it was not carried out. The MS containing a tour in "sections," of which the latest surviving part is (6), was, to judge both from the event and from the cancellations on (4), (5), and (6), returned to W for reduction and reorganization. Possibly Wilkinson and W had misunderstood each other from the outset, Wilkinson expecting commentary more closely related to the individual prints than that which W supposed that he was to supply; so that a condensed tour was a compromise for mutual convenience. Perhaps W had already decided to write a description of a tour as a result of having formed goals—to be discussed shortly—independent of Wilkinson's work. But, to return to strictly chronological considerations, while evidence is insufficient to support conjecture of a *terminus a quo* later than 17 Nov 1809, W had in fact received a number of prints by 10 May 1810 (*MY* I, 404); and a time about June 1810 would appear to remain a distinct possibility for the writing of at least (4), (5), and (6). Work for Wilkinson had probably reached a conclusion by c mid-Nov 1810. Hence (1) to (6) may be dated probably between 17 Nov 1809 and 11 Nov 1810, perhaps between c June and 11 Nov 1810 (a special problem posed by (1) will be dealt with below). Items (4) to (6), to judge from content, probably were written before (1) to (3), which seem to have been published with little revision; and (3) was probably concluded on 11 Nov 1810. The balance of evidence allows the conjecture that (4) to (6) and perhaps more materials of the sort were written c June and "Section I" and "Section II" mostly between W's return from his long absence from Grasmere, c 29 June—possibly c but by 3 Sept, and 11 Nov. Dates of publication of the prints probably nowhere offer decisive evidence of date of writing: the engraving of the bridge at Brathay (no. 14), published 1 Dec, is mentioned long before (on p. 44, line 2) the conclusion of Section II, and before materials probably composed 11 Nov (see (3) above).

W had contemplated, and was in some degree pursuing, objectives that extended beyond the needs of Wilkinson's project even before he wrote the portions of G 1810 following the "introduction." Perhaps on 17 Nov 1809 DW wrote to CCl that she had encouraged W to write a guide and to prefix it to the introduction that he had already written: "He has some thoughts of doing this; but do not mention it, as Mr. W's work should have its fair run. He mentioned to Mr. Wilkinson his scheme, to which I should think that Mr. W. would have no objection; as the Guide will, by calling Mr. W.'s publication to mind, after its first run, perhaps help to keep up the sale." (*MY* I, 372.) The time of publication of "Section I" and "Section II" of W's letterpress remains uncertain. No pertinent advertisement has been found. *Jollie's Cumberland Guide and Directory* (Carlisle, 1811) reports Wilkinson "at present engaged in publishing Select Views in Cumberland, Westmorland, and Lancaster, with appropriate Descriptions," a work "much admired" (I, 56); but the publication information is unlikely to be current. *The London Catalogue* gives the year of Wilkinson's work as 1812. SH transcribed the "Preface" (apparently the "Introduction") for Luff some time about early 1812 (*SHL* 46)—a procedure possibly required, however, by inability to obtain the letterpress independent of the engravings.

W was in any event very probably back at work on a guide again, motivated by financial objectives, c Nov 1812 (DW had thought on 18 Nov 1809 that a guide would "sell better, and bring [W] more money than any of his higher labours"). Evidence for this conclusion is neither abundant nor direct, but sufficient: the basic grounds are cited 1812:98. To remarks made there may be added the following considerations:

(a) It is quite certain, as shown, that some of the materials among the G MSS were written after late Aug 1811.

(b) The paper of (10) above appears in numerous letters of the W family, but I have been unable to find any other use prior to DW's letter to CCl of 5 Jan 1813 (the latest noted is W's letter to Hutton of 25 Nov 1816, and it was used for at least eight letters in 1813). It is unlikely that such paper was withheld from use for letters for a year or more preceding 5 Jan 1813.

(c) An octavo gathering made from the paper discussed in (b) is found in the Robert Walker folder of the W Correspondence File, DCP. On it are written memoranda drawn on by W for his biographical sketch of Walker for *The River Duddon*, 1820. The memoranda include neatly written notes, some certainly copied from elsewhere, by W and DW. Among them are the epitaphs of Walker and his wife from the Seathwaite churchyard; the memorial note about Walker in the Seathwaite

PR; and notes from PRs and other sources concerning Ulpha Kirk, "Ashdale" [Eskdale], Netherwasdale, and Loweswater. W's Memoir of Walker draws also on the Loweswater memoranda. The notes on Walker are further used by W in the G draft cited in the fourth category of MSS discussed above. Other content of the gathering consists of a copy of a hymn in the autograph of SH, "Dear Vale When Spring Thy Charms Unfold [*sic*]." W may have received some of his notes from correspondents. He visited Wastwater in 1807 and apparently attempted a description of his tour soon after (see above); and he probably visited the Duddon Valley in Sept 1808. But W fairly certainly had no note of the epitaph at Ulpha Kirk c mid-1810 (see (9) above). He visited Seathwaite and Ulpha Kirk in Sept 1811; and he was almost surely in the area of Loweswater and Borrowdale in Sept 1812. One note, however, reads: "Henry Tyson now living in Nether Wasdale. aged 81. .his wife [79 *corrected to* 78] or [78 *corrected to* 77]. They have 8 Sons & 6 Daughters all alive. never had more the eldest 51. the youngest 25 years old." Mr. Donald P. Sewell has kindly advised me, after consultation with the Rev. J. S. Whinery, incumbent at Netherwasdale, and examination of the Netherwasdale Parish Record Book, of gravestones at the Netherwasdale Church, and of Tyson family records in the Family Bible in the possession of Mrs. Sewell, that the Henry Tyson thus noted is almost certainly Henry Tyson of Whitesyke, whose tombstone records that he died 24 July 1813, aged 82. The same stone records that Tyson's wife Margaret died 7 Jan 1828, aged 90. The Family Bible records that Tyson was born 25 Dec 1730, and the Parish Records that he was baptized 1 Jan 1730/ 1731. These records also make plain that he and Margaret Tyson were parents of eight sons and six daughters, the eldest born 9 Feb 1761. Tyson would have become 81 on 25 Dec 1811, and his eldest child 51 on 9 Feb 1812. The paper of the gathering is watermarked "1810"; no visits to the appropriate areas other than those mentioned are known near this time; no other use of the paper in the W family MSS can be dated before 1813; all the notes on this paper, except perhaps the copy of the hymn, were plainly written about the same time; and these notes are drawn upon in the G MSS. It is hence reasonable to suppose that these notes and the MS that draws on them were written not before late 1812.

(d) A draft concerning Borrowdale in the fourth category above draws on information from the Borrowdale PR. Not enough of (1) survives for certainty that the draft with which it belonged did not survive. But the draft that is extant corresponds closely with *G* 1810, which itself makes no allusion to the PR. The prose draft on Borrowdale in MS 69, which is yet later than the MSS mentioned, specifically states that it was W himself who examined and took notes from the Borrowdale PR. The evidence, although mainly negative, tends to encourage the speculation that W examined the PR after writing the draft cited for *G* 1810. As stated, W is not known to have visited Borrowdale after 1810 before Sept 1812.

(e) It is improbable that W can have worked much on a guide in Dec 1812 or early 1813 (see *MY* II, 69; 1812:99–1813:4), and no available evidence points to his having worked on a guide in immediately succeeding years.

It has already been remarked that all materials not otherwise distinguished that are written on paper watermarked with a cursive "P" over "1806" appear to have been composed at about the same time. The pages concerning Grasmere and the road to Keswick appear to belong in the same sequence. While these include direct allusion to the etchings, DW had assumed in 1809 that W's enlarged guide would call to mind Wilkinson's publication. That W's work toward a guide in 1812 should mention the etchings is thus hardly surprising. The general similarity between this MS and the others described outweighs doubts: it appears likely that these materials, including (7) to (10), and those in the fourth category, including the Essay on the Sublime, all constitute work toward an expanded Lake Guide, and date from about the same time; and that that time is c Nov 1812.

The chronological interinvolvement of these MSS with MS D of *HG*, DC MS 76, and with the MSS of *Exc* is complicated. A general survey of external evidence regarding *Exc* composition from 1810 has been given, and definitive descriptions of the *Exc* MSS, which are in most cases intricately complex, are of course beyond the limits of the present study. Brief descriptions of the main MSS follow. Of these it might be remarked first and generally that they tend to indicate that composition of *Exc* from about the beginning of 1810 was proceeding under conceptions of principal characters and main themes similar to those of the poem as published, but that the final organization of the poem was fixed during the period of intense work commencing 3 Jan 1813.

The chief MSS concerned, which vividly confirm W's statement that the poem was "written with great labour" (*MY* II, 144), are DC MSS 69–71, 73–75. The Coleorton Commonplace Book contains a copy of *Exc* VII. 395–481 written between a copy of W's letter to Lady B of 21 May 1807 and copies of DW's "Peaceful Our Valley" and "There Is One Cottage" and an "Extract from the Essay on Epitaphs." The *Exc* fragment is quoted by W at the conclusion of the third Essay upon Epitaphs, and the "Extract" is the opening paragraph of the second Essay. Both essays were written by 28 Feb 1810 (see 1809:136).

MS 71, which will frequently serve as a point of reference hereafter, contains the longest surviving continuous MS of any portion of the poem, a basically complete copy of Books I to III—the MS "P" of *PW* V. The main MS commences with a moderately neat and continuous copy, subsequently heavily corrected, of *Exc* I–III.324 in the autograph of MW. At III.325 W has taken up the copying and continued more messily to line 423 with work apparently close to the original composition. Draft, of which the "MS" readings of *PW* V for lines 423 ff are fairly representative, then goes on to the close of III in the hands of W, MW, and DW. Drafts apparently made after the main copy have been written into blank spaces throughout. Drafts toward a revised reading of *Prel* I.228–38 perhaps preparatory to MS C appear near the front of the NB; and the first three lines and part of the fourth line of "Say, What Is Honour?" (probably composed between c Mar 1809 and some time in 1810) have been copied at one end of the NB, evidently before the *Exc* materials. Several leaves and gatherings written by W and MW have been sewn in as inserts, revising and replacing primary materials both before and after III.324. These inserts, almost all on laid paper watermarked with a cursive "P" and countermarked "1810," contain materials corresponding to II.39–319, III.352–423, 583–631, 793–930. The insert for II.39–319 is an expansion of the primary MS. Two leaves cut out have been replaced by eight sewn in. The last two of these, a double sheet with watermark "1798," contains lines 243–319; of these, lines 243–65 are an earlier version of corresponding materials on the inserted leaves standing before, but the remaining lines belong to the process of expansion represented by the preceding leaves of the insert. The lines thus added include the history of the Solitary's marriage and the deaths of his wife and children. The insert for III.352–423 is an expansion of lines in the basic MS running from 352–55 to three or four rejected lines to 419–23. The subject is stoic tranquillity. The insert for III.583–631 is also an expansion of basic MS materials, and contains a portion of the Solitary's account of his marriage; the materials from which came *Characteristics of a Child Three Years Old* and *Maternal Grief* are among the basic MS lines. The insert for III.793–930 replaces two leaves cut out of the main NB. The passage concerns the Solitary's journey to America. As remarked *PW* V, 419, draft toward III.584–98 appears on a draft of W's letter to LdL of 8 Jan 1813. The verse draft follows the letter, but appears to belong to about the same time. As implied *PW* V, 415, 418–19, the materials concerning the Solitary's bereavement and those contributive to *Characteristics* and *Maternal Grief* must generally date after Dec 1812, hence not earlier than 3 Jan 1813 (see 1813:5; *MY* II, 64).

The appearance of the MS would thus suggest that all the copy beyond III.324 dates after 3 Jan 1813. As all these inserts except the double sheet watermarked "1798" are of the same kind of paper, and all were plainly written at about the same time, they probably date not before late 1812. The "1798" paper was in heavy use by the Ws for letters during 1810 and 1811. The priority of the entire main MS, however, places all these inserts certainly after 3 Jan 1813 also. The basic draft beyond III.324 is no more unkempt or hurried-looking than large portions of W's MSS from all periods of his life (cf *PW* V, 419), but the conjecture of *PW* that W was working on materials used in the later parts of III in early 1813 is justified by the draft in the 8 Jan 1813 letter to LdL.

The autograph of MW, however, appears in the basic MS up to the conclusion of a version of III.549/550 *app crit* (*PW* V, 93) and in the inserts for II.39–319; and in view of the melancholy family events of the recent past W may be supposed unlikely to have employed MW early in 1813 to copy materials dealing with the Solitary's happy marriage and its tragic conclusion. It would appear safe to date the materials beyond III.324 in this MS between 3 Jan 1813 and May 1814. There appear no grounds for very confident conjecture that the basic MS materials I–III.324 were copied before Jan 1813; but it seems fair to assume in view of the kind of drafting going on c but not before 8 Jan 1813 that W would not have set forward a copy of II without the story of the Solitary's marriage—which can hardly have been treated as an important subject in the two pages cut from the original MS (these would have contained only about sixty lines) but which is so treated by the inserts—after 3 Jan 1813. So the base copy of I–III.324 probably was written by Mar 1812.

Drafts toward I and III appear also in MS 69. Drafts toward II and III appear in MS 70. And drafts toward III appear in MS 73. MS 69 is an octavo NB made of laid paper with a watermark of a trefoil over "1802"; it is without cover and much reduced by removal of pages. It contains, in addition to unidentified stubs, drafts toward I.66–111 and III.20–22, 30–47, 143–64, 303–24, clearly preceding basic MS P copy (the Book I drafts postdate MS M). Also present are stubs of leaves on which appear to have been written materials including draft of much of *Exc* III.79–81, 185–86, 265–67, 292–95; IV.9–c26, c108–329, 676–?758, and V.308–672. Drafts for most of III.1–324 were fairly certainly present at one time. Draft of IV.759–62 survives following the IV stubs, and beneath the last line is an inked "130" and a pencilled "693," both in W's hand. The numbers probably conclude line counts of a passage like that now beginning IV.631 ("Upon the breast of new-created earth"), and perhaps of a book, or portion of one, some seventy lines shorter than the final version of Book IV to that point. It seems probable that most of IV.1–762 was copied here. The Book V materials apparently preceded the Book IV materials in entry, but seem unlikely to have been written much earlier. A simile of ten lines, commmencing "As when, upon the smooth pacific deep," appears to date from about the same time. Passages of prose toward a guide have been mentioned above, and assigned to a date c Nov 1812. Appearance does not permit confident conjecture about the relative priority of entry of *G* and *Exc* materials; but as the drafts toward *Exc* I and III precede the basic MS of MS P, these probably date by Mar 1812. In seeking a *terminus a quo*, one may remark that a version of IV.109–21 (stubs show "If/[?]/day /the deep /[?]/ced /joy /with light" was at one time present, and elsewhere, perhaps in an earlier reading, "And/★And/ If/ A/ The/ [?]/ Wh/ In/ Of s/ T[?h]/"), probably derives from W's concern about the possibility of failing eyesight. Such concern seems unlikely to have troubled W before the summer of 1810 (Moorman II, 255; *MY* I, 470; 1805:3; 1810:46); so that this copy probably does not date before 12 May 1811. The general appearance of the surviving MS suggests fairly continuous use of the NB, and accordingly implies that both the IV and V drafts followed 12 May 1811.

The first page at one end of MS 70, a NB like that of MSS 38, 45, 47, and 48, contains a copy of Latin verses, written vertically in the autograph of DW, commencing "Si mihi, si liceat traducere leviter ovum." DW evidently first, when the NB was blank or nearly so, started to write these verses horizontally on the first page at the other end but found that the lines would not fit the page well; the first four words survive there, overwritten with *Exc* drafts. The NB is occupied mainly by fragmentary drafts in the autographs of W, MW, and DW comprising most of *Exc* III.367–78 (later than *TofP* and here part of drafting for Book V); most of IV. 332–825, 851–1119, 1130–47, 1307–15; and V.1–10, c100–04, 168–c225. Near the end appear also drafts toward II.153–320 (later than MS 47), fairly certainly written after the drafts toward IV and V. Although some of these materials, among them especially II.153–320, almost certainly represent transcriptions from other sources, the appearance of the drafts suggests that most were made as part of a process of fairer copying elsewhere. The drafts for II and III clearly precede the inserts in MS 71. As the draft for II includes no reference to the Solitary's marriage, it probably dates before early 1813; so, thus, do the other drafts. Comparative readings make evident that the stubs and draft of Book IV in MS 69 represent work later than that of MS 70. Possibly the drafting in MS 70 was connected with copying in MS 69. The opening words of lines 708–12, for example, which are worked out in MS 70, are copied straightforwardly in MS 69. The first word of line 760 is "After" in MS 70 but is "From," the final reading, in MS 69.

DC MS 73 is a NB made from the same kind of paper—laid, with a watermark of a trefoil over "1802"—as MS 69, and is otherwise similar to that NB in format except that MS 73 apparently originally contained about half as many leaves as MS 69. Its contents include: draft toward III.967–88; IV.83–91 followed integrally by IV.1158–1290, which contain the lines quoted *PW* V, 429–30 (1) and described p. 430 (2); VI.1–211, 275–521; and IX.293–796 (end). The draft for IV certainly precedes the draft for III, which precedes the corresponding lines in MS P. Most of the draft for IX precedes that for VI, but a fair copy of IX.682–796 appears to have been written at about the same time.

W is not very likely to have written the bulk of Book IX before late 1811. Moorman II, 179 suggests more specifically Dec 1811, a time when W was certainly busy writing and was also much preoccupied with Dr. Bell's educational theories, which surely in some degree inspired the call for national education that forms an essential part of the book. W had taken an interest in Bell's work earlier (*MY* I, 269–70, 278–79), but the impassioned character of Book IX's advocacies is particularly likely to reflect the intense concern of late 1811. Any time from late Aug would, however, appear a reasonable possibility. All of the contents of this NB may hence be assigned to a period commencing late Aug 1811. How much later they might have been written is a question that requires examination of two other MSS, 74 and 75, containing draft of Book IX as well as of many other portions of the poem.

The main NB of MS 74 appears to have been a twin of MS 73. Many of its leaves are now loose, but content and physical characteristics of the MSS allow determination of their original order. The content, variously in the autographs of W, MW, and DW, includes materials toward *Exc* V.264–365, 485–557, c897–921, c978, 1002–16 (end); VI.573–1267 (end); VII.1–268, 302–400, 482–695, 878–1057 (end); VIII.1–486, 592–601 (end) (VIII.487–591 were clearly once present); IX.3–c397; materials quoted *PW* V, 432–41 ("While here I stand," hereafter called "The Peasant's Life"); materials quoted *PW* V, 461–62 (hereafter called "The Shepherd of Bield Crag"). At the end of the NB, surrounded by drafts for Books IX and V, are drafts of

"Praised Be the Art," *Yew-trees*, and the long sentence added by W to the 1814 *Exc* text of Essay upon Epitaphs beginning "If then in a creature" (*Exc* 1814, 434; Grosart II, 30). A draft of the introductory sentence for that essay as printed in *Exc* 1814 (as a note to V.978) appears elsewhere in the NB along with line 978 itself (with "But" for "And"). The draft was apparently written in on a page previously left blank among drafts for Book V. The presence of this introductory sentence, an apology for the reprinting of the *Essay*, tends to imply, however, that the NB was in use during the late stages of preparation of the poem for press.

Few if any of the copies appear certainly first drafts, and the following materials, although sometimes heavily corrected even in the process of writing, seem among those especially likely to have been copied from other sources: VI.787–1052 (see description of MS 75); VII.320–400, 507–620, 911–75, 995–1057; VIII.97–115, 441–86 (see description of MS 75), 592–601 (end); IX.3–c200 (see description of 75); "The Shepherd of Bield Crag." The general variety and many shades of difference of the autographs in the NB make pronouncements on order and date of entry dangerous, and an exhaustive description is impossible here. Prolonged consideration leads, nonetheless, to a few speculations:

(1) "The Shepherd of Bield Crag" and VI.787–1052 (the story of Ellen) appear to have been among the first materials entered in the NB.

(2) Then, perhaps, the following were entered, beginning forward of the materials cited in (1) on the recto of what is presently the twenty-eighth leaf: V.485–557, c897–921; VI.589–99 running directly into "The Peasant's Life" 1–22, 31–45, 62–70, 74–75; V.264–94 (as *PW* V "MS" down to p. 162, 4 lines up), 292–308, 320–30; *PW* V, 163–64 *app crit*; V, 331–65, 610–19; "The Peasant's Life" 87–167. Here the drafting met the previously entered "Shepherd of Bield Crag."

(3) Then, evidently, W continued on "The Peasant's Life" well toward the rear of the book.

(4) Having finished work on "The Peasant's Life," W turned back to the conclusion of the story of Ellen and worked along on what is now Book VI from line 1053, and from what is now the conclusion of Book VI directly into what is now Book VII.1–241/42 (*app crit*) without making any noticeable division between the books other than an uncommonly large capital letter at the beginning of what is now VII.

(5) W then, after fairer copies of VII.1–97 and VI.1134–1191, worked on VI.573–786 through pages left blank in the earlier drafting of "The Peasant's Life."

(6) At some time before returning to heavy use of the pages still left blank

in the front of the book, he used facing pages and blank spaces among the Book V drafts for work on "The Peasant's Life" to line 96, and employed some of the front leaves for fairer copy and further drafting of the same materials. (Revision of these and other associated materials probably went on later.)

(7) He then used pages left blank in the front of the book for successive drafts toward VII.878–1057, VIII (all the lines now missing, as noted above, were probably once present), and IX.3–320, the IX drafts skipping around the copy toward V.485–c920, "The Peasant's Life" through line 167 (see (1) above), and "The Shepherd of Bield Crag."

The sequence of entry of drafts at the rear of the NB toward V.c978, 1002–16, VII.302–400, 482–695, and IX.281–397, appears indeterminate, except that: (a) the IX verses seem likely to have been entered after V.c978 and are certainly later than the IX materials standing before in the NB with which they overlap; (b) the V.c978 lines clearly precede the draft of the introductory sentence for the Essay upon Epitaphs note; (c) VII.395–400 are clearly later than the version of the same lines that introduces the copy of VII.395–481 at the conclusion of the Essay upon Epitaphs printed last by Grosart—a copy probably written by 28 Feb 1810. The draft toward VII.c529 in MS 75 precedes the drafting of VII.482–695 here; as will be seen, these materials probably do not date before 6 Mar 1813. The drafting of IX, as remarked above, surrounds copies of "Praised Be the Art" and *Yew-trees* (draft for IX.281–89 and 298–357 precedes "Praised Be the Art"; and draft for 355–62 and c385–c397 follows *Yew-trees*). "Praised Be the Art" was written perhaps c early June 1811. So this portion of the MS of Book IX, at least, may be supposed to follow that date. The IX drafts in the middle of the NB and at the rear seem sufficiently tied to W's concern with Dr. Bell's educational system to justify the assumption that these materials cannot precede late Aug 1811. MS 74 appears on balance, however, likely to have been filled with the bulk of its *Exc* materials within a short space of time, although a few materials (see (1) above) may have been entered earlier than the main body. One general argument for this conclusion is negative: that only by fairly constant use of the NB, once copying was well under way, was W likely to have been able to keep the whereabouts of the varied contents clearly enough fixed in his mind to make the use of the NB at all convenient. One may, therefore, assign the materials here copied to the period of composition perhaps between late Aug 1811 and c late May 1814. The *Yew-trees* draft probably dates between June 1811 and c late May 1814.

A loose group of leaves filed with MS 74 contains a fair copy by MW, corrected by W, of most of *Exc* V.1–1016, later than the Book V materials of MS 70 and of the main NB of MS 74. The leaves perhaps more properly belong with MS 75: the paper, low-quality octavo double sheets, laid, with watermark of a cursive "P" over "1806," is similar to that of MS 75 and that of most of the late G MSS described above. This MS will hereafter be referred to as MS 74A. Also filed with MS 74, apparently accidentally, is a small octavo double sheet containing notes, in an unidentified hand, of mathematical instruction for a schoolchild and neat drafts, probably all of the same general time, and in W's autograph, of "There Was a Spot" (*PW* V, 342, III) and *Prel* X.445–66 and 568–74. The *Prel* draft precedes the 1805 poem, and these materials may thus reasonably be dated, in view of the time of main work on *Prel* X, between early Oct and late autumn 1804 (see Appendix V).

MS 75 is a set of seven octavo double sheets similar to those of Verse 74A. These sheets like those appear to have been made by dividing folio sheets. The paper of two of the double sheets, however, is distinctly heavier than that of the others, and resembles the paper of MS 74A rather than the other sheets in this MS (see also the remarks above on the paper of the G MSS). These heavier leaves contain fair copy, in the autograph of MW, of VII.30–58, 201–36, and 252–85. The appearance of the writing also connects the leaves closely with MS 74A. The neatness of all these implies that they date from the late stages of preparation of the poem, perhaps early 1814. The other leaves, of flimsier paper, contain draft toward V.922–43; VI.707–825; VII.c529, c780–916, 821–30, c849–58; VIII.520–571; IX.57–92, 105–c130, c156–78; materials quoted *PW* V, 466. Despite the editorial remarks of *PW* V, 466, the last drafts cited draw on rather than precede *TofP* (as does also the inserted copy toward III.352–423 in MS P), and this draft work is in turn drawn upon in VI.787–805 and VII.277–85 and 595–631 elsewhere in MS 75. A draft of VIII.459–c516 on the same paper is in the Berg Collection, NYPL. The general appearance of the draft on the flimsier paper makes fairly certain that most or all was written at about the same time. The IX draft, especially of c156–78, suggests a time in any case not earlier than late Aug 1811. One double sheet, however, containing what was originally copy and draft by MW and W of V.922–43 (as "MS" in *PW* V, 183 *app crit*, to line 15 in the autograph of MW, thence to line 21 in the autograph of W), all seemingly of the same time (W appears to have taken up the writing directly from MW), contains also both draft for VII.c529 and a draft by W for his letter to LdL of 6 Mar 1813. The draft for VII.c529 precedes the letter, but definitely belongs to the same time: W seems simply to have reversed the paper on which he had just been drafting verse in order to draft the letter.

The Book V draft precedes corresponding work in MS 74A, and the Book VII draft precedes corresponding work in MS 74. The draft toward VII.1–268 in MS 74, however, precedes the drafts of VII.30–58, 201–36, and 252–85 mentioned above. The VI, VIII, and IX drafts precede those of corresponding passages in MS 74. Insofar as a pattern of use of the MSS is evident, it is that the drafts of flimsier paper in MS 75 precede MS 74 where they correspond, and the drafts in MS 74 precede those on heavier paper, including two sheets in MS 75 and the whole of MS 74A. The flimsier paper was in use c but by 6 Mar 1813, and it appears probable that most or all of this draft dates not before 3 Jan 1813. Since most of MS 74 seems to have been filled—with exceptions as cited—about the same time, its materials on this account perhaps generally date from a time not before 3 Jan 1813.

Available evidence accordingly tends to imply this much, summarized by MS, about the development of *Exc* beyond the *RC* MS of MS M and the 1806 MSS of *HG* (on earlier materials see GCL):

(a) *Exc* II.1–c725, 741–63
Basic copy in MS 47 remotely possibly c Sept 1806. Probably composed between c Dec 1809 and c late May 1810.

(b) *Exc* I.66–111; III.20–22, 30–47, 143–64, 303–24, 367–78
Drafts in MS 69 probably between c Dec 1809 and Mar 1812, esp. between c Dec 1809 and c late May 1810, c early May and possibly c early July 1811, late Aug 1811 and Mar 1812; but before basic copy of MS P.

(c) *Exc* I–III.324, III.325–991; II.39–319; III.325–423, 583–631, 793–930
Basic copy in MS P, MS 71, probably between c Dec 1809 and Mar 1812, within periods cited in (b) above. Basic copy of III.325–991 in MS P probably between 3 Jan 1813 and c late May 1814. III.967–88 follows corresponding material in MS 73. II.39–319; III.325–423, 583–631, 793–930, on inserts in MS P probably between 3 Jan 1813 and c late May 1814.

(d) *Exc* II.153–320; III.367–78; IV.332–825, 851–1119, 1130–47, 1307–15; V.1–10, c100–04, 168–c225
Drafts in MS 70 probably between c Dec 1809 and Mar 1812, within periods cited in (b) above.

(e) *Exc* III.967–88; IV.83–91, 1158–1290, including materials quoted *PW* V, 429–30 (1), and described *PW* V, 430 (2)
Draft in MS 73 probably between 3 Jan 1813 and c late May 1814.

(f) *Exc* IV.9–c26, c108–329, 676–?758 and perhaps more (as indicated by stubs); IV. 759–62; V.308–672 (indicated by stubs)

Draft in MS 69 perhaps between 3 Jan 1813 and c late May 1814. The IV copy postdates MS 70, and the V copy MS 74.

(g) *Exc* V.264–365, 485–557, c897–921, c978, 1002–16; VI.573–1267; VII.1–268, 302–400, 482–695, 878–1057; VIII.1–486, [487–591], 592–601; IX.3–c397; materials quoted *PW* V, 432–41 ("The Peasant's Life"), *PW* V, 461–62 ("The Shepherd of Bield Crag")

Draft and copy in MS 74, main NB probably between 3 Jan 1813 and c late May 1814. "The Shepherd of Bield Crag" and VI.787–1052 and some other materials possibly written earlier, but not before c Dec 1809. Materials corresponding to MS 75 follow MS 75 except for MS 75 drafts for Book VII up to VII.268, drafts toward which precede MS 74.

(h) *Exc* V.922–43; VI.787–805; VII.30–58, 201–36, 252–85, c529, c780–816, 821–30, c849–58; VIII.459–571; IX.57–92, 105–c130, c156–78; materials quoted *PW* V, 466

Draft and copy in MS 75 (VIII.459–c516 on leaf in Berg Collection, NYPL), probably between 3 Jan 1813 and c late May 1814. Draft for V.922–43 and VII.c529 probably c but by 6 Mar 1813. Copy of VII.30–58, 201–36, 252–85 perhaps c early 1814.

(i) *Exc* VI.1–211, 275–521; IX.293–796

Draft and copy in MS 73 probably between 3 Jan 1813 and c late May 1814. Materials corresponding to MS 74 postdate MS 74.

(j) *Exc* V.1–1016 (end)

Copy in MS 74A perhaps c early 1814.

Complete MSS thus exist only for Books I, III, and V, and of these none is the final MS. Significant gaps remain in surviving MSS of Books IV, VI, and VII. And few of the drafts can be the first of the passage concerned. Still, the MSS tend on balance to imply that the last seven books of the poems cannot have been organized in a form much like that of the present *Exc* until the final major period of composition between 3 Jan 1813 and c late May 1814. *PW* V, 371 suggests that the "subject-matter of Books V, VI, and VII of [*Exc*] . . . is clearly related to W's broodings over the general subject of epitaphs" [in the winter of 1809–1810], and it is reasonable to suspect that many of the accounts by the pastor of persons buried in the churchyard were basically composed, as was VII.395–481, c early 1810. Closely related narratives were composed for *HG* in 1806, however; and as a basis for assignment of the dates of composition of the bulk of these books, this reasoning is not firm enough for great confidence. One may hardly feel certain, that is, that the three books which DW was hoping on 28 Feb 1810 that W would finish before turning to any other labor were definitely "The Pastor" and the two books following. But the MSS seem collectively to indicate that W's work from early 1813 was being carried on vigorously within a coherent general plan for the poem corresponding to that shown by the present poem, although possibly not for some time with an exact number of books fixed. The earlier MSS—from possibly 1806, certainly c Dec 1809—show W developing the work through the interaction of the Poet, the Wanderer, the Solitary, and (from the time of DC MS 70) the Pastor, as a consideration of the nature of the responsibilities of modern man to himself and society in view of the possibilities and limitations of human life in all conditions.

Lines not otherwise accounted for may reasonably be assigned to the period between c Dec 1809 and c late May 1814.

MS D of *HG*, DC MS 76, now remains to be treated. The MS contains a fair copy by MW on two types of paper, the leaves stitched together to form a single MS of forty-two pages. Lines 1–79 and 304–end are written on blue-tinted laid paper watermarked with a crowned quartered shield and countermarked "Harris" over "1828." The MS concludes "[Thinking *corrected to* Musing] in Solitude (see Preface to the Excursion to its conclusion)." The correction, in view of the watermark, must be the consequence of a careless mistake, or of rejection of a late alteration, since "Musing" is the reading of the published *Prospectus* from 1814. The remainder of the MS is written on a kind of paper discussed above in connection with G and *Exc*, a laid paper watermarked with a cursive "P" and countermarked "1810." For reasons already cited, it is appropriate, on present evidence, to assign uses of this paper in W's MSS to a period between late 1812 and late 1816. Professor James Butler has called my attention to the fact that the lines published by W in G 1823 as *Water Fowl*—fairly surely originally composed between c late June and early Sept 1806—are here corrected to the readings of the 1823 version. W's own date for the poem, 1812, might thus look back to the time of copying or correction, or both. It looks equally possible, on the other hand, that W's date represents simply a loose recollection of the period of main work on *Exc*, and hence preoccupation with the *Recluse* generally. The *HG* MS was possibly written out as an adjunct to the copying of *Exc*.

The date of the later portion of the MS may be conjectured with some confidence, again on the basis of the paper, which is also used by MW in the copying of *Prel* III, IV, and V in *Prel* MS D: W's note at the beginning of that MS (partly a correction of words now illegible) is: "This Poem begun about 1798. greater part written about the beginning of the Century. Corrected *1832*[.]" This statement, together with external evidence (see

PREL xxiii), makes probable that *Prel* MS D was copied c early 1832 (the entire MS representing the correction to which W refers). The portions of *HG* on this paper generally bear a very close resemblance to *Prel* MS D. A date about the same time is fairly certain.

APPENDIX VII

The Printer's MS of Poems in Two Volumes

The chronology of the copying and forwarding of the printer's MS for *P2V* is more obscure than that of W's preceding book, the second volume of *LB*. External information is limited, and the MS reveals its history grudgingly. Some indirect clues are, however, provided by letters from Coleorton:

(1) W to Wrangham, 7 Nov 1806: "I think of publishing a Vol: of small pieces in Verse this winter. How shall I get a Copy conveyed to you?" (*MY* I, 89.)

(2) W to Sir GB, 10 Nov 1806: "In a day or two I mean to send a sheet of my intended Volume to the Press; it would give me great pleasure to desire the Printer to send you the sheets as they are struck off if you could have them free of expense." (*MY* I, 95. See (11) below.)

(3) W to Scott, 10 Nov 1806: "I am going to the Press with a Volume . . . .[He requests Scott to send a copy of W's verses *The Seven Sisters*] I mean if you think they would have any effect in my intended Vol: either for their own sakes or for the sake of variety. I stumbled upon the first draught of that Poem some little time since and it seemed to me sad stuff; perhaps the finished Copy which I think you said you have may turn out better. . . . I must beg of you in this case to send it soon, because it must have an early place if at all." (*MY* I, 96–97. See also (9) below.)

(4) DW to Lady B, 14 Nov 1806: "My Brother works very hard at his poems, preparing them for press. Miss Hutchinson is the transcriber." (*MY* I, 100.)

(5) DW to CCl, 24 Nov 1806: "Wm is going to publish *two* smaller volumes and is to have 100 Guineas for 1,000 Copies." (*MY* I, 104.)

(6) W to Thomas Wilkinson, probably between 10 and 30 November: "I have in press a poetical publication that will extend to a couple of small volumes, 150 pages or so a-piece. . . ." (*MY* I, 105.)

(7) DW to Lady B, 7 Dec 1806: "William has written two other poems, which you will see when they are printed. He composes frequently in

687

the grove.... We have not yet received a sheet from the printer."
(*MY* I, 108.)

(8) DW to Lady B, 19 Dec 1806: "[W's] poetical [*sic*, MS] labours have been at a stand for more than a week." (*MY* I, 110. See 1806:113.)

(9) W to Scott, 20 Jan 1807: "Many thanks to you and your Transcriber for Lord Archibald which was received in due time, and has already passed through the Press with a slight alteration or two....

"The printing of my work which is now to be extended to two small Vols of 150 pages or so each has met with unexpected delays, and as the sheets are sent down to me for correction, and three are only yet gone through, it will be three full months before it is out; for we do not get on faster than at the rate of a sheet a week." W also requests advice concerning the phrase "Lega" in *The Blind Highland Boy*. (*MY* I, 122–23.)

(10) DW to Lady B, 15 Feb 1807: "For more than a week we have had the most delightful weather; if William had but waited a few days, it would have been no anticipation when he said to you the 'songs of spring were in the grove. ...'" (*MY* I, 134.)

(11) Sir GB to W, 23 Feb 1807 (DCP): Sir GB thanks W for two packets of proof sheets. The number of sheets conveyed is uncertain.

(12) W to Scott, late Feb 1807: Thanks Scott for advice for *The Blind Highland Boy*: see (9) above. "My Printer seems to have added one more to the number of the Seven Sleepers; I have not had a Sheet these thirteen days." (*MY* I, 139–40.)

An exhaustive account of the appearance and contents of the surviving portions of the printer's copy of *P2V*, the collection of MSS that is now BM Add. MS 47,864, would require space much beyond the limits of the present study. The main progress of the preparations of these materials, and the dates for main composition of a few of the poems not datable by other means, may, however, be suggested by a more limited examination.

The printer's copy for W's volumes was prepared and sent off in lots over the late autumn, winter, and spring of 1806–1807. Individual lots were apparently intended to contain an amount of verse about equal to that of one of the printed duodecimo sheets. The larger portion of these lots were numbered as "sheets" by W, although one is actually termed "lot"; and most are numbered according to the order in which they were to be set in type by the printer. This order is evidently also the order in which the materials were sent off, although some lots may have been sent off together in packets, others alone literally as sheets. Where lots are unnumbered, their place can be identified by W's numberings of the individual poems, the order of the poems as printed and bound, or other clues. Some lots are, or began as, neat copies written out expressly for the printer in late 1806 and early 1807; others are amalgams of copies probably made before the residence at Coleorton with copies made at the later time.

The contents of the several lots may be described in general fashion as follows, in probable order of forwarding and printing:

[Lot 1]: *To the Daisy* ("In Youth") (see Hale White 53–54); *Louisa* (see Hale White 54); *Fidelity* (see Hale White 54–55); "She Was a Phantom of Delight"; *The Redbreast and the Butterfly* (see Hale White 55); *The Sailor's Mother*; and a short letter from W to Longman and Rees (the removal to Coleorton has prevented W's writing sooner; the sheets are to be sent to W for final revisal after correction by the printer). On the address panel W has written "*a single sheet.*" The postmark—the only one appearing among these MSS—is F/NOV 14/1806 (morning duty); and the address panel is also stamped [LOU]GHBOROUGH 109. This lot must thus have been complete by the morning of 13 Nov.

"2nd Sheet": General directions for the printer (the two volumes are to be printed uniform with *LB*; instructions on number of lines to be printed per page; request for speed); *To the Small Celandine*; *To the Same Flower*; *Character of the Happy Warrior* (see Hale White 51) and note; note to insert separate title page "Poems composed for amusement during a Tour chiefly on Foot"; *Beggars*, 1–24. The last two items are deleted.

The reference to "two volumes" indicates that the note, a late addition, was written after 10 Nov (see *MY* I, 96–97). W in urging speed states that the printer "will be regularly supplied with Copy" and that he will "send a sheet by the next Post." He thus implies that at least the third lot was virtually ready. The directions to the printer imply that this sheet must have gone off almost immediately after the first.

"3 Sheet": *The Horn of Egremont Castle* (see Hale White 51–52); *The Affliction of Mary—of—[sic]* (see Hale White 52, 63); *The Kitten and the Falling Leaves* with revision stitched on (see Hale White 52, 64–65).

"Sheet 4": *The Seven Sisters* (see Hale White 52); *To H.C.*, in two stitched-on fragments (see Hale White 52); "Among All Lovely Things"; "I Travelled among Unknown Men" (the last two items are stitched on in two fragments, on the verso of one of which are the first seven stanzas of *To the Spade of a Friend*, and of the other a few lines from *The Emigrant Mother*); *Ode to Duty*, very heavily revised (see Hale White 53, 66); instructions to insert separate title page, basically as p. 75 of *P2V* I; address, to Messrs. Longman and Rees. Foldings suggest that sheets 3 and 4 may have been sent off as a single packet, but the fold lines are insufficiently clear for confident conjecture.

"Sheet No 5": Instructions for separate title page, as at conclusion of fourth sheet, except that the phrase "for amusement" follows "composed"; commencement of *Beggars* (these two items are written on a stitched-on fragment; the rest are written on the main sheet); *To a Sky Lark*; "With How Sad Steps, O Moon"; *The Tinker* (see Hale White 63–68; *PW* II, 542–43); *Alice Fell*; *R&I* 1–112 (see Hale White 68; *PW* II, 238 *app crit*).

The duplication of the cancelled reading of [lot 2] for the "Tour" title page implies that this sheet was copied before the fourth, containing the final reading, was completed. *The Tinker* was not published in *P2V*, although the printer's note "97F" at what would be, on the published pages, the heads of both pp. 93 and 97—the latter now the first page of signature F—indicates that the poem, which would have occupied four pages, was probably set in print and then cancelled before the completion of the formes for sheet E.

"Sheet No 6": Note from W requesting advice if the previous sheet did not conclude with "human strength, & strong admonishment"; conclusion of *R&I*; instructions for separate title page for Sonnets; *Prefatory Sonnet* ("Nuns Fret Not"); instructions for title page of "Miscellaneous Sonnets."

W's opening note indicates that this sheet was sent off after and separately from sheet 5.

"Sheet No 7 (possibly lots 7 and 8): Sonnets numbered, but not arranged except for the first six, as in *P2V*, with instructions concerning the title page for the Second Part. The final state of the surviving MS differs in content from the printed version in the case of the last sonnets of the First Section. The MS has: 17. "Pelion and Ossa" (see Hale White 72); 18. "Brook That Hast Been" (see Hale White 61–62); 19. "The World Is Too Much with Us"; 20. "It Is a Beauteous Evening"; and 21. *To the Memory of Raisley Calvert*. The published volume has: 17. "Lady! the Songs of Spring" [*To Lady Beaumont*]; 18. "The World Is Too Much with Us"; 19. "It Is a Beauteous Evening"; 20. *To the Memory of Raisley Calvert*. "Pelion and Ossa" and "Brook That Hast Been" are omitted from *P2V*. "Brook" is deleted in MS, but no provision is made for renumbering the following poems, a fact which suggests that the deletion was made after the MS was sent off. No printer's note remains to indicate whether the poem was set in print. A copy of a version of "Degenerate Douglas" is cancelled (see Hale White 60–61), and a copy of *At Applethwaite. Near Keswick*, first numbered "10," is heavily deleted, as is an unnumbered copy of "There Is a Trickling Water." It is possible that this lot was divided in two: W would have been calculating on the basis of a poem per printed page, and at that rate this lot would be about twice normal length. No obvious indication of this division appears, but if a division existed, it must have been made about the beginning of "Part the Second."

[Lot 8 or 9]: Notes for Vol. I; directions concerning general title page; Advertisement; title instructions, including motto "Orchard Pathway," for first section (see Hale White 70–72). A note here for "Pelion and Ossa" was not used (see "Sheet No 7"). W would appear to have intended, at the time of writing, that the first section of the poems be called "The Orchard Pathway." The Advertisement, title designation, and motto do not appear in *P2V*.

Vol. II. "Sheet 1st": Last three stanzas of *Ode to Duty*, cancelled; instructions concerning title page for *Poems Written during a Tour in Scotland; Rob Roy's Grave*, with printing instructions pasted on, and the stanza commencing "For why?" also stitched on, possibly to correct an accidental omission (see Hale White 56); *The Solitary Reaper* (see Hale White 56); *Stepping Westward; Glen Almain; The Matron of Jedborough and Her Husband* (see Hale White 56–57).

On the verso of the slip pasted on appear the remains of a frank in an unidentified autograph: "ary 1807 /worth Esq /ton Hall /de la Zouch." The slip might have been sent late and pasted on at the printer's, but this is not likely. The sheet was probably not sent off before Jan 1807.

"2 Sheet": *To a Highland Girl*; "Degenerate Douglas"; *Ejaculation at the Grave of Burns* (see Hale White 57, 69), cancelled; *Yarrow Unvisited* title and prefatory note, cancelled; *Address to the Sons of Burns; Yarrow Unvisited* title and prefatory note, followed by blank space where a beginning for the poem was probably once stitched on. This sheet was probably accompanied by a copy of *Yarrow Unvisited*, on leaves of a different paper (see below).

"3d Sheet": Instructions for title page of *Moods of My Own Mind; To a Butterfly* ("Stay near Me"); "The Sun Has Long Been Set"; "O Nightingale!"; *Written in March; The Small Celandine; The Sparrow's Nest; To the Cuckoo; To a Butterfly* ("I've Watched You"); "It Is No Spirit."

Sent off after this sheet was an associated leaf containing copies of "I Wandered Lonely," "Who Fancied What a Pretty Sight," and *Gipsies*, with instructions that the first two of these were to be placed following [*Written in March*], and that the last was to precede *The Sparrow's Nest*. The first two now appear in the printed volume at the beginning of gathering D preceding *The Sparrow's Nest*, separated from [*Written in March*] by *The Small Celandine* ("There is a Flower"), and the last placed just following *The Sparrow's Nest*. Printer's notations of "49 D Vol II" at *The Sparrow's Nest* and "Vol. II 73 E" at *The Green Linnet* (see "4th lot" below) indicate that sheets D and E originally began with those poems. "I Wandered Lonely" now begins the first of the resultant gatherings, and the second begins midway in *The Blind Highland Boy* (see 4th lot). The marking "97 Vol. II F" at *To the Same Flower* corresponds to the present printed text. Thus the leaf of additions was sent off after "3d Sheet" but either with or before [lot 5]. *Gipsies* was probably composed c but not before 26 February 1807. But "O Nightingale" was probably not composed before early Feb; so the lot is not likely to have been even basically organized before early Feb.

"4th lot": *The Blind Highland Boy* (see Hale White 62) with instructions concerning title page; *The Green Linnet*.

The remaining lots, not individually numbered as such, are distinguished by means of the poet's numberings of the poems, by the relation of the order of the copies to *P2V* as finally printed and bound, by pagination, and by general appearance. W's own numberings of the poems are noted in parentheses.

[Lot 5]: *To a Young Lady* (1); *On Seeing Some Tourists* (see Hale White 57, 69–70), cancelled; [*Stray Pleasures*]; *Star Gazers* (3) (see Hale White 59); *The Power of Music* (see Hale White 59); *To a Daisy* ("With Little Here") (4) (see Hale White 57); *To the Same Flower*; *Incident Characteristic of a Favorite Dog* (5); *Tribute to the Memory of the Same Dog* (see Hale White 57); "Yes, There is Holy Pleasure in Thine Eye" (6) (see Hale White 58); "Though Narrow Be That Old Man's Cares"; *A Prophecy. Feb. 1807*; *To Thomas Clarkson* (see Hale White 58).

The unnumbered poems seem to be integral to the MS as sent off, although their appearance does not preclude their having been added after the others were written.

[Lot 6]:[*The Emigrant Mother*] (1); *Foresight* (2); *A Complaint*; [*Personal Talk* sonnets] (3); "Yes Full Surely 'Twas the Echo"; *To the Spade of a Friend* (4) (see also lot 7).

A Complaint was copied in on the verso of the leaf containing *Foresight* at a time plainly different from that of the copying of *Foresight;* but "Yes Full Surely" was equally clearly copied in after the *Personal Talk* sonnets in the same process of writing.

[Lot 7]: *Song at the Feast of Brougham Castle* (1) (see Hale White 58); "Loud Is the Vale" (2); "Rid of a Vexing and a Heavy Load" (3), cancelled; [*Elegiac Stanzas, Suggested by a Picture of Peele Castle*] (see Hale White 58); draft toward *To the Spade of a Friend*, preceding both the lines on the verso of the stitched-on leaf in Vol. I, sheet 4, as described above, and Vol. II, lot 6; *Ode* (4) through line 87 (see Hale White 61 and plate opp. 60); note to printer advising that the rest of the poem with the notes, title page, and the remainder of the materials which will conclude the book, will be sent next day.

[Lot 8]: Conclusion of *Ode*; notes to the Second Volume (see Hale White 63, 70–71).

The first two pages of the notes were originally numbered "23" and "24" (the last number was possibly "22" but the vertical stroke for a "4" seems definite) in sequence with the leaves of lot 7, but the numbers have been erased and new numbers "1" and "2" written in. (Successive pages are numbered through "7.") In the center of the last page, plainly the cover for the rest of the lot, the simple address "Messrs Longman and Rees" appears, but inconspicuously and as if an afterthought: W must have been confident that the conveyor was well apprised of the packet's destination.

The preceding description omits discussion of, among other details, the characteristics of the various papers used in the MS. This subject deserves independent attention. In this respect the MS may be divided into three kinds of materials: (1) Lots of careful fair copy, or copies begun with the intention that they be fair—written on small folio laid double sheets watermarked with a medallion containing a seated Britannia with a date 1802 at her feet and countermarked J HOLYOAKE. This is the paper of several letters of this time, including *MY* nos. 54, 59; *STCL* nos. 639, 643; SH to Joanna H, c 23 December 1806. I am unfamiliar with examples of this paper used for W family MS materials written elsewhere from Coleorton. Most of the writing is in the autograph of SH, and most is in double columns. Some fragments of the same paper but of single-column width are stitched on. (2) MSS written before the Coleorton visit, then used as printer's copy without basic re-writing. These materials are written on laid octavo paper watermarked with a crowned horn-in-shield and countermarked "1798." Some Coleorton copying has been inserted in space earlier left blank on these leaves. (3) Other MSS, none apparently written before the Coleorton residence, but on several sorts of paper, including fragments of the Holyoake paper already described.

(1) The first of these groups would appear fairly clearly to represent the work on which W and SH were engaged during Nov as indicated in quotation (4) above. Included are the first five lots of copy for the first volume and the first two of the second. All attached fragments are written on the same kind of paper except for the pasted-on slip on "Sheet 1st" of Vol. II. Appearance as well as content makes plain that these materials were worked up closely together, probably basically before printing was very far advanced. Sheet numbers, for example, have been repeatedly altered, and one or more

sheets so copied have been cut up and portions stitched on other sheets to complete them. For a more precise instance: *To H.C.*, on sheet 4 of Vol. I, has been stitched on in two fragments from what was clearly another sheet of the same sort. On the verso of the second of the two fragments are lines from *R&I*, commencing as those on the present sheet 6 commence, but with a preceding notation, "4th sheet," the number corrected to "5th." The notation would clearly have stood at the top center of the first page of the sheet from which this was cut. The present fifth sheet, containing *R&I* up to the point where the lines on the fragment just discussed begin, was originally numbered "3rd Sheet," but the notation is cancelled and an extra leaf has been stitched on above containing the beginning of *Beggars* and the heading "4 Sheet," corrected to "Sheet 5." "Sheet No 5" is later written on elsewhere. The first leaf of this once third, then fourth, and finally fifth sheet was clearly left mostly blank while portions of the later pages were filled, for the copying on the first leaf—the conclusion of *Beggars*, *To a Sky-lark*, and "With How Sad Steps, O Moon"—was filled in late, and completed by use of the stitched-on leaf; and the title "Ode" was apparently written in about half-way down the first column before other writing there, then cancelled before or during the copying of *To a Sky-lark*. Evidently this sheet and the sheet from which the *To H.C.* fragments were taken were at one stage of the copying respectively the third and fourth sheets; these were then renumbered as the fourth and fifth; and then that fifth sheet was cut up and what had been the fourth sheet was made the fifth. (The other fragments stitched on the "4th sheet" as described above contain similar copy.) None of the numberings of the present sheets 2–4 seems to result from correction.

Both the first and second sheets of the second volume have been renumbered, although heavy obliteration prevents confident discernment of the previous numbers. The first sheet commences, as already noted, with the cancelled three stanzas of the *Ode to Duty*, which must of course have preceded the copy in the present fourth sheet of the first volume. The original number can be seen to have been followed by a "th," indicating "4th" or higher. The heavy revision that the sheets underwent before finally sent off might at first seem to indicate a furious pace of activity in early Nov, and W when sending the second sheet promised another by the next post.

It is likely that something happened soon after the second sheet was sent off to slow abruptly the pace at which the later ones were forwarded. Possibly the printer or publisher requested delay, or W decided to await the return of the first proof from the printer, or other circumstances intervened. If W did actually await word from Scott about *The Seven Sisters*, the fourth sheet can of course hardly have been prepared before the latter part of Nov.

Among the corrections and additions to the *Ode to Duty* on the same sheet appears one—the fourth in Hale White's copy of the unpublished stanzas and second in the variant readings for lines 25–32 on *PW* IV, 85—which is in the autograph of STC, who cannot have had access to this part of the printer's copy of *P2V* before he joined the Ws at Coleorton on 21 Dec. (SH, that is, can hardly have participated between 25 and 29 Oct—the earliest conceivable opportunity for her to engage in such work—in the preparation of the quantity of MS necessary for STC to have been able to enter the correction then.) No sheets at all had come from the printer on 7 Dec, and only three, probably including signatures B-D of the first volume (*The Seven Sisters* is printed in D; see quotation (9) above; gathering [A] contains prefatory materials sent off later) had come back to the author by 20 Jan; these would have carried the printing part of the way through the *Ode to Duty*, and not quite through W's fourth MS sheet. The paper of the published volumes, watermarked with an "HS" over "1806," suggests that printing may not have commenced before Jan, although W might have received proof on other paper.

Some copies of *P2V* had been bound by 23 Apr, however; so that for the remaining sheets of the two volumes (that is, ten full sheets bound in duodecimo, plus probably another sheet bound in separate gatherings of eight and four leaves in Vol. I, plus five other printed leaves in Vol. II) to have been printed and corrected in appropriate time, the printer must have produced at an average rate of about a sheet a week, evidently his pace in Jan. (W can hardly be speaking on 20 Jan of a sheet-a-week average on the basis of a period of more than three weeks, since no more than three sheets had come.) Yet the printer was even less active in the latter part of Feb (see quotation (12) above). An obvious conclusion is that the printing proceeded much more rapidly from that time. (W's remark of 20 Jan that "we do not get on faster than at the rate of a sheet a week" does not, of course, make explicit whether W is referring to his own sheets or proof sheets. After preparing sheet D of Vol. I the printer would, however, have had some eleven and one-half of his sheets still to make up out of twelve or thirteen "lots" from W: W was possibly thinking of the two types of sheet as equivalent.) The fourth sheet—and possibly also the third—were sent off after 21 Dec; and while it is probable that the printer had a backlog of at least one of W's lots when W wrote to Scott on 20 Jan, he need not have had much more. Unless the more expeditious stages of the printing process were delayed improbably long after late Feb, however, W is likely to have sent off the seventh sheet of his first volume by then. Other evidence makes it likely that the seventh sheet was in fact sent off by early Feb. The sonnet "Lady! the Songs of Spring

Were in the Grove" was fairly certainly composed c early Feb. The poem
appears on the recto of leaf G1 of Vol. I (H8 is the last leaf of the volume),
but does not appear in the printer's MS (see the description of the seventh
sheet of Vol. I above).

Folding and stitching of the gathering of signature G can be seen to have
followed the procedure normal for the duodecimo gatherings in the two
volumes, by removal of G5-8 from across the foot of the printed sheet,
folding this long leaf across at the center, folding again at the center, and
binding in four between leaves G1-4 and G9-12 as formed by folding the
remaining portion of the sheet into eight by two center folds parallel with
the shorter sides. Fold marks, cuts, tears, and the like in uncut copies appear
to show that all leaves of G are portions of a single original sheet. It is thus
improbable that this gathering or sheet can have been printed before early
Feb. W, on the other hand, seems to have supposed on 20 Jan that a rate of
production of a sheet a week was effectively established; and he appears to
have received at least one sheet, and to have expected more, between 20 Jan
and mid-Feb. It is doubtful that W could have delayed sending his seventh
sheet until well into Feb and then have delayed yet beyond that time his
decision to insert the sonnet where it is now found in the published work.
Circumstances as well as probabilities appear to suggest that the seventh
sheet was sent off by early Feb and the corrections for it not long after composition of *To Lady Beaumont.*

The portion of the frank found on the first sheet of Vol. II, as remarked
above, makes plain that that sheet cannot have been completed before Jan
1807. *To Thomas Clarkson* was probably not written before 26 March 1807,
and is printed on the verso of Vol. II, leaf F6 (on the recto of which is *A
Prophecy. Feb. 1807*). The paper of uncut copies shows plainly that this leaf
too was part of the original sheet F. So the printing of F and later signatures
is unlikely to have been completed before 26 March. The MS of *To Thomas
Clarkson* is an integral part of the fourth lot of copy for Vol. II. It is improbable, therefore, that this lot or those following were sent off before late Mar.
In view of the time of the completion of the volume it does not seem likely
either that any lots can have been sent off after early Apr. W's questions to
Scott on 20 Jan about "Lega!" for *The Blind Highland Boy* imply that preparation of the fourth lot for Vol. II was in mind at that time, and corrections to
the MS which obviously reflect Scott's advice are unlikely to date before late
Feb: W does not seem to have procrastinated in thanking Scott for his help
(see *MY* I, 139). So the fourth lot is unlikely to have been sent off before that
time. *Gipsies*, a late insert among the materials of II, lot 3, was probably
composed c 28 Feb or after; although the correction was sent along to the

printer after the main lot (see description of sheet 3 above), the time at which either was sent does not seem capable of exact determination.

The negative evidence provided by the dates of later lots of MS for the second volume thus does little, in sum, to fix the time by which the first two lots were sent off. The general appearance of the basic copy on the double sheets of Holyoake paper, however, implies that the basic work on the sheets was done within a fairly short period, perhaps between 30 Oct and early Dec.

(2) Laid paper with watermark of a crowned horn-in-shield and counter-mark "1798" (or parts thereof) is used for the following:

> Vol. I, lot 7. All sonnets except "Nuns Fret Not" and the conjunct leaves containing "No Mortal Object," *To the Supreme Being*, and *Written in Very Early Youth*, and those containing *The King of Sweden* and *On the Extinction of the Venetian Republic*.
> Vol. II, lot 2. *Yarrow Unvisited*.
> lot 3. All materials except the late inserts.
> lot 4. Both poems (*The Blind Highland Boy*, *The Green Linnet*).
> lot [5]. *To a Young Lady*, *On Seeing Some Tourists*.
> lot 6. [*The Emigrant Mother*], *Foresight*, *A Complaint*, [*Personal Talk* sonnets].
> lot [7]. *Ode*.

Most of these copies seem to have been written at about the same time and to have belonged to a single MS or fairly unified process of copying, although a few have plainly been written in late—"Yes, Hope May with My Strong Desire Keep Pace" and *November. 1806* among poems intended Vol. I, and *On Seeing Some Tourists* and *A Complaint* among poems intended for Vol. II. Apart from the poems just named, only one of these works, *The Blind High-land Boy*, has recently been attributed to a time as late as the Coleorton visit (see Moorman II, 97; *PW* III, 88).[1] The poem, however, is copied in the Coleorton Commonplace Book (PML) between the *Ode to Duty* and the *Ode*, and all the copies seem to have been written in successively at about the same time. It is unlikely that Lady B had access to a set of W's MSS of the materials which he was preparing for *P2V* during the winter of 1806–07 except in the brief period 20 Oct–2 Nov, while she fairly certainly had some access to them during W's visit to London of 4 Apr–c 20 May 1806 (see especially *MY* I, 24, 100). The poem was thus probably written before the Coleorton visit and by Mar 1806, but, as it does not appear in MS M (from which its length

[1] Knight's *PW* 1882–89 date is "1803." Dowden states that the date is "uncertain," an assessment repeated by Knight in 1896. Smith's date is "probably 1806."

would fairly surely have precluded accidental omission), not earlier than late Mar 1804. *To the River Duddon* ("O Mountain Stream"), on the 7th sheet for Vol. I, also seems likely not to have been composed before c late Sept 1804 (see 1804:107).

Of the numerous instances of use of this paper among Wordsworthian documents it may be observed that none can be assigned with much probability (one earlier usage by an associate of W's will be discussed below) before very late 1805, and use in 1806 was quite heavy: over a third of the surviving letters written in that year are on such paper, as are DC MS 60 (*PB* MS 5), MS 57 (elegiac poems), *Waggoner* MS 1 (BM Ashley 4637), and MS 56 (*Waggoner* MS 2). DW was engaged c 28 Nov 1805, just before writing *Prel* MS A, in copying "some of [her] Brother's Poems" (*EY* 648); and her autograph appears frequently among these copies, as in *The Sparrow's Nest*, *To a Butterfly* ("I've Watched"), *The Blind Highland Boy*, *Yarrow Unvisited*, *The Green Linnet*, "The Sun Has Long Been Set," and *Foresight*. It seems not impossible that some of these materials might date from as early as 28 Nov 1805, although the likelihood is not great. DW was busy with the copying of *Prel* through much of Dec 1805, and with *Prel* and her *Recollections* early the next year (see 1805:108; 1806:10). RS remarked on 4 Feb, although not unambiguously, that "Wordsworth was with me last week; he has of late been more employed in correcting his poems than in writing others" (CCS III, 19). SH's autograph also appears in the materials, and she plainly took part in whatever program of copying these items represent. DW would probably not have failed to mention such work in her survey of recent copying activities on 2 Mar 1806 (*MY* I, 10) had the quantity been of significant proportions. The corrective work of c late Jan mentioned by RS may likewise have been, despite RS's phrasing, mainly on *Prel*. Still, the prospect of W's trip to London at the end of Mar 1806 would have provided strong incentive for transcribing materials of which only one MS then existed: it would have been uncharacteristically incautious for W to carry off unique copies of his works; and he certainly took copies to London (see *EY* 448, 465, 653).

Except for the evidence provided by the paper, another time would present itself as perhaps the most likely one for this work: c Mar–Apr 1805. DW reports on 11 Apr 1805 that they have been busily "transcribing some of my Brother's manuscript Poems, the work I was first able to do after John's death." I have, however, found only one instance of use of such paper by any of the W group before late Dec 1805, TCl's letter to John Wadkin from Grasmere, 26 July 1805, DCP (see H. D. Rawnsley, *Past and Present at the English Lakes*, Glasgow, 1916, 203–08). There is, of course, no reason to suppose that TCl obtained the paper for his letter from W, although the circumstances perhaps offer an indication that the paper was available in or near Grasmere. In the absence of apparent use of the paper by the Ws themselves before the end of 1805, it would on balance be unreasonable to date these MSS some three or four months before TCl's letter.

Some portion of this copying may have been based on the Ws' duplicate of MS M (see 1804:32): of the copies of the *Sonnets Dedicated to Liberty* which are written on this paper and which also appear in MS M, those from *Composed by the Sea-side near Calais* through *October. 1803* follow the order of M. This fact would in turn suggest that the four sonnets following next, although their internal order would not be the same, might have stood in the original transcription just before *Composed by the Sea-side*, their position in M. The *Miscellaneous Sonnets* and other copies on this paper do not appear to show a significant dependence on a copy like M.

(3) Of the remaining materials little need be said for present purposes. Inasmuch as W and SH were probably heavily concerned through Nov 1806 with the basic copying using the Holyoake double sheets, all materials on such paper, as already implied, probably date from that time or after; but none of this work shows any sign of having been written before the Coleorton visit.

APPENDIX VIII

The Composition of The White Doe

The early stages of composition of *WD* are fairly readily definable as abstract quantities of lines in relation to times of writing; and surviving MSS can be dated with some confidence. The history of the poem nonetheless contains broad areas of obscurity.

W fairly certainly had not begun the poem before receiving a copy of Dr. Whitaker's *History of Craven* on 16 Oct 1807 (1807:88). He had composed some kind of Introduction probably by 8 Nov, and 500 lines by 1 Dec (1807:95, 1807:101). His statement in the IF note that "the earlier half of this Poem was composed at Stockton-upon-Tees" during his Dec [1807] visit, while thus probably not technically accurate, may be taken as a sound indication that the poem was well advanced, perhaps half written, before he left Stockton. Thus some 850 to 950 lines had perhaps been composed by 19 Dec. By 3 Jan 1808 W had written "above 1200 lines" (*MY* I, 187). Probably on 16 Jan he finished "a narrative Poem of about 1700 lines" (*MY* I, 191). A MS was transferred to RS, possibly by 2 Feb (1808:7), certainly by 16 Feb: a MS was intended to go off to STC some time after 5 Feb (see *MY* I, 192–93), and RS carried this same MS away from Ambleside on 16 Feb (1808:12). He perhaps carried it on with him to London, and W probably recovered it there c late Feb. W apparently supposed that RS would take the MS to the Marshalls at Leeds, and that it would be seen in turn by Dr. Whitaker; but this expectation was not realized. (See esp. 1808:12.)

MS 1, DC MS 61, contains a plainly early MS of lines 1–856; drafts for other materials on versos include work toward lines 1761–76, 1783–92, 1811–23, unused lines related to 1823–31, the drafts quoted *PW* III, 554 as for 1010–75, work toward 1832–72, draft for the "Advertizement," and draft for *The Force of Prayer* 1–46, following which a leaf has been torn out. *The Force of Prayer* draft probably dates from c 18 Sept (*MY* I, 168); and although it stands last in the NB, it almost certainly antedates the *WD* materials. The evidence thus far cited and the appearance of MS 1 suggest that the materials through lines 856, in the autographs not only of W and MW, but also, for lines 174–593 and probably 629–63, of DW, are likely to have been copied

700

after W's return from Stockton, although the copying of 1–173 (by MW) might date any time after W's arrival there. Presumably all these verses would date by 16 Jan 1808, since the materials on the versos, which are fairly surely prior to the first completion of the poem, were clearly written in after the copying of 1–856. A date by late Jan seems almost certain.

MS 2, DC MS 62, contains efforts at neat copy, by MW, of at least 536–81, 594–795, 797–802, 878–937, 1346–63, 1570–1635; draft for 916–17, 962–72; a fair copy that became draft, headed "Fourth Canto," of 936–86, including lines quoted *PW* III, 552–54. Composition was still very much in progress when these drafts were made, and they too probably date by 16 Jan, and certainly by late Jan. "Advertizement" drafts here may be supposed of the same date (on these see esp. *STCL* III, 111–12).

Neither of these MSS can, of course, be the one that went to London early in 1808, which apparently no longer survives. The history of the poem during the next few months is outlined with general accuracy in *PW* III, 543–44. Although W was apparently determined when he departed for London—probably 23 Feb 1808—to publish *WD*, he decided by 29 Mar, possibly discouraged partly by a reading in company with CL, Hazlitt, and Sarah Stoddart, not to publish it after all (*MY* I, 207, 221–22). W evidently at some point, however, offered the poem to Longman, although he was unwilling to submit it for inspection; and when W departed London on 3 Apr STC was fairly certainly left with the understanding that he was empowered to negotiate publication arrangements and to make alterations (*STCL* III, 110–16, VI, 1021–22). By 17 Apr Longman had agreed to publish on W's terms of 100 guineas for 1000 copies (*MY* I, 225). W was apparently not prepared to be rushed into print either by publisher or by family. Writing on 17 Apr from Grasmere he had promised Wrangham a copy of the poem "if I publish it" (*MY* I, 212). On 1 May DW wrote that the family were "*very anxious*" that *WD* be published as soon as possible (*MY* I, 230). On 10 May W advised CCl "not to be in such a bustle of expectation about the poem" (*MY* I, 234); and on 11 May he was described by DW as "averse to [publication] now [but yielding] to Mary's entreaties and mine" (*MY* I, 236). On 18 May he wrote to Longman to assure that publication would not go forward. He evidently indicated also that STC had acted without authority (*STCL* III, 110–16, VI, 1021–22). The plan in W's mind on 5 June, as DW then understood it, was that the poem was "not to be published till next winter" (*MY* I, 253). Later, on 29 June W told the Rev. Mr. Pering about a poem that he had written referring to Bolton "which he intended to publish," as Pering recalled, "when it was sufficiently corrected" (Pering Diary, DCP).

Appendix VIII

The London MS evidently went on to MM and eventually reached W again some time between DeQ's departure from Grasmere, c but by 20 Feb, and 26 Mar 1809 (see 1809:17; Jordan 96; *MY* I, 302). SH wrote on 19 Apr 1809 that "William came in to me just now to read some of his additions to [*WD*] with which he is at present busy—there is to be another canto added to it . . . " (*SHL* 20). On 1 May 1809 DW wrote: "My Brother has begun to correct and add to the poem of the White Doe, and has been tolerably successful. He intends to finish it before he begins with any other work, and has made up his mind, if he can satisfy himself in the alterations, he intends to make, to publish it next winter . . . " (*MY* I, 325). On 28 Dec 1809 DW advised Lady B that W was "going to finish the Poem of the White Doe" and was "resolved to publish it, when he has finished it to his satisfaction" (*MY* I, 379). By 28 Feb 1810 further delay was in prospect: W was back at work on *The Recluse* instead. "After this Task is finished he hopes," said DW, "to complete the White Doe, and proud should we all be if it could be honoured by a frontispiece from the Pencil of Sir George Beaumont" (*MY* I, 392).

When, over three years later, on 24 Apr 1814, DW announced W's intention to publish the poem in the not-distant future, although probably not "before next winter" (*MY* II, 140), the assertion might seem, were the sequel unknown, a prefiguration of later announcements about finishing *The Recluse*. But a MS of *WD*, probably that used for printing, presently at King's College, Cambridge, was apparently prepared and conveyed to Longman by early Aug 1814, and the firm wrote to W on 5 Aug confirming an offer of £100 upon publication (Owen LLW 26–27). Although W possibly did not receive that letter, DW reported on 11 Nov that W then intended to publish the poem "in the spring" (*MY* II, 165). Longman again wrote on 28 Jan 1815, in response to a recent query from W, with an offer to commence printing immediately. About 9 Feb 1815 CW received a MS from Sir GB at Dunmow, probably the same that Longman had read in 1814, for conveyance to London. (Owen LLW 27; *MY* II, 201–02.) Proof was being corrected later in Feb (see 1815:24); and the dedicatory verses are dated 20 Apr. The Longman accounts for the volume commence under 15 May. The volume was entered at Stationer's Hall on 30 May and advertised as published on 2 June.

The specific content of the entire poem at any point before preparation of the printer's MS remains a puzzle. The final version contains over 1900 lines rather than 1700; and the version seen and criticized by STC (*STCL* III, 110–16) clearly differed from the poem as known (see discussion *PW* III, 543–47).

APPENDIX IX

The Wordsworth Commonplace Book, DC MS 26, and Certain Other Copies in W's MSS

On the contents of DC MS 26 see especially Mary Moorman, "Wordsworth's Commonplace Book," *N&Q* N.S. IV (1957), 400–05; R. S. Woof, "The Literary Relations of Wordsworth and Coleridge," Diss. University of Toronto, 1959; Betz *BN*. The following remarks make no attempt to solve all remaining questions about the identity and sources of the contents of this book and the relation of the contents to W's work. They do attempt some suggestions about the basic chronological interrelationship of the copies as already identified, especially in the examinations just cited, to which my debt in the material below is general and continuous.

As indicated by Mrs. Moorman, the book is unlikely to have been in use before the date inscribed by W on the flyleaf, "Janry 1800," and the latest entry to which an approximate date may be assigned with confidence is that standing last in the main set of copies, an extract from W's letter to Wrangham of 5 June 1808, probably copied about that date. A few other comments are possible:

A first sequence of entries may be regarded as concluding with stanzas from Robert Greene's "Ah, What Is Love?" in what is possibly the fair hand of JW.[1] This entry, if written by JW, would date by 29 Sept 1800 (see 1800:145). The preceding eleven entries are:

[1] This suggestion is made against, and subsequent to, the advice of Professors Carl Ketcham and Paul Betz. Comparison of the hand in question with that of JW's letters of 1800–1801 and the log of the *Earl of Abergavenny* (India Office Records) seems to reveal a decisive number of common characteristics in formation of letters, including a pronounced tendency to form the lower-case *s* (particularly at the end of a word) with an abrupt and only slightly curled downward stroke, and even more noticeably to make a long diagonal upward stroke to the right before the downward stroke on lower-case *t*'s and *h*'s, and often on *b*'s, *p*'s, and *k*'s as well. This long stroke, although not uncommon in contemporary autographs, seems virtually unique to JW, in combination with other features of the hand in the MSS of the W circle at this time.

Appendix IX

(1) An extract from *Robert the Devyll, A Metrical Romance* (London, 1798).

(2) A portion of a passage on pedlars from Robert Heron's *Journey through the Western Countries of Scotland* (1793), followed by a stub of a leaf cut out. The Heron passage is that referred to—and, in editions from 1827, quoted—by W in his note to *Exc* I. 341. The leaf cut out probably contained most or all of the remainder of the passage as quoted in *Exc*.

(3) Extracts from "Pennant's 1st Tour of Scotland" (*A Tour in Scotland, 1769*, Chester, 1771), including the story of "Ellen" of Kirkconnell on which W based *Ellen Irwin*.

(4) Extracts from Anders Sparrman's *Voyage to the Cape and Round the World* (1785).

(5) Extracts on "eutrapelia" from Isaac Barrow's sermon *Against Foolish Talking and Jesting*. The passage was probably a favorite of STC's as early as 1800 (see *STCL* II, 1017).

(6) On a duodecimo double sheet pasted in, two poems copied by Thomas Wilkinson, "I Love to Be Alone" and "Lines Written on a Paper Wrapt round a Moss-rose Pulled on New-years Day, and sent to M. Wilson."

(7) Extracts from Thomas Motte's *Travels to the Diamond Mines of Jumbulpoor*. These extracts, in the autograph of W and DW, have also been pasted in. They are preceded by an introductory note written by MW on the page to which the copies by Wilkinson were affixed. Ink blots on the facing pages of the opening show that MW's note was written before the pasting-in took place.

(8) An extract from the "Morte Arthur," also pasted in.

(9) A leaf, pasted in, containing, in the autograph of SH, the first three stanzas of Campbell's *The Exile of Erin*. The two concluding stanzas were written on the other side of the paper (the side pasted away from view) with a cryptic note by SH, "Take care of it"; but DW has written the final two stanzas into the next page of the book.

(10) "Fragments": (10a) one stanza, "Go Fetch to Me a Pint o' Wine," from Burns; (10b) the last stanza of *The Queen's Marie*; (10c) two stanzas commencing "O that my Father had ne'er on me smil'd"; (10d) four stanzas that had contributed to *The Thorn* from Herd's *Ancient and Modern Scottish Songs*.

(11) Extracts from *The Life of Madame Guyon*.

Except as stated otherwise all these materials are in the autograph of W or DW. Only the double sheet filled by Wilkinson seems likely to have been written or pasted in out of sequence (see below), and the book may otherwise be supposed to have been filled up to that point possibly by 29 Sept 1800. Unless MW's note introducing the Motte excerpts was itself written much later than the rest, it would probably precede her departure from DC, possibly 4 or 5 Apr; and hence so would the entry of all materials through those taken from Motte.

Entry (13), following the Greene quotation (12), is a copy of "A Lementation on the Untimely Death of Roger, in the Cumberland Dialect," copied by Thomas Wilkinson on a small quarto double sheet made from the same paper as (6), laid, with a watermark of a crowned horn-in-shield over "LVG," the V connected from its base with the base of the shield by the vertical line of a 4. The Wilkinson copy, here tipped in, would probably date after 19 Jan 1801 unless the Ws had the copy through a third party: W is not known to have met Wilkinson earlier. The same consideration would apply to (6).

Entry (14a) is a paste-in of a copy of a poem, "An unfortunate Mother to her infant a[t her] Breast," which, although written on paper seemingly like that of (13), is in the autograph of STC. Five stanzas of the original copy are visible. The concluding two stanzas have been partly cut away and partly pasted against the NB page. They are replaced by copy by W on another pasted-on slip. With the aid of a strong light a fragment of a note in STC's autograph may also be read on the verso now pasted away from view: "arrivals of Ships at Liverpool and [*word or words cut away*] the Hussar & the Speedwell from St [*blank*]." The note would appear likely at first to date not before Mar 1804, after STC had been in Liverpool but before his departure from England in the *Speedwell*, of which he shows no sign of having known anything before that month (*STCL* II, 1083–84). The notice, however, is probably irrelevant to STC's journey and perhaps is a reference to another ship of the name, since the *Hussar* was wrecked on 12 Feb, and the news published in London on 22 Feb (*Courier*, 22 Feb, 1 Mar). The poem appears in the "Fugitive Poetry" section of the *Poetical Register . . . for 1801* (London, 1802) and thus was probably copied from an ephemeral source of 1801 or from *The Poetical Register* itself, from the text of which this copy does not appear to vary significantly. W's conclusion of the verse copy is written on one side of a slip apparently taken from an old MS, unfortunately not otherwise known to have survived, containing, on the other side, a portion of draft for the Dedication of the 1793 *Descriptive Sketches*.

Below on the same page on which the slip just described is pasted are pencil copies, in a large autograph, fairly surely STC's, of (15) a three-line misquotation from Cowper's *Lines to Mrs. Unwin* (the same misquotation appears *STCNB* 1441; cf *STCNB* 2433&n) and (16) a two-line extract from Joshua Sylvester's "O Holy Peace." The same lines are copied again in ink by DW at the top of the next page, and below on the same page DW has gone on, apparently at the same sitting, to copy (17) "Lines written by Coleridge in bed at Grasmere on Thursday night October 1st or rather on the morning of Friday October 2nd 1801" (see 1801:62). Pinholes in the DC pencil MS of the same poem and in the Commonplace Book indicate that the pencil MS was pinned into the Commonplace Book after (14a) was pasted in. DW's copy was fairly certainly made from the pencil copy. The next entry is (18) a copy by DW of a portion of a letter from DeQ to W of 4 Mar [1804] (cf Jordan 35; Moorman article cited, 404). Written inversely at the foot of the page on which the copy from DeQ concludes is a copy of "Dr Beddoes' prescription sent to Mr Edmundson"—undoubtedly the prescription sent on 24 Mar and referred to by DW on 25 Mar 1804 (see *EY* 461).

Items (14) to (18) thus all appear to be associated with STC or with a time about early 1804 by 25 Mar, or both; and (16) was obviously copied in in succession from (13) to (15). More specifically, (15) and (16) are likely to date by 14 Jan 1804, and as they appear to allow space for (14a) and (14b), these are likely to have been written by that time also. The *Ode to the Rain* and immediately preceding copying probably preceded the next entry. Item (14a) is likely to date from c early Mar or after and the succeeding copies also from Mar. The copy of the Beddoes prescription is likely to date from late Mar or after, and to indicate a date by which the preceding materials were written. In the absence of other evidence, the copies by Wilkinson, (6) and (11), may be supposed to have been tipped in by this time.

Three copies in W's autograph, all plainly written by W at about the same time, follow:

(19) Three stanzas commencing "Sweet scented flower! who'rt wont to blow/On January's front severe." The Jacobean content of this lyric, which addresses a "funeral flower" that throws its "sweet decaying smell" across the "desart gloom" in the lonely tomb, makes the verses unlikely to have been copied any time within a few years after 11 Feb 1805; so the copy probably dates earlier.

(20) An excerpt from Richard Edwardes' "In Going to My Naked Bed," first published in *The Paradise of Dainty Devices*.

(21) Lord Herbert of Cherbury's Epitaph for himself.

In absence of more specific evidence, (19) to (21) may be regarded as dating between Mar 1804 and 11 Feb 1805.

The remaining copies at this end of the book, with the exception of the last (the letter to Wrangham already mentioned) look as if they had been entered in fairly steady succession, although one or two may in fact have been copied in out of order. A copy (22) of Cowper's *Yardley Oak* (see GCL 123n), lines 1–124, in the autograph of SH, and (23) extracts from Sir John Barrow's *Travels in China* (1804), in the autograph of SH and MW, appear next. Both seem to have been copied in at about the same time, and the time of the copying of Barrow is not likely to have preceded 8 Feb 1807 (*MY* I, 133). Following these appear (24) a copy by MW of three stanzas of John Mayne's "By Logan's Streams That Run Sae Deep," headed "By John Mayne Author of the Poem of 'Glasgow'" and (25) a copy by DW, "From Aristotle's Synopsis of the Virtues and Vices." The second of these was also copied by W, from a review, in his letter to Lady B of 12 Mar 1805, and was probably copied here at about that time. The copy of "By Logan's Streams" immediately preceding is quite neat. The last two lines are written at the top of the page containing "From Aristotle's Synopsis," which follows about a half-inch below separated by a short line. The appearance of the two lines, although they are written high on the page, does not indicate any concern on the part of the copyist about tightness of space, and they were probably the first materials written on the page. So the copy of the Mayne poem may be conjectured, on the assumption that it followed (14)–(21), to have been made between Mar 1804 and 12 Mar 1805.

Commencing just following the Aristotle "Synopsis" extract W has copied (26) a set of extracts from J. L. Buchanans' *Travels in the Western Hebrides* (1793). Next W and MW have cooperated in copying, fairly certainly at about the same time (W's part appears to have been written at the same sitting as the Buchanan extracts), four Blake lyrics (27): *Holy Thursday* (*Innocence*), *Laughing Song*, *The Tyger*, and "I Love the Jocund Dance." Next appear two extracts in W's autograph from Thomas Wilkinson's Journal, the first (28a) the description of a "Female who was reaping alone" that W had drawn on for his *Solitary Reaper*, and the second (28b), beginning "But take courage," drawn on by W probably later for *Exc* IV.489–504. There appears no reason to doubt that these were copied in following the Blake poems; and as Professor Betz has shown (Betz *BN*), the copying is likely to have taken place between the time that W regained access to Wilkinson's Journal upon returning to DC on 10 July 1807 (see *MY* I, 104) and W's departure for Eusemere on 25 Aug. The Blake copies fairly certainly were made at Coleorton, after the copies from Barrow, and are reasonably dated by Betz between mid-Mar and mid-Apr (when W and MW went to London) or between mid-May and 10 June 1807. The second of these two periods may be fixed more precisely as commencing 6 May (see 1807:41). Entry (26) may be assigned to the same periods.

Next follow copies, all clearly of much the same time, and in the autograph of DW, of or from six ballads. All the copies appear to have been taken from Ambrose Philips' three-volume *Collection of Old Ballads* (1733–35) (see Abbie F. Potts, *The Elegiac Mode in English Poetry*, Ithaca, 1967, 124–26). These include: (29) "Eighth Henry ruling in this land" (Philips III, 64–66); (30) *A princely Song of the Six Queens that were married to Henry the 8th, King of England* (Philips III, 67–73); (31) *Fitte of the Ballad of Lady Jane Grey and Lord Guilford Dudley* (Philips III, 81–82, from "Sweet Princes they deserv'd no blame"; DW's title is copied in after (34) below); (32) *The Lady Arabella and Lord Seymour . . . a Fragment* (Philips I, 209–10, from "Once more to Prison"); (33) *The Suffolk Miracle*, sixteen stanzas (Philips I, 266–68), with corrections by W; (34) *The Lamentable Complaint of Queen Mary for the Unkind Departure of King Philip* (Philips III, 83–90).

In the absence of evidence to the contrary, copies (29) to (34) may be dated between 10 July 1807 and c 5 June 1808. The extract (35) from W's letter of 5 June 1808 to Wrangham, in MW's autograph, closes the series of entries at this end of the Commonplace Book.

At the other end of the book are found medical recipes or prescriptions (for inflammation of the bowels, for croup, for chilblains) and a recipe for making ink; inventories of household linen (see 1802:248); accounts, with which belongs a slip on which DW notes sums received from STC (see 1804:15); and memoranda about Johnny (see 1804:36; 1804:54; 1804:57).

Here may also be noted the copying by DW of four epitaphs in DC MS 20, which contains DW's journal for 14 May–22 Dec 1800. These are (1) the epitaph of Josias (here called "Tobias") Franklin and his wife; Benjamin Franklin's epitaph; the epitaph of Sir George Vane at the parish church of Long Newton, Durham, noted as taken from [William] Hutchinson's *History of Durham* III (1794), 168 (see Essay upon Epitaphs, Grosart II, 47); and (4) an "Epitaph taken from the Parish Church-Yard of Marsk in the County of York." MS 20 physically closely resembles MSS 19 and 25, and like them contains notes dating from the W's 1798–1799 trip to Germany but shows no sign of having been in use earlier. The epitaphs are copied between stubs of leaves that apparently once contained financial accounts from the German trip, and other leaves containing drafts for *Complaint of a Forsaken Indian Woman* (see *PW* II, 475–76). The *Complaint* drafts fairly certainly date between 14 Sept 1798 and 22 Dec 1800, where the journal breaks off on account of the *Complaint* draft; but they stand in indeterminate chronological relationship to the epitaphs. The Franklin family epitaphs appeared in London editions of the *Memoir of the Life of Dr Franklin* in 1793 and 1799, as well as in the Dublin and Dundee editions of 1793 and 1796. All of these, however, name Franklin's father "Josias"; so DW is likely to be copying from a secondary source. The Vane epitaph suggests a time of copying about that of the W's Sockburn residence, as does also the "Marsk" epitaph:[2] Marske-by-the-Sea is thirty miles from Sockburn. All the copies, however, appear to have been made at about the same time and with the same pen, and on this account as well as on the basis of content all may be assigned to the period between late Apr 1799 (when the Ws returned to England from Germany) and 17 Dec 1799 (when they set off for Grasmere).

Here too may be noted a copy by W from Volney's *Travels through Syria and Egypt* concerning the "Semoum or Samiel," in DC MS 28 on an inter-leaving opposite page 158 of *Religious Musings*, where in lines 287–89 STC refers to the Simoom. W seems unlikely to have entered the note after he began to use the book (the portion now DC MS 30) for *Michael*. But one cannot be certain that the volume remained intact even in late 1800, and too little of it survives for confident conjecture respecting the length of time when W might have had an opportunity to write in it. A date more exact than between early 1796 (see *CEY* 181) and perhaps c late 1800 seems unjusti-fied. RS drew on the same passage in Volney for a note for *Thalaba* (1801, I, 100–03).

[2] The Marsk epitaph reads

> A virtues Woman I have been
> And many troubles I have seen
> When I was alive I did my best
> But now my bones are laid at rest.

APPENDIX X

A Letter from Mary Wordsworth to Mrs. Thomas Cookson

The following letter from MW to Mrs. Thomas Cookson, written on a large octavo single sheet of plain wove paper, is published with the kind permission of the Master and Fellows of St. John's College, Cambridge. A few very minor corrections, deletions, and overwritings are not described, and some short lowered dashes have been transcribed as regular dashes.

Coleorton [1806]
Saturday Nov. [3 *deleted*] 1st[1]

My dear Mrs Cookson
                        You will be glad to hear of our safe arrival—the two parties within 20 minutes of each other on Thursday evening about 9 oClock, all [tolerably *inserted over a caret*] well, except poor little Thomas whose cough was very bad all the way—& he [was *overwritten* did] & still does, suffer much in consequence of my being heated, & fagged with the journey.—Dorothy (not little D.) has got a hoarseness—Sarah was as usual very sick & unable to take any food all the way—but we are now all in the way of well-doing so I will no longer dwell upon it. as for adventures on our road I have none to speak of unless I tell you when John was unmanageable, & how often Dorothy was cross—[but *inserted above the line*] this I may in few words say, was the case the whole of the way—travelling with Children never shall have my good word.—But let me hasten my dear kind friend! to thank you in the name of myself and all of [us *overwritten* my] [friends *inserted above a caret*] for your exceeding goodness to us. I cannot fully express to you how deep an impression it has made upon us all.—I hope the pleasure we enjoyed in your society will be renewed in the spring, when we shall have more leisure to walk about, & quiet. to draw

[1] The "st" of "1st" is preceded by a curved stroke, possibly part of a partially overwritten "2."

round your fireside.—We were most kindly received by our Friends here & find every thing to promise us a comfortable home for the winter.

I ought to have told you that the chaise party slept the first night not at [*blank*] but at a very comfortable house a mile beyond—the second night at [*blank*] & about 12 oClock on Thursday as we drove up [at *overwritten* to] the inn at Derby [I *overwritten* we] had the pleasure to see our friends about to drive off in the heavy loaden Coach. this meeting as you may well suppose was a great joy to us—& gave us spirit for the rest of our journey—I have not time to say more for the letters are wanted to send [you *deleted*] to the post—I [was *overwritten* I h *deleted*] have been so fully engaged all the morning, settling [all *deleted*] our little affairs with Lady B. or I would not have written you such a hasty scrawl, but much less, would I delay another post writing at all, to you—

God bless you my dr Mrs C best love to your good Husband & kisses to all the Darlings

Yours most truly
M. Wordsworth—

Do let us hear from you—Sara will write soon

Addenda and Corrigenda for
The Chronology of the Early Years

p. ix, line 11: *for* A.H. *read* G.H.

p. 10, line 11: The names of father and son were John Pinney and John Frederick Pinney.

p. 17, line 2 of conclusion of note 3; and p. 322, line 15: *for* pages *read* leaves

p. 20, GCL 21; p. 78, 1787:26 & n; p. 82, 1788:7 & n: Professor Paul Betz has supplied convincing evidence based on textual content that the version of the *Dirge* addressed to a "maid" and dated Jan 1788 is the earliest of these poems, and was followed by the second set of verses addressed to a maid, then, in blank space remaining earlier in the NB, by the *Dirge* addressed to a boy. Another copy of the *Dirge* addressed to a boy is commenced under the title "Song" at the rear of the NB, but breaks off after two lines.

p. 23, lines 1–3: The verses were first arranged as two poems *LB* 1800, and were perhaps first divided in preparation for the volume. See 1800:73.

p. 24, note 12, line 5: *for* Christiansen *read* Christensen

————————, line 9: *for* Vicompte *read* Vicomte

p. 25, line 4: *for* to Walk *read* the Walk

——, GCL 45c, and p. 336: *Terminus ad quem* of MS 2 probably early 1800. The MW autograph revision was probably entered in preparation for *PELY* publication.

p. 27, lines 3–4: *Borderers* 1539–44 misquoted William Hazlitt, *Lectures on the English Comic Writers*, 1819; quoted *PW* 1836 IV, 46. Prefatory Essay pub. *The Nineteenth Century and After*, Nov 1926.

p. 28, line 26, and p. 339, line 12: *for* 1207–75 *read* 1207–96

——, last line: *Exc* I.500–02 pub. *Friend* 25 Jan 1810; *Exc* I.626–34 pub. *Friend* 16 Nov 1809.

p. 29, line 18: *for* 15 Sept *read* 13 Sept

p. 30, lines 22–24: "There Was a Boy" pub. *LB* 1800.

p. 31, GCL 63g4: On the dates of *Prel* MSS U, V, RV see above, 629n.

p. 32, line 21: *for* 1800 *read* 1798

p. 38, 1764:1: Mr. D. P. Sewell advises on the basis of documents in the

Record Office, Carlisle, that JW Sr. arrived to take up his duties in Cockermouth on 2 Oct 1764.

p. 47, 1799:1: On W's years at Hawkshead generally see esp. T. W. Thompson, *Wordsworth's Hawkshead*, ed. R. S. Woof (Oxford, 1970).

p. 52, 1780:8, 1781:1: Peake's headmastership concluded in mid-1781; he formally resigned on 26 June 1781. Christian resigned 18 July 1782. See Thompson 342.

p. 54, 1782:1: The Tysons probably removed to Colthouse in late 1783 (Thompson 56).

p. 55, 1782:5: On this expedition see Thompson 211–14.

p. 60, 1784:4: Tyson died on 1 Mar (Thompson 56). Concerning W at this time see also Thompson 61.

p. 61, 1784:9: On the likelihood of W's having passed the summer at Hawkshead see Thompson 373–74, note for 107. (*CEY* is apparently not an intended object of the last sentence's refutation of the view that W "both before and at Cambridge, 1787–9, ever spent the period of the actual school holidays in Hawkshead," since *CEY* allows this possibility only in the year 1784.)

p. 62, 1784:10: On this incident see Thompson 224–34.

———, 1784:13, and pp. 298–301: On W's first poetic composition see also Thompson 311–18. (*CEY* is apparently not an intended referent of the phrase "recent scholars" in the last sentence of p. 318, since it does not make the assumption—that W's earliest verses were assigned for the vacation—attributed to that group.)

p. 64, note 2, line 6: *for* second *read* school

———, note 4: Mingay was probably also W's only formal instructor in French. See E. L. Pierce, *Memoirs of Charles Sumner* (Boston, 1878), I, 356.

p. 79, note 20, line 10: *for* Telling *read* telling

p. 86, note 6, line 1: *for* 7 *read* 6

p. 87, 1788:18, and p. 93, 1789:7: W passed the nine weeks at Hawkshead referred to 1788:18 during his long vacation of 1789, not 1788. He possibly spent a longer time there in 1788, in June and after 28 July. See esp. Thompson 134–35n (which, however, fails to notice payments by Uncles Richard and Christopher to W in Oct 1788).

p. 96, 1790:3, line 4: *for* June 1794 *read* July 1792

p. 109, 1790:64: At Lucerne on 29 or 30 Aug, or 10 or 11 Sept, W probably saw a model of the Alpine country encompassing the Lake of the Four Cantons. (G, opening remarks; MW's MS Journal of 1820 Tour to Continent, DCP.)

p. 112, note 23, line 2: *for* heart *read* head

pp. 114–15, 1790:100: W and Jones probably returned via Ostend. See *Autobiography of Mrs. Fletcher* (Edinburgh, 1875), 228.

p. 115, note 29, line 3: for *Fielder* read *Fiedler*

p. 142, note 5, lines 4–5: *for* MS letter *read* transcript of letter

p. 153, 1794:10, line 1: *for* 19 *read* 20

p. 156, 1794:19, line 1: *for* 16 *read* 18 (Information from Mr. D. P. Sewell.)
——————, line 2: *for* 51 *read* 61 (Information from Mr. D. P. Sewell.)

p. 166, 1795:19, line 2: for *Osterly* read *Osterley*

p. 167, 1795:25: Between this time and Aug 1798 W often conversed, when in Bristol, with William Gilbert, author of *The Hurricane* (letter, W to John Peace, 1839, DCP).

p. 169, 1795:32, line 2: *for* Forncett *read* Halifax

p. 176: Concerning 1796 see also the last paragraph of Appendix IX above.

p. 181, 1796:25: Margaret Hutchinson died 28 Mar 1796 (M-H Book of Common Prayer, DCP).

p. 210, 1797:79, lines 1, 2, 8: *for* 12 *read* 13
——————, note 37, line 1: *for* Tuesday *read* Monday

p. 212, 1797:85, line 3: They probably departed London at 4 AM Friday and arrived in Bristol that night. (MS of *EY* letter no. 79, Rosenbach Foundation; information from Professor James Butler.)

p. 239, 1798:140, line 2: *for* DW writes *read* W and DW write
——————, 1798:141, line 4: *for* type size *read* spacing of lines

p. 258: A review of *LB* 1798 appeared in the *Monthly Mirror* VI (Oct 1798). See Ward, Hayden.

pp. 261–62: Reviews of *LB* 1798 appeared in the *New Annual Register* XIX (1798) and the *New London Review* I(Jan 1799). See Ward.

p. 264, 1799:19, last line: See also E. J. Morley, "Coleridge in Germany," *Wordsworth and Coleridge. Studies in Honor of George McLean Harper*, ed. E. L. Griggs (Princeton, 1939), 220–36.

p. 267, 1799:28: On the arrival at Sockburn see also Woof *Inward Eye* 28–29.

p. 271, 1799:42, line 6: W also thanks Cottle for a copy or copies of *LB* and the second volume of [RS's *Poems*, 1799]; declines request to supply a poem for [*Annual Anthology*]. (MS of *EY* letter no. 119, Rosenbach Foundation; information from Professor James Butler.)

p. 271, 1799:43: The letter here discussed was written in late May and postmarked 1 June 1799. (MS, Rosenbach Foundation; information from Professor James Butler, whose text of the letter will appear in a forthcoming article.)

p. 272, 1799:50: W also thanks Cottle for *Annual Anthology*; compliments Cottle on his poem *The Killcrop*; reassures him regarding verses of Beddoes'.

(MS of *EY* letter no. 122, Rosenbach Foundation; information from Professor James Butler.)

p. 276, 1799:64: Perhaps also on this day W sees an epitaph in the churchyard at the head of the lake; learns from relatives the story of the Deaf Man later recounted by W *Exc* VII.395–481 (*Exc* IF note, *PW* V, 464).

p. 282, 1799:85: Concerning composition during this portion of W's visit at Sockburn see esp. pp. 629–30 n above.

p. 283, 1799:93, line 6: The removal from Grasmere probably took place 12 May 1813 (Reed *N&Q*).

p. 285, 1799:96, line 6: *delete* of one

p. 321, last two lines of text: The Pedlar lines also include description corresponding to Prel VII.c720–29 (advice from Professor Michael Jaye; see also addendum for p. 326).

p. 322, line 28: *for* 342–45, i–viii; *read* 342–44, i–viii,

p. 325, lines 13–14: The draft "possibly from Ariosto" was probably toward W's "ballad poem never written" for which *The Danish Boy* was to have served as a prelude (see *Danish Boy* IF note). (Information from Professor Paul Betz.)

p. 326, line 24: *for* additional verses *read* additional verses contributive to *Prel* VII.c720–29

p. 327, line 22: *for* 405–07 *read* 405–08

p. 331, lines 1–3: The printer's MS of *Nutting*, not mentioned, was written c but by 13 Aug 1800. See 1800:99.

Renumbering of the Dove Cottage Papers 1785–1814

New Numbers	Old Numbers (where appropriate)
DC MS 1	MS Verse 1
DC MS 2	MS Verse 4
DC MS 3	MS Verse 3
DC MS 4	MS Verse 2
DC MS 5	MS Verse 5
DC MS 6	MS Verse 6
DC MS 7	MS Verse 7
DC MS 8	MS Prose 1
DC MS 9	MS Verse 10
DC MS 10	MS Verse 11
DC MS 11	MS Verse 12
DC MS 12	MS Verse 14
DC MS 13	MSS Verse 31, 32, 44, 46 (a)[1]
DC MS 14	MS Verse 19
DC MS 15	MS Verse 18
DC MS 16	MS Verse 18A
DC MS 17	MS Verse 33
DC MS 18	MS Verse 34
DC MS 19	Journal 5
DC MS 20	Journal 3
DC MS 21	MS Verse 40 (a)[2]
DC MS 22	MS Verse 26
DC MS 23	MS Verse 15
DC MS 24	MSS Verse 41, 47, 50, 51, 56[3]
DC MS 25	Journal 4
DC MS 26	MS Prose 31

[1] Reconstructed folio notebook of 1797–1802.
[2] *Prel*, *MS RV*.
[3] Reconstructed notebook, incl. *Nutting* fragment.

New Numbers	**Old Numbers** (where appropriate)
DC MS 27	*MS Verse 13*
DC MS 28	*MS Verse 43*
DC MS 29	*MS Verse 37A*
DC MS 30	*MS Verse 42*
DC MS 31	*Journal 6*
DC MS 32	STC misc. vol., incl. *To Rain etc.*
DC MS 33	*MS Verse 36*
DC MS 34	*MS Verse 37*
DC MS 35	*MS Verse 45*
DC MS 36	*MS Verse 46* (b)[4]
DC MS 37	*MS Verse 33A*
DC MS 38	*MS Verse 27*
DC MS 39	*STC Dejection*
DC MS 40	*Mad Moon	Tinker*
DC MS 41	*Sara's Poets*
DC MS 42	*MS Verse 49*
DC MS 43	*Journal 7*
DC MS 44	*MS Verse 25*
DC MS 45	*MS Verse 41A*
DC MS 46	*MS Verse 48*
DC MS 47	*MS Verse 28*
DC MS 48	*MS Verse 29*
DC MS 49	*MS Verse 30*
DC MS 50	*Journal 8*
DC MS 51	*Journal 13*
DC MS 52	*MS Verse 20*
DC MS 53	*MS Verse 21*
DC MS 54	*Journal 9*
DC MS 55	*Journals 10 & 11*
DC MS 56	*MS Verse 52*
DC MS 57	*MS Verse 51A*
DC MS 58	*MS Verse 38*
DC MS 59	*MS Verse 39*
DC MS 60	*MS Verse 35*
DC MS 61	*MS Verse 53*
DC MS 62	*MS Verse 63*
DC MS 63	*Journals 1 & 2*

[4] Latter part of *Manciple's Tale*.

New Numbers	**Old Numbers** (where appropriate)
DC MS 64	*Journal 14*
DC MS 65	*MS Verse 54*
DC MS 66	*MS Prose 32*
DC MS 67	*MS Prose 6*
DC MS 68	*MSS Prose 19–30*[5]
DC MS 69	*MS Verse 57*
DC MS 70	*MS Verse 58*
DC MS 71	*MS Verse 59*
DC MS 72	*MS Verse 52A*
DC MS 73	*MS Verse 60*
DC MS 74	*MS Verse 61*
DC MS 75	*MS Verse 62*
DC MS 76	*MS Verse 40 (b)*[6]
DC MS 77	*Journal 31*
DC MS 78	*MS Verse 8*
DC MS 79	*MS Verse 9*
DC MS 80	*MS Verse 62A*

[5] Reconstituted G MS.
[6] *HG, MS D.*

The above list has been prepared, and with small individual reservations accepted, by Paul Betz, Stephen Gill, W. J. B. Owen, Stephen Parrish, Mark Reed, Robert Woof, and Jonathan Wordsworth. It has the authority of the Trustees of Dove Cottage.

Index to Writings

Abbreviations:

c   composition or writing
m   manuscript, transcript, author's instruction
e   events, persons, or circumstances prompting or referred to in the work
d   distribution of copies of work, including presentation copies, sales
p   publication
q   quoted
r   review

719

Subject Index

Abbreviations:

f.a.   financial arrangements

p.c.   personal contacts

Abbotsford, 571
Abercorn, 568
Aberfeldie, 221n
Aberfoyle, 561
Acharn, Falls of, 230
Achray, Loch, 226, 232, 561
Acland, A. H. D., 339n
Addingham, 549
Addison, Henry, 448, 449, 533, 557
Addison, Isabella, 165; receives copy of *LB* 1800, 119n, 168; marries John M, 326
Addison, Jane, 415
Addison, Mary, 530, 557
Addison, Richard, 455n, 463, 514, 529, 531, 541, 552, 573, 597
Addison, Mrs., 243–44
Adye, Major R. W., 287
African, merry, 100
Aikin, Anne (Mrs. Charles), 499, 500
Aikin, Arthur, 499
Aikin, Dr. Charles, 499, 500
Aikin, Lucy, 390
Ainslie, Dr. Henry, 464
Aird, Rev. John, 224
Airey, Henry, 251
Airey Force, 261
Albano, Lake of, picture by Sir GB, 321
Alconbury Hill, 316
Ale, 104, 369
Alexander, William, 555n, 596n, 608
Alexandria, Battle of, 420
Alfoxden, 417
Allan, Bridge of, 233n

Allan Bank, 281, 360; agreement that W will occupy, 349; removal to, 388; residence, 388–475; f.a. concerning, 388n, 401; grounds, 352, 361; smoking chimneys, 398–99, 401, 436, 440, 444, 448; oilcloth sought for passages, 403, 452. *See also* Crump, John G.
Allen, John, 361
Alloa, 567; Tower, 567
Allonby, 574
Allston, Washington, 485, 494, 605; *Jacob's Dream*, 605
Almond, River, 566
Alms, Miss, 556, 557, 580, 585, 589, 592, 593
Alnwick and Alnwick Castle, 123
Alsager, Thomas Massa, 603, 605
Alvie, 565
Ambleside, *passim;* Fair, 581
Amulree, 566
Anachree, Moss of, 228
Anderson, Dr. Robert, 570
   Works of the British Poets: copies at DC, GH, 202–03n; STC note in copy, 243; W, RS, Anderson discuss additions to 570, 572–73, 574, 589–90. *See also* names of anthologized authors
Anderson, Miss, 570, 574n
Andover, Viscountess, 358n
Angerstein, Sir Julius, pictures, 376
Angle Tarn, 433–35n
Annan, 22, 558
Annual Anthology, see Southey, Robert
Annual Review, 242n, 390
Antijacobin Review, 62

739

ton, 368; health, 380; property, 393; to reside in Wales, 408; leaves for Wales, 415n; and William Johnson, 492; tours South Wales, 503; receives copy of *P* 1815, 595; letters, 61n, 63–64n, 100–11n, 136, 281n, 282n, 394n, 409n, 415, 415n, 492, 586n; letters from MH, SH, DW to, *see* names of letter-writers. *See also* Gallow Hill

Hutchinson, John, 66, 465, 471, 542, 588; visits Ws, 306, 423, 472; Ws visit, 368–70; witnesses W's wedding, 195; f.a. with Ws, 144n, 202, 423. *See also* Stockton

Hutchinson, Margaret, 714

Hutchinson, Mary: takes up residence at Gallow Hill, 64n; visits DC, 59–61; and JW, Stoddart, 60n; her and W's intention to marry, 59n, 149, 157, 174; receives copy of *LB* 1800, 11–12; presents copy of *LB* 1800, 168; GH, 127–28, 134, 139; visits Eusemere, 139–41; meets W near Penrith, 147; W meets at Middleham, 159–60; marriage, 195–96. *See also* Gallow Hill; Wordsworth, Mary

    health, 130, 135, 137

    copyist, 66, 127, 134, 137, 166n, 616. *See also* Index to Writings, *s.v.* Manuscripts

    letters, 130, 131, 134; to Joanna H, 131, 136; to SH, 128, 136; to Ws, 65, 95, 102, 103, 142, 144, 148, 149, 150, 151, 152, 153, 155, 156, 159, 160, 164, 169, 173, 174, 175, 176, 178, 179, 182, 184, 185

    letters from SH, DW, JW, W to, *see* names of letter-writers

Hutchinson, Mary (niece of MW), 468

Hutchinson, Mary Monkhouse: letter, 579n; letters from SH to, *see* Hutchinson, Sara. *See also* Monkhouse, Mary

Hutchinson, Sara: with Ws at GH, DC, 101–108; with Ws, Eusemere, 109–13; visits DC, 113; visits GH, 113–14; visits DC, 114–17; at Middleham, 159–60; at Gallow Hill, 186–87, 194–96; receives copy of *LB* 1802, 195; childhood residence, 197; at Penrith, 201; visits DC, 201–06; visits GH, 206; visits DC, 211–12, 258; at PH, visits Eusemere with DW, 261; visits DC, 268–70; proxy godmother for Dora, 269; visits Kendal, DC, 281–83, 286–89; visits GH, with W, 299; at PH or Eusemere, visits Lowther with W, DW, 305; at Threlkeld, PH with W, 308; visits DC, 310–29; visits PH, with W, 329; joins Ws, Kendal, 336; visits Coleorton with Ws, 336–58; STC fantasizes sexual intimacy with W, 345; visits London, with Ws, 351–54; visits Bury, 354; visits Halifax, Kendal, with Ws, 356–58; possibly at Appleby with W, Thomas H, 369; at Appleby, Penrith, with W, MW, 370; visits Eusemere, 370; visits DC, AB, 372–92; possibly absent, 373; to make home with Ws, 385; visits Eusemere, 392–93; visits Penrith, 409, 415; visits Duddon, perhaps GH, 396; visits Elleray, 419, 422; visits Eusemere, Penrith, 436; visits Elleray, 437; dines at Lloyds, 445; visits Hindwell, Wales, 450; returns to Ws, at Rectory, 481; visits Yewdale, 484; visits Luffs, Patterdale, 484, 486; visits Hackett, 496; visits GH, 497–500; visits Hackett, 496; visits Appleby, 511–12; absent from Rectory, returns, 514; visits Ambleside, 518–20; moves to RM, 529; visits Appleby, 525–27; visits Mary Barker, 531–33; visits Stockton, 538–45; visits GH, 554, 556; visits Scotland, 556–71; visits Kendal, Ludlow, Liverpool, Chester, Hindwell, 573; asked to join Ws in London, 599; visits London, 1815, 500–08; visits Bury, 608–09

    health, 204, 324, 337, 380, 381, 385, 392, 426n

    f.a. with Ws, 100, 204, 210, 514

    copyist, 105, 115, 116, 284, 286, 288, 289, 315, 340, 415, 440, 443, 490, 491, 492, 546, 556n, 673, 674, 704, 707; autograph, 635, 655. *See also* Index to Writings, *s.v.* Manuscripts, *esp. Poems in Two Volumes*

    letters, missives, 440n, 443, 530; to

155; meets MH at Middleham, 159–60; begins mature composition of sonnets, 170; not to live at GH, 177; visits Gallow Hill, London, France, 186–97; visits Kendal, *see* Kendal; marries, 195–96; meets Sir GB and Lady B, receives property from Sir GB, 217, 218; tours Scotland with DW, STC, 221–37; enlists in Grasmere Volunteers, 237–38; seeks important old books through CL, 246; visits PH, *see* Park House; visits Brougham Hall, *see* Brougham; tours Ennerdale, Wastdale, Duddon Valley, 271; learns of JW's death, 281; contemplates removal from Grasmere, *see* Grasmere; visits Patterdale, climbs Helvellyn with Scott, Davy, 296–97 (*see also* Patterdale); purchases Broad How property, *see* Broad How; visits London, 316–23; visits CW, *see* Wordsworth, Christopher; portrait drawn by Edridge, 322; meets Fox, 323; meets Constable, 335; meets STC in Kendal after STC's return from Malta, 337; visits Coleorton, 336–58; plans anthology, 344; takes AB for residence, 349; visits London, 351–54; visits Nottingham, Halifax, Bolton Abbey, 358; visits Appleby, *see* Appleby meets LdL, 361; tours Wastdale, Ennerdale, Whitehaven, Cockermouth, 363; meets John Wilson, 364; meets DeQ, 366; resides at AB, 369–475; visits Stockton, 369–70, 700–01; visits London, 375–81; tours Duddon and elsewhere, with SH, STC, 396; indignant at Convention of Cintra, *see* Cintra, Convention of; appears over sixty, 407n; disappointed in his country, 426; joins Wilson's fishing party, 431–32; visits Elleray, *see* Elleray; visits Sockbridge, *see* Sockbridge; visits Coleorton, Wales, 454–60; resides at Rectory, 475–524; seeks office, obtains stamp distributorship, *see* Stamp Distributorship; W visits LdL, *see* Lowther, Sir William; visits London, Wales, 493–507; visits Hackett, *see* Hackett; tours northwest

Lake District with DW, 512; resides at RM, 529–609; visits Watermillock, *see* Watermillock; offered Collectorship of Customs, Whitehaven, 599; visits London, 600–09; Haydon makes cast of face, 606

health: poor health, miscellaneous, 71, 73, 82, 85–86, 92, 98, 101, 103, 116, 120, 129, 130, 132, 134, 137, 142, 143, 145, 146, 148, 149, 150, 154–55, 162, 169n, 200, 201, 315, 373, 405, 409, 413, 414n, 492, 580; cold, 336, 373; eyes, trachoma, 336, 373; teeth, 69, 373; influenza, 546; insomnia, 131, 143, 144, 145, 153, 165, 168, 171, 173, 175, 176, 177, 178, 181, 183, 185, 578

f.a., *see* Financial arrangements

writings, *see* Index to Writings

letters, 58, 67, 71, 75, 106, 107, 108, 115, 117, 118, 121, 122, 149, 155, 174, 176, 242, 249, 253, 254, 255, 286, 289, 316, 325, 333, 335, 336, 341, 352, 375, 379, 379n, 383, 384, 390, 397, 398, 403, 404, 416, 417, 429, 434, 447, 503, 506, 508, 529, 533, 534, 535, 536, 537, 541, 545, 551, 553, 582, 583, 586, 589, 590, 591, 593, 593–94, 594, 599, 601, 657, 668, 670–71, 687, 690, 692–93; to Sir GB and Lady B, 240, 266, 269, 276, 281, 284, 285, 289, 291, 292, 294, 295, 302, 314, 325, 330, 331, 333, 341, 343, 347, 355, 374, 383, 452, 479, 485, 485–86, 513, 527, 528, 555, 652, 654, 656, 660, 675, 687, 687–88, 688; to Biggs and Cottle, *see* Index to Writings, *s.v. Lyrical Ballads* 1800, printer's MS; to CCl, TCl, 138, 283, 318–19, 385, 497, 503, 505, 506, 587, 588, 687; to STC, 67, 114, 120, 130, 134, 136, 137, 143, 145, 149, 151, 155, 161, 165, 169, 181, 201, 254–55, 259, 269, 335, 341, 373, 381, 383, 384, 385, 387, 425, 498, 662; to SFC, 149, 474; to DeQ, 218, 254, 256, 320n, 322, 325, 352, 400, 410, 411, 412, 413, 414, 416, 417, 420, 425, 426, 427, 428, 506, 518, 578, 590, 660; to MH, 104, 119, 178, 181 (*see also* letters to MW); to SH, 114, 178, 196, 495, 506, 542, 585,